聖嚴研究 | 第十三輯

聖嚴法師圓寂十週年國際研討會論文集

Studies of Master Sheng Yen **Vol.13**

Collection of Essays From the 2019 International Conference Commemorating
the 10th Anniversary of Master Sheng Yen's Passing

二〇二〇年十一月

聖嚴研究

第十三輯

目錄

專題演講

Mindful Economics and the Countdown to 2030

.... Joel Magnuson, Ph.D. 13

1. Pathological System Conditions (PSCs) 13

2. The Fall 2018 IPCC Report 14

3. Perpetual Economic Growth is Unassailable 16

4. Mindful Economics and Social Provisioning 21

5. "New Economics": Same Wine Different Bottles? 23

6. Roshi Bernie Glassman and the Greyston Mandala 26

7. Conclusion 28

   References 29

Applying Buddhist Principles to Managing People and
Organizations in the Public, Private and Nonprofit

Workplaces .... Frances Berry 31

1. Introduction 31

2. Management in Today's World 32

3. Leadership in Buddhist Writings 37

4. Summary and Brief Discussion 55

5. Conclusion 59

　全文中譯 .... 高照東方 61

Business Ethics:

Some Insights from Buddhism .... Simon S.M. Ho 89

1. Objectives 89

2. Business Ethics Problems 89

3. Re-shaping Capitalism 90

4. Common Unethical business practices 90

5. Legal Regulations, Business Ethics and Human Characters 90

6. Buddhism Offering Distinct Perspective on Business Ethics 91

7. Some Relevant Unique Doctrines of Buddhism 91

8. Relevant Buddhist Scriptures for Practical Adoption 92

9. Noble Eightfold Path 八正道 92

10. Ethical Beliefs and Spiritual Pursuit 93

11. Further Observations 94

Sociology and the Cultivation of Buddhist Wisdom

.... Richard Madsen 95

1. Sociology's Compatibility with Buddhism 96

2. Buddhism's Transcendence of Sociology 99

3. Contributions of Sociology to Buddhism 100

4. Sheng Yen's Contributions to Sociology 104

5. The Future of Transcendence? 107

　全文中譯 .... 陳維武 110

論文

經濟富足與心靈安樂
——聖嚴法師「心靈環保」思想對「佛教經濟學」理論之啟示

.... 許永河 129

一、前言 131

二、「佛教經濟學」的發展概述 134

三、聖嚴法師「建設人間淨土」的思想 144

四、聖嚴法師「建設人間淨土」思想對「佛教經濟學」理論
發展之啟示 161

五、結語 213

參考文獻 218

英文摘要 222

Sense of Interdependence and the Altruistic behavior

.... Miko Ching-Ying Yu, Tzyy-Jan Lai 225

1. Introduction 226

2. Hypothesis 231

3. Conclusion 234

Reference 235

中文摘要 236

Buddhadharma and Sustainable Development:

An Integrated Framework of Analysis .... Ching-yi Chiang 237

1. Introduction 239

2. Sustainable Development: Principles and Practice 244

3. An Integrated Framework of Sustainable Development 257

　　4. Conclusion 274

　　　　Reference 275

　　　　Appendix 278

　　　　中文摘要 283

正念影響情緒平衡之研究　　　　　　朱金池 285

　　一、前言 286

　　二、「正念」的兩種不同意涵 288

　　三、西方醫學、心理學的「正念覺察」對情緒平衡之影響 292

　　四、佛教的「正念修行」對情緒平衡之影響 ... 308

　　五、結語 323

　　　　參考文獻 329

　　　　英文摘要 332

「緣起領導」管理模式
——佛法與領導管理　　　　　　　　吳志軒 335

　　一、領導管理模式的演變 337

　　二、慈悲與智慧的領導力 339

　　三、緣起的身分認同 342

　　四、佛菩薩的領導模式 346

　　五、以修行為領導的基礎 348

　　六、「緣起」的領導力 352

　　七、「緣起領導」的實踐 354

　　　　參考文獻 359

　　　　英文摘要 363

心靈環保、企業社會責任與公司揭露與實踐永續發展目標之影響因素 李啟華 365

一、緒論 366

二、文獻探討及假說建立 371

三、研究方法 384

四、實證結果 391

五、結論 399

參考文獻 401

英文摘要 407

正念對工作家庭間情緒溢出調節功能的初探 彭奕農、陳思仔 409

一、文獻回顧 412

二、研究方法 419

三、結論與建議 433

參考文獻 437

英文摘要 444

至善社會福利基金會都市原住民照顧計畫之社會投資報酬分析 陳定銘、徐郁雯 445

一、前言 447

二、文獻探討 451

三、至善基金會個案析探 463

四、SROI 分析與討論 466

五、結論 503

參考文獻 507

英文摘要 511

Karma, Social Justice and Lessons from Anti-Oppressive
Practice for Buddhist Practitioners .... Wei Wu Tan, Ph.D. 513

1. Introduction 515

2. What is Social Justice? 515

3. The Conundrum of Karma for Buddhism 516

4. Responses to the Karma Conundrum 518

5. Doctrinal Foundation in Buddhism for Social Justice 520

6. Anti-Oppressive Practice in Social Work 528

7. Implications and Lessons for Practice and Discourse 532

8. Conclusion 536

References 538

中文摘要 541

人間性、場域性與解構性
—— 聖嚴法師論如何建設現代社會為人間淨土 .... 王宣曆 543

一、前言 545

二、人間性：人間佛教與建設人間淨土 546

三、場域性：「建設人間淨土」以現代社會為實踐場域 555

四、解構性：如何建設現代社會為人間淨土 565

五、結論 578

引用書目 580

英文摘要 584

The Social Origin of Creativity:
A Sociological Analysis of Master Taixu and Master Sheng Yen as
Buddhist Thinkers .... Rebecca S.K. Li 587

1. Introduction 589

2. The Social Construction of Master Taixu as a Great Thinker .. 590

3. Collins's Theory of Intellectual Creativity 595

4. Conditions for intellectual creativity in early twentieth-century

China 598

5. Intellectual network in early twentieth-century China 603

6. Explaining Intellectual Creativity: The Case of Master Taixu ... 608

7. Explaining Intellectual Creativity: The Case of Master Sheng

Yen 615

8. Conclusion 623

Work Cited 628

中文摘要 631

專題演講

Mindful Economics and the Countdown to 2030

Joel Magnuson, Ph.D.

An independent economist based in Portland, Oregon, USA.

1. Pathological System Conditions (PSCs)

The English word *pathological* or *pathology* derives from the ancient Greek root of *pathos*, meaning the experience of suffering. Generally, now the term applies to medical science and the study of disease but in a broader sense it simply means conditions of suffering. In terms of the Buddhist first noble truth, when we refer to pathological system conditions, we are talking about suffering that exists not just among individuals but also as embedded in our social and ecological systems. Specifically, we are entering into an era during which the pathology of global warming and climate change are palpable. This is undoubtedly the most pernicious challenge faced by humanity as we tread our way through the twenty-first century.

As we are now well aware, the global ambient temperatures are rising as a result of higher concentrations of carbon dioxide in our atmosphere. On the ground, there are real-time events coinciding with these rising temperatures. Just in the last few years the United States has experienced record temperatures, hurricanes of growing intensity, record numbers of tornadoes, devastating floods, and catastrophic wildfires. In November 2018, a small California town called Paradise was consumed in a hellish wildfire. In the span of eight ghastly hours, ninety percent of the homes in this town were burned to the ground. Government officials and rescue teams warned the local population to evacuate their community. These warnings were identical to those issued about a month earlier to members of the small community of Mexico Beach, Florida that was crushed by Hurricane Michael.

It is difficult to prove with 100 percent certainty that these environmental disasters are indeed the result of climate change, but most scientists believe they are. Moreover, they are entirely consistent with what scientists have been warning for decades, and they are growing in intensity with rising global ambient temperatures.

These pathological system conditions are causing us to drift toward what is becoming "triage economy" in which we are being forced to shift increasingly large amounts of resources to cope with this damage. In terms of the amount of money spent to repair, relocate, and reconstruct there were over fourteen billion-dollar weather and climate disasters in the United States in 2018 alone. Congress last month passed a bill authorizing the spending of another $19 billion in disaster aid funds in anticipation of more to come.

One of my concerns is that so many of us are becoming numb to all this—burying our heads in the sands of cognitive dissonance as a way of avoiding anxiety. And like so many mythological "boiling frogs" accepting these pathological system conditions as the new "normal." People are literally turning their backs on the effects of climate change. As such, they are choosing to turn their backs on the first noble truth that such conditions even exist. And as people close their eyes to reality, it becomes profoundly more difficult to open minds to the other noble truths about knowing to uncover the root causes of these conditions, and knowing to make real and positive changes in how we think and act in the world.

2. The Fall 2018 IPCC Report

In the fall of 2018, just as Hurricane Michael was trampling the southeast part of the US, the Intergovernmental Panel on Climate Change issued a new report titled, "Special Report on Global Warming of 1.5°C: Summary for Policymakers." It was also at this time that CO_2 levels had just risen above 400 ppm.

The general position held by the IPCC is that climate change is anthropogenic; that is, caused by human economic activity. It urges that immediate and comprehensive action needs to be taken to reduce concentrations of carbon dioxide and other so-called greenhouse gasses from the atmosphere in order to limit the most severe warming trends—to bring it down to 1.5°C or less over the next decade. (IPCC, 2018:18) The IPCC notes that this effort "would require rapid and far-reaching transitions in energy, land, urban and rural infrastructure (including transport and buildings), and industrial systems." (Ibid) The IPCC focus is primarily on overhauling energy production and consumption as the most significant option for global warming mitigation. The IPCC also notes that such mitigation efforts are aligned with the seventeen United Nations Sustainable Development Goals (SDGs), adopted by the United Nations in 2015. The ultimate goal is to bring carbon dioxide levels down to below the threshold of 350 parts per million by 2030. As we can see from Figure One, this is threshold was exceeded around 1990 and has been on the rise since. The goal would be to limit the warming trend in global ambient temperatures down to 1.5°C or less over the next decade. The IPCC notes that this effort "would require rapid and far-reaching transitions in energy, land, urban and rural infrastructure (including transport and buildings), and industrial systems." But the IPCC focus is primarily on overhauling energy production and consumption processes as the most significant strategies for global warming mitigation.

The IPCC report resonates as a final warning for significant efforts worldwide to overcome "socio-economic, institutional, technological, financing and environmental barriers that differ across regions." (Ibid). In other words, they are calling for nothing short of large-scale systems transitions that are "unprecedented in terms of scale." (Ibid:17) Such systems transitions would have to involve scaling down economic activity in general, but this would be at odds with the categorical imperative of ongoing economic growth.

Figure 1: Atmospheric Carbon Dioxide, 1975-2018 (parts per million (PPM))

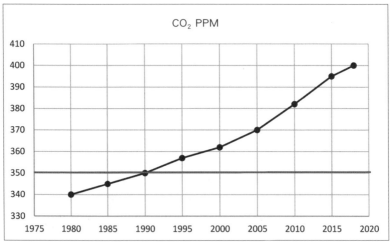

Source: National Oceanic and Atmospheric Administration, Climate Change: CO2 Breaks Record in 2017, https://www.climate.gov/news-features/understanding-climate/climate-change-atmospheric-carbon-dioxide

3. Perpetual Economic Growth is Unassailable

About a dozen years ago, it seemed as if someone had removed the lid from Pandora's Box and every possible dismal thing you could imagine about the global economy was released into the world. Government agencies took desperate policy measures—emergency bailouts, massive loans to banks, stimulus plans, and colossal debt—to restore the economic machinery back to normal. Normal means spinning on a perpetual growth trend as the *raison d'etre* of all economic activity. Yet returning things to normal also means deepening our economic and cultural attachment to this process of ongoing economic growth, and that growth remains largely powered by fossil fuels. Again, scientists have been warning us for several decades about the ecological consequences of endless growth and the excess combustion of fossil fuels; and as the data and imagery attest, those consequences are finally upon us.

The question begs. Why do people everywhere have such an attachment to economic growth? We can certainly point to population growth or the growth imperative embedded in the capitalist system. But there are some other deeper, existential drivers at work as well, and I believe Buddhists have some very compelling things to say about that.

The second noble truth in Buddhist philosophy is to come to know the root causes and origins of our suffering. There are perhaps as many root causes as there are different varieties of dislikable conditions of life, but for the project of developing what might be called "socially engaged Buddhist economics," our focus is on the kinds suffering that are of our own creation through economic production and consumption.

A consistent theme in the work of many socially engaged Buddhists that I have studied is that much of our troubles are traceable to the Three Fires: greed, hatred, and delusion.

In a society captured by greed, it is as if everyone has an internal voice in their head that keeps repeating, "more, more, not enough, faster, newer, better, more." The chase is never ending, and leaves us with a deepening sense of dissatisfaction, which eventually cuts us away from authentic wellbeing. As Zen master, poet, and author, Thich Nhat Hanh, reminds us, "you probably have a notion that there's some as yet unrealized condition that has to be attained before you can be happy… a promotion or income level. But that notion may be the very thing that prevents you from being happy." For Nhat Hanh, the first step to be taken toward wellbeing is fostering mindful awareness, "To release that notion and make space for true happiness to manifest, you first have to experience the truth that entertaining your current ideas is making you suffer." (Nhat Hanh, 2015:71) This kind of suffering, which arises from being trapped by such habits of thought and behavior that leaves us grasping continuously for more, is often depicted in Buddhist literature as the Realm of Hungry Ghosts.

In some interpretations, the Realm of Hungry Ghosts is a mythological place where people languish in a kind of hellish world of discontent. In this realm, each is trapped in a state of escalating cravings that will never be satisfied. Here people are captured by their compulsions to chase after what seems to be an illusory "good life," only to experience these fleeting moments of joy that are soon overshadowed by the heavy feelings that things are never good enough. Physician and author, Gabor Maté refers to this realm as the domain of addiction, "where we constantly seek something outside ourselves to curb an insatiable yearning for relief or fulfillment."(Maté, 2008:1-3) Maté sees contemporary Western culture, particularly in the United States, as awash with addictions: to drugs, alcohol, food, cell phones, computers, sex,and not least of which to consuming, shopping, and gambling. This condition is, of course, is not exclusive to Americans, but how can it be that so many people are captured by these afflictions?

Ken Jones, one of the pioneers of socially engaged Buddhism in the UK, notes that much of this pathology originates from the troubled conditions wrapped up in our individual sense of self, the ego. In this view, the human ego is something that is potentially constructed, sometimes monumentally so, out of fear. For many of us, we fear that if we do not have a prominent and oversized self we become, in a sense, nothing. And fear of nothingness or emptiness is tantamount to a fear of death. For Jones, people are thus compelled to aggrandize a kind of fictional self and form an attachment to it. (Jones, 2003:38)As we become self-attached, we are grasping on to a figment of our imagination like identifying with a character in a movie. A deep sense of dissatisfaction looms as we try to constantly affirm this fabricated self. It is like trying to fill a hole that cannot be filled and feeling eternally frustrated because the more we try to fill the imagined hole, the more we realize it is a bottomless pit. For Jones and others, this is where many of our troublesoriginate.

Paradoxically as we try to feel more alive in this manner, we go out of our way to mask who we really are. We cling and grasp on to impermanent, illusory things, feelings, and sensations that we believe will affirm our ego. We become figment-attached, which can only serve to make us feel even more vulnerable and thus strengthening a resolve to reject anything that seems to pose a threat—the fires of hatred, or aggression and delusion are thus inseparable from the flames of greed.

All of this begins to take on a life of its own and a sense of vulnerability builds; we cling, grasp, and covet out of worry that if we stop, everything will fall to pieces. It is almost as if the clinging itself is what makes us feel alive. On this Ken Jones notes that, "Liberation from our sense of lack is impossible as long as we evade accepting it's ultimately ego-created nature and instead go on trying to fill the imagined hole by top-loading our lives and the world with ego-affirming behavior that is needless, ineffective, and destructive." (Jones, 2003:3)

Perhaps nowhere is this more evident than in the relationships people have with money and material wealth. Jungian psychologist and financial analyst, Deborah Gregory, looks at this from the view of modern psychology and draws the same conclusions, "... when examined on the unconscious level from a psychoanalytic perspective... greed is being driven by an inner need to accumulate money... the compulsion to amass wealth is akin to an empty hole that will need continual filling." (Gregory, 2014:40) Compulsions lead to craving and hoarding and chronic dissatisfaction.

Stepping back and taking a holistic view, we can see the defilements of greed, hatred, and delusion extended beyond the individual. The realm of hungry ghosts is just that: a realm. The existence of suffering is connected to the fearful ego as well as societal conditioning. Thus, to find the root causes of our pathological system conditions, we have to look both inwardly and deeply into ourselves as well as outwardly to the conditions of our surroundings. There is much suffering that originates from the troubled conditions wrapped up in our individual sense of self, the ego, and just the same from the defiled conditions embodied in our social structures.

Zen master, Philip Kapleau, teaches us that the process of changing society first begins with work on the self, but remaining mindfully present with affecting social change, "To help people without hurting them at the same time, or hurting yourself, means that we must first work on ourselves." He uses the term *middle way* as a kind of metaphor, "A Middle Way that alternates between the life of inward meditation and the life of action-in-the-world… "(Kapleau, 2000:244)

Another Zen teacher and scholar, David Loy, has often pointed out that greed is not just a human emotion; it is an institutionalized force within the global economy, he tells us that "our economic system institutionalizes greed in at least two ways: corporations are never profitable enough and people never consume enough." (Loy, 2008:3)

In their endless drive for profits, corporations exert influence that in many ways spread the fires of greed and delusion around the world with an emphasis on conquering markets and the dispersion American-style consumerism. From this phenomenon, pathology appears inevitable. The more people are motived by the three fires, the more they feel they must manipulate their surroundings to get what they want. Manipulative behavior inevitably leads to feelings of alienation as each individual begins to see how they are being manipulated by others. Society becomes awash in mutual distrust, jealousy, and prejudiced hostility toward others. Recent studies in psychological pathology indicate that societies everywhere are moving in the direction of permitting, reinforcing, and actually valuing some of the traits listed in the "psychopathy checklist" including traits such as impulsivity, irresponsibility, and lack of remorse. In short, we make ourselves and those around us miserable. Loy concludes that, "…the problem is not only that the [three fires] operate collectively but that they have taken a life of their own." (Loy, 2008:89)

In light of this, Philip Kapleau writes about the widespread suffering that is created in our economic society, "Capitalist industrial society has created [among the human population] conditions of extreme impermanence, terrifying insubstantiality, and a struggling dissatisfaction and frustration. It would be difficult to imagine any social order for which Buddhism was more relevant and needed." (Kapleau, 2000:244) Loy similarly makes this case succinctly, "Buddhism can provide what the modern world most needs: the spiritual message that may yet awaken us to who we are and why we as a species have such a penchant for making ourselves unhappy." (Loy, 2008:3) Perhaps, therefore, a good first step toward a more mindful and sustainable economy is to go back to the fundamentals.

4. Mindful Economics and Social Provisioning

One of the things I emphasize in my own writings is that an authentic economic system should exist for the purpose of social provisioning: mobilizing resources to provide food, housing, health care, education, security in retirement, and all the other things required to sustain ahealthy population. Being mindful of this is at the very core of what I call Mindful Economics.

If people seek to have an economic society grounded in social provisioning, then this would require an established set of economic institutions that hold such provisioning as a priority. Mindfulness can help as a kind of reality check, by observing and constantly asking the very pragmatic question: *Is what we are doing in our economy helpful for social provisioning? If not, then why we are doing it?*

The pragmatic vision of American philosopher, John Dewey, is valuable in this regard as he set out to build a philosophy based on a foundation of social action put in the service of humanity. Dewey makes a case for human social behavior that springs from an existential drive, not for ego-aggrandizement, but to shape the world around them in positive ways. As people follow this drive and become engaged in social development, they can create better social structures that advance social intelligence and foster the development of education, art, health, technology, and purposeful economic activity. By doing so, communities pursue a pragmatic path towards creating opportunities for individuals to develop their own unique powers and capabilities. These powers and capabilities, in turn, will allow a person to become an effective participant in the life of the community, and can advance the project of building institutions that provide for their wellbeing. In this way, communities and the individuals who live in them coevolve. (Gruchy, 1972:127)

In this evolutionary process, everything is constantly changing. Through a course of karmic volition, we have inherited a responsibility to give shape to this process of change toward authentic wellbeing. Recall that Philip Kapleau emphasized that we must follow a middle way that alternates between the life of inward meditation and the life of action-in-the-world, one existing as a dialectic reflection of the other. Recall also that the Buddha stated succinctly that, "If you act with a corrupt mind, suffering will follow. ... If you act with a peaceful mind, peace will follow." (Sivaraksa, 2018:19) Extending the logic of this to the social realm would be to say *if you act with a corrupt mind, social institutions become corrupt, and widespread suffering will follow; if you act with a peaceful mind, social institutions become peaceful, and widespread peace will follow.*

In an article titled, "The Realism of Applying Dharma to Situations of Conflict," activist John McConnell argues that a dharma practice "... is not a set of dogma to be believed, but a way of beginning, here and now, with the mess we have made of our lives, and turning things around." (McConnell, 1999:315)

Can we see such dharma action in the world economically?

5. "New Economics": Same Wine Different Bottles?

For decades we have seen one economic initiative after another stepping forward promising to turn our social and environmental messes around. In the mid-nineteen-eighties, for example, a group of scholars convened for two conferences aimed at building a "New Economics" paradigm. The first was held in London, England in 1984 and the second, was held in Bonn, Germany the following year. The goals set out for the new paradigm were to develop and promote an economic system that is centered on social justice, the satisfaction of a wide range of human needs, sustainable use of resources, and environmental conservation. The meetings were called The Other Economic Summit (TOES) to symbolize a clean break from the business-as- usual Group of Seven meetings or World Economic Forums. TOES addressed a spectrum of economic issues that were becoming increasingly exigent such as the problem of trying to achieve endless economic growth within the confines of a finite planet, the widening income and wealth gap between the world's rich and poor, the need for economic indicators that could better assess human wellbeing than gross domestic product (GDP), chronic unemployment, access to education and health care services for the world's population, alternative business models, alternative systems of finance and trade, gender equality, and tax policies. The conference presentations were compiled, edited by conference organizer and economist Paul Ekins, and a year later published in a book titled, *The Living Economy: A New Economics in the Making* (1986).

This was followed by a host of a new economics proposals. Among the pioneers were Paul Hawken, Frances Cairncross, Amory and Hunter L. Lovins, Jonathan Porrit, Lester R. Brown, James "Gus" Speth, and others. Of the next two decades the like-minded economists launched a library of information in books: *Costing the Earth* (1992), *Ecological Commerce* (1993), *Natural Capitalism* (1999), *Eco-Economy* (2001), *Capitalism as if the World Mattered* (2005), and the *Green Collar Economy* (2009).

The core message in all this work is summarized by Yale economist and founder of the National Resource Defense Council, Gus Speth, as an articulation of the notion that "the market can be transformed into an instrument for environmental restoration; the incentives that govern corporate behavior can be rewritten; growth can be focused on things that truly need to grow and consumption on having enough, not always more; and the rights of future generations and other species can be respected." (Speth, 2009:12)

As this "new economics" vision continued to gain momentum, market-oriented eco- entrepreneurship expanded with differentiated green product identities, conventional products were rebranded as to be seen as sustainable to stay ahead of market saturation. At the same time there was an explosion of socially responsible investment funds, or SRIs, which later morphed into impact investing.

In the last decade or so, B Corporations have become a promising business model in the US. B Corporations are business models based on the principle that a corporate entity can be a blank slate and its charter can be written to be a force for social and environmental change; that is, a business that is also a force for social equity and environmental sustainability.

Similarly, among the most recent and compelling developments in the "new economics" movement in the US is an initiative spearheaded by The Sustainable Accounting Standards Board and The Climate Disclosure Standards Board. These are non-profit organizations working to provide material information for investors and financial markets through the integration of sustainability and climate change-related information into mainstream financial reporting of publicly traded corporations. In other words, they are trying to place climate and sustainability practices on equal footing as the corporate bottom line. This initiative is largely in response to what they perceive as a shifting attitude among investors, particularly professional asset managers. Institutional investors are increasingly getting pressured by their clients to find investment funds that do good and do well. As such, they are pushing for new reporting and accounting standards that will be binding for all publicly traded corporations, and to make their track records transparent to investors.

"Do good and do well" has been the mantra, and corporations, investors, and consumers alike found it irresistible. Workers were promised that now in addition to becoming information workers, they were also going to secure lucrative green collar jobs. As they make big money, they green collar professionals can afford to buy high end organic, sustainable, certified consumer goods, and the businesses that successfully market those goods will be plowing their profits back into even greener economic development. Everybody wins: producers make profits, investors get big returns, workers get jobs, and consumers save the planet by shopping conscientiously.

But is any of this really working? How do we test the veracity of these initiatives in terms of authentic social provisioning? This has been going on for four decades and the data supporting the Sustainable Development Goals, particularly #10 reducing inequality and #13 climate action, are showing a bleak picture--economic inequality is becoming more polarized and climate change more severe. Recall that the IPCC last year made its final call for large-scalesystems transitions that are "unprecedented in terms of scale" in the next decade.

All of these "new economics" initiatives over the last 30 years are very positive and doubtless are contributing, in some way or another, to a better world. But the central problem with this movement, it seems to me, is that these initiatives continue to be forged in the same cauldron of greed and delusion as were the corporations that have brought us to the brink of annihilation.

Jeanne and Dick Roy, founders of the Northwest Earth Institute, warned us about corporate greenwashing and question the veracity of businesses claims of sustainability. The Roys assert that there is asymmetry between the goals of shareholder responsibility and true sustainability. The result, the Roys write in their newsletter, is what they call "sustainability lite" or a half-hearted approach to sustainability. The Roys quote an executive with a typical business-oriented approach to sustainable practices: "I am an advocate of sustainable practices so long as they increase the bottom line. Otherwise, how would I sell this approach to management." Jeanne and Dick Roy, 2012:1-2) Green capitalism guru, Paul Hawken, also warned that the allure do-good-and-do-well economics is leading to "…the dumbing down of criteria and the blurring of distinctions between what is, or is not, a socially responsible company."

This fiduciary responsibility to shareholder value is sovereign in the corporate capitalist world. If the Three Es of sustainable business—economy, equity, ecology—are like a three-legged stool in which the "do well" leg is much longer than the other two "do good" legs, and it is virtually impossible for a corporation to cut the other two legs down to match. Corporate executives are most likely to give a salute to sustainable practices, but if these do not result in handsome bottom line returns, they'll likely pass.

It is for this reason that I turn to a completely different model developed by Roshi Bernie Glassman.

6. Roshi Bernie Glassman and the Greyston Mandala

Formerly a mathematician at McDonnell-Douglas corporation Bernie Glassman quit his lucrative job and turned to Buddhism. After becoming ordained in the Soto Zen Buddhist tradition in 1976, Glassman sought to build a particular brand of Buddhism that holds social engagement and social transformation to be as important as self-work and personal transformation. He became one of the founders of the Zen Center of Los Angeles. Perhaps most notably in terms of social change, however, is the Greyston projects he started after moving from Los Angeles to New York in the early1980s.

He developed a distinguishing style of engaged Buddhism based on, "… the creative use of traditional Buddhist metaphors and images… and the emergence of a distinctive new dharma of social service." For Glassman, meditation is an exercise in cultivating what he calls "bearing witness" as a kind of window to the wholeness of life, without judgement or preconception. It is a process of dissolving attachments in the ego-based mind, letting go of preconceived notions, and simply being. (Glassman, 1996:59-60)

Glassman found inspiration from earliest Zen masters who started placing more emphasis on daily chores. The Zen tradition began taking on a new element involving meditation not only when sitting on the cushion, but also when engaged in the tasks of everyday working life. The work itself became a kind of meditation or mindfulness practice. For Glassman, this extended to a business enterprise with Buddhist guidelines—from right mindfulness to right livelihood—to serve both as a way to support a Zen community and to positively affect social change through authentic social provisioning.

In 1982, Glassman originally opened Greyston Bakery in The Bronx, New York (five years later relocated in Yonkers). The idea of the bakery was to create a business that could support a growing community, provide training and opportunities for personal growth and spiritual transformation, and to help alleviate homelessness among the underprivileged. Glassman notes, "As a Zen community, we didn't want to engage in anything that fell outside the Buddhist definition of right livelihood. We didn't want to produce anything that would harm people.... In terms of social action, we needed a labor-intensive business that could create jobs for a lot of people." (Ibid)

Greyston continues now as a for-profit social enterprise and became the first Certified B Corporation in the state of New York. Instead of profits going to some absentee owners' pockets as would be the case of a standard C corporation, they go to the Greyston foundation to help fund social progress. As a social enterprise, Greyston pursues multiple objectives: providing baked goods for consumers and other businesses, employment, job skills and training as an anti-poverty measure, and an "open door" hiring system. According to their website, they have open door hiring policy geared toward offering employment opportunities regardless of educational attainment, work history, or past social barriers such as incarceration, homelessness, or drug use.

7. Conclusion

As we begin to feel these pathological system conditions around us, we will be forced to re-examine what we consider to be the good life. Many of us in the so-called developed world have high expectations for our career choices, our levels of income, the things we want to buy, and all the other accoutrements of a plentiful lifestyle. But this is all beginning to change.

The choices we make today as we adapt to mounting scarcity may be the most important historical events of the 21st century. We can choose to be forward thinking and work actively toward positive changes in a spirit of celebration and make this transformation in ways that are healthy, ecologically sound, economically stable, and just. Or, we can choose to be complacent, to continue treating our world as an infinite resource pipeline and an infinite waste dump, to brace ourselves for endless wars over resources, and to trudge through one debilitating crisis after another, pushing all of humanity through a long historical period of decline—a descent into a kind of Dark Ages of the third millennium. This would be a tragic downfall for humankind,but the ultimate cause of our downfall would not be the crises themselves. The cause of our downfall would be our refusal to deal with the obvious fact that the age of fossil fuels is coming to an end.

In closing, we can be hopeful that Kapleau's middle way of dharma practice—both the inner work liberating ourselves and the outer work of transforming our communities will be the path toward an authentically mindful economy. Possibly the "Right Livelihood" of Glassman is the missing piece that can be added to the economic mix and help move us in another direction.

References

Ekins, Paul , ed., *The Living Economy: A New Economics in the Making*, (NY: Routledge, 1986).

Jones, Ken, *The New Social Face of Buddhism: An Alternative Sociopolitical Perspective* (Boston: Wisdom Publications, 2003).

Glassman, Bernard and Fields, Rick, *Instructions to the Cook: A Zen Master's Lessons in Living a Life That Matters* (NY: Bell Tower, 1996).

Gregory, Deborah, *Unmasking Financial Psychopaths: Inside the Minds of Investors in the Twenty-first Century*, (NY: Palgrave Macmillan, 2014).

Gruchy, Allan, *Contemporary Economic Thought: The Contribution of Neo-Institutional Economics*, (Clifton, NJ: Augustus M. Kelley, 1972).

Intergovernmental Panel on Climate Change (IPCC), "Special Report on Global warming of 1.5°C: Summary for Policymakers," (October, 2018), http://www.ipcc.ch/.

Kapleau, Philip, *The Three Pillars of Zen* (NY: Doubleday, 1980). "Responsibility and Social Action," in *Dharma Rain: Sources of Buddhist Environmentalism*, Stephanie Kaza and Kenneth Kraft, eds., (Boston: Shambala, 2000).

Loy, David, *Money, Sex, War, Karma: Notes for a Buddhist Revolution*, (Boston, MA: Wisdom, 2008).

Maté, Gabor, *In the Realm of Hungry Ghosts: Close Encounters with Addiction* (Berkely, CA: North Atlantic Books, 2008).

McConnel, John, "The Realism of Applying Damma to Situations of Conflict, in *Socially Engaged Buddhism for the New Millennium, Socially Engaged Buddhism for the New Millennium*, (Bangkok, Thailand: The Sathirakoses-Nagapradipa Foundation, 1999).

National Oceanic and Atmospheric Administration, Climate Change, "CO2 Breaks Record in 2017," https://www.climate.gov/news-features/

understanding-climate/climate-change-atmospheric-carbon-dioxide.

Nhat Hanh, Thich, Silence: The Power of Quiet in a World Full of Noise (NY: Harper Collins, 2015).

Roy, Jeanne and Dick, "Deep Sustainability" in *Earth Matters: The Newsletter of the Northwest Earth Institute*, 12, No.1.

Sivaraksa, Sulak, *The Wisdom of Sustainability: Buddhist Economics for the 21st Century,* (Kihei, HI: Koa Books, 2018).

Speth, James Gustave, *Bridge at the End of the World*, (New Haven, CT: Yale University Press, 2009).

Applying Buddhist Principles to Managing People and Organizations in the Public, Private and Nonprofit Workplaces

Frances Berry

Professor, Askew School of Public Administration and Policy, Florida State University
Presented at the Buddhism and Social Sciences Conference commemorating the Tenth Anniversary of
Master Sheng Yen's Passing; June 29th at Dharma Drum Mountain in Jingshan, Taiwan

1. Introduction

I am very grateful to be attending the 2019 International Conference on Buddhism and Social Science in Commemoration of the 10th Anniversary of Master Sheng Yen's Passing, and deeply honored to be asked to give this morning's keynote address. I also feel humbled and inadequate to be speaking on such a complex topic, when I am but a beginner in Buddhist studies. So please forgive my errors, and remember the Buddha's four reliances: (1) Rely on the Dharma, not the person; (2) Rely on the meaning, not just on the words, (3) Rely on the real or ultimate truth, not on the conventional truth, and (4) Rely on wisdom, not on ordinary, intellect.

This talk is a journey into exploring management using Buddhist principles and making some brief comparisons to western management principles. I presented the four reliances as good advice as we listen and reflect, but also thinking that between three and four, we should rely on "practical wisdom as opposed to theories". And since much of my talk is presenting Master Sheng Yen's practical wisdom on management, we are in good hands. Let me briefly outline what I will discuss today. In the first section, I will provide a brief overview of modern private and public sector leadership principles and approaches. Next I will present Buddhist management principles as Master Sheng Yen wrote about them, as well as some writings from Chan Masters in the Song Dynasty (translated into English in the book *Zen Lessons: The art of Leadership*). I am presenting these as written and not paraphrasing them in my own words. And to conclude, I will summarize and make some comparisons between Buddhist and western leadership principles.

2. Management in Today's World

Leadership and management of complex organizations is an essential part of modern life. Whether the organizations be universities, hospitals, government agencies, monasteries, charities for disaster relief or the United Nations, each organization develops structures, institutions, rules and guidelines to accomplish their missions and work. Management is required wherever two or more people work together to achieve common objectives. President Roosevelt of the U.S.A. once said: "a government without good management is a house built on sand." The implication is that an organization can have plenty of money, staff, and good services, but without good management and leadership, it will not be effective. And master Sheng Yen has said that "to build a sangha, an institutional structure (Jhi du) definitely needs to be established".

Leadership and management can be viewed as the process of uniting people in the organization behind a common mission and common values, so they willingly commit to following rules that benefit the organization, the individuals in the organization, the broader community and beyond. But when working in bureaucracies, staff may feel they are restricted and coerced rather than voluntarily following rules and procedures. In a world where people living in democratic societies expect civil liberties and some personal freedom, there is tension between rigid bureaucracies and personal discretion. How to harmonize organizational rules and discretion for individual workers within that organization is a central question and role for leadership.

As a management scholar, I am surprised that there has not been more written on Buddhism and management, but this may be my shortcoming, in that I do not read Mandarin, and perhaps it is largely Chinese scholars who are writing on this topic. Over the past two decades there has been more study on spirituality in the work place among western social scientists. The *Journal of Management, Spirituality & Religion* is now fifteen years old, and publishes articles on how to measure spirituality in the workplace, workplace spirituality and employee engagement, and the impact of meditation on workplace productivity. To give you a short conclusion, there is some positive impact when workers practice meditation at the workplace, but primarily the practice helps workers feel more satisfied with their workplace, rather than being more productive. But I have not seen an article in this journal on how to lead and manage using Buddhist principles.

Leadership in Western Management Studies

In the earliest American public administration textbook published by Luther Gulick in the 1930s, the principles of management were captured in the acronym PODSCORB which stands for Planning, Organizing, Directing, Staffing, Coordinating, Reporting and Budgeting. Strategic management in the 1980s and beyond incorporated the important tasks of developing relationships with external stakeholders, and developing intelligence on the organization's environment to counter threats and weaknesses related to the organization, and to promote the organization's strengths and opportunities. Mark Moore (1995) emphasizes that strategic management is about adding value to what governments (or organizations) do for their citizens and communities, which requires plans, measures and capacity to deliver those plans through implementation. In the 1990s and beyond, management became evidence-based, with performance measures capturing program outputs and outcomes (de lancer Jules, et.al., 2007).

In the past sixty years, western leadership studies have gone through stages identifying what is leadership and how to be a leader. Early leadership studies focused on personal personality characteristics like being outgoing or extroverted, being decisive and willing to take risks, having charisma but by the 1990s leadership research was much more focused on behavioral functions, consisting of roles and world views that the leader uses to inspire, focus and motivate her staff and workers. Warren Bennis distinguished between leadership and management penning such pithy statements as "Leaders do the right thing, managers do things right; *The manager relies on **control**; the leader inspires **trust**. The manager has a **short-range view**; the leader has a **long-range perspective**....*

Master Sheng Yen in a writing I'll read shortly, does distinguish between a manager, and the boss (presumably not referring to managing the Sangha, but managing in ordinary government or corporate agencies. And we all understand that within a bureaucratic agency, and most of the organizations in the world are still largely structured using a bureaucratic model, people at the higher levels are primary decision makers for the organization. And senior managers need to be leaders on a more regular basis than mid-level managers or below.

But for my talk today, I am using the terms leader and manager interchangably, and will use the word leader and leadership throughout my talk to represent management and leadership.

And let me underscore, the term "leadership" in modern management applies not JUST to the top leader of an organization, but to behaviors that people at all levels of the organization can exhibit. In modern leadership textbooks, the theme is that each person can be a leader in their own work department, at any and all levels of work units in an organization. Although, in truth, primary leadership is still be centered near the top of the organization.

So for this talk today, I am merging leadership and management as one function, except when they must be differentiated. And I am adopting the modern management **notion that everyone can be a**

leader in whatever job and role they serve, because leadership is primarily based on behaviors and attitudes, and these can be learned by everyone.

In 1990, James Kouzes and Barry Posner wrote the book *The Leadership Challenge: How to Get Extraordinary Things Done in Organizations*. This book has become the best selling management book of all times in North America. They lay out five principles and roles that leaders should perform to help their organization be successful:

Fist, Leaders Need to Challenge the Process. This means they confront the status quo, look for opportunities to change and innovate to improve the organization, and are willing to experiment and take risks.

Second, Leaders must Inspire a Shared Vision, both laying out ideal scenarios for the organization's future, and also enlisting organizational members to support and carry out that vision.

Third, Leaders Enable Others to Act. They encourage collaboration, and they share power and information so all members of the organization know what they need to know in order to carry out their roles. Leaders also support discretion for workers to achieve their tasks.

Fourth, Leaders Model the Way. They lead by doing and setting an example, and they create small wins that show how the vision and mission can be carried out well.

Fifth, Leaders Encourage the Heart. They demonstrate emotional intelligence and personal caring for the staff. They recognize contributions and reward good performance. They have celebrations to recognize organizational accomplishments.

A second bestselling management and professional development books is *The 7 Habits of Highly Effective People by Steven Covey*. His seven habits include:

Habit 1: Begin with the End in Mind. Envision what you want in the future so you can work and plan towards it.

Habit 2: Be Proactive. Don't sit and wait in a reactive mode, waiting for problems to happen or resolve themselves before taking action.

Habit 3: Put First Things First. Leadership in the outside world begins with personal vision and personal leadership. A leader must tackle important and urgent priorities first, and leave unimportant and not urgent things for last.

Habit 4: Think Win/Win Genuine feelings for mutually beneficial solutions or agreements in your relationships. Value and respect people by understanding a "win" for all is ultimately a better long-term resolution than if only one person in the situation had gotten their way.

Habit 5: Seek First to Understand, Then to Be Understood. Use empathetic listening to genuinely understand a person, which compels them to reciprocate the listening and take an open mind to being influenced by you. This creates an atmosphere of caring, and positive problem solving ...

Habit 6: Synergize. Combine the strengths of people through positive teamwork, so as to achieve goals that no one could have done alone.

Habit 7: Sharpen the Saw *means* preserving and enhancing the greatest asset you have—you. It *means* having a balanced program for self-renewal in the four areas of your life: physical, social/emotional, mental, and spiritual.

These two books capture the strategic and participatory principles of leadership in large public and private organizations.

So to summarize, western management in the last thirty years has emphasized that leaders must help define a vision and mission for the organization, be proactive and confront the status quo that is not working well, encourage collaboration and team work; set a good example, or as management lingo goes—"They walk their Talk". And yes, there is some attention to caring for people and listening as well as being a decision maker.

But one difference is that caring for others in a supportive environment is NOT the first or most important principle of western management. And finally, Mr. Covey recognizes that we all need to keep a good balance of physical, mental and spiritual health.

Servant Leadership

A final paradigm of western management is Servant Leadership, created by Robert Greenleaf. His motto was: Seek to serve others rather than yourself. In Servant Leadership, a key function of leaders is to create community in the organization. Communities are characterized by social interaction, a sense of shared place, and common bonds. In this kind of community, citizens and public servants or leaders have mutual responsibility for identifying problems and implementing solutions. The absence of these community attributes contribute to self-interested and impersonal relationships between people.

Servant leadership is concerned with focusing human energy on projects that benefit humanity. Leaders do not primarily use financial incentives to get people engaged in their work. Leadership is not just seen as a prerogative of those in high office, but as a function that extends throughout groups, organizations and societies. ❶

3. Leadership in Buddhist Writings

As I understand history, in Shakyamani Buddhas's time, there

---

❶ "Leadership is no longer about telling People what to do. Instead, leadership, whether it comes from a person in a position of formal authority or from a person with little formal authority, "is concerned with aiding a group, an organization or a community in recognizing its own vision and then learning how to move in a new direction." (Heifetz, 2017)

was little structure or formal organization to manage the followers of the Buddha; nuns and monks lived simply often out in the forests, and while the Buddha taught extensively, he did not try to build a management structure or even an organization. The Buddha himself, did not act as a CEO or President of an organization to manage the community. Of course, one can speculate that the Precepts developed for monks and nuns were a management tool to help people lead virtuous lives, and to give individuals the tools to distinguish what to do and what to avoid. Interestingly, very few rules were developed to apply at the community (or group level) besides the monastic precepts. This suggests the view was that individuals would manage their own minds and actions, and could be outcast from the Sangha if they broke precepts. And community was dependent on individuals regulating themselves, based on precepts and community norms, rather than on a "boss" or a judge who embodied the laws and official pronouncements.

The Art of Leadership in the Book Zen Lessons

As Buddhism flourished, and Bodhidharma brought Chan to China by the sixth century CE. monasteries were constructed; hierarchical structures and rules and leaders, such as Abbott Presidents for Buddhist monasteries were developed and put into place.

In the Book *Zen Lessons: The Art of Leadership*, there are short writings from Chan masters of the Song dynasty (tenth to thirteenth century) on leadership and responsiveness to the community and Buddhist practitioners. One lesson on leadership I particularly like is written by Master Fushan Yuan in a letter to Master Jungyin Tai:

> "There are three essentials to leadership: humanity, clarity and courage. Humanely practicing the virtues of the Way promotes the influence of the teaching, pacifies those in both high and low positions, and delights those who pass by.
> Someone with clarity follows proper behavior and just duty, recognizes what is safe and what is dangerous,

examines people to see whether they are wise or foolish, and distinguishes right and wrong.

The courageous see things through to their conclusion, settling them without doubt. They get rid of whatever is wrong or false.

Humanity without clarity is like having a field but not plowing it. Clarity without courage is like having eyes but no legs to walk on. Courage without humanity is like knowing how to reap but not how to sow.

When all three of these are present, the community thrives. When one is lacking, the community deteriorates. When two are lacking, the community is in peril, and when there is not one of the three, the way of leadership is in ruins." (Cleary, 1989, 8-10)

Chan Master Fushan Yuan also wrote: " The leader, who is in a position overseeing others, should be humble and respectful in dealing with subordinates. If the leader is proud and haughty, and subordinates are lazy and personally careless, the minds of those above and below do not communicate. Then the path of leadership is blocked." (Cleary, 1989, 10)

Considering the Qualities of a Good and a Bad Manager

Master Sheng Yen in the book *Zen and Inner Peace*, Volume 1 has a short section on Being a Good Manager, and he begins by saying:

"The worst kind of manager is one who fawns on the boss and tyrannises the people beneath him. He takes all the credit for work done by the people under him and blames them when he makes a mistake. When he is given work from above, he passes the entire load to the subordinates and lets them take the responsibility. When they do well, he takes credit; when they perform poorly, it's their fault. When his superiors have a problem to solve, and ask him for suggestions, he is unable to contribute any wisdom. He only says, 'Boss, your thoughts, your opinions, and your perspectives are remarkable and farsighted. You have great wisdom.'

"What kind of managers do well that wise bosses like? Those who are able to offer precious advice, those who save the boss from having to wrack his brains, and allow him simply to have a firm grasp of company policies and strategic principles. The boss is not responsible for the methods involved. He does not need to tell you how to do it. The boss tells you what he wants. This is the best kind of boss." (p. 141)

What is a good manager? Master Sheng Yen writes:

"A mid-level manager is the one who does the planning for the boss. He devises strategies, does research, implements plans, then allocates and delegates the work carefully. After he allocates the work for the different levels under him, he must coordinate and harmonize the lateral relations of the departments, and provide a working systems for the company's hierarchy. He solves all problems and is caring toward everyone, all the employees. He understands and is in control of every issue, knows clearly the details of those issues. This kind of manager is the best kind of manager."

"When the boss needs advice, this kind of manager is very frank and very meticulous in analyzing things for the boss, reporting to the boss, and asking the boss for instructions. My principle is that a manager should ask for instructions beforehand specifically regarding general guidelines. After everything is done, he should make a report, which includes just the key points. If one can demonstrate these positive qualities, then one may become upper management. He can become the boss of a company; he can lead a country. He knows how to choose talented people. He knows how to train people. As for the business, he knows how to manage it. I have never studied management, so my guideline has been the principles I use to run a monastery, and care for its entirety using the Dharma."

Six Essentials of Management, as written by Master Sheng Yen

(1) Stick to the principle: The principle refers to the principle for the entire group, not that of individuals. While each of us may be able to fully contribute our talents and views, we must go by the group principle and work together so that we will not go astray.

(2) Delegate fully: The delegation is a relationship between superiors and subordinates. For those in superior positions, they must fully delegate jobs so that their subordinates can perform well. Conversely, if managers intervene in and command on everything, the lack of discretion among their subordinates may cause inefficiency and stagnation in performance.

(3) Respect others: People must be respectful and grateful to each other. It also applies to the top managers when they are interacting with subordinates.

Respect is different from sympathy. To respect someone, we are first respecting their thoughts, views, and personality. If people are not allowed to have their own views and thoughts, they are unlikely to have a sense of accomplishment at work. Therefore, do not insist other people to do things in our own way, as long as they do no harm to the group and accomplish their tasks. Second, we should have respect to others. Everyone has different capacity, with regard to their basic, learning ability and adaptability. People vary in their abilities and it is unreasonable to request them to be as capable as us. Even if someone does not perform well, we still need to have respect toward him once he is hired. Even if his work attitude is not compatible with us, we shall not bad mouth at him, as this is a fundamental and genuine respect towards others.

(4) Care for Others: Caring others is not limited to work but also extending proper care for people's emotional, physical and

mental wellbeing, and their families. Always take the initiative to care for others because our greeting and comfort may help release their entanglement. As a superior, one needs to be aware of employees' emotions and render care. A superior must avoid caring for only a small group of people and neglecting others. If not, others will feel being treated unequally.

(5) Initiate communication: When communicating with our superiors, subordinates, and peers, active communication is always valuable. Here, the word "active" is important since we are not supposed to passively wait for other people to start the conversation. It is recommended to have well-thought plans, including foreseeing any potential challenges, and developing feasible solutions and alternatives before we start communicating. This is different from throwing a problem to others for solutions. The latter can easily create conflicts and is not at all conducive to accomplishing a task. Even worse, it upsets people by making them disappointed in the work , encountering obstacles all over and having doubts on their colleagues, and eventually losing the harmony of the group.

To complete our jobs, we must work actively, have respectand communicate with others. ...Then it is about time to change our perspective or change our mind. Do not hold on tightly to the original idea and not willing to give up or make change.

Even in the worst case when finding no way out, there is still one last option, that is, to accept the dead end. Accepting the dead end is itself an option. If the problem is inevitable and unsolvable, facing reality with a brave heart may alleviate our suffering.

(6) By "review," we are talking about self-reflection but not accusing others. We should keep reviewing ourselves on occasions when facing a miscommunication problem, a work failure, an unfair treatment, a liability that does not belong to us. Do these occasions have anything to do with our own mistakes? That said, if self-reflection and continuous communication does not help us get out of these occasions, we can seek help from our supervisor. When our supervisor does not agree with us and, consequently,

cannot provide solution, we should try to understand and forgive other people. After all, they are our colleagues who work and grow together in the group.

These six principles seem to have universal application for managers, going beyond the monastic walls to apply in any public, nonprofit or private organization. We can imaging that Master Sheng Yen covered these principles in his discussion and advice giving to corporate and government leaders.

The Practical Advice on Leadership and Management from Master Sheng Yen

While in the first quotes from Master Sheng Yen, he describes in detail the good and bad qualities, and roles of a manager. He is not applying his management principles specifically to the management of Dharma Drum Mountain. In his later years, Sheng Yen also wrote extensively about management and leadership, both because he was advising political and corporate leaders, and also to share his management wisdom with leaders of DDM for when he was no longer alive to give advice. These are powerful and direct writings on how we should conduct ourselves in the Sangha. While his words were primarily written for monastics in the monastic Sangha community, I believe Master Sheng Yen's practical advice on leadership and management applies in the lay community also. And for us who are lay practitioners, I believe the words ring true and give us direction in our practice, whether it be work or personal life.

Given that these precious writings by Master Sheng Yen exist, I will quote extensively from them on various topics of leadership, so you can learn directly from his own work, without interpretation from me.

"The Sacred Zhi-shi, Management Staff, in the Sangha"
(*Dharma Drum Morning Talks* Chapter Five Section 1)

Zhi-shi, or management staff, in the Sangha community are appointed by the Abbot on behalf of the Sangha. Everyone in the Sangha has a function or job to manage or take care of a certain thing—the Abbot is no exception. Why is there a need for zhi-shi? It is because in every institution or group, when there is privilege to enjoy, there is an obligation to fulfill, a function or job. Hence, as long as there is a Sangha, all the monastics in it must take on certain management functions.

It does not matter what kind of job you do, whether it be big or small, they are all the results of cause and condition and your karma. You should accept it with a grateful, respectful and joyful mind. For those who have the functions above the basic management levels in the Sangha, you should use the opportunity to temper yourself, because it affords a great opportunity to make great contributions to the Three Jewels and it is an honorable opportunity which is difficult to come by.

When there is a problem and you think you are suffering, you should dissolve your vexation in your mind; however, the problem should still be presented to Sangha group for assistance. After discussions by several people, wisdom and methods will emerge and the problem can easily be resolved. This is also putting into practice the spirit of Sangha life—working with the Sangha, going with the flow of the Sangha, depending on the Sangha, and harmonizing with the Sangha.

The Mentalities that a Zhi-Shi Should Have (*Dharma Drum Morning Talks* Chapter Five Section 2)

Seng-zhi, monastic management staff, needs to have a concept of viewing our Sangha community as a whole, a sense of responsibility, a stable personality, a concept of timeliness, abilities to analyze and organize, and most importantly, the dao-xin (the Bodhi mind); without dao-xin, the person will merely be a staff in a business company, not a zhi-shi, management staff, among the monastics. Therefore, seng-zhi must possess the following five mentalities:

(1) Have a Concept of Viewing our Sangha Community as a Whole

The meaning of the "whole" includes all entities under the Dharma Drum Mountain organization, regardless whether it is the Sangha, the business units, the different units at this headquarter location, and the branches at other locations. All of these appear to be independent, but actually are related and in fact operated in accordance with Shifu's ideals and compassionate vows and centered on the Sangha. Hence, when we make decisions, we always take into considerations the entirety of Dharma Drum Mountain organization.

Always considering only your own view point will result in the isolation of yourself within your unit and tend to lead you to resist, reject, criticize, and produce demands on others, making it difficult to work with others harmoniously. This type of person either does not realize that everyone is so closely interrelated and thinks they can just do the work without regards to others, or thinks that he or she is the best and the busiest and works the hardest, and others just have it easy. The concept of viewing the organization as a whole is very important, as the saying, "A yanking of a single thread of the hair can jerk the entire body." We must recognize that each of us is a member of the Sangha and everyone is a representative of the organization; it is a duty and an honor as well.

(2) Have a Sense of Responsibility

When a person, who has a sense of responsibility, accepts a task, he would definitely finish it with his best efforts, because he would first evaluate his own ability, time, amounts and the nature of the work. Then, he would perform the work knowing his abilities and asking for support from others, when needed.

(3) Have a Sense of Timeliness

To complete the work, one must control the time. Besides attentive to the work at hand for the purpose of increasing efficiency, one could also use some modern tools, such as operational calendar, work planning chart and schedule chart, to control the time and progress.

(4) Have Abilities to Analyze and Organize

Having abilities to analyze and organize would enhance planning, without it would be difficult to achieve results with efficiency. Therefore, leadership and managerial level staff should cultivate the business planning capabilities of the junior staff, beginning from the simple job functions.

(5) Have Bodhi Mind

People without Bodhi mind always feel wronged, being a failure, having no alternative or no choice, angry, and not being able to settle down. Although one may be very able, but he can't help to whisper, "Been busy all days, but for whom and for what?" "Have done so much, but Shifu and Abbot don't even know. My fellow Sangha members never praise me, the superiors only demand more and show no appreciation. What I am doing this for?" "Forget it. After all, the monastics that don't do anything still got fed. Why should I work so hard?"

The ones with Bodhi mind understand that the zhi-shi today is working not for some individuals, but for the Sangha here now and monastics everywhere and for our own Dharma body and wisdom in life. It is the opportunity to build our merits, accumulate our good virtues, and cultivate our blessings and wisdom. We should do our utmost best.

Mutual Understanding among Zhi-shi—Harmony Is the Most Precious Thing Soft Touch Can Overcome Harshness, Harmony can make things work (*Dharma Drum Morning Talks* Chapter Five Section 3)

First, I should note that the meaning of "sangha" as pat of the three jewels is "community in harmony". So to take refuge in the sangha means to take refuge in harmony. To return to Shifu's words:" Sangha members can sometimes have differences of opinion or interpretation in annotating Shifu's ideals and the image of the Sangha as a whole. What should you do when encounter this situation? In fact, personalities of people can sometimes be categorized as gentle or strong. People with strong or harsh personality often seem to have the upper hand in the short term of a dispute, but the ones who can pacify people are always the gentle and harmonious ones, because gentleness or soft touch can overcome harshness and harmony can make things work. Every job in the Sangha must be carried out in harmony and. use respect to attain peace. If there is conflict and no coordination with each other, then the monastics' principles of harmony and respect would be violated."

There are two ways to resolve conflicts: first, one should fully understand the situation and if necessary, make some appropriate adjustment; next, one could invite both sides to talk it over and try to bring things into line. If there are certain dispute and argument, the coordinator must maintain neutral and keep an open mind to entertain the thoughts expressed. Try not to directly comment or criticize but give suggestions. Buddhadharma is kind and gentle, but firm.

The Principles and Methods of Carrying Out Management Functions (*Dharma Drum Morning Talks* Chapter Five Section 4)

Zhi-shi, management staff, are selected by heavenly devas to guard and uphold the Sangha for them—it is equivalent to that we ourselves uphold the Sangha. When we uphold the Sangha, we prioritize Sangha's benefits and image in our considerations. Especially, we regard Shifu's ideals as our ideals and Shifu's image as our image. What are the three principles and methods to conduct management functions?

(1) Uphold the Sangha. Everything should be based on the whole Sangha's benefit and image as the priority, not on your individual benefit as the emphasis. Otherwise, it is for certain

that there will be conflicts with Sangha and other zhi-shi.

(2) Safeguard the Image of Zhi-shi. Zhi-shi should safeguard each other's image. Even though you may not be in agreement with one of the zhi-shi's thought and way of doing things, you should never count his faults in front of other monastics or followers. If you see zhi-shi criticizing and accusing each other, you should courteously advise them and find the right channel to reflect and straighten out the problem.

(3) Uphold the Benefit of the Group. Always serve and show concerns to the Sangha with a cheerful mind. If you are a zhi-shi in charge of a department, you should even show more understanding and use an inquiring format to give guidance to the member in your group.

How to Manage People (*Dharma Drum Morning Talks* Chapter Five Section 8)

During our morning and evening services, we always chant the Three Refuges, one of which is "I take refuge in the Sangha, and I wish all sentient beings will be brought together in great harmony, without any obstructions at all." How to bring people together so they will have no obstructions? It will take constant learning and accumulation of experience.

Our main management function is to get things done. But it needs people to do it, so we must respect, be considerate of and recognize the fact that people are different. We should not require others to have exactly the same personality as that of our own, or it would be difficult to associate with others. We must know that the reason a group can grow and be strong is because of the merging of wisdoms of all others, not of just one individual.

Why can't one be considerate of others? It is because we don't look at the big picture and only stubbornly keep our own views and standby our own position—always my thought. In interacting with people, if one only uses his own considerations to require others to cooperate, it would be a very painful way of doing things.

Therefore, we should all cultivate the good virtue of not insisting on our own opinion. When we meet some roadblock, we would rather take a step back and let others go first. We must have this kind of concept.

Equality among Sangha, Distinction between Monastics and Lay Practitioners (*Dharma Drum Morning Talks* Chapter Five Section 5)

"I am not the leader. I am one of the monastics." This is what the esteemed Shakyamuni Buddha said to his disciples. Budddha regarded himself as a member of the Sangha and he should too observe the rules From the Zhi-shi's, the management staff's point of views, they should have this breath of mind towards other monastics.

Zhi-shi among the Sangha are fundamentally the same, as they all have a job to do. In other words, every organization is structured to have things taken cared of evenly by different people. Although the positions and roles are different, the work itself is equally distributed.

The ones in high positions should be considerate and respect of the subordinates and not be arrogant and high-handed in treating others, or haggling over things with and discriminating against others.

The subordinates should be respectful and go along with the will of the superior, not to resist or disobey the guidance. Always ask for direction, be communicative and cooperative, and maintain full cooperation and give full support.

Everyone is on equal footing and the work are also even. Only the functions given are different and the responsibilities can be heavy or light. Everyone has a job and a work to do in the process of offering to the Sangha and serving the sentient beings.

There is a saying that matters that happen among the

Sangha should be dealt with by the Sangha. Even though some lay practitioners at home are very devoted and enthusiastic, we should not discuss any internal matters with them, to avoid misunderstandings and loss of respect towards the Sangha and gradually erode their faith in Buddhism.

Though Buddadharma's nucleus is monastics, we cannot take lightly the importance of the lay practitioners at home, as they are our upholders and the objects of our mission of uplifting the character of humanity and the developers of a pure land on earth. We are close to the Three Jewels because of them, because we have a purpose to serve and to practice the bodhisatvas's way. Lay practitioners regard monastics as their field of blessings and monastics regards lay practitioners as their benefactors

Performing Zhi-Shi Functions is Practice (*Dharma Drum Morning Talks* Chapter Five Section 6)

"A Knife must be ground to be sharp." The work itself performed by Zhi-shi is a form of training and experience—learning to settle down your body and mind while performing work and cultivating yourself while making offerings. It is also planting seeds of blessings and developing wisdom while working. Therefore, performing Zhi-shi functions is practice—cultivating blessings, developing wisdom, and practicing meditation.

Trying to understand others' mind and character is developing wisdom; helping others is cultivating blessings; when vexation arises, taking up the Bodhi mind and using Dharma to retrieve your vexation is practicing meditation; dis-associating with evil things and doing good deeds is upholding the moral disciplines.

If one can often think this way, behave this way and be reminded of these facts; and can often have a shameful mind, a mind of repentance, and a grateful mind, it is taking advantage of the opportunity to practice. As long as our mind is along the Bodhi path, everything we do is for the Sangha from everywhere and for all sentient beings.

New Staff, New Challenge (Dealing with Change) (*Dharma Drum Morning Talks* Chapter Five Section 10)

Faced with a new future, we must try to take some new initiatives. Following established rules is to take advantage of past experiences, but sticking to conventions, standing still and being complacent will lead to no progress. People often say, "Learning is like rowing a boat upstream, advance, or be pushed back." It is simply saying when there is no progress or the progress is very slow or insignificant, it will fall behind and eventually be eliminated. Therefore, we must do and learn at the same time and try to blaze some new trails.

However, there is also a customary saying, "Now officers always start the job by starting three fires (initiating some new policies)." It is saying that many people have dreams and aspirations and that once they get an opportunity with a new responsibility, they would immediately make a full play of their ideas. "I want to do it this way, I want to do it that way. ..." But when they encounter difficulties, they would give up without a struggle. The fact is that there is a big gap between ideals and reality; whatever you dream, it will happen that way.

One must learn how to utilize and stimulate one's ability and wisdom in adapting to the ever changing situations he/she faces. Considering the organization in its totality, one can then really grow for him/herself, as well as for the Sangha members, in his/her new role as a management staff.

Being a Staff is an Opportunity to Stimulate Hidden Intellectual Capacity (*Dharma Drum Morning Talks* Chapter Five Section 11)

Every task is a good opportunity of growth for the staff, as it can stimulate you hidden intellectual capacity and enhance your growth. You should recognize the blessings of this opportunity and be grateful.

Intelligence can also be said as talent, which comes in two types: one comes with the birth and the other is cultivated after birth. Some people have very balanced intellectual development in many areas and some may be leaning towards a particular area. We often, however, do not recognize the type of endowment or qualities we have.

Leaders' intellectual abilities are not knowledge, nor are techniques. Because leaders must be able to understand and control the overall situation, his intellectual abilities need to be broad and deep. Therefore, cultivation of a leader needs to be in steps by learning and experiencing, to develop multi-facet abilities. He needs to experience, understand, and be exposed to the work in every department, every operation and at every level, in order to enrich his intelligence—he cannot be living in isolation.

Therefore, people who are inclined to develop into a particular interest, let him to be exposed to the different operations and to experience the works at different levels. He may develop a broad perspective on things and become a person very suitable as a leader. From this point of view, intelligence or abilities can be trained and stimulated. Hence, when a job is given to you, accept it with a good attitude and utilize it to develop your hidden talents and make them be useful. However, as long as one is willing to try, a person's ability is unlimited.

Zhi Shi Must View the Sangha as a Whole (*Dharma Drum Morning Talks* Chapter Five Section 13)

As long as Zhi Shi, the management staff, is to serve the Chang Zhu, they must take into considerations the benefits of the whole Sangha community or the great majority of Sangha members, not for just a few individuals. This is not an easy concept to establish.

You should not sit by yourself to reinvent the wheel and think of who should be doing this or that and which office should be doing this or that. You should understand the personality and ability of each person and the need under the circumstances for the group as a whole. Then, integrate all the elements and develop a fresh outlook of the situation—this is what "whole" means.

It is normal to have differences. What is needed is to find a common view. The key in finding a common view among the differences is to let everyone to express their own thoughts and then integrate them to let everyone have a chance to use their talents. When everyone's talents are stimulated, they will feel a sense of achievement and participation and will support to the proposal agree upon by majority of the people. This is what called seeking a common view among the differences.

As we serve the Chang Zhu (or the Sangha), it may feel that this group is kind of small, in that it is only our Sangha group. But from a broader view, it is for the whole Dharma Drum Mountain organization. And, looking out a little further, it is for Chinese Buddhism, for Buddhism in the modern world, and even for the Buddhism of the future and forever.

Hence, you should all have this view: As long as Chang Zhu has needs, whatever position I am being given, I will play the role well; it is not for myself, but to stimulate my intellectual capacity, to adapt to the environment, to serve people, and to create a fresh outlook to our life, This is to view the Sangha as a whole.

Grow while Being Criticized, Faulted, and Examined

The staff position you get is offered to you by the Three Jewels in the ten directions, past, present, and future. It is a very noble, honorable, and dignified event—do not regard it as a pressure. If you do not establish this view in your mind, before long you will feel weary and want to resign, to not finishing the job; it is also likely that when you feel a little wronged or work a little too hard, you will think of quitting or begin to complain. Regardless the position, a Zhi Shi grows on the job, while enduring criticism, being wronged, and examined, of which even though they may not necessarily be true, one must accept them with thankful and grateful mind. (*Dharma Drum Morning Talks* Chapter Five Section 12)

My Shifu told me before, "When you are in charge for three years, even your dog despises you." Why? Because when you are in charge, you are to run things and take the group's interest into considerations. In the process, there are always people who want more freedom and dislike restrictions. Even though they understand in concept that rules in a group are necessary, they subconsciously wish that they are not part of it. So, when the rules affect them, they will automatically make a stand to protect themselves. It will produce resistance and inaccurate criticisms. (*Dharma Drum Morning Talks* Chapter Five Section 14)

From their angle, when you cannot make them happy, you should feel sorry and try to make some adjustment and improvements. Therefore, the accusations, criticisms and examinations are not necessarily totally negative - they may be a stimulant of growth to learn not to be afraid, not to hate, and not to be pained. When someone is willing to criticize us, regard it as their good will, because they cannot stand to see us making mistakes. (*Dharma Drum Morning Talks* Chapter Five Section 14)

Even if you feel someone despises you and dislikes you, do not feel anger and indignation. On the contrary, humbly examine your own speech and conducts as to whether there has been any arrogance, impoliteness, conceit, disrespect, insisting on your own idea, headstrong, and speaking improperly, so you can try to adjust yourself. In this way, you can grow and people will like to be close to you and interact with you. Therefore, please do not immediately feel pained, once someone accuses, criticizes, and discuss you. (*Dharma*

Drum Morning Talks Chapter Five Section 14)

When you meet somebody or something that you do not like, but have to deal with them; in this situation, do not allow your emotional level to be upset, just immediately chant Guanyin Pusa to adjust your emotions and learn to "face it, accept it, take care of it, and let go of it."—This shows a type of growth. (*Dharma Drum Morning Talks* Chapter Five Section 14)

4. Summary and Brief Discussion

(1) Organizational Mission: Leadership assumes that leaders need to get their employees focused on similar goals and educate them about the core processes of the organization. The focus in western leadership is how leaders can provide direction for the organization and help the worker fit into its structure and purpose. In Buddhist principles, the practitioner is working on their own spiritual development, and contributing to the organization whose purpose is to promote compassion, wisdom and assist with education and spiritual development of the individual and society. This point of view resonates with the Servant Leadership Model of western management. Both western and Buddhist organizations stress the importance of having a clear mission that people inside the organization understand and use to direct their work when choices need to be made.

The mission of Dharma Drum Mountain is to "spread Chinese Chan Buddhism, with Protecting the Spiritual Environment at the core. To achieve the purification of the world through comprehensive education and extend loving care to all."

Master Sheng Yen in his 2010 teachings on Engagement in Society { (p. 90) in the book *Master Sheng Yen*, published in English in 2010} advocated the building of a pure land on earth by promoting comprehensive education and extending loving care to all, hence social and charitable works are considered indispensable and fundamental undertakings. The Master emphasized that social charity requires the spiritual more than the material aspect…In today's world, chaos and turbulence in fact result from spiritual poverty in humanity. Only through spiritual overhaul can human destiny be fundamentally improved."

It is impossible to imagine a western corporate or public sector leader writing these words.

(2) Self reflection and self-correction are paramount in Master Sheng Yen's instructions. Self-reflection from the perspective of the whole sangha (Chang zhu) is repeated in Master Sheng Yen's writings. These qualities are rarely encouraged in western management. Leaders may be urged to listen to their employees, or treat people respectfully, but rarely are they or their staff focused on developing virtue. Instead the focus is generally on the bottom line—making profits—and meeting established performance measures. These pressures sometimes lead workers to cheat, shirk, blame others and not take personal responsibility or act in non-virtuous ways in order to achieve individual recognition of company gains.

Here the leadership approach found in Buddhist masters and their teachings are radically different from western management principles.

(3) Attitudes and Values

This focus is a major difference between western and Buddhist management. Buddhist teachings stress harmony, not having strong views or being unwilling to compromise, and listening rather than judging.

The Sixth Patriarch of Chan Master Huineng from the Platform Sutra: "If you see the wrongs of others, then you yourself are wrong. " and "Discard the fault-finding mind and vexations will be gone."

(4) "The way to get along with others is to communicate effectively. When communication fails, compromise, when compromise fails, tolerate and forgive." Master Sheng Yen said.

(5) Flexibility and Nonattachment to Change. One of the three core principles of Buddhism is impermanence. We live in

a constantly changing world, and we seek to develop the attitude of nonattachment to the past or the future while living moment to moment in the present; how do you see change? Recall the Not the Wind, not the Flag koan verse. The two monks are arguing about the fluttering flag, one saying "The flag is moving" while the other argued "No, the wind is moving." The sixth ancestor gave the Buddhist teaching saying "It is not the flag moving and it is not the wind moving. It is your mind that is moving." Can we lead while keeping our mind still, and being adaptive to the people and context we work within?

(6) Taking the Big Picture of DDM's purpose and Role in Society and for Individuals

Master Sheng Yen wrote many times about DDM's purpose in an extension of consideration for the whole sangha. My teacher Guo Gu recounts a principle lesson that Master Sheng Yen taught him when Guo Gu served as his personal assistant. First, learn to take care of one person, then learn to take care of the sangha, then one can take care of the country, and then all sentient beings. So Master Sheng Yen was equating DDM's vision with the sangha's harmony and going beyond to take care of all people in society.

Master Sheng Yen laid out his vision of Protecting the Spiritual Environment, which was published in English in 2011 in the book *Living in the 21ˢᵗ Century: A Buddhist View*. In that book he stated that the Mission of DDM is "To spread Chinese Chan Buddhism, with protecting the Spiritual Environment at the core. To Achieve the purification of the world through comprehensive education and extend loving care to all.

    A. Four Steps to handling problems (individual, group or organization)

      Face it, Accept it, Deal with it, and Let go of it.

    B. Accept Causes and Conditions; think transformation. The great path is not difficult as long as you do not pick and choose.

(7) Lifelong learning and education; practice as work (Practice is not just sitting meditation--*The Platform Sutra*)

Master Sheng Yen believed that uplifting the character of humanity must start with every individual by constant learning and improvement from birth until death...so he supported holistic and lifelong learning."

Western management supports continual professional development and lifelong learning so one's skills do not become outdated, and one keeps in step with the current technology, management philosophy, service and product development, and other organizational processes.

(8) Institutional Structures: Bureaucracy has been the structure of government, nonprofit and private sector agencies for many decades. But that is changing as organizations across sectors discover that partnerships, joint action, and ongoing cross agency teams can be more effective than working in the silos of bureaucracy.

It appears that monasteries largely remain bureaucratic structures. This fact may be softened by Master Sheng Yen's instructions to treat everyone equally and that all jobs are important. But in truth, in a bureaucracy, some jobs have more power and a broader oversight than other jobs. This may restrict innovative thinking, and questioning the status quo by organizational members, and propel many mid to low level staff to be risk averse and not take much initiative.

Also in an increasingly networked society, organizational networks provide support, resiliency and resources to their members. There may be opportunities for DDM to use more networks and collaborative partnerships in furthering its mission and service provision.

Ideas DDM might consider / learn from western manage-ment

(1) Importance of external and internal integration; inclusion of external people (lay people and other stakeholders) into planning. This may be more necessary to adapt to the community and country contexts that the Chan centers exist in, so that while the teachings remain the same, the practices and programs may differ somewhat

to adapt to cultural preferences and meanings.

(2) Networked and collaborative governance structures: Western management uses a variety of matrix team structures, and horizontally networked task forces and units to accomplish goals with similar clients or overlapping resources. This can lead both to efficiencies but also strong working relationships.

(3) Marketing and branding so that people are more aware of DDM's offerings.

(4) New approaches (including non-Chinese practices) to consider how to offer Buddha dharma to people who are not yet exposed to it, or have not accepted its important in their lives.

Things western management might learn from DDM

(1) Importance of meditation and daily attention to integration of buddhadharma

(2) Importance of seeing life overall as an opportunity to practice and no split between work and other parts of life

(3) Humble attitude; all jobs are equal regardless of high or low; different tasks

(4) Each person should keep the mission and overall view of their organization's health and purpose in mind as they conduct their work.

(5) Each person should focus on their own attitude and not cause conflict or have strong opinions; do not talk negatively about other members or gossip; understand where others are coming from rather than defend yourself.

(6) Ceremony of transition into new/different jobs; a tradition of unity and openness. Acknowledging responsibility and job function while celebrating the overall health and robustness of the organization and Buddhadharma in the world.

5. Conclusion

Buddhist and western management have some key overlapping principles:

(1) The organization's mission is primary and should guide all workers in their work.

(2) Be proactive and willing to solve problems with new solutions and approaches.

(3) Encourage the heart, respect fellow workers, and seek to understand.

(4) Lifelong learning is necessary and should be supported through education & training.

Master Sheng Yen articulated a comprehensive way for individuals and organizations to live in The Fivefold Spiritual Renaissance Campaign, published in 2011 in *Living in the 21*st *Century: A Buddhist View.* If you are not familiar with this Campaign element, I highly recommend you familiarize yourself with them. If I had more time today, I would do that now.

It seems impossible to summarize all I have covered in this talk. It turns out that there are some common principles between Buddhist management and western management teachings.

Using Buddhadharma, and the lessons Master Sheng Yen has set before us in his writings, we can become better Dharma practitioners while also being leaders in our jobs. We can support each other, examine ourselves, do our best to accomplish our work with good results, help our communities, and help spread Buddhadharma in all that we do.

〔全文中譯〕

在公共、私營及非營利工作場所中運用佛教原則管理人員和組織

Frances Berry 講　高照東方譯

美國佛羅里達州立大學 Askew 公共行政與政策學院教授

「聖嚴法師圓寂十週年——佛法與社會科學國際研討會」主題演講

2019 年 6 月 29 日於臺灣金山法鼓山

一、緒論

　　我非常感激能有機會參加二〇一九聖嚴法師圓寂十週年——佛法與社會科學國際研討會。承蒙邀請做今早的演講，我深感榮幸。做為一個佛教研究的初學者，我同時亦對探討這樣一個複雜的話題感到慚愧和不足。所以，請原諒我的錯漏，並謹記佛陀的四依法：依法不依人，依義不依語，依了義不依不了義，依智不依識。

　　接下來我將探討如何使用佛教原則進行管理，並將其與西方管理原則進行簡要比較。對於剛剛提到的四依法，我認為它們是我們應當聽從與思考的箴言，我同時認為在實踐依智不依識和依了義不依不了義的過程中，我們應該依賴「和理論相對的實踐智慧」。所以，我要談到的大部分內容都涉及聖嚴法師對管理的實踐智慧。請允許我簡單概述一下我今天要討論的內容。首先，我會簡述現代私營和公共部門的領導原則和方法。之後，我會對聖嚴法師所寫的佛教管理原則

與宋代禪師的一些著作（在《禪林寶訓》中被譯成英文）進行介紹。對這部分內容，我引用了原文。最後，我會總結並比較佛教和西方的領導原則。

二、當今世界的管理學

對複雜組織的領導與管理是現代生活的重要組成部分。無論是大學、醫院、政府機構、寺院、救災慈善機構還是聯合國，每一個組織都要制定組織架構、機制、規則和指引來完成其任務和工作。只要是兩個人以上一起努力實現共同的目標，我們就需要管理。美國前總統羅斯福曾說：「一個沒有良好管理的政府就像是一座建在沙灘上的房子。」這說明一個組織可以在擁有充沛的資金、人員和良好服務的情況下，由於缺乏出色的管理和領導而運作低效。正如聖嚴法師所說，「制度對僧團來說必不可少」。

領導和管理可以被視作一個用共同任務和價值連結組織成員的過程。如此一來成員們便會自願奉行能夠惠及組織、成員、社群乃至整個社會的制度。但假如官僚主義盛行，成員們則不會自願遵守規定和程序，反而會感到被約束和壓迫。當生活在民主社會的人們期待民權和個人自由時，僵化的官僚體制和個人的自主裁量將產生對立。是故，如何協調組織規則與員工的自由裁量權是領導的核心作用，也是它的核心問題。

做為一個管理學學者，我很驚訝學界沒有更多關於佛教和管理的著作。但這可能是本人的疏漏，因為無法閱讀中文，我或許不了解華人學者對此的相關研究。在過去的

二十年中,西方社會科學家對工作環境的心靈層面有了更多的研究。《管理、靈修與宗教學報》（*The Journal of Management, Spirituality & Religion*）已有十五年的歷史,學報發表衡量工作場所靈性、員工敬業度以及禪修對工作效率的影響等相關文章。大體說來,員工在工作場所禪修會帶來一些正面影響,這種影響主要體現在員工對工作的滿意度上,而非提昇工作效率。然而,我還沒有看到這本學報有文章討論如何運用佛教思想進行領導和管理。

西方管理學中的領導

　　盧瑟·古利克（Luther Gulick）在二十世紀三〇年代出版了美國最早的公共行政書籍,在書中提出了 PODSCORB 的管理學原則,這個由首字母縮寫組成的原則代表了規畫（planning）、組織（organizing）、指導（directing）、人事（staffing）、協調（coordinating）、報告（reporting）和預算（budgeting）。二十世紀八〇年代和之後的戰略管理（strategic management）則將與組織外部利害關係人協調關係、領導組織因應威脅和不足並提昇發展機遇等重要課題納入考量。馬克·摩爾（Mark Moore, 1995）強調道,為了讓政府向市民和社群提供更好的服務,戰略管理須要計畫、評估和有實施計畫的能力。進入二十世紀九〇年代,管理學轉變為以實證為基礎（的一門學科）,用績效標準來衡量項目產出和影響（de lancer Jules 等,2007）。

　　在過去的六十年裡,西方關於領導的研究經歷了釐清何謂領導以及如何成為領導人的階段。早期的研究側重於性

格特徵，比如外向、有決斷力、敢於承擔風險、具有人格魅力等。然而到了二十世紀九〇年代，對領導的研究更多地放在了（領導者的）行為功能上，例如領袖為了鼓舞人心而用的角色和世界觀。沃倫・本尼（Warren Bennis）對領導和管理做了如下的區分：「領袖（leaders）做對的事情，經理（managers）則把事情做對；經理靠的是控制而領袖則（通過）激發（他人的）信任。經理看重短期而領袖則著眼長遠……。」

在我稍後會談到的著作中，聖嚴法師闡明了經理和老闆的不同（他所指的大概不是管理僧團，而是管理日常的政府和企業）。我們認識到在官僚機構和世界上大部分組織中，官僚模式仍是主流，為組織做決策的大體是身居高位者。高層主管比中層和基層幹部更常起領導作用。

不過在我今天的談話中，我將混用「領袖」和「經理」的概念，領導人（leader）和領導（leadership）在接下來的內容中指的是管理（management）和領導作用（leadership）。

需要強調的是，現代管理學中的「領導人」一詞並不僅僅專門指一個組織的最高領導，它同時也代表著組織各層級起領導作用的人。現今領導力研究中的一個主旨認為，每一個人都可以在他們各自工作部門發揮領導作用，不論層級。儘管在現實生活中，領導作用仍集中在組織頂層。

所以在今天的演講中，領導和管理將會是同一個功能。我也採納了剛才提到過的主旨，即每個人都能成為領導者，不管（其本身的）工作內容和角色。因為起領導作用的主要是行為和態度，而每一個人都能習得這樣的行為和態度。

　　詹姆士‧庫塞基（James Kouzes）和貝瑞‧波斯納（Barry Posner）在一九九〇年撰寫了《模範領導：領導，就是讓員工願意主動成就非常之事》（*The Leadership Challenge: How to Get Extraordinary Things Done in Organizations*）。這本書已經成為了北美史上最為暢銷的管理學書籍。二人提出了五個領導者為了組織成功而應落實的原則和角色：

　　首先，領導人需向舊習挑戰。這意味著領導人需要大膽面對現狀、為組織的發展尋找改變和創新的機遇，並勇於試錯承擔風險。

　　其次，領導人須喚起共同願景。在展現組織未來的理想的同時，促成組織成員對此共識的支持和配合。

　　第三，領導人要促使他人行動。他們要鼓勵合作、下放權力和共享訊息。這樣一來，組織的全體成員可獲得他們角色所需的內容。領導人還要支持員工為了達成任務而行使的自主權利。

　　第四，領導人要以身作則。他們要親身示範成功案例以領導大眾，而且他們也會創造一步步的勝利來向成員展現如何有效達成（組織）願景與任務。

　　最後，領導人要鼓舞人心。他們要有高情商且體恤下屬；他們要嘉獎個體的貢獻和優異表現；他們還要頌揚組織的勝利成果。

　　位居第二的管理學專業暢銷書為史蒂芬‧柯維（Steven Covey）的《高效能人士的七個習慣》（*The 7 Habits of Highly*

Effective People）。他提出的七個習慣包括：

習慣一：鎖定目標。釐清你想要達成的終極目標，可以讓你朝向目標規畫並努力邁進。

習慣二：積極主動。不要坐以待斃幻想麻煩，能夠自我解決。

習慣三：要事第一。對外部世界的領導源自自我認知和自我領導，一個領導人必須分清主次。

習慣四：雙贏思維。互利共贏、不損人利己是重視和尊重他人的體現。

習慣五：首先理解別人，再令人理解自己。真誠地傾聽他人可以使他人也變得樂於傾聽，這能營造積極解決問題的關懷氛圍。

習慣六：統合綜效。通過積極的團隊合作，集眾人之力達成個體所不能完成的目標。

習慣七：不斷更新。守護和增加你最寶貴的財富，這意味著在你生活的四個方面自我更新：身體上、社會／情感上、精神上、心靈上。

以上兩本書總結了在大型公共和私營組織中的關於領導的策略和參與原則。

簡單來說，西方管理學在過去的三十年裡一直強調領導人必須為組織尋找定位和目標，積極面對困境，鼓勵團隊合作。（他們要）樹立一個好的榜樣，或如俗話所說——「身體力行」。同時，關懷他人、傾耳細聽和果敢決策也被

強調。

但（與東方文化）不同的是，關懷他人並不是西方管理學的首要原則。最後，柯維指出我們要在身體、精神和心靈上保持健康。

僕人領導學

西方管理學的最後一個範例是僕人領導學，由羅伯・格林里夫（Robert Greenleaf）所創。他的格言是：服務他人而非自己。在僕人領導學中，領導人的一個重要作用是在組織中營造社群。社群從社交互動而來，是一種歸屬感。在這類社群中，公民與公僕（或領導者）有共同的責任來一起釐清問題並解決問題。若缺乏上述特質則會導致人際關係變得自私和冷漠。

僕人領導學關注能夠令人性受益的努力。領導者不再以財務利益為主要手段來刺激人積極工作；領導不再僅被視為上位者的特權，而是延伸到整個群體、組織和社會的一種功能。 ❶

三、佛法中的領導管理學

在我看來，在釋迦牟尼佛的時代，沒有什麼正式的組織來管理佛陀的信徒。比丘尼和僧人往往宿居於林中。儘管佛

---

❶ 「領導學不再指導人們去做什麼。不論領導來自於職位所賦予的正式權威還是非正式權威，領導學關注幫助一個群體、組織或社群來實現自己的目標然後轉向新的發展方向。」（Heifetz, 2017）

陀有諸多教誨，他沒有嘗試去建立一個管理架構或者一個組織。他不是一個組織的 CEO 或者總裁，去負責管理社群。當然，人們可以認為僧尼的戒律是一種管理手段，用來幫助人們修行和區分什麼可為、什麼不可為。但除此之外，沒有什麼其他的規定被制定出來管理社群（或群體）。這意味著人們可以管理他們各自的想法和行為，並會因為破戒而被逐出僧團。此時，社群（的管理）依靠著大家各自按照戒律和社群規範去管控自己，而不由一個「領袖」或裁判來執行法律和規則。

《禪林寶訓》的管理智慧

隨著佛教的興盛，菩提達摩在六世紀把禪帶到了中國。在寺院被修建起來的同時，階級、制度和領導，譬如寺院住持，也隨之出現。

《禪林寶訓》一書收錄了一些宋代（十至十三世紀）禪師的短偈。這些短偈有關於領導和對社群和佛教信眾的回應。其中一課我尤其喜歡。浮山法遠禪師在一封給淨因臻和尚的信中寫到：

> 遠公曰。住持有三要。曰仁。曰明。曰勇。仁者行道德。興教化。安上下悅往來。明者遵禮義。識安危。察賢愚。辨是非。勇者事果決。斷不疑。姦必除。佞必去。仁而不明。如有田不耕。明而不勇。如有苗不耘。勇而不仁。猶如刈而不知種。三者備則叢林興。缺一則衰。缺二則危。三者無一。則住持之道廢矣。（CBETA, T48, no.

2022, 頁 1018, a25-b2）

法遠禪師還寫道：「遠公曰。住持居上。當謙恭以接下。執事在下。要盡情以奉上。上下既和。則住持之道通矣。」（CBETA, T48, no. 2022, 頁 1018, b11-12）

好經理和壞經理的品質

聖嚴法師在《大法鼓》0342 集有對好經理的討論，他說：

> 最糟糕的主管是那種對上面吹、捧，而對下面欺、壓的人。把下面的功勞全部拉歸自己，當自己出了紕漏則全部推給下邊。上邊交下來的工作、責任全部往下去交。……做好了是他的功勞，做壞的是下邊的過失。如果上邊需要解決問題，請教他解決問題的時候，他不能夠提供他的智慧，而只是說：「老闆，你的思想、你的觀念、你的看法高明遠見，你的智慧真高。」

> 英明的老闆喜歡什麼？能夠提供寶貴意見的經理……老闆本身最好是不用太多的頭腦，只是掌握政策的原則、政策的方針。老闆交代的不是技術問題，老闆不是要告訴你怎麼樣子做，老闆是說我要做什麼。最好的老闆是這樣的。

那好經理呢？聖嚴法師說道：

中層次的主管就要為老闆好好的策劃、好好的設想、好好的研究、好好的執行。然後呢，分的工要分得很細，一步一步的分工以後，要對下邊的每一個部門橫的方向要給他們做協調；直的方向、直的系統要給他們一個一個的安排，處理所有的問題。關懷所有的人、所有的員工，所有的事自己瞭如指掌，而且把他們一樣一樣的都能夠清清楚楚的知道。這種經理呀，就是最好的經理。

老闆問你一些什麼事的時候，這個做經理的人要非常坦誠的、非常細膩的給老闆分析，給老闆做報告，向老闆請示。我的原則希望事前要請示，請示是原則性的；事後要報告，報告是重點性的。如果把經理這樣的角色做好的話，這個人能做大老闆，能做一個公司的老闆，也能做一個國家的領袖了。用人才，他會用；訓練人才，他會訓練；那麼做事業的時候，他會經營。我不是學管理的，我只是對於一個寺院如何的經營、一個寺院的團體如何地用佛法來照顧和關懷，我以這個原則講了今天這樣的一個主題。（《大法鼓》0342集，〈主管與員工的相處之道〉）

聖嚴法師的行事六要領

第一，堅守原則：所謂「原則」，指的不是個人的原則，而是整個團體的原則。我們每個人都有發揮自己才能、意見的空間，但必須在整個團體的大原則之下去發

揮，才不會失之偏頗。

第二，充分授權：這是指上下之間的關係。在上位者必須充分授權，以方便下屬行事，否則事事指揮、干涉，下面的人遇事無權處理，會造成事情停滯，效率不彰。

第三，尊重他人：人與人相處要相互尊重，常常心懷感恩，即使上對下也要心懷尊重。

尊重並不是同情，而是：首先、尊重對方的想法、意見和人格。如果不許對方有意見、想法，會讓對方在工作上無法產生成就感。所以，不要堅持一定要按照自己的方式做，只要不損害整個團體，能把事情完成即可。其次、尊重他人的能力。每個人的學習能力、適應能力、基本能力都不一樣，各有高低，不能要求每個人都相同，或者和自己的能力一樣。即使有人表現得不夠理想，但既然已錄用他，仍然要保持尊重。雖然對方的工作態度和我們不合，但我們千萬不可以惡言相向，這是基本人格的尊重。

第四，關懷對方：這裡指的不僅僅是工作的關懷，情緒、身心、家庭等皆需要適當的關懷。隨時主動去關懷他人，見到有人悶悶不樂，給予一點慰問，也許對方的心結就會打開。而主管對於職員的情緒應有所注意，並加以主動關懷，而且應該要普遍地關懷，不能只關懷其中一、二位，否則可能會造成其他人內心的不平衡。

第五，主動溝通：無論上對下、下對上，平行之間都要主動溝通。在此特別強調由「自己主動」溝通，而非等待、等著別人來與你溝通。主動與人溝通時，最好自己先有腹案，想好該如何做，預先設想可能遭遇到的困難，並

擬好解決或替代方案。如果只是丟個難題要別人做，這樣
不但事情做不起來，也容易產生是非。而當事情無法獲得
解決時，就很容易對環境產生不滿，覺得處處障礙，心裡
痛苦，甚而相互懷疑，如此一來，整個團體便不能和諧
融洽。

想要完成任務……如果遇到挫折……心改個方向就好
了。不要心有不甘，一直執著原來的想法。

即使到了上天下地、左右全無路時，還是有一條路──
死路一條，死路也是路啊！天無絕人之路，既然老天要我
死，也只能如此了；能夠勇敢面對現實，心也就不會感到
那麼痛苦。

第六，隨時檢討：所謂「檢討」，是檢討「自己」，不
是檢討別人。無論是溝通不良、工作不順利、別人待我們
不好，甚至把責任推給我們，都要檢討自己，是不是自己
有什麼過失才會造成這種情形。如果一再自我檢討、努力
與對方溝通，仍無法改善，可以反應給主管知道，如果主
管也不認同你，無法解決你的問題，那麼就請諒解對方、
接受對方吧！畢竟都是一起在團體成長的同事。❷

這六個原則不僅適用於寺院圍牆之內，也在經理人和各
種公共、非營利和私營組織當中有著廣泛的應用。聖嚴法師
向企業和政府領袖講解這些原則的情境好似浮現眼前。

---

❷ 引自釋聖嚴，《帶著禪心去上班──聖嚴法師的禪式工作學》，《法鼓
全集》10-14，2005 年網路版，頁 42-46。

聖嚴法師對管理和領導的實用建議

聖嚴法師講到了好經理和壞經理的品質以及經理的職責。他並沒有把他管理的原則限定在對法鼓山的管理上。在他的晚年，聖嚴法師還大量撰寫了管理和領導的內容。其中一個原因是他當時在向政治和企業領袖提供建議，另一個原因是他想在自己圓寂後依舊可以給法鼓山的管理者提供他的管理智慧。這些有力且直白的文字談到了我們應如何在僧團中行事。雖然他的思想主要是寫給寺院裡的僧眾，我相信聖嚴法師在領導和管理方面的實用建議也適用於普通人。對於我們這樣的普通信眾，我認為這些話依舊可以為我們的日常指明方向，不論工作還是生活。

鑒於聖嚴法師的思想已寫成文稿，我將會在各種有關領導的話題當中大量引用。這樣一來，你可以直接從他的話中去學習（他的思想），而不需要我的轉述。

在《法鼓晨音・第五篇　執事應有的觀念》❸ 這個篇章中，聖嚴法師寫到：

1. 神聖的僧中執事（原第一節）

僧中執事，並不是師父或方丈託付的，而是方丈代表常住付予的。

僧團中每個人都領有一份執事，方丈亦不例外。何以

---

❸ 釋聖嚴，《法鼓晨音》，《法鼓全集》8-8，2005 年網路版，頁113-146。

要有執事？因為在任何一個團體中要享有權益就必須盡義務，盡義務的工作就是一份職務。所以只要有僧團的存在，僧眾都必須擔當執事。

不管諸位領了那一種執事，責任是輕是重，都是個人的因緣福報所致；因此大家要以感恩心、恭敬心、歡喜心來領受。而擔任僧團中管理層次以上的執事，不但可藉此機會來磨練自己，對三寶的奉獻更是一份大功德，是一件難得且光榮的事。（頁113）

當發生問題時，你自以為是在受苦受難時，要將煩惱消歸自心；可是問題的解決還是要交由僧團來協同處理，經由數人集體討論後，智慧、方法自然會出現，問題即可迎刃而解。這也是僧團生活的精神——入眾、隨眾、靠眾、和眾的具體實踐。（頁115）

2. 執事者應具備的觀念（原第二節）

僧執要有整體感、責任感、穩定性、時間觀念、組織和分析的能力，最重要的是還要有道心（菩提心）；若無道心僅是一般公司行號的職員，而非僧中執事。

僧執必須具備以下五項觀念：

（1）要有整體感

所謂整體，涵蓋了法鼓山體系下的每一單位，不管是僧團的、事業體的、本山總部的、各地分支的，這些看似各自獨立卻相連屬的許多單位，實際上都是依著師父的理念、悲願在經營，都是以僧團為其中心。因此每當我們做決策時，皆需將整體考慮在內。（頁116）

本位主義，是指對內孤立自己；對外產生抗拒、排斥、指責、要求，難與人和樂共事。本位主義者要不是未能顧慮到自己與他人息息相關，各管各的工作，便是只認為自己做得最好、最辛苦、最忙碌，其他的人卻很輕鬆。

整體性的觀念相當重要，所謂「牽一髮而動全身」，我們一定要認同自己是僧團中的一份子，每個人都是全體的代表，這是一種責任，也是一種榮譽。（頁117）

（2）要有責任感

一個有責任感的人在接受所交辦的任務後，一定會盡心盡力完成該項工作，因為他首先會衡量自己的能力、時間、工作量，以及工作性質，然後量力而為。（頁117）

（3）要有時間觀念

工作的完成必須掌控時間，除專注當下的工作，以提昇工作效能外，亦可運用行事曆、工作計畫表、工作進度表等現代管理工具來掌握時效。

（4）要有組織分析的能力

有組織分析的能力就可策畫，若無此能力，則雖忙但不容易做出成果來。因此領導、管理層次者應培養清眾的企畫能力，可以從簡單的職務開始學起。（頁118）

（5）要有菩提心

沒有菩提心的人，總覺得自己很委屈、不得志、很無奈、不如意、怨氣不斷，缺乏落實感。雖然能力很強，內心難免會嘀咕：「一天忙到晚，到底為誰辛苦為誰忙？」「做那麼多，師父方丈非但不知道，師兄弟們不讚歎，上層只會要求，不會體諒，所為何來？」「算了，反正出了

家不做事也能有飯吃,何必那麼辛苦?」

有菩提心的人會明白現在所擔任的執事,不是為了某些個人做;是為了現前僧和十方僧做,為了自己修持法身慧命做,這是積功累德、修福修慧的機會,應當要盡心盡力。(頁119)

首先,我要說明僧團在三寶中的涵義是「和諧的社群」。所以皈依僧寶即是皈依了和諧。回到聖嚴法師的話:

3. 執事的共識──以和為貴(原第三節)

常住眾有時也會為了詮釋師父的理念、整體的形象,而發生知見差異的爭執,當遇上這種情況,怎麼辦?

其實人有剛、柔之分,剛強的人雖然短時間略佔上風,然而安人者必然是柔順者及和眾者,因為柔能克剛,和能成事。(頁120)

僧中的任何一項職務都必須以和成事、以敬安人,若互有衝突而不彼此協調,就有違出家人的和敬原則了。

解決衝突的方法有二,首先當充分瞭解實際的狀況,若有必要,再做妥當的調整。其次可找雙方談話並予以協調,若當事人有所爭辯,協調者務必保持中立,放寬心量加以包容,切忌直接評斷、指責或給予建議。

佛法是剛柔並濟,以退為進,以疏導代替直接的衝突。(頁121)

4. 執事的原則和方法(原第四節)

執事本身是由龍天推選出來的，代替龍天護持常住，也就等於我們自己護持常住。執事護持常住，以常住的利益及形象為優先考量，更應以師父的理念為理念，以師父的形象為形象。（頁 123）

至於從原則至方法，如何掌握與推行？

（1）護持常住。凡事應以常住全體之利益、形象為著眼，不要以你個人的利益為前提。否則，一定會與常住大眾及其他執事發生衝突。

（2）維護執事的形象。執事彼此若不互相維護形象，僧眾們會互相仿傚，而不服從所有執事的指導或勸解。對某一執事的想法及做法，即使無法認同，也萬萬不可對信徒或僧眾們數落他的過失。若遇見執事互相批評、指責，應好言規勸，當用正常的管道來反應和溝通。

（3）維護大眾的利益。時時要以歡喜的心、服務的心，來關懷常住大眾。身為組長的執事，更要以體諒的心、諮詢的方式，來輔導自己所帶領的清眾。（頁 123-124）

5. 如何統理大眾（原第八節）

早晚課誦都會念三皈依偈，其一是「自皈依僧，當願眾生，統理大眾，一切無礙。」如何才能統理大眾一切無礙呢？這就要靠不斷的學習和經驗的累積。（頁 130）

我們主要是處理事情，但事情需要人來做，所以一定要能夠尊重、包容、體諒人的差異性；不要用自己的性格來要求其他的人和自己完全一模一樣，否則將難以和人相

處。要知道，一個團體之所以能夠成長、碩壯，是因為各種不同智慧的匯集與貢獻，絕非一人獨立所成。

　　為什麼不能包容他人？因為不能往大處著想，只固守本位主義，各自站在自己的立場：我想怎樣，我認為怎樣……。在與人互動時，如果僅以自己的尺寸要求他人配合，必然是件痛苦的事。（頁 130-131）

　　因此，要養成不堅持己見的美德，假如遇到關卡，寧可先退一步，讓人先行，我們一定要有這樣的觀念。（頁 132）

6. 僧眾平等、僧俗有別（原第五節）

　　「我不領眾，我在僧中」這是釋尊對弟子們說的話，佛自己認為他是僧中的一份子，要守僧眾的規則。以執事立場而言，也應該對清眾有這等胸襟。

　　僧中執事本身都是平等的，換言之，任一組織架構本身都是平等的，雖然工作、角色不一樣，但工作本身是平等的。

　　居高位者，應體惜下情，尊重下屬，不宜趾高氣昂，或用高壓手段待人，亦不計較、分別。

　　居下位者，對上要恭敬、順從、不抗爭違逆。凡事皆應充分地請示、溝通、協調，並相互配合、支援。

　　眾生平等，職務也一樣平等，只是所領執事的不同，而有責任輕重之分。每一個人都是在某一職位上負責某項職務，為常住奉獻，為大眾服務。（頁 125）

　　所謂僧中事、僧中決，即使在家菩薩很熱忱，也不可與

之談論，以免他們對常住誤解而失去敬心，或退失對佛教
的信心。

雖然佛法是以出家眾為核心，但我們也不可輕視在家
眾。他們是我們的護持者，佛法教化的對象，人間淨土的
開墾者，我們因他們的親近三寶，而有服務、行菩薩道的
對象。俗眾以僧眾為福田，僧眾以俗眾為恩人。（頁 126）

7. 僧中執事即是修行（原第六節）

「刀不磨不利」，執事本身的工作就是一種歷練，在
奉獻之中成長自己，在做中學習安定身心，也在做中植福
報、開智慧，所以是在修福、修慧、修定。

對他人心性的瞭解是修慧；幫助他人是修福；煩惱生
起，提起菩提心，以佛法的實踐將煩惱消歸自心是修定；
諸惡莫作，眾善奉行，是持戒。

要常常如此想，如此做，如此省悟，常常起慚愧心、懺
悔心、感恩心，便是藉境修行。

只要我們的心安住在菩提道上，任何事皆是為了十方常
住及一切眾生而做。（頁 127）

8. 新的執事，新的挑戰（原第十節）

面對新的未來，必須想辦法開創，蕭規曹隨是經驗傳
遞，墨守陳規、故步自封，便無法進步。我們常說：「學
如逆水行舟，不進則退。」這是說，如果沒有進步，或進
步得很慢，就是退步，是會被淘汰的，所以必須要邊做邊
學，並且有所創新。

　　但是俗話也說：「新官上任三把火。」多半的人都有許多夢想和抱負，甫一上任就想大展抱負：「我要怎麼做，我要怎麼做……。」結果遇到挫折，馬上就無疾而終。事實上，理想與現實是有差距的，不是任你憑空想要怎麼就能怎麼的。（頁 136-137）

　　必須要善用自己的才智、激發自己的才智，來適應所面對的各種瞬息萬變的狀況，並以整體為考量，才能真正在新的執事上，為常住、為自己都得到新的成長。（頁137）

9. 執事是激發潛在才智的機會（原第十一節）

　　任何一項執事，都是一個非常好的成長機會，它可以激發你潛在的才智，使你得到成長，所以要知恩、感恩。

　　才智，也可以說是才能，分為兩種：一種是先天的，另一種是後天培養的；有的人可以全才均衡發展，有的人則偏向某一方面。不過，我們往往不知道自己有這樣的資質。

　　領導人的才智，英文為 intelligence，不是 knowledge（知識），也不是 technique（技術）。因為領導人必須掌握全局，其才智就得深遠廣大，因此領導人的培養就要逐步經驗學習，完成全方位才能的開發，每一個部分、每一個部門、每一個層次他都要去接觸、歷練、瞭解，以充實其才智，不能困於一隅。（頁 138）

　　因此，才智有偏向發展的人，如果讓他到各部門、各層次去經歷，他就會普遍地開發，變成一個非常適合擔任領

導者的人。

由此可見，才智是可以被訓練、激發的。因此，被付予
新的職務，就必須要好好地接受它，然後運用它，激發潛
在的才智，使之能夠充分地發揮。

只要願意嘗試，人的才智其實是無限的。（頁 139）

10. 執事要有整體觀（原第十三節）

既然是常住的執事，就必須考慮到全體或大多數的人，
不能僅為少數或個人著想。這個觀念相當不容易建立。
（頁 143）

不能自己枯坐一處閉門造車，光想著分派這個人做什
麼、那個人做什麼，這一組做什麼、那一組做什麼。一定
要瞭解每個人的性格、才能，以及整體的環境需求，然後
再將之整合，開創出一個新的局面來，這才叫做整體。

有差異是正常的，不過可以在差異中尋求共通之處。
而異中求同的唯一方法，就是要讓大家充分發表他們的想
法，然後再加以整合，這樣大家就可以發揮自己的才智。

當每一個人的才智被激發出來以後，他自己會覺得很有
成就感、參與感，而且會認同這意見是大家共同通過的，
這就是異中求同。（頁 143-144）

我們為常住服務，或許感覺上這個常住很小，只是我
們的僧團；但是擴大一點看，其實是為了我們整體法鼓山
組織；再擴大看，是為了中國的佛教，為了現代的世界佛
教，甚至是為了永遠的、未來的佛教。

因此大家要有這樣的認知：只要常住需要，把我擺在那

一個點上，我就扮演好我那一點上的角色，不是為自己，而是激發自己的才智，適應環境，為大眾服務，並開創新的局面，這才是為整體想。（頁144）

11. 在接受批評、指責、檢討中成長（原第十四節）

所得到的執事，就是十方三世常住三寶所付予的，是一樁神聖的、光榮的、非常莊嚴的佛事，不要把它當成是一種壓力。這個觀念如果不建立起來，做不了多久，你就會感到厭倦，想要辭職，不會有心繼續把它完成；也很可能受了點委屈，或稍微辛苦一些，就會起退心、生埋怨。（原第十二節，頁141-142）

不論擔任什麼執事，都是在接受批評、指責、檢討之中成長。這些指責、批評、檢討不一定正確，但一定要以感謝的心、感恩的心來接受。

我的師父曾經跟我講過：「當家三年狗都嫌。」為什麼？因為當家的人負責管理，是為了維護整體而設想的。但總難免有少數的人希望自由，不喜歡約束，雖在觀念上認為團體的規制是必要的，卻不喜歡把自己擺進體制。一旦體制約束到他的時候，他就會不自覺地生起抗拒的行為，為了保護他自己，他會有許多抗爭和不正確的批評。

從對方的角度看，不能夠讓他快樂，自己應該覺得很抱歉，必須要有所調整和改善。所以指責、批評、檢討並不一定就是負面的，而是一種成長的激素，不要怕、不要恨、也不要痛苦。有人願意指責我們、批評我們，那是他的善意，因為他不忍看到我們出差錯的緣故。

即使是感覺到對方討厭你、不喜歡你,也不要忿忿不平;相反地,要虛心檢討自己的言行,有沒有未曾覺察到的傲慢、無禮、自負,或對人不尊重、堅持己見、剛愎自用、說話不得體之處,然後設法調整自己,如此才能有所成長,讓人歡喜親近、往來。所以,請大家不要受到一些指責、批評、檢討,馬上就覺得很痛苦。

如果遇到一些不希望接觸到的人或事,而又非處理不可,在這種狀況下,不要有情緒上的起伏,應該馬上念觀世音菩薩,隨時調整自己的心情,也要學習著「面對、接受、處理、放下」,這便是一種成長。(原第十四節,頁145-146)

四、總結和討論

(一)組織的使命:領導學認為領導者需要讓員工專注於共同的目標,並教育他們關於組織的核心流程。西方領導學的重點在於領導者如何引領組織以及幫助員工適應其結構和目的。在佛教原則中,信眾努力修行自身,為致力於促進慈悲、智慧和有助個人與社會教育和精神發展的組織做出貢獻。這種觀點和西方管理學中的僕人領導學不謀而合。兩者都強調擁有明確使命的重要性,組織內部成員需要它來理解並指導他們工作中的選擇。

法鼓山的使命是「以心靈環保為核心,弘揚漢傳禪佛教,透過三大教育,達到世界淨化。」

聖嚴法師在社會參與的教導中(英文版《聖嚴法師》〔*Master Sheng Yen*〕,2010年,第90頁)提倡建設人間淨

土，提倡全面教育，落實整體關懷，因此社會和慈善工作被認為是不可或缺的組成部分。法師強調，社會慈善需要精神而非物質層面……在當今世界，混亂和動蕩實際上是人類精神的貧乏造成的。只有通過精神上的改革才能從根本上改善人類的命運。

西方企業或公共領導人難以寫出這樣的思想。

（二）自我反省和自我修正為聖嚴法師的重要教誨：自我反省在聖嚴法師有關僧團（十方常住）的著作中反覆出現。西方管理學很少鼓勵這樣的品質。領導者或被敦促傾聽員工、尊重他人，但他們和他們的員工很少會關注發展美德。恰恰相反，他們的關注點通常會放在結果，即營利，以及達成既定績效指標。這些壓力有時會導致員工弄虛作假、相互推諉、指責他人、不承擔個人責任或者以卑劣手段來讓自己所在的公司收益。

在領導學方面，佛教高僧和他們的教誨則與西方管理學院截然不同。

（三）態度和價值：這一點是西方和佛教管理學的主要區別。佛教教義強調和諧，不提倡強硬的觀點或不願妥協。提倡傾聽而不是評判（他人）。

《六祖壇經》中的六祖惠能說，「若見他人非，自非卻是左」、「但自卻非心，打除煩惱破」。

（四）「人與人之間的相處之道，需要溝通，溝通不成則當妥協，當妥協不成時，就原諒他和忍讓他吧。」聖嚴法師如是說。（《叮嚀》，《法鼓全集》8-3，2005年網路版，頁63）

（五）彈性與無著（Flexibility and Nonattachment to Change）：佛教的三法印之一是無常。我們生活在一個不斷變化的世界中，身處當下，我們尋找對過去和未來的無常看法；你怎麼看待變化？讓我們重溫風動、幡動、心動的故事。兩位僧人因風吹幡動而爭論，一說是幡動，一說是風動。六祖則以佛家思想看待，「不是風動，不是幡動，仁者心動。」我們能夠穩定心境並且適應周遭的人、事、物嗎？

（六）把握大局，法鼓山的願景和對社會和個人（所扮演）角色：聖嚴法師多次寫道，法鼓山的願景在於全體僧眾。我的老師果谷菩薩講述了他在擔任聖嚴法師的侍者時，法師對他的教導。首先，學會照顧一個人，然後學會護持僧團，之後就能照顧國家乃至守護眾生。所以聖嚴法師把法鼓山的理念和僧團和諧等同了起來，甚至到達了守護全人類（的境界）。

聖嚴法師在二〇一一年出版的英文書 *Living in the 21st Century: A Buddhist View*（《生活在二十一世紀：佛教觀》）一書中講述了他心靈環保的理念。他說法鼓山的使命是「以心靈環保為核心，弘揚漢傳禪佛教，透過三大教育，達到世界淨化」。

1. 解決困境的四它主張（個人，團體或組織）：面對它、接受它、處理它、放下它。
2. 接受因緣，思考轉化：至道無難，唯嫌揀擇。

（七）終身學習和教育；工作即修行（道不在坐——《六祖壇經》）

聖嚴法師相信人性的提昇必須由每個人自出生到離世不

斷學習和進步而來……所以他支持全面而終身的學習。

西方管理學支持繼續專業發展和終身學習，這樣的話，一個人的技能就不會過時，一個人也能跟上現今技術、管理哲學、服務和產品研發和其他組織進程的發展。

（八）結構制度：官僚機構幾十年來都是政府、非營利組織和私營機構的架構。但隨著各行業的組織認識到合作、聯合行動和跨機構工作團隊比孤立的官僚機構更有效率，這一情況正在改變。

寺院似乎仍保留著大量的官僚結構。聖嚴法師平等待人、工作平等的教導或許已經改善了這一狀況。但事實上，在官僚機構中，有一些工作會比其他工作享有更多的權力和更廣的監管。這可能會限制創新思維，並且引發組織成員對現狀的質疑，導致很多中低層員工採取厭惡風險而非積極主動（的怠工態度）。

此外，在一個聯繫日益緊密的社會，組織網路為其成員提供了支持、恢復和資源（的功能）。法鼓山有機會使用更多的網絡和合作夥伴關係來推進（達成）自己的使命和服務。

法鼓山可向西方管理學借鑒的內容

1. 外部和內部整合的重要性；將外部人員（非專業人員和其他利益攸關者）納入發展計畫。這意味著現存的禪宗中心應吸納所處的社群和國家的背景。如此，儘管教學精神依舊不變，實踐和項目可能會因不同的文化偏好和涵義而做出改變。

2. 網路化和協作治理結構：西方管理學使用各種矩陣型組織結構、橫向聯繫的工作組來達成那些有著相似客戶或資源重疊的目標。這既可以提昇效率，也可以增強工作關係。

3. 營銷和品牌推薦以便人們更加了解法鼓山。

4. 採用新的方法（包括使用非中文）來向未接觸過佛法或還沒認識到佛法重要性的人們傳法。

西方管理學可向法鼓山借鑑的內容

1. 禪修及每日留心將佛法和精神教育融入日常生活的重要性。

2. 視整體生活為修行的機會、不將工作與其他生活面向分離的重要性。

3. 謙虛的態度；所有的工作都是平等的，不論高低的任務。

4. 每個人在工作時應牢記組織的使命及組織健全與目的整體觀。

5. 每個人都應該注重自己的態度，不要引起衝突或有過激的意見；不要消極對待其他成員或傳播八卦；傾聽其他人的觀點而不固執己見。

6. 過渡到新的、不同的工作的儀式；團結與開放的傳統。在慶幸組織與佛法整體健全而穩健（流傳於）世間的同時，要認清責任與工作職能。

五、結語

佛教和西方管理學有一些重要的共通點：

（一）組織的使命是重要的，應該成為所有員工工作的指導原則。

（二）積極主動，願意用新的方式和方法解決問題。

（三）鼓舞人心，尊重同事，而且尋求理解。

（四）終身學習是必要的而且應該通過教育和培訓來支持。

聖嚴法師為個人和組織提供了一個「心五四運動」的全面方式，英文版詳述於二〇一一年出版的 *Living in the 21st Century: A Buddhist View*。如果你還對此運動的內容不甚知曉，我強烈建議你去了解它們。可惜時間有限，我今天不能細說。

總結我今天的演講是一項艱巨的任務。簡言之，佛教管理學和西方管理學有一些共同的原則。

運用佛法和聖嚴法師在他的著作中提到的例子，我們可以成為更好的佛法修行者、一個工作中的領導者。我們可以互相支持，反省自己，盡力完成我們的工作、達到最佳的結果，幫助我們的社群，並在我們所從事的每件事上弘揚佛法。

Business Ethics:
Some Insights from Buddhism
(Speech Outline)

Simon S.M. Ho

President, The Hang Seng University of Hong Kong

1. Objectives

To demonstrate how studies of modern business ethics, CSR and sustainability can learn from Buddhism philosophy.

To outline the basic distinct Buddhist perspective and practical applications of some basic Buddhist doctrines/principles, i.e. a Buddhist-inspired approach to business ethics.

To promote developing a more systematic research framework in applying and measuring the practice of some Buddhist doctrines such as the Noble Eightfold Path.

2. Business Ethics Problems

Many ethical breaches and corporate scandals happened in the past 2 decades: Enron, Lehman Brothers, Volkswagen, Turing Pharmaceuticals, Toshiba , ...

Maximizing shareholders' returns (and executives' compensation) at the cost of other stakeholders.

The prevention of corporate misconducts underscores the importance of business ethics, particularly in a world that is more short-term oriented and bottom-line driven.

3. Re-shaping Capitalism

After hundred years of vibrant development, capitalism or free-market economy ideals now face various challenges and predicaments, riddled with problems, i.e. rotten capitalism.

A low standard of business ethics reflects the current nature of the business environment, which itself a question on the morality of society at large.

Hence, to address the problem, we should start with the rehabilitation of the moral values of society and then re-shape capitalism.

4. Common Unethical business practices

- Labor exploitation
- Dishonesty or unfairness in gaining profits
- Conflict of interests
- Unfair competitions
- Product safety
- Untruth advertisements
- Personal privacy invasions
- bribery and corruptions
- Polluting the environment

5. Legal Regulations, Business Ethics and Human Characters

Enacting more laws would not be sufficient or effective to solve these ethical problems, and legal standard is the only the minimum standard (some laws may be even unethical).

Businesses need to formulate their own ethical standards, and such need all individual players to follow earnestly.

Business ethics is a system of moral principles and values that are applied to business activities affecting all different stakeholder groups (employees, customers, suppliers, competitors, the environment, the community, the Government, etc.).

Human characters and other factors are extremely important.

6. Buddhism Offering Distinct Perspective on Business Ethics

Different religions and philosophies have dealt with morality and ethics, and they share many common concerns and methods (e.g. not killing, not stealing, not lying, etc.).

While Buddhism shares some similar ethical concerns as Western (Judeo-Christian, Kantian) and Confucian, it offers a distinct perspective (e.g. on the inner thoughts and feelings of the individual) and approach for handling business ethics.

All forms and schools of Buddhism share similar ethical beliefs.

7. Some Relevant Unique Doctrines of Buddhism

- Compassion for all sentient beings (though humans is the main focus) as all being are our parents.
- Human beings are master of themselves, and there is no other more superior creatures, beings or forces that can determine the fate of human beings.
- All human beings (stakeholders) are equal, and they all can become a Buddha with earnest efforts.
- Karma (Causal Cycle) 因果報應
- If one can, one should try (intending) to be helpful with an altruistic spirit 利他 . If one cannot be helpful to others, at least he /she should not cause harm to others.
- In order to develop this empathy and compassion for others, one should learn to recognize and understand suffering (sorrows) in different contexts.
- It is necessary to examine one's own mind and discipline oneself until one finds oneself with a full sense of compassion.
- Focus on one's Buddhist-inspired deeply felt ethical consciousness

and eternal values.

8. Relevant Buddhist Scriptures for Practical Adoption

Four Noble Truths 四聖諦：
> Sorrow 苦
> Cause of sorrow 集
> Extinction of sorrow 滅
> Eightfold Path to remove the sorrow 道

Five Precepts 五戒：
> No killing living beings 不殺生
> No stealing 不偷盜
> No sexual misconduct 不邪淫
> No lying 不妄語
> No intoxication 不飲酒

Six Paramita 六波羅蜜：
> Charity 布施
> Morality 持戒
> Concentration 禪定
> Wisdom 智慧（般若）
> Effort 精進
> Tolerance 忍辱

9. Noble Eightfold Path 八正道

At the heart of Buddhist teachings lies in the Eightfold Path.

The life is full of suffering/sorrow and to end this suffering one has to follow the Eightfold Path.

3-fold approach 根、道、果：
• Cultivation of wisdom:
- Right view 正見

- Right intention 正思惟

• Maintaining conducts:
  - Right speech 正語
  - Right actions 正業
  - Right livelihood 正命

• Development of concentration:
  - Right efforts 正精進
  - Right mindfulness 正念
  - Right concentration 正定

Non-linear: the last 2 go into all parts of the paths.
They intertwine and intersect

10. Ethical Beliefs and Spiritual Pursuit

Spiritual can feed the hunger of mind and soul for people, besides material progress.

Ethical beliefs is considered necessary for progress on the spiritual path.

Spiritual pursuit in Buddhism refers to keeping away the negative emotion such as anger, jealousy, greed, doubt and fear. True freedom refers to states when such feelings do not arise at all.

Buddhism teaches its followers to take greater personal responsibility for their actions, to have a determined detachment when needed, and embrace a holistic perspective of their actions.

One can follow the Noble Eightfold Path to maintain an ethical, spiritual and professional life.

The principles if followed by a modern business organization, then it can have high ethical standard.

The best management is to manage one's mind and heart well.

Evidence suggest that embracing spirituality within organizations (such as awareness of self and environment, and connectedness with the community) lead to better personal development, staff management and corporate performance.

Modern management should incorporate more Buddhist thoughts to enhance the fragmented model of individual and recognize a person as a whole person.

11. Further Observations

A Buddhist perspective on business ethics takes into account the individual in a holistic manner which focuses on one's interconnected cognitive efforts, inner thoughts, feelings, and behaviour.

People adopting these Buddhism-inspired ideas do not need to limit to them as an exclusive or limiting framework. Consistent with the openness of Buddhism, people may use other principles (e.g. the 5 virtues of Junzi) in conjunction with them.

Additional research is needed to develop instruments for adopting the Noble Eightfold Path and measuring its practice and effectiveness.

Sociology and the Cultivation of Buddhist Wisdom

Richard Madsen

Distinguished Professor, Department of Sociology, UC San Diego

The world today is in crisis. Indeed, it always has been. The first noble truth taught by Sakyamuni Buddha is the existence of suffering. Although the fundamental impermanence of all things is the root of suffering, the felt form of suffering changes over time. The main human vices that cause suffering are greed, anger, delusion, and hatred. These have always been with us. But now we have capitalist greed, militarized anger (with weapons of mass destruction), technological delusion, and ethnic hatred, all globalized and causing a breakdown in our fragile systems for even imperfectly maintaining peace and threatening the ecological balance of our planet and perhaps even the survivability of the human species itself. The scope of this crisis exceeds anything that the people of Sakyamuni Buddha's time could have imagined. But these are the causes and conditions we face today. Along with other masters of humanistic and engaged Buddhism, Sheng Yen Shifu worked to engage the Buddhist tradition with this modern world in crisis. This is a task his followers must continue. As a sociologist deeply inspired by Sheng Yen Shifu, I would like to offer a few words about how the sociological imagination might help contribute to this task.

1. Sociology's Compatibility with Buddhism

Sociology is a modern science, developed in the 19th and early 20th centuries to help understand the wonderous possibilities and great dangers of the modern world—especially, to understand the possibilities for true human freedom and fulfillment in this world. Although it is a modern, secular science, its sociological imagination resonates with important parts of the Buddhist tradition. It does this more fully, I think, than the other secular social sciences of modernity, economics, political science, and psychology. One of the most basic sociological insights is that of our fundamental social interdependence—the isolated individual is an illusion. As the great French founding father of sociology, Emile Durkheim wrote when discussing the origin of religious practices among Australian aborigines, "We speak a language we did not create; we use instruments we did not invent; we claim rights we did not establish; each generation inherits a treasury of knowledge that it did not itself amass; and so on. We owe these various benefits of civilization to society, and although in general we do not see where they came from, we know at least that they are not of our own making. It is these things that give man his distinctiveness among all creatures, for man is man only because he is civilized." The sacred symbols of the aborigines were the way they expressed and brought into being this fundamental interdependence and Durkheim thought that this was indeed the basis of sacred symbols in all types of religious life throughout history.

Thus, our self-identity is dependent on the vast interdependent social world into which we were born, and indeed since Durkheim's time we have come to appreciate more deeply our interdependence not only with the social world but with the whole interconnected web of life. We know the truth of ourselves only as part of a larger social whole.

Yet that social whole has been changing, around the world, with the forces of global modernity. An important part of these changes is individuation. The old social bonds that connected people to family, community, town and nation have become attenuated. The modern self, as the sociologically-informed philosopher Charles Taylor has put it, is a "buffered self". There is a kind of shell around the self that at least partially insulates it from the influence of others. Cut off physically, and sometimes emotionally, from tight-knit family and community, people are thrown back onto their own resources. As the 19th century French philosopher and proto-sociologist Alex de Tocqueville wrote of Americans, "Such folk owe no man anything and hardly expect anything from anybody. They form the habit of thinking of themselves in isolation and imagine that their whole destiny is in their own hands....Each man is forever thrown back on himself alone, and there is danger that he may be shut up in the solitude of his own heart."

There is a strong resonance here with Buddhist warnings about the suffering that comes from being shut up in our own self-centered desires. "The primary obstacle to attaining wisdom," says Sheng Yen, "is attachment to the self. When you face people, things, and situations, the notion of 'I' rises immediately within you. When you attach to this 'I,' you categorize and judge everything else accordingly: 'This is mine; that is not. This is good for me; that is not. I like this; I hate that.' Attachment to the idea of self makes true clarity impossible."

Whether we see it or not, interdependence exists and profoundly affects us, and sociologists have seen it as their job to help us understand the interconnected interdependence, and in the end to help each of us take responsibility for building a better interconnected world.

Sociology also shows how our individual actions often have consequences that reach far beyond our immediate intentions. And it has a strong view of relentless systemic change, driven by such unintended consequences. Echoes of karma.

All of such change, sociologists—especially sociologists of culture—tell us is driven not only by material forces but by changes in the meanings that give us direction and purpose. Buddhism too focuses on meaning. I particularly remember a dharma talk given by Sheng Yen soon after the devastating earthquake of 921, 1999. Classical Buddhist teaching, he said, was that our perceptions about the world were illusions. But there was a distinction between perceptions of "hard realities" like buildings falling down in earthquakes—these were not illusions—and interpretations of the meaning of these realities. The understanding of the earthquake as a disaster was an illusion. One needed spiritual healing to understand this event in a positive light, an understanding that would comfort the afflicted and produce good karma for generations to come.

But a particularly important modern development is the collapse of common meanings. The great sociological founding father Max Weber wrote that modern people live in a world of "warring gods", that is warring values about the proper goals of life, backed up in the end by warring systems of belief. We live now in an age of competing meanings—competing ideologies about the purpose of life, our responsibilities toward others, the requirements of justice, the goals of politics. Is the purpose of life material success defined through consumerism or something more transcendent? If more transcendent, how is that defined? Are we responsible mainly to enable ourselves to come out ahead in competition with others or to weave webs of interconnection for the benefit of all? Is justice about making everybody the same or giving everyone a proper place in a hierarchical order? Is politics about creating harmony or engaging in aggression? There are coherent voices arguing for all these positions, not only outside of us but within our minds. Modern people have divided selves. Our various social roles pull us in this direction and that: How can I be both a good parent and spouse, and also a good worker, a good citizen, and a good friend? Often these different parts of our lives place contradictory demands on us. We can try to compartmentalize them but most of us still crave integrity. This is modern suffering in the modern condition and sociology helps explain how this condition has come into being.

2. Buddhism's Transcendence of Sociology

There is an important degree of compatibility, even resonance, between the sociological imagination and the Buddhist vision. In Dharma Drum University, you should teach sociology, not merely to help provide tools to "market" the dharma but to provide a way of thinking about the modern world that can help reinforce and enhance traditional Buddhist teaching. Nevertheless, sociology is by no means the same as Buddhism. Sociology is after all a modern science that draws upon the Western Enlightenment tradition to combine rational thought with empirical investigation. Buddhism goes deeper. It engages not just the brain but the whole person to seek not just accurate knowledge but true wisdom. It provides a way to not only recognize our interdependence but to embrace it, to not only acknowledge the existence of warring gods but to transcend them.

When you sit in Chan meditation or practice walking meditation or cultivate mindfulness in everyday work, you are reaching beyond scientific knowledge, and indeed beyond words. As Sheng Yen said, "you must remember that when we practice in the Chan tradition, we refrain from using words and speech....Nonetheless, you will notice that Chan masters talk a lot. They sometimes write a lot too. But the import of what we talk or write about is to convey that whatever you think or say is wrong. That is the content of all my talks. No words or description will suffice to describe a state of realization. Anyone who attempted to describe such a state would be considered by a Chan master to be a smart devil, not an awakened being."

With many words, sociology can analyze the degrees and forms of our interdependence, but it cannot go beyond cognitive awareness to accept interdependence, to find integrity, and to accept the moral responsibilities that come with that. The practice of Buddhism, especially though the guidance of a wise master and the support of a compassionate sangha, can do this. It can help us see the world not only intelligently but clearly and with a clarity that sustains compassion. Amid the flux of a turbulent ocean of modern ideologies it can also give us an anchor, albeit a weightless one. That is, Buddhist practice, especially in the Chan tradition, is a "gateless gate." It does not absolutely say this particular set of ideas is right and all others wrong. It looks to a wisdom beyond words, beyond ideologies that rejects the ultimate truth value of all of them but is open to learning some worthwhile insights from all.

3. Contributions of Sociology to Buddhism

Thus, the ancient traditions of Buddhism, especially Chan Buddhism, transcend the limited perspective of modern social sciences like sociology. Nonetheless, I believe that sociology still has something important to contribute to Buddhism, a challenge to make it to go continually deeper to heal the brokenness of our modern lives in our modern world. Like the other great religious and philosophical traditions arising in the "Axial Age" of about 2500 years ago, Buddhism represented a leap in human consciousness toward transcendence—of going beyond social relations constrained by rigid rules enforced through power and constantly pitting Us versus Them.

But very often, over centuries, the great insights brought by Sakyamuni Buddha and other great prophets have become corrupted, co-opted into systems of wealth and power and transformed into cages of rules that stifle the spirit rather than expand it. This has happened throughout the centuries. Modern sociology can help us see how bad the corruption has become today. It can show how greed is institutionalized in global capitalism. Global systems of capital demand that all kinds of producers relentlessly strive to maximize profit even if that generates widespread inequality, while justifying such arrangements through advertising that defines the good life through limitless consumerism. Even if someone isn't personally greedy, he must take part in the system of relentless profit-making if his business is to survive. And these social imperatives affect people who are not directly involved in business, even leaders of religious organizations. Too often, around the world, religious organizations have treated their message as a "product" to be marketed like a commodity designed to produce "experiences" along the lines of other items in the consumerist marketplace. If they don't do this, they think, they won't grow. Too often, leaders of major religious organizations have entered into cozy alliances with wealthy and powerful elites and compromised their spiritual message to meet the interests of such elites. If they don't do this, they think, they won't get the resources to carry out their good works. We see this for example in some of the scandals affecting the worldwide Catholic Church today. But there have been some scandals along these lines affecting some Buddhist organizations in Taiwan in recent years, which may not be based on accurate facts but on suspicions that some members of the public have come to have about all successful religious organizations. But to your great credit, Dharma Drum has not been touched by such scandals.

Sociology can also analyze the causes of growth in the militarized hatred of war. It can indeed show how religious fervor can increase the violence of war. Throughout history religious movements have too often justified military aggression, "Holy Wars." This includes some Japanese Zen Buddhists supporting the military during the Pacific War.

Sociology also dispels the delusion that the solution to our problems is simply more technology. It shows how technological development is not driven by pure disinterested science but by powerful social interests and how the benefits of technology can also be coupled with great harm. Sociology can uncover the social forces that enable both the good and bad elements of technology and point to the need to reform such social forces if we are to reap the good but not the bad.

Finally, sociology documents and at least partially explains the rise of global ethnic hatred—including the role that religion has played in fomenting this. The sacred symbols of religion have served as the foundation for ethnic identities in a way that allows the groups to dehumanize others. We see this among certain white Christian identity groups in the USA, but also in Buddhist support for atrocities against the Rohingya in Myanmar. Once again, to your credit, and to Sheng Yen's leadership, Dharma Drum has never been implicated in such things.

But sociology can provide not only a criticism of the ways that other spiritual lifeworlds have (in the words of the philosopher Jurgen Habermas) been "colonized" by systems of wealth and power, it can furnish warnings to religious practitioners too. It can show the relentless pressures and temptations that cause "charisma" to become "routinized" and the spirit to become corrupted. It can give us cautionary tales that can heighten our awareness and strengthen our resolve to avoid such things.

Beyond this, a sociological imagination can challenge Buddhists to new ways of engagement with the modern world. The practice of Buddhism—like deep practice of all kinds of religion—requires leisure time, a time of freedom separate from the pressures of making a living and from the distractions of the clamorous voices of necessity. Global inequality, both within and among nations, leaves too many people in crushing poverty and puts even the insecure middle classes under great pressure simply to maintain their precarious position in life. These are the causes and conditions of the modern world and sociology can reveal their extent and power. How should Buddhists respond?

One way to enter the zone of freedom necessary for Buddhist practice has of course always been to leave the family and enter a monastery. But only a few can do this. Others can go on retreats or pilgrimages or find time during the day for periods of meditation or study. But the structural pressures of the modern economy make this seem like an unaffordable luxury for many if not most. Moreover, meditation and mindfulness require a certain amount of relaxation, but in too many places wars and rumors of war make this impossible. The deepened awareness that comes from Buddhist practice can enable us to stand courageously in stressful and fearful times, but one first has to find the time and space to begin to develop such awareness. To enable the dharma to flourish, we need global economic structures of shared material sufficiency and political structures of stable peace.

Of course enlightenment comes from individual practice, but because of the interdependency of all things, I would advocate from a sociological perspective that Buddhists (and committed members of other religions) engage in effort to transform some of the economic and political structures that inhibit pursuit of the dharma. This would involve participating in collective action that firmly but non-violently might challenge the local manifestations of such global structures: structures of economic exploitation, racism, militarism. Of course, humanistic Buddhists in Taiwan and elsewhere have been doing marvelous work in giving compassionate care to victims of these structures, but in general Taiwan's humanistic Buddhists have not confronted the structures themselves. This approach was perhaps very correct, an application of skillful means to the causes and conditions of Taiwan in the past generation. But the causes and conditions are dynamic, constantly changing, and, faced from a sociological perspective with widespread global breakdown of systems of even fragile justice and peace and environmental sustainability, perhaps we need to consider more collective engagement with the social systems causing the crisis. There are various models for such engaged Buddhism, such as that of Thich Nhat Hanh and the Dalai Lama.

The problem, from a sociological perspective, with engagement meant to transform unjust structures of the world is that those who get engaged can end up "fighting fire with fire" and taking on themselves the very vices that are embedded in these structures. From a Buddhist perspective, the structures are polluting. Sheng Yen said that Buddhism should be engaged with the secular world but avoid being compromised by it. To that end, Buddhists and religious practitioners of all kinds must practice constant spiritual cultivation along with any engagement—meditation, prayer, and study under the guidance if possible of wise masters, that would help in understanding how compassion to change the world is shaped by the wisdom of the tradition—how religious people have unique ways of dealing with worldly problems, distinct from purely secular actors.

4. Sheng Yen's Contributions to Sociology

Sheng Yen laid the seeds for this way of thinking when he spoke about how to confront the ecological crisis into which our planet is heading.

> "The wasteful consumption of natural resources and destruction of ecology are caused by humankind's psychological craving for convenience and wealth. If we can practice the Buddha's teaching of 'leading a contented life with few desires' and 'being satisfied and therefore always happy', and if we are willing to use our intelligence to deal with problems and engage diligently in productive work, then, without having to contend with one another or fight with nature, we can lead very happy lives."

A spiritual salvation is therefore key to salvation of the material environment. But the practice of saving the planet can itself be a form of cultivation that leads to higher spiritual awareness. According to Sheng Yen:

> "The environmental tasks of general people are mostly restricted to the material aspects…. The environmental tasks we carry out have to go deeper from the material level to the spiritual level of society and thinking. Environmental protection must be combined with our respective religious beliefs and philosophical thinking into an earnest mission, so that environmentalism will not become mere slogans. So, strictly speaking, the purification of humankind's mind is free from evil intentions and is not polluted by us. However, for ordinary people, it is advisable to set out by cultivating the

habit of protecting the material environment, and go deeper step by step until at last they can cultivate environmentalism on the spiritual level."

With other religious leaders, Sheng Yen stresses that we need spiritual solutions, based on transcendent visions, to address the problems that "worldly philosophers" like the sociologists have long been describing. Although from a sociological perspective the world is in an overwhelming crisis, based on global forces so strong that it is hard to see what hope there is to overcome the crisis, we also can describe signs of hope arising in new forms of spiritual awakening, the renewal and modernization of the old Axial traditions of transcendence and the conversion of people from fatalistic despair to hopeful engagement. At the end of my book Democracy's Dharma, on religious renaissance in Taiwan, I wrote a section on a sociology of hope. Using, among others, the example of Dharma Drum Mountain, I tried to explore the conditions in which hopeful spiritual awakenings could arise.

I said that historically such awakening arose when a society has been destabilized and threatened with breakdown—but not to the point where its religious and moral traditions have been completely destroyed. There is then the opportunity for moral leaders to build on those remnants of tradition and fashion from them new visions that point toward a better future. I thought that Taiwan was a good example of such a context—a place disrupted by a century of colonialism, war, migration and dizzying social and economic change, and caught in the middle of struggles of mighty global powers, all of which condemn it to radical insecurity. Yet its basic culture was never destroyed (it was much more intact than the culture of China after Mao's Cultural Revolution) and there have arisen out of this religious leaders who have creatively developed the traditions to meet modern conditions. Sheng Yen was one such leader.

In responding in a hopeful way to the local anxieties and confusions of people in Taiwan, he built on the universal principles inherent in the Buddhist tradition to put forth a truly global vision, a vision that asks us to transcend religious and ethnic divisions to achieve world peace. For example, in a speech given at the World Economic Forum in New York on February 2, 2002, less than six months after the terrorist attacks on the World Trade Center, Sheng Yen proclaimed, "The days of monocultural societies are long gone and will not return again; and fortunately so, otherwise the destiny of humanity would be a very tragic one! Therefore, I would like to make this appeal here for all humanity: humankind must understand that the notion of the sacred is interpreted differently in a multicultural pluralistic world, and that we should strive to seek for harmony. Such harmony is not to be found in dogmatic homogenization or elimination of difference. It can only come through a grassroots discovery of commonality within difference, and difference within commonality."

There is a nod here to the sociologist Emile Durkheim's theory that sacred symbols are the foundation of human communities— a theory that helps explain the global conflicts between different ethnic-religious communities based on different sacred symbols. But while sociology can help explain this and warn us about it, Sheng Yen develops a Buddhist perspective to move it forward.

In another speech given in New York at an International Conference on Religious Cooperation just nine days after the terrorist attacks, he said: "Once on an airplane I was sitting next to a Christian missionary who was piously reading the Bible and praying. Seeing that I had nothing to do, he gave me a Bible and showed me how to read it. I praised his good intentions and enthusiasm, and agreed with his statement that Christianity is the only religion through which one can attain salvation. He immediately asked me, 'If this is the case, why are you a Buddhist monk? Isn't that a pity?' I said, 'I'm sorry, but for me Buddhism is most suitable. So I would say that Buddhism is the best religion.'" Sheng Yen can explain this paradoxical position in terms of classical Chan.

"Transcending your thoughts...is a method that consists of

maintaining an attitude of non-involvement with yourself or others. The goal of this method is roughly described as a phrase that translates as, 'Be separate, or free, from the mind, from thoughts, and from consciousness.' To be free from all this, is to be in a state of enlightenment. In such freedom of mind, it might be said that we see the world." But this freedom, it must be said, is not achieved simply by reading theories, but by following a dharma path of cultivation through ritual and meditation.

Sheng Yen's wisdom has not stopped the world's crisis. Since he made these statements, the world has continued to develop more polarization, more religiously based hostility, more suspicion toward people of different faiths and ethnicities. Thus, from a sociological point of view I would think that his successors should combine contemplation with action. We need to keep on developing ways to bring people from different ethnic groups into positive contacts with one another and we need to break down social boundaries that make this difficult. We need to facilitate respectful dialogues between believers in different faiths (as Sheng Yen was doing with the Christian missionary on the plane). Through concrete, compassionate action, we need to welcome and support refugees and migrants. Through non-violent example, we need to combat militarism.

5. The Future of Transcendence?

I would like to close with some paragraphs I wrote in a chapter on "The Future of Transcendence" which I wrote for a book on "*The Axial Age and its Consequences.*"

We are going through a period of social breakdown like the era that gave rise to Buddhism, Confucianism, prophetic Judaism, and Greek rationalism 2500 years ago—quests for spiritual unity that after initial flourishing were often subsumed by the wealth and power of ancient empires. Such disintegration, as before, can only be overcome through a renewed spiritual unity. So argued the great philosopher Karl Jaspers. But as he said, "The universality of a world order obligatory to all (in contrast to a world empire) is possible only when the multiple contents of faith remain free in their historical communication, without the unity of a universally valid doctrinal content. The common element of all faith in relation to world order can only be that everyone desires the ordering of the foundations of existence, in a world community in which he has room to evolve with the peaceful means of the spirit." As Sheng Yen put this more succinctly, "The days of monocultural societies are long gone…"

The development of humanistic Buddhism in Taiwan—of which Dharma Drum Mountain is a prime example—is perhaps one of those movements that can lead toward such an ecumenical spiritual unity. Such movements usually occur at the margins of their respective institutionalized religious traditions. They reach across doctrinal religious boundaries to create networks of concern, cross-national and cross-class affiliations of unlikely bedfellows. It is such movements that Jaspers seemed to think were the potential fabric of authentic world community: "He who would like to live in the unclosed and unorganized and unorganisable community of authentic human beings—in what used to be called the invisible Church—does in fact live today as an individual in alliance with individuals scattered over the face of the earth, an alliance that survives every disaster, a dependability that is not fixed by any path or any specific imperative."

But such movements are not a good object for standard sociological study. They cannot easily be categorized, pinned into a theoretical framework. Sociology is more at home studying the corruption of the spirit than its emergence. So perhaps we cannot "operationalize" the seeds of global transcendence; sociology in itself cannot tell us when we have encountered them. But by amply theorizing and documenting the boundary development, the alienation and dehumanization that call out for transcendence, and by starting us on a global, comparative search for the contexts in which transcendence might happen, sociology might lead us up to the point where we might actually witness it. Sociology can play what Karl Jaspers called the role of "philosophy": "Philosophy [sociology] lead us along the road to the point at which love acquires its depth in real communication. Then in this love, though the success of communication, the truth that links us together will be disclosed to those who are most remote in the diversity of their historical origin."

Buddhist wisdom—together with the wisdom of other great Axial traditions—can take us beyond the point where philosophy and sociology leave off and help us to touch, however tentatively, on the truth that links us together.

〔全文中譯〕

社會學和佛法智慧的修持

趙文詞著　陳維武譯

今天的世界處於危機之中，其實我們的世界向來都是如此。釋迦牟尼佛所教導的四聖諦，第一諦就是苦的存在。雖然諸行無常是苦的根本原因，苦的感知形式卻是隨著時代而改變的。人類造作苦的惡因主要是貪、瞋、癡，和仇恨。雖然人類社會自古以來就有這些惡因，但是在今日的世界，我們面對的是資本主義的貪、帶有大規模殺傷力武器軍事化的瞋、科技的癡，以及族群之間的仇恨。而這一切皆席捲全球，破壞了人類賴以勉強維持和平的脆弱系統，也威脅了地球生態的平衡，甚至於威脅了人類這個物種繼續生存下去的可能性。這個危機範圍之廣，不是生活在釋迦牟尼佛時代的人們所能想像的。然而這正是我們今日所須面對的因緣。與其他人間佛教及入世佛教的導師一起，聖嚴師父努力使佛教傳統介入這個危機中的世界。這是他的追隨者所當繼續的任務。身為一位深受聖嚴師父影響的社會學者，我想貢獻幾句微言，探討社會學的想像能為這個任務做出什麼樣的貢獻。

一、社會學與佛法相容之處

社會學是一門現代科學。它在十九及二十世紀這段時間發展起來，旨在幫我們了解現代世界中有哪些殊勝的機遇，又有哪些巨大的危險。它特別關注的是了解人類在這個世界中獲得真正的自由和真正圓成人生的可能性。雖然它是一門現代的世俗科學，社會學的想像與佛教的一些重要成分，相容互通能起共鳴。我認為社會學在這方面比包括經濟學、政治學和心理學等的其他現代世俗社會科學做得要更透徹充實一點。社會學的一個最基本的領悟是人類社會的根本相互依存性，也就是說，與世隔絕的個體只是一個幻象。社會學的一位偉大奠基人、法國的埃米爾·塗爾幹在討論澳洲原住民宗教活動的起源時這麼說：「我們說著不是由我們自己創造的語言；我們使用著不是我們自己發明的工具；我們宣稱擁有不是自己創設的權力；我們的每一代都繼承了不是由他們所積累的知識寶庫；諸如此類。因為有了社會，我們享有文明所帶來的各種利益。雖然我們原則上無法看到這些東西源於何處，我們最少清楚知道，這一切都不是由我們自己所創造的。正是這些東西讓人類有別於其他生物，人之所以為人，就是因為他的文明。」原住民的神聖符號是他們表達和示現這個根本的相互依存性的方式。塗爾幹認為，這也正是歷史中所有的宗教最基本的神聖符號。

因此，我們誕生於一個廣大的相互依存的社會世界中，我們的自我認同就依附著這個社會世界而起。確實，從塗爾幹的時代以來，我們就學會了更深切的珍視與社會世界、乃

至和整個相互關聯的生命網路的相互依存性。我們知道，自己只是一個更大的社會整體的一部分，這就是有關自我的真相。

　　但是，這個社會整體，循著全球的現代性力量，在世界各地不斷地改變。這些改變中的一個重要內容是個體化。曾經把人們與家庭、社群、城鎮及國家聯繫著的舊有社會鏈結已經變弱了。深諳社會學的哲學家查理斯‧泰勒就說過，現代的自我是個「緩衝的我」。意思是在這個自我的周遭，有類似外殼的一種東西，把他和他人的影響最少是局部地隔絕了起來。在形體上、甚至是情感上切斷了和家庭及社群的密切關係後，人們只能仰賴自身的資源。就如十九世紀的早期社會學家亞力西斯‧德‧托克維爾對美國人的評述：「這種人對任何人都沒有虧欠，也不期望從任何人那裡得到什麼。他們養成了一種在孤立狀態中思考自身的習慣，想像自己的命運完全操在自己手上……每個人都永遠只能仰賴自己，而危險的是，他也可能因此封閉在自心的孤寂中。」

　　佛法對於被封閉在自我中心欲望裡頭所引發的苦，給予我們警誡。托克維爾的說法和佛法的警誡互通共鳴。聖嚴師父說：「證得智慧的主要障礙，是我執。當你面對人、事、物的時候，我相在心中即刻升起。而當你執著這個『我』的時候，你就依著我相對所有東西分類，加以評判，『這個是我的，那個不是。這個對我是好的，那個不好。我喜歡這個，我討厭那個。』對於我相的執著，讓我們無法清楚了知。」

　　不管我們是否看見，相互依存性確實存在，也深深地影

響著我們。而社會學家正是把理解交織在一起的相互依存性視為己任，更希望最終能幫助每一個人為建設一個更好的相互連結的世界盡自己的責任。

社會學也解釋了個人的行動後果常遠遠超出我們當下的行動意向。它也對由這些意想不到的後果所驅動的無止息的系統變遷有一套強烈的看法。我們可稱之為業力的呼應。

社會學家、特別是文化社會學家告訴我們，驅動所有這些變遷的，不只是物質的力量，還包括了給予我們方向和目標的價值觀的改變。佛教也著重意義和價值觀。我特別記得聖嚴師父於九二一大地震後的一個開示。他說，在經典佛法裡，我們對世界的感受是虛幻的。但是在這場地震中，我們必須區分諸如在地震中倒塌的建築這種「硬現實」和我們對這些現實所賦予的意義。「硬現實」不是虛幻的，但是把地震解讀為災難確實是虛幻的。我們需要心靈的療癒才能以正面的角度理解這種事件。而這種理解方式，能夠撫慰受難者，能夠為後世帶來善業。

但是現代社會的一個重要發展是共同意義的崩潰。社會學的偉大奠基人馬克斯・韋伯就說過，現代人居住在一個「諸神交戰」的世界。也就是說，我們的世界裡有各種相衝突的價值體系，它們對生命目的的不同詮釋造成價值之爭。我們活在一個意義競爭的時代，這是各種意識型態對生命的目的、對他人的義務、正義的條件、政治的目的等等賦予不同的意義並相互競爭的時代。生命的目的是追求由消費所定義的物質成就，還是另有更為超越的目的？如果是更為超越的目的，又如何定義呢？我們的責任主要是讓自己在和別人

的競爭中勝出，還是為了眾人的利益去編織相互連結的關係網絡？正義是讓所有人都變得一樣，還是讓每個人在階級秩序中各得其所？政治是為了創造和諧還是為了相互攻擊？這些不同的立場，都各有一套條理分明的聲音在為其辯護，而這些不同的聲音不只在我們身外，也在我們心中。現代人的自我是分裂的，不同的社會角色總是把我們往不同的方向推擠。比如說，怎麼樣才能身為人父人母，同時身為人妻人夫，又同時扮演一位好的員工、好的公民、好的朋友？這些生命中不同的角色往往對我們有相牴觸的要求。雖然我們可以嘗試把這些要求區分開來處理，但是多數人仍然渴望一以貫之的整體感。這是一種現代情境中的現代之苦，而社會學有助於解釋這種狀況的由來。

二、佛法對社會學的超越

社會學想像和佛法之間，在某個程度上有重要的相容性，甚至說共鳴。法鼓大學應該要開社會學課程，其目的不只是為了提供能協助「行銷」佛法的工具，而是提供一個在現代世界中有助於加強及提昇傳統佛教的思惟方式。不過，社會學和佛法確實並不相同。它畢竟是一門從西方啟蒙運動傳統中汲取養分、結合了理性思考及實證研究的現代科學。佛法走得更深。佛法發動的不僅是大腦，而是人的整體，所追求的不只是精確的知識，而是智慧。它提供了一條道路，不只是認識我們的相互依存性，而且要是擁抱相互依存性，不是只了解有交戰諸神的存在，更是要超越諸神。

當你在打坐或經行，或者在修動中禪的時候，你已經

在嘗試超越科學知識了，甚至於在超越語言文字了。聖嚴師父說：「在禪門內修行，必須牢記我們是不用文字和語言的……話雖如此，禪師們卻說了很多話，有時還寫了很多東西。但是，我們所說所寫的，其重要的意義在於傳達，任何你所能想的或者說的東西，都是錯的。我所有開示的內容，就是如此。證悟的境界不是任何文字或語言所能描繪表達的。如果有人嘗試形容悟境，那在一位禪師眼中，這個人不會是個開悟的人，而是個聰明的魔。」

社會學假以文字，可以分析我們的相互依存性的程度和形式，但是它無法超越認知覺知，從而接受相互依存性、找到整體性，去接受與此相隨的道德責任。佛法的修行，特別是依止明師的指導以及得到慈悲僧團的扶持，卻可以做到這一點。佛法可以幫助我們，不僅是知性地去看世界，而是以一種能長養慈悲的清晰度，把世界看得一清二楚。在現代意識型態的洶湧海洋暗流中，佛法給了我們一根錨，一根沒有重量的錨。這是說，佛法的修行，特別是在禪宗裡面，是「無門之門」。它不會指認某套思想絕對是對的，而其他的全是錯的；它的目光總是望向超越語言文字、超越意識型態的智慧，這種智慧否定所有意識型態的絕對真理價值，卻又願意開放地從這些意識型態中學習值得學習的見解。

三、社會學對佛法的貢獻

所以，古老的佛教，特別是禪佛教，超越了諸如社會學等現代社會科學的有限觀點。儘管如此，我相信社會學仍然能為佛教做出一些重要的貢獻，它能挑戰佛教，使佛教在面

對現代世界中破碎的現代生命、使之療癒的路上，不斷地愈走愈深入。與其他在大約兩千五百年前出現在「軸心時代」的偉大宗教和哲學傳統一樣，佛教代表的是人類意識朝向超越性的一個跨越，超越那種由威權維持的僵化規矩所制約的社會關係及其所不斷挑起的人我之分。

但是，釋迦牟尼佛和其他偉大先知所傳下來的智慧，千百年來一次次地被腐蝕，被財富和權力體系納入其中，被轉變成規矩的牢籠，壓制著人類的精神，而不是擴展人類的精神。這種情況在歷史的各個時期都發生過。現代社會學可以幫我們看清，到了今天，這種腐蝕的程度有多嚴重。社會學可以向我們展示，貪婪是如何在全球資本主義中被體制化了。全球的資本系統要求各類生產者，即使會產生廣泛的不平等也要力求最大的利潤，更通過各種宣傳，把過上好日子等同於無節制無止盡的消費，以此為求取最大利潤的行為辯解。在這個系統中，即便個人本身不是貪婪的，如果想讓業務存活下去，他就得參與這個毫無保留的尋求利潤的系統。這種社會律令的影響所及，還包括了沒有直接涉入商界的人，甚至還包括宗教組織的領袖。在世界各地，太多宗教組織把他們所要傳達的訊息當成一種「產品」來傳銷，當成一種可以產生「體驗」的商品設計，與世間消費市場中的其他商品一樣銷售。他們的想法是，如果不這樣做，就無法成長。一些主要宗教組織的領袖常與手握財富和權力的菁英結盟取暖，降低心靈教誨的標準，來滿足這些菁英的利益。他們的想法是，如果不這樣做，就無法獲得能讓他們做好事的資源。今日全球天主教教會的若干醜聞，就是這種作法的例

證。近年來臺灣的一些佛教團體也捲入了類似的醜聞,儘管這些醜聞不一定有確鑿的證據,而是源於社會上某些人對所有成功的宗教組織所抱有的猜疑。法鼓山沒有被捲入這類醜聞中,這是值得嘉許的。

社會學也可以分析軍事化仇恨戰爭的起因。確實,社會學分析告訴我們,宗教狂熱是如何增加了戰爭的暴力。在人類的歷史中,宗教運動往往被用來為軍事侵略辯護,這就是所謂的「聖戰」,某些日本禪宗佛教徒在太平洋戰爭中對軍方的支持即屬此類。

社會學也掃除了寄希望於僅憑更多的科技來解決人類問題的妄想。社會學分析顯示,技術的發展並不是由純粹中立的科學所驅動,而是由強大的社會利益所驅動。它也顯示,技術帶來利益的同時,也帶來禍害。社會學可以揭示導致技術行善或作惡的社會力量,也指出如果想要收穫善果,規避惡果,我們就得對這些社會力量進行改革。

最後,社會學記錄了全球族群仇恨益發嚴重的現象,而且至少對其做出了部分的解釋,這包括宗教在醞釀族群仇恨中所扮演的角色。宗教的神聖符號被當作族群身分認同的基礎,甚至於使本族群不把他者當人。這樣的例子包括美國一些標榜白人基督徒身分的群體,也包括佛教徒對緬甸針對羅興亞人暴行的支持。法鼓山不曾涉入這類事件,在這方面,聖嚴師父的領導和四眾弟子的行誼,是值得嘉許的。

但是,社會學不僅能夠批判精神生活的世界被財富和權力系統「殖民」(套用哲學家約根·哈巴馬斯的話)的各種途徑,它還能為宗教修行者提供警示。社會學能揭示出使

「魅力」變成「慣例」的無盡壓力和誘惑。它所講述的警世敘事，能讓我們提高覺照，增強我們避開這些事物的決心。

除此之外，社會學的想像能激發佛教徒以新的方式和現代世界互動。與其他一切宗教的深度修行一樣，修行佛法必須有閒暇，也就是說，必須在謀生的壓力和生活中各種需求的喧囂之外有自由的時間。全球的不平等，包括國家內部的不平等和國與國之間的不平等，造成的局面是太多人生活在能壓垮人的貧困中，就連中產階級的地位也難有保障，使他們為了維持岌岌可危的地位，活在巨大的壓力中。這種狀況是現代社會中的因與緣，社會學可以揭露它們的威力和程度。那麼佛教徒應該如何因應這個局面呢？

要進入修行佛法所必備的自由之域，其中一個慣常的途徑當然是出家。但是這只有少數人能做到。其他人或許可以參加禪期、朝聖、在日常生活中撥出一些特定的時段來禪修及研習佛法。但是，由於現代經濟的結構性壓力，讓這個方法對許多人，甚至於多數人來說是不可企及的奢侈。另外，禪修及正念是以一定程度的放鬆為基礎的，而在太多的地方，戰亂和戰亂的傳言，讓放鬆成為不可能的事。佛法修行的最深覺照，讓我們能勇於面對充滿壓力和恐懼的時刻。但是，要開發這種覺照，必須具備修行所需的時間及空間。如果要讓佛法處處綻放，我們必須塑造一個共享物質豐足的經濟結構和長治久安的政治結構。

當然，開悟是個人修行之事。但是，由於萬事萬物是相互依存的，從社會學的角度，我謹倡議，佛教徒必須和其他宗教積極投入的修行者一起，參與帶動轉變有礙於追求佛

法的一些經濟和政治結構。這包括參與堅定而非暴力的群體行動，以制約諸如經濟剝削、種族主義和軍事主義這樣的全球結構在本地的推展。當然，在臺灣和其他地方的人間佛教行者，慈悲救濟這些結構的受害者，做了很多殊勝的工作。但是，總體來說，臺灣的人間佛教行者未曾直接面對並挑戰這些結構自身。這種作法或許非常正確，可以說是因應上一代臺灣社會因緣的方便法門。但是，因緣是動態的，不斷在變化。從社會學的角度來看當前的因緣，我們面對的是廣泛的、全球性的系統崩壞，甚至連脆弱的公義、和平及環境可續性都在崩壞。那麼我們或許就必須考慮以更加群體化的方式介入造成危機的社會系統。這種作法，入世佛教有一些值得借鑒的模式，例如一行禪師和達賴喇嘛的作法。

從社會學的角度看，付諸行動來轉化這個世界不公正結構的問題，是那些參與其中的人，可能最終會「以暴制暴」，沾染深植在這些結構中的惡行。從佛法的角度看，這些結構是會汙染的。聖嚴師父就說過，佛教應該涉入世俗世界，但是必須避免向其妥協。要做到這一點，佛教和各宗教的修行者必須在涉世的同時，恆常不斷地修行，禪修、祈禱，可能的話，在有智慧的老師指導下學習。這有助於修行者明瞭傳統的智慧如何形成了改變這一世界的慈悲之心，也就是說，宗教徒如何以其不同於純粹世俗之人的獨特方法處理世間的問題。

四、聖嚴師父對社會學的貢獻

聖嚴師父在提到如何面對地球正在趨近的生態危機時，

為這樣的思維播下了種子。

　　對自然資源浪費的使用以及生態的破壞，源於人類對方便和財富的心理欲求。如果我們能學習佛陀所教導的『少欲知足』及『知足常樂』，也願意運用自己的智力來處理問題，勤勞的從事生產，那麼，我們就可以在不需彼此競爭或和自然鬥爭的情況下，過著非常幸福的生活。

　　因此，心靈救贖是物質環境救贖之鑰。但是，拯救地球的行動也可以是修行的一種。做為一種修行，它也能讓我們趣向更高的心靈覺照。聖嚴師父說：

　　一般人的環保，多數是限制於物質的環保……我們所做的環保必須走得更深，從物質的層次到社會和思想的精神層次。環保必須與我們各自的宗教信仰及哲學思維結合，成為一個懇切的使命，環保才不至於只是一些口號。所以，嚴格的說，人類心靈的淨化指的是遠離惡念，不受染汙。不過，對於普通人，可以先從養成保護物質的習慣開始，再一步步的深入，直到可以在精神或心靈的層次做環保。

　　與其他宗教領袖一道，聖嚴師父強調，為了解決諸如社會學者等「世俗哲學家」很早就勾勒出的問題，我們需要基於超越觀的心靈解決方案。雖然從社會學的角度來看，我們的世界正處於一個由無比強大的全球力量所製造的大危機

中，很難想像能有什麼力挽狂瀾的希望，但是，我們看到希望的跡象，這些跡象包括嶄新的心靈覺醒形式、軸心超越傳承的復興與現代化，以及人們從認命的沮喪轉向充滿希望的參與。我所著的《民主之法》一書，內容是臺灣的宗教復興，最後一章寫的是希望的社會學。書中用了包括法鼓山在內的幾個宗教團體的例子，嘗試探索充滿希望的心靈覺醒需要具備什麼條件。

我在這一章中說，歷史上這種覺醒總是在社會已經不穩定、面臨崩壞的時刻產生，但前提是其宗教和道德傳統未被徹底破壞。在這種情況下，道德領袖有機會在這些尚存的傳統的基礎上重建，從中形成新的、面向更好未來的理念。我認為臺灣就是一個很好的例子。它經歷了一個世紀的殖民、戰爭、移民、讓人不知所從的社會及經濟轉變，並且夾在巨大的全球權力鬥爭之間。這一切讓臺灣社會面臨深切的不安。但是，它的基本文化沒有被破壞，相較於文革後中國的文化，臺灣的文化保存完整許多。在這個社會狀態中，就有宗教領袖應運而起，以創新的方式發展傳統，順應現代的因緣。聖嚴師父即是其一。

面對臺灣民眾的焦慮和迷茫，他以充滿希望的方式回應，依據佛教本具的普世原則，提出一個真正懷抱全球的理念，一個促請世人超越宗教和族群藩籬，以達成世界和平的理念。其中一個例子是他在世貿中心遭遇恐怖襲擊還不到六個月，於二〇〇二年二月二日在紐約世界經濟論壇的演講。聖嚴師父宣說：「只允許單一文化存在的社會，已經不會再來，否則人類的命運，將會非常地悲慘！因此，我要向全人

類提出建議：人類必須理解，在多元化世界裡，對『神聖』的認知是多元的，而我們必須求同存異。求同存異的和諧，不是由某種教條的霸權來消除差異。這種和諧，其唯一的途徑是在草根的層面上發現異中之同，同中之異。」

這個說法呼應了埃米爾‧塗爾幹的理論，即神聖符號是人類社群的基礎。塗爾幹的這個理論可以用來解釋根基於不同神聖符號的不同族群之間的全球性衝突。但是，雖然社會學能夠幫我們解釋這個現象，給予我們警戒，聖嚴師父則發展了佛法的觀點，使其跨前一步。

在恐怖襲擊僅九天後於紐約舉行的國際宗教合作研討會中，他發表演講，說了這一段話：「有一次，我在出國旅行的飛機上，正好和一位可敬的基督教傳教士緊鄰而坐。他非常虔誠地讀《聖經》和禱告，見我無事可做，便給我一本《聖經》，並且教我如何閱讀。我就稱讚他的善意和熱心，同時也同意他所說的，信仰基督教是世界上唯一可以得救的宗教。他便立即問我：『既然如此，為什麼做了佛教的和尚，豈不可惜！』我說：『真對不起，對我來說，佛教最適合我，我也要說，佛教是最好的宗教。』」聖嚴法師能用經典禪的觀點解釋這種矛盾的立場。

　　「離念的方法，是維持一種不與自我和他人糾纏的態度。這個方法的目的可以如下粗略的描繪：『把自己的心、意、識全部抖落，赤裸裸的，一絲不掛。』這個心無掛礙的境界，就是開悟的境界。如是心無掛礙，可以說我們真正的看到世界。」但是，必須指出的是，這個自由不

是通過研讀理論所能企及的，它必須在佛法的道路上，通過懺法和禪法的修行方能完成。

聖嚴法師的智慧沒能阻止世界的危機。在他發表上述的言論之後，世界繼續變得更加兩極化，宗教敵對狀況變得更加嚴重，不同族群和信仰的人們之間有更多的猜疑。因此，從社會學的角度，我想，他的繼承者應該要結合思想和行動。我們需要繼續開發讓不同族群的人有正面接觸的方法，也需要打破阻撓這種行動的社會藩籬。我們需要創造機會，讓抱持不同信仰的人能聚在一起相互尊重地對話，就如聖嚴師父在飛機上和基督教傳教士的對話一般。通過具體而慈悲的行動，我們需要敞開胸懷，歡迎難民和移民，支持他們。通過非暴力的方式，我們需要和軍事主義對抗。

五、超越之未來

最後，我想以自己所撰的一篇文章段落來結束今天的演講，這篇名為〈超越之未來〉的文章，是《軸心時代及其結果》一書中的一章。

我們正經歷著有如兩千五百年前一般的社會崩壞，在那個時候，佛教、儒家、先知猶太教和希臘理性主義應運而起。這些精神合一的追求，在初始的盛放後，往往就被古代帝國的財富和權力所收納。偉大的哲學家卡爾·雅斯貝說，要克服社會崩壞的情況，和從前一樣，只能復興精神的合一。但是，他也說：「只有當信仰的多元內涵在歷史的溝通中保持各自的自由，而不是訴諸大一統的教條內容時，一種

對所有人負責的（與世界帝國形成對照的）普世世界秩序才有可能。所有信仰對建立世界秩序的共同元素，只能是本著每個人對存在的基本秩序的渴望，在人人都能以心靈和平的方式演進的世界共同體中實現。」用聖嚴師父的話說：「只允許單一文化存在的社會，已不會再來……」。

人間佛教在臺灣的發展或許是能帶領我們走向這種精神上包容合一的一種運動，法鼓山即為主要案例。這種運動通常是在各宗教體制層面的邊緣產生，它們能跨越宗教教條的藩籬，圍繞焦點形成網路，促成原本毫不相干的人們跨越國族、跨越階級的歸屬。雅斯貝在思考真正的世界共同體所需的素材時，所指的或許就是這種運動。他說：「想要活在非封閉、無組織、也無法組織的一個真正的人的共同體中，一個基督教所稱的無形教會中，這樣的人必然會做為個體與分散在地球表面的其他個體為盟。這是一種能夠克服任何災難的聯盟，它具有不受制於任何道路和特定約束的可靠性。」

但是，這種運動不是標準社會學研究方便處理的對象。它們不容易被分類、被置入某種理論架構中。社會學研究更便於研究精神的墮落，而不是精神的提昇。或許我們沒有辦法把全球性的超越種子變成具體可操作的東西，因為社會學自身無法確認這些種子。但是，社會學只要豐實地記錄諸如邊界的發展、記錄呼喚超越性的異化和去人性化，並提供理論分析，通過全球性的比較研究，考察可能出現超越性的情境，那麼，社會學就有可能帶領我們走到真能見證超越性的那個點。社會學就能夠扮演卡爾·雅思貝所說的「哲學」角色。他說：「哲學（社會學）帶領我們循路而行，抵達

『愛』在真正的溝通中獲得深度的地點。在愛中,通過有效成功的溝通,把我們聯繫在一起的真理,將向歷史源頭迥異的人們展示它的真面目。」

佛法的智慧和軸心傳統的其他智慧一道,可以引導我們超越哲學與社會學帶領我們到達的那個點,有助於我們去嘗試接觸將我們所有人聯繫在一起的真理。

論文

經濟富足與心靈安樂
——聖嚴法師「心靈環保」思想對「佛教經濟學」理論之啟示

許永河
國立成功大學經濟學系教授

▌摘要

　　本文以聖嚴法師「心靈環保」與「建設人間淨土」之思想為核心，嘗試摸索其思想對近代「佛教經濟學」理論發展的可能啟發處，除一方面將佛教的基本教理整理介紹，另方面也將聖嚴法師思想的學術價值做不同角度的詮釋，最後則依據「心靈環保」的觀念，對佛教的幸福經濟學提出永續幸福發展的初步理論論述。

　　主流經濟學與佛教經濟學的差異在於對欲望或幸福的看法的不同。對主流經濟學來說，幸福或效用是來自於擁有的物質或財富的增加所致。但奉行主流經濟理論為圭臬的世界，長期以大量生產、大量消費來追求物質欲望滿足的結果，出現了資源耗竭、環境汙染，以及生產廢棄物累積所帶來的生活環境惡化等不幸福的現象。佛教經濟學之學者不認同主流經濟學的幸福觀，不同意以消費水準做為評量幸福感的依據，認為應以「最少的消費」達到「最大的滿足」才是幸福。此外，佛教經濟學主張幸福不能以物質消費為目標，而應以苦惱的減少為目的，因為苦惱的減少即是幸福感的增

加，而苦惱與貪欲有關，追逐無止境的欲望滿足是與幸福目標的達成相違背的。

　　本文中回顧主流經濟學、佛教經濟學、心理學，以及希臘哲學的幸福觀，再參酌佛教的基本教理、太虛大師「五乘教」，以及聖嚴法師「心靈環保」與「建設人間淨土」的思想，建構佛教經濟學的幸福觀。最後依據聖嚴法師「心靈環保」的理念，提出「心靈環保國富論」的初步邏輯架構，說明一個追求經濟富足與心靈安樂的社會，如何實現永續發展的經濟生活目標。本文除了將聖嚴法師的「心靈環保」理念應用在經濟學的理論之中，也補充現有佛教經濟學理論宏觀理論論述之不足。唯本文之「心靈環保國富論」構想仍在發展中，日後將繼續發展充實之。

關鍵詞：聖嚴法師、心靈環保、建設人間淨土、佛教經濟學、
　　　　　心靈環保國富論

一、前言

近代經濟學鼻祖亞當・斯密（Adam Smith）在其一七七六年出版之《國富論》中強調，經濟學是「富國富民」之學；治國之道在於增進國家財富，而國家財富是以民眾可消費的物品數量來表示，並非以一國之金銀存量多寡做衡量。❶其見解以今天的話來說，就是追求經濟成長，以產出或經濟成長做為國家富足的目標。嗣後由於古典經濟學以「勞動價值論」為基礎的生產、交易、分配理論的瓶頸，以及自然科學發展的刺激，經濟學隨科學潮流而追求「科學的經濟學」，發展出邊際效用價值論和邊際分析方法，認為社會的資源有限，但人類欲望無窮，人類福祉的增進，不是以經濟成長來展現，而是藉由經濟資源的最適配置來達成。於是經濟學的討論主軸從生產與分配問題，變成「如何用最有效率的資源配置方式或生產手段，來達到欲望滿足最大化的目標」。「邊際革命」之後的主流經濟學研究，其主要任務是探討限制條件下效用最大化或利潤最大化的目標達成之道，而以數學做為重要的分析與研究工具。❷

從學問的本質上來說，經濟學是研究人類經濟生活與生存活動的學問，但最近百餘年來以西方的市場體系或資本主義經濟制度為基礎的主流經濟學研究，在研究工具上仍擺脫不了數學，在其理論的底蘊，仍然以「自利心」為人類經濟

---

❶ 見 Smith（1776）。
❷ 見 Backhouse（2008）。

活動的動機，認為讓個人自利心充分發揮，便可達成人類社會福祉或幸福最大化的目標。然而，幸福是一種心理感受，雖可以感覺卻難以用語言描摹，而且幸福程度的高低也缺乏客觀的衡量準據。因此，西方主流的經濟學界便以消費者的「效用」（utility）代替「幸福」（happiness），認為效用最大化即是滿足程度最大化，也是幸福感的極大化。因此，主流經濟學便以限制條件下的效用（或滿足）最大化的計算與追求，做為達成「幸福最佳化」的手段。

主流經濟學的研究，探討面對「資源有限」的限制條件下，如何有效率地支配所得與支出，來達成「效用」或滿足最大化的目標。在這些的計算中，對於人在市場交易過程中所面對的人與人、人與環境的關係等，均和資源的限制一樣，被視為市場經濟的「給定條件」（given conditions），因此不予探討。

因此，從研究方法來說，主流經濟學認為人是理性的動物，人活在不得不面對的給定條件下，努力追求欲望滿足最大化的生活，這便是理性的態度。從另外的角度來說，在主流的經濟研究中，認為「幸福」是抽象的哲學議題，「幸福」也是無法量化、難以客觀衡量的質性因素，因此無法以「科學方法」來研究；然而主流經濟學並非不重視幸福，但認為人對物品的消費能產生滿足，而滿足程度完全是主觀的感覺，因此只要能夠提高所得，或者增加消費能力以及消費的內容，便能達到提高滿足度的提高，也可以達到福祉或幸福感提高的目的。基於此一邏輯，長久以來經濟學的思想轉化成經濟政策，就是設法打破環境的限制，追求「經濟成

長」或「所得增長」來達成經濟福祉的提昇。

　　主流經濟學的效用理論，說明透過消費可以帶來滿足，而每個人的消費能力受其所得限制，因此效用滿足能力也受所得限制。為了提昇效用水準，若能提高所得，進而提昇消費能力，其經濟福祉便能提高。換句話說，福祉與所得水準呈現正向相關的關係。此外，個人消費不僅帶來自身的滿足感提高，也會帶來社會總需求增加，以及國民所得水準提高，其結果也可以帶來提昇社會整體幸福感的效果。因此，一九五〇年代以來的經濟發展理論，大抵均以前述觀念為基礎追求經濟成長及經濟福祉的提昇。然而，長久以來人類社會以「人定勝天」的態度，企圖突破自然環境的限制來追求經濟成長，並以經濟成長或國民所得提昇做為幸福衡量指標的作法，其結果是現在世人所看到的環境汙染、資源耗竭、地球暖化、貧富不均，以及大量消費、大量資源浪費等現象的出現。

　　這些現象出現所帶來的問題，顯示一味追求所得成長，不必然帶來人類社會幸福的提昇。❸因此，從經濟幸福的立場來看，主流經濟理論的價值觀與政策思維固有其價值，但需要予以重新檢視，並做補充，這也是近代許多從事跨領域研究的佛教學者所努力之處。

---

❸ 近年的「綠色國民所得帳」的編制，以及許多國際組織，如聯合國（United Nations, UN）及經濟合作暨發展組織（Organisation for Economic Co-operation and Development, OECD）所發展的幸福指標（Happiness Index）或美好生活指標（Better Life Index），均說明過去獨尊「經濟成長思維」做為幸福指標之不足。

二、「佛教經濟學」的發展概述

　　佛教經濟學的出現，最早是在南亞的佛教國家。在一九五〇年代，斯里蘭卡及緬甸等國為了追求經濟成長，試圖找出適合佛教國家使用的經濟發展模式而發展出「佛教經濟學」的概念。德國裔的英國經濟學者舒馬赫（E. F. Schumacher）在一九五〇至六〇年代擔任緬甸經濟發展計畫的顧問，他認為西方主流的經濟理論與觀念並不適合緬甸經濟發展之所需，在觀察緬甸社會一段時間後，他提出「佛教經濟學」的觀念，做為緬甸經濟發展政策的思考基礎。「佛教經濟學」的觀念最初用在東南亞國家，包括斯里蘭卡、緬甸與泰國，後來由於資本主義市場經濟為基礎的社會出現貧富不均、資源耗竭、自然環境惡化等問題，佛教經濟學的論述逐漸被西方經濟學界所重視。

　　一九七〇年代是自由主義思想蓬勃發展的年代，同期間也出現許多對於主流經濟研究方法與研究方向的反思，近年更有一些研究重新檢視經濟成長、永續發展與生活幸福關係的思潮。其中，在非西方主流的領域中，舒馬赫（Schumacher, 1966）最早提出「佛教經濟學」概念，試圖以佛教的教義在物質福祉與心靈健康之間找到平衡點。❹他認為經濟學的內容，不應離開生活的意義及目的（the

---

❹ Schumacher 最早在一九六六年提出「佛教經濟學」（Buddhist Economics）的觀念，試圖解釋如何以佛教的教義來做為追求經濟成長與心靈平安的準則。該短文後來於一九七三年被收入其著作集《小即是美》（*Small is beautiful: Economics as if people mattered*）一書中。

meaning and purpose of life），而佛教經濟學的方法，應
建立在兩個原則之上，亦即「充足而非過度（sufficiency,
not surfeit）」，以及「區分可再生資源及不可再生資源
（renewable vs. non-renewable resources）的使用」原則。對
於第一個原則，他認為經濟成長的目標，只要達到夠用（或
充足）的地步即可，超越夠用之外而追求經濟成長，將產生
邪惡、破壞性的「不經濟」結果。至於第二個原則，他認為
佛教經濟應區分可再生和不可再生資源的使用；建立在可再
生資源基礎上的文明是優於以不可再生資源為基礎而建立的
文明的。此外，他認為主流經濟學以消費為導向的幸福觀是
不理性的，「因為消費僅是達到人類福祉的一種手段，真正
的目的應是藉由最少的消費來達到最大的福祉」。❺

　　一九七二年不丹國王吉格梅・辛格・旺楚克（Jigme
Singye Wangchuck）批判主流經濟思想以國民所得衡量幸福
之不當，認為不丹王國不需盲目跟從西方社會的觀念，而應
有一個更妥適的幸福指標。對於經濟成長與生活幸福的關
係，他提出「國民幸福指數」（Gross National Happiness,
GNH）的觀念，以 GNH 衡量國民福祉或幸福感，並取代
過去以國民所得或國民生產毛額（Gross National Product,
GNP）做為衡量經濟福祉標準的作法。這個 GNH 的概念與
其衍生出來的永續發展（sustainable development）理念，後

---

❺ "A Buddhist economist would consider this approach excessively irrational:
since consumption is merely a means to human well-being, the aim should be
to obtain the maximum of well-being with the minimum of consumption." See
Schumacher (1973), p. 28.

來逐漸受到各個國際組織及學界所重視。❻

　　Kolm（1985）則認為效用不能僅以消費來衡量，生活中尚有能提高生活滿意的活動，例如禪坐即是。因此，他以西方主流經濟研究之效用理論為基礎，建構一個藉由消費與禪坐來達到效用與滿足的模型。為了消費，必須花費時間去工作；但為了追求心靈的平靜，則需要花時間禪坐。工作的所得固然可以提供物質消費的滿足能力，但禪坐卻可帶來心靈的平靜，兩者都能夠帶來效用的提昇效果。然而，花費時間在禪坐之上便無法工作，因此一個佛教徒的「最適安排」是降低對消費的渴望，不需花費太多時間為了金錢而工作，如此便可挪出時間來追求靈性的生活，而在工作與靈性禪修時間的安排中，得到最大的滿足。Kolm（1985）認為在物質需求和精神生活的平靜之間找到平衡點的生活模式，即是所謂的「中道」（the "Middle Way"）。

　　泰國僧侶 Payutto（1994）提出靈性生活的經濟學，認為佛教的觀念提供了對欲望與經濟活動動機的深刻心理分析，佛教的教義可以幫助人解脫自我的束縛。由於自我覺察，因而能夠了解什麼樣的消費與生產行為是有利的或有害的。關於欲望，他認為佛教徒會辨別渴愛（tanha）與希慕（chanda）的差別；因貪欲而生的渴愛，與無明

---

❻ 請參閱聯合國永續發展目標（UN Sustainable Development Goals, SDG），網址：https://sustainabledevelopment.un.org/partnership/?p=2212。另請參考英國牛津大學 Oxford Poverty & Human Development Initiative, "Bhutan's Gross National Happiness Index" 之說明，網址：https://ophi.org.uk/policy/national-policy/gross-national-happiness-index/。

（ignorance）相應，而依於正欲而起的希慕，則是與智慧（wisdom）相應的。就經濟活動來說，經濟活動的目的，是達成善與清淨生活的手段；生產、消費以及其他的經濟活動，本身並不是目的，均僅僅是手段而已。經濟活動的目的，應該要能夠提昇個人內在的福祉，以及個人在社會及環境的福祉。

欲望有兩類，價值也有兩種，分別是真價值，以及虛假的價值；真價值是由智慧所創造，虛假的價值是因為貪欲而產生。真價值可以達成幸福追求的最終目標，虛假的價值能夠滿足人類對商品消費的欲望。因此，消費也分成正確的消費以及錯誤的消費，正確的消費是以商品或勞務來滿足真正幸福的追求，而錯誤的消費則是以財貨或勞務來滿足感官的愉悅，或自我的快樂。對佛教經濟學來說，節欲（moderation）的智慧是追求幸福的重要核心觀念；消費的目的不在滿足欲望的最大化，而是達成最高幸福的真價值實現，這與西方主流經濟學的看法是大相逕庭的。

在主流經濟學中，無窮的欲望是受制於有限的資源；但在佛教經濟學中，無窮的欲望是受制於節欲的理性，以及對最終幸福的希慕。佛教的節制智慧，可以消弭毫無節制的經濟活動所產生的不幸福。在這種理性與節制的「正確的消費」或「中道消費」來說，消費本身僅是維持色身的一種手段而已，不是為了追求口腹之欲的無限滿足。換言之，是以維持身心健康的手段，來達到追求精神或法身慧命成長的目的。在消費的過程中，佛教經濟學與主流經濟學一樣，都有選擇的問題，但佛教經濟學的消費節制，不是選擇消費或不

消費，或者欲望的最大化，而是辨別這個選擇是否達成自我
成長的目的。

此外，Payutto 認為主流經濟學的生產理論，僅考量帳
面的成本與利潤的追求，忽視生產所產生的資源破壞與廢棄
物問題，更忽視環境中其他生命被毀滅的事實。因此，他強
調生產活動的倫理，認為生產不免帶來破壞，但生產活動如
帶來環境惡化，或者自然資源大量破壞的結果，則應避免。
總而言之，Payutto 的佛教經濟學觀念，認為理想的經濟活
動內容，應該帶來每個人的自我成長與社會的整體成長，不
能淪為滿足自私欲望的工具，或成為助長社會爭端的來源，
更不應製造社會不安或生態毀滅。因此，他認為經濟學應掌
握兩個特色和原則：其一，是經濟活動的目的，必須能夠提
昇真正的福祉；其次，經濟活動應該要避免對自己和他人的
傷害，亦即不應對社會或自然環境造成傷害。

日本學者井上信一（Inoue Shinichi, 1995）認為佛教徒
經濟活動的目的，不能僅是為了自己，也應該要幫助他人。
因此，佛教徒經濟活動的主要目的，不應該是為了利潤，而
是為了服務社會。能夠抱持服務社會的宗旨，在服務的過程
中，利潤自然會出現；但利潤是個副產品，而非經濟活動的
主要目的。人為了生活，無可避免地會傷害到其他的眾生，
但佛教徒應該降低因為個人生存欲望而對其他眾生的傷害；
在生活中應該表現對其他眾生的感恩，而且對於傷害他人或
其他眾生的行為，應該要有懺悔的態度。現實生活中的生產
和消費活動，都是無可避免的經濟行為，也會對環境與社會
產生影響。因此，經濟活動應該評估生產和消費對環境的影

響程度，進而選擇能夠滿足生活必需，且對地球和環境傷害最低的方式來進行。此外，對於經濟效率的內容也應該重新評估，不應該拘泥於追求最大化的目標做為經濟效率的指標，而應思考以「不浪費」取代「最大化」，做為經濟效率的標準。

Welford（2006）則以四聖諦為基礎開展佛教經濟學的永續發展概念。他認為自我中心的欲望是無止境的，人之所以受苦，是因為被貪婪的心念所束縛之故。在資本主義社會中，成就和幸福是以財富累積的多寡來衡量的；然而財富的追求與累積，則是貪欲累積的過程。因此，資本主義社會的財富累積結果，是苦惱的堆疊，不能獲得真正的幸福。少欲知足才能遠離苦惱，並創造真正的幸福。由於欲望的降低，可以帶來消費的減少，而消費的減少則帶來非生活必需品生產減少的效果。因此，整個社會可以空出更多的資源，挪做生產落後國家所需的生活必需品，達到提昇整體人類福祉的目的。此外，人類因為欲望的降低，也不會為了刺激消費而不斷盲目開發新技術，用來生產新商品，其結果是經濟活動對環境的掠奪與傷害也因而減少。因此，少欲知足的經濟生活，不僅個人幸福感增加、對環境的破壞程度下降，也提昇了整體社會的幸福感。

Puntasen（2005）則連結了佛教的觀念與希臘哲學家亞里斯多德的哲學思想，將生活區分為維持生存之所必需，以及超越生活必需後的另一個層次的良善生活（the good life），亦即幸福人生。如同亞里斯多德，他將財富的功能或價值分成兩類，分別是使用價值（the use value）與交換

價值（the exchange value）。使用價值是財富滿足人類基本生活的有用性，而交換價值則是從市場的交易活動中所產生；使用價值來自物品的有用性，交換價值則根源於人類的欲望。在佛教來說，樂（sukha）有數個層次，分別是追求財富而得到的滿足，這是低層次的「樂」。其次則為擁有而不占有（non-acquisition）的心理狀態，這是較高一個層次的「樂」。但最高層次的樂，則是人心能夠解脫一切雜染或苦惱；若要達到這樣的最高層次心靈狀態，則須透過學習佛法來訓練自己的心，有了「慧」（paññā）才能實現。他認為佛教經濟學的生產方式不是為了市場交易，或在交易中尋求效用或享樂的最大化，而是為了追求自己和他人痛苦最大可能的減輕。這樣的生產，就是「般若主義」（paññā-ism）的生產模式，因為苦惱的減少，即是平安與福祉的增加。

Puntasen 認為在生產過程中，智慧應該被用來控制所有生產的投入，包括技術、資本、勞動，以及自然資源，而整個生產過程應該提昇人力投入的品質，也就是能夠創造勞動的技術、生產力，以及勞動過程的成就感。這個過程不應該讓勞動者感到被剝削，而應讓勞動者感受到自己的工作或生命的意義，同時創造勞動者成就其他人勞動成果的成就感。對資源的使用，應該盡可能地使用可再生的能源，而對於不可再生能源的使用應該達到最小化，生產過程所產生的廢棄物應維持在盡可能的最低水準，同時對自然資源和環境也應盡力改善。在佛教的經濟學中，消費也是適量的消費，因為適量消費的緣故，所以也不需無端擴大生產來滿足消費增長的需要。智慧主義的生產及消費模式下，可以有更多的資源

拿來捐獻給其他資源不足或缺乏智慧者，以減輕他們的生活苦惱。簡要言之，Putasen 認為佛教經濟學的目的，是追求眾生苦惱或痛苦的減少；有智慧的人以智慧來過生活，僅取其生活之所需，而將多餘的部分給其他更需要的人。

　　另有所謂的「入世佛教」（engaged Buddhism），❼主張佛法的教義應該用在社會、政治、環保、經濟之上，並對世間的不公義現象表達其看法。由於其主張與環保人士的主張相近，因此在許多環保爭議議題及活動中，都可以看到這類的激進佛教徒主張出現。❽其中一位非常重要的學者，也是社會運動者，是泰國的素拉‧司瓦拉差（Sulak Sivaraksa; 2009, 2014），他認為生態的苦難是幾個世紀以來人類對地球和環境濫用（abuse）的結果，許多先後出現的環境暴力現象，均導致生態環境的永續性遭到破壞。這些對環境的暴力現象，包括殖民主義、工業發展、戰爭、盲目追求經濟成長、軍備競賽，以及國家資本主義間的競爭等。全球資本主義制度（global capitalism）被主流社會奉為組織生產與分配的最佳制度，然而其對人類社會的禍害卻被忽視。人類社會追求物質消費的成長，卻忽視了全球資本主義貪婪擴張所帶來的問題，以及它對人類社會和生態環境所埋下的潛在災難。如果忽略全球資本主義的缺陷，同時不能正視生態災難等現象是源自全球政經體系之「系統性暴力」之事實，則人

---

❼ 較有名的組織為「國際入世佛教協會（The International Network of Engaged Buddhists, INEB）」。

❽ 因「入世佛教」團體經常參與社會運動，因此常被冠上「左翼佛教徒」或「激進佛教徒」之名。

類的生存以及資本主義制度本身，最終將被資本主義的市場
制度所摧毀。因此，所有人應當體認到一件事實，亦即人與
人、人與環境，彼此是相互連結、相互關聯的。人世間的現
象和自然界的運轉方式，也都同樣受佛法的「法輪」（the
wheel of Dharma）所支配，因此佛法的「法輪」可以用來做
為修正國家資本主義的系統性暴力行為之參考。司瓦拉差認
為他的「法輪」見解，提供了「為什麼解決環境問題需要宗
教或精神層面支持」的理由。

　　此外，司瓦拉差（Sivaraksa, 2009）在其書中，認同
「佛法現代化」（Dhammic modernity），而提出以佛使比
丘（Buddhadasa Bhikkhu, 1906-1993）的「佛法社會主義」
（Dhammic socialism）理想，做為解決當代社會危機的制度
設計藍圖。在經濟理念上，他延續 Schumacher 之「小即是
美」的見解，認為在目前的全球化環境下，生產與消費應該
以小規模、本土性❾和可持續生產的方式為目標，以之取代
資本主義的生產模式，並以佛教教義做為經濟活動的指導原
則，在以人為本、追求個人發展（individual development）
的基礎上，重建整個經濟體系。

　　美國學者 Brown（2017）將 Schumacher 之佛教經濟學
延伸，認為生活的品質不能僅是建立在物質生活內容的衡量
上，因此提出建構一個從個人、社會制度，以及環境的整體
關係模型，企圖以個人與環境的良性循環模型來衡量經濟幸

---

❾ 亦即在當地設廠生產、以當地的原料及勞動力投入生產，並以當地市場
　銷售及消費為原則。

福。在傳統的自由市場經濟學中，認為每個人都可以透過消費的增加來提高其快樂和生活滿意度，因此認為追求所得的提高是實現更快樂、更滿足生活的手段。然而在 Brown 的佛教經濟學觀念中，幸福是由人與環境的相互關聯來定義。所有的人、所有的生物都在大自然的環境中相互依存；因此，幸福是源自於人在環境中可以保持舒適感，而且能以有尊嚴的方式過活才有幸福可言。人在生活中不僅應該相互關心，也應關心自然環境，以有意義的方式過生活。其思想建構在三個觀念的次第：首先，人與人、人與環境的關係是一體而不可分割的，每個人的行為結果，均影響到他人以及環境，最後反射回來讓自己也受到影響。其次，由於人與環境的一體性，好的行為是利己又利他的；對他人及環境友善，便是對自己的仁慈。因此，在行為上應該確保自己不會對他人或環境產生傷害。最後，由於人與環境一體性的緣故，有一人受苦便是大家受苦，因此對他人的苦應該要體恤關心。人之所以受苦，是因為自私心，以及對他人的苦和環境的遭受破壞保持冷漠之故。因此，她認為幸福快樂的佛教經濟學，教導我們學習遠離無知、學習以愛與慈悲來過有意義的生活。

　　總結本小節對佛教經濟學的回顧，可以了解近年興起的佛教經濟學的研究或論述方向，主要包括生產和消費的面向。對消費活動的看法，不再強調效用最大化，而以節制欲望，達到痛苦最小化、欲望簡單化做為目標。在生產相關的論述，則以智慧主義（panna-ism）的生產模式，以社區的自給自足（self-sufficiency）及對他人、環境的關心，以及對環境非暴力（non-violence）的方式來生產。不論生產或消費

行為，都希望能與「中道」（the middle-way）相應。這些研究或論述，主要是以南傳佛教教義為基礎而延伸出來的看法，其中也有積極參與社會改革運動、追求社會正義的「入世佛教」。至於非南傳佛教地區的「佛教經濟學」論述，內容大抵離不開人與人、人與環境是相依相存的觀念，而強調利人利己、仁慈等概念的經濟生活。其中，佛教經濟學之人與生物都在大自然的環境中相互依存的觀念，也被近代環保運動者借重，做為環保訴求的理念之一。

三、聖嚴法師「建設人間淨土」的思想

聖嚴法師「建設人間淨土」思想的提出，除了他本身的修行經驗與身為宗教師對世間的使命感之外，也受當代環境保護思潮影響，因而提出符合當代生活需要的佛法觀念。

一九六二年美國生物學家 Rachel Carson 出版了《寂靜的春天》（*Silent Spring*）一書，說明農藥殺蟲劑對環境的汙染和破壞，❿成了近代環境保護議題的先驅。受該書的影響，美國政府開始對劇毒的環境殺蟲劑進行調查，並於一九七〇年成立了環境保護局，各州也相繼通過禁止生產和使用劇毒殺蟲劑的法律。一九七二年六月間聯合國在瑞典斯德哥爾摩召開「聯合國人類環境會議」，通過《人類環境宣言》（*Declaration of the United Nations Conference on the Human Environment*），又稱《斯德哥爾摩宣言》，是環境保護議題

---

❿ 見 Carson, Rachel (1962). *Silent Spring*. Boston: Houghton Mifflin; Cambridge, Mass.: Riverside Press。

正式受世界各國政府重視的開端。

　　一九八○年間，西方世界長期追求市場擴張和財富累積所帶來的諸多問題相繼出現，包括環境汙染、能源短缺、環境破壞，乃至社會的貧富懸殊等現象，引發了環境保護運動，以及許多的社會改革運動。再加上自然環境災變所帶來的苦難，導致全球社會動盪不安。許多的社運團體，面對社會或環境的問題，因為彼此立場與見解的差異而相互攻訐，更加深了社會的不安。而在國內環境方面，一九八○年代末期國內社會改革開放前後，出現社會動盪現象，也導致人心不安。

　　在這樣的一個國內外的社會氛圍下，聖嚴法師看到社會及環境災難的根本原因，是人心的問題、是欲望的問題，也是觀念、見解與生活態度的問題。為了從根本解決人心與環境的災難與紛擾，配合社會的氛圍，提出大眾容易理解與接受的解決方案，因此將佛法用淺顯易懂的觀念、以生活化的方式，提出「心靈環保」與「建設人間淨土」等主張，做為實現平安社會的綱要。此外，先後推出「四種環保」、「心五四運動」、「心六倫運動」等社會運動，希望藉由法鼓山僧俗四眾的努力，將「心靈環保」的理念，推廣到社會的各個層面，讓臺灣的社會朝向「提昇人的品質，建設人間淨土」的理想境界邁進。聖嚴法師「建設人間淨土」的理想，並不局限於臺灣或漢傳佛教弘傳的華人社會，而希望能夠將這個理想普及於全世界、全人類：「我們提倡的心靈環保，是在推動一個超越宗教、超越民族、超越國界的大運動，它是屬於全人類的心靈提昇運動，乃至於不論有沒有宗教信仰

的人，都可以一同分享。」⓫

　　聖嚴法師於一九七五年從日本取得博士學位，嗣於同年底赴美弘化。他在西方社會弘化，以禪法為接引的方便，推廣生活與禪修合一，期望大眾能夠在生活中體驗平衡身心、達成提昇人品為目的。在推廣禪法的同時，法師也全力興辦佛教的高等教育，培育佛教教育的高等人才，因為法師認為「今天若不辦教育，明天便沒有佛教」。法師一九八九年創立法鼓山，做為漢傳禪佛教的弘化中心，又在國內提倡「建設人間淨土」的理念，以大學院教育、大普化教育、大關懷教育等三大教育來實踐人間淨土的理念。為響應環境衛生、保育自然生態、珍惜自然資源的號召，同時呼籲發起「心靈環保」運動，⓬因而在國內外各種場合推廣心靈環保的理念。聖嚴法師從一九八九年起，到二〇〇九年捨報為止，先後二十年間，其弘揚「心靈環保」、推動相關理念的內容之大事記，請見表一。

表一：聖嚴法師弘揚「心靈環保」理念大事記

時間	內容
1990 年	• 於紐約東初禪寺撰寫〈與法鼓山僧俗弟子共勉語〉，後更名為〈四眾佛子共勉語〉。
1991 年	• 於護法勸募會員聯誼會中提出〈我們的共識〉。
1992 年	• 提出「心靈環保」，成為法鼓山的核心理念。

⓫ 釋聖嚴，《人間世》，《法鼓全集》8-9，2005 年網路版，頁 81。
⓬ 釋聖嚴，《聖嚴法師心靈環保‧自序》，《法鼓全集》3-5，2005 年網路版，頁 260。

1994 年	• 提出「禮儀環保」，推動佛化聯合奠祭、佛化聯合祝壽、佛化聯合婚禮。 • 繼「心靈環保」、「禮儀環保」之後，又提出「生活環保」、「自然環保」，總稱為「四環」運動。 • 於「護法信眾聯誼大會」，提出法鼓山之工作重點為「一大使命，三大教育」。
1995 年	• 總結過去提出的提昇人品方法，提出「安身、安心、安家、安業」的四安運動。
1997 年	• 訂定本年為「人間淨土年」，以推動人間淨土之主題為法鼓山年度活動重點。
1998 年	• 在「我為你祝福」祈福法會中，提出「四要」（需要、想要、能要、該要）、「四感」（感恩、感謝、感化、感動）、「四福」（知福、惜福、培福、種福）。
1999 年	• 提出「心五四運動——二十一世紀生活主張」。
2007 年	• 提出「心六倫——新時代‧心倫理運動」。 • 提出「法鼓山的四大堅持」，闡明法鼓山以此四大堅持，關懷全世界。

資料來源：作者整理自聖嚴法師《法鼓全集》及聖嚴基金會「法鼓山發展理念簡表」。**⓭**

（一）法鼓山的理念：「提昇人的品質，建設人間淨土」

聖嚴法師的修行經驗深刻、佛學思想圓融，他在世間弘化的晚期，將修行經驗與佛法以深入淺出的方式，介紹給臺灣及西方社會，對社會的影響力日增。由於因緣成熟，他在一九八九年提出「建設人間淨土」的具體弘化理念，推廣淨化人心、改善社會風氣的運動。在一九八九年之後的二十餘年間，先後將佛法的觀念以淺顯易懂的現代化語言做表達，提出許多世人易懂易行的理念，推動社會運動，來達到其全

⓭ 請參閱《法鼓山聖嚴法師數位典藏》，網址：http://www.shengyen.org/bio-thought-years.php，2019 年 4 月 25 日檢索。

面關懷世間的目標。法師追隨佛陀本懷，並以其禪修的佛法
經驗，再參考佛教經典，提出以「心靈環保」為核心價值，
以「提昇人的品質，建設人間淨土」為終極理念的佛法現代
化運動。法師的思想脈絡與悲願弘圖，在其流傳於世的著作
或演講紀錄中，均可略窺一二。為何要推動這樣的一個佛法
弘化現代化的運動？法師說：

> 佛教的根本任務，是在用佛法為人類的心理和精神做
> 救濟……我們的法鼓山，就是為了實踐這樣的理念：「提
> 昇人的品質」，是讓人人成為好人，人人都做好事，結合
> 物質和精神兩項建設的推動，便是「建設人間淨土」的工
> 程。⓮

一九九七年法鼓山假臺北市國家圖書館舉辦「第三屆中
華國際佛學會議」，其主題為「人間淨土與現代社會」，聖
嚴法師在閉幕致詞時表示，此次學術會議主要在「探討如何
將傳統的佛教，古為今用，發現它的人間性，展現它的現代
意義，以資實踐法鼓山的理念『提昇人的品質，建設人間淨
土』」。⓯嗣後，法鼓山體系於一九九九年訂定該年為「人
間淨土年」，以推動人間淨土之主題做為法鼓山年度活動
重點。

⓮ 釋聖嚴，《教育·文化·文學》，《法鼓全集》3-3，2005 年網路版，頁
116。

⓯ 釋聖嚴，《教育·文化·文學》，《法鼓全集》3-3，2005 年網路版，頁
101。

　　聖嚴法師「人間淨土」的思想脈絡，精神上固然承續佛陀本懷，但也繼承了中國佛教的淨土思想、太虛大師的人間淨土，以及印順長老的人間佛教的思想。法師的「人間淨土」理念，雖先後在許多著作及公開演講中提及，但一九九九年的〈人間佛教的人間淨土〉一文，❶是法師對「人間淨土」理念最具體而扼要的文字說明。茲摘錄法師對其「人間淨土」思想的說明：

　　本文❶除將中國淨土思想的發展，作了探源性的介紹之外，特別依據《大般若經》的成熟眾生嚴淨佛土，《法華經》的釋尊即以此界為淨土，《維摩經》的直心是淨土，太虛大師的人間淨土，印順長老的人間佛教，綜合而成法鼓山建設人間淨土的思想脈絡：眾生（人）的心清淨而行為清淨，個人的身口意清淨而影響所處的社會環境清淨。在做往生佛國、嚴淨佛土的準備工夫階段，先要在人間自利利人，便是建設人間淨土。❶

　　現在我們的法鼓山，正在提倡心靈環保，正在倡導建設人間淨土的理念。我們的理論依據，便是出於《維摩經·

---

❶ 釋聖嚴，〈人間佛教的人間淨土〉，《中華佛學研究》第 3 期，中華佛學研究所發行，1999 年 3 月出版，頁 1-17。
❶ 指〈人間佛教的人間淨土〉一文，該文為紀念日本京都佛教大學前校長水谷幸正博士七十大壽而撰。
❶ 釋聖嚴，《兩千年行腳》，《法鼓全集》6-11，2005 年網路版，頁116。

佛國品第一》所說:「若菩薩,欲得淨土,當淨其心,隨
其心淨則佛土淨。……菩薩心淨則佛土淨。」[19]

我們所提倡的「人間淨土」,它的基礎思想是依據《般
若經》、《法華經》、《維摩經》諸大乘經,以「發菩提
心」而成就眾生、淨佛國土。從人心的淨化、行為的淨化
而實現環境的淨化。以戒律規範達成清淨的生活,以禪定
安頓繁亂的身心,以智慧指導人生的方向。依據「心淨則
佛土淨」的觀點,只要一念心淨,一念見淨土,念念心
淨,念念見淨土;一人心淨一人見淨土,人人心淨人人見
淨土。那是由於人心的淨化、行為的淨化而完成人間社會
的淨化。目的是在指出,為了求生信仰中的佛國淨土或天
國淨土,必須先在現實的人間,努力於心靈的淨化、生活
的淨化、環境的淨化。[20]

(二)「建設人間淨土」的核心精神:心靈環保

聖嚴法師為什麼要提倡「心靈環保」?因為環境的汙
染是由人的行為所造成的,而人的行為是「心靈」的結果。
因此,討論環境汙染的問題,必須從根源著手,亦即從「心

---

[19] 釋聖嚴,《維摩經六講·自序》,《法鼓全集》3-5,2005年網路版,頁
297。

[20] 釋聖嚴,「第三屆中華國際佛學會議」閉幕詞,見《教育·文化·文
學》,《法鼓全集》3-3,2005年網路版,頁101-102。

靈」開始。㉑此外，一般人談到健康，僅注重身體的健康，「往往疏忽了心理是否平衡自在，連帶著也忘記了精神層面的修養」。㉒因此，法師提倡的「心靈環保」，是希望世人得以從觀念來重視身心靈一體的健康，也能夠去體驗生活中如何達成身心靈的平衡與健康。

聖嚴法師所提倡的「心靈環保」，是將佛法的觀念做深入淺出的介紹，用現代人聽得懂的平易語言，介紹「心靈環保」的觀念與方法。他提倡「心靈環保」的目的，是希望社會大眾都能維持心理的平衡以及人格的穩定。為了達到這個目的，除了需要有觀念的導正，也必須有可以練習的方法做為實踐的依據，否則就算平時能夠保持安穩，一旦遇到刺激、誘惑或不如意境界，便無法平安。

因此，聖嚴法師將基礎佛法的因果因緣觀，轉化成易懂易行的言詞，引導大眾的日常生活觀念，再輔以禪修的觀念與方法，做為生活中面對不安時的安心方法。「心靈環保」的推動，徒有觀念而無方法，將落入空談；雖有方法，但無正確觀念做指引，可能出現盲修瞎練，誤入歧途而無法平安。為了避免這些缺失，聖嚴法師提出具有先後步驟的四種觀念，以及四種方法，來達成心理平衡及人格穩定的目標。

1.四個心靈環保的觀念步驟

練習心理的平衡及人格的穩定，首先是從觀念的調整做

㉑ 釋聖嚴，《禪門》，《法鼓全集》4-11，2005年網路版，頁90。

㉒ 釋聖嚴，〈心靈環保——慈悲沒有敵人，智慧不起煩惱〉（二〇〇二年二月二十五日講於總統府「國父紀念月會」）。見《致詞》，《法鼓全集》3-12，2005年網路版，頁41。

起，它的步驟有四種：

（一）凡事應作正面的認知，便可避免負面的危機和悲觀的情緒；人生的旅途，總是有起有落的，但那都是前進的過程。（二）凡事宜作逆向思考，便可做到勝而不驕傲，敗而不氣餒；成功而升至巔峰之際，要有走向下坡的心理準備，失敗而降至谷底之時，宜有攀登下一個極峰的願景在望。（三）凡事應知進退有度，能收能放而收放自如，古人說：「達則兼善天下，窮則獨善其身」，也就是說能有機會舒展抱負，奉獻天下，應該當仁不讓，竭盡全力，積極進取，萬一時運不濟，屢戰屢敗，那就養精蓄銳，以圖未來。（四）不論成敗，宜將自我的私利和私欲看空，要將對於國家、民族、乃至全人類的安危禍福的責任，一肩擔起，這便是一個有智慧和慈悲的人了。㉓

2. 保持心靈平安的方法與四個體證階段

運用禪修的方法，從禪法修習的自我觀照中，體驗認識自我、肯定自我、成長自我、消融自我的過程，達成人品提昇及心靈淨化的目的。

光有觀念的調整，尚不能保證真的可以做到心理的平

㉓ 詳請參閱釋聖嚴，〈心靈環保——慈悲沒有敵人，智慧不起煩惱〉（二○○二年二月二十五日講於總統府「國父紀念月會」）。見《致詞》，《法鼓全集》3-12，2005 年網路版，頁 43-44。

衡及人格的穩定，必須輔以方法的練習，才能奏效。我們所用的方法，便是禪修，基本的原則是由放鬆身心、體驗身心、統一身心到放下身心的四階段。放鬆身心與體驗身心，是屬於自我肯定及自我認知的範圍；體驗身心與統一身心是屬於自我反省及自我成長的範圍；統一身心與放下身心，是屬於自我完成及自我消融的範圍。❷

「心靈環保」是一種心態與生活態度，亦即以「奉獻自我」為生活的原動力，而不以「爭取自我利益」為出發點，是「以利他的存心，達成自利的目的」。面對生活與生命的問題，眼光「從整體大局著眼，從個人的成長著手」；❷處理問題，則「以慈悲包容人，以智慧處理事」。以這些態度來生活，就是「心靈環保」的生活。

（三）心靈環保的生活實踐：「四種環保」、「心五四運動」與「心六倫」

心靈環保雖以消融自我為最高理想，但心靈環保的工作者和實踐者，並非一定得學佛修禪才行。因此，聖嚴法師在國內外推動的心靈環保，分成兩個層面與對象，分別是學佛修禪者及非學佛之一般大眾。其中，對有意願、有興趣來學佛禪修者，以學佛禪修的觀念及方法，幫助他們從認識自

---

❷ 釋聖嚴，〈心靈環保——慈悲沒有敵人，智慧不起煩惱〉（二○○二年二月二十五日講於總統府「國父紀念月會」）。見《致詞》，《法鼓全集》3-12，2005 年網路版，頁 44。

❷ 釋聖嚴，《禪門》，《法鼓全集》4-11，2005 年網路版，頁 98。

我、肯定自我、成長自我，最終消融自我、體證無我。對於
尚無意願學佛以及無暇禪修之一般大眾，則盡量不用佛學名
詞，淡化宗教色彩，以投合現代人身心和環境需要之語言，
提出以心靈環保為主軸的「四種環保」及「心五四運動」。❷❻

　　法鼓山推動「建設人間淨土」的社會運動，是以心靈
　　環保為主軸，以安心、安身、安家、安業的四安為行動；
　　又以提倡禮儀環保、生活環保、自然環保，來配合心靈環
　　保，成為四環運動，以促進人間社會的平安快樂。❷❼

　　所謂「四種環保」，是指心靈環保、禮儀環保、生活環
保、自然環保。而所謂「心五四運動」，則是指跟心靈環保
相關的五個類別，各有四點的實踐項目，其目的在實踐四種
環保。心靈環保是四種環保的核心理念，為何心靈環保不獨
立出來，而併入其餘的三種環保，並列成四種環保？因為心
是世間一切現象的根源，也是苦樂的根本原因。每個人能夠
自淨其意，平等心對待他人、慈愛心面對自然及一切生命，
則世間便是淨土。心靈環保是其他環保的核心，其他三種環
保是心靈環保的開演與實踐。聖嚴法師在許多場合闡述這四
種環保的理念，但二○○四年七月他在世界青年和平高峰會
臺北論壇演說的內容，是最具體的說明。他說：

---

❷❻ 釋聖嚴，《學術論考 II》，《法鼓全集》3-9，2005 年網路版，頁 58-
59。

❷❼ 釋聖嚴，〈《平安的人間》自序〉，《書序》，《法鼓全集》3-5，2005
年網路版，頁 316。

心靈的事實表現可有三種：那就是對於自然世界充滿了平等而無私的愛心，對於每一個生命都抱持崇高的敬意，在和任何人相遇相處之時，都能絕對的真誠與絕對的謙卑。因為對於自然世界的一切對象，有平等的愛心，便能珍惜自然資源、便能尊重各類的生命，便能願意過節儉和簡樸的生活；因為對於每一個生命都能抱持崇高的敬意，跟任何人相遇相處之時都是真誠的、謙卑的，便會以感謝心相看，便會以禮貌的言行舉止相待了。

心靈環保的內涵有四種：那就是以保護自然資源及自然生態而言，稱為自然環保；以生活的節儉、整潔和簡樸而言，稱為生活環保；以真誠、謙卑和禮貌與人相處而言，稱為禮儀環保；以上三種環保的出發點，乃是出於人的情意、觀念（思想）、精神的淨化，稱為心靈環保。因此我們法鼓山這個團體，是以心靈環保為主軸，提倡四種環保。❷❽

對於法鼓山所推動的「心靈環保」與「心五四運動」的理念關聯與發展，聖嚴法師說：

從最初只有一個「心法」，漸漸地有了「心靈環保」，再發展成「心靈、禮儀、生活、自然」等四種環保。接著就陸續出現了「心」五四運動，目的是在完成四種環保與

---

❷❽ 聖嚴法師二〇〇四年七月二十四日世界青年和平高峰會台北論壇主題演說，見《致詞》，《法鼓全集》3-12，2005 年網路版，頁 76。

三大教育。這是我歷年來佛學講座的主題，是為了淡化佛法玄深化、神奇化、流俗化的色彩，使佛法讓人一聽就懂，一懂就可以運用在日常生活中，以達成入世導俗、淨化社會的目的。❷❾

隨著法鼓山弘化活動的推廣，聖嚴法師及四眾弟子有感於臺灣社會的亂象，導致人心不安，而且社會的倫理觀及價值也逐漸式微，因此更於二〇〇七年將心靈環保的理念，推展到現代倫理觀念的建立，而提出「心六倫」，希望藉此六種倫理的推動，幫助臺灣社會與人心的淨化、平安與健康，達成「提昇人的品質，建設人間淨土」的目的。❸⓿「心六倫」是心靈環保理念的一貫延續，除了因應國內環境面因素外，心六倫也適應世界的需要，是全球性的、現代化的倫理。❸❶聖嚴法師在二〇〇〇年八月二十九日千禧年「世界宗教暨精神領袖和平高峰會議」開幕致詞中說：

　　我們相信，任何一個宗教，都會有一個永恆不變的希望，那就是神的天國，或是佛的淨土，都是為了人類而設置的。佛教雖主張眾生平等，但只有在人間，才能夠實踐

---

❷❾ 釋聖嚴，《抱疾遊高峰》，《法鼓全集》6-12，2005 年網路版，頁 117。

❸⓿ 釋聖嚴，《我願無窮——美好的晚年開示集》，《法鼓全集》10-10，2005 年網路版，頁 152。

❸❶ 釋聖嚴，《我願無窮——美好的晚年開示集》，《法鼓全集》10-10，2005 年網路版，頁 223。

佛陀的教法。因此，我們正在提倡一個運動：先把神的天國或佛的淨土，建設在人間。如果我們努力於人間天國或人間淨土的建設工程，那麼不論於何時死亡，必定能夠蒙受神的恩典及佛的接引。

不論給它什麼名稱，天國或淨土，我們不僅都是地球村的好鄰居，也都是同一個宇宙之母的同胞兒女；我們彼此之間，不僅是好朋友，根本就是同一個大家庭中的兄弟和姊妹。因此，我們除了共同用各種方法來保護這個地球的生存環境，除了撤除一切人與人之間的隔閡障礙而彼此相愛，沒有別的選擇。㉜

聖嚴法師在《我願無窮──美好的晚年開示集》一書中，對「心六倫」的時代意義，做了這樣的說明：

本來中國傳統儒家思想已有「五倫」的觀念，即是「父子、君臣、夫婦、兄弟和朋友」，可是在今天這個社會，必須要擴大倫理的範疇，因此，「心六倫」新增了幾個不同的面向，譬如自然、職場和族群的倫理，都是過去「五倫」所沒有的；而原來的「五倫」之中，如「父子」一倫的內涵，對現代社會而言也不夠完整。所謂不夠完整，是指無法概括家庭之中夫婦、親子和兄弟姊妹彼此之間的關

㉜ 請參閱《建立全球倫理──聖嚴法師宗教和平講錄》，頁35-37，《法鼓山聖嚴法師數位典藏・智慧隨身書》，網址：http://www.shengyen.org/books-grid.php?s=3。

係，因此「心六倫」也在這方面做了加強，希望能夠涵蓋
現在這個時代、這個世界，包括人與人、人與社會、人與
自然等各種各樣的關係。**❸❸**

「心六倫」所提倡的倫理，是指人與人之間，每一個
人都應該盡責、負責，自己是什麼身分、什麼立場，就要
負起應有的責任，擔當應盡的義務，如果「身在其位而不
謀其政」，即是有失其責，也就不是倫理。倫理一定是盡
責、負責，在什麼立場就做什麼事、說什麼話，這即是出
家人所說的「做一日和尚撞一日鐘」。**❸❹**

關於「四種環保」、「心五四運動」及「心六倫運動」
的內容，筆者將之濃縮整理如表二所示。

表二：四種環保、心五四、心六倫的內容

理念名稱	內容概述
四種環保	解決人類過去疏忽所遺留的問題，開創美好的未來，讓人安居樂業。
心靈環保	人的情意、觀念（思想）、精神的淨化；保持心靈的平靜與明淨。
禮儀環保	以真誠、謙卑和禮貌與人相處；保護人類社會的尊嚴與謙和。
生活環保	生活的節儉、整潔和簡樸；保障生活的整潔與儉樸。
自然環保	保護自然資源及自然生態；保全地球生態的共存與共榮。

---

❸❸ 釋聖嚴，《我願無窮——美好的晚年開示集》，《法鼓全集》10-10，
2005 年網路版，頁 326。
❸❹ 釋聖嚴，《我願無窮——美好的晚年開示集》，《法鼓全集》10-10，
2005 年網路版，頁 328。

心五四運動	二十一世紀的生活主張，以精神啟蒙運動為主的生活教育。
四安	**安心、安身、安家、安業** 安心：在生活中的少欲知足。 安身：在生活中的輕鬆自在、日新又新、勤勞儉樸。 安家：在家庭中的相敬、相愛、互助、互諒、彼此學習。 安業：在身、口、意三種行為的清淨精進。
四要	**需要、想要、能要、該要** 需要的才要；想要的不重要；能、該要的才要；不能要、不該要的絕對不要。
四它	**面對它、接受它、處理它、放下它** 面對它：正視困境的存在，不逃避不畏懼。 接受它：接受困境的體驗，不怨天不尤人。 處理它：用智慧處理事，以慈悲對待人。 放下它：盡心盡力做好，結果如何不再煩心。
四感	**感恩、感謝、感化、感動** 感恩：感恩所有讓我們成長的因緣，包括父母、師長、國家民族、大地眾生。 感謝：感謝給我們成長機會的順境、逆境。 感化：用佛法的智慧之言及慈悲之教，感化自己。知慚愧、常懺悔。學做無底的垃圾桶，效法無塵的反射鏡。 感動：凡事從自己做起。以勤勉、謹慎、恭敬、謙虛、寬容的態度，感動他人。
四福	**知福、惜福、培福、種福** 知福：知足常樂‧安貧樂道；知福才能知足常樂。 惜福：珍惜擁有‧感恩圖報；惜福才能經常擁有。 培福：享福非福‧培福有福；培福才會增長幸福。 種福：成長自己‧廣種福田；種福才會人人有福。
心六倫	**二十一世紀新倫理運動；透過心靈環保，使倫理生活化、生活倫理化。**
家庭倫理	家庭成員間彼此的互重與各盡其責；家庭和樂是社會的穩定基礎。
生活倫理	節約、簡樸、不浪費；珍惜善用生活中的各種資源、對環境給予愛護和尊重；給自己方便，也尊重其他使用者的權益。
校園倫理	教師、學生、家長三方的倫理規範，使三方各盡其職務，各盡其義務，權益受保障，以教育出品德和學養兼美的下一代。
職場倫理	人與人之間工作上的互動關係，包括：長官與部屬，勞動與資本，廠商與廠商，商家與顧客等，各盡其責，彼此成就、互相照顧，互利互榮。

| 族群倫理 | 對不同族群、文化、語言、習俗、宗教等的尊重與包容；站在尊重多元的立場，讓每個族群都能發揮自己的特色，也受同等尊重與保護。 |
| 自然倫理 | 自然倫理關懷，除了直接保護有機生態，也間接保持各種資源間的永續平衡。 |

資料來源：筆者整理自聖嚴法師相關著述。

　　聖嚴法師「建設人間淨土」的理念，是以「心靈環保」為核心，以教育為關懷的手段，藉由改變人的觀念，達到行為改善、人離煩惱的結果。這是一個從個人心靈淨化，到生活淨化，而後社會環境淨化，最後到自然環境淨化的「善法外擴」的世間淨化過程，而整體環境的淨化，也就是「人間淨土」實現。這個過程，教育是非常重要的手段，因為人心或觀念的改變，需要透過教育的手段，先修正想法，才能出現行為改變的結果。

　　在聖嚴法師「建設人間淨土」的悲願中，「教育」是極為重要的一環。透過三大教育，❸❺來達到「以關懷完成教育的功能，又以教育達成關懷的任務」，❸❻最終實現「人間淨土」的理想。他說：

　　　　我們的佛教教育的目的是在建設人間淨土，佛教教育的
　　　　範圍，是從僧團拓展到每一個人的家庭、社會的每一個階
　　　　層、學校的每一種層面，不一定勉強人人成為佛教徒，卻

❸❺ 三大教育為大學院教育、大普化教育、大關懷教育。詳請參閱釋聖嚴，《兩千年行腳》，《法鼓全集》10-11，2005 年網路版，頁 118-120。
❸❻ 釋聖嚴，《法鼓山的方向》，《法鼓全集》8-6，2005 年網路版，頁136。

願以佛法的利益，分享給人間大眾。❸

聖嚴法師一生推動的「人間淨土」理念，濃縮成為「法鼓山的共識」，共有四項：

> 理念：「提昇人的品質，建設人間淨土。」
> 精神：「奉獻我們自己，成就社會大眾。」
> 方針：「回歸佛陀本懷，推動世界淨化。」
> 方法：「提倡全面教育，落實整體關懷。」❸

前述四項共識的內容，是以佛法的慈悲與智慧，做為生活指導原則，在生活中自利利人，從個人、社會，到自然環境，都能祥和清淨，而「法鼓山的共識」的內容，也是大乘菩薩道的日用實踐。

四、聖嚴法師「建設人間淨土」思想對「佛教經濟學」理論發展之啟示

主流經濟學認為在限制條件下追求「最佳化」的滿足是人的理性態度，姑且不論這種理性是否為「完全的理性」或「有限的理性」，主流經濟學對於世間真相的探索，仍欠缺理性的整體論述，這是不爭的事實。本文第二節中回顧佛

---

❸ 釋聖嚴，《兩千年行腳》，《法鼓全集》10-11，2005 年網路版，頁 120。
❸ 釋聖嚴，《聖嚴法師學思歷程》，《法鼓全集》3-8，2005 年網路版，頁 155。另見《平安的人間》，《法鼓全集》8-5，2005 年網路版，頁 126。

教經濟學的研究，了解其將佛教的某些觀念應用在經濟發展或經濟生活的論述，但對於佛法的基礎觀念如何連結到現實經濟生活，其論述仍然不夠深入。因此，本文擬以聖嚴法師的「建設人間淨土」思想，對佛教經濟學的理論提出不同的見解，以做補充。本小節中首先介紹佛法對世間和生命的看法，其次則就聖嚴法師的「心靈環保」以及「建設人間淨土」的想法做進一步的解說，並以之做為發展「佛教經濟學」的基礎脈絡，提出個人對生活富足、心靈安樂與幸福永續發展的「心靈環保國富論」之粗淺看法。

（一）從佛法看世間與生活

因緣果報的觀念，是佛法說明世間現象的基本思想。人的生命，是果報的現象，而報相的出現，則是因緣和合的結果。有情眾生各以其過去身、口、意所造之善惡業為因，而感得苦樂之果報；善因與善緣相應，招感福樂果報，而惡因則招感罪苦報果。個人的業力固然感得個人的生命與一生之際遇，而每個人生活依存的世間也是因緣果報現象。

唯識學說有情眾生以其過去之業力為因，「共相識種，能感依報。不共識種，能感正報。」❸《菩薩瓔珞本業經》中說：「凡夫眾生，住五陰中，為正報之土。山林大地共有，名依報之土。」❹另《大智度論》中，說世間有三種：

---

❸ 明・智旭，《成唯識論觀心法要》，《卍新纂大日本續藏經》第 51 冊。（CBETA, X51, No. 824）

❹ 《菩薩瓔珞本業經・賢聖學觀品第三》：「佛子，土名一切賢聖所居之處。是故一切眾生賢聖，各自居果報之土。若凡夫眾生，住五陰中，為

「一者五眾世間，二者眾生世間，三者國土世間。」❹五眾
世間即五陰世間，指由色、受、想、行、識等五陰所形成之
世間，亦即有情的正報身；眾生世間，又稱有情世間，乃指
一切有情眾生所成的世間；國土世間，則指器世間，亦即眾
生所依存的環境。換句話說，三種世間包括個人的身心、人
與人、人與其他眾生，以及人與自然環境的關係與現象。

　　人活在世間，需要物資來養活色身，也需要精神活動
來讓生命得到活力與滿足。換言之，人的生活，需要物質與
精神的食糧。在《阿含經》中佛陀多處開示有情以「四食」
為生，以及有情對「四食」生出貪愛心，因而受無盡憂悲苦
惱。《雜阿含經》卷第十五之三七四經如是說：

　　　　爾時，世尊告諸比丘，有四食資益眾生，令得住世攝受
　　　長養。何等為四？一者摶食，二者觸食，三意思食，四者
　　　識食。
　　　　若比丘於此四食有喜有貪，則識住增長。識住增長故，
　　　入於名色。入名色故，諸行增長。行增長故，當來有增
　　　長。當來有增長故，生、老、病、死、憂、悲、惱苦集，
　　　如是純大苦聚集。
　　　　若於四食無貪無喜，無貪無喜故，識不住、不增長。
　　　識不住、不增長故，不入名色。不入名色故，行不增

正報之土。山林大地共有，名依報之土。」見《菩薩瓔珞本業經》，
《大正新脩大藏經》第 24 冊。（CBETA, T24, No. 1485）
❹ 見《大智度論·釋問相品第四十九》，《大正新脩大藏經》第 25 冊。
（CBETA, T25, No. 1509）

長。行不增長故,當來有不生不長。當來有不生長故,
於未來世生、老、病、死、憂、悲、惱苦不起,如是純
大苦聚滅。❷

　　四食中,搏食又稱段食,即現代人所稱之三餐及宵夜,
係以鼻舌分時段而食之,所食之物以香、味、觸三塵為體。
觸食,又稱樂食,以接觸喜樂之事而長養身命,此食以觸之
心所為體。思食,又稱念食,乃心中之意志作用,是對所欲
之境而生希望之念,以資助諸根;此食以第六意識及第七末
那識之作用為體。識食之識,在大乘法中指第八識,第八阿
賴耶識是有情一切生命現象的根本。此四食中,段食為滋養
生命的物質食物,觸、思、識三食則為心理及精神的食糧;
又段、觸二食可以滋養「現生」之能依、所依,思、識二食
則有能引生「後有」的功能。

　　生命,是果報的現象;果報,是從因到果的結果。由於
過去的業因,感得現在的果報。因果,是時間的先後關係,
然而果報現象的出現,除了因果的時間關係,尚須有空間的
助成條件,也就是「緣」。內在的「因」雖是果報現行的主
觀條件,但尚須有客觀的「外緣」助成,始能成就果報。因
緣互為主賓,是成就果報的空間關係。僅有因,不能成就
果;僅有外緣,也無法成就果;必須因緣和合、主客條件具
足,才能生果,故稱一切現象均是「緣起」。從緣起的觀點

---

❷ 《雜阿含經》第 15 卷,《大正新脩大藏經》第 2 冊。(CBETA, T2, No.
99)

來看，「人生，乃至所有一切眾生，在宇宙間，沒有一樣是單獨存在的，一個人的生存，必然要受他人的影響，同時也會影響他人，這種影響他人，這種影響的關係，在佛法中講，便是緣」。❸

不管有情正報的身心，或者依報世間的一切現象，莫不是緣起的。因為緣起，所以性空。緣起的一切現象，眾緣和合則生，眾緣離散則滅，所以是無常的。因為「無常」，所以身心內外的一切境界，莫不遷流不止；因為一切遷流不止，所以世間難安。世間難安，故「苦」。一切現象莫不隨因緣聚滅而遷流，因緣背後更有因緣，現象遷流中了無主宰，故「無我」；因為緣生無主、無我，所以「性空」。然而有情不能了知緣起性空的道理，執著一切境界實有，對境界生出貪愛分別，而於內外的一切境界強立有我，起我執。因為我執與貪愛，所以身心向外，便出現人際關係的「人我對立」，對內則出現前念後念相互矛盾的「自我對立」。有對立，便是煩惱，有煩惱便無法幸福。

緣起性空是世間的真理，但凡夫由於自我中心的分別執著，起貪愛心而被貪欲所牽絆，欲令智昏，不辨事理、不識自心，而致心隨境轉而不安。苦惱中雖努力想在當下求平安快樂，卻因心中缺乏正見，對境生出貪、瞋、癡等惡念，造作惡業，又招感苦果而受苦。人的動機雖然希望平安快樂，卻因為行為顛倒而招感惡果，最後落入愁憂苦惱中。簡單地說，眾生不明因果，不識因緣，妄執有我、對境貪愛攀緣，

---

❸ 釋聖嚴，《神通與人通》，《法鼓全集》3-2，2005 年網路版，頁 146。

因而受無盡的生死苦惱。

佛陀不忍眾生愚癡顛倒，長夜受苦，因而教示「離苦得樂」之法。佛陀的教法，浩瀚無涯，簡要來說，以「三法印」、「四聖諦」為基礎，繼而開展出「八正道」、「三學」、「六度」，以及三藏十二部的經教。為了接引不同根器的有情，開演出人天法、聲聞法，大乘菩薩法等「五乘共法」、「三乘共法」，以及「大乘不共法」等教法。佛陀的一切教法，均以「把人做好」的端正法為基礎，法門看似甚多，但萬法唯心，佛陀以悲智開導眾生離苦得樂，其法不離「看心、知心、調心、安心、化心」之心法，以及開展正智、正行之生死解脫法。

（二）解讀聖嚴法師「建設人間淨土」思想

前節中介紹聖嚴法師「建設人間淨土」理念提出的時間及內容概要，然而因為法師理念係在不同時間先後提出，雖然每一理念均甚具意義，但如不能仔細探索法師整體的理念架構，將落入見樹不見林之憾，也很難得出法師理念在現代社會的意義，更難以了解其可貴性與可實踐性。因此，筆者試圖建構法師「心靈環保」思想與「建設人間淨土」理念的全貌，再以之為基礎，推論法師思想對現代「佛教經濟學」理論之啟示。

聖嚴法師以「心靈環保」為核心的「建設人間淨土」理念，是以佛法的核心精神為基礎，加上他個人的禪修體驗，以及多年教授禪法、弘講佛法的經驗，綜合開展出來佛法現代化的入世行動。「心靈環保」的觀念，也是法師以宗教師

的角色，一生為續佛慧命、關懷世間眾生之悲願，所演化出來的貌似淺易，但實則寓意深遠而易行的理念。

從因緣法來看，一切法平等，一切眾生也都平等。世間的不平，都是因為人的我執與分別心而起。儘管法性平等，但因果因緣所現起的現象，確實因時空條件的差異而有不同的面貌，因此每個人在世間的福報或際遇也不盡相同。人往往攀緣外境，迷於現象而不知因緣因果的道理，貪愛境界以致對境不能看心、知心、化心，陷於「有我難安、有心難平」的狀態。因此，為了生活的平安幸福，需要有方法來安心，更需要有觀念來疏導自己的心，讓人在逆境時不陷溺於苦惱而積極向上，在順境時能夠不貪福樂，並在一切境界下，都有方法保護自己的心，避免貪欲與煩惱的染汙。因此，聖嚴法師提出「心靈環保」觀念，做為現代人平安生活的南針，因為「由人心清淨而行為清淨，由個人的三業清淨而使社會的環境清淨。……一念清淨一念見淨土，一日清淨一日見淨土；一人清淨一人居淨土，多人清淨多人居淨土。……此心由煩惱而顯菩提，此土由穢土而成淨土」。❹

西方神學認為人是最高造物者所創造，是神將人置入世間環境中。過去數百年西方科學思想的發展，對神學的思想提出挑戰，懷疑神造世人的說法，而「進化論」的思想與「產業革命」的出現，是影響近代人類社會生活的兩個重要事件。「進化論」認為物種的進化與生存，是物競天擇的結果，在進化過程中「適者生存」。此一思想不僅認為人類高

---

❹ 釋聖嚴，《學術論考》，《法鼓全集》3-1，2005 年網路版，頁 473。

於其他的物種，也認為人類社會有優秀與低劣的人種差別。而西方產業革命之後的「人定勝天」思想，也認為人的能力可以改變自然環境，並創造有利於人類生活的物質條件，增進生活幸福。受到西方優勝劣敗、人定勝天思想影響的社會，便出現為了追求物質生活的成長而不計後果的環境破壞現象，也出現種族隔離的現象，以及資源掠奪的戰爭。

凡此現象，都是人類社會文明的病態，追溯其根本原因，則是人類貪婪與自私的心性問題，以及社會變化過程中，雖累積了知識，但卻欠缺智慧之故。今日西方主流文明社會的問題，是自我主義所產生的競爭與對立問題，也是一味追求物質生活的提昇，而對環境恣意破壞所產生的問題。解決當前人類社會的問題，需要有新的觀念與作法，佛法的人生觀、世界觀與宇宙觀，不僅提供了解決當前人類社會問題的思想基礎，依著佛法來過生活，也可以緩解人類社會當前問題的惡化，並且能夠保障有限資源下的人類社會永續發展。

從佛法來說，人在世間的生命現象，是因受報而有；報有依正，個人又以其福分差異，依正二報的報相也有不同。天台九祖湛然大師在《法華玄義釋籤》中將智顗大師「迹門十妙」❹之觀心大綱攝為「十不二門」，❹而在每一門中均

---

❹ 天台智顗大師解釋《妙法蓮華經》經題之「妙」字時，謂「妙」字包含十義，而分別說迹門十妙、本門十妙，以及觀心十妙。見《妙法蓮華經玄義》，《大正新脩大藏經》第 33 冊。（CBETA, T33, No. 1716）

❹ 十不二門分別是色心、內外、修性、因果、染淨、依正、自他、三業、權實、受潤等十門。見《法華玄義釋籤》第 14 卷，《大正新脩大藏經》

以「一念三千」、「三諦圓融」的義理，歸結出「無二無礙」的結論。在其「依正不二」一門中，以一念心因本具三千諸法，由無始一念三千法中，生出眾生及五陰的二千是正報，而國土一千屬依報。「依正既居一心，一心豈分能所」❼。因此，正報與依報的五蘊世間、眾生世間，以及器用世間是一體不可分的。

人在世間，受報的當下又繼續造業，由於依正不二，其受報當下造業的行為，也會改變正報及依報的面貌。因此，從佛法的觀點來看西方主流文明的物競天擇、人定勝天的價值觀，便知觀念的問題導致人間的災難。依循人定勝天的觀念過生活，從人的自我中心欲望的滿足做出發，便出現眼前的環境破壞、地球暖化、海平面上升等現象，這些現象也將造成人類社會未來的自我毀滅。在佛法來說，世間的一切眾生均是平等的、人與環境是一體的，五蘊世間、眾生世間、器用世間也是一體不可分的。傷害環境、傷害他人，便是對自己的傷害。

人活在世間的關係，有人與人的關係，也有人與家庭、家庭與家庭、家庭與社區，以及人類社區和自然環境的關係，人的生存與幸福，與這些世間關係密不可分。在人類生存的大小環境中，沒有一個人（五蘊世間）可以獨立於眾生世間（社會）及器世間（自然環境）之外而過活。人若為自

第 33 冊。（CBETA, T33, No. 1717）

❼ 見《法華玄義釋籤》第 14 卷，《大正新脩大藏經》第 33 冊。（CBETA, T33, No. 1717）

己的利益而傷害他人，其結果會讓自己受害；人類為了物質
欲望而損毀山林、耗竭資源，並造成環境汙染，最後全體人
類終將因自己的愚癡行為而受害。因此，「三種世間」及
「依正不二」的道理，是聖嚴法師「心靈環保」及「建立人
間淨土」思想的佛法理論基礎（圖一）。

　　以佛法的慈悲對待他人及世間，以智慧消融自己的煩
惱，在生活中不因自利而害人，不自苦惱他，就不會產生自
害害他的結果。如果更能關懷他人、關懷世間，就能夠產生
自利利他，彼此福報增長的結果。因此，心靈環保就是以正
見、正行來自利利他，是以緣起性空的智慧為正見，以少欲

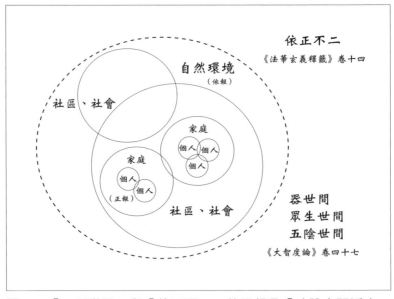

圖一：「三種世間」與「依正不二」的思想是「建設人間淨土」
的理論基礎

知足的心態來過自利利他的生活。《大乘本生心地觀經》中說：「心清淨故世界清淨，心雜穢故世界雜穢。我佛法中以心為主，一切諸法無不由心。」[48]因此，聖嚴法師說：

> 若從佛學的角度來談心靈環保，便是基於離卻貪、瞋、疑、慢等的煩惱心，而開發智慧心及增長慈悲心的立場，來面對我們所處的環境。有了智慧心，便能使自己的身心，經常處於健康、快樂、平安的狀態；有了慈悲心，便能使他人也獲得健康、快樂、平安的身心。至於如何轉煩惱而成悲智？便是勘破五蘊構成的身心，是空不是我，此有兩個結果：一是不再造作自害害人的惡業；二是當下不受苦報，縱然處身於火宅之中，猶如沐浴於清涼池內。但是尚有無數的眾生不明此理，尚被困在貪、瞋、疑、慢等的煩惱火窟之中，所以要用此五蘊身心作為工具，救世救人，稱為菩薩行者。[49]

五蘊法中，色蘊是生理的構造，受、想、行、識四蘊是心理與精神的作用。人在世間受報，報體是五蘊的整體，可是受報當下對境造業，是心動而後有行動，是心念顯露於外而成外顯的身、口、意行動。心動的緣由，就是自我中心的貪愛與想法。因此，能夠在觀念上以緣起法來疏導心中的

---

[48] 《大乘本生心地觀經》第 4 卷，〈厭捨品第三〉，《大正新脩大藏經》第 3 冊。（CBETA, T3, No. 159）

[49] 釋聖嚴，《學術論考 II》，《法鼓全集》3-9，2005 年網路版，頁 52-53。

執著，認知五蘊非我，而更能進一步照見五蘊皆空，體證無
我，智慧心與慈悲心便油然而生。

「心靈環保」要從知我、安我、化我，到成長自我，因
此「建設人間淨土」理想的實踐順序，是從個人的自我清淨
為起點，向外推展至人在家庭與社會中之「人我關係」的平
安與清淨，再到「人與其他生命體」及「人與自然環境」的
和諧清淨。換言之，也就是從心中遠離貪欲煩惱的「心靈環
保」做起，實現每個人的「五蘊世間」環保，進而實現「眾
生世間」的環保，再由眾生同心協力，完成「器世間」的環
保。簡言之，由每個人的內心清淨開始做起，最終完成淨化
人心、淨化社會、保護自然環境的「建設人間淨土」理想
（圖二）。

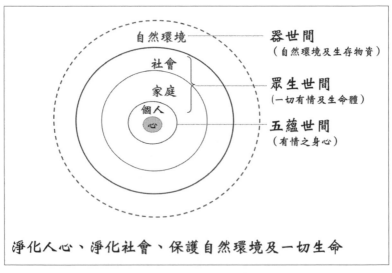

圖二：「建設人間淨土」從個人「心靈環保」做起

　　「建設人間淨土」是以「心靈環保」為核心，而為了保護每個人的心靈清淨、身心健康，必須有可行的觀念，以及實用的方法與方針。因此，聖嚴法師提出「心五四」的觀念，做為每個人心靈環保的實踐方針。「心五四」雖然是一個比較現代化的名詞，但其實質的精神和內涵依舊是佛法。這是聖嚴法師希望將深奧難懂的佛學名詞，轉化成人人易懂、也可以在生活中活用的觀念。因此，「心五四」是以人為本的佛教生活化、心靈淨化的人品提昇運動。❺⓪

　　在「心靈環保」的實踐上，每個人在生活中可以練習以「四安」來安心、安身、安家、安業，做為提昇人品、保護個人生活場域清淨與平安的方法（四安內容請詳本文表二）。面對生活中許多的欲望蠢動，以「四要」來處理欲望的誘惑，亦即以「四要」來提醒自己，需要的不多，想要的太多；能要該要的才要，不能要不該要的絕對不要。如能以「四要」來化解欲貪，便能避免落入欲望牽引的煩惱中。此外，人在生活中莫不希望幸福快樂，但福報是累世善因而感得。不管今生有福無福，要學習以知福、惜福、培福、種福等「四福」的觀念，在生活中為自己及眾生增福祉。人莫不希望一帆風順，但生命過程中難免出現許多不如意的境界，而不如意的逆境通常令人煩惱。面對生命中的不如意，練習提起「四它」的觀念，用正向的態度來面對它、接受它、處

---

❺⓪ 請參閱聖嚴法師〈心五四運動的時代意義〉一文，分兩期刊載於《法鼓》雜誌。見《法鼓》雜誌 119 期，1999 年 11 月 15 日第 2 版，以及《法鼓》雜誌 120 期，1999 年 12 月 15 日第 2 版。

理它、放下它，以「四它」來保護自己的心不落入境界的煩惱漩渦中。此外，人在世間生活，一定會有人際的互動，也難免有摩擦，對於人與人的關係，用「四感」的感恩、感謝、感化、感動來誠懇處理。

以「心五四」做為自己內心處理問題的方針，達到情意、觀念與精神的淨化，實踐「心靈環保」。以「心靈環保」為核心，落實生活的節儉、整潔和簡樸的「生活環保」；從個人的生活，外擴到與人相處的心靈環保，以真誠、相互尊重和禮貌的態度與人相處，增進人與人和睦關係的「禮儀環保」，更以「心靈環保」的生活，保護自然資源及自然生態，實踐「自然環保」。「心五四」的生活，也是為自己培福、為眾生種福的「自利利他」生活，更是大乘菩薩道法的實踐。

其次，為了將四種環保落實在依正二報的三種世間之個人生活、人際關係，以及人與自然環境的關係中，聖嚴法師進一步提倡「心六倫」的新生活，這是以「心靈環保」為基礎的六種倫理關係，包括「家庭倫理」、「生活倫理」、「校園倫理」、「自然倫理」、「職場倫理」和「族群倫理」等六種人在生活中的倫理關係。「心六倫」的提倡，是希望每個人不論在生活中扮演的是何種角色，都能守分、盡責、奉獻的正確觀念，時時做到尊重、關心他人，建立世間的和諧平安，而達成「建設人間淨土」的目標（圖三）。

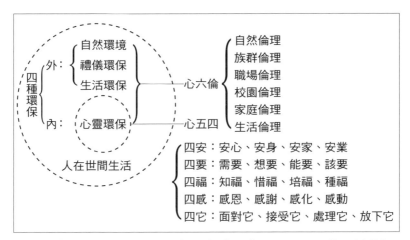

圖三：「建設人間淨土」理念的實踐：「心五四」、「四種環保」
與「心六倫」

（三）聖嚴法師「建設人間淨土」思想對「佛教經濟學」
　　之啟示：「心靈環保國富論」

　　經濟學所探討的欲望，是物質的欲望；經濟學所說的
效用（utility）或福祉（well-being），則是物質欲望滿足後
的一種愉快（pleasure）狀態。這種心中的愉悅狀態，到底
是屬於感官的滿足？或是心理的愉悅？還是幸福感？長久
以來，主流經濟理論中並未對此有所討論與說明，僅假設一
種叫做「效用」的心理感覺存在，且每個人心中對所有消費
品都有主觀的效用，每個人的生活都在追求效用的最大化。
久而久之，「效用」或「心理的滿足感」在主流經濟理論中
便被視為「幸福」的同義詞，而決定消費能力高低的所得水
準，便被視為客觀衡量滿足感或經濟福祉的重要指標。這個

觀念被推展到總體經濟面，便出現以國民所得毛額（GNP）或每人國民所得（per capita GNP）做為評比不同國家間的經濟福祉或同一國家內不同時期經濟福祉的重要指標。

主流經濟學以「自利心」做為經濟行為的動機，以「欲望的滿足」做為經濟行為的目的，認為透過市場的自由競爭，可以使得經濟體系的資源使用效率達到最佳化，同時也可以完成有限資源的「最適」分配。在所謂的「科學的經濟學」（scientific Economics）研究中，幸福感是以消費者的「消費滿足心理」及廠商「追求利潤心理」為基礎，假設這些心理存在，也假設追求心理最大的滿足是共通的人性。

主流經濟學以追求「最大化」的心理動機做為生產、消費、分配的分析基礎，但卻缺乏「滿足心理」的理論論述，這是因為「科學經濟學」受限於其分析工具，以及其強調分析邏輯的「科學性」所無法逃避的困境。主流經濟學的經濟分析，為了邏輯的完整性，或者是為了方法運用的需要，往往必須對經濟現象或行為做假設，在假設的前提之下，將複雜的現象化為簡要的因果邏輯關係。例如，主流經濟理論中常用「同質性」（homogeneity）的假設來處理勞動者效用或消費者效用的議題，然而「人性」並非齊一的，以過度簡化的假設來處理人的「欲望」或「滿足」問題，其理論對現實人生的實用性便會遭受挑戰。

主流經濟學建立在欲望滿足的基礎所發展出來物質幸福追求的理論，是近代佛教經濟學對其批判的重點。另從現實生活面來看，過去三百年來人類社會長期追求經濟成長所產生的諸多問題，包括所得分配不均、環境破壞、空氣汙染、

工業與生活廢棄物的累積，以及全球暖化等問題，更是以主流經濟學為基礎的資本主義市場經濟制度令人詬病之處。

佛教經濟學認為以市場經濟為基礎的生產、消費及分配制度，不僅產生物質豐富但精神貧窮的不幸福結果，也導致人類社會的不公義現象出現，以及破壞地球環境的永續性問題。因此，佛教經濟學批判資本主義經濟制度底蘊的主流經濟學，認為它是「不經濟」的科學，因而試圖重新探索「經濟幸福」的意義，以及可以保障人類社會幸福可持續發展的經濟生活方式。

目前已知的佛教經濟學研究大要，已如本文第二節中介紹。主流經濟學理論固然欠缺完整的經濟行為的心理論述，佛教經濟學為了修以正主流經濟學為基礎的資本主義市場制度所產生的環境破壞與貧富不均問題，提出經濟生活倫理的主張，但其內容多屬「規範性」的倫理，仍然欠缺倫理、經濟生活與人生幸福的整體論述。因此，在討論聖嚴法師「建設人間淨土」思想對「佛教經濟學」理論的啟示之前，本文將先介紹心理學者馬斯洛（A. W. Maslow）的人類生存動機階次論，說明心理學家如何看待人類生存的追求動機。其次，介紹古希臘哲學家亞里斯多德（Aristotle, 384-322 B.C.）《尼各馬科倫理學》（*Nicomachean Ethics*）一書中所討論的幸福觀，希望跳脫倫理對生活的外在「規範性」範疇，而了解倫理「內在自發性」的人性發展幸福觀。在介紹這些人類生存動機或人性發展的倫理幸福論述之後，再來看佛法的幸福觀，以及聖嚴法師以佛法為基礎所提出的「心靈環保」及「建設人間淨土」理念，藉此說明聖嚴法師佛法現

代化思想的可貴性，以及其可實踐性，同時也可看出其思想
對當代佛教經濟學理論的啟發處。

1. 馬斯洛（A. H. Maslow）之人類生存動機階次論

相較於經濟學對經濟活動欲望動機論述的不足，心
理學家對於人類行為與動機的描述無疑是更豐富而且更深
入的。其中，廣為相關社會科學領域學者引述的是馬斯洛
（A. H. Maslow）的「人類動機理論」（A Theory of Human
Motivation）。Maslow（1943）認為人類的活動，受到其內
在的心理動機所左右。Maslow 將人類的生存需求動機，自
最基本的維持生活的需求開始，從低到高，依序分為五個層
次，分別是：生理的需求（physiological needs）、安全的需
求（safety needs）、愛與歸屬感的需求（belongingness and
love needs）、自尊與尊嚴的需求（esteem needs），以及自
我實現的需求（self-actualization）等五類（圖四）。

在 Maslow 需求金字塔的底層，是最基本的生理與心理
需求，包括基本的物質生活所需、生活安全，在滿足基本需
求後，則有社會面的愛與歸屬感，和精神愉悅感等層次。位
在生存動機最上層的則是自我實現的需求，其內容是自我潛
能開發與創造力發揮的活動等。

在生命的過程中，這些需求的迫切性會有不同。生存欲
望的滿足是最基本的動機，如果生存的基本需求無法滿足，
其他的需求便沒有迫切性；一旦最基本的動機達到滿足，人
便會將心力轉向更高的動機層次去追求。

基本的物質需求及心理需求，被馬斯洛稱為「不足的
需求」（Deficiency-Needs），亦即這些動機是因生理或感

圖四：馬斯洛（Maslow, 1943）的生命需求動機階次論

圖形來源：McLeod, S. A. (2017). Maslow's hierarchy of needs. Retrieved from www.simplypsychology.org/maslow.html.

官欲樂的不滿足而產生；而金字塔頂端的需求動機則被稱為「成長的需求」，或者「生命的需求」（Being-Needs），這類頂端的需求動機係為追尋自我生命意義的實現而產生。當生命基礎的需求無法滿足時，人的心理便會產生維持生命存在的需求動機，因此基本需求與心理需求，被稱為「不足需求」的動機。然而當生活存在的基本欲求被滿足後，便會逐漸追求感官之外的上層心理滿足。一旦基本需求與心理需求逐漸滿足之後，圖四中底層的四種需求動機會逐漸減弱，自我實現的需求動機便逐漸增強。

　　相較於經濟學中僅僅強調人的活動是為追求物質欲望的滿足，心理學家馬斯洛更具體地說明了人類生存活動的基本動機，包括了物質與心理的滿足，而人的欲望尚且包括愛

與被愛,以及生命尊嚴滿足等;尤其是自我尊嚴的滿足,包括自尊、自信,以及渴望個人的能力與成就能得到社會的認同。除了社會認同的動機之外,馬斯洛的人類動機尚且包含了超越基本生存需求之後的內在生命成長動機,也就是所謂的「人性發展」(human development)動機。

就經濟學與心理學的行為動機來總結來說,經濟學的分析著重於物質生活的心理滿足,以自利心為出發點,以消費滿足為目的,並以物質的滿足做為幸福感的衡量基礎,其內涵僅屬馬斯洛人類動機中最底層的生理需求動機而已。因此,主流經濟學以自利心、效用為經濟行為動機的論述,強調生活欲求或欲樂(pleasure)的追求是經濟行為的動機,其論述欠缺對經濟行為心理動機的完整說明。馬斯洛從生命的滿足著眼,其內容包括了最基本的生理或物質需求滿足、心理層面的安全感、心理愉快、自尊等,更說明自我生命實現等較高層次的心理動機對生命活動的影響。

雖然馬斯洛的心理動機論述可以彌補主流經濟學中動機論述之不足,然而不管是主流經濟學或馬斯洛的心理學分析,對於內在「心靈」平靜所產生的另一層次的幸福感均未涉及,此為兩者不足之處。而內在心靈幸福的論述,則是宗教或哲學可能貢獻之處。

2. 亞里斯多德《尼各馬科倫理學》的幸福觀[51]

古希臘哲學家亞里斯多德(Aristotle, 384-322 B.C.)在

---

[51] 本小節內容,主要參考來源為 Ross, Brown, and Lesley (2009),以及 Kraut (2006)。

其《尼各馬科倫理學》一書中,探討「人生在世,最終目的為何?」「何謂幸福?」以及「人生在世,如何獲得幸福?」等議題。

基本上,亞里斯多德認為沒有人喜歡悲慘的生活,因此「幸福」❺是人類生活的核心價值,也是生活的最終目標。至於人能否活得幸福,則與其德行(virtue)培養的能力有關。

亞里斯多德將自然環境中的一切,分為無生命的山石礦物,以及有生命的植物、動物和人類等四大類。他認為這四大類中除了山石外,其他三類有生命之動植物均有靈魂(soul),然而有靈魂的三類生命中,僅人類具有理性推理的能力,這也是人異於其他物種之處。人在生命過程中所追求的「好」,異於動物的「好」,因為人懂得運用理性的推理,具有能力與潛力去追求更高的「好」。

人雖然具有追求感官「快樂」(pleasure)的傾向,但僅有感官的快樂並不構成「幸福」,因為「快樂」是動物所追求的,而人類比動物有更高的理性思惟能力,能夠務實地思考問題,並轉化「快樂」的追求,將之轉變成有意義的行

---

❺ 亞里斯多德以希臘字 "eudaimonia" 表達「幸福」,其涵義較英文的 "happiness" 或 "well-being" 更深遠,因此許多西方的著作將之翻成「好生活」(the "good life")。eudaimonia 內容較英文的「幸福」(happiness)更深刻,不僅是快樂的感覺,而且包含人生意義的自我實現,以及德行圓滿內化而與人格合一的狀態。eudaimonia 是生命圓滿狀態,也是美滿人生的狀態,是極致的善美人生;其內涵較英文 happiness 深遠。因此,本文討論亞里斯多德的「幸福」時,意指 eudaimonia,而非英文之 happiness。

動，去達成更好的生活目標。

亞里斯多德說「快樂」是動物所追求，並不否定人有「快樂」的事實，更不是說人生的目標就是要消滅身上的動物性生理衝動，而是說人能以理性思惟的方式，導引欲望追求的衝動，使它符合「理性動物」的特質，而達到「幸福」的目的；理性動物的特質，即是人的德行。

人類生存的最終目的，是為了追求幸福（eudaimonia），而幸福即是豐富的生活（flourishing life）。豐富不僅指物質條件的富饒，而是在其一生中，藉由能豐富生活內容的物品或人際關係，來達成人性完善的目標；能豐富生活內容之物，包括健康、財富、知識、朋友等。幸福是「人性完善的生活」，是與「圓滿德行」（complete virtue）相應的靈魂活動；因此，幸福是依據「圓滿德行」來過活的人生。亞里斯多德認為幸福的人永遠有足夠的外在物品來滿足其所需，而不是僅在某個時點的偶然豐富而已。其所謂的外在的物品（external goods），包括生理健康、物質條件和人際關係。幸福是圓滿善德的行動，而「善德」與「善福」是永遠是相輝映的。

令人幸福的德行何處來？亞里斯多德認為德行是人類理性推理的結果。當人的身心愈來愈成熟時，生活漫無目的的情況便會減少，因為人會運用推理能力，整合生活中的各種目的，使之成為一個整體性的生活計畫。這個計畫不僅可以令人的生活產生踏實感與方向感，也可以藉此實踐生命的最終目標。人類的生命活動，都是為了繁榮（flourishing）、活得好（living well），以及過「好生活」（the "good life"）而努

力。人類生活中所有的行動，都以它們為目標。然而這些目標中，有些僅是達成終極目標的手段，例如物質繁榮或感官的快樂，雖都有助於幸福的提昇，但它們本身都不是幸福，當然也不是生活的目的，而僅是達成最終目的的手段。生活最終的目的，就是幸福，就是要過「好生活」。

因此，幸福是生命過程中所發展出來的「好生活」，而「好生活」是與人性完善（或德行）的生命活動相關，也是內在的「理智德行」與外在行動一致的生活。

亞里斯多德認為「德行」是生活中一種發自內心的行為，是在「過與不及」兩種極端的「中間處」（the mean）做出主觀判斷，並在生活中維持在此一中間處。❸例如：對於財富的使用，既不致極端吝嗇，也不會過度揮霍，而知如何妥善運用；對於人事的處理，既不莽撞，也不懦弱，而能維持人際的和諧。德行是發自內心的、真誠的、自發性的、正直的人格特質，與這些內在特質相應而表現於外的行動，才是德行。偶一出現的好行為，未經過主觀的理性判斷，故不是「德行」。

不同的人對於「好生活」的認知，可能不一樣。例如：某些人的「好生活」內容可能是積累財富，但對其他人來說，可能是擁有權力，或是博得好名聲或擁有名位，但也可

---

❸ 中間處不必然是與兩端等距的中間點，而是經過理性推理後的某一個落足點，此落足點可以實現最後的幸福。"So virtue is a purposive disposition, lying in a mean that is relative to us and determined by a rational principle, and by that which a prudent man would use to determine it. It is a mean between two kinds of vice, one of excess and the other of deficiency..."

能是盡情享樂。如果每個人對「好生活」的看法都可能不一樣，如何確定所有的人最終都會尋求同樣的幸福目標？對此疑惑，亞里斯多德以「欲望」來說明。人縱然欲望不同，但並非所有的欲望都能增進「好生活」。

他認為欲望有兩種，分別是後天的欲望（acquired desires）和自然的欲望（natural desires）。後天的欲望，是對外表美好或引人注目物品所產生的渴望，而自然的欲望，則是對於生命有實質功用物品的欲求。比如說，希望得到寶石首飾，是後天的欲望，因為它與「渴望」（craving）的心理有關；對三餐食物的欲望，則是自然的欲望，因它與我們的「需要」（needs）相對應。後天的欲望在每一個體間是不一樣的，但自然的欲望則對所有的人來說都一樣。「好生活」是指人在其一生中所擁有的物品，都是真正對自己有益的物品，而對任何一個人真正有益之物，都是可以滿足其「自然欲望」的物品。總結來說，對一個人有實質利益的物品，對另外一個人也可產生實質利益，因此「好生活」是人類共同的生活目的。

人為了生活，固然需要財富、食物、衣服、居所和朋友等，物質生活豐盛和活得好都是有益於人生的，但財富等物品均僅僅是達成「好生活」目的的手段而已，不是生活的目的。「好生活」才是人類生活的最終目的，而且它不是達成其他任何目的的手段。例如，對財富理性地運用，可以涵養德行，但德行不是增進財富的手段。人追求幸福或「好生活」，並非希望透過幸福來達成其他的目標，而是因為幸福本身，就是生活的目的。

「好生活」的實現，必須在生活中擁有有益於生活的有用物品，而能夠幫助人類達成「好生活」目的的實質利益物品，共有三大類，分別是：（1）身體或生理之財貨（bodily goods），包括健康、體力、生命力和快樂等；（2）外部財貨（external goods），包括食物、飲料、住所、衣服和睡眠等；（3）靈魂財貨（goods of the soul），包括知識、技能、愛情、友誼、美學素養、自尊和榮譽感等。

　　如何才能擁有這些能增進「好生活」的實質有益之物，來幫助生活幸福目標的達成？亞里斯多德認為應該藉由理性的推理（reasoning），來培養內在的德行。然而，更重要的是在生活中培養實踐德行的行為。亞里斯多德把生活中的良好習慣稱做德行，因為一個好習慣可以讓人毫不費力就能完成某些有益的事，也可以習慣性地做出好的抉擇，不僅增進生活的「好」，也可以避免不好的結果所帶來的不利影響。

　　德行有兩類，分別是心智的德行（intellectual virtue）與道德的德行（moral virtue）。心智的德行是知識的能力，它是與生俱來的感知、理解與辨別能力；這種能力雖是與生俱來，但仍須透過不同人生階段的學習而成長，也會隨年齡增長而逐漸成熟。因此，心智的德行是自然和學習的結果。道德的德行，則是對事情做出正確選擇的能力，它是與實際事物相關的智慧；亦即面對生活的狀況，有能力辨別該如何做，並且在任何情況下，均能夠維持不落入極端的狀況而生活。道德德行的涵養，是透過後天的推理與學習而來。道德的德行對於人的「美好生活」（living well）具有關鍵的作用，因為做出正確選擇的習慣，可以決定生活過得好或

不好；如果經常做出錯誤的選擇，將不利於「好生活」的
實現。

　　培養好習慣或道德德行（moral virtue）對「好生活」
很重要，因為人在生活中面對許多後天欲望的誘惑，對於
生活必需品以外的東西經常動心，因此，需要培養道德德
行。人生中重要的道德德行，包括節制（moderation）、勇
氣（courage）和正義（justice）。節制使人不致沉溺於享樂
或尋求太多生理或物質欲望的滿足；勇氣的德行讓人能夠在
正確的時間、以正確的動機、用正確的方式做出正確的行
為，讓「好生活」得以實現；正義是德行在人際關係間的顯
現，是人對他人或社會所顯示的「道德正義」或「平等」
（equality）行為。正義之所以是德行，是因為這種德行可以
使人在人際關係中得到信任與尊重，有這種德行可以在「占
人便宜」與「被占便宜」的中間找到平衡點而讓「好生活」
可以維持。因此，正義的德行可以讓人擁有朋友，並享受合
作的好處。

　　然而，亞里斯多德認為知道「好生活」的意義，也具備
道德德行，並不必然保證活得好，因為人無法決定自己生命
起始點的條件，而且後天的生活環境也非人可完全控制。因
此，亞里斯多德認為美好生活的實現，多少還需要帶點幸運
（fortune）的成分。但一個人如果具有「好生活」的心智德
行，也具有道德德行，更具有福分，就能夠過幸福的生活。

　　總結來說，亞里斯多德從倫理的角度來談人類生活的
幸福，他認為生活的目標或生命的意義是過好的生活、活得
幸福。人的理性思惟能力，可以使人選擇朝向幸福的目標前

進。人的欲望有後天的欲望與自然的欲望，自然欲望的滿足有益於幸福或道德的提昇，而後天的欲望往往與「渴欲」相應，不利於人性德行的發展。因此，人為了活得幸福，必須發展德行或好的習慣；因為道德德行或好習慣的養成，可以使人在面對生命抉擇時做出正確的決定，得到好的結果。

在亞里斯多德的理念中，幸福的人生離不開人的生理與物質需求，離不開人與人的社會關係，以及心靈的滿足。節制的德行，使人知道如何擁有對幸福實質有益的物品；勇氣的德行令人知道生活中「行不偏執」的「中間」生活，能夠在面對恐懼或不可知的時候，在正確的時間、以正確的態度，做出好的決定。具有正直或正義的德行，便不會傷害他人來獲得自己的利益，因此可以贏得他人的信任。過幸福的生活，是人生的意義，也是人活在世間的終極目標，此終極目標的達成要靠平日在生活中不斷累積善德，朝向成就圓滿德行的目標前進。

亞里斯多德的幸福觀與馬斯洛的心理動機論相較，多出了理性思惟與道德提昇的心靈需求層次。雖然兩者心靈層次的論述，都涉及了人性發展（human development），但馬斯洛強調追求自我實現是生命的最終目的，亞里斯多德則認為幸福雖是生活的終極目標，但保障「好生活」的德行是在生活中逐漸學習而養成，圓滿德行（complete virtue）成就之時，就是最高幸福實現之日。亞里斯多德哲學思想中具備圓滿德行的幸福者，是全心全意、本能地以德行來過生活者，這是馬斯洛的心靈論述所不及之處。

亞里斯多德認為德行的「好生活」是在生活中過「遠離

「極端」生活，乍聽之下似乎與佛教的「中道」相同。然而，兩者仍有不同之處。亞里斯多德的遠離極端仍有「道德」的意識與執著，也仍有「道德之事」可以成就；但佛教的「中道」則是超絕對待的智慧，遠離苦樂、有無之兩邊執著，是「即有即空、即空即有、空有不二」，不執著兩端，也無中間可執的智慧狀態。

3. 聖嚴法師「建設人間淨土」思想對「佛教經濟學」理論之啟示：「心靈環保國富論」初探

當代主流經濟學的發展，是以資本主義的生產模式下的市場經濟制度做為研究對象，以自利心為市場經濟活動的動機，以個人追求欲望滿足最大化、廠商追求利潤最大化為經濟活動的目標，進而探討如何將有限的資源用在各種可能的用途，讓最多的人得到最大的滿足，以之做為經濟效率的指標。

佛教經濟學對當代西方經濟學的基本原則提出了挑戰，包括：（1）市場經濟制度的無效率性、廠商利潤最大化與自利心追求的不經濟性；（2）以物質欲望滿足為幸福指標的不幸福性；以及（3）資本主義市場經濟制度的生產、消費行為對環境濫用的破壞性等。針對主流經濟原則的缺失，佛教經濟學提出了其他經濟生活的原則，例如：以最少的消費達到最大的滿足、經濟活動追求痛苦的最小化、簡約欲望、生產與消費方式的非暴力原則，以及提出人與環境相依性，說明對環境的慈悲，即是對自己的慈悲；對人布施，即是增進自己幸福等。儘管這些觀點都不離佛法的觀念，但筆者認為相關的論述，對於佛法觀念的解說，都過於片段，也

欠缺佛法對世間看法的完整論述，且大部分的論述，均以佛教的倫理學或道德學（ethics）為出發點，說明當如何過經濟生活，其論述也欠缺以佛法為基礎所開展出來的經濟生活與幸福提昇的具體說明。

佛教對眾生生活關心的重點，不在物質的層面，而是生活品質。生活物資的滿足，是生而為人的維生基本需要，因此佛教不否定世間的經濟活動。然而在物質生活之外，佛教更關心「心理健康」對生活品質及生活幸福的影響。聖嚴法師的「心靈環保」及「建設人間淨土」理念，有佛法的幸福論述，包括對世間幸福、出世間幸福，以及世出世間幸福的說明。過去法鼓山體系在推動這些理念時，多偏重於人心淨化的啟發與關懷活動的推廣，較少將之與經濟生活連結，也鮮少與經濟學學術領域的理論相關聯。因此，本文大膽從聖嚴法師理念對「佛教經濟學」理論發展的可能啟發處來入手，希望對「建設人間淨土」的世間實踐，做出些許的貢獻。

釋果光（2014）《心靈環保經濟學》一書，是國內試圖將「佛教經濟學」與聖嚴法師「建設人間淨土」理念結合的先鋒。其書中以聖嚴法師「心靈環保」理念為基礎，建構現代佛法的經濟生活，分別論述僧團的經濟生活以及現代居士的經濟生活兩部分。對於居士的經濟生活，該書提出「心五四的經濟生活」主張，將聖嚴法師的「心五四」賦予經濟生活的意義，其主張為：以「四它」面對當代經濟情勢；以「四要」對治貪欲達到正念消費；以「四福」增長善欲達到正命生產；以「四安」促進「利和同均」的分配原則，以及

以「四感」獲得心靈財富。❸

　　果光法師已將「心五四」做了非常精闢到位的經濟生活應用，本文已難超越其架構，但仍設法從「心五四」的精神，以及人類經濟活動的動機、目的和生活的意義入手，嘗試解讀聖嚴法師「心五四」精神的現代意義，並提出其理念對建構「佛教經濟學」理論之可能啟發，以及對近代經濟永續發展思維的可能貢獻之處。

　　因此，本文試圖回到幾個最基本而深遠的問題來尋找「心靈環保」對「佛教經濟學」理論建構之意義。這些問題包括：「人活在世間，生命的意義是什麼？生活的目的是什麼？怎樣活才能平安快樂？」「宗教除了提供心靈慰藉，期盼來生生天國或淨土的救贖，還能為世間的苦難提供其他更積極的功能嗎？」「宗教，特別是佛教，能為地球人類的永續發展，提供何種答案？」本文期望藉由此類問題的思考，找出聖嚴法師的「心靈環保」與「建設人間淨土」思想，對西方主流經濟學及佛教經濟學理論建構之啟發處。

　　此外，資本主義市場經濟的發展雖提昇了物質的文明，但也帶來了許多難以回復的環境災難，許多國家在追求經濟成長的同時，也出現貧富不均惡化的現象。因此，「經濟成長與環境保護是否必然互相排斥？」「生活幸福是否必須大量消費？」「所得成長是否可以避免貧富不均的擴大？」「人類社會如何可以達成經濟富足與心靈安樂兼具的永續發展？」本文也希望藉由聖嚴法師的「心靈環保」與「建設人

---

❸ 釋果光（2014），《心靈環保經濟學》，頁89。

間淨土」思想的理解，提出建構人類社會永續發展的「心靈環保國富論」的經濟生活理論。

　　人活在世間，對於生活會產生多樣化的需求，包括健康的、生理的、心理的，以及精神層面的需求。如馬斯洛的人類動機階次論所說，這些需求中，圖溫飽應該是生命的最基本需求。溫飽之外，人莫不希望生活平安快樂，這種需求也是人性的共通處。然而不管生命的需求處在馬斯洛人類動機的何種階次，「欲望」應該都是需求的動機。如果從人類文明發展的歷史去考察，不難發現一個規律，亦即精神文明的興盛，通常是在經濟繁榮穩定的社會中出現。因此，人在基本欲望滿足後，便進而追求心理或精神層次的欲望滿足，這應該也是人類的共通性。亞里斯多德在《尼各馬科倫理學》所稱的德行生活，是物質與心靈均豐盛的生活，但他說有德行者的生活也未必一帆風順，而將德行者生活中的不幸遭遇，以「運氣」來解釋。亞里斯多德的幸福觀，雖較馬斯洛的人類需求動機階次論有更多形而上的心靈或人格修養的說明，但其見解對於世間的幸與不幸，仍不如佛教的三世因果因緣觀來得透徹。

　　為了說明佛教與世間心理學與哲學幸福觀的差異，先說明「幸福感」是如何產生的。幸福感來自於人在生存環境中所得到的舒適感或自在感，而生活中此類的感覺，則與生活或生命的滿足感有關。這些感覺有三個層次：其一是形而下的物質生活需求滿足，其次是精神生活的滿足，最後則是靈性生活的滿足。人活著，必須能夠從環境中得到生存物資的滿足，這是生存的最基本需求。在得到經濟安全及人身安

全之後，則進一步追求精神層次的滿足。這些生活中的安全
與稱意，離不開人對生活的滿意度、人在生存環境中與環境
互動的稱心如意感，以及生命過程的自我實現等。然而，有
一類的幸福，是片塵不染、無事罣心頭，自在無礙的智慧生
活，這部分的幸福，是佛法超越世間幸福的部分；佛法的幸
福，是智慧圓滿的德行生活，也是亞里斯多德純粹追求德行
圓滿所不及之處。

　　在討論聖嚴法師「建設人間淨土」思想對「佛教經濟
學」理論啟示之前，本文首先將簡單回顧比較主流經濟學、
馬斯洛的人類動機論、亞里斯多德的幸福倫理觀的異同，繼
則說明佛教的幸福觀，說明佛法不離世間，但也不陷泥於世
間的幸福生活。此一比較，除了用以說明主流經濟學以欲望
滿足為幸福之看法的不足，也說明佛法對欲望的態度，了解
佛法對「欲望」與「幸福」的看法，有世間知識學問所不及
之處。在了解佛法幸福法門之殊勝後，最後回到「佛教經濟
學」的討論，說明聖嚴法師依據佛教的核心思想，以及其自
身的修證經驗，所建立的「心靈環保」與「建設人間淨土」
理念在生活的應用，也據此說明其對「佛教經濟學」理論的
啟發。

　　（1）世間學問的幸福觀比較：經濟學、心理學與哲學

　　對於「欲望」的探討，是西方經濟學理論的基礎價值，
而對「欲望」與幸福關係的討論，也是區分主流經濟學、心
理學、哲學和佛教教理差異之處。在圖五中，筆者以圖形對
比說明「欲望」與「幸福」的概念，在世間學問、佛法，以
及「建設人間淨土」思想之異同。

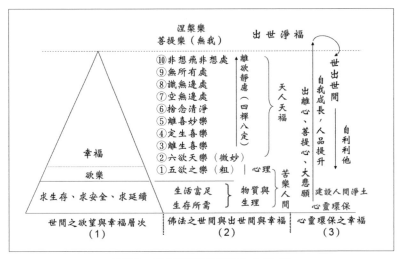

圖五：欲望與幸福概念之比較

　　圖五的幸福概念比較，分三大區塊，分別對比說明世間學問、佛法，以及「建設人間淨土」的幸福觀。在該圖最左方（1）的部分，說明世間學問（包括經濟學、心理學與哲學）對欲望與幸福看法的異同。

　　求生存，是人在世間的最基本需求；基本需求滿足後，還有求安全、求生命延續的需求。這些需求的內容，有物質、生理與心理的需求，但不管是精神或物質的需求，其基礎都是「欲望」。

　　西方主流經濟學說「欲望無窮」，主要是以「自利心」為出發點，所談是最基礎之「求生存、求安全、求延續」等欲望滿足，其內容主要是物質擁有與消費滿足的心理愉悅，因為消費滿足而產生的「快樂」（plcasurc），被稱做「效用」，而效用水準愈高，滿足感或幸福水準就愈高。因此，

主流經濟學的幸福，係以物質消費的滿足為主體；這種滿足感，是粗重的感官或生理口腹之欲滿足的快樂。因此，主流經濟學是以物質消費所得到的感官快樂為幸福。

心理學則認為人在基本生理欲求滿足之後，尚有心理上的愛與被愛、社會歸屬感，以及自尊的心理需求；在心理需求滿足後，還會產生自我實現的需求。愛與被愛的幸福、自尊得以維持的滿足與自信，以及生命探索與自我實現的幸福，都是主流經濟學中所未討論的幸福，尤其是自我實現的精神幸福，更遠非經濟學的物質與感官幸福所能比擬。

在希臘亞里斯多德的幸福哲學中，生命的最終目的是追求「幸福的極致」，而生命過程中所有的生理與心理的快樂，都是實現幸福的手段而已。相較於心理學的幸福，希臘哲學的幸福帶入了「德行」的倫理觀念，並以身心內外一致的「完全德行」所實踐的「好生活」，做為生命的目標與生命的完成。就幸福的層次來說，希臘哲學的幸福，不僅包括生理、心理與精神的快樂，尚有「完全德行」的心靈幸福。此一部分的幸福，則非心理學的自我實現動機所能比擬。

儘管主流經濟學、心理學和希臘哲學的幸福觀的內涵有差異，但三者的幸福，都需要在人群中才能實現。經濟學的幸福要在市場關係中實現，只有交易成功才能達到欲望滿足的目的。心理學金字塔頂端的幸福，也要在人際關係的和諧與被人接受（愛與被愛、社會歸屬感）之後，才會產生強烈動機去追求自我的實現。希臘哲學中的德行生活，也一樣必須在人群中培養、在人我關係中實踐，才能實現「好生活」的理想。不論三者中的「幸福」層次差異有多少，但三者所

論述的幸福，都是具有「自我意識」的幸福追求。佛法雖不否定人存在的基本需求與自我存在的感覺，但認為自我意識是束縛人的自由、令人無法得到幸福的根本原因。只有以智慧解脫自我的束縛，才有真正的幸福。佛法不否定「我」在世間的生活，有物質需要，也有人際與心理活動的滿意感，但「我」有三個層次，小我、大我與無我。小我是自我中心的「我」，大我是群體歸屬的「我」，無我則是超越世間小我、大我的自在。世間的學問追求「我的幸福」，不論其為小我或大我，都是「有我」；佛法並不否定世間「我的幸福」存在，但認為「無我」的自在才是真正的幸福，這是佛法的幸福觀與世間幸福觀差異之處。

（2）佛法的生活幸福觀❺❺

欲望是支撐人積極求生的動力，但欲望也是人在世間生死苦惱的原因。對人來說，欲望的滿足，固然感到稱心如意的快樂，如果欲求無法滿足，則是瞋恨、憂惱怖畏。因此，對人來說，幸福與不幸福，都與「欲望」相關，也都與心理的狀態相關。

《成唯識論》卷五說：「云何為欲？於所樂境，希望為性。勤依為業。」❺❻人在面對境界時，根（感官）境（外境）識（心識）三者和合而生「觸」，因觸而生「受」（感

---

❺❺ 本小節中僅討論佛法中的欲望與三界九地的幸福差別，至於佛法的經濟生活幸福的觀念，請參考許永河（2017）之〈幸福社會的經濟幸福——佛教的幸福經濟學〉一文。

❺❻ 《成唯識論》第 5 卷，《大正新脩大藏經》第 31 冊。（CBETA, T31, No. 1585）

受）。受有苦、樂、捨三種，對「受」生出分別、願求心，即是欲望。欲有善、惡、無記三性，善欲能發正勤，因而助成一切善事、善行；惡欲則因希欲而非法貪圖財色或名利，心中對所欲之事貪愛不捨，而造諸惡業。故不論善欲、惡欲，均因勤依而造業。

而《瑜伽師地論》卷八十六說：「復有三種諸受欲者，圓滿差別，由是因緣，諸受欲者，恒常戲論。何等為三？一、資產圓滿。二、自體圓滿。三、廣大殊勝有情供養圓滿。」❺生而為人，有受報的五蘊身，由於身心的存在，因此追求自己身心圓滿的「自體圓滿欲」；有了身心，就需要物資來過生活，因此就追求資產無缺的「資產圓滿欲」；有了身心，當然有父母、家庭眷屬、社會關係，有人情世故之往來，有金錢、物資與情感交流的需求，因此產生「廣大殊勝有情供養圓滿欲」。由於這三種欲求，人的起心動念，陷入欲念的追求中，而受欲念的纏縛；這種纏縛，如牛為軛所制，不得自由。因此，《阿毘達磨集異門足論》卷第八中說：「於諸欲中，所有欲貪、欲欲、欲親、欲愛、欲樂、欲悶、欲耽、欲嗜、欲喜、欲藏、欲隨、欲著，纏壓於心，是名欲軛。」❺因為欲愛貪著，欲令智昏，所以造種種的惡業，而於生死中輪迴：「眾生因欲緣欲，以欲為本故，母共子諍，子共母諍，父子、兄弟、姊妹、親族展轉共諍。彼既

---

❺ 《瑜伽師地論》，《大正新脩大藏經》第 30 冊。（CBETA, T30, No. 1579）

❺ 《阿毘達磨集異門足論》，《大正新脩大藏經》第 26 冊。（CBETA, T30, No. 1536）

如是共鬪諍已，母說子惡，子說母惡，父子、兄弟、姊妹、親族更相說惡，況復他人？是謂現法苦陰，因欲緣欲，以欲為本。」「復次，眾生因欲緣欲，以欲為本故，行身惡行，行口、意惡行，彼因身、口、意惡行故，因此、緣此，身壞命終，必至惡處，生地獄中，是謂後世苦陰，因欲緣欲，以欲為本，是謂欲患。」❺這裡所說的「欲」，是專指欲界眾生而言，特別是對貪著粗重五欲的人道眾生而說。如果能夠離欲，便可以擺脫欲軛，因此《增壹阿含經》卷第四十九云：「欲我知汝本，意以思想生；我不思想汝，則汝而不有。」❻

另《法苑珠林》卷二❻中說「欲」有四種，分別是情欲、色欲、食欲、淫欲等四欲。情欲，是對男女情愛所起的欲望；色欲，則指對男女形色所起的欲望；食欲，是對美食所起的欲望；淫欲，則是男女互相愛染而遂行欲事的欲望。三界的眾生，因欲望之差別而致受生之界地有別。欲界中的眾生有形色，也有欲境，故欲界眾生四欲全具；色界眾生則僅有微細色法，已離淫、食二欲，此界眾生雖無淫欲，但仍有微細的形色欲與情欲；無色界眾生則離淫食二欲，更無有色法，僅有情欲。

---

❺ 見《中阿含經》第 25 卷，〈（九九）因品苦陰經第三〉，《大正新脩大藏經》第 1 冊。（CBETA, T1, No. 26）

❻ 見《增壹阿含經》第 49 卷，〈非常品第五十一〉，《大正新脩大藏經》第 2 冊。（CBETA, T2, No. 125）

❻ 《法苑珠林》第 2 卷，《大正新脩大藏經》第 53 冊。（CBETA, T53, No. 2122）

　　三界中，欲界為五趣雜居地；在欲界居止的眾生，包括欲界天、人、地獄、餓鬼、畜生。在欲界中行十善者，感生人天果報；若放縱欲望而行十惡，則墮地獄、餓鬼、畜生三惡道中。欲界中人，若好靜慮而遠離粗重貪欲，修行禪定，則生禪天；色界、無色界俱屬禪天。色界的禪天有四種禪定境界，而無色界禪天亦有四種禪定境界，其眾生之禪定功夫較色界更為深細，已超越意識感受的境界。色界、無色界雖遠離粗重貪欲，但仍有微細的禪定意識貪執。

　　三界眾生均需食物以滋養身命，經論中說眾生以段食、觸食、思食、識食等四種世間食來攝持色身及精神。❷四食中，段食又稱粗摶食，需段食以維生者，僅限欲界眾生，其餘觸、思、識三食則通三界，此三種食依識而轉，隨識有無而有無。生而為人，雖需食物長養色身，但其發願出離生死者，則不以色身之欲望為念，而以禪悅食、法喜食、願食、念食、解脫食等五種出世間食，來持養善根、資益法身慧命。三界中的眾生，因為自我中心的欲望，而在世間受生死流轉之苦；出世之二乘聖人及大乘聖位菩薩，則因離欲而修善法，證入無我的智慧，而得出離生死之樂。

　　生死流轉是苦，出離生死是涅槃樂。從生死流轉到生死涅槃之間，由於對欲望的貪著輕重、品德與行為善惡差別，以及內心精神與心靈的安定深淺差異，而有不同層次快樂或幸福感受。此類差別，請見圖五中（2）「佛法之世間與出世間幸福」，以及下文的說明。

---

❷ 見《增壹阿含經》第 41 卷，另見《成唯識論》第 4 卷。

　　欲界眾生，因為淫食二欲的牽扯，心多散亂而煩惱重，故稱欲界散地；此間眾生所享福樂高低，與個人的德行有關。就人間來說，追求生存所需及生活富足、滿足五欲之樂，這部分是與世間經濟學的物質、生理與心理的快樂相通的。人是因過去所造的善惡業因交雜而感生人間，故人在世間，苦不致於重到無法承受，樂也不會好到永遠享有，因此是苦樂交雜。至於天人的福樂，則遠勝於人間。天人福樂最低的是欲界天，此界天人因為持戒行善、廣行布施，並發願求生天上而受生該處。欲界天的有情，隨其福報高低，其正報身形壽命、依報器用也有不同，但其欲樂微妙，遠非人間欲樂所可比擬。

　　欲界天之上為色界的四禪天，以及無色界的四種無色定。禪天的有情，因持戒修定、遠離欲望的擾亂而感生。色界從初禪的離生喜樂地，到二禪的定生喜樂地，一直到三禪的離喜妙樂地，均是遠離憂愁苦惱而感得微妙禪樂，相較於欲界的煩囂動亂或粗重感官快樂之歡喜，禪樂是更緩細的樂受。到了四禪捨念清淨地以上，心更無喜樂念頭生起，唯住捨受，心一境性，平和安定。色界之上的無色界，也是禪定天，定境較色界四禪更深，分別是空無邊處、識無邊處、無所有處、非想非非想處，此界禪定之樂，已非言語所能形容。

　　前述三界九地眾生，依於身心之五蘊，各有我見、我所見，而產生不同的欲望。有人因為人間太苦，所以希望死後生天。欲界天人之欲樂雖已遠非世間粗重的福樂所能比擬，而禪天靜慮之所生定心深妙、無所愛樂之心識狀態，又遠勝

欲界天之妙樂。但不論欲界天、色界天或無色界天之天人，其所享天福並非究竟之福，天人享福而未繼續造福，一旦天福享盡或定力消失，仍將墮入輪迴。只有在知見上了解三法印、四聖諦、八正道之理，勤修戒、定、慧，廣修六度萬行，積德修慧，照見五蘊皆空，悟入「無我」之理，才能出離生死，而證出世淨福，得菩提樂。

佛教不僅是宗教，而是人性淨化圓滿的生活實踐。佛法是以人為中心的教法，太虛大師說佛教之教法有五乘法：「曰人乘、曰天乘、曰聲聞乘、曰緣覺乘、曰如來乘。前二世間，後三出世，唯如來乘完全此五。」❻❸聖嚴法師說佛法依眾生發心差異，而有五道法，即人道、天道、解脫道、菩薩道、佛道等五道。❻❹不論五乘法或五道法，皆說明佛法以人類為本，佛法的修行都是從人間的端正法、端正行開始的。因此，在佛法來說，把人做好，是一切福德的基礎。佛法的人天法，通於世間的倫理道德的「世福」，以及世間宗教的「天福」觀念，但佛教「涅槃解脫」的極致幸福觀，則是不共世間，也不共世間神教的。涅槃解脫幸福的實踐，要從世間善法的倫理道德修起，❻❺再修福德增上的戒定慧三

---

❻❸ 釋太虛，《佛教人乘正法論》，《太虛大師全書》第 5 冊，頁 192。

❻❹ 釋聖嚴，《平安的人間》，《法鼓全集》8-5，2005 年網路版，頁 92-94。

❻❺ 本文前述亞里斯多德倫理學的幸福觀，認為德行圓滿的豐富生活便是幸福。若依著亞里斯多德的德行原則過生活，可以成為世間聖人，但依著佛法的戒定慧三學、六度法門過生活，則可成為出世聖人。世間聖人與出世聖人的差別，在於「有我行善」與「無我行善」之別。從「有我」到「無我」的德行修持，便可漸出世間。

學、六度法門，藉由悲智雙修雙運，破除人我五蘊的執著而出世間生死。出世間生死後，再運悲心，入世度眾，則是大乘的菩薩行。

（3）「建設人間淨土」的「心靈環保國富論」

佛法的生活幸福觀，已如前小節所述。茲依據聖嚴法師「心靈環保」與「建設人間淨土」理念，建構能保持生活幸福豐富、永續的當代經濟生活模式，此一生活模式的理論架構，本文稱之為「心靈環保國富論」。依據「心靈環保」的「心五四」及「四種環保」來生活，不僅可以使現在的生活幸福實現，也可以保障未來的幸福，更能讓人類社會幸福生活的永續發展得以持續。此處先說明「心靈環保」與「建設人間淨土」思想的生活幸福意義，再以之建構整體經濟體系的生產、消費與再生產的永續發展模型。

關於聖嚴法師「建設人間淨土」思想的幸福觀，以及世間學問的幸福、佛法的幸福觀念之對比，請見圖五之（3）「心靈環保的幸福」。人的欲望，有一部分固然來自生活的「需要」，但絕大部分是與基本生活溫飽無關的欲求，這部分的欲求稱之為「貪欲」。人生所有的煩惱或不快樂，都與「欲壑難填」有關。在大小乘經典，如《阿含經》或《禪要經》中，都可以看到「訶欲」的說法。「訶欲」並非視欲望為罪惡，而是提醒人應該了解「需要」與「貪欲」的差別，更應了解，無止境欲望的追求，是不幸福、不快樂的根源，提醒人應了解「貪欲」對幸福的危害性。

這是佛法說「欲望」與世間經濟學談「欲望」不同的地方；世間經濟學說追求個人效用或滿足的最大化，是「理性的

行為」，但卻無法認知此種理性是「有限的理性」；它僅說明欲望滿足的效用性，卻無法透視欲望追求的苦惱性。因此，生活中希望離苦得樂，應該建立少欲知足、知福惜福的態度。

在現代社會中，人無法離群索居，因此，人我關係的定位、人際關係的紛擾，都需要用智慧處理。世間無常，生命中難免出現不如人意的事，如何度過生命難關，更需要智慧。人在世間的所有不幸福，都離不開「有心難安」的困擾；心能安定清淨，便可以平安幸福。人心保持不受自我的欲望汙染、不受環境的擾動影響，便是「心靈環保」的功夫。因此，聖嚴法師很善巧地因應現代人的生活需要，將佛法的觀念現代化，提出「心五四」做為「心靈環保」的核心實踐綱要。

「心靈環保」的生活，是對生命中的一切苦樂境界，生出離心，同時發菩提心與大悲願，努力自我成長、提昇人品，達成淨化人心、淨化社會、保護自然環境的目標。在作法上，是從內而外，層層向外推展，而達成「建設人間淨土」的理想。

在心內的環保來說，要做到離卻貪、瞋、癡、慢、疑等煩惱心，開發智慧心及慈悲心；以慈悲心及智慧心來利人利己，兼顧身、心、靈健康的生活。其次，展現在外的是生活環保，生活上是少欲知足、簡樸節約的態度，以少欲知足來培養知福、惜福、培福、種福的生活態度，才是「有福」的生活。其次，向外推及人我關係的環保，實現利己利人、智慧與慈悲兼顧的社會生活，並以心儀、口儀、身儀保育社會生態。最後，推及人與自然的關係，實踐知福惜福、感恩大

地及一切生命的態度，並保護生態及自然環境免受汙染破壞（心靈環保的理念落實，請見圖六）。

「心五四」與「心靈環保」的幸福生活，與世間幸福觀的共通處是世間修福的倫理觀，而其超越世間幸福觀之處，則是與佛法教理相應的出世淨福，以及出世間再入世間，為眾生拔苦造福的慈悲與智慧（如圖五之（3）所示）。因此，「心靈環保」的幸福生活，是令眾生得「現法安、現法樂」及「後世安、後世樂」的永續幸福的方針。

了解聖嚴法師「心靈環保」理念是人類社會幸福永續發展的方針之後，筆者嘗試將「心靈環保」的理念應用在「生產與再生產」的永續經濟發展構想中。茲以簡單的生產、消費、儲蓄、投資，以及再生產的關係，說明以「心靈環保」為基礎價值的社會，其生產、消費與環境承載力的相互關

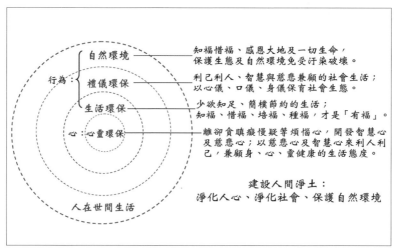

圖六：以「四環」做為「建設人間淨土」的實踐綱要

係，以及「心靈環保」如何支持此一生產與再生產的永續發展關係的實現（圖七）。對於圖七的邏輯架構，茲略做說明，由於此部分的論述邏輯仍在發展中，未來將繼續充實。圖七的理念，是建立在下述的幾個觀察基礎：

A.「心靈環保」是幸福生活的核心價值：在一個經濟體系中，決定人類生存的是生活物資與自然資源，而決定一個社會生活幸福的因素，是依於前述「心靈環保」所建構的社會價值觀。幸福社會的生活，固然需要遠離物質匱乏，需要生存物資的支持，更需要「心五四」的生活實踐。

B. 幸福生活須從教育入手：觀念影響行為，行為決定個人的生命際遇，以及與環境互動的方式。錯誤的觀念，讓人

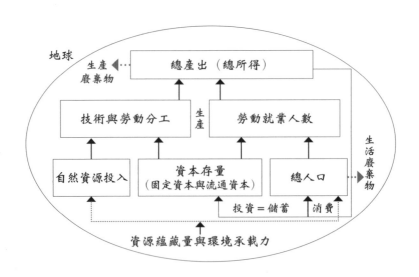

圖七：「心靈環保國富論」──幸福永續發展的生產與再生產關係示意圖

得不到心中想要的幸福，也會讓人對社會及自然環境產生破壞。幸福的生活需要正確的觀念與行為，而良好的觀念與行為的建立，需要靠教育。因此，「心靈環保」與「心五四」的生活價值觀，需要透過教育來推廣。

C. 追求物質生活而破壞環境，不利人類的生活幸福：地球的自然資源是固定的，耗竭即無法再生。生活物資是社會勞動力與生產技術的成果，必須使用資本、勞動與自然資源投入來生產。生產活動所產生的生產廢棄物、二氧化碳及廢水等，必然破壞自然環境，降低自然環境的承載力，對經濟發展與人類幸福產生不利的影響。

D. 破壞環境，將降低自然環境的人口承載力：自然環境及生活物資決定該社會之環境可以承載的人口總數；人口總數又決定社會可以投入生產的勞動數量。人口愈多，固然可以帶來勞動投入增加、產出增加與消費增加的效果，但人口增加與消費增加，帶來生活廢棄物的增加，對自然環境產生不利的影養，也會降低環境對人口的承載力。

E. 盲目追求技術進步與經濟成長，阻礙人性發展：社會的生產力提高可以提高產出水準，但生產力的提昇，受技術水準與勞動分工的細密程度所左右。勞動分工的細密度受整體社會的心智發展與勞動過程中的人性發展（human development）的程度所所決定；人性發展的程度則受整體社會「心靈環保」與永續幸福追求的意識所左右。一味追求利潤與產量提高的技術，但缺乏「心靈環保」意識的技術發展，將阻礙人性發展，產生勞資關係惡化、資源耗竭與環境破壞的結果。

F. 明智分配所得，有利幸福生活的永續性：現代的生產技術嵌入在實質的資本中，因此技術水準受資本存量高低所影響。資本存量水準高低則受儲蓄多寡所影響；儲蓄是總所得中未被消費及未被用做公益用途的餘額。因此，從社會總所得來看，家計單位的消費、社會公益與儲蓄的決策，將決定未來投入再生產的資本，以及未來的產出量。

G. 知福惜福的消費態度，可以培福增福：以「心靈環保」為基礎的經濟體，消費的需求是建立在「少欲知足」、「知福、惜福、培福、種福」的觀念上，消費品的需求是由依循「心五四」與「心靈環保」過經濟生活的家計單位所決定。家計單位的消費決策，決定市場的需求水準，而市場的需求則決定產出與就業。在「心靈環保」的經濟體中，供給是受需求所決定的；無人需求的產品不會被生產，過度大量生產的物品也會減少生產，因此資源浪費與環境破壞的情況便可減輕。

H. 具有「社會企業責任」意識的生產活動，可以減少生產對社會及環境的負面衝擊：組織生產的是廠商，在已知的生產技術下，廠商的決策決定勞動、資本與自然資源的雇用與投入。但「生產」是一個具有誤導性的術語，好似「生產」可以從無到有，產生新的東西。實際上，生產是一個破壞性的過程，因為要生產新的東西，舊有的生產形式或現有的環境必須被摧毀或破壞。從整體社會來說，生產的最終目的是為了消費，但對廠商來說，生產則是為了賺取利潤。因此，生產是一個具有廠商私人利益與社會環境整體利益間衝突的活動。一個具有「心靈環保」意識的生產者，知道其決

策對於自己、他人（勞動與其他廠商）、社會與自然環境的
影響，會以知福、惜福，創造永續幸福的態度來生產，在
「企業社會責任」意識的前提下，不是追求最大利潤，而是
以「最小傷害」為組織生產的目標。

　　I. 依正不二，故關懷弱勢，是提昇人己幸福的必要行
動：社會總人口分勞動人口及非勞動人口兩類，其中非勞動
人口包括老弱殘病或因故無法投入經濟活動的人口。可以從
事經濟活動的勞動人口中，又分就業與失業兩類。因此，總
人口中僅就業人口有所得，其餘失業或其他弱勢人口則無所
得。無所得者缺乏經濟資源來維持生計，需要社會其他人的
支持。從「依正不二」的觀念來說，人不可能完全隔絕於依
報環境之外而自求多福，因此有所得者對經濟弱勢人口的關
懷援助，是對自己幸福與他人幸福提昇的必要行動。

　　J. 以「心靈環保」為核心的經濟生活，可保障「經濟富
足」與「心靈安樂」的可持續性：以「心靈環保」為核心的
個人經濟生活的經營，在現代經濟生活中有其必要。個人的
有限時間如何在就業、休閒與靈性生活提昇間做分配，需要
智慧做指引。所得如何在目前消費、經濟安全、濟助弱勢或
其他社會公益用途間做分配，以及儲蓄應如何在現金、金融
投資或房地產等方式間分配握有，也都要以智慧的態度做抉
擇。其抉擇的結果，不僅影響個人當下的生活，也影響整個
經濟體系的生產、消費與再生產。

　　在約略說明「心靈環保」的總體經濟生活所涵蓋的面
向之後，茲就圖七內容說明維持現在、未來生活幸福永續性
的「心靈環保國富論」架構。地球只有一個，人類社會追求

經濟成長與生活幸福，不能再落入過去百年來追求無盡成長的陷阱中，因為事實證明一味追求物質的繁榮，雖能增加物質消費的豐富性，卻無法帶來真正的幸福。經濟繁榮是物質欲望追求的結果，而欲望的追求必然有得失與煩惱，有煩惱得失便失掉了幸福感。「心靈環保國富論」說明心靈安樂、經濟富足的社會，其幸福永續發展的特質，根本核心價值是「心靈環保」；在成長的追求過程中，建立「心靈環保」的社會意識，才能保證幸福永續發展的實現。換言之，物質不是財富、物質也不是幸福，僅是滿足欲望的手段；只有懂得以「心靈環保」的方式來產生的財富（物質），才有助於幸福的實現。因此，本文之「心靈環保國富論」的構想，設法從主流經濟學「財富」的生產與再生產的過程，探討人類社會幸福永續發展構想。

生產的目的是為了生活的需要，生活的目標是富足與幸福。總產出（圖七上方第一個方格）是生產的結果，但沒有勞動的投入，便無產出。因此，生產品是使用勞動與技術對原料加工的結果。決定勞動就業人數多寡的因素是這個社會有多少勞動人口可以雇用，以及現有技術需要使用多少勞動來配合生產（圖七上方第二層）。勞動就業的多寡，是受社會的資本存量水準及總人口所決定，勞動分工程度及技術之使用，則受自然資源及資本存量所影響（圖七上方第三層）。

一個社會的就業人口多寡，受人口的總數以及人口的年齡結構所左右。總人口中的倚賴人口比率低，便有更多可投入生產的勞動人口數。因此，總人口愈多、倚賴人口比愈

低,則勞動人口愈多。經濟體系的就業機會愈多,則勞動人口的就業率便愈高。然而,如果環境的人口承載力下降,總人口及勞動人口下降,帶來就業下降,其結果是總產出或可供消費的物資數量下降,生活水準必然隨之下降。

資本的內容包括機器設備等固定資本,以及原料、資金等流通資本。資本增加的來源為投資,投資資金的來源則為廠商的利潤,以及家計單位的儲蓄。資本存量的水準,不僅決定勞動雇用數量,也決定生產的技術水準與勞動分工的細密度,其結果將影響產出與所得。在一定的所得水準下,消費愈高,則儲蓄愈低,下期可供投資的資金來源減少,將降低資本累積而影響下一期的所得。如果基本消費水準不變,但所得下降,儲蓄能力下降,又影響未來的資本數量及產出。凡此變化,均對未來的經濟福祉產生不利的影響。

在主流經濟分析中,決定技術與勞動分工程度的主要因素,是市場的擴大程度;市場愈擴大,則勞動分工愈可能實現,且為了滿足日益擴張的市場需求,也愈可能帶動技術進步。但在「心靈環保」的生產體系中,自然資源有限,受限於資源的蘊藏量,生產不可能無限擴大,而且少欲知足的消費模式下,需求增加有限,市場也不可能無限擴大。在「心靈環保」的生產體系技術進步仍有可能出現,新的生產方式仍會出現,但主要的技術進步,是與人類心靈發展而產生的生活與消費方式的改變有關。在「心靈環保」的經濟體系中,心靈成長帶動相關消費與生產的成長,而非傳統的生產者與廣告、行銷業結合,以刺激感官與欲望的方式,來增加消費與生產的模式。

　　此外，由於地球對物種的承載度有其極限，因此總人口數不可能無限制增加，天然資源也不可能無限地擷取。總人口數無法無限量增加，市場的發展便有其極限；此外，自然資源有限，生產也不可無限地擴大，想藉由刺激欲望來達到擴大市場的手段也有其自然的限制。因此，傳統經濟學中藉由追求經濟成長提昇幸福，希望藉由無限的產出成長來達成幸福的無盡提昇，事實上是不可能實現之事；何況在追求產出成長過程中，對自然環境的傷害，已經造成幸福的實質傷害。因此，僅有「心靈環保國富論」的經濟成長，才有助於永續幸福的實現。

　　現行資本主義的市場經濟制度，其所顯現的是大量生產、大量消費，並藉由刺激欲望來達到市場擴充與利潤擴大的目的。但資本主義制度發展的結果，是人類社會為了掠奪有限的資源，產生國與國之間的戰爭；為了爭奪市場，出現了經濟壁壘與對立；而在生產過程中則產生了勞動者與資本家的對立，再加上生產結果所出現的所得分配不均等問題，也使得社會出現對立不安。過去人類社會追求經濟成長的結果，雖帶來物質消費的內容以及物質文明的提昇，但因為追求無盡的欲望滿足，卻帶來心靈貧窮與不安的現象。因此，市場經濟活動出現所帶來的大量消費現象，不必然帶來滿足與幸福的增加，而是不斷追求短暫物質消費愉悅感滿足的現象，帶來地球的毀滅以及人類社會自我毀滅的危機。

　　人類的理性是追求幸福的生活，在基本生活需求的滿足之後，追求精神或靈性生活的需求便告增加。這樣的經濟富足、心靈安樂的生活，不能靠無盡的物欲追求來達成。影

響經濟富足、心靈安樂的永續幸福實現的關鍵因素，是「社會共利共榮的倫理關係」。此一倫理關係，是建立在社會每一個經濟活動參與者的「覺知」意識（正念）之上，覺知我與社會環境和自然環境是一體的。不論是家計單位或廠商，均以「心靈環保」為核心價值，共同創建共利共榮的經濟關係，而且在經濟活動的相依關係中，建構安定的社會，以及對自然環境友善的互利關係（圖八）。

　　經濟活動者的「覺知」意識，是每個人或社群，均能了解在相互依存的依報世間中，彼此相依相存，且每個人的行為不僅改變環境，也會改變自己的命運。每個人為了自己的幸福，應該對自己的行為負責，不能僅是追求「自利」而傷

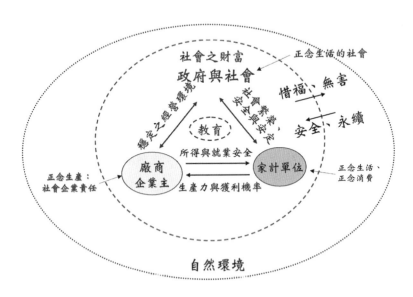

圖八：「心靈環保」與幸福永續發展的共利共榮倫理關係

害他人、傷害環境；在自利的同時，也應該以「利他」的心去關懷他人，因為每個人自己的身心，是「小身體」，環境是「大身體」，為利己而害人，以自私心傷害「大身體」，便是傷害自己，結果必然讓自己不幸福。

在經濟活動中，廠商與家計單位是經濟活動的主體，社會與自然環境則是經濟活動的場域；幸福，是人類社會共同的價值，而所有的人的經濟與非經濟活動，都是為了追求幸福。因此，生產單位的企業主與家計單位的勞動者，在覺知我與環境一體的前提下，都以「心五四」及「心靈環保」為幸福生活的方針，彼此善意相待。對勞動者來說，應該盡責盡職，努力提昇生產力，為雇主創造獲利的可能性；而雇主則提供就業機會、維持工作安全，為勞動者提供穩定的所得來源。以「心靈環保」為基礎的勞資關係中，雇主有利潤，勞動有所得，共利共榮的生產關係中，社會的生產與再生產關係便能夠持續，永續的生活幸福才能實現。

互利互榮的雇主與勞動，均在社會與自然環境的場域中出現。因此，勞動者及廠商為了自己的幸福，不僅僅是關心彼此的關係，更應該關心彼此所生活的社會；對社會的苦難或弱勢者做出關懷與付出，維持社會整體的安全、安定與繁榮。安定的社會回報給廠商與個人的是，安全的社會與繁榮穩定的經營環境。對於自然環境，不論廠商與個人在經濟活動中，都應抱持惜福與無害的保育態度，不隨意糟蹋資源、破壞環境，則自然環境回報人類社會的是自然災害的降低，以及宜居的永續地球村。永續幸福的經濟生活，就是負責任與彼此關心的「心靈環保」生活，也是聖嚴法師「心六倫」

的實踐。透過「心靈環保」與「心六倫」的實踐，維持身心內外環境的和諧與安定，保障互利互榮的富足與幸福。

我們雖不懷疑每個人都會希望過幸福的生活，但我們不能期望每個人都有「心靈環保」的意識，或者具備如何實踐「心五四」的知識與決心，因此永續幸福生活的實現，需要從大眾觀念的改變做起，而大眾觀念的改變，則需要透過教育來宣導。法鼓山的大普化、大關懷、大學院等三大教育，是人間社會的經濟富足與心靈安樂能否實現的關鍵因素。藉由普化的教育，提昇人品，遠離貪、瞋、癡對幸福的毒害。達成每個人內心遠離貪欲煩憂、人類社會繁榮和諧、自然環境舒適怡人，便是「人間淨土」的實現。

五、結語

經濟生活離不開物質與生存欲望的滿足，主流經濟學談欲望、談滿足，認為追求限制條件下「無窮欲望」的最大滿足，是人類理性的行為，而且從亞當‧斯密以來，崇尚經濟自由者認為讓每個人的「自利心」（self-interest）充分發揮，不僅每個人的幸福或福祉可以達到最大化，也會產生社會福祉最佳化（optimization）的結果。不可諱言，為了生存而追求溫飽，固然是理性的行為，但人的無窮欲望中，何者是屬於「需要」（needs）？何者是「想要」（desire）或是渴要（craving wants）？如果無法區分需要與渴要，放任自利心狂馳的結果，對個人來說，是欲求難滿的苦惱，對環境而言則是為了私欲而不計後果的破壞。因此，自利而無道德約束或智慧指引，其結果不僅自己苦惱，也會造成周圍環

境的不安與苦惱。追求平安幸福固然是人的正當欲望，但為了追求幸福卻落入苦惱，則是「貪欲」與缺乏智慧所致。人類社會無止盡的追求欲望的滿足，卻不辨別「貪欲」與「正欲」的差別，將無法得到生活的平安幸福。

佛法談幸福，雖不否定物質生活的必要性，但強調幸福感不是建立在「無窮欲望」的滿足上，而是一種遠離煩惱的心理狀態。西方經濟學或心理學的幸福感（happiness），是指來自物質的獲得或感官的滿足所產生的愉悅（pleasure）；佛法的幸福快樂，不否定感官滿足快感的存在，但強調幸福不是建立在感官愉悅或物質的滿足之上，而是建立在心靈層次的安穩與澄靜。因此，從佛法的角度來看世間的生活，雖然不否定欲望的滿足可能帶來快樂，但強調「欲壑難填」是苦惱的根本原因，而與「我執」連結的「欲望」，亦即「我愛……」或「我不愛……」等，則是造成對立矛盾的原因，也是每個人的苦惱與不幸福根源。

在一般人的觀念中佛教是著重於修證解脫、不食人間煙火的，但這是一種誤解。經論中說有情眾生以「四食」為生，❻因此不管在家、出家，獲取物資來長養色身，都是必要的。然而在必要的基礎上，如何過適確的經濟生活來提昇幸福，則需觀念的修正與行為的改變，因此生活本身就是一

---

❻ 「四食」為摶食、觸食、念食與思食，見《雜阿含經》卷十四、卷十五、卷十七、《中阿含經》卷七大拘絺羅經、卷四十九說智經、《長阿含經》卷八眾集經、卷二十世記經、《增一阿含經》卷二十一、卷四十一等。四食中，摶食限欲界，其餘三食通三界。然依據《攝大乘論釋》卷十四與《大乘阿毘達磨雜集論》卷五，四食有凡聖之四種分別。

種修行。佛教經濟學與主流經濟學的連結與分野，在於對「欲望」問題的看法，以及滿足欲望的手段與態度的差異。

主流經濟學談欲望，不分別「需要」與「想要」，通通歸入消費的欲求；然而「需要」是生活所之所需，而超過生活所需之外的欲望，則是「想要」或「渴要」的成分，也是無窮苦惱的根源。主流經濟學追求限制條件下的欲望滿足最大化，其結果雖然達到「物質富裕」的地步，但卻落入「精神貧窮」無法幸福的狀態。「心靈環保」的幸福經濟學內容，是在面對「欲望」之時，保持正念，區分「需要」與「想要」，所謂「需要的不多，想要得太多」，❻❼因此為了自身的幸福與人間的幸福，練習「少欲知足」的生活態度，在「能要」與「不該要」之間，知所取捨，以避免無窮貪欲所帶來的煩惱。

幸福是一種心靈清淨光明的安定狀態，少欲知足的幸福，要從心理、思想與精神面來培養。「心理的層面是屬於情意的，思想的層面是屬於理智的，精神的層面是屬於情意和理智的昇華，也就是把我們從自我中心的束縛之中釋放出來，所出現的慈悲和智慧，那是平等而無條件的愛。因此，心靈環保是以情意及思想為基礎的著力點，使得我們淨化或轉化成為具有高尚的品德標準，並有無限愛心的偉大人格。」❻❽

---

❻❼ 請參閱《聖嚴法師教淨土法門》：「要常常想到四福：知福、惜福、培福、種福；還有四要：需要的不多、想要的太多、能要該要才可以要、不能要不該要的絕對不要。」（《法鼓全集》10-11，2005年網路版，頁52，行12-13）

　　由於工業革命以來人類為追求物質文明而對環境及資源的破壞，因此近代出現環境保護的風潮，但也屢屢造成環境保護與經濟發展孰輕孰重的矛盾與衝突。聖嚴法師對近代環保運動發展的困境，點出環保問題的核心在於「人的觀念」，因而提出「心靈環保」的觀念，此一觀念不僅點出近代環境保護運動的盲點，也彌補了現有佛教經濟學理論基礎的不足。

　　「心靈環保」從生活面來說，包含了人與自然環境生活關係的「自然環保」、人與人生活關係的「禮儀環保」，以及人面對自己生活的儉樸知足態度的「生活環保」。前述三種環保，是以「人的情意、觀念（思想）、精神的淨化」❻❾為核心，此一情意觀念與精神的淨化，即是「心靈環保」。從觀念上的自我教育來提昇人品，再回到現實生活中將觀念落實踐履，遠離貪欲與精神匱乏的生活，當下就是平安幸福。因此，聖嚴法師的「心靈環保」觀念，不管從理論面或實踐面，都是幸福經濟生活的理論與實踐的綱要。

　　聖嚴法師一生弘揚漢傳佛教，將佛教的修行觀念與方法做深入淺出的介紹。雖然「建設人間淨土」的理念是在其晚年較為世人所熟知，但「人間淨土」思想是聖嚴法師一生修行與弘化悲願的縮影。❼⓿誠如聖嚴法師所說，「心淨國土

---

❻❽　請參閱「聖嚴法師談心靈環保」，見網址：https://www.ddm.org.tw/event/spirit/page01_03_02.html。另請參閱聖嚴法師〈認識心靈環保——闡明心靈環保的精義，以及與心靈貧窮的關聯〉一文（《致詞》，《法鼓全集》3-12，2005 年網路版，頁 75-76）。

❻❾　同前註。

淨」、「人間淨土是佛陀本懷」**❼**，但一般人認識聖嚴法師多從修行法門或佛教學問的研究來開始，較少從「人間淨土」、「心靈環保」與經濟生活實踐的關係來探討。因此，本文以聖嚴法師「心靈環保」與「建設人間淨土」之思想為核心，嘗試摸索其思想對近代「佛教經濟學」理論發展的可能啟發處。除一方面將佛教的基本教理整理，另方面也將聖嚴法師思想的學術價值做不同角度的詮釋，並對佛教的幸福經濟學依據「心靈環保」的觀念，提出永續幸福發展的初步理論論述。

本文所提之「心靈環保國富論」構想仍屬初探，整體理論仍在發展中。其具體內容，將包括與心靈環保意識相應之社會正念生活（mindfulness life）共同價值觀之建立，正念生產、正念消費之經濟生活，以及以正念生活所建構之可持續性生活幸福等，其論述將以淨化人心、淨化社會、保護自然環境為核心，探討經濟富足、人民安樂而且不破壞幸福的社會生活實踐。由於前述內容涵蓋甚廣，難以短文詳述，未來將以專書形式，詳細討論說明之。

---

❼ 聖嚴法師弘揚「人間淨土」大事年表。網址：http://old.shengyen.org/content/about/about_02_4.aspx。

❼ 聖嚴法師思想理念：「人間淨土」思想。網址：http://www.shengyen.org/bio-thought-p1.php。

參考文獻

中文部分

中華電子佛典協會（CBETA），《大正新脩大正藏經》，2011 年電子版。

釋果光，《心靈環保經濟學》，臺北：法鼓文化，2014 年。

釋聖嚴，《法鼓全集》，2005 年網路版，網址：http://ddc.shengyen.org/pc.htm。

許永河，〈幸福社會的經濟幸福──佛教的幸福經濟學〉，收入聖嚴教育基金會學術研究部編，《聖嚴研究》第九輯，臺北：法鼓文化，2017 年 11 月，頁 51-112。

英文部分

Adler, Mortimer J. (1978). *Aristotle for Everybody: Difficult Thought Made Easy.* Macmillan. May 1978.

Alexandrin, G. and C.E. Zech (1999). "Ancient futures: papal and Buddhist economics", *International Journal of Social Economics*, Vol. 26 Issue: 10/11, pp. 1344-1353.

Backhouse, Roger E. (2008). "Marginal Revolution." in *The New Palgrave Dictionary of Economics*, 2nd edition, 2008. Edited by Steven N. Durlauf and Lawrence E. Blume, New York: Palgrave Macmillan. pp. 1-5.

Brown, Clair (2015). "Buddhist Economics: An Enlightened Approach to the Dismal Science." *Challenge,* 58(1):23-28, 2015.

Carson, Rachel (1962). *Silent Spring.* Boston: Houghton Mifflin; Cambridge, Mass.: Riverside Press.

Daniels, Peter L. (2010). "Climate change, economics and Buddhism—Part I: An integrated environmental analysis framework." *Ecological Economics*. Vol. 69, Issue 5, 15 March 2010, pp. 952-961.

Daniels, Peter L. (2010). "Climate change, economics and Buddhism—Part 2: New views and practices for sustainable world economies." *Ecological Economics*. Vol. 69, Issue 5, 15 March 2010, pp. 962-972.

Diwan, R. and Lutz, Mark A. (1987), *Essays in Gandhian Economics*, Intermediate Technology (December 1, 1987).

Drechsler, Wolfgang (2019). "Reality and Diversity of Buddhist Economics." American Journal of *Economics* & Sociology. Mar 2019, Vol. 78 Issue 2, pp. 523-560.

Inoue, S. (1998). *Putting Buddhism to work. A new approach to management and business*. Translated by Duncan Williams. Tokyo, New York, London: Kodansha International Ltd.

James, Simon P. & Cooper, David E. (2007). "Buddhism and the environment." *Contemporary Buddhism*, Vol. 8, No. 2, November 2007, pp. 93-96.

Keown, Damien (2007). "Buddhism and ecology: A virtue ethics approach." *Contemporary Buddhism*, 8:2, 97-112.

Kolm, S. C. (1985). The Buddhist theory of 'no-self.' In *The multiple self*, ed. Jon Elster, 233-265. Cambridge: Cambridge University Press.

Kraut, Richard (2006). *The Blackwell guide to Aristotle's Nicomachean ethics*. Editor. Malden, MA ; Oxford : Blackwell Pub., 2006.

Le Duc, Anthony (2018). "A Framework for Buddhist Environmentalism: The Horizontal and Vertical Dimensions." *International Journal of Buddhist Thought & Culture*. Vol. 28. No. 1 (June 2018): 177-203.

Lennerfors, Thomas Taro (2015). "A Buddhist future for capitalism? Revising Buddhist economics for the era of light capitalism." *Futures*. Vol. 68, April 2015, pp. 67-75.

Loy, David R. (2014). "Why Buddhism and the Modern World Need Each Other: A Buddhist Perspective." *Buddhist-Christian Studies*. Vol. 34 (2014), pp. 39-50

Magnuson, Joel (2017). *From Greed to Wellbeing: A Buddhist Approach to Resolving Our Economic and Financial Crises*. Chicago, IL: Policy Press, 2017.

Maslow, A. H. (1943). "A Theory of Human Motivation." Psychological Review, 50(4), 370-96.

Pathompituknukoon, Pakpicha (2014). "Dynamic Optimization with Simulations How to Achieve Maximized Utility under Buddhist Economics." *International Journal of Intelligent Technologies and Applied Statistics*. Vol.7, No.2 (2014), pp. 127-146.

Pathompituknukoon, Pakpicha, and Suriya, Komsan (2014). "Mathematical proofs of the middle path in Buddhist economics as a pathway to the maximum of happiness." *The Empirical Econometrics and Quantitative Economics Letters*. Vol. 3, No. 1 (March 2014), pp. 25-32.

Payne, Richard, *ed.* (2010). *How Much Is Enough? Consumerism, Buddhism, and the Human Environment*. Boston: Wisdom Publications, 2010.

Payutto, P.A. (1994). *Buddhist economics: A Middle Way for the market place*. Bangkok: Buddhadhamma Foundation.

Puntasen, A. (2005). *Buddhist economics: Evolution, theories and its application to various economic subjects*. Bangkok: Amarin Publisher.

Puntasen, A. (2007). "Buddhist economics as a new paradigm towards happiness." *Society and Economy* 29(2):181-200. August 2007.

Ross, W. D. & Brown, Lesley (2009). *The Nicomachean Ethics*/Aristotle; translated by David Ross; revised with an introduction and notes by Lesley Brown. Oxford World's Classic. New York: Oxford University Press Inc.

Schumacher, E.F. (1973). *Small is beautiful*. London: Abacus.

Sivaraksa, Sulak (2009). *Wisdom of Sustainability: Buddhist Economics for the 21st Century quantity*. Koa Books Inc.

Sivaraksa, Sulak (2014). "Ecological Suffering: From a Buddhist Perspective." *Buddhist-Christian Studies*, Vol. 34 (2014), pp. 147-153.

Varela, F.J. (1999). *Ethical know-how. Action, wisdom, and cognition*. Stanford: Stanford University Press.

Waldau, Paul. (1998). "A Review of Buddhism and Ecology: The Interconnection of Dharma and Deeds; Buddhism and Ecology: Balancing Convergence, Dissonance, and the Risk of Anachronism." *Journal of Buddhist Ethics* 5 (1998): 374-383.

Welford, R. (2006). "Tackling greed and achieving sustainable development." In *Business within limits: Deep ecology and Buddhist economics*, Laszlo Zsolnai and Knut J. Ims, eds., 25-53. Oxford: Peter Lang.

Zsolnai, L. (ed.). (2011). *Ethical Principles and Economic Transformation—A Buddhist Approach*, Issues in Business Ethics 33, Springer Science Business Media B.V.

Economic Prosperity and Happy Life:
On Master Sheng-Yen's "Building Pure Land on Earth" and Its Inspiration on Buddhist Economic Theory

Yuan-Ho Hsu

Professor of Economics, National Cheng Kung University

▌ Abstract

The mainstream neoclassical economics has "self-interest" and "competition" as its foundations for the analysis of market efficiency in the capitalist economy. Utility maximization and profit maximization are the axioms for the valuation of market efficiency. In mainstream economics theories, "utility" is a synonym of life satisfaction or happiness. Therefore, pursuing non-stopping economic growth becomes a major strategy to meet the insatiable desires and to attain consumption gratification. However, the deficiency of the mainstream economic theories is to blame for the development of various adverse outcomes of the market economy, such as global warming, natural resources depletion, and income inequality in the world. Moreover, the mainstream economics theories are also incapable of solving these problems.

The Buddhist economics criticizes the deficiency of mainstream economics and introduces economic theories based on the ethics of Buddha's teaching. Contrary to the mainstream economics, the Buddhist economics claims that happiness does not lie on material consumption, but on the status of mind. Also, the mainstream economics proposes the principle of maximizing consumption with the optimal pattern of production, but Buddhist economics treasures maximizing human satisfaction with the optimal consumption pattern. Moreover, Buddhist economics proposes alternative principles of economics activities, such as minimizing suffering, simplifying desires, non-violence, compassion and genuine care, instead of the mainstream economics' self-interest and competition.

This study aims to develop an alternative framework for the Buddhist Economics study, based on Master Sheng-yen's preaching of "Protecting the Spiritual Environment" and "Building Pure Land on Earth." The theoretical framework has consumption, production, employment, social environment, and natural environment in the integrated setting. The aim of this work is to develop a conceptual framework for a society that could achieve sustainable happiness and maintain economic prosperity. The core value of economic activities for people in this society is to protect their spiritual environment, so that the society can attain the quality of life and preserve the purity of the living environment at the same time.

Keywords: Rev. Sheng-Yen, Pure Land on Earth, Protecting Spiritual Environment, Buddhist Economics

Sense of Interdependence and the Altruistic behavior

Miko Ching-Ying Yu

Assistant Professor, College of Management, Yuan Ze University

Tzyy-Jan Lai

Associate Professor, College of Management, Yuan Ze University

▌ Abstract

This study try to investigate and answer two questions, first, would it or is it beneficial for one to take altruistic behavior? Second, how or what factor will lead to more altruistic behavior? This study used sample questionnaire and proved the following two hypothesis: When one has higher sense of interdependence between self and others, perceived social distance is small and will participate more in altruistic activities. When one participate more (measured in frequency) or in depth (measured in variety of activities) in the altruistic activities, it will lead to higher individual utility, and a more coherent community.

Therefore, if we enhance our sense of interdependent with others within our society, which will motivate altruistic behavior and result in a benefit to ourselves, to others, and to the community or society as a whole. This is consistent with Master Sheng-Yen's "The six ethics of the mind", it is our nature and everyone own the capacity to do it.

Keywords: Altruistic activities, Social distance, Sense of interdependence, The six ethics of the mind

1. Introduction

The behavior economics observe a typical individual's behavior and come to the conclusion that given the prices of goods and income one will try to consume goods accordingly to maximize one's utility. And it also induces the conclusion that if everyone maximizes own utility the social welfare will reach the highest level.

In this study, we ask the question: even it has to cost money or other resources, would it or is it still beneficial for one to take altruistic behavior? What factor cause some people spend their own money and resources to invest in benefit others than self? Our observation is that if people consider and perceive close social distance to others, that is if one perceive there is strong interdependence between oneself and others, then one's optimal behavior will be more empathetic and more willing to engage in helping others.

In other words, if our choice is rational, consider our own benefit, even it has cost, people still engage in activities that benefit others. Because at the same time they also perceived that such behavior will result in more happiness in terms of intangible or non-material to their own utility.

The perception about the social distance measures our sense of interdependence with others and also measures the perceived degree of own utility or welfare related to others. One may argue that altruistic behavior may use up part of our resources, such as income or time, which may reduce our consumption of goods and reduce our own utility. By taking into account all tangible and intangible benefits, invest in altruistic behavior may still be rational optimal choice. Hence, further implication is more altruistic behavior will result in a higher level of social or community welfare.

So the next question is to ask is there a lot difference among people's sense of social distance? And what factor causes the difference? If everyone perceive all of our happiness are further or closer connect to each other, then no one can maximize his/her happiness without take others welfare into account, which will lead to a higher total welfare. The closer the perceived social distance the less difference between self and others, more altruistic behavior will be involved and higher utility will be reached.

In this study, we are not going to build a formal model to prove altruistic behavior will result in higher total utility equilibrium. Instead, this study tried to illustrate that sensing of the interdependence among us will lead to higher involvement in altruistic behavior and will directly increase other and indirectly our own happiness and benefit, in addition, enhance the coherence of our community as a whole.

In fact, almost no one will disagree that everyone should be kind and nice to people and which will lead to a more peaceful mind. But in many times when come to the reality in daily life and workplace, what commonly observed are competition, selfish, inconsiderate, even harmful behaviors. Why? In this study we would like to point out the factor that mislead by individualism let us undermine the degree of our interdependence with others and misunderstanding selfishness can bring more benefits. And by realize that fact can motivate one's altruistic behavior and further increase our own happiness as well as the whole community. This is also consistent to what Buddhism assertion that if we can reduce the sense of selfness and cultivation our sense of interdependence with others, it will help us to build our compassion toward others and obtain our own peaceful mind and ultimate happiness.

Especially given modern world's labor division, not one task can be completely done just by one person. Therefore, actually we are more and more depend on each other and the degree of interdependence among us is getting higher and higher.

WHY? Or Should we have compassion (more than just be nice and kind?) Which means, should we take other people's happiness and welfare as part of our own welfare and happiness? So it becomes the motivation and responsibility to help each other. And this is the compassion we discuss in this study, that is not just be kind and nice but be actually try to take altruistic actions. Because only after we take into account other people's welfare or happiness as our responsibility or as part of our own welfare and happiness then the altruistic behavior can be motived and not always consciously or unconsciously be replaced by selfish consideration instead.

So, as live in a community no one will disagree that we should help each other and be nice to others. Almost all will consider be nice, be kind, and try to be helpful is a good thing, which will benefit others benefit the community and as a result will benefit ourselves. But many times we are not able to actually be compassionate, and have empathy on others.

Why? When consider carefully, many times we think that helping others involve spending our money, time, efforts, or other resources. Since resources is limited, so our compassion ends up be kind and nice, or become "sympathy."

This is only because we consider happiness always come from outside, from our sight looking at pleasant seen, from our hearing hear pleasant sound or wards, from we taste the good food, from we feel the pleasant sense, ect.. And all these come from the material world and need spend resources to produce, to obtain them. But we always ignore or forgot the fact that the degree of happiness you got is not always proportionate to the wealth you have, the goods consumed, or the money spend. In many times, rich people seemed even more difficult to feel content than the poor people. When considering happiness is based upon a peaceful, tranquil, equilibrium mind, then it becomes more obvious that self interest and altruistic behavior need not be competitive to each other. Further more, it is possible to lead to benefit self, benefit others, and benefit community as a whole.

CAN we have compassion?

After understand the benefit of altruistic behavior, the next question is can we or are we able to do it?

Can we reduce our selfish and ignore the difference between ourselves and others, and always think of benefiting others?

If we put kids with different races, countries, communities, and families, many times they have no problem to play with each other. While we grow up, we cultivate the sense of individuality and is affected by the outside world more and more and distance us to others. We build our own value systems according to different culture, family, or educational system. But forgot that no matter poor or wealthy, white, yellow, or black, male or female, we all are human beings that hope to obtain happiness and avoid pain. To the extent of human beings, all of us are not different from each other. More over, as a human, our nature is loving and kind, and everyone has a capacity to help, to love others.

Within the island Taiwan, many people would make a huge distinction between those who came from mainland China during the World War Two or whose ancestor originated move from Mainland china. But it is obvious that when we travel to a different country one will be very happy to meet anyone from Taiwan and glad to share information with each other. On other cases, it is also very happy to hear someone who can speak Chinese and will easily and glad to help each other out. That means, the circle of 'we', is able to expand or shrink all depends on the circumstances or depends on how we perceived who is 'us' and who isn't. Considering this, then it is revealed that as long as we can expand the circle of 'we', as long as we perceive the difference between ourselves and others are not that different, then we can easily and we are able to helping people and behave empathetically. It all depends how we perceive the difference and the distance between others and ourselves. The broader range is considered as the same group as us, each individual take a less weight and become less important. Since it seems nature to help the member in the same group, it is easier for one to help other and help more people. Because we also have the tendency of distance our team and other teams.

HOW do we cultivate compassion:

Everyone should be kind! No one will object to that! Everyone will also encourage the altruistic behavior. But not many people and not time, people will be helpful and compassion to others. Instead, we are more used to behave selfishly and not thinking of anyone else and some time even harmful to others. Why? And how can we cultivate the altruistic behavior?

All religions emphasize love and compassion, but without wisdom, they are just a "good-hearted person" and a compassionate person. Therefore, there is a limit to altruistic behavior. You will pity the poor but will not be compassionate to the rich. And we always think that self-interest and altruism are in conflict.

Almost all religions emphasize love or compassion is a unique human quality that can be explored to obtain a harmonic society or family life.

But with love or a good heart without wisdom may end up being a good-heart or kind person but with very limited good results. Because we usually think that benefit others and benefit self are contradict and incompatible! We perceived that self interest and benefit others is competing for our limited resources such as time and efforts, or our income like money or other.

The difference between Buddhism and other religions is to emphasize that others and I are equal and identical. To reduce the difference between yourself and others, to raise yourself to altruism.

A. The compassion of Buddhism includes: metta is hoping that others can be happy, compassion is hoping that others will stay away from pain and increase their happiness; this responsibility will be fulfilled and completed by me. Therefore, he has practical ingredients, which are very different from other religions.

B. Meaning (motivation) of the master, and all the foundations of good deeds are in Bodhicitta, not for self-interest; for the benefit of others, not for accumulating their own fortune.

Also echoing the six ethics of mind from Master Sheng Yen.

In addition, how to distinguish between good heart and Bodhicitta heart? Be Nice: he/she is pitiful, I hope he can get better. Generally, Bodhicitta especially in Mahayana Buddhism school is try to help all sentient being to relive from pain and obtain persistent or ultimate happiness.

Also, how to benefit people is a true altruistic? Put yourself in other people's shoes. So your motivation is: if I were he/she, what can I do to relive from this pain or obstacle? That's why education or training is better than just give money to a child or young man. Company and relieve their pain is more important than try to give more treatment for.

In order to cultivate the sense of altruistic mind, we have tried to raise the importance of others in our mind, and to reduce the importance of self. So as to eliminate the difference between I and else, and then we are able to treat others as same as ourselves. So we will truly understand other's need. Most of time we are too judgmental to. Therefore, Buddhism advocates: "Equality is equal", it is necessary to reduce the difference between oneself and others, and to see others as important as themselves (the method of cultivating Bodhicitta in the "On-the-God Theory" by Silent Bodhisattva: "Change from Him") It will be beneficial to his behavior.

2. Hypothesis

Based on the discussion in the previous paragraph, we used the well-known social distance to explore the sense of altruistic mind from self to others.

Although many of the same mechanisms that explain the effects of social distance are also used to explain the identifiability effect (Small and Loewenstein, 2003). Recognizable targets evoke more empathy (Kogut and Ritov, 2005) and make it easier to perceive targets psychologically from the perspective of a single beneficiary (Slovic, 2007).

Ida and Yu (2016) used psychosocial distance to measure the extent of donations. We continue this research method, trying to find the psychosocial distance and how it affects the amount of donations. Then go on to explore the development of altruism.

H1: When one has higher sense of interdependence between self and others, perceived social distance is small and will participate more in altruistic activities;

H2: When one participate more (measured in frequency) or in depth (measured in variety of activities) in the altruistic activities, it will lead to higher individual utility, and a more coherent community.

Here, we use different social distance (Jones and Rachlin, 2006) to considering the donation on them. We apply field experiment method (Treatment group and control group) of dictator game in social distance (Bohnet,1999). In this case, in asking participants about social distance that is defined as the degree of reciprocity that respondents believe exists within social interactions. Therefore, indicates the closeness of subjects as

A. Family members ;
B. Same-gender friends;
C. Estranged same-gender friends; and
D. Strangers.

Subjects were recruited from the undergraduate student body at the Yuan-Ze University, Chung-Yuan University, Jin-Wen University and Feng-Chia University Taiwan in the spring and summer of 2016. A baseline and two treatments with watching the video and discussion were conducted.

Then, we follow two social preferences: inequality aversion and social distance. Each respondent made 2 choices in donation under different situation. Given that we included alternatives, attributes, and levels are as follows; respondent divided 1000 with different social distance: family members, close same-gender friends, estranged same-gender friends and strangers.

The result (Table 1) from dictator game, that our willingness to share goods and resources with other individuals is influenced by social distance. In echoing the H1 hypothesis: when one has higher sense of interdependence between self and others, perceived social distance is small and will donate (participant) more in altruistic activities.

Table 1: Social discounting for Taiwan

Taiwan Treatment Group	Average offer rate
Family members	**29%**
Close same-gender friends	26%
Estranged same-gender friends	18%
Stranger	12%

Moreover,the random utility (McFadden,2000) that O obtains from choosing alternative i can be expressed in this inequality aversion model (Ida, 2012) as follows: Where denotes an independently and identically distributed extreme value (IIDEV) term. Note that we have assumed that own utility is the log of own payoff (lnx_{Di}) and have normalized its coefficient to 1. It is usually assumed that the utility function is linear in inequality aversion. The inequality aversion model (1) predicts, therefore, that the dictator makes a fifty-fifty offer.

$$U_{Oi} = lnx_{Oi} - \alpha * lnq_{Ri} - \beta * s_{Ri} + \varepsilon_{Oi} \quad (1)$$

To test H2: When one participate more (measured in frequency) or in depth (measured in variety of activities) in the altruistic activities, it will lead to higher individual utility, and a more coherent community. The result from inequality aversion model as table 2. From the weights (the importance of social distance) attached to the social distances, the importance(utility) were as our exception from family members to strangers, respectly.

Table 2: Weights (the importance of socail distance) attached to the social distances

	Treatment group (Watching the video and discussion)	Control group (None)
Taiwan		
Family members	0.48	0.48
Close same-gender friends	0.30	0.29
Estranged same-gender friends	0.04	0.06

3. Conclusion

Ethics is a kindness, a kind of compassion for Bodhisattva. In addition to the self-interested demands, he must be altruistic; only his own self-interest is the most secure. If you only think about self-interest and don't consider altruism, then your own interests will not be stable, because other people will come and fight for it. In the more chaotic environment, the more ethical education and ethics are needed.

If we enhance our sense of interdependence with others in society, this will stimulate altruistic behavior and bring benefits (positive test in H1,H2) to ourselves, others, and society as a whole. his is consistent with Master Sheng-Yen's "The six ethics of the mind". This is our nature, and everyone has their own abilities. This is the best value and the true meaning of happiness and happiness.

Reference

B. Jones., H. Rachlin. "Social discounting." *Psychological Science*, 17, 2006, 283-286.

C.Y. Yu., T., Ida." Empathy Diffusion - NGO Sustainable Development." ISPIM, 2016, Portugal.

D. Kahneman., J.L. Knetsch., R.H. Thaler. "Fairness And The Assumptions Of Economics." *The Journal of Business*, 59, 1986.

D. McFadden.,K. Train,"Mixed MNL Models for Discrete Response." *Journal of Applied Econometrics*, 15, 2000, 447-470.

D. A. Small., G. Loewenstein. "Helping a victim or helping the victim: Altruism and identifiability." *Journal of Risk and Uncertainty*, 26(1), 2003, 5-16.

I. Bohnet,, B.S.Frey."Social distance and other-regarding behaviour in dictator games: comment." *American Economic Review*, 1999, 335-339.

T., Ida, Ogawa., K. "Measuring the inequality aversion rate, the social discount rate, and the time discount rate using a hypothetical dictator game." *International Journal of Social Economics*, 39(5), 2012, 314-329.

T. Kogut., I. Ritov. "The identified victim effect: An identified group, or just a single individual?." *Journal of Behavioral Decision Making*, 18(3), 2005, 157-167.

相互依賴覺知與利他行為

尤淨纓
元智大學管理學院國企學群助理教授

賴子珍
元智大學管理學院國企學群副教授

▌摘要

　　此篇論文嘗試回答兩個問題：利他行為是否「是」或「能」利己？以及，哪些因素會引發更多的利他行為？本文利用問卷調查檢驗兩項假設：當對自己及他人具有較高的互相依賴的覺知（sense of interdependence），所認知的社會距離（social distance）就會較小，就會參與較多的利他活動。當參與次數（以參與頻率衡量）較多，或參與程度較深（以參與種類衡量)，會引發較高的個人效用（utility）以及群體的和諧度。

　　因此，在社會群體中加強人們對於彼此互相依賴程度的覺知，就可誘發個人較多的利他行為，從而社會、他人、自己都將獲益。以上的假設與推論，與聖嚴法師所提倡的「心六倫」內涵是一致的，這樣的認知及利他行為是符合人的天性（nature），而且是每個人都可依自力做到。

關鍵詞：利他行為，社群距離，相互依賴，心六倫

Buddhadharma and Sustainable Development:
An Integrated Framework of Analysis

Ching-yi Chiang

Assistant Professor, Department of Economics and Finance, Ming Chuan University

▌ Abstract

Sustainable Development is a very important modern concept and practice for solving global problems. There are many frameworks for sustainable development which are useful for us to understand the world and put our efforts into actions. But I find there is a very important element which is missing in these frameworks. If we want to effectively solve social, economic, and environmental problems, we should have a healthy mind first. Hence, I think that the Buddhist doctrine, which is about the teaching of the mind, should be added into any models. If so, we not only have a better understanding of the roots of problems but also can effectively solve the global problems. Then people can enjoy higher well-being, having genuine happiness. This paper explores the sustainable path for development in accordance with the essence of Buddhist doctrines. Firstly, we introduce the principle of the modern concept of sustainability, and showing the inherently damaging and unsustainable features in our economic system. We then reason that the principles in Buddhism are sustainable in nature. The paper also offers an integrated framework of sustainable development by combing the material and spiritual aspects together. The resulting model possesses very desirable features that can simultaneously deal with human's problems from the inside and outside of people and guarantee sustainability and higher well-being for every human and nonhuman species right now and in the future.

Keywords: sustainable development, sustainability, development, buddhadharma, Master Sheng Yen

1. Introduction

Our world is faced with unsustainability in many ways which would cause human beings and other living beings to suffer now and in the future. The members of the United Nations have implemented a plan of action to combat the problems and improve the wellbeing for all the stakeholders since 2015 (United Nations, 2015). With the vision to transform our world into a sustainable one, 'The 2030 Agenda for Sustainable Development provides a global blueprint for dignity, peace and prosperity for people and the planet, now and in the future.' (United Nations, 2015). The agenda includes 17 sustainable development goals and 169 targets aiming at achieving sustainable development in three dimensions—economic, social and environmental—in a balanced and integrated manner. It promises that no one will be left behind.

What are the challenges we are facing? To name a few, poverty, hunger, disease, unemployment, inequality of opportunity, wealth, and power, conflict, violent extremism, terrorism and related humanitarian crises and forced displacement of people, natural resource depletion, greenhouse gas emissions, adverse impacts of environmental degradation, including desertification, drought, land degradation, freshwater scarcity and loss of biodiversity, increases in global temperature, sea level rise, ocean acidification, more frequent and intense natural disasters,... (Robertson, 2014; Roorda et al., 2012) 'Climate change is one of the greatest challenges of our time and its adverse impacts undermine the ability of all countries to achieve sustainable development.' (United Nations, 2015)

Scientists have been warning that we are overshooting the limits of Earth's support capacity. Meadows and coauthors spent 30 years to tell us this fact. It means that if we do not change the trend our future would be so grey. In 1972, the best seller *Limits to Growth* (*LTG* thereafter) (Meadows et al., 1972) reported that global ecological constraints (related to resource use and emissions) would have significant influence on global developments in the twenty-first century. The authors adopted a "system" method to understand the severity of the ongoing global problems. It gave a strong warning, saying that population and production growth would collapse in uncontrolled manner if the present growth trends in world population, industrialization, pollution, food production, and resource depletion continued unchanged, and the limits to growth on this planet would be reached sometime within the next 100 years. *LTG* pleaded for profound, proactive, societal innovation through technological, cultural, and institutional change in order to avoid the possible crisis. 20 years later, in 1992, these authors published the update book *Beyond the Limits* (Meadows et al., 1992). Their study showed that the warning became a reality, that is, humanity had already overshot the limits of Earth's support capacity. According to the estimation of Wackernagel and his colleagues (Wackernagel et al., 2002), human resource use exceeded the global carrying capacity by 20 percent.❶ Scientific

---

❶ In their paper "Tracking the Ecological Overshoot of the Human Economy', the authors develop an accounting framework to measure the extent of humanity's current demand on the planet's bioproductive capacity, creating comprehensive measures of human impact on the biosphere. By integrating and modifying the contributions of earlier studies, this study demonstrates an aggregated approach to natural capital accounting in biophysical units. A wide variety of human uses of nature are identified, measured, and expressed in units that enable direct comparison of human demands with nature's supply of ecological services. When area demand can exceed area supply, it is called "ecological overshoot". There are 6 impact components measured in their accounting system, which are six human activities that require biologically productive space. They are (i) growing crops for food, animal feed, fiber, oil, and rubber; (ii) grazing animals for meat, hides, wool, and milk; (iii) harvesting timber for wood, fiber, and fuel; (iv) marine and freshwater fishing; (v) accommodating infrastructure for housing, transportation, industrial production, and hydro-electric power; and (vi) burning fossil fuel. Wackernagel et al. build a 40-year (1961-1999) time series for humanity's

consensus and meteorological data both suggested that the global climate was altered by human activity. The world was moving into unsustainable territory. A decade later, in 2005, they published *Limits to Growth: the 30-Year Update*. They expressed much more pessimistic about the global future than they were in 1972 "since humanity squandered the past 30 years in futile debates and well-intentioned, but halfhearted, responses to the global ecological challenge." The global footprint gets larger day by day.

The severity of the world's ongoing crisis may be better summarized by "*World Scientists Warning to Humanity*" signed by more than 1,600 scientists, including 102 Nobel laureates, from 70 countries (Meadows et al., 2006):

> Human beings and the natural world are on a collision course. Human activities inflict harsh and often irreversible damage on the environment and on critical resources. If not checked, many of our current practices put at serious risk the future that we wish for human society and the plant and animal kingdoms, many so alter the living world that will be unable to sustain life in the manner that we know. Fundamental changes are urgent if we are avoid the collision our present course will bring about.

With deep globalization, these problems affect all the people and countries in the world, as a matter of fact, everyone may play a part to the cause. The UN's *Sustainable Development Goals* recognize those goals are linked to each other and interdependent. To successfully eradicate poverty, combat inequality, preserve the planet, and create sustained, inclusive and sustainable economic growth, and foster social inclusion, people and nations need to

---

ecological demand. Their graph (Fig.1 , p.9269) shows "human demand over the last 40 years exceeds nature's total supply from the 1980s onwards, overshooting it by 20% in 1999."

act in an integrated manner and devote collectively to the pursuit. However, *The Sustainable Development Goals Report 2018* (United Nations, 2018) reviews the progress in the third year of implementation of the 2030 Agenda and found that the rate of global progress is not keeping pace with the ambitions of the Agenda. Hence, it urges for immediate and accelerated action by countries and stakeholders at all levels.

Sustainability seems a positive concept to us and probably made us to hold a bright view about the future and forget about the ongoing global crisis. Huge amount of scientific evidence shows clear signs that we are overshooting the planet's limit, but cold figures, graphs, statistics of all kinds just do not scare people in any way. The growth oriented policies are still popular worldwide. Since the economies are still growing although slowing down a little bit, we people just do the business as usual and enjoy the comforts from the material growth, ignoring the possibility of a breakdown of our system. The pictures of starved skinny polar bears, a dead whale with full of stomach of plastics, and many other forms of suffering are caught by our eyes, but not our hearts. Perhaps, we may say that those problems and the victims caused by human activities seem too far away and irrelevant to us, here and now, or we may feel that we don't mean to hurt or cause any disaster and damage to happen. True, nevertheless, it is fair to say that, the most serious problem is that we do not know the fact that we are suffering in one way or another and that we are acting out of ignorance, blindness, and self-centeredness with all the information revealed to us. It seems that there are some fundamental systematic problems in the coordination of human's collective efforts toward sustainability. And that prohibits us, both individually and collectively, from moving onto the right path.

The predicaments we face are all consequences of our behavior and the ways we have organized ourselves socially, politically, and economically; these, in turn, motivated by our values, perceptions, judgments and emotions. It appears that we need a global ethics that can guide people to act responsibly, righteously, justly, virtuously, mindfully, and compassionately. We also need a more complete, paradigmatic approaches which can help us transform our mind and heart from within to lead our understanding, motivation and actions. Buddhist doctrines are all about the teaching of mind and Buddhism has a delicate structure of concepts, methods and practices that can help us to uplift human's characters and build a flourishing environment. It is promising that, if we fit the mentality and spirit elements into any modern sustainable program and framework, which are more material-oriented or of outward pursuit, we can have a very powerful and effective comprehensive sustainable development model. The resulting model would possess very desirable features that can simultaneously deal with human's problems from the inside and outside of people and guarantee sustainability and higher well-being for "all"-every human and nonhuman species-"right now" and the future. It is also easy for people to understand and apply in the daily life without a sense of sacrifice or compromise, or losing our freedom and choices. The people, planet, and ecosystem would be all sustainably flourishing, across space and time. ❷

Hence, this paper aims at integrating the Buddhist sustainable development model, such as *The Four Kinds Spiritual Environmentalism* (Master Sheng Yen, 2004) and the general

---

❷ The anonymous referee pointed out "the paper failed to provide definite reasons and strong evidences to explain suggested result is a worthwhile and viable one for us." As to the issue about the evidence supporting the Buddhist theories, it is truly a promising field of future research. As far as I know, in the happiness research more and more studies are exploring the factors of spiritual wellbeing (Chaing, 2019). Many findings which are consistent with the Buddhist doctrines may provide some evidence to verify the Buddhist teachings (for example, see His Holiness the Dalai Lama, Archbishop Desmond Tutu, and Douglas Abrams, 2016; Yongey Mingyur Rinpoche, 2013.) Considering the space of the paper, I leave this topic out of this paper. I thank the referee for bringing this issue out.

sustainable development frameworks, such as *The 2030 Sustainable Agenda* (United Nations, 2015), and *The Human Development Approach* (UNDP, 2016), by putting crucial components for sustainability together. The former mainly focuses on the spiritual development, and the latter emphasize the material development. For sustainable development being practical and effective, we need both. The resulting model emphasizes both features. However, the paper does not claim that the Buddhist doctrine is "the only" global ethics that we can adopt. The paper holds that any framework of sustainable development should possess both material and spiritual aspects. So the paper tries to find something in common in both the general frameworks and the Buddhist doctrine. The two complement each other. I suggest that any other frameworks, spiritual ones or material-oriented ones may do as long as they possess the features that are identified in the paper (section 3.3.1). As a matter of fact, the material-oriented frameworks are based on some values or ethics (such as the Charter of the United Nations and the Universal Declaration of Human Rights etc.) and the spiritual ones do not exclude the material development in any way.

The remaining paper is arranged as follows. Section 2 introduces the principle of the modern concept of sustainability and Buddhist doctrines. Section 3 we first integrate the Buddhist human development model and two modern sustainable development models and then sketch a comprehensive framework. The steps of an empirical practice in the daily life are also suggested in this section. Section 4 is the conclusion.

2. Sustainable Development: Principles and Practice

2.1 Modern concepts and methods

2.1.1 Concepts

Robertson (2014) notes that the word "sustainability" refers to systems and processes that are able to operate and persist on their own over long periods of time. The Oxford English Dictionary defines the ecological meaning of "sustainability" as "Of, relating to, or designation forms of human economic activity and culture that do not lead to environmental degradation, especially avoiding the long-term depletion of natural.

Sustainability can be as an idea and as a professional discipline. As an idea or concept, sustainability has multiple aspects. Sustainability is a way to see and recognize the dynamic, cyclical, and interdependent nature of all the parts and pieces of life on earth. It also indicates the direction that human's efforts are guided to and the urgent action needed to take to restore what is damaged in an innovative manner. Furthermore, it shapes the humanistic view that sets the equitable principle of allowing every living being, including the unborn of the future, to live and thrive. As a professional discipline, "sustainability" is one academic field of study and is interdisciplinary or multidisciplinary in nature (see Robertson, 2014, Ch.1).

In 1970s, the concept of "sustainable development" was brought up to deal with a global-scale environmental, social and economic crisis (Robertson, 2014, Ch.1). As to the definition of sustainable development, Roorda et al. (2012) noted that there are over a hundred of them. The most often-quoted one is given by the Brundtland report *Our Common Future* (UN, the World Commission on Environment and Development, WCED, 1987). It defined sustainable development as "development that meets the needs of the present without compromising the ability of future generations to meet their needs." (WCED, 1987)

The most important feature of the sustainable development is to adopt the "system" method to deal with global problems. There are three primary areas of attention for sustainable development. The so-called "the three pillars" or "triple bottom line" of sustainable development are "people, planet, and prosperity," or the three "Es" "environment, economics, and equity." Our planet has many problems that are connected, including poverty, health, overpopulation, resource depletion, food and water scarcity, political instability, and the destruction of the life support system we depend on. We cannot fix one problem in isolation because they are all interconnected and inderdependent. In order to live sustainably, we 'need to foster communities that are healthy, safe, and secure, with economic opportunity for everyone while keeping Earth's life support system in good shape.' To be on a sustainable development path, we must understand their meanings and take appropriate action or inaction in a whole system context, not partial or local one. As Robertson (2014, pp. 5-6) points out:

> The first "E" represents environment (or ecology), and it refers to preserving and storing the health of living systems. All life on the planet depends on ecosystems to purify air and water, pollinate crops, provide food, recycle waste, and to circulate atmospheric gases, chemical elements, and energy; this process is referred to as ecosystem services. In order to create a planetary condition that is sustainable we must understand how these processes work, not just as individual pieces but as systems. We must see our own species as neither victims nor masters but as active members of the interconnected webs of all living beings. We need to learn to live within our means ecologically, to recognize that there are built-in limits to any system known as its carrying capacity. ...

> The second "E" represents economics. In order for systems to continue over the long term, resources must be distributed fairly, with each individual able to meet their own basic human needs. Unlimited economic growth is not sustainable, although increasing the quality of life is (Daly and Farley, 2003, 12). Economic growth that uses up natural resources, pollutes the soil, air, and water, and depletes ecosystem services will eventually lead to a decline in quality of life. ...

> The third "E" represents equity, that is, social equity or equality (Edwards, 2005, 23). Equity includes freedom from unhealthy living conditions and equal access to food,

water, employment, education, and healthcare. Equity means providing opportunities for all people, not just a privileged few, to grow and flourish in their own way.

Equity also includes intergenerational concern: acknowledging the impact our decisions today will have on future generations. Some writers refer to these future people we have not met year as "our neighbors in time." ...

It indicates that these three Es will ensure an overall improvement in the well-being for human and nonhuman species, right now and in the future by humans' kind and wise actions. And the environment and society will be sustainably developed into one with endless nourishing elements and mechanisms.

From above, we may learn that sustainable development concerns the relationship between people, society, and environment across space and across time. It attempts to deal with global problems in a more integrated manner, rather than a partial manner. It aims at promoting well-being for all in our planet, now and in the future.

2.1.2 Unsustainability and sustainable practice

The threat of unsustainability results from climate change, which is mostly manmade. It arises from our modes of economic activity which is motivated by growth oriented practice and policy. We produce massive quantities goods and services by burning fossil fuels. As a consumer, we "prefer" more consumption to less, although consuming more may not really increase our well-being. With deep globalization, the markets become bigger and bigger and then this expands scale of production even more. All of these encourage economic growth. Unfortunately, these in turn leave a large impact on the environment.

We can see it by the *IPAT* equation. Environmental scientists summarize the drivers of environmental degradation with a formula called "*IPAT*" (Ehrlich and Holdren, 1972). It says that environmental *Impact* is a product of the size of human *Population*, their *Affluence* or consumption per capita, and *Technology* that determines the environmental impact of each dollar spent. *IPAT* can be extended to *IPANT* by disaggregate the "technology" (*T*) part of the original equation into: *N* the nature, or pattern, of consumption and production, and, *T* the technology-environment relation for each specific type of production or consumption (Daniel, 2010).

To become more sustainable, societies and countries can make efforts to reduce those drivers. There will be substantial improvement in environmental impact if developing countries can reduce *Population*, and if industrial countries to reduce their *Affluent* and *Nature* of consumption pattern. As to *Technology*, the work can be focused on renewable energy, building and site design, product design, and industrial ecology (for sustainable strategies and practices, see Robertson, 2014; Roorda et al., 2012).

The growth model is the mainstream in modern economic thoughts and policy making. It cares about an increase in size or an increase in production. Growth is a quantitative concept. However, pursuing sustainable "growth" is physically impossible because the biosphere is finite. On the contrary, development is qualitative; sustainable development involves an increase in quality without a quantitative growth in consumption or production; it brings about an improvement in well-being. Well-being includes both human quality of life and the health of all other parts of the biosphere. Sustainable development would keep natural capital intact, living off nature's income rather than consuming its capital (Robertson, 2014, Ch.4).

The growth model has many flaws that prevent a sustainable development. It results in inequities; it cannot brings about higher well-being; it does not account for all of real costs; it does not recognizes that natural system have limits; it does not set a value on ecosystem and on ecosystem services; market prices underestimate the real value of goods and services and are kept artificially low through inappropriate subsidies (Robertson, 2014, Ch.4). In short, the growth model sees that the economy operates in a one-way traffic manner, not a cyclical and an integrated manner (Roorda et al., 2012, Ch. 2-Ch. 3).

We also need to recognize the flaws in use of GDP as a measure of "well-being", or "development". GDP (gross domestic product) is the market value of domestically produced final goods and services within a period of time. GDP is just a measure of economic activity. It omits some goods and services that are beneficial to individuals and societies, such as nonmarket activities, like volunteer work, home-services, leisure, moral or virtuous act etc. Besides, it does not differentiate a good or bad, wholesome and unwholesome activity either. For example, if natural or manmade disaster causes damage, then the cost of repairs would count as a contribution in GDP. However, it is indeed a deduction in well-being (for details, see Frey and Stutzer, 2002, Ch.2). This well-established fact is often played down or intentionally ignored by the public, politicians or policy makers. In order to promote genuine well-being and sustainable development, we should not overemphasize GDP in the social decision making. Instead, it's wiser to look at some more indicators to analyze the problems and then we can make a right move.

2.2 Buddhist views of sustainable development

Are Buddhist doctrines consistent with the idea of sustainable development? Absolutely yes. Buddhism has a delicate structure of concepts, methods and practices to help humankind to sustainably develop themselves in order to attain the Buddhahood (Figure 1). To obtain Buddhahood means to attain perfect wisdom, compassion, and blessings, by practicing the Bodhisattva path. Everyone possesses Buddha-nature and then has potentiality to become a buddha. Buddhists first generate a great Bodhi mind and make the four great vows to purify themselves, both mind and behavior, and help others to do so. The aim of Buddha's appearing in this world is to help all of sentient beings liberate themselves from all kinds of sufferings and then obtain genuine happiness. Of course, on the path toward ultimate liberation, the environments and surroundings will be purified simultaneously. Hence, people, society, and the world can be sustainably developed if Buddhadharma is applied and practiced. This is the Buddhist view of sustainable development.

How is the Buddhist doctrine related to the sustainable development? We will illustrate the points from three perspectives, namely, adopting a system method, promoting well-being for all in the harmonious world by purifying three activities, and acting out of loving-kindness and compassion.

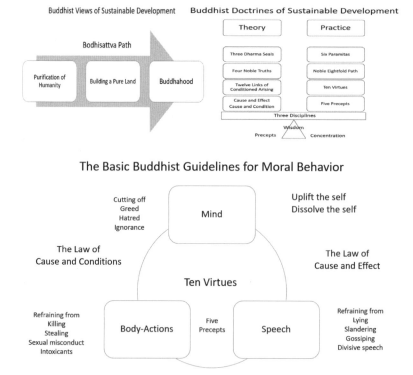

Figure 1: The Buddhist Framework of Sustainable Development

(1) Adopting a system method

Buddha's teachings equally emphasize theory and practice methods (Figure 1). Theoretical teachings give people right views to look at the myriad things in the world. And practical methods allow people to remove wrong doings with regard to mind, action, and speech that lead to sufferings. This is consistent with the core idea of sustainable development which aims at promoting well-being for "all" by applying sustainable practices in a "systematic" manner. While the modern practice focuses more on the "symptoms" of the problems, the Buddhist directly points to the roots. The roots are three poisons, greed or desire, hatred or aversion, and ignorance or delusion. These are deep-rooted defilements of the mind that lead to unwholesome states and activities.

With regard to the theoretical dimension in the Buddhist doctrine, the Four Noble Truths first articulate the truth of the existence of suffering, the truth that the origin of suffering is ignorance, the truth that suffering can be ceased, and the truth that cessation of suffering comes through following the Noble Eightfold Path, which begins with Right View, Right Intention, Right Speech, Right Action, Right Livelihood, Right Effort, Right Mindfulness, and Right Concentration (Master Sheng Yen, 2010, p. 183; for details see Master Sheng Yen 2003, pp. 87-103). We may summarize the cycle of suffering as a sequence of ignorance, unwholesome actions, and sufferings. And this sequence even goes on and on across space and time. Nevertheless, if we can eliminate ignorance bit by bit through practicing the path, our actions will turn wholesome gradually, and then we will suffer less. From another perspective, we can learn more about the origin and elimination of suffering. The Twelve Links of Conditioned Arising straighten out the truth of the cycle of birth and death which lock sentient beings in endless sufferings. It begins with fundamental ignorance, and then action, consciousness, name-and-form, the six sense faculties, contact, sensation, desire, clinging, becoming, birth, and aging-and-dying.

All kinds of suffering come from fundamental ignorance, which is the basic confusion as to how things are and operate. We misbelieve there is a separate, independently existing "self". This belief in self is the source of suffering. Buddhist teachings aim to help sentient beings realize the illusory nature of "self". So, what are the truths about the working of phenomena, both material and mental?

Three Seals of Dharma lay down the principles of the phenomena; all phenomena are impermanent, all dharmas are selfless, nirvana is quiescent. Phenomena are according to the law of causes and conditions and that of causes and effects; the former is regarding phenomena in space, the latter in time. Any phenomena arises through the interplay of myriad causes and conditions and it also perish through causes and conditions. It is both the result and cause of another phenomenon. Things are all interconnected and interdependent in a subtle manner. Hence, any phenomenon is constantly changing without a fixed entity. Its true nature is impermanent and selfless. However, humankinds mistakenly think the opposite, believing that things can exist forever as we hope. It is this wrong view that causes us so much suffering and motivates us to plant even more seeds of suffering. In short, ignorance prompts wrong deeds and then brings about suffering. Suffering in turn hinders us to see the truth and get us trapped in the web of afflictions even deeper and then start endless cycle of three hindrances.

This is how people understand the world through Buddhist doctrines. Obviously, it is consistent with the concept of sustainability, which looks at things in an integrated and cyclical manner, and recognizes that things are ever-changing and interdependent. Specially, the Buddhist doctrine, such as karma (action, deed), points out that all our actions, words, and thoughts have consequence that manifest as retribution in the present, and future lives, from causes laid down in the past lives. While wholesome and virtuous actions, words, and thoughts yield rewards, unwholesome and unvirtuous actions yield negative retribution.

We then recognize that, in order to achieve a desirable result, we should add favorable conditions, or to remove undesirable causes. We can easily see how powerful of any single action can arouse a big multiple effect sequentially. That is, even a small individual ill action can lead to a huge damage to society if everyone does so. On the contrary, a small good deed can collectively bring about a big blessing, and also can easily reverse a vicious cycle. Speaking of sustainable development in economic, social, and environmental dimensions, it follows that human's cooperation is essential for sustainable development and that everyone should participate in the process since our fates are all bound together.

Furthermore, we should also recognize that any human being is just a tiny entity in the whole ecosystem, hence we human beings should not act like the master of our planet, doing whatever we want at cost of other species. The living beings and the environment are inseparable, hence harming other living beings or the environment is just like harming ourselves. Instead, we should be feel grateful for our mother nature, and be a guardian for other living beings and the environment.

(2) Promoting well-being for all and building a harmonious world by purifying three activities

The goal of sustainable developments is meant to build a world in which every living being can flourish. This likens to the idea of building a pure land in Buddhism. Both advocate to promote the well-being of human beings and non-human beings. But there are fundamental differences between the two.

While the modern ideal cares more about the improvement of the physical conditions to make people live better and longer, Buddhism focuses on the quality of mind, spirits and actions, i.e. human characters. Buddhist teachings emphasize enlightenment and accumulate merits by practicing the bodhisattvas path to accomplish Buddhahood, that is to attain perfection of wisdom, compassion, and blessings. Buddhadhamas teach people not only to truly liberate themselves from suffering and then achieve genuine happiness but also to vow to deliver sentient beings. It seems the Buddhist doctrine is more spiritually oriented, or of less materially pursuit. Does it mean that the Buddhist's world cannot have a prosperous society?

From Buddhist sutras, we learn that pure lands are not only materially abundant but also free from all kinds of disasters, mishaps, hardships and suffering. Pure lands are depicted as being abundant, prosperous, peaceful, secure, stable, pure, clear and cool, etc. People in pure land enjoy a stable climate and nice weather, flat and smooth lands formed with jewelry, a beautiful nature, exquisite houses and palaces, jewelry trees, jewelry ponds, heavenly sounds of music, cozy breeze, having something to eat, wear, live…whenever and whatever they wish, virtuous and enlightened companions, Buddha, saint, sage, bodhisattvas, etc…; the only thing people are fond of doing is to devote themselves in practicing buddhadharmas. There are well-known examples of buddha lands in the Buddhist sutras, such as Amitabha Buddha's Western Pure Land of Utmost Bliss, Buddha Medicine's Pure and Illuminous World, The World of Hwa-Zan, and our world in the future when Maitreya Buddha comes to the human realm to achieve buddhahood.

Buddhas' pure lands are ideal places at which human beings dream of being reborn. Obviously pure lands do not come out from nothing. They are built and realized by Buddhas' great vows, their long-term efforts, and devotions of people on the pure lands as well. People on the pure lands are all virtuous people who practice buddhadharma. We should know that pure lands and human's characters are interconnected and interdependent and that they are causes and effects for each other. So the Buddhist doctrine singles out the human's virtues as the most important cause in building a flourishing an ideal world.

Buddhas' lands depicted in the sutras may sound like fairy tales to us, unreal and remote. We may regard them as ideals. Can we build a pure land on earth? That's for sure. Buddhist practitioners build a pure land by practicing Buddhadharma. And how? They purify the mind and behaviors by practicing three disciplines-precepts, concentration, and wisdom- and six paramitas-generosity, morality, patience, diligence, meditation, and wisdom. The foundations of all the Buddhadharma are five precepts-not to kill, not to steal, not to engage in sexual misconduct, not to speak falsehoods, and not to indulge in intoxicants-, and ten virtues (refraining from killing, refraining from stealing, refraining from sexual misconduct, refraining from lying, refraining from slandering, refraining from gossiping, refraining from divisive speech, cutting off greed, cutting off hatred, and cutting off ignorance). The five precepts and ten virtues are the basic guidelines of moral behavior (Figure 1).

In accordance with Buddhadharma, people will strive to do good deeds that would promote the health of body and mind for themselves and others, preventing evil deeds that would harm their own and other's well-being. We may infer that there would neither be much pollution to environment nor conflicts of any kinds to societies. People produce right kinds and right amount of products, consumers wisely choose what and how much to buy. Hence, even with deep globalization, there would be no harm to the environment. The well-being for all would truly be raised.

Simply speaking, Buddhist lifestyles would promote both material and spiritual well-being simultaneously. Because people cultivate virtues and blessings, they enjoy the fruits of good deeds. It is not like our modern thoughts that encourage material pursuits and ignore spiritual development. The modern practice causes so much adverse effects to humans and our ecosystem. Building a pure land should start with purifying our deeds and thoughts. Buddhist sutras give us some clues as to how to build a desirable world (see Chiang, 2018).

(3) Acting out of loving-kindness and compassion

In order to attain the Buddhahood, Buddhists make the Four Great Vows, that is, to help innumerable sentient beings without discriminating between them, to cut off endless vexations, to master limitless approaches to Dharma, and to reach supreme buddhahood. These vows generate the motivation towards enlightenment and buddhahood, which is bodhi-mind. It is the mind of wisdom which represents both the altruistic mind and selfless action. The Ten Great Vows of Bodhisattva Samantabhudra in Avatamsaka Sutra (Hua-yen Jing) says: "Since every Buddha Tathagata has the body of great compassion. The great compassion arises for the sake of sentient beings and gives birth to the Bodhi-mind. Because of this Bodhi-mind, perfect enlightenment is then attained." So the buddhist doctrines promote universal loving-kindness and compassion, encouraging the practitioners to bring happiness to people and eliminate their sufferings.

In today's society, social equity is so much advocated. It concerns about the welfare of the disadvantaged. The society calls for a system to promote the general well-being. A good social institution is designed to reallocate the wealth from the rich to the poor. This mechanism comes out of human's loving-kindness and compassion. People recognize that they are interconnected and interdependent. We all live on nature's resources and other people's help as well. The fact that we devote a little but receive so much also encourages us to repay the kindness received. Besides, men are born as equal. Every life, no matter how wealthy or poor, how fortunate or unfortunate, is precious, having its own mission in this world. If every individual improves himself in this lifetime, he would be transformed to a better life in the future. As a matter of fact, we are all brothers and sisters, parents and children of the same family, not only in this lifetime, but also we were in the previous lives and will still be in the future.

Hence, we all have the privilege and obligation to assist others; it, in turns, would promote our own development. If we keep this belief in mind and put it into practice, we can earn the rights to social assistance and enjoy karmic reward of blessings as well; these privileges come naturally without eagerly pursuit. According to the Buddhist teachings, making great vows to deliver sentient beings is the first of the Four Great Vows for bodhisattvas. This compassionate vow and action not only helps us to get rid of greed and desire, broadening our mind and heart, but also brings peace, joy and fortunes. Besides this loving-kindness and compassion also extend to the future generations because of the seed of blessings.

To sum up, we may say that the aim of Buddhism's sustainable development is to develop dharma body and wisdom-life, and also to construct a pure land for sentient beings to flourishingly develop themselves (Chiang, 2018).

3. An Integrated Framework of Sustainable Development

3.1 Examples of the framework of sustainable develop-ment

The world is faced with challenges in all three dimensions of sustainable development—economic, social and environmental. There has been great efforts made globally to fix the global scale of problems. The grandest project is the 2030 Agenda for Sustainable Development. In 2015, the members of the United Nations declared that the 2030 Agenda is a global plan of action for the next 15 years in areas of critical importance for humanity and the planet (Figure 2 below and Table A1 in the Appendix). "In adopting the 2030 Agenda for Sustainable Development, world leaders resolved to free humanity from poverty, secure a healthy planet for future generations, and build peaceful, inclusive societies as a foundation for ensuring lives of dignity for all. This collective journey has at its heart a promise to leave no one behind. The 2030 Agenda is deliberately ambitious and transformational, with a set of 17 integrated and indivisible sustainable development goals and targets to guide us. Crucially, it is a universal agenda, applying to all countries; even the richest have yet to fully ensure women's rights, conquer inequality or safeguard the environment." (United Nations, 2017, p. 2).

The plan is highly humanistic and compassionate; there must be many people who will benefit from the realization of the Agenda. However, we can see that all the goals focus more on the improvement on the physical environment, but the humankind's spiritual world or ethical dimensions are not touched on the surface. For this issue, we may turn to another approach, Human Development, for further reflection.

Since 1990 the United Nations Development Programme (UNDP) has published a series of global *Human Development Reports* to discuss major development issues, trends and policies. Researchers' caring about human development has shifted peoples' focus from the material concern to well-being. It puts people at the center of the development discourse, changing the lens for assessing development policies and outcomes.

> The first Human Development Report, in 1990, presented human development as a people-centred approach to development. The human development approach shifted the development discourse from pursuing material opulence to enhancing human well-being, from maximizing income to expanding capabilities, from optimizing growth to enlarging freedoms. It focused on the richness of human lives rather than on simply the richness of economies, and doing so changed the lens for viewing development results (UNDP, 2016, p. 2).

The UNDP defines that human development is about enlarging freedoms so that all human beings can pursue choices that they value. It is about expanding their freedoms, enlarging their choices, enhancing their capabilities and improving their opportunities. It is both an outcome and a process.

> "Human development is a process of enlarging people's choices. But human development is also the objective, so it is both a process and an outcome. Human development implies that people must influence the processes that shape their lives. In all this, economic growth is an important means to human development, but not the end. Human development is the development of the people through building human

capabilities, by the people through active participation in the processes that shape their lives and for the people by improving their lives. It is broader than other approaches, such as the human resource approach, the basic needs approach and the human welfare approach. (UNDP, 2016, Box 1, p. 2)

In order to measure the level of human development, the composite Human Development Index (HDI) has been complied and reported regularly. The Basic HDI includes three basic dimensions of human development, namely, life expectancy, education, and income. The four more indexes consider the problems of inequality, that is, the inequalities of income, gender, and non-income factors.

It appears that the HD approach is similar to the sustainable development approach; they are concerned with the material world. The two have common analytical links (UNDP, 2016, p.45): (1) Both are anchored in universalism—the human development approach by emphasizing the enhancement of freedoms for every human being and the 2030 Agenda by concentrating on leaving no one behind. (2) Both share the same fundamental areas of focus— eradicating extreme poverty, ending hunger, reducing inequality, ensuring gender equality and so on. (3) Both have sustainability as the core principle.

These two approaches are aimed at promoting people's wellbeing and focus on the objectives wished to achieve. They are very helpful for countries and organizations to design polices and regulations to guide collective actions. However, with regard to the individual action, these goals seem too big and impossible for a person alone to accomplish. For example, how can a person do to achieve the goal of ending poverty, eliminating hunger, having a healthy body, enjoying a decent life, combating the climate change…etc.? It appears that there needs more mechanisms in the integrated model to direct individual efforts toward these goals. This mechanism may present the motivations and actions that individual can take to move onto the sustainable path in an integrated manner. And the spiritual approach can fill in to enrich the model, making it more practical and effective.

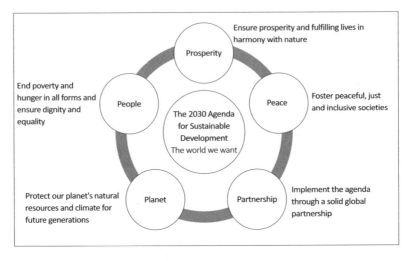

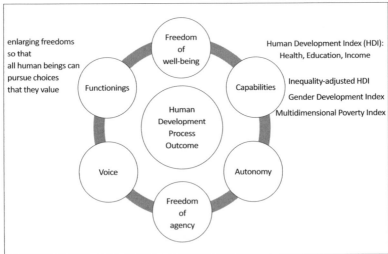

Figure 2: Examples of Framework of Sustainable Development

3.2 A spiritual approach of sustainable development

The founder of the Dharma Drum Mountain (DDM), Master Sheng Yen (2004) proposed a set of ideas and method for people to adjust their views, develop their minds and improve the quality of life. They are called the *Four Kinds of Environmentalism* and the *Fivefold Spiritual Renaissance Campaign* aimed at spiritual enlightenment (Figure 3 below and Table A3, A4 in the appendix). They provide the education that modern people need to live their lives, titled as *"A Proposition for Living in the 21ˢᵗ Century"*. Compared with the general approaches to sustainable development above, the spiritual approach appears consistent with these models in some ways but with more spiritual concerns and being action oriented. Specially, the core idea behind the spiritual approach is that the environment changes with our mind.

The *Four Kinds of Environmentalism* set four pillars supporting sustainable development, namely, (1) the protection of the spiritual environment, (2) the protection of social environment, (3) the protection of living environment, and (4) the protection of the natural environment. Its foundation is the "spiritual environmentalism". These four echo the three dimensions regarding the economy, society, and environment in the general framework for sustainable development but with one more key element-spirits or mind-added. And the *Fivefold Spiritual Renaissance Campaign* is a project for practicing and actualizing the *Four Kinds of Environmentalism*. There are five propositions in the campaign, namely, (1) proposition for uplifting the character of humanity, (2) proposition for calming the mind, (3) proposition for resolving the difficulties of life, (4) proposition for getting along with others, and (5) proposition for increasing blessings. These guidelines are rooted in the Buddhist doctrines and enable individuals to develop themselves sustainably.

Can this Proposition for Living help to resolve the global problems? Poverty, hunger, pollution, climate change...etc.? After all, those guidance are all "spiritual". Unlike the general approaches to sustainable development focusing on the problems themselves,

Master Sheng Yen looked at the roots of the environmental, economic and social problems, directly pointing out the poverty of mind as the cause. He advocated the "spiritual environmentalism" as the solution.

> "Many people emphasize raising their quality of life in material terms, to the neglect of raising the quality of their spiritual life. This is one of the main reasons for environmental pollution."(Master Sheng Yen, 2015, p. 122).

> "An unhealthy mind is a disease. Protecting the spiritual environment treats causes, while protecting the living, natural, and ecological environments treats symptoms. If the mind does not acknowledge the idea of protecting the environment, all other efforts will fail. Only with a healthy and wholesome mind can environmental protection work take root, and become effective, long-lasting, and widespread (Master Sheng Yen, 2015, p. 321).

These are the methods to realize two missions of DDM: Uplift the Character of Humanity, Build a Pure Land on Earth. The two missions are not independent of each other, but being the cause, effect and conditions for each other, and then reinforcing each other. Since not only environment changes with the mind, but also the mind changes with the environment. For ordinary people, these two missions are equally important. Broadly speaking, these methods are not just for DDM, they also highlight the method and direction that any individual, family, community, society, and the whole world can adopt to develop themselves and promote their own wellbeing.

Can it also give one more freedom, choices, security, and peace…etc. to promote human development? It certainly can. We can also see the importance of purifying the mind in promoting material and mental well-being in the following paragraphs.

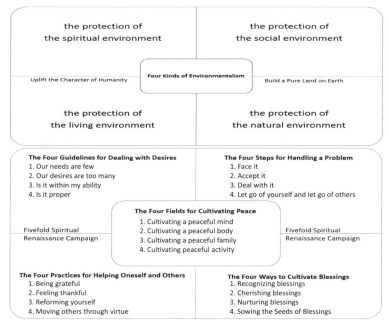

The protection of the spiritual environment | the protection of the social environment

Uplift the Character of Humanity | **Four Kinds of Environmentalism** | Build a Pure Land on Earth

the protection of the living environment | the protection of the natural environment

The Four Guidelines for Dealing with Desires
1. Our needs are few
2. Our desires are too many
3. Is it within my ability
4. Is it proper

The Four Steps for Handling a Problem
1. Face it
2. Accept it
3. Deal with it
4. Let go of yourself and let go of others

The Four Fields for Cultivating Peace
1. Cultivating a peaceful mind
2. Cultivating a peaceful body
3. Cultivating a peaceful family
4. Cultivating peaceful activity

Fivefold Spiritual Renaissance Campaign

Fivefold Spiritual Renaissance Campaign

The Four Practices for Helping Oneself and Others
1. Being grateful
2. Feeling thankful
3. Reforming yourself
4. Moving others through virtue

The Four Ways to Cultivate Blessings
1. Recognizing blessings
2. Cherishing blessings
3. Nurturing blessings
4. Sowing the Seeds of Blessings

Figure 3: A Spiritual Approach of Sustainable Development

"When speaking of the problem of humankind's poverty on earth, everyone will think of the regions that are ravaged by natural disasters and wars. So we should offer assistance to those regions and appeal for peace. But as you may also know, even the United States is not free from the problem of poverty. So I wish to point out a fact, whereas poverty of material things threatens the lives of people, whereas poverty of the spirit and heart deprives people's living environment of security and happiness. Therefore, our organization, Dharma Drum Mountain, is promoting a movement called "spiritual environmentalism", where individuals start by purifying their mind, filling it with gratitude, kindness and compassion for life. In this way, they will devote the fruit of their efforts to others. As long as one continuously works hard to improve one's living conditions, one will be able to overcome material poverty; as long as one feels grateful and compassionate, one will be able to enrich oneself spiritually and mentally.

Enrichment of the spirit is a more precious wealth than material possessions. Chinese Ch'an (Zen) Buddhism is characterized by a simple way of life. Ch'an practitioners can gain freedom and peace of mind because they have little desire for material things in their lives. When one's spirit is calm and stable, one will not be stimulated or tempted by the external material environment, neither will one harm others and damage the natural environment." (Master Sheng Yen, 2008, pp. 8-9)

The spiritual approach takes an all-in-one strategy to solve economic, social and environmental problems. It also guarantees genuine fortunes and happiness. Since it motivates an individual to act in accordance with wisdom and compassion, this approach is effective whenever the action starts. The good action not only benefits the individual himself but also benefit for other people, a whole society, world and environment as well. Particularly, we will feel free and peaceful at any circumstances, favorable or adverse.

For example, how can we get out of poverty? how to become rich? We can start by practicing "Four Ways to Cultivate Blessings". First we need to recognize the blessings we have, and cherish them, not to waste them. We also keep nurturing them by giving and sharing blessings. The equally important thing is to recognize that enjoying blessings is not a blessing and then to sow the seeds of blessings whenever possible. In this way, we will be content with few desires and feel calm all the time. Then we can have a peaceful mind and healthy body. Knowing that we are blessed, we will feel grateful and thankful; this, in turn brings us a good relationship with others. Furthermore, we may wish to repay the kindness received and then will become active to work hard for public benefits. So for us there is no such thing called as unemployment. In addition, if we know that we have more than we deserve, we will cherish resources and respect any kinds of lives; then the ecosystem will flourish and there would not be more pollution, deterioration of environment, species endangering, injustice, inequality, un-satisfaction, conflict, war,....

From above, we can see that one virtuous act stimulates subsequent similar actions and effects, creating a virtuous cycle. If any individual can accumulates merits in accordance with these guidelines, he or she may become wealthy and also feel meaningful and accomplished at all times. If more people can take the same action, the economy, society, and environment will develop in a more sustainable manner that we wish.

It is worth noting that, by practicing these four ways of cultivating blessings, we are simultaneously practicing four other methods in the *Fivefold Spiritual Renaissance Campaign* and realize the *Four Kinds of Environmentalism* at the same time. Practicing any other method in these guidelines brings about the benefits from all other methods. These guidelines and methods are complements to each other, creating multiple beneficial effects.

It is obvious that the spiritual approach to life is sustainable development not only in the human development sense, but in a broader sense. The mind, body, and environment can all be sustainably developed.

3.3 An integrated framework of sustainable development

3.3.1 The features of the integrated model

Scientists try hard to discover the causes and facts about the unsustainability in the material world. Many people and organizations also make great efforts to discover the strategies to live sustainably. Social arrangements and institutions are set up to meet with sustainability... They are all very helpful. Nevertheless, the efforts are not big and effective enough to turn around the ongoing global crisis. Most people feel indifferent or powerless to the problems. Perhaps it is because of lacking right values and ethics.

In 1990, Master Sheng Yen made it clear: "An unhealthy mind is a disease. Protecting the spiritual environment treats causes, while protecting the living, natural, and ecological environments treats symptoms. If the mind does not acknowledge the idea of protecting the environment, all other efforts will fail. Only with a healthy and wholesome mind can environmental protection work take root, and become effective, long-lasting, and widespread (Master Sheng-Yen, 2015, p. 321). In 1993, the *Parliament of the World's Religions* proposed *the Declaration toward a Global Ethic*. It made the similar point. The declaration outlines the principles of a global ethics and called for emphasis on transformation of consciousness and on the issues of values, and ethics. It pointed out "Historical experience demonstrates the following: Earth cannot be changed for the better unless we achieve a transformation in the consciousness of individuals and in public life...." (Figure 4).

We all want to be happy and to avoid suffering; obviously, what we are doing is just the opposite. What went wrong? In *The Book of Joy* (His Holiness the Dalai Lama, Archbishop Desmond Tutu, and Douglas Abrams, 2016), the Dalai Lama also points to worldwide materialistic values and lack of inner values, such as kindness and compassion, as the roots of global problems.

"Now we are in the twenty-first century. We are improving on the innovations of the twentieth century and continuing to improve our material world. While of course there are still a lot of poor people who do not have adequate food, generally the world is highly developed. The problem is that our world and our education remain focused exclusively on external, materialistic values. We are not concerned enough with our inner values. Those who grow up with this kind of education live a materialistic life and eventually the whole society becomes materialistic. But this culture is not sufficient to tackle our human problems. The real problem is here ...and here...Mind and heart. Materialistic values cannot give us peace of mind. So we really need to focus on our inner values, our true humanity. Only this way can we have a peace of mind-and more peace in our world. A lot of the problems we are facing are our own creation, like war and violence. Unlike a natural disaster, these problems are created by humans ourselves. (pp. 29-30)

"Something is lacking. As one of the seven billion human beings, I believe everyone has the responsibility to develop a happier world. We need, ultimately, to have a greater concern for others' well-being. In our words, kindness or compassion, which is lacking now. We must pay more attention to our inner values. We must look inside. (p. 30)

"In order to develop our mind, we must look at a deeper level. Everyone seek happiness, joyfulness, but from outside-from money, from power, from big car, from big house. Most people never pay much attention to the ultimate source of a happy life, which is inside, not outside. Even the source of physical health is inside, not outside (p. 31).

The solution to our problems lies in training our mind and heart. The two great spiritual leaders, the Dalai Lama and Archbishop Tutu, both agree that helping others is the source of greatest lasting happiness. As Archbishop Tutu remarked in the book that: "...that ultimately our greatest joy is when we seek to do good for others." (p. 59) and they invited us to experience joy by cultivating our mind and heart (The Eight Pillars of Joy).

"Every day and each moment, we are able to create and re-create our lives and the very quality of human life on our planet. This is the power we wield.

Lasting happiness cannot be found in pursuit of any goal or achievement. It does not reside in fortune or fame. It resides only in the human mind and heart, and it is here that we hope you will find it." (p. ix)

We now recognize that the global problems arise from human's inappropriate actions and practices, which in turn are motivated by human's wrong concepts and values. So the world reflect the things we think and we do accordingly, like a mirror reflects things with exactness. It appears that in order to effectively live our life in a sustainable manner, it would be better to integrate the material approach and the spiritual approach. While the former indicates what goals and ideals we want to achieve, the latter gives us the practical ways how to realize them.

How can we integrate the material approach and spiritual approach to sustainable development? Figure 5 illustrates the rationale for an integrated model of sustainable development. When the mind is purer, our thoughts will be purer, and so will be our behaviors. It brings about a healthier body, balanced emotions, and better characters. This brings forth a more harmonious and just society. The economy will be more prosperous and flourishing. It forms a virtuous cycle. On the contrary, if our mind is deluded, full of scattered thoughts, vexations, we will not see the truth of things, and we will act in the wrong way and suffer a lot. A vicious cycle is then started.

This model is based on the Buddhist doctrine which puts emphasis on the mind. The mind has the material aspect and spiritual aspect. The material mind refers to the heart and the brain. The spiritual mind includes emotions, reason, thoughts, and concepts. These two together bring about the functions of the mind. "In Buddhism "mind" refers to the afflicted mind as well as to the pure mind. States associated with you, I, they, greed, anger, ignorance, impermanence, suffering, and the like are expressions of afflicted mind. What we call "you," "I," and "they" denote the function of discrimination, and the reactions generated upon coming into contact with people, affairs, and things." (Master Sheng Yen, 2014, p. 116). As Buddhist sutras point out: "All dharmas are created by the mind alone." "All dharmas arise from

Figure 4: Declaration Toward a Global Ethic (Parliament of the World's Religions, 1993)

the thinking of mind" "The mind is like a skillful painter, it draws many kinds of five aggregates." "When the mind arises, all things arise; when the mind perishes, all things arise."

As a matter of fact, the nature of mind is pure. For sentient beings, what we experience as mind is an illusion or deluded mind, scattered mind, full of afflictions. For enlightened sages or saints, they can experience the state of no mind, which is the nature of Buddha mind. As long as people can train the mind and change the behavior by practicing Buddhadharma, people will attain Buddhahood and building a pure land simultaneously.

The resulting integrated model share the same global ethics as the other models; it also will integrate the modern strategies and ancient practices. So it will help the society, economy, and environment to develop sustainably. The model possesses the following features.

(1) The goal is to build a pure land on earth.

It pursues a world without much suffering. While it is important to build an environment, society, and economy that would promote welfare for all by adopting sustainable strategies, it is more important to purify our spiritual world by eliminate all kinds of vexations and afflictions, and all of wrong deeds as well. The latter directs people to move onto the right path, the former manifests all of collective efforts. No matter what kinds of pursuing are, they must ensure to liberate people from suffering.

(2) The global ethics is wisdom and compassion.

The methods we adopt to realize the goal must to be wise and compassionate. The wise have no vexations and afflictions since they know the true nature of things, and the compassionate have no enemies since they would treat others as themselves. So the methods adopted by people like this are not only non-violent, causing no harm, but also be kind, just and beneficial to all. They definitely enable everyone to freely develop themselves as much as possible. If people can practice wisdom and compassion in everything they do, there would be no greed, hatred, ignorant, killing, wars, compression, discrimination, and all kinds of mistreatment, etc... On the contrary, peace, stability, security, friendships, fortunes, prosperity, joy, and happiness... would ensue naturally.

For example, the Buddhist doctrine takes five precepts and ten virtues as the foundations for all virtues, and three disciplines and six paramitas are areas that practitioners need to learn to realize wisdom and compassion (Figure 1) . *The Declaration toward a Global Ethic* declares that every human being must be treated humanely, which is a fundamental demand. It sets out the principles to meet this criteria, that is, (a) commitment to a culture of non-violence and respect for life; (b) commitment to a culture of solidarity and a just economic order; (c) commitment to a culture of tolerance and a life of truthfulness; (d) commitment to a culture of equal rights and partnership between men and women. If everyone takes responsibilities to uphold these duties, then it would ensure the corresponding rights to actualize (Figure 4).

(3) The method is action oriented and aimed at stimulating individual and collective efforts.

It urges the right actions to promote wellbeing for oneself and others. It is easy to say than to do. It is important to recognize the urgency that we should act right away. Since whatever we do now will impact us and others both at this instant and in the future and the effects grow bigger and bigger. If we don't take an appropriate action, we suffer right away and even more in the future. While a small problem can turn into a disaster, a big crisis can easily be reversed and stopped by a small single action if everyone takes appropriate actions. Everyone is responsible for the global ongoing crisis and needs to take more responsibility.

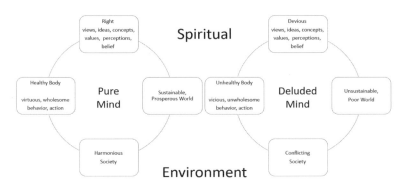

Figure 5: An Integrated Framework of Sustainable Development

(4) The theory and practice adopt a system method, highlighting the principle of inter-being and interdependence.

The model articulates the truth of the world. It reminds us that we live in an interdependent manner, i.e., people, other living beings, things depend on each other. If we live in a good, right way, other livings and things will be affected in a beneficial way. On the contrary, our unwholesome actions will have a significant harmful impact on others and surroundings. The fact that our living is of inter-being prompts us to appreciate others' contributions and assistance at all times and to repay the kindness we receive whenever possible. Because this arises, hence that arises; because this perishes, hence that perishes. So we must realize the law of cause and effect. If we hope for a desirable result, we first need to know the "right" cause. In addition, we also need to realize the law of cause and conditions, adding "right" conditions to make the efforts bear fruits.

It should be noted that these four features are compatible with and enhance each other. If anyone or society adopts any model with these features, people and society could develop in a sustainable manner and enjoy genuine happiness with least effort.

3.3.2 Empirical Practices

How can we put sustainable principles into our daily life in an integrated manner? It is easy. There suggests a few steps.

(1) Make vows to live sustainably.

The goal of our pursuit is to reach a healthy state of body and mind. Making vows would make us more determined to fulfill the vows. Not just to make vows once, but make vows every day. We do it not only for our own benefit but also for others' benefits.

(2) Adopt a simple way of life and be content.

As a Buddhist sutra says "Having too much desire causes us suffering. Life-death and tiredness result from greed and desire. Be content with less desire will bring about a healthy body and mind and being at ease." (Sutra of Eight Great Enlightening Principles for People). After all, what we need is few, what we want is bottomless. Pursuing fortune, fame, position, status, … puts ourselves in an unsatisfied and endless state of poverty.

(3) Be active in public affairs for others' benefits.

Generously giving our wealth, our belongings, our knowledge, skills, intelligence… not only would help others in need but also can cure the mind of greed for ourselves.

(4) Uplift characters by practicing virtuous deeds.

This will help us to eliminate three poisons, greed, anger, and ignorance, which are the roots of all kinds of attachments and afflictions. It, in turn, transforms our characters to be wiser and more compassionate. We will have a more harmonious life and social relationships.

(5) Be a vegan or a vegetarian.

We would not eat meat by killing lives. Instead we will save other lives and protect other species. As a result, our body will turn healthier and our life span would also be lengthened. Because of loving-kindness and compassion, there would be no conflicts, killings and wars in the world. At the same time, there is no need to raise more animals by cutting trees in order to expand farmland to raise crops to feed them. More resources will then be saved and the greenhouse emission will be greatly reduced. The climate change can be reversed in time.

(6) Be mindful whenever possible and keep track of what we do and what we think.

We will know more about ourselves by being aware of our shortcomings and then can effectively improve ourselves. We will work hard and be responsible in what we do.

(7) Integrate modern knowledge and ancient value systems to turn human's wisdom in a most beneficial way.

We now enjoy a remarkable technological civilization, but at the same time, we are facing so many threats from these technological advances. It may seem that humans are smarter than before. However, the fact is that human is not wiser though. So the kinds of suffering are increasing more and more. It appears that we need to relearn the ancient values and ethics which have evolved for a long time and been used by many people across time and space.

(8) Practice meditation and cultivate peace of mind.

The goal of life is to prevent suffering and obtain happiness. The most effective way to enjoy enduring happiness is to live wisely and compassionately. Although Buddhist sutras point it out that the nature of our mind is of compassion and of wisdom, ordinary people's minds are clouded by ignorance, anger, and greed that constantly keep us away from being happy and cause us suffer a lot. By practicing meditation to train our mind and then to turn the vexed one into calmer one, we can know ourselves better and then be able to improve ourselves, helping us to uplift our characters. When the self becomes less attached and self-regarding, one can experience peace of mind and enjoy more lasting happiness. This in turn brings more joy to others and the surroundings. Hence practicing meditation and keeping our mind calm in each moment would effectively transform ourselves to be wiser and more compassionate.

These steps would promise a sustainable development for everyone, and of course the society on a whole would also be on a sustainable development path.

4. Conclusion

This paper proposes an integrated framework for sustainable development. The model tries to link the general framework and the spiritual model together. The rationale behind the model reflects the fact that the mind changes with the environment and the environment changes with the mind. On the one hand, the general models are more of material pursuit, focusing on the arrangements and institutions in social, economic, and environmental dimension and collective efforts. Since they set up visions and goals, they adopt a kind of top-down approach to analyze the problems and take actions to solve. On the other hand, the spiritual models emphasize the roots of problems which come from the mind and actions. So it is a kind of bottom-up approach, focusing on right values, ethics and quality of action. In order to effectively solve for global wide problems, we need both features. In the paper, I argue that the integrated model has these very desirable features. The model integrates the theoretical and practical aspects, combing material and spiritual aspects together. The message from the model is: by purifying human's characters, we can surely build a prosperous and peaceful world in a sustainable manner.

Reference

Chiang, Ching-yi (2018), 'Sustainable Development and Building a Pure Land: A Global Ethic Framework,' *Studies of Master Sheng Yen*, 10, 369-422, Taipei: Dharma Drum Publications.

Chiang, Ching-yi (2019), 'Things We Need to Know for Building a Happy Economy: Subjective Well-being and Reflections,' *Studies of Master Sheng Yen*, 12, 235-324, Taipei: Dharma Drum Publications.

Dalai Lama, Desmond Tutu, and Douglas Abrams (2016), *The Book of Joy: Lasting Happiness in a Changing World*, New York: Avery.

Daly, Herman and Joshua Farley (2003), *Ecological Economics: Principles and Applications*, Washington, DC: Island Press.

Daniels, Peter L. (2010), 'Climate Change, Economics and Buddhism — Part I: An Integrated Environmental Analysis Framework,' *Ecological Economics,* 69, 952-961.

Edwards, Andrés R. (2005), *The Sustainability Revolution: Portrait of a Paradigm Shift*, Gabriola Island, BC: New Society Publishers.

Ehrlich, Paul R., and John P. Holdren (1972), 'Critique: One Dimensional Environmental Policy', *Bulletin of the Atomic Scientists*, 28 (3), 16-27.

Frey, Bruno S., and Alois Stutzer (2002), *Happiness and Economics: How the Economy and Institutions Affect Human Well-being*, Princeton and Oxford: Princeton University Press.

Master Sheng Yen (2003), *There is No Suffering: A Commentary on the Heart Sutra*, New York: Dharma Drum Publications.

Master Sheng Yen (2004), *A Proposition for Living in the 21st Century*, Taipei: Dharma Drum Mountain Foundation.

Master Sheng Yen (2008), *Establishing Global Ethics*, New York: Dharma Drum Mountain Buddhist Association.

Master Sheng Yen (2010), *Things Pertaining to Bodhi - The Thirty-Seven Aids to Enlightenment*, Boston: Shambhala Publications, Inc.

Master Sheng Yen (2014), *Chan and Enlightenment*, Taipei: Dharma Drum Publishing Corporation.

Master Sheng Yen (2015), *The World of Chan*, Taipei: Dharma Drum Publishing Corporation.

Meadows, Donella H., Dennis L. Meadows, and Jorgen Randers, William W. Behrens III (1972), *The Limits to Growth*, New York: University Books.

Meadows, Donella H., Dennis L. Meadows, and Jorgen Randers (1992), *Beyond the Limits*, Post Mills, VT: Chelsea Green Publishing Company.

Meadows, Donella H., Jorgen Randers, and Dennis L. Meadows (2006), *Limits to Growth: The 30-Year Update*, London: Earthscan.

Robertson, Margaret (2014), *Sustainability: Principles and Practice*, Oxon: Routledge.

Roorda, Niko, Peter Blaze Corcoran, and Joseph P. Weakland (2012), *Fundamentals of Sustainable Development (Eds.)*, New York: Routledge.

UNDP (the United Nations Development Programme) (2016), *Human Development Report 2016,* New York: The United Nations Development Programme.

United Nations (2015), 'Transforming Our World: the 2030 Agenda for Sustainable Development,' the seventieth session for action during the United Nations summit for the adoption of the post-2015 development agenda to be held from 25 to 27 September 2015, the General Assembly, United Nations, 2015.

United Nations (2017), *The Sustainable Development Goals Report 2017,* New Yok: United Nations.

United Nations (2018), *The Sustainable Development Goals Report 2018,* New Yok: United Nations.

Wackernagel, Mathis, Niels B. Schulz, Diana Deumling, Alejandro Callejas Linares, Martin Jenkins, Valerie Kapos, Chad Monfreda, Jonathan Loh, Norman Myers, Richard Norgaard, and Jørgen Randers (2002), 'Tracking the Ecological Overshoot of the Human Economy,' *Proceedings of the Academy of Science*, 99, no. 14: 9266-9271, Washington, DC, 2002. Also available at www.pnas.org/cgi/doi/10.1073/pnas.142033699.

World Commission on Environment and Development (WECD) (1987),

Our Common Future (The Brundtland Report), Oxford: Oxford University Press.

Yongey Mingyur Ringpoche (2013), *The Joy of Living: Unlocking the Secret and Science of Happiness*, Taipei: Acorn International Publishing Ltd.

Appendix

Table A1: The 2030 Agenda

17 Goals	
Goal 1 No poverty	Goal 10 Reduced inequalities
Goal 2 Zero hunger	Goal 11 Sustainable cities and communities
Goal 3 Good health and well-being	Goal 12 Responsible consumption and production
Goal 4 Quality education	Goal 13 Climate action
Goal 5 Gender equality	Goal 14 Life below water
Goal 6 Clean water and sanitation	Goal 15 Life on land
Goal 7 Affordable and clean energy	Goal 16 Peace, justice and strong institutions
Goal 8 Decent work and economic growth	Goal 17 Partnerships for the Goals
Goal 9 Industry, innovation and infrastructure	

Source: 1. The United Nations (2018).

Table A2: Human Development

Human development[2]		
Key Concept	Aspects	Rationale
Human development is about enlarging freedoms so that all human beings can pursue choices that they value.	* Human development is about acquiring more capabilities and enjoying more opportunities to use those capabilities. * With more capabilities and opportunities, people have more choices, and expanding choices is at the core of the human development approach	* Human development is also a process. * Anchored in human rights, it is linked to human security
Freedoms	having two fundamental aspects	HD's ultimate objective is to enlarge human freedoms.
*Freedom of well-being	*functionings	the various things a person may value being and doing— such as being happy, adequately nourished and in good health, as well as having self-respect and taking part in the life of the community
	*capabilities	Capabilities are the various sets of functionings (beings and doings) that a person can achieve.
*Freedom of agency	*voice *autonomy	Agency is related to what a person is free to do and achieve in pursuit of whatever goals or values he or she regards as important.

Source: UNDP (2016). Excerpt by the author.

Table A3: Four Kinds of Environmentalism

Propositions / Movements	Focus / Practice	Importance / Rationale
Four Kinds of Environmentalism	a plan of action	living Buddhadharma
1. the protection of the spiritual environment	mind	the essence of the Buddhadharma
2. the protection of the social environment	etiquette: * following the vinaya * maintaining deportment * keeping precepts	the basic foundation of Buddhism
3. the protection of the living environment	making Buddhism relevant to daily life	
4. the protection of the natural environment	* Direct and circumstantial retribution form one's place of practice * Every person uses her direct retribution to practice within her circumstantial retribution	A person's body and mind are direct karmic retribution and the environment she lives in is circumstantial retribution

Source: Master Sheng Yen (2004). Excerpt by the author.

Table A4: Fivefold Spiritual Renaissance Campaign

Fivefold Spiritual Renaissance Campaign	Development of spirit	A project for practicing the Four Kinds of Environmentalism
1. Four Fields for Cultivating Peace	Mind, Body, Family, And Activity	A proposition for uplifting the character of humanity
* Cultivating a peaceful mind	Having few desires	
* Cultivating a peaceful body	Working and being thrifty	
* Cultivating a peaceful family	Loving and respecting	
* Cultivating peaceful activity	Being honest and upright	
2. The Four Guidelines for Dealing with Desires	Need, Wants, Ability, And Propriety	A proposition for calming the mind
* Our needs are few.	Needs	People cannot acquire what they want. As a result people feel restless and uneasy and social problems crop up endless.
* Our desires are too many.	Wants	
* Is it within my ability?	Ability	
* Is it proper?	Propriety	
3. The Four Steps for Handling a Problem	Face it, Accept it, Deal with it, and Let it Go	A proposition for resolving the difficulties of life
* Face it	Being aware that a material body comes karmic retribution and with that comes obstacles	Karmic retribution and obstacles don't necessarily have to lead to affliction.
* Accept it	Don't avoid.	Karma must manifest in accordance with conditions.
* Deal with it	Dealing with problems involving emotion, it is to advisable to use reason; dealing with problems regarding family, ethics.	Continue to work diligently to bring condition to fruition.
* Let go of yourself and let go of others	Giving rise to a mind of sympathy and respecting towards all people	Clinging to yourself betrays a lack of wisdom; clinging to others a lack of compassion.

Source: Master Sheng Yen (2004). Excerpt by the author.

Table A4 (continued): The Protection of Spiritual Environmentalism

Propositions / Movements	Focus / Practice	Importance / Rationale
4. Four Practices for Helping Oneself and Others	Feeling Thankful, Reforming Yourself, Moving Others Through Virtue	A proposition for getting along with others
* Being grateful	Contributing and repaying kindness without seeking anything in return	
* Feeling thankful	Good and ill fortune are both our benefactors	
* Reforming yourself	Knowing shame, repenting often, and improving oneself through compassion and wisdom	
* Moving others through virtue	Reforming yourself, then using compassion and wisdom to move others	
5. The Four Ways to Cultivate Blessings	Recognizing Blessings Cherishing Blessings Nurturing Blessings Sowing The Seeds Of Blessings	A proposition for increasing blessings The doctrines and practices of Buddhism aim to cultivated blessings and wisdom.
* Recognizing blessings	Knowing contentment and being happy, and being at peace with want and delighted in the way	If you can recognize our blessings, we will know contentment, and if we know contentment we will always be happy.
* Cherishing blessings	Treasuring what we have with gratitude and hoping to repay the kindness we've received	
* Nurturing blessings	Living the good life is not a blessing, nurturing blessings is a blessing	
* Sowing the Seeds of Blessings-	Through one's own growth, one can broadly sow the seeds of blessings so that all maybe blessed	

Source: Master Sheng Yen (2004)

佛法與永續發展
——整合的分析架構

江靜儀

銘傳大學經濟與金融學系助理教授

▌摘要

　　永續發展是解決全球問題的一種重要觀念與方法。有許多永續發展的架構非常有用，能幫助我們了解世界和付諸行動。然而，這些架構中遺漏了一個重要的元素。若我們想要有效地解決社會、經濟、與環境問題，首先需要有健康的心靈。因此，我認為佛法教導的心法應該加入任何的永續發展模型中。若能如此，我們不僅能更了解問題的根源，而且也能有效地解決全球性的問題，並能享有更高的福祉，以及真正的快樂。本篇研究探討符合佛法的永續發展路徑。首先介紹現代永續發展的原理，並指出目前經濟體系中內具的破壞性與不永續性。文中申論佛法的原則本質上是永續的概念。本文也提出一個整合型的永續發展分析架構，同時結合物質與精神面向的要素。此模型具有很好的特性可以讓我們由內、由外同時處理人類的問題，使所有人類和其他物種即刻和未來都能達成永續性與更高的福祉。

關鍵字：永續發展、永續性、發展、佛法、聖嚴法師

正念影響情緒平衡之研究

朱金池

中央警察大學行政警察學系教授兼警政管理學院院長

▌摘要

　　傳統佛教的正念修行（mindfulness）是佛法八正道之一，意指繫念於聖道的實踐，心不旁騖，意不散亂。其修行的目的在收攝身心，以期達到解脫煩惱的開悟境界。其修行的方法是透過發菩提願心，以及修習次第禪觀與默照禪觀，使心念安定，甚至達到放捨諸相，休息萬事的境地。自一九七九年以來，西方借用佛法有關正念的禪修觀念與方法，積極開發以正念減壓及療癒心理疾病的課程（如正念減壓及正念認知療法等），強調專注在當下且不帶評價的覺察，對減少身心壓力與病痛，以及治療心理疾病上有明顯的幫助，因而普遍流傳於西方的主流社會。本文首先探討傳統佛法的正念修行與西方醫學、心理學的正念覺察練習二者在意涵上之區別，次再分析二者對情緒平衡的影響情形，最後在結語中，從跨學科的觀點對正念之研究，提出三點看法。

關鍵字： 正念修行、正念覺察、情緒平衡、正念減壓、正念認知療法

一、前言

原始佛教的根本思想之一是由佛陀在菩提樹下，親證實悟的四聖諦：苦、集、滅、道等四諦。其中道諦是指由修行而證悟寂滅（涅槃）之道的方法，也就是斷「集」、離「苦」、入「滅」的修行法門。道諦主要有八大項目，稱為八正道，包括正見、正思惟、正語、正業、正命、正精進、正念及正定等項目。其中「正念」的意思，聖嚴法師認為是：「繫念於聖道的實踐，心不旁騖，意不散亂」（釋聖嚴，2013：79）。

正念（mindfulness）是佛教靜觀修行的核心，並漸漸應用到各個領域中。過去兩千六百年來，正念的培育盛行於亞洲許多國家的寺院和俗世中。一九六〇與一九七〇年代，這類修行方法普及到世界各地。由於正念靜觀的精髓是普世的，因此正念愈來愈快速地進入了西方的主流社會（胡君梅，黃小萍譯，2013）。而且，正念的培育正廣泛應用在醫學、神經科學、心理學、教育及企業等領域。特別是在一九七九年，分子生物學家 Jon Kabat-Zinn 博士於美國麻州大學醫學中心建立了「正念減壓課程」（Mindfulness-Based Stress Reduction Program, MBSR）。從此之後，興起了大量的研究，探討正念如何有效處理壓力、沮喪、藥物濫用、痛苦，以及疾病等之問題（Stahl & Goldstein, 2010）。

Jon Kabat-Zinn 在其所著《正念療癒力：八週找回平靜、自信與智慧的自己》一書致中文版讀者的序中，提及他探討正念及其潛在的強大力量，是淵源於中華文化中道家

「無為」及禪宗的思想。而且，正念進入美國主要是經由禪宗。在他的觀念裡，禪宗思想是人類歷史中最優異的智慧體系之一。禪宗與中國文化和道教的相遇，為這世界激盪出既獨特又深刻的方法，超越所有的二元論，通往智慧與慈悲（胡君梅，黃小萍譯，2013：10）。

　　Jon Kabat-Zinn 認為：覺察，是關乎我們如何使用自己的心思、如何能接納事情的真實樣貌、能接納到何種程度。覺察不是消極順從，而是帶著智慧、慈悲和幽默與周圍的世界互動。他又提到：在臺灣，聖嚴法師的教導和著作清晰且充分地體現覺察，這些教導和文字深植於禪宗與佛教語彙。然而，正念減壓課程所採用的語彙和方法，獨立於各個宗教、傳統和信念體系，因此是更普世通用的。雖然，本質上，它們其實都是一樣的（胡君梅，黃小萍譯，2013：10）。所以，Mulligan（2017: 19）作證地說到：Jon Kabat-Zinn 博士巧妙地用現代非宗教的語言，將佛法禪修的方法，應用在他所創建的正念減壓課程中，已是公開的祕密。因此，這項正念減壓課程可以讓成千上萬的西方人受益。

　　本文取材涵括傳統佛法的觀念、方法，以及西方心理學、醫學上有關正念在減壓，與在情緒平衡上的應用文獻等。本文之內容，主要在探討正念在傳統佛教及西方心理學、醫學上的兩種不同意涵，並分別說明各自的運作機制，及其對情緒平衡的影響。最後，提出三點結語：1. 在理論比較方面，傳統佛法的正念修行與西方醫學、心理學的正念覺察練習，在目的、觀念、方法，以及對情緒平衡的效果上均有所不同；2. 在推廣策略方面，傳統佛法的正念修行法門可

朝生活化及可操作化的方向推廣；3. 在跨域研究方面，可結合佛教與醫學、心理學等之正念研究，建立一套兼具有深厚理論與實踐方法的修行法門或練習課程。

二、「正念」的兩種不同意涵

由於正念對人們身、心帶來的好處，已漸漸成為東西方社會所重視的價值。而且，正念的意涵，可從佛教、醫學及心理學等多重觀點來理解。然各個觀點對正念的觀念與方法之詮釋，有很大的差異。佛教所談的「正念」，不僅重視聖道的修行，亦重視心念的覺察；而醫學與心理學上所稱的「正念」，則較偏重在心念的覺察，較少觸及聖道的修行。茲分述如下：

（一）佛教的「正念修行」之意涵

正念的梵文是 sati，是基本佛法「八正道」（aryastangika-marga）中的一個條目，是指如實憶念諸法之性相，令不忘失之意。若以四念處為例，即是憶念觀照「身、受、心、法」的自相及共相，以對治淨、樂、常、我的四種顛倒；若以六念法門為例，一心憶念「念佛、念法、念僧、念戒、念天、念施」，便是正念；又若以淨土法門的念「南無阿彌陀佛」的六字洪名為例，念佛念至臨命終時，能夠心不顛倒，意不錯亂，便名之謂不失正念。因此，正念是與無漏慧相應的，故又名為「諦意」。❶從而，聖嚴法師（2013：79）對正念下的定義是：「繫念於聖道的實踐，心不旁騖，意不散亂。」在佛經中有多處提到正念如下：

　　《佛說大乘菩薩藏正法經》卷三十七，〈勝慧波羅蜜多品 11〉：「云何正念？謂於是念安住正道，離諸諂曲輪迴過失，乃至見涅槃道於如是念亦當遠離，而於聖道無有迷亂。是名正念。」❷

　　《大方等大集經》卷三十：「云何正念？若念不失不動於法，正直不曲，見生死過進向涅槃，繫心不忘不失正道，是名正念。」❸

　　《佛說法乘義決定經》卷二：「云何正念？謂憶過去所修善法，念念攝持，而無錯謬。是名正念。」❹

　　由此可見，佛教所稱的正念，是著重在修行的層次上。又正念修行如何才能安住於正道？或可修習「不忘念」的工夫。印順導師（2007：318）有偈云：「正念曾習緣，令心不餘散，明記不忘念，安住而明顯。」意指：在修止時，使心在同一境相上安定下來。使心繫住一境的，是正念的力量。使心念繫住什麼境呢？印順導師講的是「曾習緣」，指曾經習慣了的境相。例如，修習念佛的人，先要審視觀察佛

---

❶ 釋聖嚴，〈八正道講記──何謂八正道？〉，《七葉佛教書舍》，2016年 7 月 1 日，網址：http://www.book853.com/show.aspx?id=160&cid=91。檢索日期：2020/5/25。
❷ CBETA, T11, no. 316, p. 878, a7-9。
❸ CBETA, T13, no. 397, p. 210, a14-16。
❹ CBETA, T17, no. 763, p. 657, b25-26。

相，修習時可用憶念佛相的方法，使佛相在心上顯現起來。如此就能令心不向餘處馳散，心就漸漸安定了。而且，明白地記憶所緣之境相，不忘記正念，才能使正念安住又明顯。因此，「不忘念」的工夫，就是要念念繫於修習的方法和方向，沒有任何雜念妄想來打斷或干擾，也就是「制心一處」，心不再游離而失去正念（釋聖嚴，2010：118）。誠如《佛遺教經》所云：「汝等比丘，求善知識，求善護助，而不忘念，若不忘念者，諸煩惱賊則不能入。是故汝等，常當攝念在心。若失念者，則失諸功德；若念力堅強，雖入五欲賊中，不為所害，譬如著鎧入陣，則無所畏。是名不忘念。」

聖嚴法師進一步說❺：「妄念與正念有關係，從正念能夠看出妄念來。如果你專注於現在做的這項工作，就叫做正念。比如說，我們正在吃飯的時候，你想到寫文章，那寫文章這個念頭就是妄念；吃飯的時候我知道吃飯，這是正念。」《修習止觀坐禪法要》提及：「起信論云：若心馳散，即當攝來住於正念。是正念者，當知唯心，無外境界。即復此心，亦無自相，念念不可得。」寶靜法師（2003：131）的詮釋是：「正念者，無念也，無念之念，名為正念，因此正念能破除一切妄念。」亦即正念的實踐，在心不攀緣外境，因為外境乃唯心所現，是無目性的。

---

❺ 釋聖嚴，〈如何去除煩惱：妄念與正念〉，《大法鼓》0729 集。

（二）西方醫學、心理學的「正念覺察」之意涵

　　Jon Kabat-Zinn 博士於一九七九年正式將根源於佛教的正念，引入西方醫學界。Kabat-Zinn（2011）巧妙地想將佛教的「業力」和「苦」的概念，與臨床所談到的「壓力」進行聯結，因此，他設計出一套正念減壓的八週訓練課程（徐名敬，2019）。Kabat-Zinn 認為：「正念是一種特殊的專注方式，連同以此專注方式而帶出的覺察，即以一種探索及認識自我的精神態度，觀察深層的自我（胡君梅，黃小萍譯，2013：032）」。在 Kabat-Zinn 設計的正念減壓課程中，強調有七個態度是正念練習的主要支柱，包括：非評價（non-judging）、耐心（patience）、初心（beginner's mind）、信任（trust）、非用力追求（non-striving）、接納（acceptance），以及放下（letting go）等。在正念減壓的方法上，強調正念呼吸有助於讓自己的身體與心裡平靜下來，以較平靜的心與敏銳的眼光，覺察自己的想法與感受，面對事情可以看得更清晰，也更有洞見（胡君梅，黃小萍譯，2013：069，083）。因此，西方對正念的定義是：「時時刻刻不帶評價的覺察❻（Stahl & Goldstein, 2010: 15；胡君梅，黃小萍譯，2013：013）。」此西方簡化版的正念，

---

❻ Stahl & Goldstein (2010: 15) 對正念的定義原文為："Mindfulness is about being fully aware of whatever is happening in the present moment, without filters or the lens of judgment. 而 Mulligan (2017: 79) 對正念的定義是："Wise Mindfulness: whole body-and-mind awareness." 乃指：對整體身與心的覺察。

涵括了兩個要素，一是對當下（此時此刻）的體驗的覺察，另一是對當下的體驗抱持著開放與接納的態度。

此外，Shapiro 等人（2006）從心理學的觀點，將正念分解成三個要素，包括意圖（intention）、專注（attention）與態度（attitude），而且此三個要素息息相關，無法分開，是同時在剎那間的念頭中運作著。❼亦即西方的正念在運作上，必須具有意圖、專注當下念頭或感受的覺察，以及對所浮現的念頭或感受採取不評價的態度。

因此，西方所稱「正念」中的「正」具有兩個意涵，一是表示現在進行式，正念總是在當下，也就是如何讓念頭停留在每一個當下的具體方法；「正」的另一意涵，是表示不會東倒西歪，亦即正念就是如何讓念頭時時刻刻維持清明持穩的方法（胡君梅，黃小萍譯，2013）。

綜上所述，傳統佛教的「正念修行」與現代西方醫學、心理學上的「正念覺察」之意涵有所不同。佛教的正念修行是繫念於聖道的實踐，強調如實憶念諸法之性相，而使心不旁騖，意不散亂；而西方的正念覺察是強調透過當下的覺察與不評價的態度，以減輕身心壓力及療癒疾病為目的。

三、西方醫學、心理學的「正念覺察」對情緒平衡之影響

本節先介紹情緒與情緒平衡的意涵，次再說明西方醫學、心理學的正念運作機制，如何對情緒平衡產生影響，最

---

❼ Shapiro 等人（2006）稱此正念的模式為「IAA 模式」。

後再說明此類正念的測量及相關的研究。

（一）情緒與情緒平衡的意涵

　　情緒（Emotions）是指：「當人們察覺某些攸關自身重要福祉的事情發生時，會依個人過去的發展經驗，自動地對這些事情給予評價的一種過程，並因而引發一套生理上的變化及情緒上的行為，以應付該情境（Ekman, 2003: 13; Cullen & Pons, 2015: 21）。」因此，情緒反應演變成人們生存的機制。這種對情境「自動評價」的過程，會使人們的情緒反應變為標準化。例如，當人們害怕時，會自動產生逃跑或嚇住的情緒反應；當人們生氣時，會自動去掃除障礙等。由於情緒的反應常是自動產生的，所以常未經大腦的同意和覺察。人們的情緒反應有些是具有共同性的，例如，當人們看到迎面撞來的車子時，幾乎每個人都會感到害怕；但並不是所有人在高處都有懼高症，也不是所有人看到蜘蛛都會感到害怕（Cullen & Pons, 2015）。

　　情緒反應具有正面與負面的功能。例如，人們看到迎面撞來的車子時，因害怕而自動產生轉向的生理反應，是具有正面的功能；但是，如果人們因擔心可怕的事情會發生，而一直不敢離開家裡的情緒反應，則具有負功能。事實上，情緒對有知覺的生物而言，是很重要的一種生理作用。人們需要靠情緒的作用，去覺知外在的環境，去設定行為的優先次序，以及集中能量往有意義的目標前進等（Cullen & Pons, 2015）。

　　Gilbert（2009）認為：人們有三個主要的情緒管理系統

（emotion-regulation systems），包括 1. 威脅和保護的情緒管理系統（the threat system），2. 欲求、尋找資源及刺激的情緒管理系統（the drive system），以及 3. 滿足、撫慰及安全的情緒管理系統（the soothing or calming system）等，茲簡要說明如下（Cullen & Pons, 2015: 23）：

1. 威脅和保護的情緒管理系統：負責覺知外在環境的風險，且當面對攸關生存的事件發生時，會有爆炸性的應急反應。例如生氣、焦慮、厭惡的情緒反應。

2. 欲求、尋找資源及刺激的情緒管理系統：負責追求外在環境的資源，包括食物、性欲、結盟等，以獲得物質上或非物質上的滿足，例如生理上或尊榮感的滿足。

3. 撫慰及平和的情緒管理系統：此系統攸關知足常樂、放鬆及社會安全的感覺，不僅希望遠離威脅，而且希望獲得內心的平靜與快樂。接受過有關正念、靜坐或同理心等練習的人，比較能增強此撫慰及平和的情緒管理，而降低前述威脅和保護，以及欲求、尋找資源及刺激等的情緒管理系統的作用。

人類行為觀察者曾經一再指出，有一組有害的人類核心傾向會阻礙快樂。這些心智狀態不僅會讓我們在靜心時分心，也是我們生活中的絆腳石。它們是最令人痛苦的五種情緒，包括貪婪、執著、乖戾、怠惰、焦躁和猜疑等（李芸玫譯，2015：164）。又根據理性情緒心理學的研究指出：情緒是源自當事人對真實事件所做的內言推論和評價，情緒的產生大部分是基於人對已發生事件的解釋，以及對這些解釋所抱持的信念。而且，負面的情緒可分為建設性的

（constructive）／健康的和非建設性的（unconstructive）／
不健康的負面情緒等兩種。例如，不健康的負面情緒包括：
焦慮、沮喪、罪惡感、羞恥、氣憤、受傷、悲觀的、猜疑的
嫉妒和不健康的羨妒等；健康的負面情緒則包括：擔心、傷
感、遺憾、後悔、失望、關心人際的關係和健康的欣羨等
（武自珍譯，1997）。

此外，從情意神經科學（affective neuroscience）的研
究觀點而言，情緒型態是指我們對生命經驗的一致性反應，
受到大腦某些特定神經迴路的影響，可以用實驗室客觀的
方式測量到。情緒型態有六個向度如下（洪蘭譯，2013：
20-21）：

1. 回彈力：你多快或多慢能從困境中回復過來。

2. 展望：你能保持正向的情緒多久。

3. 社會直覺：你能從身邊的人身上得到多少社交的訊
號，知道別人在想什麼。

4. 自我意識：你多會感覺到自己身體對情緒的反應。

5. 情感敏感度：你有多能調節自己的情緒反應，使你對
所處的情境做出恰當的回應。

6. 注意力：你的聚焦點有多清晰。

綜合上述，情緒是人們對外在事件的生理或心理上的反
應，其樣態包括正面的、健康的或建設性的，以及負面的、
不健康的或非建設性的等兩種截然不同的情形。而且，人們
對自己的情緒之覺察與調節，因人而異。因此，當人們面對

外在事件時，如何才能產生正面而健康的情緒，以及當產生
負面而不健康的情緒時，應如何敏銳地去覺察和面對它、處
理它，乃是情緒平衡的重要課題。

（二）西方醫學、心理學的正念覺察之運作機制與情緒的平衡

首先，在西方醫學的研究領域中，過去幾十年來的最
重要發展之一是：「我們不把健康視為各自獨立的身體狀況
或心理狀態，身心其實是完全交互關聯的。」醫學正在發展
的新模式認為，生活型態、思惟慣性、感覺、習慣、人際關
係、環境因素等，都會對個人的健康狀態產生交互影響，醫
學界稱這種轉變為典範轉移。以情緒的平衡為例，當負面情
緒升起時，若能以正念的覺察，真正地體驗與了解它，就更
能看清痛苦的本質，協助我們縮短混亂與受傷的感覺，撫平
動盪的情緒。因為這些心理的苦可能來自於我們自己的錯誤
認知、膨脹誇大，或一味渴望事情依照我們的想法進行。其
實真正讓我們成為受害的是自己的慣性反應，而非事件本身
（胡君梅，黃小萍譯，2013：190，373-374）。

西方醫學界應用佛法有關正念禪修的方法，所開發的正
念減壓課程，特別強調要活在當下（live in the moment）。❽
亦即於當下，對於心中浮現的各種想法，你不需要拒絕、排

---

❽ Jon Kabat-Zinn 博士有次和某位記者談話時，記者說：「喔，你指的是
為當下而活（live for the moment）。」他立即反駁說：「不，不是這樣
的。為當下而活有一種享樂主義的氛圍，我指的是活在當下（live in the
moment）（胡君梅，黃小萍譯，2013：056）。」

斥、緊抓、壓抑或控制它們，只需要集中注意力，將注意力投入於觀察呼吸與內在的覺察。該課程提及：生命中沒有任何一分一秒是一模一樣的，每一秒都是獨特的，蘊涵了各種可能。而且，練習正念時，心中一旦升起任何評價，必須能加以辨識且刻意採取更廣闊的觀點、暫時停止評價、保持不偏不倚的觀察（胡君梅，黃小萍譯，2013：60，70，72）。此種正念的練習之所以具有減壓和療癒的功能，主要是因其強調專注在當下，並以接納的態度來看待情緒，和以問題導向的因應之道來面對處境。亦即當感覺到混亂與痛苦的情緒時，可以同時採用情緒導向（即關注你的想法和感覺），以及問題導向（即著眼於局勢本身）的作法。這兩種方法是同等重要，就像火車的兩條平行軌道（胡君梅，黃小萍譯，2013：383）。

Jon Kabat-Zinn 博士的正念減壓的八週課程內容主要包括有：練習覺察呼吸的靜坐、身體掃瞄、正念瑜伽，以及行走靜觀等。其中，專注於呼吸，是進入正式靜觀練習的第一步，並且透過覺察呼吸，領受呼吸時所浮現的各種感覺；其次，透過靜坐練習，覺察自己的想法與感受，並領悟到你的想法只是想法，想法不等於「你」，也不等於「事實」；再次，練習身體掃瞄靜觀，確實感受當下所專注的身體部位，讓心停留於該部位，感受該部位的表層與裡層，然後放掉一切，讓肌肉組織所累積的緊繃隨之釋放。接著，練習正念瑜伽與行走靜觀，透過緩慢的瑜伽伸展與平衡練習，以及走路或其他運動，可以在動靜之間感受到身體的流動（胡君梅，黃小萍譯，2013：85，87，105，139，114-115，507-508）。如此每天反覆練習，則

能讓自己的身心安定下來，自然而然就能減輕壓力與平衡負面的情緒。

其次，在西方心理學的研究領域中，根據心理學者 Shapiro 等人的研究，正念的運作會產生「再覺知」（reperceiving）的反應，「再覺知」的反應會使情緒往正向發展，而達到情緒的平衡。正念的運作過程及結果（如圖一所示），分述如下：

1. 正念的運作會產生「再覺知」的反應

人們面對一個會引起情緒反應的事件時，若能有意圖地使用正念的方法，在此時此地不帶評價且專注地覺察每一個相續而生的念頭與感受，則自然而然會產生心理學上所稱的「再覺知」（reperceiving）的反應。再覺知的反應，乃指觀點的改變（shift in perspective）；再覺知的概念類似於西方心理學上的一些概念，如「去中心化」（decentering）、「去自動化」（deautomatization）、「分離」（detachment）等概念。所謂「去中心化」是指：使自己脫離當下直接的感

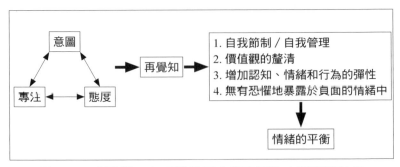

圖一：西方醫學、心理學的正念覺察運作之過程與結果

資料來源：筆者參照 Shapiro et al., (2006) 繪成

受，因而改變該直接感受的一種能力；所謂「去自動化」是指：對於覺知和認知的自動化過程之中止而言；至於所謂「分離」則指：與所注視之物保持距離之意。上述「去中心化」、「去自動化」及「分離」等心理學上的概念，均指觀點的改變而言。而且，觀點的改變乃由於透過正念的運作結果（Shapiro et al., 2006）。

2.「再覺知」的反應會使情緒往正向發展，而達到情緒平衡的結果

再覺知的反應可描述為：從主觀意識轉動為客觀意識的過程。根據發展心理學的說法，人們從幼童到成人的心理發展過程中，會從主觀的意識發展為客觀的意識。因此，透過正念的練習，會藉由產生再覺知的反應，進而使得人們的情緒往正向、成熟的方向發展，包括：（1）自我節制（Self-Regulation）／自我管理（Self-Management）、（2）價值觀的釐清（Values Clarification）、（3）增加認知、情緒和行為的彈性（Cognitive , Emotional and Behavioral Flexibility），以及（4）無有恐懼地暴露（Exposure）於負面的情緒中等四種情緒（Shapiro et al., 2006）。

（1）自我節制／自我管理

由於正念的運作會產生再覺知的反應，當引起情緒的事件或想法發生時，比較不會有自動化的反應，而較能自我節制或自我管理（Shapiro et al., 2006），亦即我們的情緒比較不會受到外境所影響。

（2）價值觀的釐清

再覺知的反應會使我們認知到，什麼才是對我們有意義

的事，什麼才是具有真正的價值？人們的價值觀通常會受到其社會文化或家庭的制約所影響，比較不會去反思這些習以為常的價值觀。而且，常以這些信以為真的價值觀，反射性地去處理周遭的事務。如果我們修習正念而產生再覺知的反應時，對於平日所抱持的價值觀，較能加以審視與反思而選擇正確者行事（Shapiro et al., 2006）。

（3）增加認知、情緒和行為的彈性

透過正念所產生的再覺知作用，對於外境的反應方式較具有彈性和適應性，比較不會被過去的觀念所制約而做出自動化的反應。好比，一個人在海面上被波浪衝擊時，是無法看清海面上的東西，但若能潛入海面下，則能平靜而清楚地看清楚海面上的東西。再覺知的反應就是能讓一個人從不同的角度看事物，亦即能以內觀的態度看清楚外境及自己當下所浮現的想法，較能增加認知、情緒和行為的彈性（Shapiro et al., 2006）。

上述透過正念或靜坐的練習，比較能增強撫慰及平和的情緒管理作用，進而增進內心的平靜與快樂。因為，人們在正念或靜坐的練習中，會專注在當下念頭（thoughts）的覺察。清楚地覺察這些念頭產生的流程，並視這些念頭只是念頭而已，❾不會加以評價與執取（Mulligan, 2017: 165; Cullen & Pons, 2015: 79）。所以，不斷練習正念或靜坐的

---

❾ 原文為："By noticing that a thought is a thought, we begin to see the transparency, fluidity, and relativity of thoughts."; "It's simply noticed as a thought" (Cullen & Pons, 2015: 78-79); "Oh, it's one of those thoughts"; "It's just a thought." (Mulligan, 2017: 165)

結果，愈能夠清楚看到這些念頭的輪廓外圍（contour），而不會去在意這些念頭的內容（content）。好比靜坐時，只在意數著呼吸，而不在乎呼吸的長短、深淺一樣。如此，我們的心念自然不再用力執取這些念頭，因而，我們的心識裡就能騰出很多空間來，而且可以節省很多執取的能量，進而能夠預防及克服情緒上的不平衡（Cullen & Pons, 2015: 78-79）。

（4）無有恐懼地暴露於負面的情緒中

透過正念而產生的再覺知反應，能使人們客觀地觀察自己心意識的內容，而且對於強烈的情緒反應如恐懼、害怕等，較能客觀、冷靜地面對。亦即再覺知的反應，能使自己暴露在負面的情緒中，而且在經歷這些情緒時，會頓覺這些恐懼、害怕的情緒並沒有想像中的可怕，進而能與它相處，不再逃避它（Shapiro et al., 2006）。

上述心理學的觀點認為，正念的運作機制，能產生再覺知的反應，進而發展出正向的情緒，包括：自我節制／自我管理、價值觀的釐清、增加認知、情緒和行為的彈性，以及無有恐懼地暴露於負面的情緒中等四種情緒，使得人們面對外境及自己內心的不愉快經驗或想法時，較能理性、不受制約、客觀地做出反應，而達到情緒的平衡。

此外，在西方認知心理治療的研究領域中，亦有多人應用正念覺察的方法，開設靜心冥想的課程，幫助人們平衡負面的情緒。例如，英國牛津大學臨床心理學的榮譽教授 Mark Williams 等人應用正念覺察的方法，發展出一套「正念認知療法」（mindfulness based cognitive therapy，簡稱

MBCT），幫助人們治療負面的情緒。Williams 等人認為一個人的情緒是由身體的感覺、想法、感受及衝動等四者交互作用下的綜合反應（Williams & Penman, 2011: 20）。例如，當一個人的想法以為自己走投無路時，會有不愉快的感受，胃部也會常常作痛，以及會有躲進棉被的衝動等，此時即產生了負面的情緒。Williams 等人進一步認為當一個人有了負面情緒時，通常會用理性的思維去了解產生情緒的原因，並試圖去解決負面的情緒，此稱為「行動」的模式（Doing mode）。但是，這種「行動」的模式，並無法停止負面情緒的產生。因此，Williams 等人設計一套八週有關正念覺察練習的課程，認為「存在」的模式（Being mode）可以取代「行動」的模式，亦即以純粹的覺察（Pure awareness）取代理性的思考。例如當負面情緒產生時，不要去想如何解決負面的情緒，而是要用心覺察「你正陷入情緒的漩渦中」、「你正在思考如何解決負面情緒」的情境。此種「存在」的模式，強調讓自己有意圖地、專注在當下、對實際發生的事物不帶任何評價地去面對，則自然而然地會產生正念覺察（Williams & Penman, 2011: 30-31; 35）。以正念覺察為基礎的「存在」模式在處理負面情緒上，比「行動」的模式更為殊勝之處有下列七點（Williams & Penman, 2011: 36-44）：

（1）「有意識的選擇」（conscious choice）優於「自動的行為反應」（automatic pilot）：正念覺察的「存在」模式可以使人充分地具有意識地覺察人的生活，並對各種行為方式做出有意圖的選擇；相反地，「行動」的模式會以自動

化的方式過生活,並養成習而不察的生活習慣。

(2)「感覺」(sensing)優於「分析」(analysing):
正念覺察的「存在」模式強調感官當下的看、聽、觸、聞、味
等的感覺,對外在世界充滿好奇,且能清楚地覺察自己內在的
想法和外在世界的情況;相反地,「行動」的模式強調思考、
分析、回憶、計畫及比較等心智的活動,常使自己活在自己的
想法世界中,而未能直接地去感受外在世界的存在。

(3)「接受」(accepting)優於「對抗」
(striving):正念覺察的「存在」模式暫時不用既有的想
法去評價外在事物,而接受外在世界的現況;相反地,「行
動」的模式是用自己的想法與夢想,去評價和比較真實的世
界,因此容易造成以管窺天的問題。

(4)「視想法是心智的產物」(treating thoughts as
mental events)優於「視想法是可信賴的、真實的」(seeing
thoughts as solid and real):正念覺察的「存在」模式視想法
只是心智的產物而已,認為「你的想法」並不等於「你自
己」,也不等於「真實」,因此不會受到自己的想法所束
縛;相反地,「行動」的模式認為想法是心智所創生的,是
值得信賴的,而且是真實的,可以解決現實的問題。但是,
往往有些錯誤的想法卻宰制了一個人的行為,而卻不自知。

(5)「面對負面的情緒和覺受」(approaching)優於
「逃避負面的情緒和覺受」(avoidance):正念覺察的「存
在」模式對於負面的情緒和覺受時,會直接面對它,最後自
然而然地化解它;但是相反地,「行動」的模式對於負面的
情緒和覺受,會盡量想辦法去逃避它,最後反而更加深此負

面的情緒和覺受。

（6）「活在當下」（remaining in the present moment）優於「受制於過去與現在的心智之旅」（mental time travel）：正念覺察的「存在」模式能夠清楚地看到此時此刻現前的想法，因此能活在當下，並能覺察出過去的記憶與未來的計畫，只是過去的記憶與未來的計畫而已，不會與當下的想法做過度的連結；相反地，「行動」的模式會讓自己現在的想法，去連結過去的記憶與未來的計畫，且易產生負面的情緒。例如，現在處於壓力狀態時，就會想起過去曾處於壓力狀態時的痛苦情形，而更加深現在的壓力，亦即理性去「做」的模式，會使現在的想法受制於過去的心智之旅。

（7）「從事健康的活動」（nourishing activities）優於「陷於耗能的活動」（depleting activities）：正念覺察的「存在」模式能夠清楚覺察哪些活動會讓人身心健康，哪些活動會讓人耗竭能量，並能有技巧地平衡處理這些不同性質的活動。例如，當因照顧幼兒或老年親人而身心疲憊時，若能覺察仍須保持有適當的休閒活動，且有技巧地利用時間和空間從事休閒活動，則有助於身心的健康。相反地，「行動」的模式，會認為這些正當的事（如照顧幼兒或老年親人）只是暫時性的，因此可以放棄例行的休閒活動，終於導致身心陷於耗竭的狀態。

綜上，正念認知療法（MBCT）以正念覺察為基礎的「存在」模式，強調有意識的選擇、感覺、接受、視想法是心智的產物、面對負面的情緒和覺受、活在當下，以及從事健康的活動等練習，能有效地平衡情緒。此與正念減壓課程

所強調的從「行動」模式轉向「存在」模式的說法一樣，亦即正念覺察的練習重在「練習與自我同在」，練習如何為自己騰出時間、如何慢下來以培養內在的寧靜與自我接納、如何觀察自己每一瞬間的起心動念、如何觀察並放下自己的念頭、想法而不受其控制等體驗（胡君梅，黃小萍譯，2013：57）。由此可知，此種以正念覺察為基礎的「存在」模式，就是要讓自己慢下腳步，讓自己安靜地與內在的自我相處，並進一步覺察自我、接納自我。

另外，在美國開設有關靜心冥想課程的 Sharon Salzberg，提出以正念處理情緒的四個步驟：包括承認（Recognition）、接納（Acceptance）、調查（Investigation）和不予認同（Nonidentification）等。❿其中第一個步驟是必須先承認正在經歷的感受；第二個步驟是以開放的態度接納任何浮現的情緒；第三個步驟是以公正無私的興趣來觀察它，就會發現這股強烈或痛苦的情緒並沒有那麼難解；第四個步驟則是對目前所感覺到的羞窘或沮喪不予認同，因為這只是暫時的狀態，而不是我們人生履歷的全部（李芸玫譯，2015）。此以承認、接納、調查和不予認同等四個步驟來處理痛苦的情緒，跟聖嚴法師所講的「四它」方法，有相通之處。聖嚴法師說：「生活中難免出現逆境，應該坦然地面對它、接受它、處理它、放下它；也就是說，遇到任何困難、艱辛、不平的情況，都不逃避，因為逃避不能解決問題，只有用智慧

---

❿ 此承認（Recognition）、接納（Acceptance）、調查（Investigation）和不予認同（Nonidentification）等四個步驟，縮寫為 RAIN 的步驟。

把責任擔負起來，才能真正從困擾的問題中獲得解脫（釋聖
嚴，2016b：28）」。

綜合上述，西方醫學、心理學及認知心理治療等研究領
域，已普遍將傳統正念修行法門中的正念覺察方法，善巧方
便地應用在減輕壓力和平衡情緒的臨床上，而且已有相當的
成效。

（三）西方對正念覺察的測量及相關研究

近年來，正念覺察的概念已被廣泛應用在醫學、教育、
輔導及心理治療等領域，並已發展出相關的測量工具。其
中，最被廣泛使用的是由 Brown 和 Ryan 等人（2003）設計
的「正念覺察注意量表」 ❶（Mindful Attention Awareness
Scale，簡稱 MAAS）。國內學者張仁和等人（2011）並
對 MAAS 加以翻譯與研究，建立了中文版的「正念覺察注
意量表」（Chinese Mindful Attention Awareness Scale，簡
稱 CMAAS）。此 CMAAS 量表的題目共十五題（如表一所
示），可供華文世界測量止觀的有效工具。

學者 Creswell 等人（2007）利用「正念覺察注意量表」
（MAAS）及腦部造影技術（fMRI）探討正念特質對於認
知、情緒與神經的關聯。他們發現 MAAS 的程度，與個體在
面對負面情緒圖片時的杏仁核活化量（amygdala activation）

---

❶ 此 MAAS 量表為單向度量表，聚焦於測量個體對自己行為的覺知狀
態。共十五題，六點量表。為目前引用率最高的正念測量工具。量表之
Cronbach's α 為 .81，對幸福感相關指標為正相關，與憂鬱、焦慮為負
相關（張仁和等人，2011：238）。

表一：中文版的「正念覺察注意量表」（CMAAS）題目

題號	量表題目
1	有些情緒可能早已發生，但我卻過了一段時間後才覺察到它們。
2	我會因為粗心大意、不專心或心不在焉，而打破或打翻東西。
3	我覺得持續專注於當下發生的事情是很困難的。
4	我通常一路直奔到目的地，而沒有注意一路上的種種景物。
5	我不容易注意到身體上的緊繃或不舒適的感覺，除非這種感覺嚴重影響到我。
6	別人才告訴我某人的名字，我馬上就把它忘記了。
7	我做事情常像反射動作一樣，而沒有意識到自己正在做什麼。
8	我倉促完成許多活動，但卻沒有真正關注它們。
9	我太專注於想要達到的目標，因而沒完整考慮自己正用什麼作法來達成目標。
10	我會不自覺地做著事，而沒有注意自己正在做什麼。
11	我會邊聽別人說話，同時邊做其他事。
12	我會不自覺地騎車前往某處，然後才去想自己為何前來。
13	我當被過去跟未來占據心思。
14	我發覺自己會做事心不在焉。
15	我會不自覺地吃著零食。

資料來源：張仁和等人（2011：246）。

達到高度負相關。同時，與前額葉腦區的活化量則達顯著正相關。由於杏仁核主要是處理負面情緒的活動中樞，前額葉則為理性監控的處理區塊，因此結果凸顯出，正念特質對於情緒調節與認知調控的正面效果（張仁和等人，2011：252）。

此外，長期研究情意神經科學（affective neuroscience）的 Richard J. Davidson ⓬於一九九九年與 Jon Kabat-Zinn 合

⓬ Richard J. Davidson 長期研究情意神經科學、大腦影像與行為科學，是大腦與情緒研究的先驅。享譽國際。他目前為美國威斯康辛大學麥迪遜校

作實驗，研究八週的「正念減壓課程」是否會對情緒及免疫力產生影響？此研究結果發現：實驗組（有受過正念減壓課程者）的焦慮程度下降了百分之十二，而控制組（未受過正念減壓課程者）反而稍微上升了些；正念減壓組大腦的活動也移轉到左側前額葉，相較於他們沒有上課之前的腦波EEG，左邊的活動增加了三倍；正念減壓組在注射流感疫苗後，他們的抗原濃度升高了百分之五，表示他們的免疫系統比控制組對疫苗的反應更有效（洪蘭譯，2013：277）。由此可見，正念減壓的訓練可以強化左前額葉的活化，降低焦慮的情緒，並明顯提高了免疫力。

綜合上述，西方醫學及心理學對正念覺察的研究與應用結果，普遍認為：修習西方意涵的正念，可以產生心理上再覺知的反應，可以緩衝人們對外境及負面想法的自動化反應，並能理性、客觀地予以覺察，所以能使情緒得到平衡。

四、佛教的「正念修行」對情緒平衡之影響

從前述佛教「正念修行」的意涵可知，佛教正念的修行，依次第可分為三個步驟。首從發願繫念於聖道的實踐，自度度人做起；次再修習次第禪觀，使心不旁騖，意不散亂；最後，透過修習默照禪觀，以達到「放捨諸相，休息萬事」的境界，則不僅能平衡情緒，更可解脫煩惱（如圖二所示）。

區健康心智研究中心主任、心理學和精神醫學研究教授，他同時也是心靈與生命研究院（Mind and Life Institude）的董事，此機構致力於提昇西方科學家與達賴喇嘛的對話。他著有《情緒大腦的祕密檔案》及《禪修的療癒力量》等書。

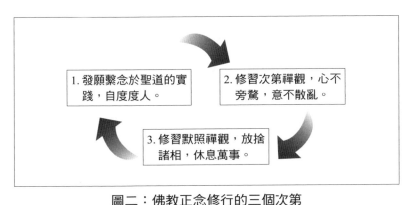

圖二：佛教正念修行的三個次第

資料來源：作者自繪

（一）發願繫念於聖道的實踐，自度度人

修習正念，首先要發菩提願心，自度度人，做為修習正念的目標與方向。例如，佛門弟子在禪修前禮佛及發四弘誓願的儀軌，即是要認清禪修的目的是要先解脫自己的煩惱（煩惱無盡誓願斷），再幫忙別人解脫煩惱（眾生無邊誓願度）；禪修的觀念與方法則是要在無量的法門中，精進修習，只要一門通，就能門門通（法門無量誓願學），如此，當煩惱斷盡、智慧圓滿、慈悲無限、福德圓滿之時，必將成佛（佛道無上誓願成）。

智顗大師在《修習止觀坐禪法要》提到修禪者必須先發弘誓願，自度度人。他說：「夫行者初學坐禪，欲修十方三世佛法者，應當先發大誓願，度脫一切眾生，願求無上佛道，其心堅固，猶如金剛，精進勇猛，不惜身命。若成就一切佛法，終不退讓。」誓願者，即四弘誓願也；謂：眾生無

邊誓願度，煩惱無盡誓願斷，此二為下化眾生，屬利他大悲；法門無量誓願學，佛道無上誓願成，此二為上求佛道，乃屬自利大智，即是發上求下化、自利利他之心（釋寶靜，2003：95-96）。

此外，宋朝的「坐禪儀」亦提到禪修者如果希望開發般若智慧，應先發起大慈悲心，和發弘誓願：「夫學般若菩薩，先當起大悲心，發弘誓願，精修三昧，誓度眾生，不為一身，獨求解脫（釋聖嚴，2004：207）。」

因此，修習正念若能發願繫念於聖道的實踐，自度度人，則不僅不會受到負面的想法和覺受所影響，同時亦能在觀照中產生智慧。

（二）修習次第禪觀，心不旁鶩，意不散亂

修習正念，特別強調專注於當下的想法及覺受，而且清清楚楚。因此，可透過次第禪觀工夫的練習，使心不旁鶩，意不散亂。次第禪觀的修習法門包括智顗大師在《修習止觀坐禪法要》，以及傳統佛教的五停心及四念住等法門。

首先，依智顗大師在《修習止觀坐禪法要》的說法，要修習止觀，必須先具有五緣、訶去五欲及揚棄五蓋❸，然後再調和五事。所謂具五緣，是指必須具備五個修行的條件，

---

❸ 「所言棄蓋者，謂五蓋也。一棄貪欲蓋，二棄瞋恚蓋，三棄睡眠蓋，四棄掉悔蓋，五棄疑蓋。……此五蓋中，即具有三毒等分。是故除此五蓋，即是除一切不善之法。……除此五蓋，其心安隱，清涼快樂。如日月以五事覆翳，煙、塵、雲、霧、羅睺阿修羅手障，則不能明照。人心五蓋亦復如是。」（釋寶靜，2003：73-94）

包括持戒清淨、衣食具足、閒居靜處、息諸緣務，以及近善知識等。所謂訶五欲，是指修行者必須先去除色、聲、香、味、觸、法等五種欲望。至所謂棄五蓋者，則指修行者必須排除五種阻撓修行的因素，包括貪欲、瞋恚、睡眠、掉悔及疑心等。然後再調和身心五事，包括調飲食、調睡眠、調身、調息和調心等。

其中，調息的要領，在將呼吸調整到沒有「風」、「喘」、「氣」等三種相，而能達到「息」相的境界。所謂風相，是指坐時鼻中氣息出入，感覺有聲音；所謂喘相，是指坐時氣息雖無聲音，但出入結滯不通；所謂氣相，是指坐時氣息雖無聲，亦不結滯，但出入的氣息不夠細微；而所謂息相，則指呼吸時沒有聲音、不會結滯，也不會太粗，而能感覺到氣息出入綿綿，若存若亡，且有資神安穩，情抱悅豫的覺受而言（釋寶靜，2003）。因此，坐禪時，如果呼吸有風、喘、氣三相的情形，就表示尚未調好呼吸。如果呼吸的氣息未調好，自然會影響心境的平穩。

當調好呼吸後，接著必須調整心念，亦即調伏心中亂想雜念，讓心念不會昏沉和浮動。調心的方法，在對治昏沉方面，要把心念收攝在鼻端；而在對治浮動方面，則要把心念收攝在肚臍下的丹田裡。如智顗大師在其所著《修習止觀坐禪法要》中所提（釋寶靜，2003：107）：

何等為沉相？若坐時心中昏暗，無所記錄，頭好低垂，是為沉相。爾時當繫念鼻端，令心住在緣中，無分散意，此可治沉。何等為浮相？若坐時心好飄動，身亦不安，念

外異緣，此是浮相。爾時宜安心向下，繫緣臍中，制諸亂念，心即定住，則心易安靜。舉要言之，不沉不浮，是心調相。

此外，聖嚴法師從修禪定的方法而言，調心可以用以下的數類對象做觀想：1. 觀想身外的東西，如月觀、日觀、因緣觀、不淨觀等；2. 觀想地、水、火、風的功德，例如觀想水能洗淨諸垢，匯百川成大海，滋養萬物，而又不爭功、不諉過；3. 以身體的官能接受身外的對象，其中以觀照用鼻子呼吸的方法最為基本有效；4. 觀想身內的五臟，例如觀想以金、木、水、火、土的五行相濟相生的方法，導引臟器的功能，增長肉體的健康。5. 觀想身體的某一部位，例如觀想鼻端，以修數息法來調心（釋聖嚴，2016a）。

聖嚴法師（2005：33-34）認為：「處在一個令人不舒服的情境時，與其希望改變環境來配合自己，倒不如回過頭來體驗自己的身心，體驗自己的不舒服。這時應該把自己當下所感受到的，也就是所謂的「念頭」轉移，比如轉移到念佛、拜佛上面。試著念佛至少具有轉移目標的效果，可以讓情緒降溫；降溫以後再反省，就可以讓情緒逐漸平靜下來。」因為：「念佛、拜佛及拜懺等方法可以把我們的心，不讓它向外亂攀緣，而讓心集中起來，然後安定下來。心安定以後，就好像一缸渾水，如果用明礬打過，這缸水漸漸沉澱之後，水裡就非常清爽，非常清澈透明。」❶❹至於念佛，最簡單的就是念「阿彌陀佛」。佛教徒念了「阿彌陀佛」，心裡感到平靜，就不會那麼生氣了。就好比基督徒一遇到

各種狀況時，自然而然就會說：「My God!」（釋聖嚴，2005）

　　聖嚴法師又提到：「佛法講調心，就是制衡我們的情緒。我們每一個人都有惡質的情緒，叫做煩惱心。因此，要用觀念來疏導，用方法來練習。觀念是指：要認定兩個人的想法、立場及需求等是不一樣的。所以，若站在自己的立場來評斷、猜想人和事，是不公平的。所以，我們要心平氣和。如果心不能平，氣不能和，那就要用方法。最簡單的方法是念阿彌陀佛，心向內看，不要老是對著外面放不下，這樣的話，情緒會平靜下來。另外，還有一個很好的方法是：注意和享受自己的呼吸，你的氣就是和的，氣和就心平，心平你的智慧就會出現。」⑮

　　綜上，調息為修定的入門，調心則是修定的主要方法。因為氣息和順舒暢，心境才能平靜安穩。心情與呼吸的關係是極為密切的，並且要想調心，必先從調息入手。因為人體生理的動靜以及心理的動靜，與呼吸的氣和息，有著依存的關係（釋聖嚴，2016a：24）。

　　調息可調整呼吸到細長均勻的地步，調心可以把浮動和散亂的心念，收攝起來。如此，就能清清楚楚當下的每一個念頭，心念不會攀緣外境，而能保持寂靜的狀態，好比鏡子

---

⑭ 釋聖嚴，〈放下攀緣〉，《大法鼓》0207 集，網址：https://www.youtube.com/watch?v=jzaWLq0Hqmw。檢索日期：2019/6/20。

⑮ 釋聖嚴，〈現代人在職場在職場需要什麼樣的 EQ，與佛法的異同〉，《大法鼓》0850 集，網址：https://www.youtube.com/watch?v=uYDP94HcZ-4(0850。檢索日期：2019/6/20。

的鏡面雖會映出鏡外的種種景物，但鏡面本身卻是靜寂不動的。因此，透過調息和調心的方法，可以培育正定與正念。

此外，要降伏貪欲心和瞋恚心，平衡情緒，可從修習止觀著手。因為修習止觀，可以培育正念，由粗而細地覺察每一個貪念和瞋念，使心不旁騖，意不散亂。修習止觀的方法有二種，一種是於坐中修止觀，另一種是歷緣對境修止觀。

1. 坐中修止觀

坐中修止觀的法門包括：對治初心粗亂修止觀、對治心沉浮病修止觀、隨便宜修止觀、對治定中細心修止觀，以及均齊定慧修止觀等五種。茲針對第一種，有關對治初心粗亂修止觀而言，說明其修止和修觀等二種方法如下（釋寶靜，2003：123-142）：

（1）修止：包括繫緣守境止、制心止，以及體真止等三種，依智顗大師的《修習止觀坐禪法要》的內容說明如下：「一者繫緣守境止，所謂繫心鼻端、臍間等處，令心不散。故經云：繫心不放逸，亦如猿著鎖。二者制心止，所謂隨心所起，即便制之，不令馳散。故經云：此五根者，心為其主，是故汝等當好止心。三者體真止，所謂隨心所念一切諸法，悉知從因緣生，無有自性，則心不取。若心不取，則妄念心息，故名為止。」

（2）修觀．包括①對治觀，如不淨觀，對治貪欲；慈心觀，對治瞋恚；界分別觀，對治著我；數息觀，對治多尋思等。②正觀，觀諸法無相，並是因緣所生，因緣無性，即是實相。先了所觀之境一切皆空，能觀之心自然不起。

以上是在禪坐中，修止和修觀的具體方法，屬於靜態

的修行，以下則再針對動態的情境中，進行歷緣對境的修習止觀。

2.歷緣、對境修止觀

（1）歷緣修止觀：當人們在行、住、坐、臥、做事及言語等六種機緣中，修習止觀。以在「行」中修止觀為例，即於行路時，修習止觀。例如在開步行走時，要問為何事而行？若此行是為煩惱所驅使，或做殺、盜、淫、妄之不善事而行的話，即不應行；若此行是為善事，如布施、修行或聽聞佛法而行的話，即應行。《修習止觀坐禪法要》云：「若於行時，即知因於行故，則有一切煩惱善惡等法，了知行心，及行中一切法，皆不可得，則妄念心息，是名修止。……即當反觀行心，不見相貌，當知行者及行中一切法，畢竟空寂，是名修觀（釋寶靜，2003：147）。」

（2）對境修止觀：包括眼對色境、耳對聲境、鼻對香境、舌對味境、身對觸境、意對法塵境中，修習止觀。例如，以眼對色境修止觀時，《修習止觀坐禪法要》云：「隨見色時，如水中月，無有定實，若見順情之色，不起貪愛；若見違情之色，不起瞋惱；若見非違非順之色，不起無明及諸亂想，是名修止。……即當反觀念色之心，不見相貌，當知見者及一切法，畢竟空寂，是名修觀（釋寶靜，2003：157，159）。」

修習「止」與「觀」，常被比喻為鳥的雙翼和車的兩輪。「止」讓「觀」照見根本煩惱，並加以拔除；但「觀」拔除根本煩惱以後，又可以反過來加深「止」的方法。

其次，在修習傳統佛教「五停心」及「四念處」的法門

方面，做為一種促進「止」的方法，「五停心觀」❶可以帶來「一心」的體驗或「定」的境界。而做為一種促進「觀」的方法，「四念處」可以去除我執，帶來「無心」的體驗。因此，「五停心觀」乃是「四念處」的前導，而「四念處」則是修慧的主要方法（梁永安，2015：106-107，147）。止後能「定」，觀後能得「慧」，止觀要同時修習，才能同時獲得定慧。若有定無慧，則為癡定；若有慧無定，則為狂慧。

聖嚴法師（1998：9）說：「修五停心觀，是為了平息、淨化心的騷亂和混濁的狀態，使心念集中，以達正定。由五停心得定，進而觀四念處開發智慧，此即解脫生死輪迴之要道。」四念處就是身、受、心、法四種觀想，是一種很複雜、很不容易修的修行方法（釋聖嚴，1998：58）。四念處修行法門的特色，在於觀照「當下」的覺受。例如，在觀「身念處」時，要覺察身體當下的動作，或是觀呼吸當下的狀況，或是觀身體當下的反應等；「受念處」所觀的是根塵相遇那一剎那心裡的苦樂等感受；「心念處」所觀的則是觀在苦樂感受下，心中隨之而生起的欲念、瞋恚與愚癡等法；至於「法念處」則是觀察心念處所生起的那些「法」的生、

---

❶ 五停心觀的五種法門雖歷來釋義略有不同，但通常界定為：一、數息觀，二、不淨觀，三、慈悲觀，四、因緣觀，五、界分別觀。漢文的佛教典籍中，亦有以念佛觀取代界分別觀的。所有這些方法皆針對一般人深重難除的習氣、障礙而設。如數息觀對治散亂，不淨觀對治貪欲，慈悲觀對治瞋恨，因緣觀對治愚痴煩惱，界分別觀對治我見，念佛觀對治罪重及障深等人。止惑除障後，才能夠純淨、專一而有信心願心，更進一步修行（釋聖嚴，1998：10）。

住、異、滅等變化。總之，修習正念的要領，就是覺察當下
那一剎那的身體、感受、心念及法相的變化。簡言之，聖嚴
法師提出禪修的心法：「身在那裡，心在那裡」，就是強調
當下的覺察工夫。意即：身體在做什麼，心就在做什麼；手
在做什麼，腳在那裡，你的心就在那裡，強調身心不可分
離，身心一致和身心統一。❶由此可知，四念處的修行法門
可以在日常生活的行、住、坐、臥中，任何一個起心動念處
做練習，久而久之自然能平衡情緒，進而解脫煩惱。

《雜阿含經》卷十一：「彼善男子難陀勝念正知者，
是善男子難陀觀察東方，一心正念，安住觀察；觀察南、
西、北方，亦復如是。一心正念，安住觀察。如是觀者，世
間貪、愛、惡不善法不漏其心。彼善男子難陀覺諸受起，覺
諸受住，覺諸受滅，正念而住，不令散亂；覺諸想起，覺諸
想住，覺諸想滅，覺諸覺起，覺諸覺住，覺諸覺滅，正念心
住，不令散亂，是名善男子難陀正念正智成就。」❶

舉例而言，《正念戰役：從軍人到禪師的療癒之旅》一
書的作者 Thomas 成功地透過次第禪觀的正念修行方法，有
效地控制其暴躁的情緒。Thomas 曾參與越戰，並在幾次驚
險的戰役中死裡逃生。他退伍後，發現自己仍活在殘酷的戰
役中，深陷在恐懼、憤怒與絕望的地獄深淵。之後，他在一
次一行禪師的禪修營中，接觸到佛法正念的教誨後，活出不

---

❶ 摘自聖嚴法師《禪的世界》，搜尋自法鼓山「以禪心過好生活：2013 法
鼓山萬人禪修」活動網站，網址：https://cfe.ddm.org.tw/page10.htm。檢
索日期：2019/6/23。

❶ CBETA, T02, no. 99, p. 73, b20-28。

同的人生。他從軍人成為比丘，並在世界各地與戰區宣揚和平與非暴力。他自述說（陳敬旻譯，2007：86-87，95）：

> 　　我與佛教的相遇引領我有意識地生活，注意念頭、感覺、觀點中最小的細節，而定義這種生活方式的名詞便是「正念」。正念這種生活方式幫助我甦醒，走出毀滅與苦難的循環。正念表達所有靈性教誨的核心，而所有靈性教誨的核心便是正念。正念只是完全處於當下——此時此地，認定除了此刻之外，別無其他。他們教導我，置身於當下的一種方法是覺察呼吸。只要呼吸，同時察覺到我在呼吸。如果我完全察覺到自己的呼吸，我就不可能在其他地方，只能在當下。如果我活在正念之中，深入觀照自己的本性，碰觸自己的苦，我就能學習和我的恐懼、我的疑慮、我的不安、我的困惑，和我的憤怒共處。

　　綜合上述，修習正念必須以次第禪觀的工夫為基本功。依照智顗大師修習止觀法門的次第，先具有五緣、訶去五欲、揚棄五蓋、調和五事後，再進行坐中修止觀，以及是歷緣對境修止觀的修行，則能達到「制心一處，無事不辦」的境界。此外，五停心觀與四念處的禪修法門亦屬於基礎的修行方法，尤其以「五停心觀」幫助修行者收攝散亂心，培養定力，更是修習「四念處」解脫智慧之基礎。

（三）修習默照禪觀，放捨諸相，休息萬事

　　默照禪法不需要像次第禪觀那樣，一個次第一個次第

地修。次第禪觀，是先修五停心，然後修四念處，是從觀呼吸、觀身體、觀心念入手，是次第的修行方法。而默照禪法，也是從呼吸入手，也是從觀身受著力，但是，默照禪是從有次第到無次第。有次第是身體放鬆，心情放鬆，體驗呼吸，體驗身、受、心、法，這是結合五停心的觀息和觀身法門，進一步修四念處的。默照禪不落次第，面對身、受、心、法的任何現象，都採取不要管它的態度，只是清楚知道自己是在打坐。放捨我執是「默」，清清楚楚是「照」，這就是默照禪（釋聖嚴，2004：19，34-35）。

聖嚴法師（2004：29-33）認為：修習默照禪必須遵守的基本態度有三：發大悲心、放捨諸相，休息萬事。首先是發大悲心，大悲心就是菩提心，也是能夠讓我們徹悟成佛的心。發起大悲心的目的，在於找到自己的本來面目[19]，以及體驗到各人的本地風光[20]。其次是放捨諸相，就是不執著任何現象，實際上就是無住心。心不住於心理現象、不住於身體現象、不住於環境現象。不住於任何一種現象，就是「默」；知道所有的現象都是正在發生中，那就是「照」。第三，要休息萬事，對於凡夫而言，修行和煩惱都是事，凡在心中有所牽掛的，就叫做「事」。隨時隨地要把心中的牽

---

[19] 所謂「本來面目」，是指離開生死現象，既不生也不死，既無生也無滅的本來面目，是人人本具的，也是不可思議的真如佛性（釋聖嚴，2004：19-20）。

[20] 所謂「本地風光」，是指在沒有任何執著的狀況下，還有智慧及慈悲的一切功能。風光，是春光明媚的風景，悟後的心地，稱為本地，是如實的自在清淨，能攝一切善法，能生一切功德（釋聖嚴，2004：21）。

掛停止，心裡沒有任何牽掛之時，雖也照常過生活，但那就是休息萬事。發現心中有事，就是「照」；不去討厭它，不去管它，休息心中所有的事，則是「默」。聖嚴法師傳授的默照工夫，特別強調「先照後默，默其所照」。亦即要先觀照自己在做什麼、在想什麼，也清楚地知道心裡所產生的種種反應是怎樣。然後，再用默的工夫，默掉那些所知、所覺、所想、所受的身心狀況，不再被它們影響下去，也就是默其所照（釋聖嚴，2004：23-24）。

　　默照禪觀的修行方法除了要調身和調息外，最重要的是要調心。依照聖嚴法師（2004：27-29）的教法，默照修行法有四個調心的層次：1. 收心：把心從緣過去境以及緣未來境的狀況，收到緣現在境的這一點上。捨下過去境及未來境是「默」，緣現在境是「照」。2. 攝心：是將收回的心攝於現前正在用的方法上。不跟雜念、妄想、瞌睡纏鬥是「默」，把心用在方法上是「照」。3. 安心：是將心念安住於正在用的方法上。清楚知道就是「照」，平穩安定則是「默」。4. 無心：是指放下一切攀緣心，既不執妄境也不求真境，但仍如常人一般地生活，這便是《金剛經》的「無住生心」，亦即《六祖壇經》的「無念心」、「無相心」。綜上，默照禪觀的調心，必須先經過收心的層次，捨掉過去與未來；次經過攝心的層次，要捨雜念、妄想；再經過安心的層次，要捨身心環境正在發生的狀況；最後到達無心的層次，要捨妄、捨真，不執著有無兩邊，也不執著中間。由此可見，修行的過程重在調心，透過方法使散心變成集中心，再把集中心變成統一心，包括身心統一、內外統一，以及前

念與後念的統一，最後再把統一心放下，達到「放捨諸相，休息萬事」的無心之境界。

由於人們的六根和六塵一接觸，立即會起心動念，甚至容易起了惡念而造了惡業。所以，修行者要在當下覺察每一個念頭與情緒的起伏變化，並且不要受到外境的影響。聖嚴法師認為：行者在日常生活中，對於身、心、環境不受任何刺激而有情緒反應，這叫做妄念不生，萬緣不拒，但是身、心、環境還是照樣地存在。這是要練習的，練習也需要有層次如下（釋聖嚴，1999：98-99）：

（一）外在的環境，聽到了，看到了，這時心裡要馬上想：這是外境在動，是外境的動作，不是我的動作，是他的事，跟我沒有關係。

（二）練習著沒有外境的對象，這必須把自我中心放下來，唯有沒有自我中心的執著，才不介意外境的對象。所以《金剛經》說：無我相，才能夠無人相。

（三）練習放下「自我」，怎樣練習沒有「我」呢？人家罵我的時候，一定有一個名字或是一個代號，你要想：這個名字不是我，這個身體也不是我，跟我沒關係。然後，只注意自己的呼吸，不介意外境的好壞；並且觀想，呼吸的人不是自己，僅是身體在呼吸，不是我在呼吸。

聖嚴法師（2010：10，17-18）說：「衝突的產生，往往是因為過度強調自我中心。」「面對生氣，要學會反觀自照，照一照自己的心念，問一問為什麼要生氣？」「如果心

裡打結了，最好能向內觀看自己的起心動念處。」因此，透過正念的修習，較能反觀自照既有的價值觀，是否行不通？是否過度執著自己的想法？上述放下自我，就是「無我」，若能以無我的精神去觀照自己的任何念頭和覺受，自然就不會受到外境的影響。

綜上，從理論上論述修習默照禪觀對解脫煩惱的幫助，此處則從一項實證上的研究發現加以驗證。亦即楊蓓（2012：387-388）在「默照禪修對心理健康影響之初探」一文中，以質性的研究方法❷，以生命經驗觀照的觀點，檢視默照禪修的影響與效能。其研究發現，默照禪修方法對禪修者大致有四種面向的改變，包括：1. 身體部分：（1）透過覺察與放鬆自己，身體症狀得以治療；（2）提昇睡眠品質。2. 心念部分：（1）調伏負向情緒，減少負向思考；（2）覺察習性、模式；（3）懂得如何轉念。3. 人際部分：（1）互動較為柔軟，減少固執己見；（2）情緒控制較好，人際對立衝突較少；（3）尋找真誠說話卻不傷人的可能性。4. 生命態度：（1）找到生命的著力點；（2）培養以自然的態度面對生死。因此，楊蓓（2012：388）認為：默照禪修對禪修者生

---

❷ 該項研究採用質性研究的方法，以立意取樣（禪修經驗超過三年，至少參加「默照禪七」三次以上），在不帶有理論預設立場的情況下，以當事人主觀生命經驗的陳述為核心，邀請十二位禪修學員，以焦點團體方式蒐集研究資料，再以現象學內容分析，歸納其禪修歷程中的生命轉折。焦點團體的訪談係由接觸禪修時的身心狀況談起，對照其禪修歷程中自我認知的改變與生活變化，來探尋默照禪修的影響脈絡（楊蓓，2012：387）。

命歷程所造成的影響具有正面效果。因為默照禪法的練習培養出「覺知的智慧」，使禪者得以在身心靈全人觀照下處理自己的困境。由此可見，藉由默照禪的修習，觀照當下浮現的任何念頭和覺受，可以化解不必要的煩惱與壓力，讓身心自在。

綜上所述，修習佛教正統的正念，必須持守三個重要的步驟：首從發願繫念於聖道的實踐，自度度人做起；次再修習次第禪觀，心不旁騖，意不散亂；最後，進一步修習默照禪觀，放捨諸相，休息萬事，而達到解脫煩惱的開悟境界。而且，無論透過漸悟式的次第禪觀或頓悟式的默照禪觀，都是屬於佛法的正念修行法門，確實可以處理人們負面的情緒。

五、結語

綜合本文對傳統佛法的正念修行與西方醫學、心理學的正念覺察練習二者的意涵，以及二者對情緒平衡的影響分析，筆者提出以下結語：

（一）在理論比較方面，傳統佛法的正念修行與西方醫學、心理學的正念覺察練習，在目的、觀念、方法，以及對情緒平衡的效果上均有所不同。

傳統佛法的正念修行與西方醫學、心理學的正念覺察，二者在情緒平衡上，雖都具有正面的幫助。但二者在目的、觀念、方法，以及對情緒平衡的效果上，均有所不同（如表二所示）。從目的上言，傳統佛法的正念修行是八正道的其中一項，強調正知、正見與收攝身心，以期達到解脫煩惱的

開悟境界；而西方醫學、心理學的正念覺察練習，則以減少身心壓力與病痛，以及治療心理疾病為目的。次從觀念言，傳統佛法的正念修行意指：「繫念於聖道的實踐，心不旁鶩，意不散亂。」而西方醫學、心理學對正念覺察的界定為：「時時刻刻不帶評價的覺察」。再從方法上言，傳統佛法的正念修行法門著重：發願繫念於聖道的實踐，並且落實修習次第禪觀與默照禪觀，不僅能做到心不旁鶩，意不散亂，更希望達到放捨諸相，休息萬事的無心境界；而西方醫學、心理學的正念覺察方法，比較簡單，著重在覺察自我與接納自我，並專注在覺察呼吸的靜坐、身體掃瞄、正念瑜伽，以及行走靜觀等課程的練習。最後，在平衡情緒的效果上，二者均有一定程度的效果，但因為傳統佛法的正念修行涵括了佛法的正知、正見，並且須具五緣、訶五欲和棄五蓋等基本工夫，所以對情緒平衡和解除煩惱，具有治本與治標

表二：傳統佛法的正念修行與西方醫學、心理學的正念覺察之比較

	傳統佛法的正念修行	西方醫學、心理學的正念覺察
目的	收攝身心，以期達到解脫煩惱的開悟境界。	減少身心壓力與病痛，以及治療心理疾病。
觀念	正念意指：「繫念於聖道的實踐，心不旁鶩，意不散亂。」	正念意指：「時時刻刻不帶評價的覺察。」
方法	1. 發願繫念於聖道的實踐，自度度人。 2. 修習次第禪觀，心不旁鶩，意不散亂。 3. 修習默照禪觀，放捨諸相，休息萬事。	1. 以純粹的覺察取代理性的思考，覺察自我、接納自我。 2. 練習覺察呼吸的靜坐、身體掃瞄、正念瑜伽，以及行走靜觀等課程。
效果	對情緒平衡有治本與治標的效果	對情緒平衡有治標的效果

資料來源：作者自行彙整。

的效果；然而由於西方醫學、心理學的正念覺察練習是簡化
版的佛法的正念修行，未有如上述佛法正念修行的基本工
夫，只直接練習調身、調息和調心，對情緒平衡的效果言，
較難標本兼達，頂多達到治標效果而已。

（二）在推廣策略方面，傳統佛法的正念修行法門可朝生活化及可操作化的方向推廣

傳統佛法的正念修行法門殊勝之處，在於能根本地解
脫煩惱，平衡情緒。例如，聖嚴法師經常提及《金剛經》裡
的兩句話：「應無所住而生其心」、「凡所有相，皆是虛
妄」，就是對正念做了最好的詮釋。聖嚴法師又引《六祖壇
經》中，六祖惠能將「煩惱即菩提」這句話，引申為：「前
念著境即煩惱，後念離境即菩提。」聖嚴法師的詮釋是：
「前念如果執著境界，對所面臨的環境產生好或壞、有或無
等反應，那就是煩惱；如果念頭一轉，下一念離開前念所產
生的種種分別、執著、計較，這就是智慧。」因此，聖嚴法
師經常勸煩惱中人一句話：「山不轉路轉，路不轉人轉，人
不轉心轉（釋聖嚴，2017：56-57）。」由此可見，佛法的
正念修行，有助於消除煩惱，增長智慧。

雖然佛法的正念法門如此之好，但是由於佛法的義理難
懂，法門難修，所以，聖嚴法師常有「佛法這麼好，但知道
的人這麼少」之慨嘆。因此，如何能將佛法上正念的義理，
用大家聽得懂的話語，甚至若能如西方醫學、心理學的正念
覺察練習課程一樣簡單易操作，且能應用在日常生活上的
話，則將更為普遍地推廣給世人。例如，聖嚴法師（2010：

3，6-7，8-9，18）提出淺顯易懂的「一○八自在語」如下，
正可應用在日常生活中，實踐正念的理念：

1. 「用平常心面對不平常的事。」
2. 「任何狀況下，都要照顧好自己的心，保持內心的平穩與安定，就是心靈的健康，就是心靈環保。」
3. 「生氣，可能是身體上、觀念上或其他因素引起的煩惱，不一定代表修養不好。如果能夠向內心觀照，用智慧來化解煩惱，也就不會自害害人了。」
4. 「遇到不舒服、不愉快的事要調心，調心是調我們自己的心，不是調別人的心。」
5. 「處理問題要心平氣和，心不平、氣不和，則容易說錯話，讓問題更複雜。」
6. 「心裡如果『打結』了，最好能向內觀看自己的起心動念處。」

（三）在跨域研究方面，可結合佛教與醫學、心理學等之正念研究，建立一套兼具有深厚理論與實踐方法的修行法門或練習課程

佛教在正念修行的義理與方法，已有豐富的經典與相關著作，對人的身、心、意、識等諸現象有鞭辟入裡的分析，若能結合西方醫學、心理學及認知科學等跨學科的相關研究，將有助於建立一套兼具有深厚理論與實踐方法的正念修行法門或練習課程。

楊蓓（2019：397-398）在〈佛法與心理治療典範轉移

可能性之探討：從 MBSR 的發展經驗省思〉一文中，提到其透過文獻整理及訪談四位受訪者❷的結果發現摘要如下：

> 以 MBSR 的發展經驗為例，研究者由文獻及訪談中觀察到一些動力，包括了對這門以佛教為基礎的新興心理治療有著矛盾情感，即樂見佛教能發展出一種入世的助人模式而廣為民眾所接受，同時卻也基於佛教信仰而對於將佛教觀念置入科技理性模式下的心理治療典範感到不安；更進一步地，這個不安相當接近於孔恩的不可共量性（incommensurability），認為佛教與心理治療處於不同的知識典範，即便講述著相近似的名詞、概念，其意涵終究是不同的，直接引用或簡化佛法，在佛教徒眼中是存疑的；最後，我們想望未來的發展，佛教與心理治療間典範轉移的歷程該怎樣走，使彼此能相互學習、尋找交集甚或創造，而非僅流於機會主義式的一個方便借用，研究者身為一個佛教徒的心理治療工作者，試圖提出一些省思與建議。

筆者同意楊蓓（2019）上述見解，姑不論佛教與心理治療間是否具有典範不可共量性的關係，筆者認為可透過跨學科或學科整合的途徑，使佛教與西方醫學、心理學等領域

---

❷ 楊蓓（2019）以立意取樣的方式，訪談四位曾接觸佛教或禪修有十年以上經驗的心理治療專業人員，訪談有關西方正念減壓課程（MBSR）的發展，以及佛法與心理治療的典範轉移與結合等議題。

間彼此相互學習、尋找交集，甚或創造出有助於人們平衡情緒、解脫煩惱的修習方法。

參考文獻

一、外文

Brown, K. W., & Ryan, R. M., 2003, "The Benefits of Being Present: Mindfulness and Its Role in Psychological Well-being." *Journal of Personality and Social Psychology.* 84(4), 822-848.

Creswell, J.D., Way, B. M. Eisenberger, N. I., & Lieberman, M. D., 2007, "Neural Correlates of Dispositional Mindfulness during Affect Labeling." *Psychosomatic Medicine,* 69(6), 560-565.

Cullen, Margaret and Gonzalo Brito Pons, 2015, *The Mindfulness-Based Emotional Balance Workbook: An Eight-Week Program for Improved Emotion Regulation and Resilience*, Oakland, CA: New Harbinger Publications, Inc.

Ekman, Paul, 2003, *Emotions Revealed: Recognizing Faces and Feelings to Improve Communication and Emotional Life.* New York: Times Books.

Gilbert , Paul. 2009, "Introducing Compassion-Focused Therapy." *Advances in Psychiatric Treatment*, 15: 199-208.

Kabat-Zinn, J. (2011). Some reflections on the origins of MBSR, skillful means, and the trouble with maps. *Contemporary Buddhism*, 12 (1), 286-288.

Mulligan, Beth Ann, 2017, *The Dharma of Modern Mindfulness: Discovering the Buddhist Teachings at the Heart of Mindfulness-Based Stress Reduction*, Oakland, CA: New Harbinger Publications, Inc.

Shapiro, Shauna L., Linda E. Carlson, John A. Astin, and Benedict

Freedman, 2006, "Mechanisms of Mindfulness", *Jounaal of Clinical Psychology*, Vol. 62(3), 373-386 (2006), DOI: 10.1002/jclp.20237.

Stahl, Bob & Goldstein, Elisha, 2010, *A Mindfulness-Based Stress Reduction Workbook*, Oakland, CA: New Harbinger Publications, Inc.

Williams, Mark & Penman, Danny, 2011, *Mindfulness: A Practical Guide to Finding Peace in a Frantic World*, London: Piatkus.

二、中文

釋印順，《成佛之道》，新竹：正聞出版社，2007 年。

李芸玫譯，Sharon Salzberg 原著，《靜心冥想的練習：28 天在家自修的正念課程》，臺北：橡實文化，2015 年。

武自珍譯，Windy Dryden 原著，《理性情緒心理學入門》，臺北：心理出版社，1997 年。

洪蘭譯，Richard J. Davidson & Sharon Begley 原著，《情緒大腦的祕密檔案：從探索情緒形態到實踐正念冥想改變生命的旅程》，臺北：遠流出版公司，2013 年。

胡君梅、黃小萍譯，Jon Kabat-Zinn 原著，《正念療癒力：八週找回平靜、自信與智慧的自己》（卡巴金博士二十年經典增訂版），新北：野人文化，2013 年。

徐名敬，〈正念訓練之心理運作機制歷程探究〉，《國防大學通識教育學報》第 9 期，2019 年，頁 129-147。

張仁和，林以正，黃金蘭等人，〈中文版「止觀覺察注意量表」之信效度分析〉，《測驗學刊》，正向心理特質的測量專刊，2011 年 4 月，頁 235-260。

梁永安譯，釋聖嚴、Dan Stevenson 原著，《牛的印跡──禪修與開悟見性的道路》（三版），臺北：商周出版，2015 年。

陳敬旻譯，Claude Anshin Thomas 原著，《正念戰役──從軍人到禪

師的療癒之旅》，臺北：法鼓文化，2007 年。

楊蓓，〈默照禪修對心理健康影響之初探〉，收入聖嚴教育基金會學術研究部編，《聖嚴研究》第三輯，臺北：法鼓文化，2012年，頁 387-416。

楊蓓，〈佛法與心理治療典範轉移可能性之探討：從 MBSR 的發展經驗省思〉，收入聖嚴教育基金會學術研究部編，《聖嚴研究》第十二輯，臺北：法鼓文化，2019 年，頁 397-438。

釋聖嚴，《五停心，四念處》，臺北：法鼓文化，1998 年。

釋聖嚴，《動靜皆自在》，臺北：法鼓文化，1999 年。

釋聖嚴，《聖嚴法師教默照禪》，臺北：法鼓文化，2004 年。

釋聖嚴，《做好情緒管理：憤怒抓狂 Stop! 》，臺北：法鼓文化，2005 年。

釋聖嚴，《自在樂活（一）：108 自在語》，臺北：財團法人聖嚴教育基金會，2010 年。

釋聖嚴，《因果與因緣》（增訂版），臺北：法鼓文化，2013 年。

釋聖嚴，《坐禪的功能》（增訂版），臺北：財團法人聖嚴教育基金會，2016 年 (a)。

釋聖嚴，《心五四運動：法鼓山的行動方針》，臺北：財團法人聖嚴教育基金會，2016 年 (b)。

釋聖嚴，《公案一〇〇》（四版），臺北：法鼓文化，2017 年。

釋寶靜，《修習止觀坐禪法要講述》（修訂版），臺北：財團法人佛陀教育基金會，2003 年。

A Study on the Impact of Mindfulness on Emotional Balance

Chin-Chin Chu

Professor, Dean of College of Justice Administration, Central Police University, Taiwan.

▌ Abstract

From the perspective of traditional Buddhism, mindfulness is one of the Eightfold Paths of the Dharma. It means that in order to practice the Dharma, every thought should be fully aware, and the mind is not distracted in the present moment. The purpose of mindfulness is to integrate one's body and mind in order to achieve an enlightened state of liberation. The methods of mindfulness include making bodhisattva wish and practicing serene contemplation and silent-illumination meditation. Hence, one may even reach the situation of letting go of all things. Since 1979, the Western society has borrowed the Buddhist concepts and methods of mindfulness to actively develop some programs concerning stress reduction and healing of mental illness (such as Mindfulness-Based Stress Reduction (MBSR), and Mindfulness-Based Cognitive Therapy (MBCT) programs etc.). Through emphasizing living in the moment with non-judging and non-striving attitude, MBSR and MBCT programs have obviously helped in reducing physical and mental stress and pain, as well as in the treatment of mental illness, so it is widely prevailing in the mainstream society in the West. This article first discusses the difference in meaning between mindfulness practice of traditional Buddhism and MBSR and MBCT programs, and then analyzes the impact of those on emotional balance. Finally, in the conclusion, from a cross-disciplinary perspective on Buddhism, three points of view are proposed in the study of mindfulness.

Keywords: Dharma, Mindfulness, Emotional Balance, Mindfulness-Based Stress Reduction (MBSR), Mindfulness-Based Cognitive Therapy (MBCT).

「緣起領導」管理模式
——佛法與領導管理

吳志軒 *

香港大學佛學研究中心名譽助理教授

▌摘要

　　領導管理的課題在多個學術和應用領域上均有深入的研究，但在宗教與公共管治方面，特別是在實踐和應用上的研究仍有待補充。本篇研究嘗試從佛法的角度去探討領導管理，從根本「緣起」和「無我」的義理出發，剖析領導管理的性質和在組織內的身分認同，為領導和管理者的角色重新

---

* 吳博士現任香港大學佛學研究中心客席助理教授，為本科及研究生教授佛學經濟學。他曾於瑞瑩資本擔任首席投資總監、摩根士丹利自營投資部門任副總裁，在投資銀行和資產管理擁有超過十五年經驗。工餘熱衷於可持續發展、傳統智慧與市場經濟融合的研究和教育，曾多次獲海內外傳媒和大學邀請做資產管理、正念和佛學方面的訪問、演講、嘉賓主持和專欄作者。吳博士現任東蓮覺苑行政總監。

吳博士在二〇〇〇年以 Phi Beta Kappa 畢業於芝加哥大學，獲經濟學學士和國際關係學碩士學位、在二〇〇七年於香港大學獲佛學碩士、二〇一六年於香港大學獲哲學博士、二〇一七年成為歐洲 SPES 學者。

吳博士重視年輕人和未來領袖的培訓，近年成為香港多間大學的導師及 Sustainable Finance Initiative 擔任顧問。二〇一五年至二〇一九年香港大學佛學研究中心校友會擔任主席，現任名譽顧問，著有《幸福「槓桿」》及佛學經濟學教科書 *Introduction to Buddhist Economics* 等。

定位。通過剖析佛和菩薩廣大的慈悲與智慧，呈現佛法在領導管理上的無私大願、自利利他的精神。論文亦以《心經》及《金剛經》的智慧，去檢視可持續的「緣起領導」管理模式，落實佛菩薩的願景、教化和修習。「緣起領導」模式特別切合在情商和智商有持續和深入虛耗的商界、社會服務界和其他專業，讓領袖除了在技術上，在「心術」上亦能夠得以提昇和淨化。本文亦以聖嚴法師倡議的「心五四運動」、「心六倫」及「四種環保」為例，探討部分實踐「緣起領導」模式的可能性。從每一個人的心開始，去轉化一個家庭、團體、企業、社會的管治。

關鍵詞：緣起領導、管理、身分認同、佛法

一、領導管理模式的演變

人類在追求物質和精神需求的過程中，群居在同一個空間，通過不同的領導結構組織起來。領袖能夠讓零散的個體力量進行溝通和協作，結集零散的力量，共同應對自然環境強大的挑戰和不確定性。它亦推動在社區內開發和傳播知識，讓所積累的經驗和技術可持續分享和繼承。雖然領導素質是多方面的，但決定領導者成敗的共通關鍵是要洞悉團體應該走向何處，踏上通往各個里程碑和最終目標的道路。領導者必須積累必要的資源和運用適當的戰略和決策，引導團體實現某些共同目標和任務。

當團體內的溝通條件不成熟，自上而下的專制（autocratic）或主權（sovereign）領導模式似乎無可避免，通過最嚴格的指揮和控制實現無縫執行。若然組織內成員的體力或智力條件差異很大時，專制領導者亦會以優越的體力或智力獲得認同去施行管治。即使團體內的每一個人都重要，但專制的領導者可能會將追隨者的個體視作可被替代、被利用的工具，為謀取更大的共同利益而犧牲個人的福祉。專制領導可以為實現社區、少數特權或少數群體的目標，對其追隨者進行戰術性、計算性和操縱性的考量。

許多領導者採取建基於自我、權力和控制，自上而下的專制或主權領導模式。有時候領導者和追隨者之間的關係模糊，讓人懷疑領導背後的真正動機，並將傾向社會的（pro-social）關係扭曲為工具使用。與僕人式領導（servant leadership）的模式相反，領導者可能會質疑他們的員工只是

出於自利的動機而不是真正的利他動機，容許自己利用員工做為達到目的工具。❶僕人式領導模式的創始人 Greenleaf 闡述，僕人式領導者將傳統的由上而下、由領袖主導的關係轉變成對追隨者真誠的、有意識的專注：明白團隊內不同人的動機、能力、及潛能。❷ Cable 的研究表明，由權力和控制欲驅動的家長式管治會讓人欠缺積極性。為了激勵團隊，他認為領導者必須持著僕人式領導的謙遜心態，培養謙卑、勇敢和洞察力，承認自己可以從下屬的專業知識中受益。❸領導者積極了解每個員工的想法和獨特貢獻，真心關懷、具人性化、關注共同利益及願景。要融合領導者和僕人的角色，自信和謙遜的性格，洞察力和好奇的能力，的確是很有回報，但在實踐中卻又充滿挑戰。

　　本文針對領導管理的性質和在團隊內的身分認同，探討了佛教教義的潛在貢獻。佛教教義的一個顯著貢獻是超越了「僕人」和「領導者」身分的概念。基於佛教的核心教義：1.「緣起」（paṭiccasamuppāda）和 2.「無我」（anatta），

---

❶ Inesi, ME, Gruenfeld, DH, Galinsky, AD 2012, 'How power corrupts relationships: Cynical attributions for others' generous acts.' *Journal of Experimental Social Psychology*, vol. 48, no. 4, pp. 795-803.

❷ Greenleaf, RF 2018. *The servant as leader—A journey into the nature of legitimate power and greatness*, Paulist Press, viewed 1 May 2018, https://www.essr.net/~jafundo/mestrado_material_itgjkhnld/IV/Lideran%C3%A7as/The%20Servant%20as%20Leader.pdf.

❸ Cable, D 2018, 'How humble leadership really works.' *Harvard Business Review*, April, viewed 1 May 2018, https://hbr.org/2018/04/how-humble-leadership-really-works.

僕人式領導的性質可以通過另一個視角去理解。正如本文中闡述，佛教教義可以為領導和下屬的關係提供了新的意義，消除兩者之間的隔礙，進而解決僕人式領導的矛盾——即將僕人和領導身分二合為一的矛盾，更充分地體現僕人式領導的理想。二十一世紀的網絡效應在加強人與人的連結的同時，個人身分變得比以往更加獨特、個人意識更強烈。僕人式領導的領導者要為每個下屬提供度身定制的管理更具挑戰。然而，通訊和網絡技術的進步亦使信息的交流更快更易。如果領導者知道如何準確地滿足其團隊成員的需求，可以發揮不可估量的鉅大潛能。

二、慈悲與智慧的領導力

Van Dierendonck 和 Patterson 提出，以智慧為基礎的慈愛應該成為僕人式領導的基石，值得深入探討智慧和慈悲的特質和培養的方法。❹在大乘佛教中，佛陀和菩薩是慈悲和智慧圓滿的體現，以無私的使命和不懈的努力來教導和治癒所有眾生，是僕人領袖的模範。他們的理想、動機和實踐在經典中都有深刻的見解和詳細的闡述，例如在《般若波羅蜜多心經》（簡稱《心經》）和《金剛般若波羅蜜經》（簡稱《金剛經》）的佛教教義和哲學基礎上，可以啟發更完善和可持續的領導模式。《心經》指出，修行成就的菩薩深刻認

---

❹ Van Dierendonck, D & Patterson, K 2015, 'Compassionate love as a cornerstone of servant leadership: An integration of previous theorizing and research,' *Journal of Business Ethics*, vol. 128, no. 1, pp. 119-131.

識到由五蘊所組成的世界是因緣和合，明瞭緣起性空的義
理，因此在他的心中再沒有任何牽掛和障礙：

> 觀自在菩薩。行深般若波羅蜜多時。照見五蘊皆空。

> 以無所得故。菩提薩埵。依般若波羅蜜多故。心無罣
> 礙。無罣礙故。無有恐怖。遠離顛倒夢想。究竟涅槃。
>
> （《心經》）

修行成就的菩薩的慈悲和智慧圓滿成就，竭力將所有
眾生「我們」從困苦的「此岸」接引到困苦熄滅涅槃寂靜的
「彼岸」。雖然這個無窮盡的願景和使命不可思議，但菩薩
的心是真正的自由、無所畏懼、無所罣礙。因為他可以明白
菩薩和眾生都是緣起無我，所以無所求亦無所得。他超越了
菩薩和眾生、領袖和下屬的身分認同，超越任何二元論的
妄念。

佛陀在《金剛經》中進一步探討這種覺醒，他教導須菩
提：「善男子善女人發阿耨多羅三藐三菩提心。應如是住。
如是降伏其心。」「所有一切眾生之類……我皆令入無餘涅
槃而滅度之。如是滅度無量無數無邊眾生。實無眾生得滅度
者。」菩薩令人難以置信的成就是他可以真正踐行無我、無
相的領導和使命，引領無量的眾生脫離困苦：菩薩沒有執取
於任何外在的假相：他自己、任何人、任何有情的眾生、任
何時間概念，否則就不能成就圓滿的慈悲和智慧而證菩薩的
果位：「若菩薩有我相。人相。眾生相。壽者相。即非菩

薩。」由於菩薩不著相，他亦不會執著於自己為他人布施和慈悲的行為：

> 復次。須菩提。菩薩於法。應無所住。行於布施。所謂
> 不住色布施。不住聲香味觸法布施。須菩提。菩薩應如是
> 布施。不住於相。何以故。若菩薩不住相布施。其福德不
> 可思量。
>
> （《金剛經》）

　　佛陀和菩薩對領導模式的啟發在於，領導者不必自視為領導者或照顧者。他們應通過領導、慈悲和智慧以利益他人，明瞭他們所提供的關懷、慈悲和領導實際上是緣起和無我的，他們的能力亦是不可思量、無法估量的。佛陀在《金剛經》中教導，引發阿耨多羅三藐三菩提心的菩薩，應如何安住他的心。佛陀闡述道：

> 是故須菩提。菩薩應離一切相。發阿耨多羅三藐三菩
> 提心。不應住色生心。不應住聲香味觸法生心。應生無所
> 住心。
>
> （《金剛經》）

　　更重要的是，佛陀在《金剛經》澄清說即使發阿耨多羅三藐三菩提心的大願亦是緣起和無我的：「須菩提。菩薩亦如是。若作是言。我當滅度無量眾生。即不名菩薩。何以故。須菩提。實無有法。名為菩薩。」關於領導力模式討

論，《金剛經》的重要啟發是即使服務或領導或做為下屬或領導者的動機，也可能成為真正領導和服務的障礙。

三、緣起的身分認同

為了解釋這個世界上事物的生起和壞滅，佛陀駁斥當時其他思想流派所倡導的二元論觀點。他宣稱緣起法：「此有故彼有，此生故彼生」和「此無故彼無，此滅故彼滅」。❺ Karunadasa 指出緣起法意味著現象的產生依賴於其他現象的產生，而現象背後沒有任何不變的實質。❻

在個人身分認同方面，佛陀闡明「不論精神或物質上，沒有獨立永恒不變的自我實體」。❼通過將緣起法應用於了解自我和外在世界的關係，我們可以認識到外在世界的核心是無常（anicca），而自我的本質實際上是無我（anatta）。我們通過五種感知的積集（「五蘊」）去認識外在世界和建立自我認同，五蘊是物質（色：rūpa）聚合以及心理的聚合，心理的聚合包括感受／感覺（受：vedanā），認知（想：saññā），心理形成／妄作（saṅkhāra）和意識（viññaṇa）。《滿月大經》說明自我的認同源於我們對感知的執著，進而根據五蘊而構建自我的存在。因為我們誤以為有「感知」就

---

❺ 《自說經》第 1 卷，〈第一品　菩提品〉，《漢譯南傳大藏經》第 26 冊（CBETA, N26, no. 10）。網址：http://tripitaka.cbeta.org/N26n0010_001。

❻ Karunadasa, Y 2001, 'The early Buddhist teaching on the practice of the moral life.' *The Numata Yehan Lecture in Buddhism*, University of Calgary, delivered in Fall 2001, p. 3.

❼ 同前註，頁 3。

應該有「我」的存在去證明合理的連續性。❽《五三經》解釋說自我認同是對感知的根本和自我存在的執取的表達。❾苦難和矛盾的產生正是因為我們以無常（anicca）和非我所能控制的我（anatta）去定義為我。❿這是以無我為實我的錯誤觀點。

一旦我們理解緣起和無我的義理，我們就應該能夠理解菩薩如何以不同的身分和角色去領導、服務和布施。「領導者」身分的概念依賴於「追隨者」而建立，同樣「追隨者」身分的概念也取決於「領導者」的概念而建立——正如教師和學生，醫護者和病患者等等的二元概念的同共生起一樣。值得注意的是，佛教的「無我」指的是遠離對我的執著，既不是對自我的否定，也不是對更大的「非我」的執取。如果我們不理解無我出離二邊的超然意義，即使是僕人式的領導和烈士式的自我犧牲領導行為也可能讓大眾遭受痛苦。

菩薩「無我」的另一個意義是超越任何形式主義：社會地位、工作、種族、性別、年齡、每個人不同的體格、情感和心理能力等等。因為菩薩沒有依繫任何標籤、概念或感

---

❽ 《第一〇九　滿月大經》，《漢譯南傳大藏經》第 11 冊第 12 卷（CBETA, N11, no. 12, p. 297 a03, p. 302 a09）。　網址：http://tripitaka.cbeta.org/N11n0005_012。

❾ 《第一〇二　五三經》，《漢譯南傳大藏經》第 11 冊第 12 卷（CBETA, N11, no. 12, p. 243 a03, p. 251 a10）。　網址：http://tripitaka.cbeta.org/N11n0005_012。

❿ Karunadasa, Y 2015a, Early buddhist teachings: *The middle position in theory and practice*, Centre of Buddhist Studies, The University of Hong Kong, Hong Kong, p. 74.

受，菩薩可以真正與眾生接觸，並以眾生需要的任何方式滿
足他們的需求。正如本文進一步闡述，當菩薩的慈悲和智慧
沒有被任何地方或任何形式所束縛時，他可以真正與所有眾
生接觸。❶

　　緣起的依他起性在《大方廣佛華嚴經》（簡稱《華嚴
經》）中以帝釋天的因陀羅網說明，網中的每一個反映都是
彼此「互即互入」，相互成就，亦成就了整體。每一個眾
生、每一顆微塵都是同樣重要，由一微塵中可以攝入大千世
界。大乘佛教的啟示是我們要超越「追隨者」和「領導者」
的二元性，明瞭兩者之間的依賴性和相互關係：「領導者」
中有「追隨者」，「追隨者」中有「領導者」，你中有我、
我中有你。真正的合作意味著整體的行動和覺醒。一行禪師
建議，要實現任何有意義的改變，我們必須超越「你」和
「我」的二元性。他以因陀羅網來說明互即互入的微妙和真
實意義，如果仔細觀察網上的任何一顆寶珠，我們都可以看
到其表面上反射着所有的其他珠寶。在其他珠寶的反射中，
我們亦可以看到原來的珠寶，及其承載的反射再次被反射，
構成了無窮無盡的反射網。❷由於個體和團體互即互入，我

❶ Dhammajoti, KL 2013, *Reading Buddhist Sanskrit texts: An elementary grammatical guide*, 2nd edn, The Buddha-dharma Centre of Hong Kong, Hong Kong, p. 308.

❷ Thich, NH 2014. *The Diamond Sutra* (A Buddhist Library), http://www.abuddhistlibrary.com/Buddhism/G%20-%20TNH/TNH/The%20Diamond%20Sutra/Dharma%20Talk%20given%20by%20Thich%20Nhat%20Hanh%20on%20December%202014%20IV.htm.

們必須承諾和從自身出發改變，而不是指責或依賴他人或其他有組織的機構。一行禪師寫道：

現在是時候讓我們每一個人覺醒，為自己的生命行動。我們有力量去決定我們地球的命運。如果我們能真正認識現實的情況，我們有能力去改變我們的集體認知。我們要一起行動，去讓大眾一同覺醒。❸

緣起性或相即的作用意味著所謂的領導者和追隨者是相互依存和不可分割的。雖然領導者可能因自身某些質素的成就而被肯定：例如溝通技巧、魅力、技能知識、智慧、道德權威、紀律和堅持不懈等等，但他們的領導力沒有追隨者的存在就無從發揮。最近的一項縱向研究調查身分認同在領導力的發展中的重要作用。❹該研究邀請皇家海軍陸戰隊新招募的軍官，在三十二週內評估他們各自在領導者或追隨者角色上的身分認同。結果表明，雖然自稱為領導者的新軍官獲得了指揮官更高的領導力評級，但那些認同並願意以追隨者身分參與的反而更獲同袍尊重，被視為更具領導力。領導者需要超越「你」和「我」，擁抱「我們」，超越傳統的「領

❸ Thich, NH 2010, 'The bells of mindfulness', in KD Moore & MP Nelson (ed.), Moral ground: Ethical action for a planet in peril, Trinity University Press, Texas, pp. 79-81, esp. p. 80.

❹ Peters, K & Haslam, SA 2018, 'I follow, therefore I lead: A longitudinal study of leader and follower identity and leadership in the marines', *British Journal of Psychology*, vol. 2018, pp. 1-16.

導者」身分。由 Steffens 等學者進行的實地研究，也表明創業家領導者的身分認同（即團隊之間「我們」和「我們的」認同）與更大的工作投入、以及較低的後續工作過勞和離職傾向等等，存在直接的關係。**⓯**

四、佛菩薩的領導模式

佛陀的領導風格或許亦能為我們帶來進一步的啟示。值得注意的是，佛陀從未將自己定位為領袖，更不用說要成為救世主了。然而，他確實致力於深入探索和教導關於生命的重要題目：「四聖諦」── 苦是什麼、苦的根源、苦的止息、以及讓苦止息的道路。佛陀在他生命的早期已展開了對真理的追求，其他人也被他的智慧所吸引去尋求啟蒙。正如 Wijebandara 所揭示一樣，佛陀擁有明確自利利他的願景，以及建基於慈愛和智慧的使命 ── 引領自己和眾生脫離痛苦。**⓰**

佛陀領導的特色亦在於，他以一位善良老師的角度去協助和向他的學生展現眾生成為佛的平等性和可能性。他的領導力是低調和沉穩。因為他理解緣起無我的智慧，他真正謙

⓯ Steffens, NK, Yang, I, Jetten, J, Haslam, SA, Lipponen, J 2018, 'The unfolding impact of leader identity entrepreneurship on burnout, work engagement, and turnover intentions', *Journal of Occupational Health Psychology*, vol. 23, no. 3, pp. 373-387.

⓰ Wijebandara, C 2016, 'The Buddha's concept of leadership', *The Nation* (Thailand Portal), 21 May, viewed 1 May 2018, http://www.nationmultimedia.com/opinion/The-Buddhas-concept-of-leadership-30286428.html.

虛、不受領導者身分認同的影響：

> 我如良醫，知病說藥，服與不服，非醫咎也。又如善
> 導，導人善道，聞之不行，非導過也。
>
> （《佛遺教經》）

Wijebandara 認為，佛陀所展示的領導模式是一種「建立在信任、愛和理解之上的優良領導，需要高度的個人誠信」。❶佛陀通過他自己圓滿的慈悲和持戒、禪定、智慧三無漏學的成就去影響教化他人。因為他正直如實地實踐他所教導的，他備受尊重、信任和敬佩。正如《阿含經增支部‧四集二十三》〈世界經〉所宣稱：「諸比丘！如來行如所說，言如所行，唯行如所言，言如所行，故名如來。」在《本生經‧五三四》〈大鵞本生譚〉中佛陀教導，一個正義之王者有十種美德，這些品質是：

> 布施（dāna）持戒（sīla）更施捨（pariccāga），
> 平直（ajjava）溫和（maddava）且自制（tapa），
> 身體無恚（非憤怒 akkodha）更無害（非暴力 ahimsā），
> 堪能忍辱（khanti）及無對（avirodhana）……

佛教教義中另一個典型的領袖是菩薩。他們是施予者的模範，不會錯過任何機會去竭力踐行本初慈悲和智慧的誓

---

❶ 同前註。

願。正如上文《心經》和《金剛經》中所分析，菩薩以緣起性空、諸法無我的覺知，超越了領導中「領導者」和「追隨者」的身分。菩薩在救度眾生出離困苦的六度（paramita）圓滿成就：布施（dāna）、持戒（śīla）、忍辱（kṣānti）、精進（vīrya）、禪定（dhyāna）、智慧（prajñā）。除了六度圓滿之外，他們亦實踐四攝法（catuḥ-saṃgraha-vastu）：布施（dāna）、愛語（priyavacana）、利行（arthakṛtya）、同事（samānārthatā）。菩薩通過他們富有同情心的行為，深刻的溝通和共享的經驗，與其他眾生深入地聯繫。沒有無我的證悟去容納巨大的慈悲和智慧，去接受眾生所遇到的種種挑戰和困難，這些深入的聯繫是不可能的。

　　為了發展這些個人和領導者的品質，佛陀所教導的戒、定、慧三種學習是基本的修行。在不斷自我修行的過程中，佛陀的核心教義代代相傳，亦按照不同人的發展需要和背景，允許進行定制和多樣化，具有度身定制和真正以人為本的靈活性。這種靈活性讓佛教「依法不依人」、「依義不依語」，不受個人主義或教條主義所局限束縛，與佛教無常和無我的理解互相呼應。下文簡要地介紹戒、定、慧三種學習，這對培養和發展超越個人認知的領導模式至關重要。

五、以修行為領導的基礎

　　佛教中的道德規範，「戒」是道德生活的行（do-s）或不行（don't-s）。它是指導我們內部思惟的過程、外在語言和行為的指南針和價值原則。正如 Karunadasa 所闡明，佛教道德不是至高無上的神祇或佛陀的一項發明。佛陀只是發現

了它，告訴我們去做「你們自己應該做應做的事」。**⑱**外在語言和行為在戒律上的錯犯可能更有害，但比內部思惟的錯犯更容易控制。因此，外在語言和行為在戒律應該是道德生活實踐的前線。**⑲**

道德規範不僅確保了內在心理和外在行為的和諧，它也確保了社區內的和諧。它的建立應該是建基於對人類思想和行為經驗的理解，以及它們對我們身心發展的影響。因此，它應該有利於個人和社會的幸福，是培養穩定的心靈和智慧的基礎。在聖賢人所推崇的的八正道上，道德紀律的實現是以「正語」、「正業」、「正命」去培養圓滿的思想和行為，去改變我們的語言和謀生方式。

道德規範有助歇止道德上不善巧的品質以語言和行為的形式向外呈現，佛教再以兩方面的禪修練習對應：1.「全面生起」的不善巧品質，這種品質由精神上的波動，如負面情緒和激動感受所喚醒；及 2. 在「潛伏」水平，即在表面意識下「睡著」的精神活動。**⑳**這兩方面禪修方法分

---

⑱ Karunadasa, Y 2015a, *Early buddhist teachings: The middle position in theory and practice*, Centre of Buddhist Studies, The University of Hong Kong, Hong Kong, p. 85.

⑲ Karunadasa, Y 2001, 'The early Buddhist teaching on the practice of the moral life.' The Numata Yehan Lecture in Buddhism, University of Calgary, delivered in Fall 2001, p. 17.

⑳ Karunadasa, Y 2015b, 'The role of meditation in the threefold scheme of Buddhist mental culture', in KL Dhammajoti (ed.), Buddhist meditative praxis: Traditional teachings & modern applications, Centre of Buddhist Studies, The University of Hong Kong, Hong Kong, pp. 117-122, esp. p. 119.

別是：1.「止」（samādhi）對「定」（samatha）的修習和2.「觀」（vipassanā）對「慧」（paññā）的修習。我們的思想通常是有分別的。「定」意味著思想專注和心一境性（cittassaekaggatā），是禪那的經驗中（jhānic）的高階部分。佛陀說「定」亦只是一種手段，最終的目標是智慧的實現。**㉑**

在躁動不定、繁雜模糊的 VUCA（volatile, uncertain, complex, and ambiguous）世代，我們受到各種信息和刺激的轟炸。這些信息和刺激以視覺、聲音、氣味、味覺、觸覺和意識型態呈現。我們的精神感官在與外界的接觸當中，通過內在意識對不同感知所接收的信息進行翻譯。但是要真正了解世界，我們不能簡單地以平常的方式思考和行動——即以如常複雜的、無休止的行動和心理過程，不斷去和外在的世界相互作用和擴展。沒有「定」（samādhi）的思惟就有如透過一杯混濁的泥水去看世界一樣。「定」是高度的集中和靜慮的過程，平靜而清澈，所有的灰塵和雜質都沉澱到只剩下清澈透明的水在頂部。在「八正道」中，通過「正精進」、「正念」、「正定」實現心理活動的集中。換句話說，這意味著心理上的專注需要正確的努力（方法論和勤奮），以正確的正念（將心念放在正確的對境所緣），應用正確的定力（焦點）。

智慧在佛教中是對現實世界正確理解的能力，對事物的生起和止息（包括我們的心理和身體活動）的準確和

㉑ 同前註。

如實見解。它「不是某種超出現實經驗的知識……相反，它是對境象存在的最終覺醒」。❷這些正確理解，如無常（anicca），苦（dukkha）和無我（anatta），具有深刻的經驗性。因為它是對境象真實的因果法則，它可以指導我們決策和解決問題，有能力做超越時間和空間的觀察。

在佛教中智慧可以通過「觀」（vipassanā）的禪修清楚地覺察。智慧是「離開判別、編輯、解釋、合理化和證明所觀察到的東西。所有形式的判別和編輯都涉及掌握和執著」。❸佛陀說「看見」的內容或對象是五蘊執取的和合體，它代表了人類對存在和外部現象感知的錯誤概念。❹佛陀在《阿含經中部第九·正見經》中教導通過緣起法對十二因緣（dhātu）的精銳觀察來開發智慧、培養「正見」。

佛教對領導力有兩方面的重要貢獻：1. 詳細解釋「自我」和世界的本質和複雜性；2. 提供洞晰複雜情況的方法——不是通過處理所有節點和變量，而是看清整個系統的相互依存——明白理解所有現象的法則。在「八正道」中，實現智慧是通過「正見」和「正思惟」。「正見」是對世間關係因果法則的理解，一旦我們建立了「正見」，保持不受障礙或干擾影響的「正思惟」則非常重要。

---

❷ 同前註，頁 120。
❸ 同前註，頁 121。
❹ 同前註，頁 119。

六、「緣起」的領導力

　　佛陀和菩薩的領導模式建基於對緣起無我的深刻理解之上，以戒、定、慧和慈悲的圓滿成就去呈現。Kemavuthanon 和 Duberley 的案例研究反映，佛教的領導觀是一個由內到外的過程，培養和連繫我們的思想和行動取向，貫徹我們的心（動機、關懷和愛）、腦（分析能力和智慧）和手（執行能力）。㉕這是從個人利益的第一層面，延伸到利益他人的第二層面，最後是互惠利益的第三層面。㉖

　　現代的社會和科技發展讓「無領導者」的社會運動和合作社㉗有可能、促進「自下而上」、「參與」、「共享」、「謙遜」等領導模式。㉘ Ross ㉙和 Kellerman ㉚等研究分析了領導力的演變，甚至預測了領導力的終結：集中權力的再分配和解散。正如 Ross、Kellerman 和 Kelly ㉛所示，合作

㉕ Kemavuthanon S & Duberley J 2009, 'A Buddhist view of leadership: the case of the OTOP project', *Leadership & Organization Development Journal*, vol. 30, no. 8, pp. 737-758, esp. p. 751.

㉖ 同前註，頁 748-750。

㉗ Ross, C 2012, *The leaderless revolution: How ordinary people will take power and change politics in the twenty-first century*. Blue Rider Press, New York.

㉘ Owens, BP & Hekman, DR 2012, 'Modeling how to grow: An inductive examination of humble leader behaviors, contingencies, and outcomes', The Academy of Management Journal, vol. 55, no. 4, pp. 787-818, esp. p. 810.

㉙ Ross, C 2012, *The leaderless revolution: How ordinary people will take power and change politics in the twenty-first century*. Blue Rider Press, New York.

㉚ Kellerman, B 2012, *The end of leadership*, Harper Business, New York.

㉛ Kelly, M 2012, *Owning our future*, Berrett-Koehler, San Francisco.

社、共同組織和其他公司的各種例子證明了廣泛分散的所有權和領導結構的可行性和優勢。然而，Kelly 和 Ovans ❸並沒有低估傳統領導層在建立願景和使命，以及組織內部協調方面的重要性。

這些「自下而上」的模式與建基於佛法的領導模式不同。雖然「領導者」做為教師、模範、明智的導師、引領者甚至是傳統意義上的領導者等的貢獻都很重要，但是每個成員的貢獻同樣重要。佛法啟發的「緣起領導」模式是一個「相互依存」的領導模式。「相互依存」可以做到真正謙虛，不僅是因為領導放棄了做為教師或領導者的個人化貢獻，亦是因為他們看到緣起無我的關鍵。他們通過在戒、定、慧方面的成就來建立「領導」的合法性和權威。因為他們沒有任何固定的想法或身分認同，他們的領導力充滿同情心和無法估量的可能性。

一行禪師建議：「我們需要一種真正的覺醒和覺悟，去改變我們思考和看待事物的方式。」❸對於如何將自私自利的爭鬥心轉化成同理心，佛教的慈悲和智慧是關鍵。一行禪師提出，實質的改變需要大家出離各種二元分別的觀念，照見互即互入（interbeing）、不一不二的慈悲和智慧。真正

---

❸ Ovans, A 2012, 'When no one's in charge.' *Harvard Business Review*, May, viewed 1 July 2018, https://hbr.org/2012/05/when-no-ones-in-charge.

❸ Confino, J 2012, 'Beyond environment: Falling back in love with mother earth', The Guardian, 20 February, viewed 1 May 2018, http://www.theguardian.com/sustainable-business/zen-thich-naht-hanh-buddhidm-business-values.

的覺醒超越山頭主義或對立面：人類與環境之間、你和我、領導者和追隨者、高收入和低收入者、個人和社會等等。這些二元分別對立的觀點只會讓人們想到兩個獨立的對立體。我們要一同改變，就必須超越這些對立的想法。真正的協作是我中有你、你中有我的。無論是在家庭還是工作上，團結和合作的最大障礙始終是私心。佛法指出我們放不下對自我的執着，由我的妄見而生起「人」和「我」的對立，再而是屬於我的貪愛和執着等等。如果能夠從緣起法認真分析，一個團隊的上司和下屬的關係亦是「此有故彼有」，一個家庭的親屬關係亦是相互依靠而存在。正如市場的供應方和需求方，人和周邊的環境都一樣，只有共贏和共輸。

七、「緣起領導」的實踐

按照上文闡述「緣起領導」的管理特性，佛菩薩的願景、教化和修習可以通過具體的管理模式得到落實。在根本理念上，「緣起領導」由緣起的義理出發，重視因果以及人與人、社會和大自然之間的關係。由於無我，所以在身分上的認同、橫向（即同一階層之間）、縱向（即上級與下級之間）、內外（即團體內部與對外）的關係有不一樣的理解，摒棄自我中心或「山頭主義」的纏縛。模式特別切合在情商和智商有持續和深入虛耗的商界、社會服務界和其他專業，讓領導管理能夠除了在技術上，在「心術」上亦能夠得以提昇和淨化。「緣起領導」模式的權力和領導力建基於內在的修行和道德力量，以無私的「慈悲」與無我的緣起「智慧」，應對世間的種種利益計算和謀略。正如佛、菩薩以無

量的慈悲與智慧去教化眾生，「緣起領導」模式下的領袖亦應以無我的慈悲和智慧去帶領團隊，協助團隊在工作中克服種種的無常和困阻，為團隊內的個人、整體乃至社會及環境的福祉做出貢獻。正如佛教中慈悲、道德和智慧的培養是建基於緣起性空和無我的正見，在八正道、戒定慧三無漏學、止觀雙修和菩薩六度四攝等修學方法上多聞、思惟和修習；「緣起領導」模式的培訓亦需要符合和體現上述的特點，否則不能彰顯「緣起領導」的獨特貢獻。雖然佛教在「緣起」、「道德」、「慈悲」、「智慧」等義理上有獨特的詮釋，但「緣起領導」模式在具體運作中，不需要以佛教的形貌呈現。意思是只要符合「緣起領導」模式的原理，不同宗教、文化、社會背景的領袖都可以運用「緣起領導」，甚至配合其他模式運用。然而，「緣起領導」管理模式和現今社會的領導價值亦有不相容性，例如「緣起領導」模式與自我中心、唯利是圖、自私自利的業務不相容，與可持續發展、具社會責任和重視價值的企業理念和運作較契合。

聖嚴法師在「心五四運動」、「心六倫」及「四種環保」等方面的理論和實踐，正是以人心為本「緣起領導」的部分呈現。當中不但符合「緣起領導」模式建基於緣起性空和無我的正見，在實踐中亦符合八正道、戒定慧三無漏學等修學方法上多聞、思惟和修習的要旨，邀請大眾重新了解自己與社會和環境和關係，可以做為「緣起領導」模式的實踐參考案例，啟發「緣起領導」模式在當今社會實踐的種種可能。聖嚴法師在「心五四運動」、「心六倫」及「四種環保」放下了佛教的標籤，但是沒有遠離佛教的精神。法師指

「心五四運動」中，❸❹「四安」是「提昇人品建立新秩序的主張」、「四它」是「解決人生困境的主張」、「四要」是「面對煩惱安定人心的主張」、「四感」是「幫助自己成就他人的主張」、「四福」是「增進全人類福祉的主張」。❸❺聖嚴法師提倡的「四種環保」亦是從每一個人的「心術」出發，以「心靈環保」保持心靈環境的純淨與安定；「禮儀環保」以心儀、口儀、身儀的淨化，促進他人和我之間的和諧；「生活環保」則提出少欲知足、簡樸自然的生活方式；「自然環保」鼓勵大眾以知福惜福、感恩大地的心態，保護自然環境免受汙染破壞。總括而言，「四種環保」是由個人內心到外在環境的的淨化，是《維摩詰所說經》「隨其心淨，則佛土淨」的實踐。法鼓山提倡「心六倫」是「誠心誠意的心來實踐倫理的觀念和倫理的道德」。

聖嚴法師指出「心六倫」講的倫理，「是講人與人之間，每一個人都應該盡責、負責，自己在什麼身分、什麼立場，就要負起自己應有的責任，擔當自己應盡的義務來……倫理一定是盡責、負責，在什麼立場就做什麼事，是什麼立場的人就說什麼話。」這種角度表面上與和本文所說的超越身分認同有衝突，但佛菩薩能夠做到《妙法蓮華經・觀世音菩薩普門品》所說應以何身得度者，即現何身而為說法，背

---

❸❹ 四安（安心、安身、安家、安業），四要（需要、想要、能要、該要），四它（面對它、接受它、處理它、放下它），四感（感化、感動、感恩、感謝），四福（知福、惜福、培福、種福）。

❸❺ 釋聖嚴，〈心五四運動的時代意義〉，《法鼓》雜誌 120 期，1999 年 12 月 15 日，第 2 版，網址：https://www.ddm.org.tw/maze/120/2-1.HTM。

後的道理就是不執著身分認同的迷思，隨順因緣以不用的角色和眾生的所需調整。在「心六倫」的家庭、校園、生活、自然、職場和族群當中，我們每人都身兼數職，要在不同角色的協同或衝突中保持有效和可持續的領導力，領導者必須超越「領導者」和「追隨者」的二元思維，超越自我身分認同的迷思。特別是在科技和互聯的年代，他們必須看到超越自我、身分和組織概念的所有可能性，並與所有可用資源聯繫起來，以實現其共同願景和使命的最終成功。如果不超越山頭主義、地理位置和時間的人造界限，他們的胸襟和能力只會受到對自身施加的界限所限制。聖嚴法師在「心五四運動」、「心六倫」及「四種環保」的教導有助大眾體現人和社會與環境之間的關係，可說是「緣起領導」模式在社會實踐的入門基礎範例。正如佛菩薩的修行有不同的階次和成就，「緣起領導」模式對領袖來說，隨著在戒定慧三無漏學、八正道、六度四攝等修習的不同層次體現亦有不同成就。在家庭的層面可以成就一家之主、在機構中可以成就首席執行長、在國家政治上成就一國元首、在人類歷史中成就跨越時空的聖者。

　　共享經濟時代需要的不再只是資源的掌控，而是將心比心的慈悲與智慧。因為當知識技術再沒有藩籬，地域時間不再是障礙，剩下的關鍵只是人的「心」。本篇研究嘗試從佛法的角度去探討領導管理，從根本「緣起」和「無我」的義理出發，剖析領導管理的性質和在組織內的身分認同，為領導和管理者的角色重新定位。從每一個人的心開始，去檢視可持續的「緣起領導」管理模式，讓領導管理能夠除了在技

術上，在「心術」上亦能夠得以提昇和淨化，去轉化一個家庭、團體、企業、社會的管治。

參考文獻

一、中文論著

姚秦・鳩摩羅什譯，《金剛般若波羅蜜經》第 1 卷，《大正藏》第 8 冊（CBETA, T08, No. 235）。網址：https://tripitaka.cbeta.org/ja/T08n0235_001，檢索日期：2019 年 3 月 1 日。

唐・三藏法師玄奘譯，《般若波羅蜜多心經》，《大正藏》第 8 冊（CBETA, T08, No. 251）。 網址：https://tripitaka.cbeta.org/ja/T08n0251_001，檢索日期：2019 年 3 月 1 日。

唐・實叉難陀譯，《大方廣佛華嚴經》第 1 卷，《大正藏》第 10 冊（CBETA, T10, No. 279）。 網址：https://tripitaka.cbeta.org/ja/T10n0279_001，檢索日期：2019 年 3 月 1 日。

姚秦・鳩摩羅什譯，《妙法蓮華經卷第七・觀世音菩薩普門品第二十五》，《大正藏》第 9 冊（CBETA, T09, No. 262, p. 56c03）。網址：https://tripitaka.cbeta.org/T09n0262_007，檢索日期：2019 年 3 月 1 日。

姚秦・鳩摩羅什譯，《佛垂般涅槃略說教誡經》（亦名《遺教經》）第 1 卷，《大正藏》第 12 冊（CBETA, T12, No. 389, p. 1112a14）。 網址：https://tripitaka.cbeta.org/T12n0389_001，檢索日期：2019 年 3 月 1 日。

姚秦・鳩摩羅什譯，《維摩詰所說經》第 1 卷，《大正藏》第 14 冊（CBETA, T14, No. 475）。網址：https://tripitaka.cbeta.org/ja/T14n0475_001，檢索日期：2019 年 3 月 1 日。

關世謙譯，《阿含經增支部・四集二十三經》，〈優樓比螺品三〉（世界經），《漢譯南傳大藏經》第 20 冊（CBETA, N20, No. 7, p. 44a05）。網址：http://tripitaka.cbeta.org/N20n0007_004，檢

索日期：2019 年 3 月 1 日。

悟醒譯，《本生經》第 23 卷，〈五三四　大鷲本生譚八八〉，《漢
　　譯南傳大藏經》第 40 冊（CBETA, N40, No. 18, p. 54a04）。網
　　址：http://tripitaka.cbeta.org/ko/N40n0018_023，檢索日期：2019
　　年 3 月 1 日。

通妙譯，《阿含經中部》，〈第九　正見經〉，《漢譯南傳大藏經》
　　第 9 冊（CBETA, N9, No. 5, p. 60a03）。網址：http://tripitaka.
　　cbeta.org/N09 n0005_001，檢索日期：2019 年 3 月 1 日。

釋聖嚴，〈心五四運動的時代意義〉，《法鼓》雜誌 120 期，1999
　　年 12 月 15 日，第 2 版。網址：https://www.ddm.org.tw/maze/
　　120/2-1.HTM。

釋聖嚴，〈心六倫〉，國防部「國軍九十七年重要幹部研習會」，
　　講於國防大學，2008 年 10 月 21 日。網址：http://ethics.ddhsif.
　　org.tw/ethics1.aspx?id=6。

釋聖嚴，《法鼓法音 3：法鼓山的實踐　四種環保》，臺北：財團
　　法人聖嚴教育基金會，2015 年 4 月，二版一刷。網址：http://
　　www.shengyen.org/freebook/pdf/9-3.pdf。

二、西文論著

Cable, D 2018, 'How humble leadership really works.' *Harvard Business
　　Review*, April, viewed 1 May 2018, https://hbr.org/2018/04/how-
　　humble-leadership-really-works.

Confino, J 2012, 'Beyond environment: Falling back in love with mother
　　earth', *The Guardian*, 20 February, viewed 1 May 2018, http://
　　www.theguardian.com/sustainable-business/zen-thich-naht-hanh-
　　buddhidm-business-values.

Dhammajoti, KL 2013, *Reading Buddhist Sanskrit texts: An elementary
　　grammatical guide*, 2nd ed., The Buddha-dharma Centre of Hong

Kong, Hong Kong.

Greenleaf, RF 2018, *The servant as leader—A journey into the nature of legitimate power and greatness*, Paulist Press, viewed 1 May 2018, https://www.essr.net/~jafundo/mestrado_material_itgjkhnld/IV/Lideran%C3%A7as/ The%20Servant%20as%20Leader.pdf.

Inesi, ME, Gruenfeld, DH, Galinsky, AD 2012, 'How power corrupts relationships: Cynical attributions for others' generous acts.' *Journal of Experimental Social Psychology*, vol. 48, no. 4, pp. 795-803.

Karunadasa, Y 2001, 'The early Buddhist teaching on the practice of the moral life.' *The Numata Yehan Lecture in Buddhism*, University of Calgary, delivered in Fall 2001.

Karunadasa, Y 2015a, *Early buddhist teachings: The middle position in theory and practice,* Centre of Buddhist Studies, The University of Hong Kong, Hong Kong.

Karunadasa, Y 2015b, 'The role of meditation in the threefold scheme of Buddhist nental culture', in KL Dhammajoti (ed.), *Buddhist meditative praxis: Traditional teachings & modern applications*, Centre of Buddhist Studies, The University of Hong Kong, Hong Kong, pp. 117-122.

Kellerman, B 2012, *The end of leadership,* Harper Business, New York.

Kelly, M 2012, *Owning our future,* Berrett-Koehler, San Francisco.

Kemavuthanon S & Duberley J 2009, 'A Buddhist view of leadership: the case of the OTOP project', *Leadership & Organization Development Journal*, vol. 30, no. 8, pp. 737-758.

Ovans, A 2012, 'When no one's in charge.' *Harvard Business Review,* May, viewed 1 July 2018, https://hbr.org/2012/05/when-no-ones-in-charge.

Owens, BP & Hekman, DR 2012, 'Modeling how to grow: An inductive examination of humble leader behaviors, contingencies, and outcomes', *The Academy of Management Journal*, vol. 55, no. 4, pp. 787-818.

Peters, K & Haslam, SA 2018, 'I follow, therefore I lead: A longitudinal study of leader and follower identity and leadership in the marines', *British Journal of Psychology*, vol. 2018, pp. 1-16.

Ross, C 2012, *The leaderless revolution: How ordinary people will take power and change politics in the twenty-first century*. Blue Rider Press, New York.

Steffens, NK, Yang, J, Jetten, J, Haslam, SA, Lipponen, J 2018, 'The unfolding impact of leader identity entrepreneurship on burnout, work engagement, and turnover intentions', *Journal of Occupational Health Psychology*, vol. 23, no. 3, pp. 373-387.

Thich, NH 2010, 'The bells of mindfulness', in KD Moore & MP Nelson (ed.), *Moral ground: Ethical action for a planet in peril*, Trinity University Press, Texas, pp. 79-81.

Thich, NH 2014, *The Diamond Sutra* (A Buddhist Library), http://www.abuddhistlibrary.com/Buddhism/G%20-%20TNH/TNH/The%20Diamond%20Sutra/Dharma%20Talk%20given%20by%20Thich%20Nhat%20Hanh%20on%20December%202014%20IV.htm.

Van Dierendonck, D & Patterson, K 2015, 'Compassionate love as a cornerstone of servant leadership: An integration of previous theorizing and research,' *Journal of Business Ethics*, vol. 128, no. 1, pp. 119-131.

Wijebandara, C 2016, 'The Buddha's concept of leadership', *The Nation* (Thailand Portal), 21 May, viewed 1 May 2018, http://www.nationmultimedia.com/opinion/The-Buddhas-concept-of-leadership-30286428.html.

Interdependent Leadership Management Model
—Buddhist Perspectives on Leadership and Management

Ernest C. H. Ng, Ph.D.

Adjunct Assistant Professor, Centre of Buddhist Studies, The University of Hong Kong

▌ Abstract

In the fields of leadership and management studies, there have been substantial research in both academic theories and applied case studies. However, specifically in relation to the management and governance of religious and social organizations, much more practical research is required. By building upon the Buddhist doctrines of "dependent arising" and "selflessness", this research attempts to analyze leadership and management models from the Buddhist perspectives, look into the nature of leadership and management, as well as the sense of identity. By illustrating the realizations of compassion and wisdom of the *Buddha-s* and *Bodhisattva-s*, the Buddhist spirit of selfless vow and genuine care is explained. With reference to the teachings of the *Heart Sutra* and the *Diamond Sutra*, Interdependent Leadership Management Model (ILMM)—a sustainable management model is introduced to exemplify the ideals, teachings and practices of the *Buddha-s* and *Bodhisattva-s*. ILMM is particularly relevant in corporates, social services, other professional fields demanding perseverance against emotional and intellectual drain. Accordingly, leaders can achieve transcendence and purification through not only technical but also "mind" skills. Using the "Fivefold Spiritual Renaissance Campaign", "Six Ethics of the Mind Campaign" and "Four Kinds of Environmentalism" taught by Venerable Sheng

Yen as illustrations, this research further explores the possibility of implementing ILMM to transform the governance of a family, an organization, a corporate and a society beginning from each of our minds.

Keywords: Interdependent Leadership, Management, Sense of Identity, Buddhist Teachings

心靈環保、企業社會責任與公司揭露與實踐永續發展目標之影響因素

李啟華

天主教輔仁大學會計學系副教授

▍摘要

　　一九九二年聖嚴法師提出法鼓山的核心理念「心靈環保」，與之後提出的四種環保、心五四及心六倫，共成一個具有精神理念、具體作法及影響力的體系，也與企業社會責任（CSR）的概念相呼應。聯合國於二〇一五年發布 17 項永續發展目標（SDGs），讓企業能在 CSR 目標設定及履行上有所依循。本研究探討心靈環保與 CSR 及 SDGs 間的呼應關係，也蒐集公司二〇一七年 CSR 報告書中 SDGs 揭露情況與其實踐程度，探討董事會特質、股權結構及利害關係人等因素，是否影響公司揭露及實踐 SDGs。實證結果指出，當公司董事會獨立性高、董事持股質押比率低、員工人數多、公司規模較大及財務績效較佳時，較可能揭露 SDGs 相關資訊，且實踐程度較高；另與供應商的關係較緊密，其 SDGs 實踐程度也較高；然而，當公司負債比率較高時，其 SDGs 實踐程度較低。

關鍵字：心靈環保、企業社會責任、永續發展目標、公司治理

一、緒論

本文探討心靈環保（protecting spiritual environment，以下簡稱 PSE）❶與企業社會責任（corporate social responsibility，以下簡稱 CSR）間的關聯性，也說明近年在 CSR 領域引起風潮的永續發展目標（sustainable development goals，以下簡稱 SDGs），與 PSE 的對應關係。最後，再以實證資料測試公司揭露與實踐 SDGs 的影響因素。

法鼓山創辦人聖嚴法師在一九九二年提出「心靈環保」為法鼓山核心理念（林其賢，2016），也將當年訂為心靈環保年。「心靈環保」❷為運用慈悲及智慧，於生活中面對無常的一切現象，是一種心清淨、行為清淨、語言清淨，而眾生也隨之清淨的，利人利己之價值觀。《維摩詰所說經》所言：「若菩薩欲得淨土，當淨其心；隨其心淨，則佛土淨。」❸，

---

❶ 本文以 PSE 表示心靈環保整體系統，以「心靈環保」表示四環中之一的心靈環保觀念。

❷ 聖嚴法師（2005）說：「觀察無常、體驗無常，若能同時運用《金剛經》的『應無所住而生其心』，便是積極的心靈環保，認知一切現象是無常，包括自然現象、社會現象、生理現象、心理現象，都是無常。……因此，凡事凡物，時時處處，都是在說無生無滅、悲智具足的實相法。一切現象既然都是諸佛的無聲說法，便不會見到跟自己有矛盾的事，也沒有得失利害的事，但有尊重生命，珍惜資源，為眾生的利益、為眾生的苦難，而生起慈悲救濟的事。這是心靈環保的最高境界。」

❸ 《維摩詰所說經·佛國品》：「……菩薩隨其直心，則能發行；隨其發行，則得深心；隨其深心，則意調伏；隨意調伏，則如說行；隨如說行，則能迴向；隨其迴向，則有方便；隨其方便，則成就眾生；隨成就眾生，則佛土淨；隨佛土淨，則說法淨；隨說法淨，則智慧淨；隨智慧

若我們要求得能永續發展的淨土，則須從淨化自心做起，才能
影響環境、影響他人及影響這個世界（聖嚴法師，1997b）。
《華嚴經》言「心佛及眾生，是三無差別」，指出佛的心與
眾生的本心是相同無別的，而佛心就是清淨心；《華嚴經》
又言「心如工畫師，畫種種五陰」、「應觀法界性，一切唯
心造」及「罪性本空由心造，心若滅時罪亦亡」，這三句經
典法語提醒我們，一切的種種虛妄皆由眾生的垢心而生，也
造成世界上的種種災禍，清淨自心讓眾生的本心顯現，則能
成就永續發展之淨土（聖嚴法師，1999）。在創造淨土時，
除有「心靈環保」下的「直心」❹外，也需要具體的實踐方
法。因此，聖嚴法師在一九九四年提出以「心靈環保」為
核心的四種環保（四環）❺，一九九九年的「心五四」❻運
動，及二〇〇七年的「心六倫」❼，則為 PSE 的具體實踐方
式（辜琮瑜，2017；釋果光，2014）。

淨，則其心淨；隨其心淨，則一切功德淨。是故寶積！若菩薩欲得淨
土，當淨其心；隨其心淨，則佛土淨。……」
❹ 聖嚴法師（1997b）說直心是指「心中沒有一定要表現的意見，沒有自我
的成見。沒有要表達什麼，只是隨緣應化，隨機攝化」。
❺ 四種環保：心靈環保、生活環保、禮儀環保及自然環保。
❻ 心五四包括：
　四安：安心、安身、安家、安業。
　四要：需要、想要、能要、該要。
　四它：面對它、接受它、處理它、放下它。
　四感：感恩、感謝、感化、感動。
　四福：知福、惜福、培福、種福。
❼ 心六倫包括家庭倫理、生活倫理、校園倫理、自然倫理、職場倫理及族
群倫理。

聖嚴法師（2011）指出，倫理是人與人之間的互動，而每個人會同時扮演多元的角色，若能善盡每個角色的本分、責任，即為倫理觀念的落實。雖然「心六倫」以人為主體，但以非自然人之企業的角度觀之，也依然適用。過去企業是以追求股東利益極大化為存在目的（Friedman, 1970），而逐漸轉向也重視員工、股東、債權人、顧客、供應商及社會大眾等利害關係人（stakeholders）的權益（Freeman, 1984）。就如同「心六倫」觀念，在追求自利的同時，也尊重及關心他人權利及利益（聖嚴法師，2011），善盡每個角色的本份。因此，隨著保障企業之利害關係人權益的觀念日漸興起，CSR 也成為公司營運上的關注項目。

依據經濟合作發展組織（Organization for Economic Cooperation and Development, OECD）的定義，CSR 是指企業對所有利害關係人，實踐經濟、社會、及環境上的利益，以達成永續發展的商業營運方式。這種 CSR 的定義觀點是源自三重盈餘（triple bottom line, TBL）的概念，此概念是一九九〇年代論述一個公司、消費者及環境的三贏策略（Elkington, 1994），而後發展成衡量 people、planet 及 profit（three Ps）相關績效的會計架構。後續學者將 TBL 分成社會、環境及經濟三部分，而在這三個面向平衡地發展的公司得以永續發展，所以也需將社會及環境績效納入會計報表中衡量公司的整體績效（Slaper and Hall, 2011）。雖然會計報表並未包含社會及環境績效，而是以 CSR 報告書的方式呈現公司的非財務性績效，但依然可以產生正面的效果（Chen et al. 2018; Church et al., 2019）。

　　臺灣法規要求符合產業別或規模條件的公司強制發布 CSR 報告書❽，且須依循全球報導倡議組織（Global Reporting Initiative, GRI）的 GRI Standards 編製，在報告項目、內容及管理方針上以一致方式的呈現，對於應揭露的重大性主題也有規範。然而，各公司在辨認重大性主題後，如何減少負面衝擊及強化正面衝擊上，則較難看到公司間一致性的目標及對全球的影響力。在二○一五年聯合國成立七十週年之際，「聯合國高峰會」17 項永續發展目標（sustainable development goals, SDGs）外及 169 項追蹤指標（target），讓全世界對於未來永續的努力方向有一致的目標。除國際發展組織及國際大型會計師事務所已發布相關應對指南（GRI et al., 2015; KPMG, 2018; PWC, 2018），國際大型會計師事務所 KPMG 調查全球 250 大公司，指出在二○一六年已有 43% 公司將 SDGs 融入於 CSR 報告書之中（KPMG, 2018），國際大型會計師事務所 PWC 在二○一七年針對全球 729 家公司進行調查，發現已有 72% 公司的 CSR 報告書揭露 SDGs（PWC, 2018）；永續報告平台（2020）報告指出，二○一九年臺灣已有 54% 的 CSR 報告揭露 SDGs 相關資訊，顯示將 SDGs 融入 CSR 報告書是編製 CSR 報告書的重要趨勢。

　　過往 CSR 績效決定因素相關文獻指出，董事會特質影

---

❽ 「上市（櫃）公司編製與申報企業社會責任報告書作業辦法」規定，當公司為食品工業、化學工業及金融業者；餐飲收入占其全部營業收入之比率達百分之五十以上者或股本達新臺幣五十億元以上者，皆需編製與申報中文版本之 CSR 報告書。

響 CSR 績效。洪雪卿等（2013）及甄友薇（2016）指出，當公司的董事會規模愈大、設立獨立董事席次、董監持股比率愈高、董事長未兼任總經理及董監事持股質押比率愈低時，公司的 CSR 績效愈好。文獻也指出回應利害關係人為公司是否提供 CSR 資訊的重要因素，所以當公司的外資持股比率、員工人數、同業競爭程愈高時，公司愈可能發布 CSR 相關資訊（甄友薇，2016；吳幸蓁與廖蕙儀，2017；Heal, 2005；Harjoto and Jo, 2011）。另外，身為公司利害關係人之一的會計師，其專業性也影響公司 CSR 的績效表現（杜榮瑞等，2017；Pflugrath et al., 2011; Sun et al., 2017）。此外，公司特質如公司規模、公司成立年數、成長性及環境敏感產業等，也都影響公司是否揭露 CSR 相關資訊（甄友薇，2016；吳幸蓁與廖蕙儀，2017；McWilliams and Siegel, 2001）。

過往文獻以公司出具 CSR 報告書、獲得天下、遠見及臺灣企業永續獎的 CSR 相關獎項，來判斷公司 CSR 績效衡量指標（李秀英等，2011；林怡君，2011；陳彩稚等，2015）。但法規要求二〇一五年起，公司資本額高於 50 億之公司須發布 CSR 報告書，而天下、遠見及臺灣企業永續獎獲獎公司數量少，且需公司主動參賽及繳交報名費，又具有不同類別，不宜直接進行比較。然而，SDGs 是二〇一五年由「聯合國高峰會」提出，有許多全球性組織支持（GRI et al., 2015），且全球企業也積極將其納入 CSR 報告書中（KPMG, 2018; PWC, 2018）。再者，SDGs 是公司自願性採用的以規畫 CSR 策略及表達 CSR 作為及績效的方式之

一，表示公司在 CSR 觀念跟上國際趨勢，也注重其他利害關係人之權益保障。所以本研究以 CSR 報告書揭露 SDGs 與否及其實踐程度，衡量公司的 CSR 績效，探討董事會特質、股權結構及回應利害關係人等因素，如何影響公司於 SDGs 上之表現。

　　本研究由心靈環保的角度詮釋 CSR，藉以補足過往文獻之不足；再者，本研究將對 CSR 之詮釋再延伸至 SDGs，也為過往文獻少見的作法；最後，再以實證結果指出，心靈環保若能善用於公司經營上，更能在 CSR 上發揮公司的能力貢獻於社會之中。因此，本文嘗試將心靈環保對人的行為影響，推論至對公司於 CSR 上的影響，更能具體展現《維摩詰所說經》所示之「隨其心淨，則佛土淨」情境，提供另一種佛法對世間影響力的詮釋角度。

　　本研究後續章節安排如下：第二部分回顧 PSE 與 CSR 呼應關係、臺灣 CSR 揭露相關規定、SDGs 介紹及與 PSE 間的對應關係，及回顧 CSR 揭露之決定因素相關文獻及建立假說；第三部分為研究方法、樣本選取說明；第四部分為研究結果；第五部分為結論。

二、文獻探討及假說建立

　　本研究第二部分將探討聖嚴法師提及之心靈環保與 CSR 間的關係，說明臺灣目前 CSR 相關法規，介紹 SDGs 及其與 PSE 的對應關係，及回顧 CSR 揭露之決定因素。

（一）心靈環保與 CSR

聖嚴法師於一九八九年提出「環保，從心做起」的觀念，隨著「四眾佛子共勉語」提出及「法鼓山的共識」建立後，將一九九二年訂為心靈環保年，向社會大眾推動「心靈環保」（辜琮瑜，2017；釋果光，2014；Shi, 2014）。聖嚴法師（1997a）說，若人心受到汙染，環境也必定被汙染，也連帶汙染精神環境，所以我們不但保護物質環境，更重要的是淨化人心。推動心靈環保是推廣核心精神理念，須藉由四環、心五四及心六倫這些具體行動方針來達成，與《維摩詰所說經》的方式一致。

CSR 大致上可分成環境、社會及治理（ESG）三個層面。環境層面是指對生物多樣性、溫室氣體排放、廢水排放等環境汙染與控制事項，而四環的「自然環保」與「生活環保」及心六倫的「自然倫理」與「生活倫理」都提醒大眾對自然環境的大地、空氣及水的珍惜及善用。四福的「知福」、「培福」及「種福」勸請大眾一同友善十方一切眾生，創造良好的環境給下一代。一九八七年世界環境與發展委員會（World Commission on Environment and Development, WCED）將永續定義為「滿足當代的需要，而同時不損及後代子孫滿足其本身之需要之發展」，與四要的「能要」及「該要」的精神相同。

社會層面包括，勞工的工作環境與安全、社區及其住民與顧客的共好、同產業公司間之互動。心六倫的「家庭倫理」可延伸至社區，「生活倫理」也告訴我們除了自我的方

便，也要顧及他人的感受。校園倫理指出對學生能因材施教，而職場倫理則指導創造有益員工成長及發揮所長的工作環境，也要生產好的產品來回饋大眾。而四福的「培福」及「種福」則引導生產者能「正命生產」，生產有利於顧客的產品，賺取合理的報酬（釋果光，2014）。四福的「培福」及「種福」也說明，應善待員工、社區及其他利害關係人，創造未來良好互動的因緣。

　　治理則為資訊透明度、公司績效及兼顧不同股東之權益。四安的「安業」指出，每個人都應在自己的工作上盡心盡力，利人利己；四要的「能要」及「該要」也提醒在工作只拿取應該領取的合理報酬，不正當的報酬則應予拒；而四福的「培福」及「種福」，則是說明當我們在逆境之中，表示我們的福報不足，更需了解「培福」及「種福」的重要性。

　　在以四它、四感的「感恩」、「感謝」及「感化」、四福的「知福」、四要的「需要」與「想要」、四安的「安心」、「安身」及「安家」為精神，以 CSR 之環境、社會及治理相關的四環、心五四及心六倫為方針，而四感的「感動」則呼應對社會的影響力。因此，本研究認為 PSE 與 CSR 的精神、作法及效果的方向有許多相呼應之處。本研究依 CSR 過程及要素種類，將心靈環保精神及具體方針，整理如表一。

表一：CSR 與 PSE

CSR	PSE
態度及理念	四環—心靈環保 四它—面對它、接受它、處理它、放下它 四福—知福、惜福 四要—需要、想要 四安—安心、安身、安家
環境層面	四環—自然環保、生活環保 心六倫—自然倫理、生活倫理 四福—培福、種福 四要—能要、該要
社會層面	心六倫—家庭倫理、校園倫理、生活倫理、職場倫理 四福—培福、種福
治理層面	四安—安業 四要—能要、該要 四福—培福、種福
影響力	四感—感動

資料來源：本研究整理。

（二）CSR 相關法規

　　金融監督管理委員會（金管會）以漸進的方式推動 CSR，讓臺灣資本市場與國際接軌。二〇一〇年二月臺灣證券交易所（證交所）及證券櫃檯買賣中心（櫃買中心）共同製定「上市（櫃）公司 CSR 實務守則」。此守則的目標為協助上市上櫃公司實踐 CSR，並促成經濟、環境及社會之進步，以達永續發展之目標。以落實推動公司治理、發展永續環境、維護社會公益及加強 CSR 資訊揭露為原則，協助公司實踐 CSR。（李秀玲，2010）

　　為提昇公司實踐 CSR 之強度，金管會於二〇一四年九月督導證交所及櫃買中心製定「上市（櫃）公司編製與申

報 CSR 報告書作業辦法」。此作業辦法規定，符合規定之上市櫃公司須編製與申報二〇一五年版中文版之 CSR 報告書。「上市（櫃）公司編製與申報 CSR 報告書作業辦法」之第二條規定，依據「上市（櫃）公司產業類別劃分暨調整要點」，分類為食品工業、化學工業及金融業者；餐飲收入占其全部營業收入之比率達百分之五十以上者；股本達新臺幣一百億元以上者，皆須編製與申報中文版本之 CSR 報告書。為了擴大適用範圍，讓更多公司能提供非財務資訊予利害關係人，也藉此讓公司檢視 CSR 的善盡程度，二〇一五年修改為股本 50 億元以上之公司，須發布二〇一六年版之 CSR 報告書。

依永續報告平台（2017）指出，以營運據點為臺灣之臺資企業、外商及其他組織機構，在二〇一五年度及二〇一六年度共發布 384 及 485 本 CSR 報告書。以二〇一六年度 CSR 報告書為例，首次、第二次及第三次發布者為 65、186 及 72 家公司，顯示約 300 家公司，為因應法規及利害關係人而開始發布 CSR 報告書，占全部報告書的 70%。因為發布 CSR 報告書的公司數量大幅增加，未來已不適合以公司發布 CSR 報告書與否來衡量公司的 CSR 績效，所以公司的 CSR 報告書也從重量逐漸進入重質的階段。

（三）SDGs 之重要性及其與「PSE」之關係

「聯合國發展高峰會」二〇一五年積極實踐平等與人權的前提下，提出 17 項「永續發展目標」❾及 169 項指標，此方針同時兼顧經濟成長、社會進步及環境保護等三大面向，做

為全球在二○三○年期望達成之 SDGs 方針。SDGs 的提出，讓公司在執行 CSR 時有較具體對應的努力目標，同時全球型組織及大型會計師事務所也推出相關的實務操作手冊❿。協助公司能藉由 SDGs 之架構，分析出合適公司的 CSR 目標，進而將這些目標融入營運策略中，而在提昇股東權益的同時，也兼顧利害關係人權益、環境保護及提昇全球人類的生活品質。

至二○三○年 SDGs 的達成過程中，將創造關於 12 兆美元的產值及數以百萬計的工作機會（PWC, 2018）。在 KPMG（2017）的報告中指出，全球 250 大公司的 40% 已在二○一六年發布的 CSR 報告書中揭露 SDGs；PWC（2018）以全球 729 家大型公司為調查對象，指出 72% 的公司在 CSR 報告書中提及 SDGs。臺灣公司在二○一六、二○一七、二○一八及二○一九年報告書中揭 SDGs 之比率分別為 8.4%、28%、44% 及 59%，呈現逐年大幅度成長之趨勢，足見 SDGs 之重要性（永續報告平台，2018、2019、2020）。

---

❾ SDGs 的 17 項目標分別為，SDG1：消除貧窮、SDG2：終結飢餓、SDG3：健康與福祉、SDG4：優質教育、SDG5：性別平等、SDG6：乾淨水資源、SDG7：可負擔能源、SDG8：良好工作與經濟成長、SDG9：工業化、創新及基礎建設、SDG10：消弭不平等、SDG11：有韌性的城鄉、SDG12：責任消費及生產循環、SDG13：氣候變遷對策、SDG14：海洋生態、SDG15：陸地生態、SDG16：公平、正義與和平、SDG17：全球夥伴關係。

❿ GRI、UN 及 WBCSD 提供 SDGs Compass；GRI 及 UN 提出 Integrated the SDGs into corporate reporting: a practical guide；KPMG 提供 How to report on the SDGs: what good looks like and why it matters；PWC 提供 From promise to reality: Does business really care about the SDGs?。

另外，在二〇一八年臺灣也參考聯合國於二〇一五年公布之SDGs，根據臺灣現況及需要，訂定適合臺灣的 SDGs（張理國，2018）。因此，SDGs 之採用、評估方式及達成水準，對實務探討及學術研究都具有相當之價值，是需深入探討之重要議題。

SDG1：消除貧窮，二〇一五年全球約有 7.3 億人口生活在極度貧窮的條件下（UN, 2019），不只需要國際的及時援助，也需要幫助這些國家能擺脫貧窮。SDG2：終結飢餓，全球有將近 8 億人活在飢餓之中，尤其以發展中國家情況更為嚴重。協助的方式上除了捐助糧食外，也可以智慧及友善環境的方式協助這些國家的農業永續經營。為達成以上二項目標需要擁有者珍惜資源及食物，再將超過所需的部分與有需要的人分享，與四福相關。SDG3：健康與福祉，因為貧窮及營養不良，再加上對於健康及醫療的知識不足，開發中國家的健康情況差於其他國家，也造成原可預防的疾病對這些地球同胞造成不可逆的損害。他們需要醫療用品外，也需要推廣醫療相關知識的協助。為達成 SDG3，除四福的精神及作為可幫助醫療資源的分享外，心理層面的健康則可藉由四它及四安來達成。SDG4：優質教育，教育是傳遞 SDGs 知識的基礎，不論是提昇農業生產率，尋求合理報酬的工作，甚至愛護環境等素養，也都需要優質教育來協助才能達成。最好的教育是「心靈環保」，而要每個人不分性別、貧富及種族都能有平等的受教權，則需推廣「家庭倫理」、「校園倫理」及「族群倫理」等觀念來精進。

SDG5：性別平權，不論性別應受到一致的對待，也都

應承擔相同的責任。然而在許多開發中國家，女生依然受到不平等待遇。SDG10：消弭不平等，人類除了財富上的差異外，在年齡、性別、身障、種族、人種、出身及宗教都有差別，如何讓我們能一視同仁看待每一位，才能促進一個更和平的未來世界。不論性別、年齡、身障、種族、人種、出身及宗教都能受到平等的對待，人類則可依心六倫而行，再加上具有「心靈環保」的理念，則能無二地平等待人。

SDG6：乾淨水資源，全球處於水資源不足的情況，而且也常因汙水未妥善處理而汙染水源，造成疾病至甚至死亡。再者，氣候變遷也造成水資源不易保留。SDG7：可負擔資源，全球依然有數億人過著無電以供日常烹煮、取暖、工作及學習的生活；在有電可用的地方，主要以石化燃料發電，排放溫室氣體及加劇氣候變遷。SDG12：責任消費與生產循環，隨著地球人口增加及各國經濟成長，人類的消費量也隨之增加，然而地球都無法支撐如此的消費及廢棄方式。SDG13：氣候變遷，因大量使用化石燃料，碳排放的日漸增加造成氣候暖化及極端氣候，其對應策略分成減少石化燃料使用及調適準備二類，以減緩人類受到氣候變遷的衝擊。為達成以上四個SDGs目標除需大家「知福」及「惜福」善用資源外，也可藉由了解「想要」及「需要」的差異，減少不必要的消費，也減緩氣候變遷的衝擊。再者，「自然環保」也提醒我們需愛惜大自然，善用而非濫用。

SDG8：良好的工作與經濟成長，在追求經濟成長的同時，也出現員工過勞及童工問題，讓我們思索如何在永續的狀況下追求經濟發展。企業可能因節省薪資的考量，而導致

過勞及童工現象，若能重視「職場倫理」，也能「感恩」及「感謝」員工的付出，及重視員工的家庭及下班後生活品質，則應提供合理的工作環境及薪資，也能減少童工的情況。

SDG9：工業化、創新及基礎建設，開發中國家迫切需要基礎建設來推動經濟成長，而已開發國家應強化災後盡速恢復的基礎設施的能力，也要讓所有人都能公平地參與產業，及以創新的方式創造永續的產業。SDG11：有韌性的城市，城市化人口比率逐漸提昇，導致住宅不足、建物老化、公安、空氣汙染、垃圾、貧富差距等待解決的問題，另外，也需減低災害的衝擊，打造一個具有韌性的城市。這二項目標都關於城鄉及貧富之間的差距，PSE 在此處的指導作法是四福，即得利益者應惜福，也可以「培福」及「種福」地協助有需要的人。

SDG14：海洋生態，海洋是生命的起源，也具有吸收碳排的重要功能。目前海洋遭受重大汙染外，海中的魚類也被濫捕。SDG15：陸地生態，隨著陸地被開發的面積逐漸擴大，也有愈來愈多的生物滅絕，然而生物多樣性的喪失卻使人類的生存受到威脅。這二項關於大自然的議題，與「自然環保」及「自然倫理」相關，也可以運用想要與需要的觀念減少對大自然的破壞，取所當取及應取的份量。

SDG16：公平、正義與和平，地球上有人生存在司法相對公平，環境相對和平的國度，但也有許多人遭受到暴力、政治迫害及司法不公。對他人的遭遇要感同深受，不因自己的私利而迫害他人，需要「心靈環保」、「能要」、「該

要」及「職場倫理」等觀念的熏陶，才能達成這項目標。最後一項目標 SDG17：全球夥伴關係，SDGs 的達成除需要個人及各國的努力外，也需要國家、企業、消費者、研究者等的共同合作才能達成，有效的夥伴關係才能創造永續的全球生存環境。現時的狀態是因緣和合而成，非只是單人或單方面之力就能達成，應以「感恩」及「感謝」的心態看待已達成的成就。因曾受助於人，也要集合眾人之力一起為全球的人類、動植物及大地之永續發展而努力，需以「感化」及「感動」的方式邀請大家一起盡己之力，達成全人類二〇三〇年的共同目標。

表二：心靈環保與 SDGs

心靈環保	SDGs
四環：心靈環保、生活環保、禮儀環保及自然環保	SDG4、SDG5、SDG6、SDG7、SDG10、SDG12、SDG13、SDG14、SDG15、SDG16
四安：安心、安身、安家、安業	SDG3
四要：需要、想要、能要、該要	SDG6、SDG7、SDG12、SDG13、SDG14、SDG15、SDG16
四它：面對它、接受它、處理它、放下它	SDG3
四感：感恩、感謝、感化、感動	SDG8、SDG17
四福：知福、惜福、培福、種福	SDG1、SDG2、SDG3、 SDG6、SDG7、SDG9、SDG11、SDG12、SDG13
心六倫：家庭倫理、生活倫理、校園倫理、自然倫理、職場倫理及族群倫理	SDG4、SDG5、SDG8、SDG10

資料來源：本研究整理。

（四）揭露 CSR 報告書決定因素相關文獻及假設建立

本研究探討公司 CSR 報告書揭露之影響因素，分成董事會特質、股權結構、利害關係人及其他控制變數進行文獻分析，並依此建立公司揭露及實踐 SDGs 影響因素的研究假說。

董事會為公司治理的重要機制，可以適時監督公司及給予公司合適營運建議（Fama and Jensen, 1983）。當董事會規模較大時，個別董事依其不同專長來協助及監督公司外，也較能分工善盡董事職責，除保障股東的權益外，也可監督公司是否善盡 CSR（洪雪卿等，2013；甄友薇，2016；陳振遠等，2017）。獨立性是董事會的一個重要特質，Armstrong 等（2012）研究指出，因獨立董事需較透明的資訊以執行職務，所以可能因聘任獨立董事而提昇公司的資訊透明度；陳振遠等（2017）也指出，獨立董事席次較多時，公司 CSR 績效也較佳；且 Baldenius 等（2018）也指出、一個友好的董事會易造成管理階層進行損害公司價值的行為。換言之，當公司董事會獨立性增加時，公司的 CSR 績效較佳，且 CSR 相關資訊揭露也較多。本研究推論董事會獨立性能提昇公司於非財務資訊之透明度，也提昇 CSR 報告書揭露程度。總經理對公司的 CSR 政策具有重大影響力（Davidson et al., 2019），而董事長兼任總經理除削弱董事會的獨立性及監督功能，也影響公司的揭露政策（Gul and Leung, 2004），損及公司內部治理機制（Core et al., 1999），故推論公司可能因此減少 CSR 資訊之揭露。基於

上述文獻分析，本研究建立假說一如下：

H1. 董事會特質影響公司 SDGs 揭露及其實踐程度

Yermack（1996）指出，董事持股比率高時，其對公司績效的依存度較高，也因此較注重公司整體利益。而公司進行 CSR 活動可以提昇客戶忠誠度、減少公司風險（Dhaliwal et al., 2011; Albuquerque et al., 2019）及產生保險效果（Godfrey et al., 2009），所以董事持股高可能為公司利益而進行 CSR 活動。然而，Morck 等（1988）認為，董事持股與公司價值間並非為線性關係，所以董事股持增加時，也可能因自身私利而損害公司價值。但是當董事持股質押比率高時，公司較可能因私利而損害公司價值（Yeh et al., 2003），且公司的 CSR 績效較差（洪雪卿等，2013）。因此，本研究認為董事持股對 SDGs 效績效及揭露有影響，但無法確認其影響方向，而董事持股質押比率，則會造成較差的 SDGs 績效及揭露。

機構投資人為專業性投資人，具有較高之專業技能使用公司相關資訊進行分析，所以對於資訊的需求性較高（Velury and Jenkins, 2006）；而且，Dhaliwal 等（2012）指出，公司揭露 CSR 報告書將有助分析師降低盈餘預測誤差。另外，Dyck 等（2019）的實證結果指出，機構投資人對公司揭露環境及社會等財務性資訊具有正向影響。因此，本研究預期機構投資人持股高之公司，為回應其資訊需求，較可能揭露及實踐 SDGs。綜合上述文獻分析，本研究建立假說二如下：

H2. 股權結構影響公司 SDGs 揭露及其實踐程度

衝突解決假說（conflict-resolution hypothesis）認為，公司為減緩股東與非股東之利害關係人間的利益不一致，所以公司實行 CSR 活動以滿足所有的利害關係人之需求（Jensen 2001; Scherer et al., 2006）。Harjoto 與 Jo（2011）實證結果說明，經理人利用 CSR 這項工具，減少利害關係人間的利益衝突，以極大化股東價值。所以當公司的股東與非股東間之利益衝突愈大時，公司較可能實踐 CSR 活動（洪雪卿等，2013；甄友薇，2016；吳幸蓁與廖蕙儀，2017；Heal, 2005; Huang and Kung, 2010; Harjoto and Jo, 2011）。而且公司、股東及其他利害關係人間的信任感，也能促使公司成長及提昇公司獲利（Lin et al., 2017）。因此，本研究探討顧客、供應商、債權人、競爭者及員工等對 CSR 資訊之需求，對公司揭露及實踐 SDGs 之影響。

H3. 回應利害關係人資訊之需求影響公司 SDGs 揭露及其實踐程度

另外，公司規模較大時，其 CSR 花費能加惠於較多之不同產品，具有較低之平均 CSR 單位成本，故較願意投入資源於 CSR 活動（McWilliams and Siegel, 2001）。而且，大公司的政治成本❶較高，較受到社會大眾關注（Watts and Zimmerman, 1986），所以也較有誘因善盡 CSR。Harjoto 與

---

❶ Watts and Zimmerman（1986）在說明規模假說（size hypothesis）指出，當公司規模愈大，愈具有政治敏感度，也被附加較多財富移轉，例如透過租稅的方式進行，所以這類型公司的政治成本也較高。

Jo（2011）研究發現，公司獲利能力較佳時，公司較願意投入資源於 CSR 活動，另也發現投入 CSR 公司具有較高之成長率。另外，吳幸蓁與廖蕙儀（2017）發現公司屬於敏感性產業時，自願揭露 CSR 資訊的可能性較高。因此，本研究加入公司規模、總資產報酬率、營收成長率及敏感性產業等變數，以控制公司特質對 SDGs 揭露及其實踐程度之影響。

三、研究方法

（一）研究樣本與資料來源

　　本研究以臺灣上市櫃公司為研究樣本，探討公司揭露 SDGs 及其實踐程度之決定因素。「聯合國發展高峰會」於二〇一五年發布 17 項之 SDGs，公司可於二〇一六年的社會責任報告書中採用；然而，永續報告平台（2017）指出，二〇一六年版之 CSR 報告書，僅有 40 家公司在報告書回應 SDGs，回應比率僅 8％，而較不具代表性，所以本研究以二〇一七年版報告書為研究樣本。此期間臺灣上市櫃資本額達 50 億元以上之公司，都被強制要求發布 CSR 報告書，包括自願編製 CSR 報告書之公司，計有 458 家上市櫃公司發布 CSR 報告書。

　　本研究至公開資訊觀測站及公司網頁逐一蒐集 CSR 報告書，並以人工方式檢視報告書，判斷公司對 SDGs 的揭露及其實踐程度。在 458 本 CSR 報告書中，有 155 本 CSR 報告書揭露 SDGs；換言之，大約 34% 的 CSR 報告書關注 SDGs，表示臺灣上市櫃公司重視 SDGs 的程度已大幅提昇。

其他財務資訊、公司治理及會計師資料，皆取自臺灣經濟新報社（TEJ）資料庫。經刪除相關財務資料不全樣本後，共計有 375 個觀測值進行後續測試及分析。

　　表三為公司 CSR 報告書揭露 SDGs 與否之樣本產業分布情況，整體樣本有近 35% 之 CSR 報告書揭露 SDGs 相關資訊。以全部樣本為比較基礎，電子業及金融業揭露 SDGs 公司家數（比例）分別為 49 家（13.07%）及 18 家（4.80%）。若以產業 CSR 報告書總數為基礎⓬，提及 SDGs 比例較高之產業為塑膠工業（55%）、航運業業（50%）、金融業（46%）、電子業（38%）及食品業（38%），此五產業之 CSR 報告書提及 SDGs 比例高於全樣本平均值（35%）；然而，觀光業（9%）、生技醫療（13%）、化學工業（17%）、貿易百貨（27%）、建材營造（27%）及鋼鐵工業（27%），則是產業 SDGs 揭露比例低於全樣本平均值。可見產業特性影響公司於 CSR 報告書上的呈現方式及揭露資訊上的選擇。

⓬ 為避免產業總家數過少造成百分比不具參考價值，本研究針對產業總家數 10 筆以上之產業進行比較。

表三：CSR 報告書揭露 SDGs 之樣本產業分布狀況

產業代號	產業名稱	CSR 報告書是否揭露 SDGs 之觀測值筆數						
		有揭露 SDGs（公司數）	比例（％）	未揭露 SDGs（公司數）	比例（％）	合計（公司數）	產業比例（％）	產業揭露 SDGs 比例（％）
1	水泥工業	2	0.53	3	0.80	5	1.33	40.00
2	食品工業	8	2.13	13	3.47	21	5.60	38.10
3	塑膠工業	6	1.60	5	1.33	11	2.93	54.55
4	紡織工業	2	0.53	7	1.87	9	2.40	22.22
5	電機機械	4	1.07	8	2.13	12	3.20	33.33
6	電器電纜	1	0.27	1	0.27	2	0.53	50.00
8	玻璃陶瓷	1	0.27	0	0.00	1	0.27	100.00
9	造紙工業	3	0.80	1	0.27	4	1.07	75.00
10	鋼鐵工業	3	0.80	8	2.13	11	2.93	27.27
11	橡膠工業	1	0.27	3	0.80	4	1.07	25.00
12	汽車工業	4	1.07	0	0.00	4	1.07	100.00
14	建材營造	4	1.07	11	2.93	15	4.00	26.67
15	航 運 業	5	1.33	5	1.33	10	2.67	50.00
16	觀 光 業	1	0.27	10	2.67	11	2.93	9.09
17	金 融 業	18	4.80	21	5.60	39	10.40	46.15
18	貿易百貨	3	0.80	8	2.13	11	2.93	27.27
21	化學工業	6	1.60	30	8.00	36	9.60	16.67
22	生技醫療	2	0.53	14	3.73	16	4.27	12.50
23	油電燃氣	1	0.27	0	0.00	1	0.27	100.00
24	電 子 業	49	13.07	81	21.60	130	34.67	37.69
32	文化創意	0	0.00	1	0.27	1	0.27	0.00
20	其 他	7	1.87	14	3.73	21	5.60	33
	合計	131	34.93	244	65.07	375	100.00	

（二）應變數定義

本研究以逐一檢視 CSR 報告書判斷公司是否揭露 SDGs，當公司有回應 SDGs 時，SDG_D 為 1，其餘為 0。除公司是否揭露 SDGs 相關資訊外，本研究另探討公司實踐 SDGs 程度。參考永續報告平台（2019）的評分標準，本研究將公司「提及 SDGs」時，設定為 1 分；有說明「相關作為」時，設定為 2 分；有說明此目標的「展現績效」時，設定為 3 分；有針對 SDGs「設定目標」時，設定為 4 分；有提出「未來改善計畫」時，設定為 5 分。SDGs 的實踐上，應以與公司營運活動最相關的目標為焦點，讓其發揮最大的影響力，而非項目愈多愈好（GRI et al., 2015; KPMG, 2018; PWC, 2018）。因此，本研究將 1 分以上的項目，取平均分數，獲得公司實踐 SDGs 程度之指標（SDG_{AVE}）。

（三）自變數定義

本研究自變數分成四類，分別是董事會特質、股權結構及利害關係人三類，另外也包括一些控制變數。董事會協助公司擬定大方向之策略，也對管理階層進行監督。當董事會人數較多時，能聚集不同特長的專業人士為公司尋求永續發展的不同方案；然而董事會人數多時也可能造成議事不易取得共識，造成議事效率不佳（Yermack, 1996），所以本研究預期董事會規模（$BDSIZE$）影響公司揭露及其實踐 SDGs 的程度，而不預期其影響方向。Armstrong 等（2014）指出當公司董事會獨立性較高可降低公司資訊不對稱，以顧及財務

報表使用者的權益。而臺灣上市櫃公司以家族企業居多數，為平衡董事會兼顧其他股東及利害關係人的利益，主管機關引入以專業為考量的獨立董事制度，藉由獨立董事的獨立性及專業性提昇公司治理之成率，所以本研究預期董事會獨立性（INDDIR）有利於公司揭露及其實踐 SDGs。然而，總經理兼任董事長將減弱董事會的獨立性及監督功能，而影響公司的揭露政策（Gul and Leung, 2004），所以本研究預期總經理兼任董事長（DUALITY）將不利於公司揭露及其實踐 SDGs 程度。

　　股權結構變數包括董事持股比率、董事持股質押比率及機構投資人持股比率。董事持股較高時，會注重公司整體利益（Yermack, 1996），但也可能因顧及自身利益而損及公司價值，所以本研究將董事持股比率（BDHOLD）視為影響因子之一（Morck et al., 1988），然而不預期其係數方向。而當董事持股質押比較高時，則董事會作為較可能損及公司價值（Yeh et al., 2003），在 CSR 作為上較不積極（洪雪卿等，2013），所以本研究預期董事持股質押比（PLEDGE）對公司揭露及其實踐 SDGs 有負向影響。另一個股權結構對公司在實踐 SDGs 上有影響的變數為機構投資人持股，因其對資訊的需求較高（Velury and Jenkins, 2006），公司為回應此項需求，較可能提供 SDGs 的相關資訊，本研究預期機構投資人持股（INTHOLD）對公司揭露及其實踐 SDGs 具有正向的影響。

　　除董事會特質及股權結構外，本研究另探討利害關係人對公司揭露及其實踐 SDGs 程度的影響。顧客是公司的重

要利害關係人，對於零售及顧客導向的公司更重視顧客的觀感，尤其是銷售差異化商品的公司更加重視（Albuquerque et al., 2019），所以較願意從事慈善公益等 CSR 活動（Gautier and Pache, 2015）。本研究以廣告費用率衡量顧客與公司間的緊密程度，預期廣告費率（ADV）較高的公司，其揭露意願及實踐 SDGs 的程度較高。本研究以存貨週轉率衡量公司與供應商之間的緊密程度（INVTURN），預期對揭露及實踐 SDGs 具有正向影響（Huang and Kung, 2010）。為激起員工的熱情，以提昇對公司的向心力，公司的 CSR 活動從只是提供資源的冷貢獻（cold contribution），轉換成讓員工參與公益活動的暖貢獻（warm contribution）（Gautier and Pache, 2015），而且員工滿意度也能提昇公司價值（Edmans, 2011），所以本研究預期員工人數（EMP）愈多時，公司揭露及其實踐 SDGs 的程度愈高。公司負債比（DEBT）愈高時，公司運用資金的限制愈高，較不會投入報酬率不確定的 CSR 活動（Krüger, 2015），所以公司的代理問題較小。因此，公司較不需要藉由 CSR 活動來減緩與利害關人間的衝突程度，本研究預期負債比率對公司揭露及其實踐 SDGs 程度有負向影響。Huang 與 Kung（2010）指出，產業競爭程度（HHI）愈高，會促使公司揭露較多的環境相關資訊供利害關係人決策之用，本研究預期 SDGs 實踐程度有正向影響。本研究也另外控制公司規模（SIZE）、公司績效（ROA）及敏感產業（SIND）對公司揭露及其實踐 SDGs 程度之影響（吳幸蓁與廖蕙儀，2017；Huang and Kung, 2010）。

自變數定義如下：

BDSIZE ：董事會規模，本研究以董事會董事席次衡量董事會規模。

INDDIR ：董事會獨立性，以獨立董事席次占全體董事席次比率計算。

DUALITY ：董事長是否兼任總經理，當公司董事長兼任總經理時，其值為1，其餘為0。

BDHOLD ：董事持股比率，董事持股占總流通在外股數之比率。

PLEDGE ：董事持股質押比率，董事設質股數占董事持股數之比率。

INTHOLD ：機構投資人持股比率，機構投資人持股占總流通在外股數之比率，機構投資人包括政府機構、本國金融機構、本國信託基金及外國法人持股（外資）。

ADV ：客戶關係，以廣告費用率衡量企業與客戶間的緊密程度，廣告費用除營業收入。

INVTURN ：供應商關係，以存貨週轉率衡量企業與供應商的關係緊密程度。

EMP ：員工人數，企業員工人數取自然對數衡量員工對公司 CSR 的影響。

DEBT ：債權人影響力，以負債比率衡量債權人對公司的影響力，負債比率為總負債除總資產之比率。

HHI ：產業競爭程度，以 HHI（Herfindahl-Hirschman Index）衡量產業的競爭程度。

SIZE ：公司規模，以公司總資產取自然對數衡量公司規模對實行 CSR 之影響。

ROA ：營運績效，以總資產報酬率衡量公司營運績效。

SIND ：敏感產業，因為水泥、化學、造紙、鋼鐵及油電燃氣等產業者，生產過程產生較大的環境成本，而電子業為臺灣的龍頭產業，較受社會大眾關注，所以本研究將水泥、化學、造紙、鋼鐵、電子及油電燃氣等產業，設定為敏感性產業。當公司屬水泥、化學、造紙、鋼鐵、電子及油電燃氣等產業時，其值為1，其餘為0。

（四）研究模型與變數定義

本研究探討公司揭露 SDGs 及其實踐程度之決定因素，建構下列迴歸模型，式中相關變數之定義說明如後。當應變數為指示變數 SDG_D 時，下式則為 logit 迴歸模型；當應變數為 SDG_{AVE} 時，為最小平方法迴歸模型。

$$SDG_i=\alpha+\sum_{(j=1)}^{3}\beta_j\,BoardCharacteristics_i+\sum_{(k=1)}^{3}\beta_k\,ShareholdingStructure_i$$
$$+\sum_{(l=1)}^{5}\beta_l\,StakeHolders_i+CV_i+\varepsilon_i$$

其中 $BoardCharacteristics_i$ 為董事會特質變數，包括董事會規模、董事會獨立性及董事長兼任總經理；$ShareholdingStructure_i$ 為股權結構變數，包括董事持股比、董事持股質押比及機構投資人持股；$StakeHolders_i$ 為利害關係人緊密程度，包括公司與顧客、供應商、員工、債權人及競爭對手間的緊密程度；控制變數（CV_i）有公司規模、公司財務績效及敏感產業等。

四、實證結果

實證結果部分包括，探討變數敘述性統計量，公司揭露 SDGs 與否的分組變數差異比較，最後說明迴歸結果。

（一）敘述性統計量及自變數差異檢定

表四為變數之敘述性統計量，SDG_D 的平均數為 0.349，表示近 35% 的 CSR 報告書揭露 SDGs 相關資訊。SDG_{AVE} 表示 CSR 報告書揭露 SDGs 之分數為 0.727；若以有揭露 SDGs 之報告書為樣本，公司揭露 SDGs 之分數為 2.08，表示平均而言揭露 SDGs 之 CSR 報告書有說明實際作為，而非僅是提及 SDGs 而已。公司董事平均席次為 8.957，董事會之獨立董事次比率平均為 0.324，總經理兼任董事長的公司比率 0.261，外資持股比率約為 55%，敏感性產業占全整

表四：敘述性統計量

變數 [a]	平均數	標準差	最小值	Q1	中位數	Q3	最大值
SDG_D	0.349	0.477	0.000	0.000	0.000	1.000	1.000
SDG_{AVE}	0.727	1.137	0.000	0.000	0.000	1.000	5.000
$BDSIZE$	8.957	2.758	5.000	7.000	9.000	10.000	20.000
$INDDIR$	0.324	0.088	0.143	0.273	0.333	0.400	0.600
$DUALITY$	0.261	0.440	0.000	0.000	0.000	1.000	1.000
$BDHOLD$	0.216	0.166	0.017	0.092	0.174	0.294	0.878
$PLEDGE$	0.083	0.159	0.000	0.000	0.000	0.106	0.754
$INTHOLD$	0.551	0.216	0.019	0.382	0.579	0.718	0.996
ADV	0.003	0.009	0.000	0.000	0.000	0.002	0.081
$INVTURN$	13.538	44.431	0.000	3.290	5.495	8.515	442.150
EMP	7.482	1.603	3.178	6.310	7.388	8.726	10.507
$DEBT$	0.478	0.214	0.032	0.315	0.466	0.624	0.963
HHI	0.150	0.165	0.023	0.062	0.091	0.172	0.792
$SIZE$	16.966	1.888	12.683	15.562	16.714	18.060	21.434
ROA	0.052	0.068	-0.288	0.017	0.043	0.085	0.353
$SIND$	0.429	0.496	0.000	0.000	0.000	1.000	1.000

註 a：變數定義，SDG_D 為公司是否揭露 SDGs 的指示變數，當公司有回應 SDGs 時，$SDG_D=1$ 其餘為 0；SDG_{AVE} 為公司實踐 SDGs 程度，將 1 分以上的 SDGs 項目分數，取平均分數；$BDSIZE$ 為為董事會規模，本研究以董事會董事席次衡量董事會規模；$INDDIR$ 為董事會獨立性，以獨立董事席次占全體董事席次比率計算；$DUALITY$ 為董事長是否兼任總經理指示變數，當公司總經理兼任董事長時，其值為 1，其餘為 0；為董事持股比率，$BDHOLD$ 董事持股占總流通在外股數之比率；$PLEDGE$ 為董事持股質押比率，董事設質股數占董事持股數之比率；$INTHOLD$ 為機構投資人持股比率，機構投資人持股占總流通在外股數之比率，機構投資人包括政府機構、本國金融機構、本國信託基金及外國法人持股（外資）；ADV 為客戶關係，以廣告費用率衡量企業與客戶間的緊密程度，廣告費用除營業收入；$INVTURN$ 為供應商關係，以存貨週轉率衡量企業與供應商的關係緊密程度；EMP 為員工人數，企業員工人數取自然對數衡量員工對公司 CSR 的影響；$DEBT$ 為債權人影響力，以負債比率衡量債權人對公司的影響力，負債比率為總負債除總資產之比率；HHI 為產業競爭程度，以 HHI（Herfindahl-Hirschman Index）衡量產業的競爭程度；$SIZE$ 為公司規模，以公司總資產取自然對數衡量公司規模對實行 CSR 之影響；ROA 為營運績效，以總資產報酬率衡量公司營運績效；$SIND$ 為敏感產業指示變數，因為水泥、化學、造紙、鋼鐵及油電燃氣等產業者，生產過程產生較大的環境成本，而電子業為臺灣的龍頭產業，較受社會大眾關注，所以本研究將水泥、化學、造紙、鋼鐵、電子及油電燃氣等產業，設定為敏感性產業。當公司屬水泥、化學、造紙、鋼鐵、電子及油電燃氣等產業時，其值為 1，其餘為 0。

樣本之 43%。其中，因金融業公司未有存貨，所以存貨週轉率之觀測值只有 336 筆。因此，本研究分別以全體樣本、非金融業及金融業進行迴歸分析，其中只有非金融業樣本放置 *INVTURN* 變數進行測試。

　　本研究依 CSR 報告書是否揭露 SDGs 分組，進行自變數的差異檢定，結果如表五。初步發現，當公司董事會席次較多、董事持股較低、外資持股較高、員工人數較多、負債比率較高及規模較大時，其 CSR 報告書較可能揭露 SDGs 相關

表五：CSR 報告書揭露 SDGs 之決定因素之差異檢定

自變數 [b]	揭露 SDGs n=131		未揭露 SDGs n=244		差異檢定 [a] 平均數 t-value	中位數 z-value
	平均數	中位數	平均數	中位數		
BDSIZE	9.832	9.000	8.488	7.000	4.62***	4.52***
INDDIR	0.322	0.333	0.324	0.333	-0.21	0.48
DUALITY	0.214	0.000	0.287	0.000	-1.54	-1.54
BDHOLD	0.185	0.135	0.233	0.185	-2.68***	-2.02**
PLEDGE	0.077	0.000	0.086	0.000	-0.58	1.25
INTHOLD	0.608	0.639	0.521	0.530	3.79***	3.61***
ADV	0.003	0.000	0.003	0.000	-0.01	0.84
INVTURN	18.516	6.670	11.016	5.110	1.21	2.42**
EMP	8.393	8.537	6.993	6.938	8.86***	7.07***
DEBT	0.540	0.511	0.445	0.432	4.15***	2.96***
HHI	0.161	0.113	0.144	0.089	0.99	2.31**
SIZE	18.110	17.987	16.352	16.188	9.58***	6.42***
ROA	0.058	0.044	0.049	0.042	1.26	0.36
SIND	0.397	0.000	0.447	0.000	-0.93	-0.93

註：[a] ***、** 與 * 分別代表達 1%、5% 及 10% 顯著水準。
　　[b] 變數定義請詳表四附註。

資訊。而存貨週轉率只在中位數檢定具有顯著差異，而平均數未達顯著差異。在此差異檢定結果可初步發現，公司治理程度、董事持股及利害關係人關注程度影響 CSR 報告書揭露 SDGs 的可能性。

（二）迴歸結果分析

本研究分別以 SDG_D 及 SDG_{AVE} 為應變數進行迴歸分析，探討影響公司是否揭露 SDGs 相關資訊之影響因素。因為樣本及變數上的特性，分別以全樣本、非金融業及金融業三組樣本進行測試，非金融業樣本包括存貨週轉率變數，以衡量供應商對公司 CSR 決策的影響；而金融業樣本公司之皆未有董事長兼任總經理，故未包含 DUALITY 變數。

　　本研究以 CSR 報告書是否揭露 SDGs 相關資訊，判斷公司運用 SDGs 設定公司 CSR 目標與否，進而探討公司運用 SDGs 的決定因素。表六呈現 SDG_D 的迴歸結果，其 LR 統計量皆達 1% 顯著水準，R^2 界於 0.208 至 0.552 之間，表示迴歸模型對應變數具有解釋力，解釋程度為 20% 至 55% 之間。董事會特質變數部分的結果指出，董事會獨立性（INDDIR）之係數，顯著為正，表示董事會中獨立董事的席次比例愈高，其 CSR 報告書愈可能揭露 SDGs 相關資訊。換言之，可能因獨立董事兼顧利害關係人之權益，且獨立董事的專業性也能為公司提供 CSR 新知識，所以公司的 CSR 報告書自願揭露 SDGs。在股權結構部分，全樣本及非金融業樣本的結果指出，董事持股質押比率（PLEDGE）之係數顯著為負，表示董事持股質押比率高時，可能因為私利

表六：CSR 報告書揭露 SDGs 之決定因素——SDG_D

自變數[a]	全樣本		非金融業		金融業	
	係數	χ^2 值[b]	係數	χ^2 值	係數	χ^2 值
Intercept	-13.323	42.50***	-13.360	35.00***	-13.283	43.54***
BDSIZE	0.082	1.54	0.096	1.64	0.090	1.91
INDDIR	3.402	3.04*	3.378	2.83*	3.462	3.21*
DUALITY	-0.225	0.51	-0.248	0.62	0.000	
BDHOLD	-0.426	0.22	-0.725	0.53	-0.310	0.12
PLEDGE	-1.599	3.02*	-1.970	3.81*	-1.386	2.38
INTHOLD	-0.841	1.11	-0.830	1.02	-0.811	1.07
ADV	2.486	0.03	7.440	0.20	4.348	0.09
INVTURN			0.004	1.59		
EMP	0.338	7.91***	0.263	4.14**	0.328	7.95***
DEBT	-0.945	1.27	-0.338	0.14	-0.911	1.20
HHI	1.287	2.73*	1.087	1.90		
SIZE	0.524	13.61***	0.546	11.80***	0.522	13.68***
ROA	4.917	4.40**	4.528	3.74*	5.282	5.24**
SIND	-0.052	0.04	-0.097	0.12		
n	375		336		39	
McFadden R^2	0.220		0.208		0.552	
LR statistics	106.50***		89.13***		103.32***	

註：[a] 變數定義請詳表四附註。
　　[b] ***、** 與 * 分別代表達 1%、5% 及 10% 顯著水準。

而損及其他利害關係人利益，而較不注重 CSR 報告書的資訊揭露。利害關係人部分，EMP 係數在三組樣本的結果都顯著為正，表示當公司員工人數較多時，其 CSR 報告書較可能揭露 SDGs 相關資訊。代表公司為回應員工之需求，提供

較多資訊之 CSR 報告書。而在全樣本的結果中，產業競爭
程度（*HHI*）之係數顯著為正，表示產業競爭程度較大時，
提昇 CSR 報告書揭露 SDGs 之可能性。另外，公司規模
（*SIZE*）及公司財務績效（*ROA*）之係數都顯著為正，表示
大公司及獲利率較高之公司，較有資源進行 CSR 報告書之
編製，所以也較能取運用 SDGs 等新觀念規畫及表達 CSR 相
關活動。

　　根據 GRI 等（2015）、KPMG（2018）及 PWC（2018）
關於企業運用 SDGs 於 CSR 活動的指引，企業較佳運用 SDGs
的方式為依據企業的營運活動，選出最攸關的數個 SDGs，
再針對這些攸關的 SDGs 來規畫策略及進行相關活動。所以
SDGs 的實踐程度是以一家企業運用 SDGs 的深度來衡量，
而非其涉及的目標個數。換言之，企業實踐 SDGs 的程度是
以公司是否將目標納入策略、提出績效、設定目標及提出改
善計畫來判斷，而非其提及之目標數而定。因此，本研究
另以 SDG_{AVE} 為應變數，探討影響公司 SDGs 實踐程度的因
素，迴歸結果呈現於表七。

　　表七中迴歸模型的 *F*value 皆達 1% 的顯著性，R^2 界於
0.1914 至 0.4802 之間，表示自變數對應變數具有解釋力，
解釋程度為 19% 至 48% 之間。董事會特質變數結果指出，
董事會獨立性（*INDDIR*）的係數顯著為正，達 1% 顯著水
準，表示獨立董事有助於企業提昇實踐 SDGs 程度，可能原
因為獨立董事的獨立性較能兼顧所有利害關係人的權益，也
較有相關知識協助公司推展 SDGs 於 CSR 規畫及活動中。
股權結構部分指出，在全樣本及非金融業樣本中，董事持股

表七：CSR 報告書揭露 SDGs 之決定因素——SDG_{AVE}

自變數 [a]	全樣本			非金融業			金融業		
	係數	t-value[b]	VIF	係數	t-value	VIF	係數	t-value	VIF
Intercept	-4.569	-7.01***		-4.477	-6.39***		-13.289	-6.87***	
BDSIZE	0.026	0.99	2.21	0.024	0.79	2.07	0.223	3.43***	3.16
INDDIR	2.116	2.61***	1.68	1.779	2.09**	1.64	10.144	4.80***	2.64
DUALITY	-0.119	-0.96	1.14	-0.123	-0.98	1.11			
BDHOLD	-0.136	-0.41	1.43	-0.199	-0.58	1.49	0.900	0.95	2.25
PLEDGE	-0.747	-2.83***	1.11	-0.883	-3.19***	1.09	0.370	0.53	1.59
INTHOLD	-0.166	-0.57	1.77	-0.197	-0.65	1.75	-0.603	-0.64	1.99
ADV	1.552	0.27	1.07	0.014	0.00	1.15	1.564	0.14	1.28
INVTURN				0.002	2.05**	1.14			
EMP	0.138	3.23***	2.15	0.105	2.29**	2.29	0.080	0.56	4.82
DEBT	-0.689	-2.28**	1.91	-0.481	-1.44	1.45	-2.170	-1.85*	6.56
HHI	0.229	0.77	1.05	0.190	0.64	1.04			
SIZE	0.223	4.20***	4.20	0.239	4.12***	3.45	0.501	3.59***	9.60
ROA	1.167	1.40	1.14	1.122	1.35	1.11	6.870	1.08	4.75
SIND	-0.005	-0.04	1.16	-0.026	-0.23	1.10			
n	375			336			39		
R²	0.2142			0.1914			0.4802		
F value	8.84***			6.66***			4.51***		

註：[a] 變數定義請詳表四附註。
　　[b] ***、** 與 * 分別代表達 1%、5% 及 10% 顯著水準。

質押比率（PLEDGE）之係數顯著為負，達 1% 顯著水準。表示董事質押比率高時，董事可能因私利而較少提供其他利害關係人相關資訊，所以公司 SDGs 的實踐程度較低。在利害關係人的結果指出，存貨週轉率（INVTURN）、員工人數（EMP）及負債比率（DEBT）都顯著影響企業 SDGs 實踐程度。表示公司於供應商關係愈緊密，及員工人數愈多時，

公司較關注利害關係人權益，其 SDGs 的實踐程度較高，提供較佳的 CSR 相關資訊供利害關係人參考；而當公司負債比率愈高，公司有較高的償還利息負擔，而限縮資金運用的空間而減低公司從事 CSR 的能力與動機（Krüger, 2015），所以減少公司 SDGs 實踐程度。另外，控制變數部分，公司規模也影響公司的 SDGs 實踐程度，可能因大公司的政治成本較高，或是公司較有足夠資源，所以其 SDGs 的實踐程度較高。

綜合本研究表六及表七迴歸模型結果而言，董事會獨立性較高、董事持股質押比率較低、員工人數較多及公司規模較大時，公司較可能揭露 SDGs，且其揭露程度較高。表示公司董事若能因「安業」，而善盡自己的職責，因四要的「能要」及「該要」，只拿取工作應得的合理報酬，對於不正常的金錢予以拒絕；因「培福」及「種福」善待員工，顧及其他利害關係人該有的權利，就能提昇揭露 SDGs 的可能性，也促使公司 SDGs 實踐程度往上提昇。另外，實證結果指出公司績效較佳時，公司較可能揭露 SDGs，表示公司「感恩」及「感謝」，在獲利之時，採實踐 SDGs 的方式顧及其他利害關係人的利益。存貨週轉率較高時，表示公司對供應商的依賴程度愈高，公司與供應商關係愈緊密，可能反應心六倫的「生活倫理」傳達在自己享受便利的同時，也要顧及供應商的感受，而提昇 SDGs 的實踐程度。最後，公司因負債比率高，償還利息的金額也高，限制資金的運用範圍或是代理問題較小，而使得公司 SDGs 實踐程度較低。表示公司因理性地考量資金及代理問題的反應外，若能因「感

恩」及「感謝」其他利害關係人對公司的貢獻，應能善盡兼顧所有利害關係人的權益，提昇公司 SDGs 的實踐程度。

另外，細究表六及表七的相異處發現，公司績效佳有益於公司揭露 SDGs 的願意，但對 SDGs 的實踐程度無顯著影響，可能是公司有穩定獲利時，才有能力去顧及 SDGs 等較新的 CSR 趨勢，但對其實踐程度沒有影響。與供應商緊密關係對於公司是否揭露 SDGs 無顯著影響，然而可助於公司提昇 SDGs 實踐程度；當公司具較多負債時，可能因資源受限，公司的 SDGs 實踐程度較低，但對是否揭露 SDGs 沒有顯著影響。

五、結論

本研究探討 PSE 與 CSR 間的關聯性，發現 PSE 的精神理念、具體作法及其影響，與 CSR 的態度及理念、環境、社會及治理三個層面及影響力是彼此相呼應的二套系統。而且以心靈環保的精神理念出發，公司以自利利他的態度執行 CSR 活動，更能提昇 CSR 整體的品質。本研究也探討 PSE 與 SDGs 間的相關性，以了解二者間的呼應情況。

本研究另以 SDGs 實踐程度來衡量公司投入 CSR 的程度，測試董事會特質、股權結構及回應利害關係人等因素，是否影響公司揭露及其實踐 SDGs 程度。研究結果指出，當公司董事會獨立性高、董事持股質押比率低、員工人數多、規模較大及績效較佳時，公司較可能揭露 SDGs 相關資訊，且其實踐程度也較高。此外，當公司與供應商關係較緊密時，公司的 SDGs 實踐程度也較高。

　　董事會獨立性高時，能提昇公司注重四要的「能要」及「想要」的程度，也注重四安的「安業」，所以聘任較多的獨立董事，讓董事會更能發揮監督及建言的功能，提高公司價值外，也顧及其他利害關係人的權益。董事持股押質比率高及負債比率高時，意指董事及公司有資金上的需求，此時，董事及公司較無心力維護其他利害關係人的權利，而導致未善盡個人職責。然而，四福中的「培福」及「種福」提醒我們，當我們遇到逆境及逆行菩薩時，表示是個人的福報不足，應多「培福」及「種福」，與他人結善緣，讓自己及他人都成為有福之人。公司員工人數多、產業競爭較大，為了回應利害關係人，而有較多公司揭露 SDGs，表示兼顧心六倫的「生活倫理」及「職場倫理」，還有四福的「培福」及「種福」。公司規模較大，對社區及環境的影響也較大，也較注重履行四環的「自然環保」及「生活環保」、心六倫的「家庭倫理」、「自然倫理」及「生活倫理」、四福的「培福」及「種福」，所以揭露 SDGs 相關資訊。而公司績效佳，較可能揭露 SDGs 相關資訊，以維護其他利害關係人知的權利，也是「培福」及「種福」的實踐。

　　本研究以法鼓山的核心理念「心靈環保」及其整體體系（PSE），探討與 CSR 間的關聯，並研究影響 SDGs 揭露及其實踐程度之因素，但並未深入地探討「心靈環保」相關的佛典及佛法觀念，期待未來能有研究在此領域進行更深入的探討，讓大眾在學習佛法時，也善盡個人及企業的社會責任。

參考文獻

一、中文

永續報告平台，《2017 台灣永續報告現況與趨勢》，2017 年。

永續報告平台，《2018 台灣永續報告現況與趨勢》，2018 年。

永續報告平台，《2019 臺灣暨亞洲永續報告現況與趨勢》，2019 年。

永續報告平台，《2020 臺灣暨亞太永續報告現況與趨勢》，2020 年。

吳幸蓁、廖蕙儀，〈自願性揭露企業社會責任資訊之決定因素與其資訊後果〉，《中山管理評論》第 25 卷第 1 期，2017 年 3 月，頁 13-62。

李秀玲，〈淺談「上市上櫃公司企業社會責任實務守則」及相關配套機制推動情形〉，《證券暨期貨月刊》第 28 卷第 5 期，2010 年 5 月，頁 5-18。

李秀英、劉俊儒、楊筱翎，〈企業社會責任與公司績效之關聯性〉，《東海管理評論》第 13 卷第 1 期，2011 年，頁 77-112。

杜榮瑞、許文馨、鄧雨賢，〈企業社會責任報告書之確信服務提供者、確信程度及產業專家與可信度之關聯：實驗研究〉，《中華會計學刊》第 12 卷（特刊），2017 年，頁 503-536。

林其賢，《聖嚴法師年譜》，臺北：法鼓文化，2016 年。

林怡君，〈企業永續經營報告書之揭露品質與財務績效之關聯性研究〉，國立臺北大學會計學系碩士論文，2011 年。

洪雪卿、陳薇如、傅雁鈴，〈影響企業社會責任績效之重要因素為何？〉，《商管科技季刊》第 14 卷第 4 期，2013 年 12 月，頁

405-441。

張理國，〈賴揆：2030 年為期程研訂我國永續發展目標〉，《中國時報》，2018 年 12 月 14 日。

陳振遠、王健聰、洪世偉，〈公司治理對於企業社會責任、公司價值之影響〉，《中山管理評論》第 25 第 1 期，2017 年 3 月，頁 135-176。

陳彩稚、許永明、張智媛，〈企業社會責任對於股東價值之風險管理效果〉，《台大管理論叢》第 26 第 1 期，2015 年，頁 153-180。

辜琮瑜，《心靈環保講座選輯（二）：心靈環保心地圖》，新北：法鼓文理學院，2017 年。

甄友薇，〈企業社會責任報告書揭露品質之決定因素及其與公司績效之關聯性〉，國立臺灣大學財務金融學研究所碩士論文，2015 年。

釋果光，《心靈環保經濟學》，臺北：法鼓文化，2014 年。

聖嚴法師，〈心靈環保的教育〉，《師友月刊》第 361 期，1997 年 7 月 (a)，頁 10-15。

聖嚴法師，《修行在紅塵——維摩經六講》，臺北：法鼓文化，1997 年 (b)。

聖嚴法師，《心靈環保》，臺北：法鼓文化，1999 年。

聖嚴法師，《學術論考 II》，臺北：法鼓文化，2005 年。

聖嚴法師，《我願無窮——美好的晚年開示集》，2011 年。

二、外文

Albuquerque, R., Y. Koskinen, and C. Zhang. 2019. Corporate social responsibility and firm risk: Theory and empirical evidence. *Management Science* 65 (10): 4451-4469.

Armstrong, C. S., J. E. Core, and W. R. Guay. 2012. Do independent directors cause improvements in firm transparency? *Journal of Financial Economics* 113 (3): 383-403.

Armstrong, C. S., J. E. Core, and W. R. Guay. 2014. Do independent directors cause improvements in firm transparency? *Journal of Financial Economics* 113 (3): 383-403.

Baldenius, T., X. Meng, and L. Qiu. 2018. Biased boards. *The Accounting Review* 94 (2): 1-27.

Chen, Y.-C., M. Hung, and Y. Wang. 2018. The effect of mandatory csr disclosure on firm profitability and social externalities: Evidence from china. *Journal of Accounting and Economics* 65 (1): 169-190.

Church, B. K., W. Jiang, X. Kuang, and A. Vitalis. 2019. A dollar for a tree or a tree for a dollar? The behavioral effects of measurement basis on managers' csr investment decision. *The Accounting Review* 94 (5): 117-137.

Core, J. E., R. W. Holthausen, and D. F. Larcker. 1999. Corporate governance, chief executive officer compensation, and firm performance. *Journal of Financial Economics* 51 (3): 371-406.

Davidson, R. H., A. Dey, and A. J. Smith. 2019. Ceo materialism and corporate social responsibility. *The Accounting Review* 94 (1): 101-126.

Dhaliwal, D. S., L. Oliver Zhen, A. Tsang, and Y. Yong George. 2011. Voluntary nonfinancial disclosure and the cost of equity capital: The initiation of corporate social responsibility reporting. *The Accounting Review* 86 (1): 59-100.

Dhaliwal, D. S., S. Radhakrishnan, A. Tsang, and Y. Yong George. 2012. Nonfinancial disclosure and analyst forecast accuracy: International evidence on corporate social responsibility disclosure. *The Accounting Review* 87 (3): 723-759.

Dyck, A., K. V. Lins, L. Roth, and H. F. Wagner. 2019. Do institutional investors drive corporate social responsibility? International evidence. *Journal of Financial Economics* 131 (3): 693-714.

Edmans, A. 2011. Does the stock market fully value intangibles? Employee satisfaction and equity prices. *Journal of Financial Economics* 101 (3): 621-640.

Elkington, J. 1994. Towards the sustainable corporation: Win-win-win business strategies for sustainable development. *California Management Review* 36 (2): 90-100.

Fama, E. F., and M. C. Jensen. 1983. Separation of ownership and control. *Journal of Law and Economics* 26 (June): 301-325.

Freeman, R. E. 1984. *Strategic management: A stakeholder approach.* Boston, MA: Pitman.

Friedman, M. 1970. The social responsibility of business is to increase its profits. *New York Times Magazine*, 32–33, 122, 124, 126.

Gautier, A., and A.-C. Pache. 2015. Research on corporate philanthropy: A review and assessment. *Journal of Business Ethics* 126 (3): 343-369.

Godfrey, P. C., C. B. Merrill, and J. M. Hansen. 2009. The relationship between corporate social responsibility and shareholder value: An empirical test of the risk management hypothesis. *Strategic Management Journal* 30 (4): 425-445.

GRI, UN, and WBCSD. 2015. SDG compass: The guide for business action on the SDGs.

Gul, F. A., and S. Leung. 2004. Board leadership, outside directors' expertise and voluntary corporate disclosures. *Journal of Accounting and Public Policy* 23 (5): 351-379.

Harjoto, M., and H. Jo. 2011. Corporate governance and CSR nexus.

Journal of Business Ethics 100 (1): 45-67.

Heal, G. 2005. Corporate social responsibility: An economic and financial framework. *The Geneva Papers on Risk and Insurance - Issues and Practice* 30 (3): 387-409.

Huang, C.-L., and F.-H. Kung. 2010. Drivers of environmental disclosure and stakeholder expectation: Evidence from taiwan. *Journal of Business Ethics* 96 (3): 435-451.

Jensen, M. C. 2001. Value maximization, stakeholder theroy, and the corporate objective function. *Journal of Applied Corporate Finance* 14 (3): 8-21.

KPMG. 2017. The road ahead: Survey of corporate responsibility reporting 2017.

KPMG. 2018. How to report on the SDGs: What good looks like and why it matters.

Krüger, P. 2015. Corporate goodness and shareholder wealth. *Journal of Financial Economics* 115 (2): 304-329.

Lin, K. V., H. Servaes, and A. Tamayo. 2017. Social capital, trust, and firm performance: The value of corporate social responsibility during the financial crisis. *The Journal of Finance* 72 (4): 1785-1824.

McWilliams, A., and D. Siegel. 2001. Corporate social responsibility: A theory of the firm perspective *Academy of Management Review* 26 (1): 117-127.

Morck, R., A. Shleifer, and R. W. Vishny. 1988. Management ownership and market valuation: An empirical analysis. *Journal of Financial Economics* 20: 293-315.

Pflugrath, G., P. Roebuck, and R. Simnett. 2011. Impact of assurance and assurer's professional affiliation on financial analysts' assessment of credibility of corporate social responsibility information. *Auditing: A*

Journal of Practice & Theory 30 (3): 239-254.

PWC. 2018. From promise to reality: Does business really care about the SDGs?

Scherer, A. G., G. Palazzo, and D. Baumann. 2006. Global rules and private actors: Toward a new role of the transnational corporation in global governance. *Business Ethics Quarterly* 16 (4): 505-532.

Shi, G. 2014. PSE economics-from inner peace to global peace. *Dharma Drum Journal of Buddhist Studies* (15): 109-149.

Slaper, T. F., and T. J. Hall. 2011. The triple bottom line: What is it and how does it work? *Indiana Business Review* 86 (1): 4-8.

Sun, W.-C., H.-W. Huang, M. Dao, and C.-S. Young. 2017. Auditor selection and corporate social responsibility. *Journal of Business Finance & Accounting* 44 (9-10): 1241-1275.

UN. 2019. The sustainable developemnt goals report 2019. Working paper.

Velury, U., and D. S. Jenkins. 2006. Institutional ownership and the quality of earnings. *Journal of Business Research* 59 (9): 1043-1051.

Watts, R. L., and J. L. Zimmerman. 1986. *Positive accounting theory*: Prentice-Hall.

Yeh, Y. H., C. E. Ko, and Y. H. Su. 2003. Ultimate control and expropriation of minority shareholders: New evidence from Taiwan. *Academia Economic Papers* 31 (September): 263-299.

Yermack, D. 1996. Higher market valuation of companies with a small board of directors. *Journal of Financial Economics* 40 (2): 185-211.

Protecting the spiritual environment, corporate social responsibility and the determinants of disclosing and implementing sustainable development goals by firms

Chihua Li

Associate Professor, Department of Accounting, Fu Jen Catholic University

▌ Abstract

Master Sheng Yen introduced the protecting spiritual environment (PSE), the core concept of Dharma Drum Mountain in 1992. The composition of Protecting the Four Environments, the Fivefold Spiritual Renaissance Campaign and the Six Ethics of the Mind is a sound system that includes concepts, practical guides and impacts. This system is in concert with the concept of corporate social responsibility (CSR). In 2015, the United Nations adopt the sustainable development goals (SDGs). That provide a guidance to help firms to set up CSR goals and direction of CSR implementation.

This study investigated the consistence between PSE and CSR and SDGs, and collected disclosure levels of SDGs from the CSR reports of the year 2017 to measure firms' CSR performance. Then this research investigated whether characteristics of the board of directors, ownership structure and responses of stakeholders affect the firms' decision of the disclosure of SDGs. The empirical results indicated that when firms have higher independence of the board of directors, a lower rate of share collateralization by directors, more employees, a bigger firms' size and better financial performance, they are more likely to disclose information of SDGs and implement a higher levels of SDGs. In addition, while firms have close relationships with suppliers, they had a higher implementing level of SDGs. However, firms that burden more liabilities achieve lower implementing level of SDGs.

Keywords: protecting the spiritual environment; corporate social responsibility; sustainable development goals; corporate governance

正念對工作家庭間情緒溢出調節功能的初探

彭奕農

國立臺北大學企業管理學系助理教授

陳思仔

國立臺北大學企業管理學系碩士

▌摘要

本研究針對正念（Mindfulness）對於工作與家庭間情緒溢出（Mood Spillover）的調節效果進行研究。51 位受試者透過智慧型手機，利用 surveycake 雲端問卷服務，連續 5 天在 4 個時刻（7am/12pm/5pm/10pm）即時提供他們當下正負面情緒的即時報告。每個填答的時刻，我們利用 LINE 通訊軟體，提醒每位受試者填答。結果顯示，不論個人是從家庭場域轉換到工作場域亦或是從工作場域轉換到家庭場域，個人的正面和負面情緒都有顯著的溢出效應。另外，個人的正念程度顯著調節個人在轉換場域時的負面情緒溢出。通過這項研究我們得到正念對於場域情緒溢出的確有調節效果，為工作和家庭平衡研究做出貢獻。

關鍵字： 情緒溢出、正念

　　正念一詞源自於巴利語的 Samma-sati，包含 Samma
「正」以及 sati「念」。sati，有念、憶念、記憶、正念之
意。正念概念源於二千五百年前的佛教經典，屬佛陀主要
基礎教法四聖諦中導致苦滅的八正道中的第七支，是認識
實相的方法。此定義是由菩提長老詮釋，他以巴利聖典為
主要資料，探討正念（mindfulness）的真正意義和功能。
菩提長老指出：正念是佛教的禪修系統，即是念住修行
（Satipaṭṭhāna）的最核心要素。正念（Samma-sati）位於八
正道❶裡正精進與正定之間，意把心的精勤運作（正精進）
和心的寧靜（正定）連接起來（溫宗堃等譯，2014）。

　　在西方第一位將「sati」英譯為「mindfulness」的人是
巴利語學者托馬斯・威廉・里斯・戴維斯（Thomas William
Rhys Davids, 1843-1922）。戴維斯（1881）將正念定義
為：記憶、回憶、回想、覺察，其中最重要的是意識到所有
身體和心理現象的無常，皆取決於關係緣起和滅絕。

　　因應當代西方社會的發展與需求下，卡巴金博士
（Kabat-Zinn, 1994）刻意將正念去除了宗教色彩，藉由
結合自身的專業知識與禪修經驗，開發出正念減壓療法
（Mindfulness-based stress reduction，簡稱 MBSR），做為
管理壓力、疼痛、疾病、情緒、身體之苦的良藥。卡巴金博
士根據自身的理解，在《當下，繁花盛開》一書將正念定義
為：「一種有意識的、當下的，不管過去和將來，不加以批

---

❶ 八正道包括：正見、正語、正業、正命、正念、正定、正思惟、正精
　進。

判的注意方式，而這樣的注意方式可讓個人有更多正知、清明智慧。」目前也是學術界最常引用的代表性論述（雷叔雲，2008）。

近來，各領域的學者們已視正念（Mindfulness）為一種可以科學檢驗的狀態，並對此進行廣泛的實證研究。例如，在教育（Napoli, Krech, & Holley, 2005）、法律、監獄、政府（Riskin, 2002）、醫療（Carmody & Baer, 2008）及心理（Auty, Cope, & Liebling, 2017）等各領域，學者們皆發現正念對於個人及組織都有利益。

此外，對於個人身體健康方面，研究亦發現，正念使個人能夠有效地減輕情緒或身體的痛苦（Baer, 2003; Broderick, 2005; Shapiro, Carlson, Astin, & Freedman, 2006）。另一方面，Allen 與 Kiburz（2012）發現正念程度較高者在工作與家庭平衡表現得更好，擁有更好的睡眠品質。

在商管領域，近年來國際大型商業機構，為期增益組織績效，也將個人正念相關訓練帶入商業組織（Hayes, 2014; Hughlett, 2013; Pinsker, 2015; Tan, 2012）。而商學學者甚至開始將正念的觀念運用於組織層級（Weick & Sutcliffe 2006, Ray, Baker, & Plowman, 2011），可見正念在商管實務及學術界也有蓬勃發展。

而在商管領域中，人力資源領域針對員工情緒及工作、家庭關係多有著墨（Edwards, J. R. & Rothbard, 2000; Williams & Alliger, 1994）。而「情緒溢出」（Mood Spillover）即是在工作家庭關係研究中探討的內容之一。

「情緒溢出」係指個人從一個生活場域轉換到另一個

生活場域時的正、負面情緒流動現象（Demerouti, Bakker, & Schaufeli, 2005; Eckenrode & Gore, 1990; Edwards & Rothbard, 2000; Larson & Almeida, 1999），而本研究亦採用此定義進行研究。情緒溢出研究中，常探討工作場域和家庭場域間的情緒溢出，因為工作場域和家庭場域是個人一生中最重要的兩個場域（Grandey, Cordeiro, & Crouter, 2005）。而人資領域亦常關注工作家庭關係研究，因其與員工之工作情緒相關。

現有情緒溢出文獻主要以了解其對個人與家庭之正面與負面影響（Kinnunen, Geurts & Pulkkinen, 2006; Larsen & Ketelaar, 1989; Demerouti, Bakker & Schaufeli, 2005）以及成因（Williams and Alliger, 1994）如角色衝突為主。但，對於減少情緒溢出之方法，較少著墨。

另一方面，正念相關研究，目前仍以個人心理相關研究為主，尤以壓力管理為業界及臨床心理領域為方向。未曾與情緒溢出研究領域，有所連結。我們認為，若能將正念程度與情緒溢出研究結合，不但能開拓雙方研究領域，更有可能找出減少情緒溢出的負面影響，對於企業、員工、社會皆會有所助益，此即為本研究之目的及學術重要性。

一、文獻回顧

以下謹對相關文獻進行探討，並將討論方向專注於「情緒溢出」、「正念與情緒」以及「正念與情緒溢出」進行討論並建立相關假說。

（一）情緒溢出（Mood Spillover）

如前文所述，「情緒溢出」係指個人從一個生活場域轉換到另一個生活場域時的正、負面情緒流動現象（Demerouti, Bakker, & Schaufeli, 2005; Eckenrode & Gore, 1990; Edwards & Rothbard, 2000; Larson & Almeida, 1999）。情緒溢出理論（Spillover theory）指出，個人在工作場域中的情緒感受可能延續到家庭，反之亦然，個人在家庭場域中的情緒感受亦可能延續到工作中（Crouter, 1984; Zedeck, 1992），如圖一所示。

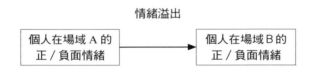

圖一：個人在場域轉換時之情緒溢出

例如，當個人的工作負荷過重、在工作上受到不公平待遇時，個人很可能會把緊張、擔憂的負面情緒帶回家中，導致回家後仍持續處在負面情緒當中（Eby, Casper, Lockwood, Bordeaux, & Brinley, 2005）。目前已有許多研究發現情緒溢出效應的證據（Allen, Herst, Bruck, & Sutton, 2000; Amstad, Meier, Fasel, Elfering, & Semmer, 2011; Ford, Heinen, & Langkamer, 2007）。

為了進一步了解個人在轉換場域時的情緒溢出的現象，

研究者開始用衝突理論（Conflict theory）的角度去看情緒溢出的現象。衝突理論指出，工作和家庭環境是不相容的，因為它們各自有不同的規範和要求（Zedeck & Mosier, 1990），更精確地來說，工作與家庭衝突被定義為個人在家庭和工作中扮演不同角色時經歷的角色壓力、衝突與矛盾，因此衝突分為兩種：

一、從工作到家庭的衝突（work family conflict，簡稱 WFC），指的是個人在工作中的角色壓力妨礙家庭的情況。

二、從家庭到工作衝突（family work conflict，簡稱 FWC），指的是個人在家庭中的角色壓力妨礙工作的情況。

在情緒溢出的文獻中，包括了正面情緒的情緒溢出之研究（Kinnunen, Feldt, Geurts, & Pulkkinen, 2006; Song, Foo, & Uy, 2008），也有關於負面情緒的情緒溢出研究（Song et al., 2008; Williams & Alliger, 1994），因此，我們把情緒分為正負面情緒分別討論。

但如上所述，現有情緒溢出文獻主要以了解其對個人與家庭之正面與負面影響（Kinnunen, Geurts & Pulkkinen, 2006; Larsen & Ketelaar, 1989; Demerouti, Bakker & Schaufeli, 2005）以及成因如角色衝突（Williams and Alliger, 1994）為主。但對於減少情緒溢出之方法，較少著墨。若能找出減少情緒溢出的負面影響，對於企業、員工、社會皆會有所助

益。故在了解正念對個人身心的影響後，發現正念對於情緒溢出或可有所調節。此為本研究對於現有文獻最有貢獻之處以及研究之初衷。為達此目的，我們對於正念與情緒之關係進行簡短討論。

（二）正念（Mindfulness）與情緒

現今研究中發現，正念對於個人之正面與負面情緒皆有影響。一般來說，正念可增加個人之正面情緒。例如，正念能增加個人生命活力、自信心、樂觀態度（Brown & Ryan, 2003; Keng, Smoski, & Robins, 2011）、正念能增加個人的自覺性（Giluk, 2009; Thompson & Waltz, 2007）、活力（Brown & Ryan, 2003）與自尊（Brown & Ryan, 2003）。

另一方面，一般而言，正念可降低各種負面情緒。例如，正念能夠降低抑鬱（Brown & Ryan, 2003; Cash & Whittingham, 2010）、神經質（Dekeyser, Raes, Leijssen, Leysen, & Dewulf, 2008; Giluk, 2009）、社交焦慮（Brown & Ryan, 2003; Rasmussen & Pidgeon, 2011）以及情緒調節困難（Baer, Smith, Hopkins, Krietemeyer, & Toney, 2006）。

綜上所述可知，正念可增加正面情緒與降低負面情緒。因為「正念」就是一種全心全意活在當下，如實以及不評價地覺察當下情況與自身情緒狀態，當個人不斷地練習專注當下，覺察能力也會隨之變得敏銳，當能夠隨時隨地如實地覺察到身體的感受、情緒的感覺、想法的起伏，那就代表我們多了一些彈性可以做出更好的情緒反應的選擇。

因此我們認為正念具有協助個人如實地活在當下，不受

過去干擾的特性。因此正念應可協助個人在工作和家庭間轉換場域時，減緩個人的情緒溢出，亦即個人在工作時的情緒不會受前一場域家庭生活的干擾。同時，個人在家庭中的情緒亦不會受到前一場域工作中的干擾。

而欲了解正念特質程度與情緒溢出之關係，必須先確認情緒溢出之存在。為了驗證個人在工作和家庭場域間轉換時有正負面情緒溢出的存在，我們提出下列四個假說：

H_{1a}：受試者在家庭場域的正面情緒會移轉到工作場域
H_{1b}：受試者在家庭場域的負面情緒會移轉到工作場域
H_{2a}：受試者從工作場域的正面情緒會移轉到家庭場域
H_{2b}：受試者從工作場域的負面情緒會移轉到家庭場域

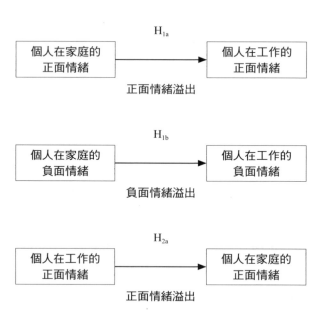

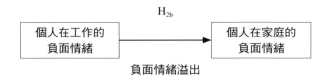

負面情緒溢出

亦可將以上關係以迴歸數學式表示如下：

$$y_{\text{mood in locatin B}} = \beta_1 x_{\text{mood in locaion A}} + \varepsilon$$

其中 $x_{\text{mood in locatin A}}$ 為起始場域之正面或負面情緒；而 $y_{\text{mood in locatin B}}$ 為終止場域之正面或負面情緒。故若情緒溢出存在時，$\beta_1 \neq 0$。

（三）正念特質程度與情緒溢出

正念具有特質（Trait）與狀態（State）兩種特性，並且可由訓練將短期的狀態轉為個人特質（Kiken et al., 2015）。此研究中由於未有相關訓練故以「特質」之觀點進行研究。

而在假說推導方面，一如前述，協助個人如實地活在當下，不受過去干擾。在此狀況下，個人不論是在前一個場域的正、負情緒高的狀況之下，在到達下一場域時，其情緒應會回復到較穩定狀態，因而減緩個人面臨家庭與工作間場域轉換時之情緒溢出。故我們認為正念可以協助穩定個人情緒，降低過去情緒之干擾。因此在此提出以下假說：

H₃ₐ：受試者的正念特質程度愈高，受試者在家庭場域的正面情緒移轉到工作場域的程度愈低。

II₃ᵦ：受試者的正念特質程度愈高，受試者在家庭場域

的負面情緒移轉到工作場域的程度愈低。

H_{4a}：受試者的正念特質程度愈高，受試者在工作場域
　　　的正面情緒移轉到家庭場域的程度愈低。

H_{4b}：受試者的正念特質程度愈高，受試者在工作場域
　　　的負面情緒移轉到家庭場域的程度愈低。

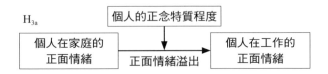

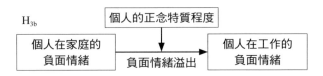

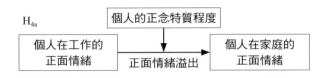

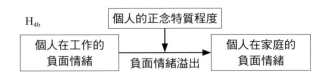

而以上相關的關係以廻歸數學式表示如下：

$y_{\text{mood in locatin B}}$

$= \beta_1 x_{\text{mood in locaion A}} + \beta_2 x_{\text{mindfulness}} + \beta_3 x_{\text{mood in location A}} \times x_{\text{mindfulness}}$

$+ \varepsilon$

其 中 $x_{mood\ in\ locatin\ A}$ 為 起 始 場 域 之 正 面 或 負 面 情 緒；$y_{mood\ in\ locatin\ B}$ 為 終 止 場 域 之 正 面 或 負 面 情 緒；$y_{midfulness}$ 為 個 人 之 正 念 特 質 程 度。故 若 正 念 特 質 程 度 調 節 能 力 存 在 時，$\beta_3 \neq 0$。

二、研究方法

此研究我們運用「手機事件抽樣法」（Cell Phone Event Sampling）（Song, Foo and Uy, 2008）進行研究，抽樣方法亦類似。

（一）樣本（Sampling）

樣本參與者主要來自便利抽樣，來自身旁的親朋好友，大部分受試者的職業為公務人員，以及 16 位法鼓山的禪修人士，邀請法鼓山禪修人士填答問卷的目的，為確保我們在測試個人的正念特質程度對於個人在工作場域和家庭場域轉換時的正負面情緒溢出，是否在負面調節時能有更顯著的調節效果，因為一般而言，沒有受過正念禪修訓練的人正念特質程度普遍不高，所以我們需要正念特質程度較高之人協助檢驗。

我們透過 LINE 通訊軟體散布邀請函，共 53 人自願參加，中途有 2 人退出，最後有符合資格的 51 人參與研究。受試者中，男性占 28 位，女性 23 位；受試者的平均年齡為 26 歲（標準差 7.57）。學歷分布上，26.4% 的受試者擁有研究生學位，69.8% 擁有學士學位，其餘為高中或以下學歷。職業方面，28.3% 為軍公教，20.7% 為金融業，15% 為服務

業，其餘受測者職業較分散占 37%。最後，73.5% 受測者未婚，26.5% 已婚。

（二）研究程序（Processures）

在正式請受試者填答問卷前，我們先請 3 位非受試者的作者親友協助填答問卷，提供建議加以修正問卷內容，以確保問卷內容正確無誤。所有的受試者都必須在正式調查之前接受一天的測試，以確保他們能夠正確使用智慧型手機填答問卷，以及有 LINE 帳號能隨時聯絡填答。

受試者需要先完成前測：關於個人基本資料，正負面情感、正念程度、工作、家庭傾向的調查。我們要求受試者隨身攜帶智慧型手機，連續 5 天每天 4 次完成調查。在每個工作日，受試者在四個時間段（上午 7 時、中午 12 時，下午 5 時和夜間 10 時）收到四條 LINE 通訊軟體的提醒，調查的目的是要及時記錄（Surveycake 網站）受測者當下的情緒狀態，詳細變數測量之內容與時機如圖二。

因此我們要求受試者每次填答時須在 LINE 通訊軟體的提醒後 2 分鐘內完成，上午 7 時和中午 12 時的個人即時情緒填答，用以判定個人從家庭場域轉換到工作場域的情緒溢

圖二：變數測量之內容與時機

出。下午 5 時和夜間 10 時的個人即時情緒填答，用以判定個人從工作場域轉換到家庭場域的情緒溢出。在調查結束後，每位受試者皆得到超商二百元禮卷的報酬。

我們一共發出 1,020 條通訊軟體訊息提醒，收到 854 條報告，回覆率為 83.7％。平均每位受試者在即時家庭情緒狀態提供 8.82（1-10）條回覆，即時工作情緒狀態提供 7.92（1-10）條回覆。

（三）量表

我們總共使用兩個量表，其中完整版的「正負面情感量表」、「止覺觀察注意量表」在前測時一併測量。另，縮減版的「正負面情感量表」需要每一受試者連續測量五天，每天測量四次。

1. 正負面情緒測量

為測量受測者情緒，我們依 Song、Foo 與 Uy（2008）文章，使用正負面感情量表（The Positive and Negative Affect Schedule，簡稱 PANAS）（Watson, Clark, & Tellegen, 1988）來評估正、負面情緒，中文翻譯版採用（鄧閔鴻、張素凰，2006）翻譯的中文版正負面感情量表。為了讓受試者每次填表時在 2 分鐘內完成，因此採用縮減版，其中共有 10 個項目，5 個表示正面情緒（熱忱的、感興趣的、果決的、興奮的、易受鼓舞的），5 個表示負面情緒（沮喪的、苦惱的、害怕的、羞愧的、神經質的）。

我們依據（Watson et al., 1988）之研究，選擇具有五個最高因了負荷的項目來選擇正面、負面情緒項目，本量表填

答方式採取李克特氏五點量尺進行評量，受試者被要求輸入從 1（非常少或一點也不）到 5（極度）範圍內的數字，以描述他們當時經驗的情緒強烈程度。縮簡版的測量和最開始測量的 20 項的正負面情緒量表 PANAS 是高度相關的，正面情緒和負面情緒的 α 係數分別為 0.91 和 0.93。

2. 正念特質程度測量

我們採用 MAAS 量表（Brown & Ryan, 2003）之中文翻譯版，止觀覺察注意量表（Chinese Mindful Attention Awareness Scale，簡稱 CMAAS）（張仁和、林以正、黃金蘭，2011），在此止觀是正念的同義詞。

量表完全參照 MAAS 的題項，共 15 題。所有題目均為反向題，為李克特氏六點量尺，主要是詢問個人注意力與覺察不集中的頻率。其中 1 分表示「幾乎沒有」，6 分表示「幾乎總是」，經反向計分後表示個人正念的程度，分數愈高代表正念程度愈高。在此謹將本研究探討之變數定義與量表羅列如下：

表一：本研究探討之變數定義與量表

變數	定義	使用量表
正、負面情緒	短期的感受或情感（Watson, 2000）	中文版正負面感情量表（PANAS）（鄧閔鴻、張素凰，2006）
正念（特質程度）	一種有意識的、當下的，不管過去和將來，不加以批判的注意方式，而這樣的注意方式可讓個人有更多正知、清明智慧。（雷叔雲，2008）	止觀覺察注意量表（CMAAS）（張仁和、林以正、黃金蘭，2011）

（四）統計分析工具及分析結果討論

我們使用 SPSS Statistics 19 軟體，將蒐集到的數據進行描述性統計分析及迴歸分析。

1. 信度分析

信度是指測驗結果的穩定性及可靠性。為了解本研究是否具有內部一致性，我們研究採用 Cronbach's α 係數來檢定，α 值愈大，顯示該構面內部一致性愈高。Cuieford（1965）認為 α 值大於 0.7 為高信度，α 值介於 0.7 和 0.35 之間為尚可，α 值若小於 0.35 為低信度，應予以拒絕。本研究的分析結果顯示如表二所示，故本研究無信度問題。

表二：各變數之信度

變數	Cronbach's α
個人的正面情緒	0.866
個人的負面情緒	0.844
個人的正念特質程度	0.842

2. 效度分析

我們利用因素分析做為效度證明之手段。效度是指衡量的工具是否能真正衡量到研究者想要衡量的問題，我們利用 KMO（Kaiser-Meyer-Olkin）與 Bartlett 球形檢定（Bartlett's Test of Sphericity）來做取樣適當性的檢定。KMO 主要是用來看取樣的適切性，由於題組間的相關性若是太高，則有可能會造成多重共線性的狀況。因此 KMO 值大於 0.6 較為適合進行因素分析，KMO 值介於 0.7 至 0.8 表示尚可、KMO

值介於 0.8 至 0.9 間表示很適合。

3. 正負面情緒效度

在縮減版正負面情緒測量變數中，利用 10 題進行因素分析，結果如下表所示。KMO 取樣適切性量數為 0.835，屬於很適合進行探索性因素分析的範圍，也代表變數所包含的題項很適合進行後續的探索性因素分析。此外，在 Bartlett 球形檢定顯著性結果亦達 0.00。

表三：正負面情緒量表 KMO 與 Bartlett 球型檢定結果

Kaiser-Meyer-Olkin 取樣適切性量數		.835
Bartlett 的球形檢定	近似卡方分配	4154.463
	df	45
	顯著性	.000

根據（J. F. Hair, Black, Babin, Anderson, & Tatham, 1998）所提出之萃取標準，擷取特徵值大（Ei-genvalue）於 1 的因素，然後以最大變異數轉軸法進行旋轉後，共分析出兩項元件（Component）。對應至兩項構面：正面情緒、負面情緒。每個構面的特徵質皆大於 1.0，觀察變項題項可解釋之累計百分比為 65.39%。各題項之因素負荷量（factor loading）愈大（一般以大於 0.5 為準），則愈具備「收斂效度」，結果顯示各題項的因素負荷量皆 > 0.5，表示將正負面情緒測量分成正面情緒、負面情緒是具備建構效度的。如表三、四所示，故本研究正、負面情緒測量無效度問題。

表四：正、負面情緒測量之因素負荷量

題項	元件	
	1	2
感興趣的	.869	
易受鼓舞的	.853	
興奮的	.845	
熱忱的	.828	
果決的	.607	
害怕的		.824
沮喪的		.821
煩躁的		.797
神經質的		.768
羞愧的		.731

4. 正念特質程度效度

在個人的正念特質程度測量中，我們利用 15 題題項進行因素分析，結果如下表所示。KMO 取樣適切性量數為 0.742，屬於很適合進行因素分析的範圍，也代表變數所包含的題項很適合進行後續的因素分析。此外，在 Bartlett 球形檢定顯著性結果亦達 0.00。

表五：止觀（正念）覺察注意量表 KMO 與 Bartlett 球型檢定結果

Kaiser-Meyer-Olkin 取樣適切性量數		.742
Bartlett 的球形檢定	近似卡方分配	305.731
	df	105
	顯著性	.000

根據（J. F. Hair et al., 1998）所提出之萃取標準，擷取特徵值大（Ei genvalue）於 1 的因素，然後以最大變異數

轉軸法進行旋轉後，共分析出五項元件（Component），與
（Brown & Ryan, 2003）的研究結果為單一因素結構不同，
其中一個可能的原因是樣本數過小（N=51），導致題項的因
素負荷量值過小，不具備建構效度（B. Hair & Babin）。

表六：止觀（正念）覺察量表的因素負荷量

題項	元件				
	1	2	3	4	5
題項 14	.776				
題項 10	.740				
題項 13	.714				
題項 9	.653	.413			
題項 2	.620				
題項 5		.882			
題項 4		.611			-.471
題項 8	.434	.553			
題項 15		.527	.517		
題項 7	.455	.523	.412		
題項 6			.913		
題項 3				.823	
題項 12				-.731	
題項 11					.715
題項 1	.537				-.558

5. 描述性統計分析

表七顯示了研究變量的平均數和標準差。圖三和圖四
顯示受試者在 5 天內正負面情緒的平均趨勢。受試者的平均
正面情緒（M=13.61）高於平均負面情緒（M=8.96），與
（Watson, 2000）的結論相一致，一般而言，大部分個人的
情感生活體驗整體上是快樂的而不是悲傷的。

表七：描述性統計：變數的平均數、標準差、變數間的相關性

變數	平均數	標準差	1	2	3	4	5
1. 正念特質程度	63.5294	9.66717	—				
2. 正面情感	26.7647	6.19222	.00	—			
3. 負面情感	16.9804	6.49766	-.41	.13	—		
4. 正面情緒平均值	13.5098	6.19222	-.36	.19	.17	—	
5. 負面情緒平均值	9.3235	6.49766	-.66	.15	.45	.40	—

N=51

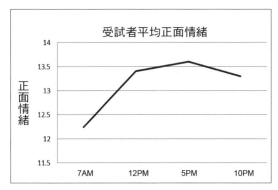

圖三：受試者平均正面情緒

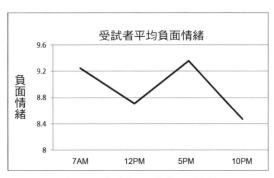

圖四：受試者平均負面情緒

6. 迴歸分析

本研究利用迴歸分析來檢驗受試者在工作場域和家庭場域轉換時是否有正、負面情緒溢出發生。並利用迴歸分析的交互作用項（interaction effect）來檢驗受試者的正念特質程度是否對受試者在工作場域和家庭場域轉換時，正、負面情緒溢出有顯著的調節效果。

此外我們也檢驗 R 平方改變量 R^2（R square），R^2 稱為決定係數（coefficient of determination），是總變異中可被迴歸模式解釋的百分比，用以判斷一組自變項可以聯合預測依變項之變異的程度（百分比），反應了以自變數（X）去預測依變數（Y）時的預測力，即 Y 變項的總變異中可被自變項所解釋的比率，因此可以反應由自變項與依變項所形成的線性迴歸模式的配適度（goodness of fit）。R^2 愈接近 1.0，代表此模式愈有解釋能力。

此外我們也檢驗共線性是指由於自變項的相關太高，造成迴歸分析之情境困擾。一般而言，允差（tolerance）小於 0.2 有共線性問題、變異數膨脹因素（Variance inflation factor, VIF）大於 10 有共線性問題。

檢驗受試者在工作場域和家庭場域轉換時是否有正、負面情緒溢出發生（H_{1a}, H_{1b}, H_{2a}, H_{2b}）。表八至十一顯示與正負面情緒溢出效應有關的結果。為了檢驗 $H_{1a} \sim H_{2b}$，我們將受測者同　天中的　個場域（工作或家庭）中對前　時期另一個場域（家庭或工作）的正負面情緒分別進行迴歸分析。

據數據結果，我們觀察到顯著的溢出效應。其中，從家庭到工作場域有顯著的正面情緒溢出效應（β=.194, $p<.01$）

（表八步驟 1）和負面情緒溢出效應（β=.248, p<.01）（表九步驟 1）；從工作到家庭亦然，有顯著的正面情緒溢出效應（β=.301, p<.01）（表十步驟 1）和負面情緒溢出效應（β=.308, p <.01）（表十一步驟 1）。因此，H_{1a}, H_{1b}, H_{2a}, H_{2b} 得到充分的支持。

表八至十一的步驟 1 中，4 條迴歸式的 R^2 分別為 0.845、0.883、0.926、0.827，皆很接近 1，代表模式有解釋能力；4 條迴歸式各自變量的允差均 >0.2，VIF 均 <10，表示 4 條迴歸式皆不存在共線性的問題。

檢驗受試者的正念特質程度是否對受試者在工作場域和家庭場域轉換時，正、負面情緒溢出有顯著的調節效果（H_{3a}, H_{3b}, H_{4a}, H_{4b}）。表八至十一同時也表示個人的正念特質程度對個人從工作場域轉換到家庭場域、從家庭場域轉換到工作場域的正負面情緒溢出的調節作用，為了檢驗 H_{3a}、H_{3b}、H_{4a}、H_{4b}，我們加入個人的正念特質程度做為調節變數進行迴歸分析，結果表示只有在負面情緒溢出中觀察到個人的正念特質程度有顯著的調節作用，包含個人從家庭場域轉換到工作場域的負面情緒溢出（β=-1.45, p<.01）（表九步驟 2），以及個人從工作場域轉換到家庭場域的負面情緒溢出（β=-1.25, p<.01）（表十一步驟 2）。在正面情緒溢出部分，個人的正念特質程度則沒有顯著的調節效果，個人從家庭場域轉換到工作場域的正面情緒溢出（β=.06, ns）（表八步驟 2）、個人從工作場域到家庭場域的正面情緒溢出（β=-.38, ns）（表十步驟 2）。

在表八至十一的步驟 2 中，4 條迴歸式的 R^2 分別為

0.839、0.914、0.928、0.879，皆很接近 1，代表模式有解釋
能力；4 條迴歸式各自變量的允差均＞0.2，VIF 均＜10，表
示 4 條迴歸式皆不存在共線性的問題。

> 因此假說 3a：受試者的正念特質程度愈高，受試者從
> 　　家庭場域的正面情緒移轉到工作場域的程度愈低
> 　　不被支持。
>
> 假說 3b：受試者的正念特質程度愈高，受試者從家庭
> 　　場域的負面情緒移轉到工作場域的程度愈低得到
> 　　充分的支持。
>
> 假說 4a：受試者的正念特質程度愈高，受試者從工作
> 　　場域的正面情緒移轉到家庭場域的程度愈低不被
> 　　支持。
>
> 假說 4b：受試者的正念特質程度愈高，受試者從工作
> 　　場域的負面情緒移轉到家庭場域的程度愈低得到
> 　　充分的支持。

表八：個人的正念特質程度對個人從家庭場域轉換到工作場域時
的正面情緒溢出的調節

變數	在工作的正面情緒					
	步驟 1			步驟 2		
	β 值	R^2	共線性統計量	β 值	R^2	共線性統計量
			允差　　VIF			允差　　VIF
正面情感	.772**	.845	.476　2.101	.770**	.839	.472　2.117
在家的正面情緒	.194*		.476　2.101	.195*		.437　2.291
正念程度				.019		.936　1.069
在家的正面情緒×正念程度				.006		.816　1.225

表九：個人的正念特質程度對個人從家庭場域轉換到工作場域時的負面情緒溢出的調節

變數	在工作的負面情緒							
	步驟 1				步驟 2			
	β 值	R^2	共線性統計量		β 值	R^2	共線性統計量	
			允差	VIF			允差	VIF
負面情緒影響	.732**	.883	.384	2.607	.563**	.914	.274	3.651
在家的負面情緒	.248*		.384	2.607	.359**		.331	3.019
正念					-.130*		.758	1.320
在家的負面情緒×正念程度					-.145**		.904	1.107

表十：個人的正念特質程度對個人從工作場域轉換到家庭場域時的正面情緒溢出的調節

變數	在家庭的正面情緒							
	步驟 1				步驟 2			
	β 值	R^2	共線性統計量		β 值	R^2	共線性統計量	
			允差	VIF			允差	VIF
正面情緒影響	.689**	.926	.240	4.159	.699**	.928	.237	4.212
在工作的正面情緒	.301*		.240	4.159	.297**		.237	4.224
正念					-.048		.821	1.218
在工作的正面情緒×正念					-.038		.795	1.258

表十一：個人的正念特質程度對個人從工作場域轉換到家庭場域時的負面情緒溢出的調節

變數	在家庭的負面情緒							
	步驟 1				步驟 2			
	β 值	R^2	共線性統計量		β 值	R^2	共線性統計量	
			允差	VIF			允差	VIF
負面情緒影響	.690**	.867	.498	2.008	.573**	.879	.312	
在工作的負面情緒	.308**		.498	2.008	.396*		.384	
正念					-.067*		.695	
在工作的負面情緒×正念					-.125**		.863	

從圖五和圖六可看出正念特質程度較高之人相比於正念特質較低之人更不容易經歷負面情緒溢出，不論是從家庭到工作的場域轉換，亦或是從工作到家庭的場域轉換皆然。

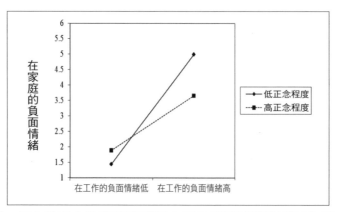

圖五：個人的正念特質程度對個人從家庭場域轉換到工作場域時的負面情緒溢出的調節

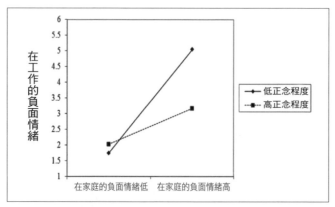

圖六：個人的正念特質程度對個人從工作場域轉換到家庭場域時的負面情緒溢出的調節

根據上述檢驗結果，將假說整理如下所示：

表十二：各假說檢驗結果

假說	內容	實證結果
H_{1a}	受試從家庭場域的正面情緒會移轉到工作場域。	支持
H_{1b}	受試從家庭場域的負面情緒會移轉到工作場域。	支持
H_{2a}	受試者從工作場域的正面情緒會移轉到家庭場域。	支持
H_{2b}	受試者從工作場域的負面情緒會移轉到家庭場域。	支持
H_{3a}	受試者的正念特質程度愈高，受試者從家庭場域的正面情緒移轉到工作場域的程度愈低。	未獲支持
H_{3b}	受試者的正念特質程度愈高，受試者從家庭場域的負面情緒移轉到工作場域的程度愈低。	支持
H_{4a}	受試者的正念特質程度愈高，受試者從工作場域的正面情緒移轉到家庭場域的程度愈低。	未獲支持
H_{4b}	受試者的正念特質程度愈高，受試者從工作場域的負面情緒移轉到家庭場域的程度愈低。	支持

三、結論與建議

（一）研究結果與討論

在本研究中，我們研究個人在工作場域和家庭場域轉換時的正負面情緒溢出效應。研究結果表明，如我們所預期的，個人不論是從家庭轉換到工作場域亦或是從工作場域轉換到家庭場域，皆有顯著的正負面情緒溢出，與前人（Song et al., 2008）的研究結果相符。

在探討個人的正念特質程度是否對於個人在工作場域和家庭場域轉換時的正負面情緒溢出效應有顯著的調節效果時，我們發現個人的正念特質程度只對個人在工作場域和家

庭場域轉換時的「負面」情緒溢出有顯著的調節效果，對正面情緒溢出的調節效果則不顯著。

我們認為其中一個可能的原因是個人在工作場域和家庭間轉換時較容易糾結於負面情緒而不自知，而有較高正念特質程度的個人則更能清楚地意識到自己正處在上一個場域導致的負面情緒困擾中，因而個人的正念特質程度愈高的人，愈不容易受負面情感情緒影響，也更不容易把家裡的負面情緒帶到到工作，同時也不容易把工作的負面情緒帶到家裡，這使得個人的正念特質程度對於個人在工作場域和家庭場域轉換時的負面情緒溢出有顯著的調節效果。

而個人的正念特質程度對個人在工作場域和家庭場域間轉換時的正面情緒溢出沒有顯著的調節效果，我們認為是因為一般而言，個人不會對於處在正面情緒下感到困擾與排斥，因而較難清楚地意識到自己的正面情緒仍受到上一個場域的影響，這使得個人的正念特質程度很難對個人在工作場域和家庭場域間轉換時的正面情緒溢出有顯著的調節效果。

（二）管理意涵

對於企業管理者而言，如果可以藉助有效的方法提昇員工的正念特質程度，對於企業與員工而言是雙贏的策略，企業可以獲得更大的商業利益，而員工因為工作家庭平衡的提昇，更能在工作時全心投入，達到工作績效。

卡巴金博士（Kabat-Zinn, 1994）當初為了在西方推廣正念，不得已刻意移除宗教色彩，但也因此失去更深入學習佛陀教法的機會，對正念有更深層的認識與理解，在臺灣的我

們很幸運的是身旁就有中國禪宗的正統傳承，提供更貼近佛陀正念原意的正念禪修方法。

臺灣有很多宗教團體提供正念學習的機會，例如法鼓山提供高品質且免費的正念正信禪修資源，提供世人更完善的提昇正念特質程度的方法以利我們學習，建議企業的管理者能善用就近的法鼓山正念禪修資源以提昇員工的正念特質程度，藉此改善員工常面臨必須兼顧家庭與工作而造成的心理衝突。

（三）研究限制與建議

我們研究的兩個可能的局限性來自於我們的樣本相對較小且相對缺乏多樣性，樣本大多來自公務人員，期許未來的研究能夠採用更大且更嚴謹的樣本，並針對更多不同職業和組織背景的員工做測試。

為了確定此次研究的有效性，剔除了與填答時間相隔超過 1 小時的數據，未來的研究可以採用更大的樣本規模，條件允許的話可以長期追蹤有高度正念特質的個人相較於一般人的表現，藉此更深刻地了解個人的正念特質程度對於個人在工作、家庭平衡的影響。希望這項研究能夠鼓勵更多研究人員在不同的生活場域和不同的個人之間進行更為嚴謹的正負面情緒的流動過程檢測。

這次的樣本大多來自於公務人員，有鑑於公務人員的生活型態上下班時間固定，生活品質較高，因而相較於其他行業的人更能在工作中同時兼顧家庭生活，所以對於在家庭時經歷的事件、情緒更在意、更投入，因而更有可能將家庭中

的負面情緒帶到工作，這使得個人從家庭轉換到工作場域時有更多的負面情緒溢出。

此外，「正念」（Mindfulness）在現今西方主導之潮流之下，已非純然根據傳統佛教對於其之定義與操作（溫宗堃等譯，2014）。因為目前西方主流探討與練習正念的目的是入世甚至是順應世俗的，而非與解脫生死直接相關，這與卡巴金博士在七〇年代末期為助「正念」為西方大眾所接受而退下其宗教外衣（Willson, 2014）不無關係。但也因此可幫助大量世人離苦（溫宗堃等譯，2014）。

故雖目前西方對於正念在學術上以及實務上的觀點，與佛陀以解脫為目標而教導之正念不盡一致。但個人認為在佛陀教導居士的方向上以及慈悲的觀點下，還是非常有價值的。另一方面，若是佛教徒，實應學習「八正道」，而正念需在正見的指導下方能達到正定而開啟無漏的智慧（釋聖嚴）。若只將正念局限於降低壓力、增進身心健康，或許限制了「正念」對人的助益，甚至會導致對於正面情緒的追求，而產生反效果，著實可惜。

參考文獻

一、中文參考文獻

溫宗堃等譯，Bodhi, B. 原著（2011），〈正念的真正意思為何──巴利聖典的觀點〉，《福嚴佛學研究》第 9 期，2014 年 4 月，頁 1-22。

雷叔雲譯，Kabat-Zinn, J. 原著（2005），《當下，繁花盛開》，臺北：心靈工坊，2008 年。

鄧閔鴻、張素鳳，〈廣泛性焦慮疾患與憂鬱疾患共病現象的階層病理模式〉，《中華心理學刊》第 48 卷第 2 期，2006 年 6 月，頁 203-218。

釋聖嚴，〈八正道的地位〉，《八正道》，《法鼓全集》7-14 之 5，2005 年網路版，臺北：法鼓文化。網址：http://ddc.shengyen.org/pc.htm。

二、英文參考文獻

Allen, T. D., Herst, D. E., Bruck, C. S., & Sutton, M. (2000). "Consequences associated with work-to-family conflict: a review and agenda for future research." *Journal of occupational health psychology*. 5(2), pp. 278-308.

Allen, T. D., & Kiburz, K. M. (2012). "Trait mindfulness and work–family balance among working parents: The mediating effects of vitality and sleep quality." *Journal of Vocational Behavior*. 80(2), pp. 372-379.

Amstad, F. T., Meier, L. L., Fasel, U., Elfering, A., & Semmer, N. K. (2011). "A meta-analysis of work–family conflict and various outcomes with a special emphasis on cross-domain versus matching-domain relations." *Journal of occupational health psychology*, 16(2), pp. 151-169.

Auty, K. M., Cope, A., and Liebling, A. (2017). "A systematic review and meta-analysis of yoga and mindfulness meditation in prison: Effects on psychological well-being and behavioural functioning." *International journal of offender therapy and comparative criminology*, 61(6), pp. 689-710.

Baer, R. A. (2003). "Mindfulness training as a clinical intervention: A conceptual and empirical review." *Clinical psychology: Science and practice*, 10(2), 125-143.

Baer, R. A., Smith, G. T., Hopkins, J., Krietemeyer, J., and Toney, L. (2006). "Using self-report assessment methods to explore facets of mindfulness." *Assessment*, 13(1), pp. 27-45.

Broderick, P. C. (2005). "Mindfulness and coping with dysphoric mood: Contrasts with rumination and distraction." *Cognitive Therapy and Research*, 29(5), pp. 501-510.

Brown, K. W., & Ryan, R. M. (2003). "The benefits of being present: mindfulness and its role in psychological well-being." *Journal of Personality and Social Psychology*, 84(4), 822.

Carmody, J., & Baer, R. A. (2008). "Relationships between mindfulness practice and levels of mindfulness, medical and psychological symptoms and well-being in a mindfulness-based stress reduction program." *Journal of behavioral medicine, 31*(1), pp. 23-33.

Cash, M., & Whittingham, K. (2010). "What facets of mindfulness contribute to psychological well-being and depressive, anxious, and stress-related symptomatology?" *Mindfulness, 1*(3), pp. 177-182.

Clark, S. C. (2000). "Work/family border theory: A new theory of work/

family balance." *Human Relations*, 53(6), pp. 747-770.

Cooke, R. A., & Rousseau, D. M. (1984). "Stress and strain from family roles and work-role expectations." *Journal of Applied Psychology*, 69(2), pp. 252-260.

Crouter, A. C. (1984). "Spillover from family to work: The neglected side of the work-family interface." *Human Relations*, 37(6), pp.425-441.

Davids, T. W. R. (1881). *Buddhist suttas*. In Muller F. Max (Ed.) *The Sacred Books of the East V.11*. London: Clarendon Press.

Dekeyser, M., Raes, F., Leijssen, M., Leysen, S., & Dewulf, D. (2008). "Mindfulness skills and interpersonal behaviour." *Personality and Individual Differences*, 44(5), pp. 1235-1245.

Demerouti, E., Bakker, A. B., & Schaufeli, W. B. (2005). "Spillover and crossover of exhaustion and life satisfaction among dual-earner parents." *Journal of Vocational Behavior*, 67(2), pp. 266-289.

Eby, L. T., Casper, W. J., Lockwood, A., Bordeaux, C., & Brinley, A. (2005). "Work and family research in IO/OB: Content analysis and review of the literature (1980–2002)." *Journal of Vocational Behavior*, 66(1), pp. 124-197.

Eckenrode, J., & Gore, S. (1990). "Stress and coping at the boundary of work and family." In Eckenrode, J. & Gore S. (Eds.), *Stress between work and family*. New York: Plenum. *Stress between work and family* (pp. 1-16): New York: Plenum.

Edwards, J. R., & Rothbard, N. P. (2000). "Mechanisms linking work and family: Clarifying the relationship between work and family constructs." *Academy of management review*, 25(1), pp. 178-199.

Ford, M. T., Heinen, B. A., & Langkamer, K. L. (2007). "Work and family satisfaction and conflict: a meta-analysis of cross-domain relations." *Journal of Applied Psychology*, 92(1), pp. 57-80.

Giluk, T. L. (2009). "Mindfulness, Big Five personality, and affect: A meta-analysis." *Personality and Individual Differences*, 47(8), pp. 805-811.

Grandey, A. A., Cordeiro, B. L., & Crouter, A. C. (2005). "A longitudinal and multi-source test of the work-family conflict and job satisfaction relationship." *Journal of occupational and Organizational Psychology*, 78, 305.

Hair, J. F., Black, W. C., Babin, B. J., Anderson, R. E., & Tatham, R. L. (1998). *Multivariate data analysis* (Vol. 5): Prentice hall Upper Saddle River, NJ.

Hayes, E. (2014). "Ommmmm... Intel employees use mindfulness and meditation to cut stress, enhance focus." *Portland Business Journal*, from http://www. bizjournals.com/portland/blog/health-care-inc/2014/01/ommmmm-intel-employees- use.html?page=all (Retrieved June 2018)

Hughlett, M. (2013). "Mindfulness arrives in the workplace." From http://www.startribune.com/lifestyle/health/233176121.html (Retrieved June 2018)

Helmreich, R. L., & Spence, J. T. (1978). "The Work and Family Orientation Questionnaire: An objective instrument to assess components of achievement motivation and attitudes toward family and career." *JSAS Catalog of Selected Documents in Psychology*, 35(8).

Kabat-Zinn, J. (1994). "Catalyzing movement towards a more contemplative/sacred-appreciating/non-dualistic society." Paper presented at the Meeting of the Working Group.

Keng, S.-L., Smoski, M. J., & Robins, C. J. (2011). "Effects of mindfulness on psychological health: A review of empirical studies." *Clinical psychology review*, 31(6), pp. 1041-1056.

Kiken, L. G., Garland, E. L., Bluth, K., Palsson, O. S., Gaylord, S. A. (2015). "From a state to a trait: Trajectories of state mindfulness in meditation during intervention predict changes in trait mindfulness." *Personality and Individual Differences*, 81, pp. 41-16.

Kinnunen, U., Feldt, T., Geurts, S., & Pulkkinen, L. (2006). "Types of work-family interface: Well-being correlates of negative and positive spillover between work and family." *Scandinavian journal of psychology*, 47(2), pp. 149-162.

Larson, R. W., & Almeida, D. M. (1999). "Emotional transmission in the daily lives of families: A new paradigm for studying family process." *Journal of Marriage and the Family*, 61(1) pp. 5-20.

Lobel, S. A., & Clair, L. S. (1992). "Effects of family responsibilities, gender, and career identity salience on performance outcomes." *Academy of Management Journal*, 35(5), pp. 1057-1069.

Lodahl, T. M., & Kejnar, M. (1965). "The definition and measurement of job involvement." *Journal of Applied Psychology*, 49(1), pp.24-33.

Napoli, M., Krech, P. R., & Holley, L. C. (2005). "Mindfulness training for elementary school students: The attention academy." *Journal of applied school psychology*, 21(1), pp. 99-125.

Pinsker, J. (2015). "Corporations' newest productivity hack: Meditation." from https://www.theatlantic.com/business/archive/2015/03/corporations-newest-productivity-hack-meditation/387286/ (Retrieved June 2018)

Rasmussen, M. K., & Pidgeon, A. M. (2011). "The direct and indirect benefits of dispositional mindfulness on self-esteem and social anxiety." *Anxiety, Stress, & Coping*, 24(2), pp. 227-233.

Ray, J. L., Baker, L. T., & Plowman, D. A. (2011). "Organizational mindfulness in business schools." *Academy of Management*

Learning & Education, 10(2), pp. 188-203.

Riskin, L. L.(2002). "The Contemplative Lawyer: On the Potential Contributions of Mindfulness Meditation to Law Students, Lawyers, and Their Clients." *Harvard Negotiation Law Review*, 7(1), pp. 1-66.

Shapiro, S. L., Carlson, L. E., Astin, J. A., & Freedman, B. (2006). "Mechanisms of mindfulness." *Journal of clinical psychology*, 62(3), pp. 373-386.

Song, Z., Foo, M.-D., & Uy, M. A. (2008). "Mood spillover and crossover among dual-earner couples: A cell phone event sampling study." *Journal of Applied Psychology*, 93(2), pp. 443-452.

Tan, C. M. (2014). *Search inside yourself: The unexpected path to achieving success, happi- ness (and world peace)*. New York, NY; HarperOne.

Thompson, B. L., & Waltz, J. (2007). "Everyday mindfulness and mindfulness meditation: Overlapping constructs or not?." *Personality and Individual Differences*, 43(7), pp. 1875-1885.

Watson, D. (2000). *Mood and temperament*. New York, NY; Guilford Press.

Watson, D., Clark, L. A., & Tellegen, A. (1988). "Development and validation of brief measures of positive and negative affect: the PANAS scales." *Journal of Personality and Social Psychology*, 54(6), pp. 1063-1070.

Weick, K. E., & Sutcliffe, K. M. (2006). "Mindfulness and the quality of organizational attention." *Organization Science*. 17(4), pp.514– 524.

Williams, K. J., & Alliger, G. M. (1994). "Role stressors, mood spillover, and perceptions of work-family conflict in employed parents." *Academy of Management Journal*, 37(4), pp. 837-868.

Wilson, Jeff (2014). *Mindful America: The Mutual Transformation of*

Buddhist Meditation and American Culture. Oxford University Press. p. 35.

Zedeck, S. (1992). "Introduction: Exploring the Domain of Work and Family Concerns." In: Zedeck, S., Ed., *Work, Families, and Organizations*, San Francisco; Jossey Bass, pp. 1-32.

Zedeck, S., & Mosier, K. L. (1990). "Work in the family and employing organization." *American Psychologist,* 45(2), pp. 240-251.

The Impact of Mindfulness on Mood Spillover between Family and Work settings: An Exploratory Study

Yi-Nung Peng

Assistant Professor, Department of Business Administration, National Taipei University

Sz-Yu Chen

Master student, Department of Business Administration, National Taipei University

▌ Abstract:

We studied how individual's level of mindfulness impacts his or her mood spillover while switching environments, from work to family or from family to work. Based on the literature, we expected that mindfulness moderates the mood spillover between environments. We recruited 51 participants. They were remind 4 times a day (7am, 12pm, 5pm, and 10pm) by a smartphone social communication App (LINE) to fill out an online survey (on SurveyCake) to record their mood in specific time. Results confirmed the phenomenon of mood spillover between family and work. We also verified the moderating effect of individual mindfulness on negative mood spillover between family and work. We shed some light on how mindfulness may help individual to achieve work-family balance.

Keywords: Mood Spillover, Mindfulness

至善社會福利基金會都市原住民照顧計畫之社會投資報酬分析[*]

陳定銘

法鼓文理學院人文社會學群教授兼學群長

徐郁雯

國立中央大學客家學院客家語文暨社會科學學系博士生

▎摘要

　　聖嚴法師倡導「心靈環保」，面對人心浮動、政治對立與競爭的社會，心靈環保與社會價值愈顯重要。本研究採取英國社會價值學會推動的社會投資報酬（social return on investment，簡稱 SROI）分析，探討非營利組織的社會價值與影響力，並以財團法人至善社會福利基金會的都市原住民照顧計畫「汐止花東新村原住民住宅」為範圍。透過 SROI 的六項步驟與七項原則，具體描繪及衡量公益活動投入、產出與成果之間因果關係，並以貨幣為統一衡量單位

---

*　本論文改寫自陳定銘（2018）計畫主持的科技部研究計畫「工作整合型社會企業之社會投資報酬（SROI）分析：以財團法人社會福利基金會兩個案為例」（MOST107-2410-H-655-001-MY2），感謝科技部經費之補助；以及陳定銘、徐郁雯（2019 年 6 月 29 日），發表於財團法人法鼓山佛教基金會在法鼓文理學院舉辦「法鼓山創辦人聖嚴法師圓寂十週年——佛法與社會科學國際研討會」之論文。

加以表達。本研究針對都市原住民計畫利害關係者的深度訪談與問卷調查，藉由 SROI 的原則與步驟分析，計算其社會價值與社會影響力。研究發現，當我們將這些成果轉換為具體數字或貨幣時，每投入新臺幣 1 元，可以創造 2.04 元社會價值；另對於不確定性進行敏感性分析時，其社會價值在 1.53 元至 5 元之間。歸納各類利害關係者之社會價值比重依序為：家長／主要照顧者（48%）、孩童（35%）、行政人員（14%）與長者（3%）。顯示此計畫實施者（家長／主要照顧者，行政人員）與受益者（孩童與長者）同蒙其利。亦如佛法的「所謂布施者，必獲其利益」，也佐證聖嚴法師所說：「培福有福」，「布施的人有福，行善的人快樂」，以及學會心與境的重新對待方式，體會心不隨境轉的微妙心法，實踐心靈環保的精神。整體而言，本研究具有實踐佛法和利益眾生之功能，並有實務的參考價值。

關鍵字：至善基金會、都市原住民照顧計畫、社會投資報酬分析、社會影響力、心靈環保

一、前言

　　二〇一九年為緬懷法鼓山創辦人聖嚴法師圓寂十週年，舉行佛法與社會科學國際研討會。聖嚴法師倡導心靈環保，將佛法精神的「淨化人心」轉化成日常生活的具體行動，實踐「提昇人的品質，建設人間淨土」的理念。面對人心浮動、政治對立與競爭的社會，心靈環保與社會價值愈顯重要。釋惠敏（2018）認為社會價值的源頭是「利他」的道心，並引用日本最澄大師說明具「慈悲心──道心」菩薩是國寶，而提出「寶，道心也」的定義，也可以說是「寶（社會價值），道（利他）心也」。

　　而呼應聖嚴法師心靈環保理念，陳定銘（2018）在研究非營利組織與社會企業時指出，在非營利組織或社會企業的文獻報告中，強調從課責（accountability）逐漸移轉至影響力，影響力是一種非實質的概念，往往需要組織藉由處理一些複雜的社會性議題，如貧窮、人權、不公義、環境正義等，才得以展現。在社會企業蓬勃發展的同時，現代社會所重視的不僅僅是經濟產出，更重視對於社會價值與環境和社區產生的影響力。由於社會企業家是以社會信仰與價值為核心，如願景、同理心、價值、信仰等心靈智能的認同，透過社會企業的社會價值實踐，改變社會環境與系統，發揮積極正向、公益慈善的社會價值與社會影響力。

　　至於聖嚴法師（2012）根據《維摩經》❶「唯其心淨，

---

❶　《佛說維摩詰經》：「若菩薩欲得淨土，當淨其心。隨其心淨，則佛

則國土淨」的觀念，提出了「心靈環保」的理念，並陸續提出「心五四」、「心六倫」等實踐方法。聖嚴法師為了接引尚沒有意願學佛，以及無暇禪修的一般大眾，盡量不用佛學名詞，並且以淡化宗教色彩的方便法，來投合現代人的身心和環境的需要，提出了以心靈環保為主軸的「三大教育」、「四種環保」及「心五四運動」、「心六倫運動」❷（釋果鏡，2010）。基此，聖嚴法師（2017）認為，在價值觀混淆的現代社會，如何找到人生的立足點？如何確定自己的價值觀未迷失？如果家人間能夠心意相通，就能相互點亮心燈。家是一個人的根本所在，無論是人生價值觀、個性品德、生活態度，都是從家庭扎根與培養來的。

　　本研究透過衡量社會價值與社會影響力常用的社會投資報酬分析（Social Return on Investment, SROI），並以財團法人至善社會福利基金會（以下簡稱至善基金會）都市原住民照顧計畫做為分析範圍。至善基金會長期耕耘臺灣原住民部落，足跡遍及新竹尖石鄉、臺中和平區、高雄那瑪夏區、屏東霧台等原鄉，從事原住民幼兒照顧、學校教育與部落人才培力等服務工作。至善基金會耕耘原住民兒少照護工作二十餘年，服務範圍除了偏鄉部落之外，亦將服務的觸角延伸

土淨。」《大正藏》第 14 冊。（CBETA, T14, no. 474）

❷ 三大教育是大普化教育、大關懷教育、大學院教育。四種環保為心靈環保、禮儀環保、生活環保、自然環保。心五四運動是指跟心靈環保相關的五個類別，各有四點的實踐項目，四安：安心、安身、安家、安業。四要：需要、想要、能要、該要。四它：面對它、接受它、處理它、放下它。四感：感恩、感謝、感化、感動。四福：知福、惜福、培福、種福。心六倫，涵蓋家庭、生活、校園、自然、職場和族群六種倫理。

至落腳於都市地區的原住民，主要服務大臺北範圍，包括協助五股伯特利全人關懷協會、汐止花東新村原住民住宅❸，以及快樂大掃，參與的對象以原住民家庭的孩童、婦女及長者為主。此亦呼應聖嚴法師提出「心五四」之中，以四安是其中極為重要的一項運動，「四安」就是從「安心」開始的，「安心」之後，就能夠「安身」，也才能夠做到「安家」、「安業」。

原住民族是臺灣相當具有特色的族群，也可以說是最早生活在臺灣這塊土地的人群。然而，隨著漢人自大陸渡臺之後，帶來不同的生活型態、社會制度與風俗文化，對於原住民族的文化與族群性具有相當深遠的影響，而族群間的互動也隨著工商業社會的發展，以及全球多元文化潮流的影響下而有所轉變。如以多元文化觀點來看，文化是人們不斷適應的過程，並配合歷史背景做為自己生存的條件，同時，學習以不同的觀點來理解與適應這不斷變動的世界（Watson, 2000）。對臺灣而言，原住民族是在地歷史與多元文化的重要根源，但在社會變遷的歷史背景之下，也必須學習以不同於舊有的觀點來看待，並面對不斷變動的社會。而如以臺灣社會族群關係之變遷來看，尹章義（1989）曾將臺灣由「先住民社會過渡成為漢人社會」的過程分為五個階段，分別為：（一）番人社會；（二）番人優勢、漢人劣勢期；

---

❸ 二○一八年四月，擴大成為「汐止 Wawa 森林——至善兒少發展中心」，是一個在大臺北都市叢林裡，扎根於汐止樟樹灣地區的都市原住民兒童與少年發展培力的社區空間。網址：https://www.facebook.com/pg/2018wawa/about/?ref=page_internal。檢索日期：2019/9/8。

（三）番漢均勢期；（四）番人劣勢、漢人優勢期；（五）漢人社會。足以顯見原住民族在臺灣社會變遷的過程中，在政治經濟勢力的邊緣化與文化勢力的弱化。

近年來，隨著族群意識興起以及文化權利抬頭，為回應原住民族社會之需求，並順應世界保障原住民族權利之潮流，行政院於一九九六年十二月十日成立原住民族委員會（中央部會層級）。至今已逾二十年，過去原住民族委員會的施政重點主要在於原住民族的政治發展、教育文化、衛生福利、經濟及公共建設、土地管理等五項。而後有感於全臺有近半數的原住民族設籍在非原住民族地區，因此，乃將其生活適應與發展等相關問題與需求視為原住民族之重要施政項目之一，並特此擬訂二○一八年至二○二一年都市原住民族發展方案❹，以就業、教育及文化為政策軸心。由此可知，都市原住民的需求受到政府相當的重視。

本研究目的在於了解至善基金會投入於都市原住民之照顧方案，所扶助的受助者們有哪些改變與成果展現，由於 SROI 方法相當重視利害關係人的轉變與過程。因此，乃以 SROI 做為研究途徑，期能以貨幣化的方式，具體描繪出至善基金會都市原住民照顧方案之成果。擇取的研究範圍，考量五股伯特利全人關懷協會已為一個成熟自立的單位、快樂大掃將以轉型成為社會企業為目標。而汐止花東新村原住民住宅，為政府於一九九一年提供原住民的社會住宅，主要給

---

❹ 原住民族委員會都市原住民族發展方案（107 年－110 年），網址：http://statis.moi.gov.tw/micst/stmain.jsp?sys=100。檢索日期：2019/9/8。

原住民族居住租用，但原住民族所需要的除了政府提供的硬體設備之外，尚有許多心理需求，如教育與社會適應問題、文化傳承等。至善基金會深知此類的需求亦不可忽視，故針對原住民族的主要居住場域及聚集區──花東新村，提供孩童與老人之照顧、文化尋根以及各類藝術、音樂與資訊等課程，並在二〇一八年四月，擴大成為汐止 Wawa 森林──至善兒少發展中心。誠如聖嚴法師提倡的「心六倫」運動，涵括「家庭」、「生活」、「校園」、「自然」、「職場」和「族群」等六種倫理，這六倫是環環相扣的。在同一個人身上，很可能就具有六種倫理的互動關係，每一種倫理關係之間，都應各盡其責任、各守其分際。而且主張「心」六倫，是從心出發，從我們自己做起。其中族群倫理則是強調尊重多元族群，互助、包容、共榮，求同而存異（釋果鏡，2010）。

總之，本研究擇取至善基金會都市原住民照顧方案中的汐止花東新村原住民住宅為個案（2017 年 1 月 1 日至 12 月 31 日止），針對各類利害關係人進行成果分析，做為都市原住民相關政策與計畫之參考。

二、文獻探討

（一）臺灣原住民族之族群關係發展

有關族群的討論相當廣泛，而針對族群一詞的定義，王甫昌（2003）總括一般研究者對於族群所下的定義為「族群是指一群因為擁有共同的來源，或者是共同的祖先、共同的

文化或語言,而自認為、或是被其他的人認為,構成一個獨特社群的一群人。」Cohen(1978)認為族群不能脫離族群關係而存在。透過進一步的觀察,族群關係的型態亦能用相對性的角度來理解,包括競爭與合作、衝突與和諧,在歷史軌跡的形塑下,各族群對彼此之間已埋下種種偏見與刻板印象,而當要面臨資源獲取的情況下,對於族群之間的關係如同注入一劑催化劑,引起族群關係的微妙變化。

以原住民族在臺灣的社會地位發展歷史來看,王甫昌(2003)認為歷經各種移入政權挾其強勢武力進入臺灣,因為統治利益對於臺灣的需求不同,而在政策上不斷擺盪的結果,造成原住民的土地受到剝奪、生活方式也逐漸被破壞。也由於原住民族的傳統生產方式不同於漢人以資本主義為導向的經濟型態,導致原住民族進入工商業社會之後常面臨社會排除的困難,長久之後,進而變成社會邊緣化的一個群體。依據孫大川(2000)的觀察,原住民族的發展面臨四個難以克服的問題,分別是民族人口縮減、生存空間狹窄、語言流失及社會與風俗瓦解。而觀察原住民族在臺灣的現況,對於主流社會而言,原住民族有較高的失業率與貧窮率、較低的教育水平和所得、較短的平均壽命。再加上酗酒問題、隔代教養、貧窮、依賴人口比例高以及原鄉地區福利、醫療資源和就業機會少(黃源協、詹宜璋,2000;莊曉霞,2012)。

綜言之,原住民運動近三十年來,縱使政府回應了原住民族的需求設立了族群代表性機關、立法保障原住民族權益,且投注了相當的資源於原住民族相關政策。但社會上對

於原住民族長期以來的偏見與刻板印象，以及原住民族在漢人的強勢文化之浸潤下，原住民族的處境相較於漢人，仍處於弱勢地位，顯見政策不足以彌補社會落差，而非營利組織的投入則期能填補這中間的裂隙。

（二）社會影響力

影響力一詞，可視為個人或組織的任何一項行為對他者所造成的影響，除了程度大小之外，也應將人、事、時、地、物等因素均考量在內，包括對哪些人、事、物造成影響？影響的範圍有多廣？影響的時間有多長？以及所造成的影響是正向或負向？綜言之，社會影響力所描述的是一種集合體，用來表示個人或組織為了達到想要的結果而投入了各種資源，在各種投入並經過中間過程，以及相關政策的導引下，所產生的實質效益（Latane, 1981; Emerson, Wachowics, & Chun, 2000; Reisman and Giennap, 2004）。

而在社會企業的研究領域中，社會影響力評估（Richmond, Mook, & Quarter, 2003; Nicholls, 2009; Smith and Stevens, 2010）則被大量地討論，對於努力達成社會使命的組織來說，社會影響力評估，能夠協助其衡量在完成社會使命的過程中，造成了哪些影響（Grieco, 2015）。就社會企業組織而言，相較於對盈餘的關注，社會企業更重視社會使命。因此，將社會效益涵括入財務報表中對社會企業至關重要，因為這將幫助他們更全面地透視本身的表現（Asutin, Stevenson, & Wei-Skillern, 2006）。但事實上，社會企業所進行的事務，常是無形且無法貨幣化的項目，而這類的項

目通常被財務報表排除在外（Richmond, Mook, & Quarter, 2003）。基此，社會影響力評估的目的之一，即是做為與外部利益相關者溝通的工具，其評估內容不再僅限於環境和經濟指標，而是關注於非經濟性的產出和組織整體的目標達成程度（Grieco, 2015）。

此外，對於組織來說，透過評估的過程，將會產生兩個層面的效益。首先，可以做為內部營運工具，幫助資源配置，也協助社會企業家管理組織；其次，可以做為一種匯報工具，讓企業股東了解目標的達成率，並進行後續的評估與調整（Grieco, 2015）。總之，可以將社會影響力評估（Social Impact Assessment, SIA）理解為一種管理工具，讓組織能用來引導目標、完成預測的過程，並且讓組織的行動可以更加朝向優質化發展（陳定銘，2016）。

（三）社會投資報酬分析

社會投資報酬（SROI）方法，主要用來衡量利害關係者，所感受或者體驗到產出的價值，是一個整合社會、環境、經濟成本與收益的工具，是從社會面出發，但卻應用在市場面的評估方法。它強調以質化的訪談對話，得到可量化或可貨幣化的「改變」事實（吳宗昇、周宗穎、張抒凡，2013）。

最早關於 SROI 的研究，可追溯至一九九七年由美國的羅伯特企業發展基金會（Roberts Enterprise Development Fund, REDF），為了衡量其資助的非營利組織及社會企業，所投入的成本與達成的效益，而研擬的評估工具。至二〇〇四年，

Social Value UK 及 Social Value International 兩個單位開始提倡 SROI，並於二〇〇五年發布 SROI 架構書（Framework Document），後續在英國政府內閣辦公室第三部門（Office of the Third Sector）的資助下，完成 SROI 的正式指南，二〇〇九年《社會投資報酬率指南》（*A Guide to Social Return On Investment*，簡稱 SROI 指南）出版，並於二〇一二年再版，成為目前最新的流通版本。而 SROI 的計算方式與財務分析上常用的投資報酬率（ROI）十分相近，都是以投資所獲得的回報除以投資金額而得，但 SROI 不同於 ROI 的地方在於所關注的不僅是財務的帳面數值，更關心的是投入資源所產生的影響與改變，包括有形的及無形的影響與改變，並嘗試將這些影響與改變量化，最後將計算的結果以社會價值的概念來表示（李宜樺、吳佳餘、朱恩言，2017）。

了解 SROI 的發展歷程及內涵之後，以類型來看，SROI 可分為預測型及評估型兩種，前者在活動規畫階段尤其有用，用以測量活動達到預期成果所能創造的社會價值，能夠幫助顯示如何讓社會投資影響最大化，也能在項目啟動和運行時確認哪些內容需要被測量；後者則是基於以發生成果、對干預行為的回溯（台灣影響力研究院譯，2016）。而在實際操作方面，SROI 指南提出六項步驟以及七項原則，讓評估方能夠依據這些步驟及原則，逐步計算出社會影響力，就六項步驟及七項原則進行論述。在六項步驟方面分別為：

1. 確定 SROI 的分析範圍並識別利害關係者：在開始進行 SROI 的分析前，需明確知道分析的範圍，及進行此次分析的目的是什麼，可以透過與利害關係人的議

和，界定分析的範圍，以及辨識參與其中的利害關係人（李宜樺、吳佳餘、朱恩言，2017）。

2. 描繪成果：成果（Outcome）是 SROI 主要衡量的影響力主體，在透過第一步驟確立分析範圍與利害關係人之後，透過問卷、訪談、焦點座談等方式，向利害關係者蒐集進一步的資訊，包括「投入」（Input）、「產出」（Output），以及兩者與成果之間的鏈狀關係。

3. 證明成果並將其貨幣化：在掌握了成果之後，須找到相關數據與指標來證明成果確實發生，之後再以貨幣形式為其評估價值（李宜樺、吳佳餘、朱恩言，2017）。

4. 確認影響力：將影響力貨幣化之後，仍須檢視是否有重複計算、非由本專案所造成之影響等不應計算在內的因素，主要歸納為無謂因子（Deadweight）、移轉因子（Displacement）、歸因因子（Attribution）以及衰退因子（Drop-off）等四項。無謂因子代表的是即使利害關係人不參與方案，仍然會發生的成果比例；轉移因子代表的是方案可能會在利害關係人產生多種成果，但成果與成果之間的可能會有所替代，轉移因子即用來表示成果之間相互替代的比例；歸因因子代表的是對利害關係人而言，現在有的改變成果，或許有一定比例來自其他地方，也就是非現有方案所帶來的成果比例；衰退因子則代表對利害關係人而言，方案所帶來的某些成果不可能無限遞延，一定會

有所衰退，這是計算成果在未來幾年的衰退比例（張抒凡，2013）。

5. 計算 SROI 值：彙總活動過程中所產生的所有效益、減除相關的非影響因素，考慮折現後計算投資所獲得的實際結果（李宜樺、吳佳餘、朱恩言，2017）。這階段可以同時測試成果的敏感度。

6. SROI 報告、應用和嵌入組織：最後一步非常重要，而又容易被遺忘。與利害關係人分享研究成果並做出回饋，SROI 在組織應用以及報告（台灣影響力研究院譯，2016）。

而除了上述進行 SROI 的六項步驟之外，指南中並進一步要求使用者在演算過程中應遵守以下七項原則（台灣影響力研究院譯，2016）：

1. 利害關係者的參與：將參與的受益人以及其他利害關係者納入計畫當中，並識別哪些需要被評估以及如何評估。

2. 理解發生的何種變化：這一項原則的主要目的是為了了解改變是如何發生的。

3. 僅納入重要訊息：將所有具有相關性以及重要性的事情報告出來，也就是應考慮事件的重要性，將利害關係者體驗到重要改變的決定和成果相關信息列為重要材料進行分析，以便將真實的影響力地圖描繪出來，並使利害關係者對影響力做出合理判斷。

4. 為關鍵成果定價：藉由評估經濟、社會與環境的受益程度與成本，將不同的成果訂定出重要性（並非只是

彙整現有的財務及帳面價值），並加以定價。

5. 不誇大成果：將您的結果與事實相比較，只要列出那些由機構干預活動所帶來的價值。

6. 保持透明公開：清楚地說明您所有的證據與假設。

7. 審核成果：請其他人來檢驗您的結果。

透過對於 SROI 評估方法的了解可知，SROI 評估方法具有明確的操作步驟，以及運用原則，能夠逐步地盤點研究個案之改變。以本研究個案來說，汐止花東新村原住民住宅的服務主要包括三個面向，在推動都市文化聚落營造的工作，持續培力婦女經營社區照顧，讓長者健康安全老化，孩子們的文化成長，並帶動族人的居住權及文化權意識。透過 SROI 評估方法，能夠仔細地檢視利害關係者的改變與所經歷的過程，並將這些改變以貨幣化的方式呈現，讓至善基金會與社會大眾，能夠以一種普及且具有代表性的衡量單位，理解汐止花東新村原住民住宅照顧計畫產生的社會價值有多少。

（四）相關文獻檢閱

本研究透過國家圖書館期刊文獻資訊網、華藝線上圖書館及臺灣博碩士論文知識加值系統、Social Value UK 通過認證之報告等資料庫平台，採用「都市原住民」、「社會投資報酬」、「社會影響」做為關鍵字，於二〇二〇年四月十日檢索結果所得，期能從中對本議題當前的研究情形有所了解，以做為本研究基礎。透過關鍵字詞之檢索可知，有關都市原住民之期刊論文為數不少，但目前尚未有針對都市原住

民進行 SROI 分析之期刊論文，因此，僅擇取對於本研究具有參考價值者（參閱表一）。而 Social Value UK 通過認證之報告資料庫中，與原住民、弱勢照顧相關的有十四篇，再加以檢閱後，擇取相關議題之報告四篇。將擇取之論文摘要歸納如表二。

表一：都市原住民相關文獻摘要表

作者 （年分）	著作篇名	相關內容摘要	實證研究概念
劉佑彰 （2001）	傾聽被忽視的聲音——都市原住民學生的學習	都市原住民學生面臨了族群文化差異、教材內容片面、家長的教育觀念較放任等困難，作者透過自身做為教育者的角度，提出對於都市原住民學童在教育面的觀察與建議。	文中提出都市原住民學童之成績偏低、缺乏學習動機與興趣，而家長則缺乏時間與學術能力指導子女之課業，因此學校教師的角色相當重要，應以多元文化的觀點對都市原住民學生提供積極正面的協助，同理都市原住民學童的學習適應問題，以整體改善其面臨的困難。
卓石能 （2010）	都市原住民學童族群認同與其自我概念生活適應之關係研究	本文使用普查方式進行問卷調查研究，以了解都市原住民學童的族群認同與自我概念、生活適應之關係及相關因素。	研究結論指出都市原住民學童的族群認同、自我概念、生活適應之「同儕適應」與人際互動等在不同年齡、家庭背景等因素下有不同的發展情形。並透過研究結果提出在教育行政機構、國小、教師等，在教育場域中的相關建議。

魏淑卿、陳淑美（2018）	談都市原住民幼兒教育——一個幼兒園教師的觀點	透過教育場域的觀察可知，都市原住民幼兒由於家庭在經濟資本上的不足，無法在孩童教育上多做投資，因此面臨了經濟資本與文化資本不足的學習困境。本文針對這方面的教育困境，提出相關建議。	透過研究提出對於都市原住民幼兒的教育建議，包括教師多元文化教育的增能、加強親師溝通及親職教育、提供原住民職訓及人才培育機會，透過親師合作，共同提昇學校與家庭之功能，改善幼兒之學習困境。
蘇翠涵（2018）	都市原住民兒少服務經驗——以汐止 F 原住民社區為例	透過社工在地服務的經驗累積與深入觀察，彙整原住民在都市居住所面臨的困境與孩童的生活現況，以及為當地社區所開展的服務及策略，並反思陪伴這些孩子與自我生命意義的連結。	透過觀察可知，在多方的偏見壓力下，影響社區內部孩子的自信心不足，而不穩定之家庭關係也無法做為孩子尋求慰藉的場域，因此，兒少照顧據點的同儕團體獲得當地原住民兒少強烈的認同。此外，由於孩童的生活與傳統文化的斷裂，也缺乏認識自我文化的動機，因此安排了耆老學，讓長者與孩童有機會進行文化的交流與互動，讓孩童很自然地接觸文化，進而讓整體社區成員能夠重新認識自我、肯定自我。最後研究者也將服務經驗與自我的生命歷程連結，進而產生了自我覺察以及療癒的過程。

表二：原住民、弱勢族群／地區之社會投資報酬分析報告彙整表

著作篇名 （年分）	相關內容摘要	實證研究概念
Social Return On Investment Forecast of Teulu Ni-Early intervention that creates value in the lives of vulnerable families (2016)	為一篇對於 Teulu Ni 計畫進行的 SROI 預測分析。Gwynedd 為英國一個相當貧困的地區，Teulu Ni 計畫主要針對 Gwynedd 地區複雜境遇家庭進行相關的預防與保護措施。期望透過對家庭提供相關支援，以預防情況惡化，主要的目標包括：主動提供綜合性和具目的性的深入支持、提昇育兒技能以及促進成人健康。	透過研究顯示，家庭關係是安定社會的核心。透過 Teulu Ni 計畫，使得家長得以提高當父母的自信心，進而促進家庭關係、改善心理健康。在子女的改變方面，則包括促進家庭關係、自我認同、增加自信、改善健康、更喜愛上學等。顯見 Teulu Ni 計畫有持續的必要性，但報告亦提出要避免受助家庭持續地依賴 Teulu Ni 計畫，並逐步地靠自己的力量改善境遇，此外，亦建議整合第三部門的力量共同投入後續的輔導與追蹤機制，以期成果能持續，進而避免再次落入複雜境遇的家庭處境當中。
Ngā Tau Mīharo ō Aotearoa, Incredible Years Parenting (IYP) programme (2019)	Incredible Years Parenting（IYP）計畫旨在解決兒童偏差行為的問題。紐西蘭的原住民毛利人兒童當中，具有行為問題的占 15-20%，高於非毛利人兒童的 5-10%，因此該計畫針對毛利人兒童之行為問題進行改善。並將毛利人的傳統文化概念如歌曲、歸屬關係、相互支持等融入計畫當中，以期執行得更加順利。	本報告中的研究結果表明，透過計畫的執行，兒童在情感發展、認知表達與社會互動等方面確實得到改善，而家長／照顧者則具有變成更好的父母、改善親子關係、家庭觀念、減輕壓力、感到更有自信……等十項改變，顯見家長／照顧者對於家庭教育的影響甚鉅，並會反映在兒童行為上。因此，得以證實在育兒行為教育、家庭

		功能教育等早期介入的有效性與重要性，既可以改善家庭整體關係，亦能降低政府的財政和社會成本（如兒童福利成本、減少犯罪和暴力、降低社會服務成本等）。
Value Creation by Taitamariki Programme（2019）	Taitamariki 計畫是由 Te Whānau o Waipareira（Waipareira）組織所提出，是針對 10-13 歲青少年的提前預防計畫，教導青少年遠離毒品和酒精，使其具有正向的意念，保有健康、快樂的生活。	本報告中的研究結果表明，透過計畫的執行，青少年產生了增加自信心、自我意識增強、改善心理健康等成果，而其家人亦產生了改善人際關係、減少濫用毒品與酒精兩項改變，對政府而言則是降低了相關的社會支出。因此可以證實，此計畫的有效性與重要性。
CTBC Foundation for Arts and Culture 2018 Love & Arts for Dreams Initiatives Project（2019）	CTBC 藝術文化基金會行政組進行討論，以優化項目。我們希望整合專業藝術家，當地社區和公司的支持，以找到最佳的協作開發模型並最大程度地發揮項目的影響力。愛與夢想藝術計畫致力於將藝術資源傳播到臺灣的每個角落，此次於臺東縣東河鄉東河小學提供舞蹈課程，將藝術帶至偏鄉。	透過研究發現，愛與夢想藝術計畫提高了參與學生的自我認同感和文化素養、擴大了生活視野，並改善了人際關係與學習能力。而舞者透過教學過程提昇了耐心和毅力，並獲得滿足感和成就感。而透過研究報告亦建議基金會能夠整合藝術家、當地社區和各項資源，以找到最佳的合作模型，並最大化計畫的影響力。

在擇取的報告當中，大多數均為對於原住民教育所面臨的困境所做的觀察與現況彙整，最後提出相關建議與解決方案，但並未針對原住民族照顧方案進行成效評估與分析，在 SROI 報告的部分，大多數是針對該地區的少數或特殊族

群所進行的協助方案，或對於偏鄉地區之資源挹注計畫進行
SROI 之分析。而不論是期刊論文或 SROI 報告，對於原住
民議題的探討相當多元，顯見原住民議題具有重要性，從而
應對於各項政策與計畫之施行效果，進行評估並予以動態調
整。而在都市原住民議題漸受重視時，仍少有針對都市原住
民計畫施行專案評估之相關報告，更未見 SROI 分析，從而
顯見本研究之特殊性。

三、至善基金會個案析探 ❺

　　財團法人至善社會福利基金會於一九九五年成立，創辦
人是善山師父，因一個善念而成立。至善是立足於臺灣的亞
洲兒少發展實踐家，服務地區包括臺灣、越南、雲南與緬甸
等亞洲四地，逾二十年來幫助 85,000 名孩子吃飽、上學、獲
得照顧，讓他們成長之路不孤單。在臺灣的計畫主要以原住
民培力與照顧為主，一九九八年至善有感於臺灣原住民族因
地處偏遠，社會資源匱乏和文化差異影響，造成原住民兒童
求學的種種限制與瓶頸，於是在新竹縣尖石鄉後山四校開展
「貧童助學」計畫，幫助原民孩童順利就學。而後又在新竹
尖石鄉各級學校和部落長期而穩定地推動教育培力工作，並
將服務據點延伸至宜蘭、高雄、屏東等原鄉，開展以陪伴、
照顧二至十八歲原住民兒少為主要工作內容的「陪你長大」
計畫。在陪伴孩童的過程，看見原鄉就業困難與發展不穩

---

❺ 資料來源：至善基金會官方網站：http://www.zhi-shan.org/；至善 FaceBook
網址：https://www.facebook.com/cit2009/。檢索日期：2018/8/31。

定，讓部落青年不得已離鄉謀生，造成原鄉孩童缺乏家庭及社區照顧，因此，至善自二〇〇五年開展了「培我原夢」計畫，支持渴望返鄉和留在部落的原住民青年，投入部落發展工作，以促進在地經濟活動與社會支持照顧系統。

近年來，隨著原住民生活型態改變，為獲取更好的工作與教育機會，許多原住民移居到都市生活，卻面臨龐大的經濟壓力與文化差異。為此，至善開展「都市原住民照顧發展」計畫，服務生活在大臺北地區的原住民朋友，提供就業服務、家庭支持、社區培力及成人教育等。根據內政部統計，全臺灣已有過半的原住民生活在六都為主的都會區裡❻，顯見都市原住民照顧的重要性。而至善基金會都市原住民計畫範圍位於大臺北地區，以協助五股伯特利、汐止花東新村原住民住宅，以及原住民婦女家事清潔服務。

（一）五股伯特利

緣起於來自屏東霧台的魯凱族婦女盧秋月，多年來關心都市幼兒照顧問題，不分族群身分，照顧的幼童包括原住民、新住民與漢人，平均每年照顧近百名的孩童，即使大部分的家長因收入不穩定而經常繳不出學費，盧秋月仍然無私地投入照顧幼童的工作，而自二〇〇七年起在至善基金會的資源挹注下，除了支援照顧空間與課輔班的設置與運作之外，並輔導伯特利立案登記為全臺第一間設立於都會區的

---

❻ 根據內政部人口統計，截至二〇一九年九月，臺灣原住民族總人口為570,074 人，其中山地原住民族 302,976 人、平地原住民族 267,098 人。

「社區互助式教保中心」，持續地為需要的孩童提供基本的餐食以及課後照顧的服務，讓孩童有較好的課後照顧的環境，並能夠讓孩子的課業維持一定的水平。

（二）汐止花東新村原住民住宅

汐止花東新村原住民住宅是都市原住民的出租國宅，成年人為生活與工作打拚之餘，常忽略了孩子們的文化教育。由於孩子們在都市長大，生活周遭早已與都市完全融合，原住民文化只剩下在學校的鄉土教學與族語認證，徹底與自己長輩的原鄉部落的連結斷裂，更沒有都市聚落原住民文化可依循。由於原住民家庭教養模式與都市家庭有所差異，讓孩子的學歷基礎跟不上主流教學的節奏，造成孩子們自身價值與自信心無所適從。因此，至善基金會於二〇一三年投入當地之照顧服務，提供課後輔導工作，除了協助孩童❼完成學校課業之外，也希望能提昇孩童對學校教育的適應能力，並自二〇一八年起擴大服務範圍至樟樹地區，改名為「汐止Wawa森林——至善兒少發展中心」。而除了兒少的工作之外，也希望能帶動長者的文化傳承能量，提昇孩子對於原住民身分的自我認同與文化意識。

---

❼ 依據聯合國《兒童權利公約》適用於全世界的兒童，即十八歲以下的所有人。因此，本研究以孩童做為統稱幼兒、兒童與青少年三類受益的利害關係人。

（三）快樂大掃

「快樂大掃」是一支由都會區原住民婦女組成的家事清潔團隊，於二〇一五年在至善基金會支持下組成。根據至善基金會對於原住民長期的照顧與觀察，不論是在原鄉或是都會區，原住民婦女總是將老幼的照顧責任一肩扛，至善基金會透過增加原住民婦女們的知識、工作收入等方式，協助婦女穩定生計，邁出經濟自立的第一步。然而，在都會區的原住民婦女常常在家庭照顧與就業之間選擇，都會區生活缺乏親族間互助與支持網絡的協助，致使弱勢、單親、低收以及離婚婦女這一群經濟弱勢婦女，因缺乏工作機會、沒有穩定收入，或是工作能力不足而被勞動市場淘汰，亦或是需負擔家務照顧的責任而陷入貧窮（至善基金會，2017 年報）。而快樂大掃是專為都會區原住民婦女組成的家事清潔服務團隊，提供為期四週的訓練課程加上一週的學科訓練之後，進行實地訓練操作四十小時，完成以上的家事培訓課程後，再通過老師評估與測驗後才能成為「家事人員」。透過扎實的訓練課程提供就業培訓讓婦女們具有就業能力，協助原本處於弱勢的她們能夠靠自己的力量翻轉就業困境、改善經濟狀況，進而提昇家庭整體的和諧與穩定。

四、SROI 分析與討論

本研究根據 SROI 的六項步驟進行，透過與利害關係人充分的溝通與了解，盡可能以同理心理解各類利害關係人真實的感受與改變，以完成預測型之社會影響評估與分析。以

下針對汐止花東新村原住民住宅原住民照顧方案進行 SROI
分析。

（一）確定 SROI 的分析範圍並識別利害關係人

1. 研究範疇

本研究以至善基金會之都市原住民專案計畫中，汐止花
東新村原住民住宅原住民照顧方案服務，做為本研究之分析
範圍。並以二○一七年一月一日至十二月三十一日止，各項
投入所產生之改變與成果，做為社會影響力預測期間，透過
跟參與汐止花東新村原住民住宅原住民照顧方案的利害關係
人議和，以及參考國內外原住民族照顧之 SROI 案例，做為
本研究 SROI 比率衡量及計算的依據。

依據至善基金會二○一七年成果報告書可知，於汐止花
東新村原住民住宅之主要工作項目包括三項，分別為對長
者、孩童與婦女之照顧。在長者部分，主要針對生活起居之
照顧提供長者供餐服務並試辦老人照護服務，另外，舉辦長
青課程以及參訪活動；在孩童部分，提供學童課後照顧服務
以及文化共學團體，並擴及家庭層面辦理社區家長座談會、
暑期親子共遊等活動，促進親子關係之和諧並扭轉教育態度
與理念；在婦女部分，除了連結汐止國泰醫院社區醫學部的
教學資源，學習社區長者照顧，進行照護工作的學習之外，
也提供電腦文書處理軟體之學習課程，培養不同的技能。本
研究依據工作項目進行後續之影響力分析。

2. 識別利害關係人

SROI 方法非常重視利害關係人的參與，透過充分地了

解其投入（Input）、產出（Output）及成果（Outcome）之間產生的改變，以辨別專案確實影響的對象，是進行 SROI 步驟中相當關鍵的過程。本研究之研究範圍中，因利害關係人之類別多元，故透過不同的議和管道及方式，確認利害關係人之參與及改變。議和過程如圖一表示：

圖一：利害關係人議和流程圖

　　經由焦點團體的討論過程，討論預期會受到影響的主要利害關係人，再藉由書面資料、初步訪談之後，依據 SROI 的七項原則之識別利害關係人及僅納入重要資訊之原則，排除部分利害關係人。此外，將納入的利害關係人群體歸納為原住民族委員會與至善基金會、行政人員、孩童、家長／主要照顧者及長者五類，並自各類利害關係人當中，以立意抽樣的方式進行訪談。利害關係人之辨識結果與原因，如表三：

表三：利害關係人辨識結果彙整表

利害關係人（數量）	是否納入分析	原因
原住民族委員會（1）	是	透過訪談得知，原住民族委員會主要在挹注資源協助基金會進行原住民照顧方案，但並非都市原住民照顧計畫的主要改變對象，因此，僅呈現其投入的部分，而不做結果分析。

至善基金會（1）	是	透過訪談得知，基金會對本身的工作充滿熱情且獲得成就感，但並非都市原住民專案計畫所改變的主要對象，因此，僅呈現其投入的部分，而不做結果分析。
行政人員（8）	是	透過訪談得知，投入汐止花東新村原住民住宅工作之社工、行政助理、廚工、課程媽媽等，透過參與工作獲得經濟支援以及成就感，且參與者之族群屬性都是原住民，為本研究要探討之主要利害關係人之一，因此，予以納入計算。
孩童（22）	是	依據至善基金會投入於汐止花東新村原住民住宅之主要工作項目可知，孩童為主要受扶助的對象，故為本研究要探討之主要利害關係人，予以納入計算。
家長／主要照顧者（30）	是	透過訪談得知，為促進親子關係，至善基金會亦辦理親子共學、共玩、共遊課程，因此，家長亦為本研究要探討之主要利害關係人，從而予以納入計算。此外，透過訪談得知有部分孩童並非與家長同住，而是由具有親屬關係者照顧，此類別的利害關係人身分別包括家長及主要照顧者。
長者（35）	是	依據至善基金會投入於汐止花東新村原住民住宅之主要工作項目可知，長者為主要受扶助的對象，為本研究要探討之主要利害關係人，予以納入計算。
志工（8）	否	主要投入在孩子的課業輔導、陪伴等，為實習性質並非長期駐點，且參與者並不固定，故予以排除。
村里辦公室（1）	否	訪談時由利害關係人提及，有關辦理老人供餐服務，供餐的時間與至善基金會錯開，但參加的族群不分原住民與否，與本研究之成果無關，僅有納入敏感性分析當中，而不做結果分析，故予以排除。
山光天主堂（1）	否	教會為大多數原住民之信仰中心，提供心靈上的支持與輔助，但並非都市原住民照顧計畫的主要改變對象，因此，予以排除。
樟樹國小（1）	否	接受課後輔導之孩童主要來自該國小，但經訪談得知，其功能主要在於提供正規教

		育，與本研究之成果無關，僅有納入敏感性分析當中，而不做結果分析。
國泰醫院（1）	否	為專案活動之互動協力單位，基於影響對象不特定且程度小，故不納入考量。

（二）投入與產出

1. 投入

藉由至善基金會之二〇一七年成果報告書及內部會計資料可知，該年度在汐止花東新村原住民住宅之投入總金額為新臺幣（以下同）1,742,862 元，其中分為政府補助經費865,154 元、自籌經費 877,708 元兩項，其中政府補助經費主要來自原住民族委員會，經費補助主要用於專案管理社工員之人事費、共餐服務之餐費及助理的工作津貼、長者照護服務之工作津貼，以及辦理長青課程之相關支出費用。

此外，除了物質性的投入之外，依據利害關係人之屬性，除了勞動力之外亦有非物質性的投入如時間，而為了遵循 SROI 方法之不重複計算的原則，在此將行政人員之人事費用、工作津貼等一律納入原住民族委員會及至善基金會之投入金額當中一併計算，以免有重複計算的情形。

而孩童、家長／主要照顧者及長者的部分，三者均為都市原住民照顧計畫之主要扶助對象，孩童參與的時間為學校放學之後的時間，且孩童都是自願參與，並無其他外部成本的產生，故推測其時間投入的價值為零；家長／主要照顧者的部分主要是在參與活動的時間，均運用放假休息日的時間參與，故無其他機會成本的產生，因此，推測其時間投入的價值為零；長者的部分則是由於長者大多賦閒在家中，也無

其他單位提供與至善基金會相同的服務，加上有同一族群屬性的親切感，長者會自願性地參加至善的供餐服務，故推測其時間投入的價值為零。有關投入之資源彙整如表四所示。

表四：投入資源彙整表

利害關係人	投入項目	投入金額／換算之貨幣價值 （單位：新臺幣）
至善基金會	金錢	877,708
行政人員	時間、勞動力	0
孩童	時間	0
家長／主要照顧者	時間	0
長者	時間	0
原住民族委員會	金錢	865,154
合計		1,742,862

　2.產出

　　透過至善基金會及原住民族委員會經費的支持、社工及行政助理的投入及學童和家長／主要照顧者、長者的參與，汐止花東新村原住民住宅的原住民照顧工作得以推展，並產生後續的影響力，依據二〇一七年服務內容之產出場次及受服務之人次數彙整如表五所示。

表五：產出彙整表

內容	數量／單位
1.提供長者共餐的社會服務	2,903 人次／年
2.試辦老人照護的服務	24 人次／年
3.舉辦長青課程	1,612 人次／年
4.社區照顧的婦女共學	100 人次／年
5.學童課後照顧	3,557 人次／年

6. 青少年聚會團體	241 人次／年
7. 文化成長共學團體	610 人次／年
8. 兒少保護工作，個案研討	15 次／年
9. 都市聚落文化採集，辦理都市生活紀錄展	1 次／年
10. 舉辦居住相關的法規政策說明會	4 場／年

（三）證明成果並將其貨幣化

1. 成果與改變

與利害關係人的深度訪談及實地的參與觀察，本研究歸納各項利害關係人的主要成果如表六，並就各項成果進行論述。

表六：成果彙整表

利害關係人		成果／改變
孩童	幼兒	提昇自信心
		增進親子關係
	兒童	自主學習
		提昇自信心
		提昇社交能力
		增進親子關係
	青少年	自主學習
		提昇自信心
		提昇社交能力
		增進親子關係
家長／主要照顧者 增進親子關係		改變教育態度
		增進親子關係
長者 文化傳承		維持社交聯繫
		文化傳承
行政人員	課程媽媽	技能提昇
		自信心

	長者用餐／一般行政助理	技能提昇（籌設協會、照顧知能）
		自信心
		擴展人際網絡
	社工	提昇反思與自省的能力
		提昇社交能力（表達與溝通協調）

　　在孩童方面，將事件鏈區分為幼兒、兒童與青少年三部分來檢視，主要由於幼兒的年齡層介於 0 至 2 歲之間，在生、心理方面的成熟度與其他階段的兒童、青少年有所區別，在產生成果的路徑上也有所不同。在幼兒階段，仍然相當依賴主要照顧者，不論是在情感依附上或是生活照顧上，與主要照顧者之間具有緊密的連結。而藉由參與照顧據點的活動，能夠與其他年齡的孩童有所互動，並在模仿學習與接受外來刺激之下，促進認知、人格、人際互動等各項發展，且照顧據點為一個友善孩童的環境，幼兒在此接受到主要照顧者以外的肯定與鼓勵，因而提昇了自信心。而多樣化的活動則增加了幼兒與主要照顧者的互動模式，使得親子關係更加緊密。幼兒成果事件鏈參閱圖二。

　　在兒童與青少年方面，由於至善基金會觀察到花東新村的孩童不一定與父母同住，而是交由親屬照顧，或是因工作繁忙無暇陪伴孩子，孩子在放學後也不一定會直接回家，而是在外遊蕩。因而汐止花東新村原住民住宅設立一個據點，讓孩子們在放學後有個能夠歸屬之處，除了能夠認識許多新朋友之外，汐止花東新村也不定期的邀請外界師資或與鄰近大學社團合作，到照顧據點進行如吉他、網頁設計、手工藝、家政等活動，讓孩子在照顧據點擁有多元的學習（至善

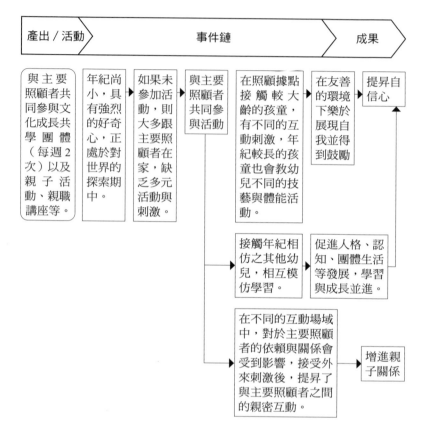

圖二：幼兒之成果事件鏈

基金會，2018）。

　　透過訪談得知孩子在參與了多元課程之後，表示其非常喜歡樂器和音樂這兩項，學到新的樂器也會很開心，甚至開始練習音樂創作。而另一個孩子則是在參與了電腦資訊的課程之後，開始學習拍攝影片，並設立 youtube 頻道，在訪談過程中更不斷展示自己的頻道，並展現出相當的自信心。而

在寒暑假期間，孩子們也主動地分工查資料，設計一日小旅
行的路線規畫與內容，對於人際互動、合作分工都有長足的
進步。透過多元課程的刺激，孩童們除了能夠找出自我興趣
之外，也會主動進一步地學習，更從中得到自信。有關孩童
部分之兒童、青少年成果事件鏈參閱圖三。

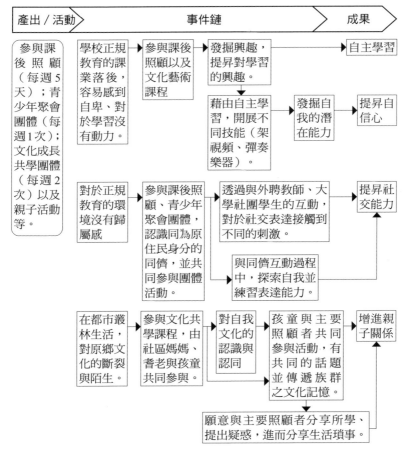

圖三：兒童、青少年之成果事件鏈

除了孩童的照顧之外，至善基金會也察覺親子教育是非常重要的一塊，因此，不定期地舉辦親子教育課程，鼓勵社區中的家長與孩童一起來參加。而透過訪談得知，孩童與家長在參加相關活動之後，孩童比較願意與主要照顧者分享生活瑣事、或願意邀請照顧者一同來參加照顧據點所舉辦的活動，至於家長／主要照顧者透過課程，了解各階段孩童發展的變化與應對，並較願意聆聽孩子的表達，而非以往權威式的教育態度，進而改善了親子關係與家庭氣氛（參閱圖四）。

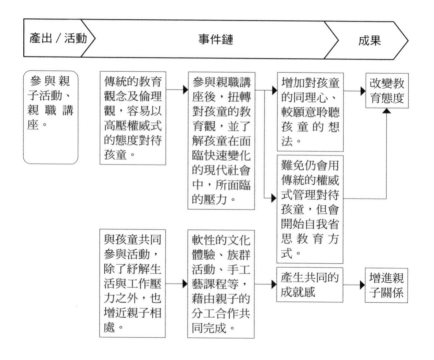

圖四：主要照顧者之成果事件鏈

　　在長者的部分，至善基金會則認為社區中的長者除了需要被照顧之外，更富有相當深厚的文化內涵。因此，在長者照護方面，與鄰近的醫院合作或聘請師資，針對社區中的婦女進行培訓與教育課程，讓婦女具備照護能力，在社區中建立互助網絡，並開辦老人共餐，提供社區中的長者一個共同相聚的時間與空間，飯後之餘也聘請師資，教導長者簡單的舞蹈，活絡身體。在共餐時間，長者之間也會閒話家常，成為一個凝聚情感的場所。

　　此外，至善基金會認為文化傳承也是不可忽視的部分，因此規畫了文化共學、耆老課程，邀請社區中的長者教導孩子各類文化技藝，包括母語、歌唱、編織、習俗、舞蹈等，讓生活在都市中的原住民孩童也能夠貼近文化，進而能夠對自我的族群更加理解與認同。長者透過訪談表示：「我們這裡會分享，只要來這裡就很快樂。」而一向重視文化的基金會理念，也安排課程媽媽與耆老合作課程，帶社區的青少年製做豐年祭的服裝配飾與舞蹈教學，藉由製作過程的參與，說明服裝圖騰所代表的意義、各類編織技法的練習以及舞步內涵，強化孩童對於族群文化的印象（參閱圖五）。

　　至於課程媽媽與長者共餐之行政助理方面，由於照顧據點除了不定期聘請外部師資之外，也邀請社區的媽媽一同參與課程教學。由各媽媽自行安排課程主題並設計課程內容，課程媽媽透過訪談表示在課程之前除了需要構思課程內容之外，也需要蒐集資料並練習如何為孩童上課，故提昇了個人的技藝知能，而在講解的過程及與孩童的互動中，也獲益許多並提昇了個人的自信心。對於協助長者用餐的助理來說，

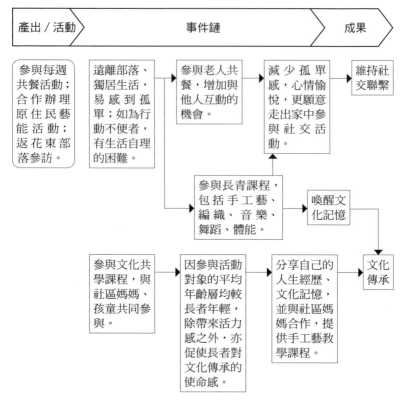

圖五：長者之成果事件鏈

至善基金會提供與鄰近醫院或相關單位的照護課程，提昇了個人的照護知能。而在課程中也認識相關領域的教師、同學與照顧者，藉此擴展了社交網絡，並可針對照護相關的實務與經驗進行交流。行政助理更表示：「這是我原本不會接觸到的領域，像是寫計畫書、核銷，這些我看來很複雜的東西，透過請教基金會還有大家提供意見，到現在慢慢我可以獨當一面寫計畫書，這是我自己覺得很不可思議的事情。」顯見其在

參與照顧據點之後,有顯著的影響與改變(參閱圖六)。

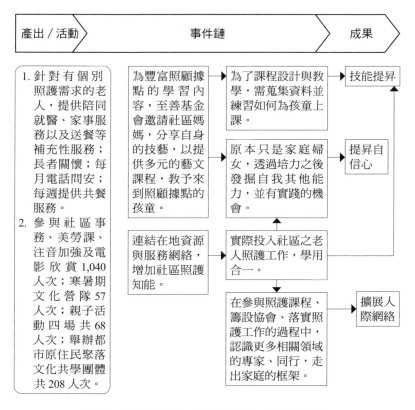

圖六:課程媽媽、行政助理之成果事件鏈

最後,在社工方面最大的改變在於提昇反思與自省的能力,以及提昇社交能力。由於第三部門組織的投入也有其專業性,如何跳脫自我中心的觀點,深入地去了解服務對象的背景與文化,才能夠找到一套合適服務對象的機制。美國社會工作人員協會(National Association of Social Workers,

NASW, 2007；黃盈豪，2016）即提出文化能力（cultural competence）的概念，意指一套能肯認及尊重不同文化、語言、階級、種族及族群身分、宗教之個人、家庭、社區價值，並保護及維持其尊嚴的過程。

由於原住民族已經受到許多刻板印象、歧視、被標籤化的經驗，因此，社工對於來到照顧據點的孩童抱持開放的態度，在服務的過程中逐步累積反思與自省的能力，對於孩童多予聆聽、少予框架，給孩童一個自在舒適的空間。透過訪談，社工表示：「我們很少談成績，比較多的是刺激思考，像是勞動節為什麼放假？然後會談一下勞動節的脈絡緣由、那為什麼孩童的父母沒有放假之類，用日常生活中的事情促使孩子們思考進而探究。」也由於擔任照顧據點的社工，接觸的對象相當多元如長者、社區民眾、家長、孩童，故也會讓社工調整與不同對象的溝通方式，提昇了溝通與表達的能力（參閱圖七）。

2. 指標（Indicators）選擇

透過與利害關係人之議和可知，利害關係人在參與至善基金會之汐止花東新村原住民住宅原住民照顧計畫後，產生在行為、心靈感受以及價值觀的改變，這些改變會受到利害關係人的個人背景因素而有所差異。因此，針對每一項成果提出至少一個指標，用以證明成果確實發生，且將指標納入問卷當中，只有當利害關係人勾選任一指標時，才代表該項成果發生，透過問卷統計結果分析做為成果發生依據。針對不同利害關係人成果指標彙整如表七。

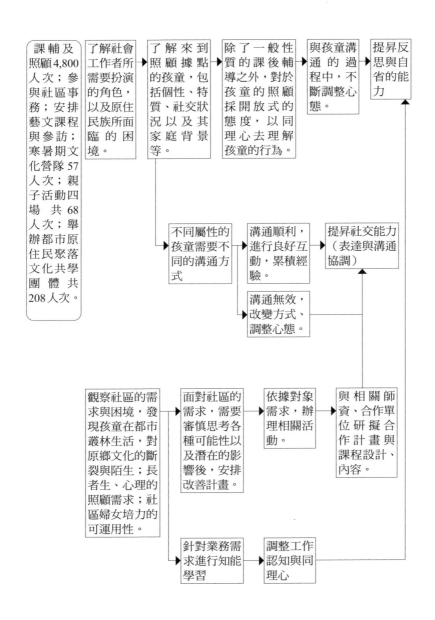

圖七：社工之成果事件鏈

表七：利害關係人成果指標彙整表

利害關係人		成果／改變	指標
孩童	幼兒	提昇自信心	1. 認為自己的自信心增加 2. 願意學習或嘗試不同（新）的事物 3. 透過家長／主要照顧者或老師的觀察，認為孩子們的自信心增加。
		增進親子關係	1. 願意跟父母分享生活瑣事 2. 遇到困難或者有事情時願意向父母諮詢 3. 一起參與活動的次數增加 4. 在家中跟父母衝突的次數減少
	兒童	自主學習	1. 能夠妥善安排時間將功課做完 2. 對於陌生的事物具有好奇心並能夠進而思考形成的原因與過程 3. 圖書館借閱書目之數量增加
		提昇自信心	1. 認為自己的自信心增加 2. 願意學習或嘗試不同（新）的事物 3. 透過家長／主要照顧者或老師的觀察，認為孩子們的自信心增加。
		提昇社交能力	1. 交到更多（3 個以上）朋友 2. 有更多人可以一起分享生活瑣事
		增進親子關係	1. 願意跟父母分享生活瑣事 2. 遇到困難或者有事情時願意向父母諮詢 3. 一起參與活動的次數增加 4. 在家中跟父母衝突的次數減少
	青少年	自主學習	1. 能夠妥善安排時間將功課做完 2. 對於陌生的事物具有好奇心並能夠進而思考形成的原因與過程 3. 圖書館借閱書目之數量增加
		提昇自信心	1. 認為自己的自信心增加 2. 願意學習或嘗試不同（新）的事物 3. 透過家長／主要照顧者或老師的觀察，認為孩子們的自信心增加。
		提昇社交能力	1. 交到更多（3 個以上）朋友 2. 有更多人可以一起分享生活瑣事

		增進親子關係	1. 願意跟父母分享生活瑣事 2. 遇到困難或者有事情時願意向父母諮詢 3. 一起參與活動的次數增加 4. 在家中跟父母衝突的次數減少
家長／主要照顧者		改變教育態度	1. 願意跟孩子一起學習、閱讀 2. 願意用比較理性的方式跟孩子溝通
		增進親子關係	1. 孩子變得比較願意跟自己分享生活瑣事 2. 若孩子遇到困難或者有事情時願意向自己諮詢 3. 一起參與活動的次數增加 4. 在家中跟孩子衝突的次數減少
行政人員	課程媽媽	技能提昇	1. 認為自己學到了以前不會的技能 2. 鍵盤輸入（電腦打字）速度變快
		自信心	1. 認為自己的自信心增加 2. 願意學習或嘗試不同（新）的事物
	長者用餐／一般行政助理	技能提昇	1. 認為自己學到了以前不會的技能 2. 鍵盤輸入（電腦打字）速度變快
		自信心	1. 認為自己的自信心增加 2. 願意學習或嘗試不同（新）的事物
		擴展人際網絡	1. 交到更多（3 個以上）朋友 2. 有更多的朋友可以一起分享生活瑣事
	社工	提昇反思與自省的能力	1. 變得更了解自己 2. 更有同理心
		提昇社交能力	1. 交到更多（3 個以上）朋友 2. 有更多人可以一起分享生活瑣事 3. 願意學習或嘗試不同（新）的事物

3. 財務代理變數（Financial Proxy）

SROI 方法最大的特點在於將非物質性的事件予以貨幣化，並以財務代理變數做為貨幣化的價值標準。考量本研究之研究對象類別眾多，所包含的年齡層分布非常廣泛，為利於利害關係人理解並降低因溝通落差所導致的研究偏誤，

因此，在綜合利害關係人之訪談資訊並參考諸多文獻、經
SROI 核定之成果報告之後，採用市場比較法為各項成果列
出一至三個替代方案，近似於利害關係人所表述的成果價值
且具有市場價值者，並透過訪談及議和的方式向利害關係人
確認最合適的財務代理變數。羅列各利害關係人的財務代理
變數於表八。

表八：各利害關係人的財務代理變數

利害關係人		成果／改變	財務代理變數	計算價值	資料來源
孩童	幼兒	提昇自信心	潛能開發夏令營	10,000	社會福利基金會網路資料
		增進親子關係	2018 年國人海外旅遊平均價格	48,529	中華民國 107 年國人旅遊狀況調查報告
	兒童	自主學習	一場知名歌手演唱會門票	3,000	演唱會平均票價
		提昇自信心	潛能開發夏令營	10,000	社會福利基金會網路資料
		提昇社交能力	卡內基兒童青少年人際溝通課程	27,000	卡內基訓練
		增進親子關係	2018 年國人海外旅遊平均價格	48,529	中華民國 107 年國人旅遊狀況調查報告
	青少年	自主學習	一場知名歌手演唱會門票	3,000	演唱會平均票價
		提昇自信心	潛能開發夏令營	10,000	社會福利基金會網路資料
		提昇社交能力	卡內基兒童青少年人際溝通課程	27,000	卡內基訓練
		增進親子關係	2018 年國人海外旅遊平均價格	48,529	中華民國 107 年國人旅遊狀況調查報告

家長／主要照顧者		改變教育態度	雲門舞集親子律動課程	15,000	雲門舞集
		增進親子關係	2018 年國人海外旅遊平均價格	48,529	中華民國 107 年國人旅遊狀況調查報告
長者		維持社交聯繫	臺北至花蓮之來回機票票價	3,500	航空公司
		文化傳承	阿美族民俗中心文化套票	650	阿美族民俗中心
行政人員	教室媽媽	技能提昇	電腦課程之平均價格	4,960	巨匠電腦
		自信心提昇	卡內基人際溝通課程	29,000	卡內基訓練
	長者用餐／行政助理	技能提昇	中度需求全日照顧之長照費用	27,600	中華民國老人福利推動聯盟
		自信心提昇	卡內基人際溝通課程	29,000	卡內基訓練
		擴展人際網絡	2018 年國人國內遊平均價格	2,203	中華民國 107 年國人旅遊狀況調查報告
	社工	提昇反思與自省的能力	卡內基人際溝通課程	29,000	卡內基訓練
		提昇社交能力	卡內基人際溝通課程	29,000	卡內基訓練

　　以孩童的自主學習為例，由於參與照顧據點的孩童中，大多數對於學校課程的學習意願較低，透過照顧據點提供的多樣化課程，發掘了自我的興趣，並提高了學習意願與求知欲，進而產生了自主學習的動機。而照顧據點所提供的課程包括電腦資訊、吉他與音樂相關課程等，其中多數孩童對於音樂具有極高的興趣，且該階段的孩童容易產生偶像崇拜的現象，對於孩童來說，將參與一場演場會視為夢想的實現以及學習音樂的成果展示，因此，透過議和以一場知名歌手演

唱會門票做為自主學習的財務代理變數。以通過 SROI 認證的報告 CTBC Foundation for Arts and Culture 2018 Love & Arts for Dreams Initiatives Project 為例，強化學習動機的財務代理變數，為一個年度當中課後活動、獎學金或獎品等能夠增加學生的學習動機並保持專注度等相關財貨的總值。

在增進親子關係方面，對於家長／主要照顧者來說，能夠陪伴孩子的時間瑣碎且短暫，而海外旅遊時會將家庭成員聚集在一起從事共通性的活動，且進行旅遊時的心情較放鬆，在排除平日的生活壓力後，家長／主要照顧者對於孩童的行為會更具有包容心與耐心，減少了教養問題與爭執，促進了彼此的關係與緊密程度，因此，以二〇一八年國人海外旅遊平均價格做為此項成果的財務代理變數，旅遊費用之資料參考自「中華民國 107 年國人旅遊狀況調查報告」。而以通過 SROI 認證的報告「Ngā Tau Mīharo ō Aotearoa, Incredible Years Parenting (IYP) programme」為例，親子關係的財務代理變數為親子治療課程之價格。

此外，在本研究所參考的四篇 SROI 通過認證之報告中，均有改善社交互動此項成果，但各自以不同的財務代理變數做為代表，包括家庭治療課程、社交課程、團隊合作類型的活動費用與人際關係諮詢課程等，由此可見，財務代理變數並沒有一個標準或範本，僅能找出最貼近利害關係人心目中各項改變的價值。

（四）確認影響力

透過影響力指南可知，將影響力貨幣化之後，仍須檢視

是否有重複計算、非由本專案所造成之影響等不應計算在內的因素，避免誇大成果，並增加報告的信度，這些因素主要有四項，分別為無謂因子（Deadweight）、移轉因子（Displacement）、歸因因子（Attribution）以及衰退因子（Drop-off）❽。

在 SROI 指南中提出在影響力這一部分，如無法得到各因子精確的比例，能以 10% 做為粗估。本研究透過參考相關的學術文獻以及與利害關係人的訪談得知，各項因子的百分比，如因利害關係人之個別因素，導致同一類別中的利害關係人之各項各因子的百分比落差非常大時，則剔除極端值後，以平均數表示。而若透過問卷、訪談、議和等各種方式，仍無法得知各項因子的百分比，則以指南中建議的 10% 做為估計值。各利害關係人的影響力因子與百分比彙整，如表九所示：

---

❽ 無謂因子（Deadweight）代表的是即使利害關係人不參與方案，仍然會發生的成果比例；移轉因子（Displacement）代表的是方案可能會產生多重或意外的成果，在此特別指對非利害關係人所造成的負面影響，移轉因子即用來表示成果之間相互替代的比例；歸因因子（Attribution）代表的是對利害關係人而言，現在有的改變成果，或許有一定比例來自其他地方，也就是非現有方案所帶來的成果比例；衰退因子（Drop-off）則代表對利害關係人而言，方案所帶來的某些成果不可能無限遞延，一定會有所衰退，這是計算成果在未來幾年的衰退比例（張抒凡，2013）。

表九：影響力因子彙整表

利害關係人	成果	影響力因子百分比 (%)				說明
		無謂因子	移轉因子	歸因因子	衰退因子	
孩童 幼兒	提昇自信心	0	0	0	0	考量幼兒的表達能力尚不充足，故由家長或主要照顧者代為回答，透過議和得知各項因子的影響力。此外，幼兒的年齡層為 0 至 2 歲，此階段尚屬非常依賴主要照顧者的時期，因此，不論是否有至善基金會之介入，原本的親子關係即已良好，透過議和確認無謂因子為40%。
	增進親子關係	40	0	0	0	
兒童	自主學習	0	0	20	0	兒童的年齡層為 7 至 12 歲，此階段的孩童屬於社會探索期，學校、家庭與自我感受對其價值觀具有相當程度的影響，因此透過問卷及議和確認各項因子之影響力。
	提昇自信心	0	0	10	25	
	提昇社交能力	0	0	15	0	
	增進親子關係	0	0	26	0	
青少年	自主學習	0	0	5	0	青少年的年齡層為 13 至 18 歲，此階段的孩童已具有獨立思考能力且同儕的影響逐步提昇，因此，透過問卷及議和確認各項因子之影響力。
	提昇自信心	0	0	10	25	
	提昇社交能力	0	0	5	0	
	增進親子關係	0	0	5	0	
家長／主要照顧者	改變教育態度	0	0	25	15	透過問卷與訪談可知，在其他單位如學校與教會對於成年人具有部分的影響力，如學校辦理之家長座談會、教會舉辦之各項家庭活動，對於改變教育態度以及增近親子關係方面均有影響，而透過問卷與議和確認各項因子之影響力。
	增進親子關係	0	25	0	0	
長者	維持社交聯繫	20	0	10	0	在無謂因子的部分由於個人因素的影響如個性、健康與體能狀況、家庭氣氛等均會受到影響，因此，透過與利害關係人議和擬定各項因子之影響力。在歸因因子的部分，則由於村里辦公室、社區發展協會、

		文化傳承	10	0	0	0	其他老年人關懷協會亦有辦理共餐活動,但參與者並非花東新村之成員,凝聚力不如至善基金會提供之共餐活動,聯誼效果有所受限,故透過問卷與議和確認各項因子之影響力。
行政人員	課程媽媽	技能提昇	10	0	0	0	由於教室媽媽本身有孩童需要照顧,也會嘗試學習不同的教育方式與技能,故透過問卷與議和,確認無謂因子為 10%。
		自信心提昇	0	0	0	0	
	長者用餐／行政助理	技能提昇	0	0	10	10	由於至善基金會提供許多婦女培力課程,提供婦女的自我成長並擴展人際網絡,但培力課程大多為一次性,後續的技能純熟度、自信心與人際網絡透過個人而得,故透過問卷與議和確認各項因子之影響力。
		自信心提昇	0	0	10	10	
		擴展人際網絡	0	0	40	0	
	社工	提昇反思與自省的能力	0	0	50	5	由於擔任社工需具有特定的教育背景與訓練,在參與擔任汐止花東新村原住民住宅之社工之外,亦有與其他組織互動交流,故透過問卷與議和確認各項因子之影響力。
		提昇社交能力	0	0	50	0	

(五)成果價值計算

在探知利害關係人改變之成果事件鏈、彙整成果並找出相對應的財務代理指數,以及確認四大調整因子之後,在整體成果價值計算之前,還需要確認各項成果的持續時間,並以郵政儲金一年期定期存款利率約 1.06% 加以計算後,才能得出貨幣化之現值。

在存續期方面,本研究依據 Social Value UK 目前最新版本的影響力地圖,對於存續期的邏輯設定為,持續時間的起始可分為計畫中或計畫結束之後兩種,如果是從計畫中就

產生的成果，則會納為 year 0 的計算總值，並從 year 1 開始加入衰退因子與貼現率計算，若成果在計畫結束後才開始才產生，則會從 year 1 開始計算成果價值並納入貼現率，且從 year 2 開始加入衰退因子與貼現率計算，依此類推。本研究透過訪談利害關係人得以了解，各項成果均於專案計畫中即產生，例如，家長參加親子教育課程返家後，對於教育觀念即開始有所轉變、孩童的社交能力亦在專案計畫進行中有所成長、課程媽媽在每一次的教學之後獲得經驗累積，彙整各項利害關係人對於成果產生時間的描述，本研究將各項成果之發生期定在專案進行期間，而各項成果之持續期亦透過問卷、訪談以及與利害關係人議和而得。

最後，在彙整各項資訊後，成果價值的計算過程為利害關係人數量（代碼 A），與各項成果（代碼 O1、O2、O3……以此類推）之財務代理變數（代碼 B）相乘，並依據不誇大的原則扣除無謂因子（代碼 C）、移轉因子（代碼 D）與歸因因子（代碼 E），計算總數即為成果的價值（代碼 G），而在專案計畫後的第一年起納入衰退因子（代碼 F）及貼現率（代碼 I）來計算。將各項成果的影響力價值（Year 0 各項成果代碼為 G0O1、G0O2、G0O3……，Year 1 各項成果代碼為 G1O1、G1O2、G1O3……）相加之後得到各年度影響力總現值（代碼 Y0、Y1、Y2……依此類推），各項資訊與代碼彙整如表十。

表十：各項資訊之代碼彙整表

項目	代碼
成果	O1、O2、O3…
利害關係人數量	A
財務代理變數	B
無謂因子	C
移轉因子	D
歸因因子	E
衰退因子	F
貼現率	I
成果的價值 (G0，year0)	G0O1、G0O2、G0O3… 以此類推
成果的價值 (G1，year1)	G1O1、G1O2、G1O3… 以此類推
成果的價值 (G2，year2)	G2O1、G2O2、G2O3… 以此類推

計算公式如下：

$$G0O1 = A \times B \times (1-C) \times (1-D) \times (1-E)$$

$$G1O1 = A \times B \times (1-C) \times (1-D) \times (1-E) \times (1-F) / (1+I)$$

$$G2O1 = A \times B \times (1-C) \times (1-D) \times (1-E) \times (1-F) / (1+I)^2$$

而各年度的影響力價值分別為：

$$Y0 = G0O1 + G0O2 + G0O3 + \ldots$$

$$Y1 = G1O1 + G1O2 + G1O3 + \ldots$$

$$Y2 = G2O1 + G2O2 + G2O3 + \ldots$$

將各年度的影響力價值相加得到總現值（代碼 V），計算公式如下：

$$V = Y0 + Y1 + Y2 + Y3 + \ldots$$

以家長／主要照顧者的改變教育態度此一成果之影響力現值

為例，其計算方式為利害關係人數量 30 乘上財務代理變數 15000，扣除無謂因子 0%、移轉因子 0% 與歸因因子 25% 後得到成果 O1 於 year 0 的影響力價值為 337,500，計算公式為：

$$30 \times 15000 \times (1-0\%) \times (1-0\%) \times (1-25\%) = 337,500$$

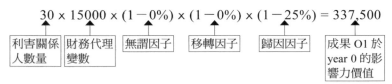

而由於此項成果之存續期具有兩年，因此次年的成果價值需要扣除衰退因子 15%，並進行折現（折現率為 1.06%），由此可得次年的成果價值為 283,866，計算公式為：

$$337,500 \times (1-15\%) / (1+1.06\%) = 283,866$$

最後，家長／主要照顧者的改變教育態度此一成果之影響力現值為兩年度的總合，亦即：

$$337,500 + 283,866 = 621,366$$

本研究將利害關係人之各項成果、成果價值、存續期以及計算後的影響力現值等，彙整如表十一所示。

表十一：社會價值計算彙整表

利害關係人		成果	成果價值計算 （利害關係人數量與各項成果之財務代理變數相乘，A x B，A 得自表三、B 得自表八）	存續期 （年）	影響力現值 （新臺幣元）
孩童	幼兒	提昇自信心	潛能開發夏令營每期約 10,000 元（9 人 x $10,000）	1	90,000
		增進親子關係	2018 年國人海外旅遊平均價格 48,529 元（9 人 x $48,529）	1	262,057
	兒童	自主學習	一場知名歌手演場會門票平均 3,000 元（8 人 x $3,000）	1	12,000
		提昇自信心	潛能開發夏令營每期約 10,000 元（8 人 x $10,000）	3	103,180
		提昇社交能力	卡內基兒童青少年人際溝通課程每期約 27,000 元（8 人 x $27,000）	1	160,650
		增進親子關係	2018 年國人海外旅遊平均價格 48,529 元（8 人 x $48,529）	1	179,557
	青少年	自主學習	一場知名歌手演場會門票平均 3,000 元（5 人 x $3,000）	1	14,250
		提昇自信心	潛能開發夏令營每期約 10,000 元（5 人 x $10,000）	2	78,396
		提昇社交能力	卡內基兒童青少年人際溝通課程每期約 27,000 元（5 人 x $27,000）	1	128,250
		增進親子關係	2018 年國人海外旅遊平均價格 48,529 元（5 人 x $48,529）	1	230,513
家長／主要照顧者		改變教育態度	雲門舞集親子律動課程，每期約 15,000 元（30 人 x $15,000）	2	621,366
		增進親子關係	2018 年國人海外旅遊平均價格 48,529 元（30 人 x $48,529）	1	1,091,903
長者		維持社交聯繫	臺北至花蓮之來回機票票價 3,500 元（35 人 x $3,500）	1	88,200
		文化傳承	阿美族民俗中心文化套票 650 元（35 人 x $650）	1	20,475
行政人員	課程媽媽	技能提昇	電腦課程之平均價格每期約 4,960 元（5 人 x $4,960）	1	22,320

		自信心提昇	卡內基人際溝通課程每期約29,000元（5人 x $29,000）	1	145,000
長者用餐/行政助理	技能提昇		中度需求全日照顧之長照費用27,600元/每月（2人 x $27,600）	2	98,839
	自信心提昇		卡內基人際溝通課程每期約29,000元（2人 x $29,000）	3	154,963
	擴展人際網絡		2018年國人國內 遊平均價格2,203元（2人 x $2,203）	1	2,644
社工	提昇反思與自省的能力		卡內基人際溝通課程每期約29,000元（1人 x $29,000）	3	43,045
	提昇社交能力（表達與溝通協調）		卡內基人際溝通課程每期約29,000元（1人 x $29,000）	1	14,500
合計					3,562,108

（六）計算 SROI 值

透過 SROI 的分析步驟至此，已得到相當完整的資訊，能夠用來計算社會投資報酬的價值。透過前述的計算式，加總所有的成果價值並將四大因子、持續期與折現率等考量在內，得到各年度之社會投資報酬，彙整如表十二。

表十二：社會投資報酬彙整表　　　　　　　　單位：新臺幣元

階段	Year 0	Year 1	Year 2
現值	3,006,198	470,755	92,013
總現值（PV）	3,006,198	465,817	90,093
總現值合計	3,562,108		
總投入	1,742,862		
淨現值	1,819,246		

備註：折現率以 2019 年度中華郵政一年期定期儲金機動利率（未達五百萬元）1.06% 為計算標準。

而最終要計算的社會價值則為成果的總價值與投入的總
價值相除，至善基金會投入在汐止花東新村原住民住宅的總
價值為新臺幣 1,742,862 元，而各項成果之總價值，經由研
究得知為新臺幣 3,562,108。因此，至善基金會之汐止花東新
村原住民住宅都市原住民照顧計畫二〇一七年之社會價值為
2.04，算式如下。（本研究之影響力地圖，請詳參考文獻）

$$社會價值 = \frac{3,562,108}{1,742,862} = 2.04$$

（七）敏感性分析

由於進行 SROI 分析的過程中，需要將許多無形的事物
／改變加以量化，並以貨幣化的方式呈現，且由於 SROI 分
析相當重視利害關係人之主觀感受，即使本研究已與利害
關係人進行了深入的了解與溝通，但仍無可避免地以估量
的方式進行，因此，透過敏感性分析，能夠了解在部分因
素的調整下，對於影響力的改變程度為何。依據 SROI 指南
建議，SROI 分析需要檢查幾個要素的變化情況，包括：無
謂因子、歸因因子和衰退因子；財務代理變數、成果數量
與投入。為符合 SROI 可驗證的原則，本研究進行了相關的
調整，調整內容分為三類，第一類為 SROI 值本身，第二類
包括持續期、財務代理指數等數值，第三類為四大因子的比
重。各項調整項目與說明，彙整如表十三。經過部分項目之
調整後，本研究之 SROI 敏感性分析，其成果在 1.53 元至 5
元之間。

表十三：敏感性分析彙整表

項目	調整內容	SROI 值	說明
SROI 值	原計算結果增加 2 倍	4.08	參考 SROI 通過認證之報告「Social Return On Investment Forecast of Teulu Ni-Early intervention that creates value in the lives of vulnerable families」敏感性分析的作法，將各項數值調整 50% 的幅度進行分析。本研究運用於將 SROI 值增加 2 倍來進行敏感性分析。
原住民兒童之財務代理指數	「自主學習」之財務代理指數改為才藝課程平均一期之價格 15,000 元	2.06	次要的財務代理變數
長者之財務代理指數	「文化傳承」之財務代理指數改為原住民語文競賽第一名獎金 3,000 元	2.09	次要的財務代理變數
課程媽媽與行政助理之成果持續期	「自信心提昇」持續期改為 5 年	2.43	透過訪談，利害關係人表明該項成果將會維持非常久、甚至一輩子，而為了不誇大成果，將利害關係人所表述的持續期設訂為 5 年做為敏感性分析。
原住民兒童成果持續期	「自信心提昇」持續期改為 5 年	2.06	
成果持續期	各項成果之持續期均改為 3 年	5	參考通過認證之報告「Ngā Tau Mīharo ō Aotearoa, Incredible Years Parenting (IYP) programme」，其表明在 The New Zealand Incredible Years Follow up Study 其中一項的研究成果顯示，家庭行為的變化能夠維持 30 個月且不會衰退，因此以 3 年做為各項成果之持續期。本研究以此為參考，進行敏感性分析。

無謂因子	原為 0% 之影響改為 10%	1.99	由於各因子為透過訪談調查得到的估計值，且會受到各利害關係人之主觀因素的影響，因此，透過敏感性分析以呈現研究結果的誤差區間，而為了呈現這些區間，我們將目前假定為 0% 之因子，小幅調整為 10% 以及較大幅的調整為 30% 以表現 SROI 之可能區間。
	原為 0% 之影響改為 30%	1.59	
移轉因子	原為 0% 之影響改為 10%	1.96	
	原為 0% 之影響改為 30%	1.53	
歸因因子	原為 0% 之影響改為 10%	2.01	
	原為 0% 之影響改為 30%	1.95	
衰退因子	原為 0% 之影響改為 10%	2.17	
	原為 0% 之影響改為 30%	2.14	
	所有的衰退因子均改為 20%	2.13	參考 SROI 通過認證之報告「Ngā Tau Mīharo ō Aotearoa, Incredible Years Parenting (IYP) programme」針對改善紐西蘭原住民兒童行為問題之計畫進行的研究，在利害關係人表示成果均不會衰退的情況下，為了避免言過其實，在與利害關係人議和之後將衰退因子設定為 20%。

（八）綜合分析

根據研究結果可知，至善基金會都市原住民照顧計畫，在汐止花東新村原住民住宅二〇一七年的社會價值為 2.04，表示投資於汐止花東新村原住民住宅原住民照顧計畫，每新臺幣 1 元將產生新臺幣 2.04 元的社會價值。進一步分析各類利害關係人之成果所產生的價值，如表十四及圖八，可以得知其所占的比重由高至低依序為：家長 / 主要照顧者（48%）、孩

童（35%）、行政人員（14%）與長者（3%）。

表十四：各類利害關係者之社會價值比重表

利害關係人	影響力現值（單位：新臺幣元）	社會價值百分比
家長／主要照顧者	1,713,269	48%
原住民孩童	1,258,853	35%
長者	108,675	3%
課程媽媽、長者用餐／行政助理與社工	481,311	14%
合計	3,562,108	100%

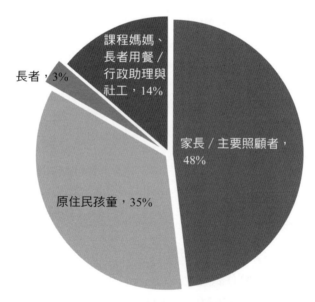

圖八：成果價值分析圓餅圖

　　由此可知，雖然至善基金會投入汐止花東新村原住民住宅原住民照顧工作最初的主要扶助者為孩童與長者，但也

間接讓孩童的家長／主要照顧者也一同產生成果與改變，可說是預期外的成果。而家長／主要照顧者的成果雖然只有改變教育態度，以及增進親子關係兩項，但家長／主要照顧者對整個家庭氣氛及對孩童的照顧是主要的營造者，當家長／主要照顧者的態度轉變時，對家庭的營造具有非常深遠的影響。至善透過舉辦家長座談會、親子共遊野餐等活動，讓家長了解孩子在成長各階段可能面臨的轉變，減少親子間隔閡與衝突，而透過親子共遊、共玩的活動，促進親子之互動，並提昇親子間親密感與信賴感，進而有助於提昇整體家庭的和諧及品質。透過訪談得知，對家長／主要照顧者這一類的利害關係人而言，認為增進親子關係這樣的轉變具有相當高的價值。因此，如以單一類別利害關係人的成果價值來看，對於家長／主要照顧者來說，增進親子關係的成果價值，占64%，顯見本專案的執行內容當中如親子共玩、共遊野餐、文化成長共學等活動，對於家長／主要照顧者確實造成相當大的影響，並且有助於整體家庭關係的改善，家長／主要照顧者之成果價值分析參閱表十五。如以整體專案來看，即使家長／主要照顧者之成果只有兩項，但社會影響力價值，占汐止花東新村原住民住宅整體社會價值的 48%。

表十五：家長／主要照顧者之成果價值分析表

成果類別	成果	成果總價值（單位：新臺幣元）	比重（單位：%）
個人方面	改變教育態度	621,366	36
家庭方面	增進親子關係	1,091,903	64

其次，原住民孩童所產生的社會價值占整體社會價值的35%。主要由於孩童除了參加課後照顧外，至善基金會亦透過課程媽媽及志工團隊開設多元課程，如數學加強班、英文伴讀班、線上英語互動、桌遊課、勞作課、煮飯課、體育課、勞動課、暑期兒少音樂班等，豐富課後輔導的多樣化，提昇孩童的學習意願並降低與正規教育之間的落差，進而能夠跟得上正規教育的學習程度。此外，辦理如冬令營隊、青少年團體聚會、文化成長共學團體等，促進與家長／主要照顧者以及社區長者間的互動，進而達到自我探索以及文化傳承的目的。

以單一類別利害關係人的成果價值來看，對於孩童來說，成果可分為個人、社交及家庭三個方面，以成果價值的比重來看，由高至低依序為：增進親子關係53%、提昇社交能力23%、提昇自信心22%，以及自主學習2%。透過活動的參與，孩童增加了與家長／主要照顧者之間共通的話題，並願意開啟與家長／主要照顧者的對話，增進了親子關係；並在參與活動的過程中接觸不同的互動對象，提昇了自我的社交能力；而在多元活動的刺激之下，有助於發掘自我能力的成長與改變，進而提昇了孩童的自信心並能夠自主學習。孩童之成果價值分析參閱表十六。

表十六：孩童之成果價值分析表

成果類別	成果	成果總價值（單位：新臺幣元）	比重（單位：％）
個人方面	自主學習	26,250	2
	提昇自信心	271,576	22
社交方面	提昇社交能力	288,900	23
家庭方面	增進親子關係	672,126	53

社會價值比重第三位為行政人員，而若以單一類別利害關係人的成果價值來看，對於行政人員來說，成果可分為個人與社交兩方面。以成果價值的比重來看，由高至低依序為：提昇自信心 62%、技能提昇 25%、提昇反思與自省的能力 9%、提昇社交能力 3%，以及擴展人際網絡 1%。

由於至善基金會投入婦女培力工作，培植社區婦女經營社區照顧工作，扭轉經濟弱勢並增加家庭經濟來源。此外，舉辦社區的婦女共學活動，在老人照顧方面之合作單位包括汐止國泰醫院、老五老基金會，而在專業課程方面則包括會計專業及電腦課程，提昇婦女專業能力。透過這些活動，讓課程媽媽具備教學能力並儲備經驗，並透過課程之間的互動提昇個人的自信心；對於協助長者供餐之行政助理方面，則透過行政專業知能的培訓，進而能夠具備獨自籌組協會的能力，對於個人的自信心提昇相當有幫助，且行政助理也因參與相關活動而得以拓展自身的人脈，延展人際網絡，進而豐富相關經驗與交流；對於社工來說，由於在服務的過程中會面臨各種狀況，需透過經驗的累積以適當的態度面對與處理，並在後續進行檢討改進或自我鼓舞，因而提昇了反思與自省的能力，而這樣的成果對於從事社會工作者來說，是相當重要的。行政人員之成果價值分析參閱表十七。

表十七：行政人員之成果價值分析表

成果類別	成果	成果總價值（單位：新臺幣元）	比重（單位：%）
個人方面	技能提昇	121,159	25
	提昇自信心	299,963	62

	提昇反思與自省的能力	43,045	9
社交方面	擴展人際網絡	2,644	1
	提昇社交能力	14,500	3

最後，對於長者來說，受到年齡與生理的限制，能夠從事的活動範圍與型態均受到先天上的限制，因此，能夠外出活動對於長者來說，具有相當大的吸引力與心理價值，最後透過議和決定以返鄉的交通工具費用，以及具有族群代表性的教育場所門票做為財務代理變數，而這兩項受到市場競爭以及公部門補助的影響，價格均不高。因此，在所有利害關係人的成果價值分析中，長者的社會價值所占比重最低，主要乃由於透過議和所決定的財務代理變數價值，相較於其他利害關係人的財務代理變數價值，低了許多之緣故。

但長者所展現的成果與轉變仍不可忽視。除了日常的社區長者供餐與關懷訪視之外，至善基金會於二〇一七年舉辦長者衛教講座、長青課程、參訪活動如參訪新北市原住民家庭關懷協會、花蓮縣春日部落老人文化健康站以及淡水八里一日遊等，除了投入日常照護的工作之外，亦透過老人聚會與活動提供長者們心靈上的支持；此外，透過手工藝、舞蹈、音樂班的開設，邀集社區家庭共同參加，讓長者的文化財產這一項無形資產得以延續，達到文化傳承之目的。長者之成果價值分析參閱表十八。

表十八：長者之成果價值分析表

成果類別	成果	成果總價值（單位：新臺幣元）	比重（單位：%）
社交方面	維持社交聯繫	88,200	81
文化方面	文化傳承	20,475	19

五、結論

　　聖嚴法師提倡心六倫，包括：家庭倫理、生活倫理、校園倫理、自然倫理、職場倫理、族群倫理。而族群倫理重視從「心」做起，尊重每個人，在這片美麗的福爾摩沙土地，每一個新、舊臺灣人都是臺灣的一份子，每一個人都要從「心」不分你我、接受對方、尊重彼此地共創臺灣的榮景。多元化的族群已經是臺灣社會的必然趨勢，因此，更應該以包容的心胸，融合各族群的文化特色，讓臺灣變得更活潑，更有生命力❾。本研究至善基金會投入原住民照顧工作二十餘年，範圍不僅限於偏鄉更擴及都市地區，而自二〇一三年起於汐止花東新村原住民住宅提供兒少及長者照顧工作，由於汐止花東新村原住民住宅是都市原住民的出租國宅，居民同質性高且來自相近的原鄉，社區內部具有相當程度的凝聚力，對於至善基金會所辦理的計畫均具有相當高的參與程度，且由於原住民部落具有共享的概念，對於社區事務與鄰里需求能夠不求回報地付出，這是現代工商社會中相當缺乏的部分。

---

❾　〈甚麼是心六倫〉，《法鼓山人文社會基金會》，網址：http://ethics.ddhsif.org.tw/ethics_contents.aspx?cat_id=20&id=45。檢索日期：2018/9/8。

　　然而，也由於與都市一般居民之文化與習性的不同，以及基礎條件的差異，使得大多數都市原住民的生活品質與都市一般居民相較為低。至善基金會投入汐止花東新村原住民住宅逾四年以來，於各類活動與計畫的執行過程中，透過動態調整計畫方向與服務內容之外，也從中深入觀察與了解在地民眾的需求，從而辦理相關活動。並在二〇一七年陸續辦理連結在地資源與服務網絡、長者共餐服務、試辦老人照護服務、長青多元班、婦女共學、學童課後照顧、青少年團體聚會、文化成長共學團體、兒少保護工作以及都市聚落文化採集等多項工作，除了成果豐碩之外，也為汐止花東新村原住民住宅注入活力與動能，並呼應汐止花東新村原住民住宅照顧計畫之目標：婦女培力、老人照護、孩童輔導。並在二〇一八年擴大為「汐止 Wawa 森林——至善兒少發展中心」。

　　本研究歸納汐止花東新村原住民住宅照顧計畫之目標及 SROI 分析成果，可以發現，由各項利害關係者所產生的成果，均可對應至計畫目標，顯見照顧計畫的資源投注項目與目標一致，並確實產生了影響。在婦女培力方面，透過與在地資源的連結，培養婦女照護專長，除了提供社區的照顧需求之外，亦提昇了婦女的自信心，而課程媽媽也因為投入社區共學課程，而提昇了相關技能與自信。在老人照顧方面，藉由共餐服務、長青班、文化成長等活動，串連社區老人的社交互動，並藉由老中青三代共同參與的共學活動，實踐了文化傳承的目標。最後，在孩童照顧方面，藉由多元活動的體驗，引發孩童自主學習，並建立孩童的自信、促進了社交

技能的發展。

　　而各類利害關係者之社會價值比重依序為：家長／主要照顧者（48%）、孩童（35%）、行政人員（14%）與長者（3%）。顯示此計畫實施者（家長／主要照顧者，行政人員）與受益者（孩童與長者）同蒙其利。亦如佛法的「所謂布施者，必獲其利益」，也佐證聖嚴法師所說：「培福有福。」「布施的人有福，行善的人快樂。」以及學會心與境的重新對待方式，體會心不隨境轉的微妙心法，實踐心靈環保的精神（釋聖嚴，2012）。換言之，至善基金會在汐止花東新村的原住民照顧計畫，以在地需求出發，營造友善的居住環境、提供多元的學習課程、提昇家長育兒能力、促進家庭關係，讓老幼婦孺的身心均得以獲得安定的力量，呼應了聖嚴法師所提倡的四安「安心、安身、安家、安業」。

　　此外，透過本研究之 SROI 分析也意外地發現，家長／主要照顧者因為參與親子共學、共玩、共遊活動，而逐漸改變教育態度並促進了與孩童的親子關係，顯見家庭為安定社會的重要基礎，未來在汐止花東新村照顧計畫，建議可提高家長教育的比重，如增加父母育兒知能、促進親子關係之教育課程、情緒教養課程等，並教導父母與孩子共同學習以提昇孩童的學習動機，針對高風險或境遇特殊之家庭，導入社會資源與正規教育的支持。藉由父母對自我認知、自信的提昇，傳遞予孩童正向的能量，朝著家庭和樂、社會共好邁進。汐止花東新村計畫目標與 SROI 成果分析如圖十三。

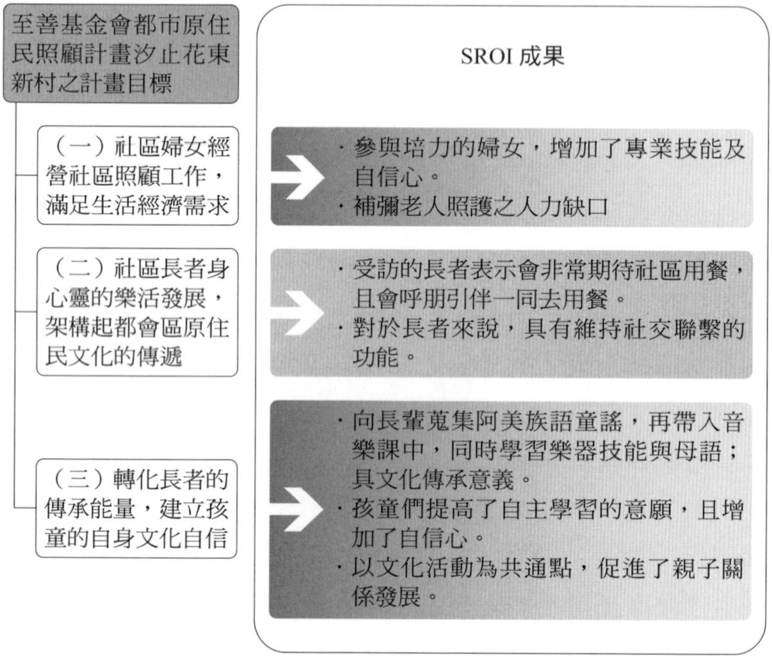

至善基金會都市原住民照顧計畫汐止花東新村之計畫目標	SROI 成果
（一）社區婦女經營社區照顧工作，滿足生活經濟需求	‧參與培力的婦女，增加了專業技能及自信心。 ‧補彌老人照護之人力缺口
（二）社區長者身心靈的樂活發展，架構起都會區原住民文化的傳遞	‧受訪的長者表示會非常期待社區用餐，且會呼朋引伴一同去用餐。 ‧對於長者來說，具有維持社交聯繫的功能。
（三）轉化長者的傳承能量，建立孩童的自身文化自信	‧向長輩蒐集阿美族語童謠，再帶入音樂課中，同時學習樂器技能與母語；具文化傳承意義。 ‧孩童們提高了自主學習的意願，且增加了自信心。 ‧以文化活動為共通點，促進了親子關係發展。

圖十三：汐止花東新村計畫目標與 SROI 成果分析圖

　　總之，本研究除了提供至善基金會，進一步檢視該原住民照顧計畫的成效之外，亦期能喚起社會大眾對於原住民之關懷與援助，並期待至善基金會原住民照顧計畫持續創造社會影響力，促進整體社會發展，以及社會大眾對原住民相關政策之關心與實踐。整體而言，本研究具有實踐佛法轉化心念成為自利利他法寶，和體驗心靈環保多元的內涵、觀念與方法之精神，並有實務應用的參考價值。

參考文獻

一、中文部分

尹章義，〈臺灣開發史的階段論和類型論〉，《漢聲雜誌》第 19
期，1988 年 12 月，頁 84-95。

王甫昌，《當代台灣社會的族群想像》，臺北：群學，2003 年。

台灣影響力研究院譯，Jeremy Nicholls, Eilis Lawlor, Eva Neitzert,
Tim Goodspeed 著（2012 年版），《社會投資報酬率指南》（*A
guide to Social Return on Investment*），臺北：台灣影響力研究
院，2016 年。

至善基金會，《2017 年報》，臺北：至善基金會，2017 年。

至善基金會，〈來交朋友一起來練功〉，《至善基金會會訊》第 85
期，2018 年 9 月，頁 17。

至善基金會都市原住民照顧計畫汐止花東新村原住民住宅 2017 年度
之影響力地圖，下載網址：https://drive.google.com/file/d/17mY8j
Q9gYld6QtRYk3b5OZGWF4iuVCqZ/view?usp=sharing。

吳宗昇、周宗穎、張抒凡，〈公益創投的嘗試與探索：公益 2.0 案
例的 SROI 成效評估〉，《社區發展季刊》第 143 期，2013 年
9 月，頁 95-127。

李宜樺、吳佳餘、朱恩言，〈公共服務影響評估工具——「社會投
資報酬率（SROI）」介紹〉，《國土及公共治理季刊》，第 5
卷第 1 期，2017 年 3 月，頁 30-41。

卓石能，〈都市原住民學童族群認同與其自我概念生活適應之關係
研究〉，屏東：國立屏東師範學院國民教育研究所碩士論文，
2010 年（未出版）。

孫大川，《夾縫中的族群建構：臺灣原住民的語言、文化與政

治》，臺北：聯合文學，2010 年。

張抒凡，〈如何評估社會企業的績效？社會創新方案的 SROI 評估〉，新北：輔仁大學社會學系碩士論文，2013 年（未出版）。

莊曉霞，〈原住民社會工作文化能力內涵之初探〉，《社會政策與社會工作學刊》第 16 卷第 1 期，2012 年 6 月，頁 133-182。

陳定銘，〈社會企業之社會價值與社會影響力評估〉，《科技部 105 年度專題研究計畫書》（MOST105-2410-H-008-011），2016 年。

陳定銘，〈臺灣社會企業社會影響力評估指標之分析〉，《第三部門學刊》第 22 期，2018 年 9 月，頁 1-35。

黃盈豪，〈從大安溪部落共同廚房的在地實踐反思文化照顧〉，《長期照護雜誌》第 20 卷第 3 期，2016 年 12 月，頁 213-228。

黃源協、詹宜璋，《建構原住民社會工作體系之研究》，行政院原住民族委員會委託研究報告，臺北：行政院原住民族委員會，2000 年。

釋聖嚴，《好心‧好世界——聖嚴法師談心靈環保》，臺北：法鼓文化，2012 年。

釋聖嚴，《福慧傳家——修福修慧，安心安家；六度萬行，傳心傳家》，臺北：法鼓文化，2017 年。

劉祐彰，〈傾聽被忽視的聲音——都市原住民學生的學習〉，《師友月刊》408 期，2001 年 6 月，頁 30-33。

謝國斌，〈台灣族群研究的發展〉，載於施正鋒編，《原住民族研究》，花蓮：東華大學原住民民族學院，2010 年，頁 57-90。

魏淑卿、陳淑美，〈談都市原住民幼兒教育——一個幼兒園教師的觀點〉，《臺灣教育評論月刊》第 7 卷第 5 期，2018 年 5 月，頁 154-159。

蘇翠涵，〈都市原住民兒少服務經驗——以汐止 F 原住民社區為

例〉，《東吳社會工作學報》第 35 期，2018 年 12 月，頁 127-137。

釋果鏡，〈聖嚴法師淨土思想之研究——以人間淨土為中心〉，收入聖嚴教育基金會學術研究部編，《聖嚴研究》第一輯，臺北：法鼓文化，2010 年，頁 69-112。

釋惠敏，〈心靈環保與社價值：以社區為基礎之社會營銷與變革理論的關聯〉，《第三部門學刊》第 21 期，2018 年 3 月，頁 1-18。

二、英文部分

Richards. A. (2006). Social Return On Investment Forecast of Teulu Ni. Retrieved April 10,2020, from http://www.socialvalueuk.org/app/uploads/2016/08/Teulu-Ni-report-FINAL.pdf.

Austin, J., Stevenson, H., & Wei-Skillern, J. (2006). Social and commercial entrepreneurship: Same, different, or both? *Entrepreneurship theory and practice, 30*(1), 1-22.

Cohen, R. (1978). Ethnicity: Problem and focus in anthropology. *Annual Review of Anthropology, 7*, 379-403.

Emerson, J., Wachowics, J., & Chun, S. (2000). *Social return on investment: Exploring aspects of value creation in the non-profit sector.* San Francisco: The Roberts Foundation.

Grieco, C. (2015). *Assessing social impact of social enterprises: Does one size really fit all?* New York: Springer.

Lakhotia,S. (2019). Ngā Tau Mīharo ō Aotearoa, Incredible Years Parenting（IYP）programme. Retrieved April 10,2020, from http://www.socialvalueuk.org/app/uploads/2019/05/Assured-SROI-Report-Incredible-years.pdf.

Latanè, B. (1981). The psychology of social impact. *American*

Psychologist, 36(4), 343-356.

National Association of Social Workers. (2007). *Indicators for the achievement of the NASW standards for cultural competence in social work practice.*Washington, DC: NASW.

Nicholls, A. (2009). We do good things, don't we? : Blended value accounting in social entrepreneurship. *Accounting Organizations and Society, 34*, 755-769.

PricewaterhouseCoopers Taiwan (2019). CTBC Foundation for Arts and Culture 2018 Love & Arts for Dreams Initiatives Project .Retrieved April 10,2020, from http://www.socialvalueuk.org/report/17026/.

Reisman, J., & Giennap, A. (2004). *Theory of change: A practical tool for action, results and learning, organizational research services.* Rotterdam, Netherlands: Erasmus University.

Richmond, B. J., Mook, L., & Quarter, J. (2003). Social accounting for non-profits: Two models. *Non-profit Management and Leadership, 13*(4), 308-324.

Smith, B. R., & Stevens, C. E. (2010). Different types of social entrepreneurship: The role of geography and embeddedness on the measurement and scaling of social value. *Entrepreneurship and Regional Development, 22*(6), 575-598.

Te Whānau o Waipareira (2017). Value Creation by Taitamariki Programme. Retrieved April 10,2020, from http://www.socialvalueuk.org/app/uploads/2017/08/Value-Creation-by-Taitamariki-Programme-Social-Return-on-Investment.pdf.

Watson, C. W. (2000). *Multiculturalism.* Buckingham: Open University Press.

Analysis of Social Return on Investment of the Project of Social Care Development in Urban Indigenous of Zhi-Shan Foundation Taiwan

Ting-Ming Chen

Professor and Dean of Graduate School of Humanities and Social Sciences,
Dharma Drum Institute of Liberal Arts

Yu-Wen Hsu

Ph.D. student of Department of Hakka Language and Social Sciences, National Central University

▌ Abstract

Master Sheng Yen advocates spiritual environmental protection, in the face of a society where people are floating, politically opposed and competitive, protecting the spiritual environment and social value are becoming more and more important. This article adopts the social return on investment (SROI) analysis promoted by the Social Value UK to explore the social value and influence of non-profit organizations, and to use the urban indigenous care plan of the Zhi-Shan Foundation Taiwan. " Indigenous House of Xizhi Hua- Dong New Village" in the Taipei area, after expanded into "The Wawa Forest: the Good Child Development Center". Through the six steps and seven principles of SROI, the relationship between change and outcome is reflected and measured. The theory of change is expressed in terms of currency. In this paper, in-depth interviews and questionnaire surveys of urban indigenous stakeholders, through the SROI principles and steps analysis, calculate their social value and social impact. The study found when we converted these outcomes into concrete figures and currency, that for every NT$1 invested, it can create a social value of NT$2.04, and for sensitivity analysis of uncertainty, the outcomes are between NT$1.53 to NT$5. The social value of the various stakeholders can be summarized as follows: parents/ primary caregivers (48%), children (35%), administrative staff (14%) and elders (3%). Shows that the applicant (parents/ primary caregivers, administrative staff) and recipients (children and elders) of this project share the same benefits. Therefore, it supports what the Dharma said: "The so-called donors must benefit from it," as well as what Master Sheng Yen said: "Nurture blessings and you will be blessed," "The charitable are blessed; the virtuous, happy." And learn how to retreat the mind and the environment, the subtle mind work that the mind does not change with the situation, and practice the spirit of spiritual and environmental protection. Overall, this article has the functions of practicing Buddhism and benefiting sentient beings, and has practical reference value.

Keywords: Zhi-Shan Foundation Taiwan, The Project of Social Care Development in Urban Indigenous, Social Return on Investment, Social Impact, Spiritual Environmental Protection.

Karma, Social Justice and Lessons from Anti-Oppressive Practice for Buddhist Practitioners

Wei Wu Tan, Ph.D.

Research Fellow, Department of Social Work, the University of Melbourne, Australia

▌ Abstract

Traditional Buddhist narratives on inequality are based on the doctrine of karma. While the doctrine of karma or the belief in some universal moral law spanning the past, present and future is an inalienable and essential part of Buddhism, conventional narratives of karma tend to be reductive. When used unskilfully, such narratives could be construed in sociological terms as victim-blaming, as many studies have shown. Moreover, these narratives are often conservative in that they could be seen as order or status-quo preserving. This article reviews the karma conundrum and modern Buddhist responses to the challenges it poses. It is argued that in modern societies where social justice is increasingly becoming the dominant discourse and where the struggle against inequality is being carried out across all differentiating categories that may lead to discrimination and oppression, a more nuanced Buddhist discourse on inequality and social change is necessary. To this end, it builds on past attempts to find a doctrinal basis for social justice from the Buddhist perspective by exploring a Buddhist narrative of social justice based on the doctrine of equality in terms of Buddha nature, the doctrine of change in terms of conditional arising, and the doctrine of action in terms of Samantabhadra's 9th Vow. Within such a narrative, effecting changes towards a world without oppression is imperative. It then explores the relevance of anti-oppressive practice (AOP) in social work to Buddhist practitioners, focusing on the concept of intersectionality—multiple and intersecting aspects of identity. It examines how the concept of intersectionality may be used to bring unconscious biases to our awareness and force us to confront our privileges. Finally, it places the eightfold path within the context of AOP and argues that judicious use of ideas and practices from AOP can inform Buddhist practitioners of the need to examine their roles in perpetuating oppressive social relations. Such an awareness may help them deepen their practice of selflessness and better realize the bodhisattva path.

Keywords: karma, social justice, Engaged Buddhism, buddha nature, conditional arising, Samantabhadra, anti-oppressive practice, social work, noble eightfold path

1. Introduction

That the world is facing an existential crisis seems to be getting more apparent by the day. It is now firmly established that anthropogenic climate change will wreak havoc to the world unless nations band together quickly to cut the emission of greenhouse gases. With the rise in global temperature and sea levels, and with the changes in extreme weather patterns, the poor is expected to bear the brunt of the climate disaster.

On a different front, social inequality has been on the rise, and more rapidly so with the rich getting an ever increasing proportion of wealth and resources. With the rapid advances in automation and artificial intelligence driven technology, economists and social scientists are predicting large scale job loss, starting in the near future. With low-skilled workers expected to be hit the hardest, this will exacerbate the already grave situation of social inequality.

In order to alleviate large scale sufferings and hardship resulting from impending climate change and social upheavals, it is clear that we must act now to change our system of economy and governance, making it serve all people equally, instead of favoring the privileged. In other words, we need a world in which social justice prevails.

Traditionally, Buddhism is known as a religion which is mainly concerned with soteriological issues. While kindness and compassion towards all sentient beings are championed, especially from the perspective of bodhisattva paths, Buddhism is yet to offer a coherent teaching on issues such as social justice. This article explores the issues of social justice by examining the concept of karma, doctrinal basis for a Buddhist narrative of social justice, and the anti-oppressive practice (AOP) in social work.

2. What is Social Justice?

Social justice is a relatively modern concept although some scholars have traced its origin to the time of Plato and Aristotle, when the issue of allocating scarce resources were discussed (Jackson, 2005). However, such a deliberation on just resource allocation, known as distributive justice, is only one dimension of social justice. Synthesizing past philosophical treatments, Jost and Kay (2010) define three dimensions of social justice, namely the dimension of allocation principle for the distribution of burdens and benefits, the dimension of procedures or norms governing decision making that preserves fundamental rights, and the dimension of dignity afforded to individuals by both institutional and individual social actors. These three dimensions correspond to distributive, procedural, and interactional justice, respectively.

Young, by applying the lens of domination and oppression, defined social justice more broadly, as "the elimination of institutionalized domination and oppression" (1990, p. 15). This broad definition was borne out of her criticism of the distributive notion of social justice, in which the importance of social structure and institutional context was often overlooked, and the importance of social relations and processes in shaping nonmaterial social goods was often neglected. While it can be argued that the multi-dimensional definition of social justice essentially converges with the broad definition based on domination and oppression, in terms of grassroot movements which seek to break the barriers of social inequality, the latter was more potent and easily graspable.

3. The Conundrum of Karma for Buddhism

Of concern is how social justice is viewed in Buddhism. This is especially relevant since traditional Buddhist narratives on inequality are based on the doctrine of karma. While the doctrine of karma or the belief in some universal moral law spanning the past, present and future is an inalienable and essential part of Buddhism, conventional narratives of karma tend to be reductive. It is not uncommon to hear statements which attribute single cause to an undesirable life situation. For example, when mistreated by another person, many Buddhists in traditional societies often attribute the maltreatment as retributions of similar maltreatments perpetrated by the victims in past lifetimes. Likewise, people who find themselves in oppressed classes in traditional societies often believe that their life situations cannot be changed since these situations are fully determined by past karma.

When used unskilfully, such a reductive narrative could be construed in sociological terms as victim-blaming in many situations. Works by practitioners of Engaged Buddhism and studies by scholars on Buddhist societies have shown that the idea of karma, or more precisely, the distorted popular interpretation of karma, has indeed led to much injustice in these societies. For example, in her works with women in many traditional Buddhist countries, Khuankaew (2007) found that karma has indeed been used to justify the oppression of women, minorities, and people with disabilities. In fact, she pointed out that in Thailand, teachings by monks had perpetuated the misinterpretation of karma, resulting in reinforcement and sustainment of violence against women.

In a similar vein, King (2017) identified different ways that karma is problematic for Engaged Buddhism, including stigmatization of disabled people, justification of caste systems, rationalization of tradition practices which are immoral and unfair, promotion of fatalism and passivity, and discrimination based on gender identity.

In fact, such a traditional narrative on inequality or understanding of social differences based solely on a reductive interpretation of karma presents a significant difficulty for traditional Buddhist communities. It could be easily used, and has indeed been mis-used, as a means to preserving existing social order, regardless of the oppressive nature of the status-quo. Such fatalism and passivity may lead to the lack of motivations and efforts in developing social systems which are more progressive and just.

4. Responses to the Karma Conundrum

The difficulties described above call into question the compatibility of Buddhism with the quest for social justice. Obviously, if life situations are fully determined by past karma, it is easy to fall into a reductive interpretation that oppression is "just", and that people "deserve" their misfortunes. If that is indeed the case, why then, should we strive for "the elimination of institutionalized domination and oppression"? That will be a futile effort.

Such questions have prompted various responses to address the karma conundrum. These responses can be broadly divided into two categories. The first category includes attempts to fundamentally reform traditional understanding of karma. The great reformer and champion of the Dalit, B.R. Ambedkar, is a proponent of such a view. As a counter-narrative to a fatalistic view of karma which was used to justify the caste system, Ambedkar suggested that "the Buddha's Law of Karma applied only to Karma and its effect on present life" (Ambedkar, 1957, Book IV, Part II, Section II, Question 2, Sentence 3). More recently, contemporary proponents of this type of attempts often argue that karma was merely a conventional concept that the Buddha had accepted for the sake of conforming to prevailing cultural understanding. They propose an interpretation of karma which is agnostic, naturalistic, or psychological in nature (e.g. Goodman, 2017; Loy, 2007). Their arguments often invoke the incompatibility of karma and rebirth with the scientific worldview (Goodman, 2017).

Naturalistic views of karma may indeed make it more "palatable". However, they ignore the very fact that Buddhism as a spiritual discipline is predicated on ultimate liberation from cyclic existence, of which karma and rebirth are essential and inalienable (Bhikkhu Bodhi, Ajahn Brahmali, & Bhante Sujato, 2014). These interpretations of karma are often partial and are based on highly selective readings of the Buddhist Canon. For instance, when examining the Buddha's position on past karma, Ambedkar cited the Cula Dukkhakhanda Sutta (Thanissaro Bhikkhu, n.d.) in which the Buddha questioned the Niganthas regarding their practice of self-mortification as a means to dispel karmic retributions (Ambedkar, 1957). Ambedkar suggested that since the Buddha questioned the Niganthas on the certainties of past existence, he was in fact casting doubt on past karma. However, in the same sutta, the Buddha clearly stated that when people engaged in misconducts driven by sensuality, after death, they might reappear in the plane of deprivation (Thanissaro Bhikkhu, n.d.). Another example is the selective psychological readings of karma. While there is no doubt that there is indeed a psychological interpretation of karma in canonical literature, to selectively cite these sources and neglect the other dimensions of the Buddha's portrayal of human conditions doesn't give the full perspective of the Dharma (Bhikkhu Bodhi et al., 2014).

In fact, scholar monks such as Bhikkhu Bodhi have consistently pointed out that based on a holistic reading of the Pali Canon, the Buddha could not have accepted the concept of karma merely because of the need to conform to prevailing cultural norms. Rather, karma and rebirth are quite central to the Buddha's world view (Bhikkhu Bodhi et al., 2014). What is more essential is the Buddha's rejection of the fatalistic view of karma (Federman, 2010).

The second category of responses accept the traditional Buddhist view of a karmic force which spans past, present, and future lifetimes. In accordance to the Buddha's rejection of the fatalistic view of karma, these responses deemphasize the past and in turn, emphasize the open nature of karma and that changes to one's life situations or social conditions can be made (e.g. Bhikkhu Bodhi et al., 2014; King, 2017). Other responses in this category include viewing people who undergo hardships and sufferings due to life situations not under their control as bodhisattvas who show others the precariousness and vicissitude of life, as Master Sheng Yen did during the devastating earthquake in Taiwan on September 21, 1999 (1999).

While karma or the law of causality is an important doctrine that underpins the path of liberation, both in the sense of the need to transcend cyclic existence and the effect of proper actions leading towards liberation, it has to be viewed within the context of conditionality. In fact, the doctrine of conditionality or conditional arising is what distinguishes Buddhism from earlier spiritual traditions. It is precisely this doctrine or truth of conditional arising that reveals the potential for changes. In the context of social changes, it means oppressed conditions can be changed and a non-oppressive system can be built, as long as we work towards creating the necessary conditions for such changes.

However, very often, in Dharma discourse to the populace in traditional Buddhist societies, only karma and the idea of karmic retributions are stressed. While the doctrine of conditional arising is also taught, it has mostly been done in relation to non-self or emptiness, in the sense of the emptiness of self or phenomena. Few had connected it to the possibility and potential for changing social institutions. This is perhaps not surprising as traditional Buddhist literatures were developed in premodern social contexts in which governing systems and social structures were not amenable to change. As a result, traditional narratives on helping people to change their lot have focused on advising them to practice good deeds and accumulate merits, in the hope of gaining a more favourable rebirth, presumably in a society of a similar structure, or for many Mahayana Buddhists, in a pure land where there is indeed equality.

5. Doctrinal Foundation in Buddhism for Social Justice

All these efforts in dealing with the conundrum of karma are important. In modern societies where social justice is increasingly becoming the dominant discourse and where the struggle against inequality is being carried out across all differentiating categories that may lead to discrimination and oppression, a more nuanced

Buddhist discourse on inequality and social change is indeed necessary.

To this end, efforts have been made in citing canonical sources which touch on social issues and obligations of rulers (Bhikku Bodhi, 2019). For example, it can be read from the Cakkavattisihanada Sutta that a period of decline ensued when a king in the sutta failed to provide just protection and security, and to eradicate poverty, leading to social disintegration (Bhikkhu Sujato, n.d.). A ruler should rule with just law and it can be inferred that a ruler has the obligation to eradicate poverty. Another relevant sutta is the Kutadanta Sutta in which the Buddha recounted a past life as a king, when he was advised to provide for material well-beings of his subjects (Bhikkhu Sujato, n.d.-b).

In contrast to the modern notion of social justice consisting of the three dimensions of distributive, procedural and interactional justice (Jackson, 2005), which seeks to eliminate all forms of institutionalized domination and oppression (Young, 1990), the brief discourses touch only on material social goods and do not go beyond the concept of distributive justice.

Other efforts emphasize the teachings on interdependence and selflessness in combination with the model of active engagement based on the bodhisattva ideal to provide an underpinning for social action (e.g. Cho, 2000). In a similar vein, engaged Buddhists have emphasized the paramount importance of loving kindness and compassion, in that when looking at people who suffer from social inequality and oppression, there is no need to even mention karma, as loving kindness and compassion trump all (King, 2017).

Here we build on these efforts in constructing Buddhist narratives of social justice by considering three important and interrelated doctrines—the doctrine of fundamental equality based on the teaching on tathagatagarbha and buddha nature, the doctrine of change based on the teaching on conditional arising, and the doctrine of action based on Samantabhadra's 9th vow in the Avatamsaka Sutra.

5.1 Buddha Nature and Fundamental Equality

Buddha nature or tathagatagarbha, used synonymously in this article, is one of the most important doctrines in Mahayana Buddhism in that it affirms the fundamental equality of all sentient beings and that all sentient beings can attain Buddhahood. In this regard, Master Sheng Yen argues that when viewed with the fundamental understanding of conditional arising and emptiness, tathagatagarbha is of utmost relevance to contemporary Buddhism due to the inclusivity and adaptability afforded by it (Master Sheng Yen, 2001).❶ For Master Sheng Yen, the importance of tathagatagarbha lies in its potential for philosophical deliberation and for serving as a basis of religious faith. Moreover, it is a doctrine that bridges the fundamental teaching on conditional arising and the teaching on ultimate reality (Master Sheng Yen, 2001).❷ He further points out that accepting the teaching of tathagatagarbha means that all who aspire to tread the bodhisattva path must willingly accept that all sentient beings are bodhisattvas and future buddhas. They would thus treat others with respect and dignity. As such, faith in tathagatagarbha is of utmost importance in the quest of building a pure land on Earth (Master Sheng Yen, 2001).❸

---

❶ "我更相信如來藏思想,並不違背緣起的空義,而具有其寬容性……而不論日本的禪,西藏的密,都跟如來藏的信仰有關,因為有其適應不同文化環境的彈性,比較容易被各種民族所接受。"(Master Sheng Yen, 2001b, foreword)

❷ "因此我敢相信,適應未來的世界佛教,仍將以如來藏思想為其主軸,因為如來藏思想,既可滿足哲學思辨的要求,也可滿足信仰的要求,可以連接緣起性空的源頭,也可貫通究竟實在的諸法實相。"(Master Sheng Yen, 2001b, foreword)

❸ "如來藏思想能使發心菩薩,願意接受一切眾生都是現前菩薩未來佛的觀念,也能使發心菩薩,願意尊敬、尊重每一個人……我們要推動人間淨土的建設工程,佛性如來藏的信仰就太重要了。"(Master Sheng Yen, 2001b, foreword)

Granted, the idea of buddha nature is not without ethical contradictions that need to be resolved, e.g. the issue of anthropocentricism (Matsuoka, 2005). But if we are to look for a doctrinal basis for a narrative of equality in Buddhism, buddha nature is a good place to start.

5.2 Conditional Arising and Changes

In pre-modern societies, social order and social institutions were not amenable to changes. In modern societies, especially in democratic societies, not only are changes possible, changes in social institutions and the ways we organize our society are imperative and urgent. This is especially so if human beings are to effectively deal with the increasing pace of change brought to us by rapid technological advances, all-pervasive reach and domination of finance capital, and impending environmental calamities.

To construct a change narrative, Buddhists should emphasize the doctrine of conditional arising, which distinguishes Buddhism from earlier spiritual traditions. One can say that it is by re-discovering the truth of conditional arising that the Buddha transformed the fatalistic and status-quo preserving interpretations of karma. It is precisely this doctrine or truth of conditional arising that reveals the potential for changes. In the context of social changes, it means oppressed conditions can be changed and a non-oppressive system can be built, as long as we work towards creating the necessary conditions for such changes.

For this purpose, connecting the doctrine of conditional arising to the possibility and potential of changing social institutions could be made a dominant discourse when teaching Dharma at all levels. Insofar as social changes are concerned, we can look up to Master Tai Xu for inspiration. Master Tai Xu is best known for originating the idea of Humanistic Buddhism and he had shown a great concern and engagement with social and political issues throughout his life. As a young monk in his early twenties, he was involved in the revolutionary movement to overthrow the Qing Dynasty and was sympathetic to the social revolutionary and anarchist cause (Master Yin Shun, 2008). While his views on revolutionary movements and ideas had changed in the later years of his life, he had shown a consistent admiration of Peter Kropotkin and his ideas of anti-domination, cooperation and mutual aid through the years. It is not the particular ideas with which he found resonant that is of relevance here, but his progressive attitude towards social changes and new ideas. His willingness to explore radical ideas of social changes and reforms, and his willingness to be involved in political discourses have set a precedence on how a major leader of Buddhism may advocate for fundamental changes. But of course, it should be pointed out that, to him, such secular endeavours are not adequate, only Buddhadharma presents an ultimate solution to the human predicament.

5.3 Samantabhadra's Vow and the Imperative of Respect and Dignity

Merely suggesting that the doctrine of buddha nature may serve as a basis of equality is not enough. People can pay lip service to buddha nature and yet engage in discriminatory and oppressive actions in practice. This has indeed been the experience of many female teachers. For example, a Tricycle article has pointed this out, citing Tenzin Palmo (Tricycle, 2011):

> Jetsunma replies: It is interesting that even most realized male teachers do not appreciate the gender bias that permeates the Dharma at all levels (except the ultimate). They say, 'Buddha nature is beyond male or female—we are all equal' and yet deny women the opportunity for study and training and routinely relegate nuns to the back of the temple (or outside). If we point out this discrepancy we are told that we are lacking 'the view'. However awareness is growing and the double standard—once seen—is slowly being redressed.

Such double standards are incompatible with the imperatives of actions as described in many teachings on the bodhisattva path.

In Chinese Buddhism, Bodhisattva Samantabhadra is known as the Bodhisattva of Great Action. This designation is based mainly on the Vows and Actions of Samantabhdra fascicle in the forty-fascicle version of the Avatamsaka Sutra translated by Prajna. Among the ten vows of Samantabhadra, the ninth vow—to always be in accord with sentient beings, is particularly relevant to a Buddhist narrative of social justice. In the passage on the ninth vow, we find the following instructions given by Bodhisattva Samantabhadra to the young boy Sudhana:

> The following is the meaning of always being in accord with sentient beings. Throughout the dharma realm and to the end of space, of all kinds of sentient beings in world systems as vast as the ocean, different in all sort of ways, I will work with whoever I come upon by being in accord with them all. I will serve them in all varieties of ways and with all sorts of offerings, respectfully just as I respect my parents. I will serve them as I serve my teachers and elderlies, the arahats, and even the Tatagatha, equally and with no discrimination. To the sick, I will be their good doctor; to those lost on their journey, I will show them the right way. I will be the bright lamp in the dark night. I will guide the poor to the hidden treasure. A bodhisattva should in this way benefit all sentient beings equally. Why is that so? If bodhisattvas are in accord with sentient beings, they are in fact being in accord with all buddhas and making offerings to the buddhas. If they serve sentient beings with respect, they are in fact serving all buddhas with respect. If they make sentient beings happy, they are in fact making all buddhas happy. Why is that so? That's because all buddhas have as their essence the mind of great compassion. It is because of sentient beings that great compassion arises; it is because of great compassion that the bodhi mind arises; it is because of bodhi mind that one attains ultimate enlightenment. Just like a kingly tree growing in the vast desert, if its roots absorb water, branches,

leaves, flowers and fruits will grow and flourish. The kingly
tree of bodhi in the vast wilderness of samsara is the same.
All sentients beings are its roots; bodhisattvas and buddhas
are its flowers and fruits. When we nourish sentient beings
with the water of great compassion, the wisdom flowers and
fruits of bodhisattvas and buddhas are the outcomes. Why
is that so? It is by nourishing sentient beings with the water
of great compassion that bodhisattvas attain supreme and
perfect enlightenment. Therefore, bodhi belongs to sentient
beings. Without sentient beings, bodhisattvas will not be able
to attain supreme enlightenment. Virtuous son! You should
thus understand this teaching. Receive all sentient beings
with the mind of equality, and you will attain the perfection
of great compassion. Be in accord with sentient beings with
the mind of great compassion, and you will truly complete
your offerings to the buddhas. Thus should a bodhisattva be in
accord with sentient beings: even if the realm of space were
limited, the realm of sentient beings were limited, the karma
of sentient beings were limited, and the afflictions of sentient
beings were limited, my acts of being in accord with sentient
beings are inexhaustible and unlimited. Thought after thought,
I will continue without a break, never to grow weary in body,
speech, and mind. ❹ (translation by author)

---

❹ "復次，善男子！言恒順眾生者：謂盡法界、虛空界十方剎海，所有眾
生種種差別，所謂：卵生、胎生、濕生、化生，或有依於地、水、火、
風而生住者，或有依空及諸卉木而生住者，種種生類、種種色身、種種
形狀、種種相貌、種種壽量、種種族類、種種名號、種種心性、種種知
見、種種欲樂、種種意行、種種威儀、種種衣服、種種飲食，處於種種
村營、聚落、城邑、宮殿，乃至一切天龍八部、人、非人等，無足、二
足、四足、多足，有色、無色，有想、無想、非有想、非無想，如是等
類，我皆於彼隨順而轉，種種承事，種種供養，如敬父母，如奉師長，
及阿羅漢乃至如來，等無有異。於諸病苦為作良醫，於失道者示其正
路，於闇夜中為作光明，於貧窮者令得伏藏，菩薩如是平等饒益一切眾

In other words, when putting the bodhisattva vow into action, one should not only provide sentient beings with material goods and serve them in the way that suit them, but should also treat all sentient beings, regardless of their identities or life situations, with the utmost respect and dignity, as if one served one's parents and even the Buddha. In a way, this is the basis on which the three dimensions of social justice in the modern sense can be explored. By extension, in the context of modern societies, such actions of being in accord with sentient beings can only be achieved by creating social systems that are free of domination and oppression. In fact, this standpoint renders the karma conundrum obsolete as action to benefit sentient beings should be given regardless of existing differences, be them physical, mental, or social.

If we accept that based on the fundamental equality of sentient beings and the imperative to treat all beings equally and with utmost respect as we treat our own parents or even the Buddha, we all need to work on creating positive social changes in the here and now. This is precisely the aim of various engaged forms of Buddhism, be it Engaged Buddhism, Humanistic Buddhism, or many other forms of contemporary Buddhism that seek to make the world a better place, although not all these forms of practice have

---

生。何以故？菩薩若能隨順眾生，則為隨順供養諸佛；若於眾生尊重承事，則為尊重承事如來；若令眾生生歡喜者，則令一切如來歡喜。何以故？諸佛如來以大悲心而為體故。因於眾生而起大悲，因於大悲生菩提心，因菩提心成等正覺。譬如曠野沙磧之中有大樹王，若根得水，枝葉、華果悉皆繁茂。生死曠野菩提樹王，亦復如是。一切眾生而為樹根，諸佛菩薩而為華果，以大悲水饒益眾生，則能成就諸佛菩薩智慧華果。何以故？若諸菩薩以大悲水饒益眾生，則能成就阿耨多羅三藐三菩提故。是故菩提屬於眾生，若無眾生，一切菩薩終不能成無上正覺。善男子！汝於此義應如是解。以於眾生心平等故，則能成就圓滿大悲，以大悲心隨眾生故，則能成就供養如來。菩薩如是隨順眾生，虛空界盡、眾生界盡、眾生業盡、眾生煩惱盡，我此隨順無有窮盡，念念相續，無有間斷，身、語、意業無有疲厭。"（Prajna, n.d.）

emphasized the perspective of social justice.

6. Anti-Oppressive Practice in Social Work

To operationalize the ninth vow's imperative on treating the myriad types of sentient beings with respect, we need to be aware of all the conscious and unconscious prejudices and biases lurking in our mind. To this end, we may borrow some lessons from the anti-oppressive practice (AOP) in social work, especially the use of the notion of intersectionality in examining our privileges and roles in perpetuating existing social inequality.

Many contemporary Buddhist explorations of the issue of social justice have come from the area of sociology, especially social psychology. Few have explored the relevance of contemporary social work. While social work and sociology are intimately related, the practice orientation of the former may make it more relevant to Buddhist practices in terms of skilful means and methods of effecting changes, alleviating inequality, and creating a just society. In fact, works being done by engaged Buddhists around the world overlap much with social work practices, albeit engaged Buddhist practices have the advantage of a spiritual basis and personal cultivation, and are not bound by the problems of professionalism. On the other hand, social work has examined social issues much more extensively and deeply, with a wide range of perspectives.

Regardless of the differences between the two, there is a lot that engaged Buddhists can learn from contemporary social work theories, perspectives and practices. Likewise, what is developed in Buddhist practices may provide new perspectives and ideas for social work. It is in this spirit that we explore the lessons Buddhist practitioners can learn from AOP.

Within the spectrum of social work theories, AOP is located on the progressive end. It is informed by the conflict perspective and is based on critical social theory (Mullaly, 2010). It explicitly links critical analysis of changing complex patterns of social relations with action, leveraging an explicit narrative and inquiry on oppression when working with service users to help them navigate difficult life situations.

Informed by Black feminist and other non-dominant perspectives, AOP was developed in the 1990s. A comprehensive definition of the term "anti-oppressive" is given by Clifford (1995, p. 65):

> ...indicate an explicit evaluative position that constructs social divisions (especially 'race', class, gender, disability, sexual orientation and age) as matters of broad social structure, at the same time as being personal and organisational issues. It looks at the use and abuse of power not only in relation to individual or organisational behaviour, which may be overtly, covertly or indirectly racist, classist, sexist and so on, but also in relation to broader social structures for example, the health, educational, political and economic, media and cultural systems and their routine provision of services and rewards for powerful groups at local as well as national and international levels. These factors impinge on people's life stories in unique ways that have to be understood in their socio-historical complexity.

This reflective stance is particularly relevant for those who engage in the bodhisattva path as it helps to bring into awareness practitioners' tacit assumptions and beliefs, as well as unconscious prejudices and biases. It enables practitioners to have a more profound understanding of structural barriers faced by people in difficult life situations and thus help them to cultivate empathy without taking a moral high ground or assuming the position of a know-it-all teacher. It also enables practitioners to better understand their own privileges and how such privileges may create oppression against others. Without these understandings, it is difficult to effectively practice the bodhisattva path in the contemporary world.

Instead of exploring the AOP approach in depth, we provide a snapshot of AOP in its use of intersectionality as a tool for critical reflection. Intersectionality refers to "the interactivity of social identity structures such as race, class, and gender in fostering life experiences, especially experiences of privilege and oppression." (Gopaldas, 2013, p. 90) In AOP, the concept is often operationalized using the so called wheel or web of oppression diagram, which is a visualization tool that helps one examine social inequality and oppression across different dimensions of social identity structures, including race, class, gender, and other differentiating categories (see Vanderwoerd, 2016 for example).

For illustration purposes, we construct a web of oppression using a simple and imaginary context not unlike the persecution of the Rohingya people in Myanmar. In Figure 1, the spokes of the web or wheel represent the differentiating categories or identity aspects that define a person's identity. These include race, gender, religious faith, socio-economic status, sexual orientation, etc. In a traditional religious society, an important identity aspect is whether one is a monastic or a lay person. Within each segment on the web, privilege and power decrease from the center of circle to the perimeter. For example, a disabled female Rohingya refugee would have faced multiple oppressions by the dominant group due to her ethnicity, faith, and language. She may also face further in-group discrimination due to her gender and disability as a refugee.

Another example is the Rakhine Buddhists. Being of the same faith with the dominant ethnic group, the Bamar, did not spare them from persecution. Yet, ethnic Rakhine have shown little interest in the suffering of the Rohingya, despite both being persecuted by the Myanmar military (Beech, 2019). This points to the importance of context when analysing oppression.

These patterns of oppression and privilege are relatively well understood but they may not be well considered in one's daily interaction with others.

An important aspect of the web is that when we try to locate ourselves on such a web, we may find that we are in both oppressed and privileged situations simultaneously. For example, a female Buddhist from a well-off family may suffer discrimination as a female, yet, she enjoys privilege as a Buddhist and a wealthy person. If she happens to have a hard-line view against non-Buddhist, and does not have much sympathy for the poor due to a distorted view of karma, she may well be perpetuating the oppression of others even as she herself is oppressed.

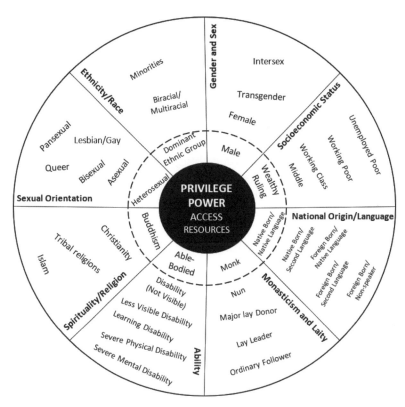

Figure 1: Intersectionality / Web of Oppression

We have described the web somewhat in the generic sense of privileges and oppression for illustration purposes. In actual AOP application, it is applied to a particular social context associated with the actual life situation of individuals. As such, the analysis is not static. For example, if a Bamar woman were to move to another Buddhist country or a country in which Buddhism is a minority faith, her situation would instantly change.

When one examines the context of oppression and privilege more critically, one would see that a meritocratic narrative is problematic. Such a narrative assumes that a person's access to resources and success is due mainly to his or her skills and efforts. An analysis of the multiplicity of identity makes it clear that resources and power are not randomly distributed or equally accessible by all people. Instead, the political and economic structures have been systematically favoring the dominant groups. The privileges of the dominant groups are institutionalized and protected, at the expense of minority groups which are marginalized (Vanderwoerd, 2016).

Perhaps the most important thing about AOP is that it is not just an intellectual analysis of oppression and privilege without practice relevance. Without putting such an analysis into actual practice, the "P" in the acronym would have remained just a "perspective", instead of "practice". When applying AOP, what is important is how social workers interact with others in a multiple dimensional web of their daily relationships, including service users, colleagues, supervisors, professionals in other disciplines, friends, family members, and others. The ultimate task is to interact with others in a way that does not unconsciously maintain or perpetuate the patterns of oppression and privilege revealed in our contextual analysis. As a practice approach, AOP has been put into practice over the years by social workers in working with various populations in a variety of practice areas (Vanderwoerd, 2016).

7. Implications and Lessons for Practice and Discourse

Based on the brief description of AOP given above, a few implications and lessons can be drawn for Buddhist practitioners, both in perspective and practice.

7.1 Understanding Merits as Privileges

As we have seen, one of the fundamental ideas in AOP is that social privileges are associated with multiple identities and that these privileges are associated with oppressions. Going back to the conundrum of karma, when examining our roles in perpetuating social inequality, Buddhists should look at the idea of merits through the lens of privileges. Regardless of whether one believes in past karma or not, when one occupies fortunate positions or encounters fortunate situations in life, be it membership in dominant groups, social economic status, educational attainments and so on, one should clearly recognize one's privileged position or situation. By viewing blessings or merits through the lens of privilege, we may create an inner awareness that may on one hand, passively protect ourselves against unconscious biases, and on the other hand, actively spur us to use our privileged position to create a world which is just and free of discrimination.

7.2 Anti-oppressive Perspective as a Means of Intro-spection

Too often, Buddhists who engage in philanthropic actions also consciously or unconsciously engage in actions that create sufferings, perpetuate injustice, and maintain inequality in the society. For example, business people who proclaim themselves to be Buddhists and may even be major donors or supporters to Buddhist organizations may engage in practices that pollute the environment in order to cut cost; they may pay non-living wages; they may buy shares of companies that destroy the environment and exploit people; they may engage in illegal actions in the name of doing good, etc. Examining one's actions and life situations using the idea of intersectionality in AOP will help us obtain clarity and implications of our actions.

The current approach of Buddhist charitable works is compatible with conventional social works which sees individual problems and social disorganization as the main problems, and thus seek to fix these problems instead of looking at structural issues. By adopting an anti-oppressive perspective, one is forced to examine structural problems. By doing so, one has a better chance of alleviating suffering of both the oppressor and the oppressed— first by changing the bad karmic actions of the oppressor, and second by alleviating the oppressed of suffering.

The truth is that conscious and unconscious biases are ubiquitous. Without a tool and conscientious efforts to bring these biases to the forefront of our awareness, we may not be able to recognize how these biases function in our daily life.

7.3 Integrating AOP into the Noble Eightfold Path

Finally, it is possible to borrow from AOP and integrate the notion and practice of anti-oppression into the noble eightfold path. Table 1 shows the association of anti-oppressive elements with the noble eightfold path. Note that these elements do not replace the conventional content of the noble eightfold path but supplement it from the perspective of AOP.

First and foremost, a reductive and fatalistic interpretation of karma, and a passive acceptance of oppressive interactions and social structures are incompatible with a holistic understanding of fundamental Buddhadharma informed by interdependence and Buddha nature. This can form an integral part of Right View which should then serve as the basis of Right Thought or Right Resolution. As a practitioner of the bodhisattva path, an important dimension of Right Diligence is to diligently bring about social changes and alleviate sufferings in the here and now of the human realm. In Right Livelihood, one must distinguish between oppressive and non-oppressive means of livelihood, and seek to transform oppressive practices in one's livelihood into non-oppressive ones. In Right Action and Right Speech, one should conscientiously engage in ethical and non-oppressive conducts and non-violent communication, and use non-oppressive language. Right Mindfulness involves applying critical thinking in accordance with Right View when interacting with others. It also involves applying mindfulness practice in recognizing one's privileges and be aware of oppressive situations across all differentiating categories or identity aspects in one's daily life. Finally, in relation to Right Samadhi, one should maintain the stability of mind, and be steadfast in upholding non-oppressive practice without giving in to anger and hatred.

Table 1: Anti-oppressive Elements in the Noble Eightfold Path

Right View	A reductive and fatalistic interpretation of karma, and a passive acceptance of oppressive interactions and social structures are incompatible with fundamental Buddhadharma. Buddha nature, interdependence and non-self should form the basis our interaction with sentient beings.
Right Thought	One should resolve on non-oppression as bodhisattva actions towards the liberation of others.
Right Diligence	One should work diligently to bring about social changes and alleviate sufferings in the here and now of the human realm.
Right Livelihood	One must distinguish between oppressive and non-oppressive means of livelihood, and seek to transform oppressive practices in one's livelihood into non-oppressive ones.
Right Action /Conduct	One should engage in ethical and non-oppressive conducts.
Right Speech	One should engage in non-violent communication and use non-oppressive language.
Right Mindfulness	One should apply critical thinking in accordance with Right View when interacting with others and examining social issues; one should recognize one's privileges and be aware of oppressive situations across all differentiating categories or identity aspects, applying mindfulness practice to such a recognition in one's daily life.
Right Samadhi	One should maintain the stability of mind, and be steadfast in upholding non-oppressive practice without giving in to anger and hatred.

8. Conclusion

In moving towards more nuanced narratives of social difference and social justice, Dharma teachers, both monastic and lay teachers, should lead the way by emphasizing why we need to critically examine the social situations in which we find ourselves and avoid reductive narratives when teaching doctrines such as karma and rebirth. In accordance with what many scholars, monastic and lay teachers, and engaged Buddhist activists have shown, it is important to adopt an outlook of open future. When looking at karma as a cosmic "force" that spans past, present and future lifetimes, one should view it together with the inconceivability of conditionality or conditional arising and avoid taking a reductive position which points fingers at those who undergo misfortunes.

Moreover, judicious use of ideas and practices from AOP can inform Buddhist practitioners of the need to examine their roles in perpetuating oppressive social relations. Such an awareness may help them deepen their practice of selflessness and better realize the bodhisattva path. Some Buddhists may argue that the use of words such as oppression and social justice may incite anger and animosity among people. However, it is precisely this and the fact that the world is increasingly polarized that bringing in a Buddhist perspective is important in enriching existing AOP conversations.

The following quote from two social work practitioners are intimately relevant to Buddhist practice (Burke & Harrison, 2003, p. 135):

> The anti-oppressive principle of reflexivity demands that workers continually consider the ways in which their own social identity and values affect the information they gather. This includes their understanding of the social world as experienced by themselves and those with whom they work.

Substituting the word "workers" with "Buddhist practitioners" and the quote might as well come from a Dharma talk of a teacher of Engaged Buddhism.

References

Ambedkar, B. R. (1957). *The Buddha and His Dhamma*. Retrieved from http://www.ambedkar.org/buddhism/BAHD/45D.Buddha%20and%20His%20Dhamma%20PART%20IV.htm#a24

Beech, H. (2019, March 3). Shared Buddhist Faith Offers no Shield from Myanmar Military. *The New York Times*. Retrieved from https://www.nytimes.com/2019/03/02/world/asia/myanmars-rakhine-buddhsts-rohingya.html

Bhikkhu Bodhi, Ajahn Brahmali, & Bhante Sujato (2014, December). Interview with Bhikkhu Bodhi. Retrieved April 26, 2019, from Sutta Central website: https://discourse.suttacentral.net/t/interview-with-bhikkhu-bodhi/64

Bhikkhu Sujato (n.d.-a). Cakkavattisihanada Sutta. Retrieved April 27, 2019, from DN 26: The Wheel-Turning Monarch—Bhikkhu Sujato website: https://suttacentral.net/dn26/en/sujato

Bhikkhu Sujato (n.d.-b). Kuṭadanta Sutta. Retrieved April 27, 2019, from DN 5: With Kūṭadanta—Bhikkhu Sujato website: https://suttacentral.net/dn5/en/sujato

Bhikku Bodhi (2019). Interview with Bhikkhu Bodhi. *Humanity Magazine*, 429, 70-75.

Burke, B., & Harrison, P. (2003). Anti-Oppressive Practice. In S. Barrett, C. Komaromy, M. Robb, & A. Rogers (Eds.), *Communication, Relationships and Care : A Reader* (pp. 131-138). London, UNITED KINGDOM: Routledge.

Cho, S. (2000). Selflessness: toward a Buddhist Vision of Social Justice. *Journal of Buddhist Ethics*, 7, 76-85.

Clifford, D. (1995). Methods in Oral History and Social Work. *Oral History*, 23(2), 65-70.

Federman, A. (2010). What Kind of Free Will Did the Buddha Teach? *Philosophy East and West*, 60(1), 1-19.

Goodman, C. (2017). Modern and Traditional Understandings of karma. In J. H. Davis (Ed.), *A Mirror Is for Reflection*.

Gopaldas, A. (2013). Intersectionality 101. *Journal of Public Policy & Marketing, 32*(1_suppl), 90-94.

Jackson, B. (2005). The Conceptual History of Social Justice. *Political Studies Review, 3*(3), 356-373.

Jost, J. T., & Kay, A. C. (2010). Social Justice: History, Theory, and Research. In S. T. Fiske, D. T. Gilbert, & G. Lindzey (Eds.), *Handbook of social psychology, Vol. 2, 5th ed.* (pp. 1122-1165). Hoboken, NJ, US: John Wiley & Sons Inc.

Khuankaew, O. (2007). Buddhism and Violence against Women. In D. C. Maguire & S. Shaikh (Series Ed.), *Violence against Women in Contemporary World Religions: Roots and Cures* (pp. 174-191). Cleveland, Ohio: Pilgrim Press.

King, S. B. (2017). The Problems and Promise of Karma from an Engaged Buddhist Perspective. In J. H. Davis (Ed.), *A Mirror Is for Reflection.*

Loy, D. R. (2007). The Karma of Women. In D. C. Maguire & S. Shaikh (Series Ed.), *Violence against Women in Contemporary World Religions: Roots and Cures* (pp. 49-65). Cleveland, Ohio: Pilgrim Press.

Master Sheng Yen (1999, October 15). Rang Xin Ling Ping Jing, Rang Tong Ku Bu Zai (May Their Minds Be at Peace and May They Be Free from Suffering). Retrieved May 2, 2019, from Dharma Drum Megazine website: https://www.ddm.org.tw/maze/118/1-2.htm

Master Sheng Yen (2001). *Zi Jia Bao Zang: Ru Rai Zang Jing Yu Ting Yi Shi (Our Own Treasure: an Exposition of the Tathagatagarbha Sutra in the Modern Chinese Language).* Retrieved from http://ddc.shengyen.org/mobile/toc/07/07-10/index.php

Master Yin Shun (2008). *Tai Xu Da Shi Nian Pu (Chronological Record of Master Tai Xu)* (Digital). Retrieved from http://www.nanputuo.com/nptlib/html/200707/1812143485802.html

Matsuoka, M. (2005). The Buddhist Concept of the Human Being: from the Viewpoint of the Philosophy of the Soka Gakkai. *The Journal of Oriental Studies, 15*, 50-65.

Mullaly, R. P. (2010). *Challenging Oppression and Confronting Privilege: A Critical Social Work Approach* (2nd edition). Don Mills, Ont. :

Oxford University Press.

Prajna (n.d.). Ru Bu Si Yi Jie Tuo Jing Jie Pu Xian Xing Yuan Pin (Entering into the Inconceivable Realm of Liberation through Samantabhadra's Realization of Vows). In *Avatamsaka Sutra (T10, No.293)*. Retrieved from http://tripitaka.cbeta.org/mobile/index. php?index=T10n0293_040

Thanissaro Bhikkhu (n.d.). Cuḷa Dukkhakkhandha Sutta. Retrieved April 27, 2019, from MN 14 Cūḷa Dukkhakkhandha Sutta | The Lesser Mass of Stress website: https://www.dhammatalks.org/suttas/MN/MN14.html

Tricycle (2011, July 13). Gender Inequality in Buddhism. Retrieved April 27, 2019, from Gender Inequality in Buddhism - Tricycle: The Buddhist Review website: https://tricycle.org/trikedaily/gender-inequality-buddhism/

Vanderwoerd, J. R. (2016). The Promise and Perils of Anti-oppressive Practice for Christians in Social Work Education. *Social Work & Christianity*, *43*(2), 153-188.

Young, I. M. (1990). *Justice and the Politics of Difference* (Vol. 2). Princeton University Press.

業力、社會正義與社會工作
反壓迫實務供佛教行者的借鑒

陳維武
澳洲墨爾本大學社會工作系研究員

▌摘要

　　佛教對不平等的傳統論述以業力為基礎，雖然業力或者說貫穿三世的因果律是佛法的核心理論，傳統的業力論述往往過於簡化。社會研究顯示，這種過於簡化的論述在許多境況中有可能被解讀為責怪受害者，也易於被視為是對現有制度和現狀的合理化，因此是相對保守的。本文首先綜述現代社會中業力詮釋的難題，以及現代佛教徒對此難題的回應，並指出在社會正義已經儼然成為主流視角的現代社會裡，對不平等的抗爭已漸漸遍及任何可以帶來歧視和壓迫的分別層面，佛教對不平等和社會變革必須有更為細緻的論述。本文以前人的研究為基礎，嘗試通過佛性的平等觀、緣起的變革觀、以及普賢菩薩第九願恆順眾生的行動觀，建構佛教對社會正義的論述。在此論述架構中，致力於社會變革，建立一個沒有壓迫的世界是菩薩行者必須履行的責任。社會工作的反壓迫觀點和實務，特別是其對多元交織性的運用，可做為佛教行者之借鑒，以其為工具，檢視自身潛意識中的偏見，自身所擁有的特權，及這些特權的社會意義。而反壓

迫的觀點亦可融入佛法的八正道中。反壓迫觀點和實務的審慎運用，是佛教行者反思自身在延續壓迫性社會關係中所扮演角色的工具，這種反思的覺照對佛教行者在入世的菩薩道中深化無我的行持，以及落實契理契機的菩薩行，有增上的作用。

關鍵詞：業力、社會正義、入世佛教、佛性、緣起、普賢菩薩、反壓迫實務、社會工作、八正道

人間性、場域性與解構性
——聖嚴法師論如何建設現代社會為人間淨土

王宣曆

美國哥倫比亞大學宗教學博士

▎摘要

聖嚴法師提倡建設人間淨土，除了攝化人群以成熟眾生、提昇人品之人間性，更點出佛法以現代社會為實踐場域之場域性；而聖嚴法師以「心靈環保」心法所開展之人間淨土建設方法，則帶有對治煩惱、解構汙染，以「淨化人心，關懷社會」來重構清淨場域之解構性。

本文首先就聖嚴法師人間佛教理念，論述其推動漢傳佛教之現代轉型，主張正信的佛教「不是世俗化，但是人間化」，回歸佛陀「成熟眾生，莊嚴淨土」之本懷，走向人間（人群、世俗社會），攝化人類，在現代世俗化社會中發揮佛法化俗、導俗之功能。

其次，本文將指出聖嚴法師建設人間淨土乃以現代社會（尤其是歷經工業化、都市化之資本主義社會）為其實踐場域，分析聖嚴法師面對現代化所開展的現代社會場域結構，觀察現代人於此結構中受苦、煩惱之因由，提出以「心靈環保」為核心之人間淨土實踐，以解構內境與外境之煩惱與染汙，轉化、重構現代社會為人間淨土，使現代人自在解脫。

　　最後，本文結論將指出，聖嚴法師「建設人間淨土」之
人間佛教理念，以其人間性、場域性與解構性，已由漢傳佛
教之現代化追求，邁向後現代性之解構與重構。

關鍵字：聖嚴法師、建設人間淨土、解構

一、前言

漢傳佛教自二十世紀太虛法師之改革理念以來，即以漢傳佛教現代化為目的，以大乘入世精神，與現代社會接軌，開展人生佛教與人間佛教之踐履。聖嚴法師提倡建設人間淨土，除了攝化人群以成熟眾生、提昇人品之人間性，更點出佛法以現代社會為實踐場域之場域性；而聖嚴法師以「心靈環保」心法所開展之人間淨土建設方法，則帶有對治煩惱、解構汙染，以「淨化人心，關懷社會」來重構清淨場域之解構性。

本文以人間性、場域性與解構性來析論聖嚴法師「建設人間淨土」理念，旨在揭示該理念乃以現代社會為實踐場域，期能淨化人心、淨化環境，解構內境之煩惱與外境之染汙，使現代人自在解脫，化萬丈紅塵為人間淨土。

本文首先就聖嚴法師人間佛教理念，論述其推動漢傳佛教之現代轉型，主張正信的佛教「不是世俗化，但是人間化」，回歸佛陀「成熟眾生，莊嚴淨土」之本懷，走向人間（人群、世俗社會），攝化人類，在現代世俗化社會中發揮佛法化俗、導俗之功能。

其次，本文將論述聖嚴法師「建設人間淨土」乃以現代社會（尤其是歷經工業化、都市化之資本主義社會）為其實踐場域，分析聖嚴法師面對現代化所開展的現代社會場域結構，觀察現代人於此結構中受苦、煩惱之因由，提出以「心靈環保」為核心之人間淨土實踐，以解構內境與外境之煩惱與染汙，轉化、重構現代社會為人間淨土，使現代人自在

解脫。

　　最後，本文結論將指出，聖嚴法師「建設人間淨土」之人間佛教理念，以其人間性、場域性與解構性，已由漢傳佛教之現代化追求，邁向後現代性之解構與重構。

二、人間性：人間佛教與建設人間淨土

（一）轉向「人間」：人間佛教之發展

　　聖嚴法師推廣建設人間淨土之理念，係承繼自人間佛教思想，代表著人間佛教在臺灣傳播之新發展，亦呈現臺灣佛教之新面貌。就人間佛教之發展脈絡而言，已有相當之研究成果，相關回顧概述，可參見學者林建德〈近二十年來臺灣地區「人間佛教」研究發展概述〉❶（2011）、學者李玉珍〈人間佛教研究之回顧與前瞻〉❷（2015）。

　　人間佛教（Humanistic Buddhism）係當代臺灣佛教最受人矚目的新發展，代表著大乘佛法適應現代社會之入世／淑世實踐。白德滿（Don A. Pittman）研究指出，人間佛教之發展可溯及太虛法師「人生佛教」（Buddhism for human life）之佛教改革理念，以漢傳佛教現代化為目的；而太虛法師高弟印順法師之提倡人間佛教，及後來臺灣佛教現代化

---

❶ 林建德，〈近二十年來臺灣地區「人間佛教」研究發展概述〉，收於《佛教圖書館學刊》52 期（2011 年 6 月），頁 6-17。
❷ 李玉珍，〈人間佛教研究之回顧與前瞻〉，收於慈惠法師總編輯，《二〇一四人間佛教高峰論壇輯二：人間佛教宗要》（高雄：佛光山人間佛教研究院，2015 年），頁 161-167。

教團如佛光山、慈濟、法鼓山推動人間佛教之踐履，均承繼
了太虛法師之改革理念❸，而開展出人間佛教之不同面向。❹

　　就理論層次而言，太虛法師與印順法師提供了人間佛教
運動之指導理念，Charles Brewer Jones 研究指出，太虛法師
與印順法師改革理念之差異，在於對「阻礙漢傳佛教現代化
之因素」提供了不同的診斷❺。如 Stuart Chandler 所指陳，
太虛法師將漢傳佛教之衰微歸因於過於強調葬儀及超度死者
之法事，故其改革理念係企圖將漢傳佛教重新導向對於「人
生」（human life，人類生命）之現世關懷；而印順法師則
批判傳統漢傳佛教之鬼神教傾向，將佛與神祇混同，故其提
倡人間佛教，強調佛教不應只將重心放在生者（人生），而
更應積極地參與到人類社會中（人間，human domain，即人
類領域之中、人群之間）❻。

---

❸ Don A. Pittman, *Toward a Modern Chinese Buddhism: Taixu's Reforms*, Honolulu: University of Hawai'i Press, 2001, p. 263. 該書中譯參見鄭清榮譯，《太虛 —— 人生佛教的追尋與實現》（臺北：法鼓文化，2008年）。

❹ 如丁仁傑以「僧俗關係」說明臺灣人間佛教教團之不同特色：慈濟為「出家者與在家者之間在組織結構上的互補和相互增強」；佛光山乃「以出家者為主力來進行積極入世的實踐」；而法鼓山則是「以在家眾為主體而試圖將佛教精神內化在其日常生活世界中」。見氏著，《當代漢人民眾宗教研究：論述、認同與社會再生產》（臺北：聯經，2009年），頁 283。

❺ Charles Brewer Jones, *Buddhism in Taiwan: religion and the state, 1660-1990*, Honolulu, HI: University of Hawai'i Press, 1999, p. 133.

❻ Stuart Chandler, *Establishing a Pure Land on Earth: the Foguang Buddhist Perspective on Modernization and Globalization*, Honolulu: University of Hawai'i Press, 2004, p. 43.

　　聖嚴法師「建設人間淨土」理念之提出，乃承自太虛法師「實行大乘佛法，建設人間淨土」、東初法師繼承太虛提倡「人生佛教」及印順法師「人間佛教」理念，為人間佛教又一新發展：一九八九年聖嚴法師創立法鼓山，以「提昇人的品質，建設人間淨土」為其兩大組織目標❼，至一九九二年，聖嚴法師提倡「心靈環保」，將兩大目標結合起來，吸收環保運動於人間佛教理念內涵，賦予人間佛教全球化之新面貌，與世界環保潮流接軌。

　　人間佛教以「轉向人間」做為追求漢傳佛教現代化之方式，已成為當代臺灣佛教最具代表性之特色，充分顯現其關懷現代社會生活之「人間性」。而隨著臺灣社會的民主化，人間佛教也在全球層次傳播，彰顯著臺灣佛教之自主性與活力。

（二）正信的佛教：不是世俗化，但是人間化

　　近代漢傳佛教，面對西方現代性之衝擊與國難、法難之雙重打擊，亟思轉型以續佛慧命；推動漢傳佛教現代化之先行者，面對艱困的時代環境，因所關注的時代挑戰不同，而採取了不同的護教（apologetic）策略，然皆期為佛教開創新局，復振（revitalize）佛教化世之社會功能。

　　以上述太虛法師與印順法師為例，太虛法師面對「佛教只對超度死鬼有用，對人生無用」的質疑，提出「人生佛

---

❼　Don A. Pittman, *Toward a Modern Chinese Buddhism: Taixu's Reforms*, p. 283.

教」的改革理念；另一方面，印順法師面對「佛教是迷信，不只對人生無用，抑且有害」之質疑，故批判傳統漢傳佛教與鬼神教混同的迷信傾向，而提倡「人成即佛成」之「人間佛教」。

有關佛教與鬼神教混同的迷信傾向，係佛教失去「化俗」功能後之「俗化」現象。印順法師說：

> 世間是緣起的，有相對性、副作用，不能免於抗拒或俗化的情形，但到底是越減少越好！❽

聖嚴法師曾將所見佛教界沉痾概括為「僧尼世俗化、法門鬼神化、信眾庸俗化」❾，唯正信的佛教，「不是世俗化，但是人間化」❿，聖嚴法師「建設人間淨土」之「人間性」，並非混於傳統俗信（conventional beliefs）而「俗化」，而是通於現代世俗語言及世俗合理性（modern secular language and rationality），以接軌現代性，發揮轉化人心、建設現代社會為人間淨土之「化俗」功能，展現佛教「人間化」之理念。

然而，具體的淨土方案，其內容如何不是世俗的同流？

---

❽ 釋印順，〈契理契機之人間佛教〉，《華雨集第四冊》，印順文教基金會推廣教育中心印順法師佛學著作集網站，頁 50。

❾ 釋聖嚴，《法鼓山的方向 II》（臺北：法鼓文化，1999 年），頁 71。

❿ 釋聖嚴，《動靜皆自在》（臺北：法鼓文化，2005 年）頁 27 指出正信的佛教「不是世俗化，但是人間化」、「不是鬼神教，但有人天教」、「不是厭世的，但是出世的」、「不是戀世的，但是入世的」。

執實而論，在具體作法上，「避免世俗化」當以守戒、持戒為核心。

所謂「避免世俗化」，即在避免因為參與世俗事務，迷失了自己的方向和立場，導致失去清淨身、口、意三種行為的精神，⓫而戒律恰正為清淨身、口、意而制。是知失戒、破戒乃至戒法斷絕，乃是佛教界之所以世俗化、法門之所以衰微不振的根本原因，令有識之士莫不嘆惋。有鑑於此，聖嚴法師十分重視戒律學，並且專攻戒律學，⓬於小乘比丘比丘尼戒及大乘菩薩戒均有紹述推廣，「從『信仰的實踐』之側面來學習戒律與佛法，也能為信仰提供『理論的基礎』，更透過『學術的研究』來提供論述，以相應於多元的現代化社會」。⓭

而在〈戒律與人間淨土的建立〉一文中，聖嚴法師指出，戒律原來是相當簡樸和親切的，而且本來就是具有彈性的，具有時空的適應性及人間性，⓮而營造人間淨土，必須遵守戒律：

佛制的戒律，不僅是為使佛教徒適應所處時空環境的

⓫ 釋聖嚴，《法鼓山的方向》（臺北：法鼓文化，1999 年），頁 154。

⓬ 釋聖嚴，《我願無窮──美好的晚年開示集》（臺北市：法鼓文化，2011 年），頁 68。

⓭ 嚴瑋泓，〈聖嚴法師戒律思想之倫理學義蘊〉，收入聖嚴教育基金會學術研究部編，《聖嚴研究》第六輯（臺北：法鼓文化，2015 年，頁 413-448），頁 442。

⓮ 釋聖嚴，〈戒律與人間淨土的建立〉，收於氏著，《學術論考》（臺北：法鼓文化，1999 年，頁 404-445），頁 444。

風土人情，以及社團的公約、國家的法令，更進一步是為
促成每一個人，身口意的淨化，並且保障這三種行為的不
斷淨化，也用此淨化的功能，奉獻給他人、影響到他人，
以達成由淨化個人而淨化社會、淨化國家的目的。也就是
說，營造人間淨土，必須要從行為的淨化開始，要想淨化
人的行為，必須遵守佛的戒律。❶

　佛陀及其大比丘弟子們，經常「遊行人間」，用清涼的
佛法，來淨化人間大眾的身、心、語言三類行為，建立人
間佛教；我們現在推廣人間淨土的理念，就是要這樣，呼
籲大家，一點一滴、日積月累，共同努力，來實現它。❶

　佛制的戒律有其人間性及實用性，就消極層面言，乃防
止因失去身、口、意清淨而導致佛教的世俗化；就積極層面
言，乃淨化人心、淨化社會，達成「化俗」的目標。❶

（三）建設人間淨土，回歸佛陀本懷

　聖嚴法師「建設人間淨土」之「人間性」，除了「避免
世俗化」之意義外，尚有「避免遠離人群」之第二層意義。
二者合觀，所謂「人間性」即是「以出世的心，做入世的工
作」，正因出世，所以能避免世俗化；正因入世，所以能走

---

❶ 釋聖嚴，〈戒律與人間淨土的建立〉，頁433。
❶ 釋聖嚴，〈戒律與人間淨土的建立〉，頁405。
❶ 本段有關戒律與人間淨土的建立，感謝匿名審查人寶貴意見。

入人間、走入人群。

果樸法師指出，印順法師由《增壹阿含經》「諸佛皆出人間，終不在天上成佛也」（佛世尊皆出人間，非由天而得也），⓲以及《阿含經》以「人間」處六道中央為樞紐之說得到啟發，以「人間」不但對治偏於死亡與鬼，也對治了偏於神和永生，故提倡「人間佛教」，而聖嚴法師提出「建設人間淨土」的切入點，則是佛陀及其弟子積極「在人間化世」的「人間佛教」。⓳

再者，由「建設人間淨土」理念提出之時間點考察，一九八九年四月聖嚴法師購得金山道場，同年六月正式命名為法鼓山；九月二十四日，聖嚴法師於農禪寺對全體僧眾早齋開示「法鼓山理念」，首次對「提昇人的品質，建設人間淨土」之理念提出完整說明：「佛陀出現在人間，是以人類

⓲ 《增壹阿含經》第 26 卷，〈等見品第三十四〉：「爾時，有一比丘白世尊言：『三十三天云何得生善處？云何快得善利？云何安處善業？』世尊告曰：『人間於天則是善處。得善處、得善利者，生正見家，與善知識從事，於如來法中得信根，是謂名為快得善利。彼云何名為安處善業？於如來法中而得信根，剃除鬚髮，以信堅固，出家學道；彼以學道，戒性具足，諸根不缺，飯食知足，恒念經行，得三達明，是謂名為安處善業。』爾時，世尊便說此偈：『人為天善處，良友為善利；出家為善業，有漏盡無漏。』『比丘當知：三十三天著於五欲，彼以人間為善趣；於如來得出家，為善利而得三達。所以然者，佛世尊皆出人間，非由天而得也。是故，比丘！於此命終當（＊勿）生天上。』」《大正藏》第 2 冊，頁 693c19-694a5（CBETA, T2, no. 125）。

⓳ 釋果樸，〈聖嚴法師「建設人間淨土」理念根源——法師大陸出家學習與近代中國佛教興革〉，收於林煌洲等合著，《聖嚴法師思想行誼》（臺北：法鼓文化，2004 年，頁 345-504），頁 457-458。

為主要的攝化對象。」[20]果樸法師據此分析，聖嚴法師所云佛陀「在人間」，意思是「佛陀遊化人間」，以攝化人類為主。[21]

進一步，果樸法師指出，依聖嚴法師之論述，「走向人間」即是「佛陀的本懷」，[22]聖嚴法師說：

> 各位都曾閱讀過《釋迦牟尼佛傳》，知道釋尊在鹿野苑度化五比丘，度過一夏之後，便指示五人各自分頭，走向人間，各化一方，這就是佛教的根本精神。[23]

是知佛陀教法，本意在走向人間，而攝化人類，更是所有佛教皆從事的目標。然而，如何特別需要人間淨土的教化呢？

其故在於，佛教在傳播過程中，不免因世間緣起法的相對性、副作用，而或產生偏離佛陀本懷的差誤，因而遠離人群、與社會脫節而陷入危機。

由歷史脈絡考察，漢傳佛教傳衍至近代所生大弊之一即在遠離人群、與社會脫節，亟需有識之士起而改革，以回歸

---

[20] 林其賢，《聖嚴法師年譜》（臺北：法鼓文化，2016 年），頁 655；另參見釋聖嚴，《法鼓山的方向》，頁 27。

[21] 釋果樸，〈聖嚴法師「建設人間淨土」理念根源——法師大陸出家學習與近代中國佛教興革〉，頁 354。

[22] 釋果樸，〈聖嚴法師「建設人間淨土」理念根源——法師大陸出家學習與近代中國佛教興革〉，頁 355。

[23] 釋聖嚴，《法鼓山的方向》（臺北：法鼓文化，1999 年），頁 153-154。

人間、回歸佛陀本懷，此即近代人間佛教運動之核心精神。

學者林其賢指出，聖嚴法師少年出家，觀察到當時（1940年代）一般對佛法的認識水平，多是對佛教採取歧視及批評的態度，把佛家的因果觀說成了宿命論，使得佛教的人生觀變得非常消極、厭世、逃避。然而法師卻非常特別地能辨識出那是變了質的信仰，並非佛陀的本懷，認為真正的佛教應該是活用、實用、積極、入世且為關懷人間疾苦而設。❷❹

因此，聖嚴法師據佛陀及弟子之化行，開展建設人間淨土之「人間性」義理，回歸「遊化人間，攝化人類」之佛陀本懷。具體而論，「人間性」展現在聖嚴法師所創建法鼓山「一缽千家飯」之宗風：

> ……「一缽千家飯」，便是要我們從一般社會大眾出發，平等接引每一個階層，為他們服務、給他們照顧，讓他們都能各取所需，得到佛法的利益，如此，佛法才會常住世間。佛法其實就是靠大眾，釋迦牟尼佛自己出身貴族，他雖化度王臣長者，但他接觸的人大多是平民，因此大家要掌握這個原則。❷❺

綜上，聖嚴法師建設人間淨土之理念，係承繼自人間

---

❷❹ 林其賢，〈聖嚴法師人間淨土思想的實踐與弘揚〉，收入聖嚴教育基金會學術研究部編，《聖嚴研究》第一輯（臺北：法鼓文化，2010年，頁153-205），頁160-161。

❷❺ 釋聖嚴，《我願無窮──美好的晚年開示集》，頁89-90。

佛教思想，以力挽佛教世俗化、與社會脫節之弊，回歸平等接引、普化人間的佛陀本懷。聖嚴法師所提出「提昇人的品質，建設人間淨土」，前句係承繼太虛法師、印順法師「人成即佛成」之理念，後句則更明顯指向人間佛教以「人間」為實踐場域之場域性，以下述論之。

三、場域性：「建設人間淨土」以現代社會為實踐場域

（一）走入現代社會為必要條件

聖嚴法師建設人間淨土之「人間性」，據上節分析，已蘊涵以「人間」為實踐場域之場域性，而就人間佛教「契理契機」之原則而論，[26]「建設人間淨土」若能切合時代所需，則其「人間」所指涉者為現代社會，走入現代社會，乃為「建設人間淨土」之必要條件，聖嚴法師強調：

> 處於現代的我們，再也不可能回到「離開人間而終老山林」的生活形態去了。
> 我們毫無選擇的餘地，已不可能捨棄人間隱入山林。[27]

> 過去的叢林是山居生活、農村社會的型態，現在則是都市生活；而在今天的社會，就算是住在山裡，所接觸

---

[26] 參見釋印順，〈契理契機之人間佛教〉，《華雨集第四冊》，頁 1-70。
[27] 釋聖嚴，《法鼓山的方向》，頁 153。

到的物資和人事，都和城市沒有兩樣，所以臺灣、日本、美國的山林佛教，都已經都市化了。修行人的生活是不可能再回到一百年前的模樣，歷史是永遠不會重演的，雖然有一定的規律在運作，但方式是不一樣的，也經常需要改善。㉘

　　如學者林其賢所指出，聖嚴法師「人間淨土」之入世理念，先後有來自太虛法師「人生佛教」及印順法師「人間佛教」之啟發，人生佛教主要是和度亡佛教做區分，人間佛教則是要和山林佛教做區分㉙；與山林佛教做區分的人間佛教，即聖嚴法師上引文所強調「我們毫無選擇的餘地，已不可能捨棄人間隱入山林」。

　　聖嚴法師具有強烈的時代感與使命感，深知歷史不會重演，漢傳佛教必須與時俱進，不再可能離開人間，反而必須走入現代社會，以現代人為佛法弘化之受眾，以現代人心為佛法弘化的對象，「建設人間淨土」之實踐場域，既在現代社會，也在現代人心。

　　上引文提及「臺灣、日本、美國的山林佛教，都已經都市化了」，或可推知聖嚴法師「建設人間淨土」之提出，主要是觀察、參照臺灣、日本、美國等歷經工業化、都市化之資本主義現代社會而發。學者楊郁文說：

㉘ 釋聖嚴，《法鼓晨音》（臺北：法鼓文化，2005 年），頁 175-176。
㉙ 林其賢，〈聖嚴法師人間淨土思想的實踐與弘揚〉，頁 160。

　　人類是非常特殊的聚集群居的社會性動物，從古代採擷
為主的合群生活模式，經由漁獵、農牧、現代機械化的工
業、服務性為主的後工業，乃至國際性的資訊工業社會。
物質生活條件在改變，社會組織形態在變化，然而做人的
道理及原則不變，靈性的需求及人格的圓滿並無差別。

　　現代人物質生活豐富，感官的刺激繁多，動物性的要求
尚可滿足；然精神生活貧乏，在現代工業化、商業化與國
際化的社會環境，對智性、靈性的成長，人格的健全，反
而增加許多障礙。現代人生活於現代社會，比起古人生存
於其人之時代，可能更加難過。❸

　　人生是苦，生命、生活自古即不容易，而現代化資本主
義社會之運作邏輯所建構的場域結構，使現代人承受新型態
的苦惱，障礙著靈性的成長、人格的健全，不得自在解脫，
如上引文所述「現代人生活於現代社會，比起古人生存於其
人之時代，可能更加難過」。

　　依聖嚴法師觀察，現代社會所製造的複雜生活問題，包
含生活步調緊張、資訊爆炸、積極過度及環境汙染等，以下
分析之。

（二）現代社會之生活問題

　　現代社會生活緊張，放鬆身心是重要的事，然而，放鬆

---

❸　楊郁文，〈佛法的人間性與現實性〉，收於林煌洲等合著，《聖嚴法師
　　思想行誼》（臺北：法鼓文化，2004 年，頁 113-149），頁 147-148。

身心與縱情娛樂並不相同，後者往往導致空虛的疲累感，使
人累上加累：

> 本來是工作上的疲累，為了解除工作疲累，跑去跳舞狂
> 歡，喝酒買醉，到第二天則會得到空虛感的疲累。原本是
> 由於工作上的疲累才跑去玩，盡情地玩累了再去工作。就
> 這麼忙著工作又忙著玩，累來累去，循環不已的人，不知
> 道活著是為什麼，也不知道為什麼要做一個人，這就叫作
> 醉生夢死。㉛

　　現代資本主義社會將休閒納入生產性邏輯，使得休閒不
再是「什麼都不做」（do nothing），而是「做些什麼事」
（do something）。在資本主義社會，休閒轉變為生產活
動，導致社會愈現代化，休閒產業愈發達。㉜休閒，相對於
工作而言，是放鬆身心、調劑生活的重要手段，在現代社會
忙碌工作之餘，適時而適量的休閒確有其必要性。然而，過
度休閒，將導致空虛感的疲累，使得工作也累，休閒也累，
進入累的循環，無暇正視生活的意義，成為現代緊張生活的
犧牲品。
　　另一方面，現代社會步調快速，時間寶貴，適時而正確
的資訊能協助縮短決策時間，然而資訊爆炸帶來的不是判斷

㉛ 釋聖嚴，《法鼓鐘聲》（臺北：法鼓文化，1999 年），頁 103。
㉜ 參見蘇碩斌，〈休閒、運動與觀光〉，收於章英華等著，《中華民國發
展史──社會發展》（臺北：聯經，2011 年），頁 621-653。

加速、明快，而是導致思考與行動混亂，浪費時間：

> 　資訊爆炸的結果，使我們的頭腦充斥著各式各樣的人、
> 事、物，令人應接不暇。本來知識愈豐富，觀察力愈敏
> 銳，應該更能夠做出正確的判斷，其實不然，這些不相干
> 的資訊，在思考與行動時，反而成為干擾，導致猶豫困
> 惑，不知該如何決定，如此一來，又浪費許多寶貴的時
> 間。❸❸

　　資訊產業發達的結果，訊息流通迅速，多重管道、不同
來源的消息，本應能收「兼聽則明」之效，唯真假難辨、疲
勞轟炸之下，往往阻滯正確判斷，陷入誤區。

　　再者，「積極」本為正面力量，使人奮發向上，然而現
代社會「太積極」、「過度積極」，反而產生負面效應：

> 　「積極」這兩個字，我們通常都會把它和樂觀、開
> 朗、進取連在一起。既然積極是這麼正面的，如果我說
> 太積極也不好，可能會有人不以為然了！事實上，積極
> 到了某一個程度，是會形成壓力的。很多人雖然做事很
> 積極，可是卻積極得很緊張、積極得很憂愁、積極得很
> 痛苦，不管到最後是失敗還是成功，過得都不是很快
> 樂。這都是因為得失心太重的緣故，本來只希望工作完

---

❸❸ 釋聖嚴，《工作好修行——聖嚴法師的 38 則職場智慧》（臺北：法鼓文化，2008 年），頁 67。

成就好的，接著又要求更好，等到達頂峰了，又擔心會
有不好的情況發生，隨時隨地都在擔憂、憂慮。即使成
功了，也還是在緊張的情緒和緊繃的壓力下，當然不會
快樂，也稱不上樂觀或開朗。所以，積極雖然會帶來事
業的成功，但成功以後呢？如果不懂得保持平常心，反
而會失去快樂和應有的開朗。❸

生活壓力本已使人緊張、憂愁、痛苦，若以積極態度承
擔面對，本應能養成樂觀進取的人生觀，唯刻意積極、過度
積極，反而加深緊張、憂愁、痛苦，內心糾結不開朗，生活
充滿不快樂，其病根，乃在於不能保持平常心之故。

又，大量生產、大量消費，刺激需求再擴大產能的資
本主義邏輯，在提高生產力、累積豐裕物資、創造富裕社會
的同時，已造成大量浪費與汙染的環保問題，如各種大量製
造、搶新求變的電子產品，除了因更換速度快而造成大量廢
棄物外，生產過程中更製造許多環境債，毒害自然及人體健
康，產生現代資本主義社會「為快速丟棄而加速製造」、
「科技始終來自人命」等怪象。❸站在人間佛教之立場，聖
嚴法師指出：

---

❸ 釋聖嚴，《找回自己》（臺北：法鼓文化，2005 年），頁 76。另參見
韓炳哲（Byung-chul Han）著，莊雅慈（正文）、管中琪（講稿）譯，
《倦怠社會》（*Müdigkeitsgesellschaft*）（臺北：大塊文化，2015 年）。
❸ 杜文苓，〈電子產品製造的環境代價〉，《科學發展》484 期（2013 年
4 月），頁 6-11。

　　大家都知道這些問題必須改善，可是到目前為止，似乎還是束手無策，縱然有改善，但改善的速度卻遠不如破壞的速度。其實，若要使得人類的生活環境不被汙染，最重要的根本，是在人類的心念，建立惜福儉樸的觀念，生活單純，物質欲望減少，心靈受到的汙染也就少，自然環境受到破壞的程度也會減低了。㊱

　　環境汙染問題使得清淨土離現代社會愈來愈遠，「建設人間淨土」以現代社會為實踐場域，其出發點在於現代人心，淨化人心，使心靈受到的汙染減少，方能改善環境汙染之問題。

（三）於現代社會建設人間淨土之契機

　　現代社會雖有種種問題，使得人間淨土之實現顯得似乎遙不可及，然而我們也需觀察到現代社會同時也提供了種種展開人間淨土建設之契機。

　　社會的現代化，帶來生活環境的改善與生活品質之提昇，使人類有更多餘暇思考精神層面的需求與靈性的追求，而傳媒科技之進展與交通之便利，亦使資訊的流通與理念的傳播更加迅捷，社會大環境之開放通達，更使人間佛教有奉獻社會之機會，凡此皆為建設現代社會為人間淨土提供良好條件。

　　就現代社會環境之通達而言，聖嚴法師曾詮解「達則兼善天下」，指出「達」並不是說自己多麼了不得，而是指社

㊱　釋聖嚴，《動靜皆自在》（臺北：法鼓文化，2005 年），頁 60。

會環境已經「通達」了，能夠讓我提供自己的力量❸。聖嚴
法師並以自己為例，說明「時勢造英雄」之理：

> 如果現今的環境仍然像過去那樣，是非常封閉的時代，
> 是威權偏執的社會，我就不可能成為一個公眾人物。我之
> 所以成為公眾人物，完全是由於整個大環境的改變，大環
> 境需要像我這樣的人，大時代允許我有奉獻心力的機會，
> 於是我就應運而成了具有相當知名度的宗教師。因此，我
> 應該感謝大時代、大環境的改變，我的成功與成就，不應
> 該歸功於自己，而是屬於這個時代環境中的全體大眾。❸

　　現代社會的民主化進程，使得時代氛圍已由威權偏執
走向寬容開放，宗教自由之人權保障提供宗教師走入人群，
貢獻於現代社會之機會。如若當今社會仍是敵視宗教，以政
治力威逼，切斷社會與宗教教團之聯繫，讓宗教「不可見」
（invisible），從世俗社會生活退卻消失，則佛教求走出山
林尚不可得，何能以現代社會為其實踐場域乎？社會大環境
的改變，是社會大眾共同努力而來，故需感恩這個時代環境
中的全體大眾，提供了建設人間淨土之契機。
　　如學者楊曾文所指出，應當看到現實世界人間是存在很
多積極的因素，有諸多美好的東西，有無數待開發的方面，

---

❸ 釋聖嚴，《是非要溫柔──聖嚴法師的禪式管理學》（臺北：法鼓文
化，2010年二版），頁19-20。
❸ 釋聖嚴，《人間世》（臺北：法鼓文化，2005年），頁50-51。

如發達的科技、高度發展的經濟生活、豐富的物質與精神財富、緊密聯繫的國際關係等，從中可以看到令人鼓舞的未來，乃是建設人間淨土的出發點。**㊴**

（四）於現代社會建設人間淨土之理據**㊵**

如上所述，現代社會製造出種種複雜的問題，使得人們過度緊張、壓力重重；現代社會雖也提供了種種展開人間淨土建設之契機，然而究實而言，在現代都市化的制度與生活方式底下，人心淨化如何保證？人間淨土建設如何可能？如無堅實理據，上節所討論的「契機」是否將只是一種一廂情願的樂觀幻想，而所謂「令人鼓舞的未來」亦無兌現之可能？

《維摩經》言：「隨其心淨，則佛土淨。」由心淨而行淨，由行淨而感動他人，使眾生淨；眾生淨而能共同建設，發揮集體力量，進而改變社會，使環境清淨。此為「心淨則土淨」之因果律，乃建設人間淨土之理據，保證了人間淨土實現之可能性。**㊶**

㊴ 楊曾文，〈人間淨土思想與不二法門〉，收於釋聖嚴等著，釋惠敏主編，《人間淨土與現代社會──第三屆中華國際佛學會議論文集》（臺北：法鼓文化，1998 年，頁 181-205），頁 203。

㊵ 本節「於現代社會建設人間淨土之理據」之修正補充，感謝匿名審查人寶貴意見。

㊶ 「自心淨」→「有情淨」（眾生淨）→「佛土淨」之因果關係分析，見釋惠敏，〈「心淨則佛土淨」之考察〉，收於釋聖嚴等著，釋惠敏主編，《人間淨土與現代社會──第三屆中華國際佛學會議中文論文集》（臺北：法鼓文化，1998 年），頁 221-246。

是知佛教的因果律，不是宿命論也不是定命論，而是不折不扣的「努力論」：❷我們所做的任何努力絕對不會白費，一定會有它的功能，只要我們願意付出，一定會有所影響。❸面對現代都市化的制度與生活方式，個人仍有努力空間，建設人間淨土依據「心淨則土淨」之因果律，其在現代社會實現的可能性，要靠我們每個人的共同努力。

然而，我們每個人可以如何努力呢？如前文提及，資訊發達或使人更有機會接觸佛教學習教法，但是同時人們也面對負面資訊轟炸的競爭，人間淨土如何突破重圍？

現代社會生活節奏快速緊張，面對資訊轟炸，能快速反應似乎是一種必要的求生手段。然而，隨資訊起舞，拚命追著新消息跑，又往往是造成精神疲勞與判斷出錯之主因。

聖嚴法師指出，從佛法立場來講，伶俐、反應快的人，並非真正聰明人。任何事情發生，最好能「慢半拍」，先不要馬上下判斷做反應，先等一會兒緩一緩。表面看來，「慢」好像遲鈍，其實它就是慎重、謹慎，就是一種智慧。❹聖嚴法師說：

> ……日常生活中凡遇任何事物發生，先不要馬上處理，經過冷靜客觀分析，同時抽取出「我」的因素，再慢慢去處理，則效果一定更好。「我」的成分務必要排除，才做

---

❷ 釋聖嚴，《正信的佛教》（臺北：法鼓文化，1999 年），頁 77。
❸ 釋聖嚴，《真正的快樂》（臺北：法鼓文化，2008 年），頁 129。
❹ 釋聖嚴，《聖嚴法師心靈環保》（臺北：法鼓文化，1999 年），頁 99。

得到客觀。㊺

　　在日常生活中，採取「慢半拍」的生活態度，面對資訊轟炸，以從容、客觀的「無我」心態，冷靜下來，再慢慢處理，是我們大家可以著手努力的方向。

　　綜上所述，「建設人間淨土」乃基於「心淨則土淨」之因果律，而現代社會環境之通達亦提供佛法弘化之契機，故知建設人間淨土契理、契機，唯其實現的可能性，在於我們願意為其實現而付出努力，有努力，有付出，在「無我」的方向上解行並重、精勤不懈，「心淨則土淨」之因果律方不致落空。

四、解構性：如何建設現代社會為人間淨土

（一）心靈環保

　　如前所述，一九八九年聖嚴法師創立法鼓山，以「提昇人的品質，建設人間淨土」為其兩大組織目標，至一九九二年，聖嚴法師提倡「心靈環保」，將兩大目標結合起來，吸收環保運動於人間佛教理念內涵，賦予人間佛教全球化之新面貌，與世界環保潮流接軌。

　　據學者林益仁之研究，一九九○年代臺灣出現的大量環保論述及環保抗爭之社會運動，可視為全球環保省思潮流之在地化，並促使聖嚴法師著手思考環保議題。㊻聖嚴法師

㊺ 釋聖嚴，《聖嚴法師心靈環保》，頁 99-100。
㊻ 林益仁，〈環境實踐的「全球」與「在地」辯證：以法鼓山的「環保」論述為例〉，《台灣社會研究季刊》55 期（2004 年 09 月），頁 1-46。

由佛教之因果法則觀察環境汙染現象，將環境汙染歸因於人類活動，再進一步將我們汙染地球環境的活動溯源至我們受汙染／製造汙染的心。針對環境汙染之因果，聖嚴法師提出了以佛法淨化心靈來做為治癒生病地球的方法，即「心靈環保」：

> 為什麼要講「心靈環保」呢？因為環境的汙染是由人造成的，「環境」本身不會製造任何汙染，植物或礦物也不會為人類環境帶來汙染。唯有人類會製造髒亂，不但汙染物質環境更是汙染精神環境，從語言、文字、符號，種種形象以及各種思想觀念等都會為人類的心靈帶來傷害。物質環境的汙染不離人為，而人為又離不開人的「心靈」。如果人們的「心靈」清潔，則我們的物質環境不會受到汙染。因此，我們討論環境的汙染，就必須從根源著手，也就是要從「心靈」開始。❹

透過心靈環保，以淨化心靈、淨化環境，即是聖嚴法師所提出將現代社會建設為人間淨土之方法。

首先，所謂的「淨化」，在現代社會的具體落實處即是「環保」。以環保觀點來看佛法之淨化，一念與環保相應、停止製造垃圾的心，即為一念心淨的「環保心」，以念念「環保心」建設起來的「環保土」，就是人間淨土。

其次，就心、境關係而言，境可區分為客觀情事之「外

---

❹ 釋聖嚴，《禪門》（臺北：法鼓文化，1999），頁90。

境」與主觀心理活動之「內境」，一般以為外境不清淨，造成內心煩惱，連帶使心靈不清淨。實際上，內境之情緒紛擾與波動，才是使心、境俱無法清淨之主因，聖嚴法師說：

> 內境是指心中的妄想、煩惱；外境是環境中的人事。大多數的人認為煩惱來自外境，為此對外境產生佔有、排斥或對立。其中，事雖不會惹來煩惱、困擾，但因為有人心的作用，因為加進了「人」，啟動了妄念，「事」就變得複雜，就會衍生出很多令人煩惱不已的問題來。❹❽

> 《維摩經》中說：「隨其心淨，則佛土淨。」心的行為能夠主導身體和語言的行為，每一個人的行為都能影響整體的環境……。
> 因此，如果心中沒有安全感，你就不得安全，心中不為安全問題煩心，就是安心的人，而且你所處的這個世界，就是佛國淨土。❹❾

停止製造垃圾的「環保心」，是停止製造內心煩惱的情緒垃圾，減少心靈的汙染，同時能主導身體和語言的行為，停止製造語言的垃圾與汙染外在環境的垃圾，從而能造就清境的環保土，這就是《維摩經》中所說：「隨其心淨，則佛土淨。」也是建設人間淨土之理據。

---

❹❽ 釋聖嚴，《法鼓晨音》（臺北：法鼓文化，2005 年），頁 35。
❹❾ 釋聖嚴，《平安的人間》（臺北：法鼓文化，2005 年），頁 123-124。

（二）解構性心靈資本：人間淨土資糧

就現代社會之結構而言，學者偉特（Bradford Verter）由布迪厄（Pierre Bourdieu）文化理論進路分析指出，❺⓪現代社會之各場域，如教育、宗教、藝術、科學等，各自具有不同的資本種類與運作邏輯，稱為場域的「結構性自律」；各類資本在諸場域中，以生產、累積、繼承、交換等經濟性模式運作，而資本運作之政治性目的，則在於再生產該場域之支配性結構，故總體而言，現代社會之各場域俱為權力場域所籠罩。

偉特主張，行動主體所擁有之宗教知識、宗教技能或對宗教之抉擇偏好，構成了「心靈資本」（spiritual capital），「心靈資本」做為「文化資本」❺①之一形式，同樣也是地位性商品（positional goods），可提昇持有者在場域中之地位。

另一方面，偉特強調，由於現代社會諸團體間有互動性連結，且現代人同時棲居於多個場域，具有重疊身分，故各種自律性場域的資本可流通互換，以心靈資本為例，其具

---

❺⓪ Bradford Verter, "Spiritual Capital: Theorizing Religion with Bourdieu Against Bourdieu", *Sociological Theory* 21:2 (June 2003), pp. 150-173.

❺① 偉特指出，在布迪厄之前的文化理論已認知到，對於高檔文化產品（古典樂、美術品、美食等）之消費，乃社會地位之標誌，而布迪厄進一步指出，美學品味之傾向亦屬文化資本，用以再製社會階級。學者、批評家及其他文化產品之生產者、分配者及媒介者，競逐定義品味的權力，以做為維持或調整其社會地位之策略。見 Bradford Verter, "Spiritual Capital: Theorizing Religion with Bourdieu Against Bourdieu", p. 152。

有跨域性質，不只在宗教領域有效，且以不同資本形式樣貌出現在不同場域。重點在於，場域間的互動及資本的跨域散布，使得某一場域的評價會影響另一場域，故「心靈資本」之估價，會隨著時間及場域結構之不斷變遷而波動起伏，對於特定「心靈資本」評價之升跌，可以解釋宗教上的改宗（conversion）、信仰折衷（devotional eclecticism）❷、宗教衰退及社會流動現象。

如借用偉特所提出「心靈資本」之概念，或可說面對現代社會既成之場域結構，以「心靈環保」為核心之建設人間淨土，其實踐所累積之人間淨土資糧，係淨化心靈、提昇人品之「心靈資本」，其運作之目的不在於提昇個人在場域中之支配性地位，而在於提昇心靈品質，以轉化、改變、解構既有之煩惱心、汙染心的運作模式，重新生產清淨性、解脫性之淨土思維與實踐以奉獻於社會，就此而言，聖嚴法師「建設人間淨土」之人間佛教理念，已由漢傳佛教之現代化追求，邁向後現代性之解構與重構。

如上所述，聖嚴法師具有強烈的時代感與使命感，面對當前社會由現代到後現代之變遷，聖嚴法師〈後現代佛教〉由佛法觀點指出：

> ……佛教的基本原則是不能離開因果論及因緣觀的，也不能離開慈悲心與智慧心的。相信因果便不會怨天尤

---

❷ 信仰折衷意指：在信仰層面，依個人之偏好，把各種不同宗教傳統的元素摻雜揉合起來。

人，相信因緣便能夠積極努力而又能看破放下；關懷普天
下的眾生，卻不以自我中心為出發點，便是悲智雙運。這
就是現代化的佛教所要實踐的，而這也正是我們社會所需
要的。

現代主義的西方社會，強調個人與自我；所以後現代主
義是以個人為立場，對社會提出批判與解構。如果從這個
角度來看，佛教則是以無我為立場，一旦解構了每一個立
場，豈不就是無我的立場呢！佛教教我們要不斷打破舊有
的框架，不斷融入現代不同文化的社會，這似乎就跟後現
代哲學接軌了。❸

聖嚴法師認為，佛法中可與後現代性接軌者，乃無我的
立場，無我的立場，即不斷解構每一個舊有的、既成的立場，
而能不斷融入異質化、多元化的後現代社會。❹就佛法的實

---

❸ 釋聖嚴，〈後現代佛教〉，《人間世》（臺北：法鼓文化，2005 年），
頁 41-42。

❹ 有關佛法之接軌於後現代性，巴徹勒（Stephen Batchelor）指出佛法
的「空性」（emptiness）相應於後現代哲學對於大敘事之懷疑不信
（incredulity toward grand narratives）；馬提斯（Susan Mattis）則由後
現代哲學對於「邏各斯中心主義」（logocentrism）之批判導入佛教中觀
學派之觀法，可資參照。見 Stephen Batchelor, "The Other Enlightenment
Project - Buddhism, Agnosticism and Postmodernity", in U. King ed., *Faith
and Praxis in a Postmodern Age* (London: Cassell, 1998), pp. 113-127；Susan
Mattis, "Introducing Buddhism in a Course on Postmodernism", in Victor
Sōgen Hori, Richard P. Hayes, James Mark Shields ed., *Teaching Buddhism
in the West: From the Wheel to the Web* (London: RoutledgeCurzon, - Curzon
critical studies in Buddhism, 2002), pp. 141-152。

踐而言，無我的立場，即不間斷地消融自我，「關懷普天下的眾生，卻不以自我中心為出發點」，而生悲智雙運之大用。

聖嚴法師說：「心是我們的老師，我們的心隨時隨地與當下所做的事、所處的環境合而為一，就是在淨土之中。」**⑤** 能隨時隨地與環境相合的心，不生人我、物我對立煩惱的心，即是無我的清淨心，由無我的立場放下自我中心之執著，不斷解構既有的煩惱心、汙染心，而能生起慈悲心、大願心、感恩心，不斷生產清淨性、解脫性之人間淨土思維與實踐以服務社會，就是在累積並奉獻心靈資本，愈奉獻愈累積，愈累積愈奉獻，在人間淨土資糧累積與奉獻於現代社會大眾之相互回饋中，相應於阿彌陀佛的慈悲與智慧，則心靈環保得以落實，人間淨土得以實現。聖嚴法師說：

> 念佛能使我們生起慈悲心、慚愧心、懺悔心、大悲願心、感恩迴向心，而這些都是成佛、修菩薩行的基礎，也是求生西方淨土不可缺少的資糧。所以，我們一定要不斷發願、練習生起慈悲心、慚愧心、懺悔心、感恩迴向心，如果練習純熟，在平常生活時，就能以慈悲心、感恩心、慚愧心來對待周遭所有認識或不認識的人。這樣我們所提倡的人間淨土就會在我們這個環境出現，完成了建設人間淨土的目的與任務。**⑤**

---

⑤ 釋聖嚴，《聖嚴法師108自在語合輯（中文繁體平裝本）》（臺北：財團法人聖嚴教育基金會，2009年），頁65。

⑤ 釋聖嚴，《聖嚴法師教淨土法門》（臺北：法鼓文化，2010年），頁288。

（三）解構性態度：奉獻與捨得

就心靈資本之制度層面言，法鼓山教團弘揚建設人間淨土之人間佛教理念，以團體的力量生產清淨佛法，推動三大教育，同修人間淨土資糧，即是累積制度化的心靈資本（institutionalized spiritual capital），奉獻給社會全體，為淨化人心、淨化社會而服務；而推廣理念的過程中，仍秉持無執無我的解構性態度，解構搶地盤的可悲心態與強迫推銷的偏執立場，而代之以無私的奉獻與無執的捨得。

聖嚴法師說：

> 我們不要把市場看成是固定不變的，不要老是跟著同一形式走，以我們佛教徒來說，就算全台灣兩千三百萬人都信了佛教，也只不過是兩千三百萬人，跟全世界比起來，可說微乎其微，何況台灣的佛教團體這麼多，每個團體都在用心推廣，希望能影響更多的人，這個時候，如果我們只想搶信徒、搶機會，就太可悲了。企業要做的，應該是提供「市場」裡的「消費者」更便利、更有用的東西。例如，看看哪些服務是別人沒有提供的？哪些商品是大家都需要卻還沒有出現的？我們應該設法把它們創造出來。說穿了，人類的文明、文化，也就是這麼推動、創造累積起來的。
>
> 我現在在做的，也只是把「理念」和「方向」分享出去而已。例如我講的「心靈環保」、「人間淨土」這些觀念，現在已經有很多地方在沿用，並不只限於佛教界，這

對我來說是很安慰的。我不會說「這是我的專利」，不准
別人使用，這就太自私了。我提出這些理念的目的，就是
要別人去用它、接受它，至於是不是我們團體的專利特
色，就不是那麼要緊了。❺

聖嚴法師提出「建設人間淨土」之理念，目的並非在利
用之以為搶地盤、搶信徒之資本，而是將佛法智慧予以現代
性詮釋，以無私的態度分享、奉獻於全人類社會，使該理念
跨域流通，「不只限於佛教界」，而能貢獻於全人類文明之
創造與推動。

在奉獻中，尚須釐清「執著」與「捨得」的分際，聖嚴
法師說：

為自我的利益而放不下，就是「執著」；為他人的需
要而奉獻，就是「捨得」。為他人奉獻而堅持到底，叫作
「毅力」，而非「執著」⋯⋯

當然也很可能會有這種情況：某人認為他的理念是最
好的、也對社會最有利，於是堅持、執著於自己的想法。
但這是僅就他自己的立場來看，並不是「同理心」。他自
己認為這個社會需要的東西，未必是社會真正的需要。例
如：我有一雙鞋，穿在腳上很舒服，就強迫別人也一定要
穿，還覺得不肯穿這雙鞋的人都對不起我：「這麼舒服的
鞋，你居然不穿！」像這樣的「執著」，這樣的堅持己

---

❺ 釋聖嚴，《是非要溫柔——聖嚴法師的禪式管理學》，頁 14-15。

見，在現在的台灣經常可以看到。**❺**

　　為社會需要而奉獻到底，是行願的毅力；建設人間淨土誠然需要毅力，但毅力不是「執著」，如執著於「建設人間淨土」之理念而強迫他人接受，他人不接受則生瞋恚，反而是製造更多紛爭與情緒垃圾，完全顛倒於清淨無私的心靈環保。「建設人間淨土」是一種奉獻，需以「捨得」的態度從事之，千萬不要拿自己的鞋子叫別人穿，當知「心淨土淨」，如態度不正確，則自心尚不能清淨，何談淨土乎！若然，則「建設人間淨土」理念之推動，當由何處著手呢？

　　究實而言，「建設人間淨土」理念之推動，當由「感化」及「感動」出發：我們要先用佛法感化自己，然後再用行動去感動人，如此才能使社會大眾漸漸地接受法鼓山的理念，**❺**建設現代社會為人間淨土。聖嚴法師說：

> 　　感化自己就是要知慚愧、常懺悔。慚愧是因為自己做得不夠好，希望能夠做得更好、更努力；懺悔是因為知道自己有做錯的地方，提醒以後不要再犯錯……有人會抱怨家庭裡的成員不夠好、不能滿自己的願；或覺得社會混亂，人心不安定。總認為別人都變好，自己就安全了，其他人都變得認真、負責，自己就幸福了；總是期待他人，認為只要別人都好，自己就有福報，但卻忘了自我要求，反省

❺　釋聖嚴，《是非要溫柔——聖嚴法師的禪式管理學》，頁 18-19。
❺　參見釋聖嚴，《法鼓山的方向》，頁 200。

一下自己是否也滿了別人的願？

　　佛法提醒我們，修行應該從自己做起，以自己修學佛法，學習到的慈悲與智慧來感動他人，而不是要求他人，這才是最可靠的。❻⓪

（四）未來展望：建設人間淨土與現代社會制度的解構與重構❻①

　　就聖嚴法師「建設人間淨土」議題，學者鄧偉仁指出，建設人間淨土不僅是宗教課題（個人煩惱雜染的淨化、菩提的證得、三界的解脫），它更是「社會改造」工程。在此面向上，「建設人間淨土」必須正視結構性、制度性的社會問題，因為人心的不善雖是所有問題之根源，但社會問題的解決必須回歸制度性公平合理之考量。因此，現代人間淨土之建設除了心靈淨化，應該重視社會制度與社會行為。❻②

　　如上所述，聖嚴法師「建設人間淨土」之理念，本身為解構性的心靈資本，具有跨域流通特性，其影響層面不僅只是宗教場域，更外溢到現代社會各場域，發揮其解構與重構之功能，這就是為何「建設人間淨土」之理念由「淨化人

---

❻⓪ 釋聖嚴，《法鼓山的方向》，頁 469-470。

❻① 本節「未來展望：建設人間淨土與現代社會制度的解構與重構」之修正補充，感謝匿名審查人寶貴意見。

❻② 鄧偉仁，「佛教倫理與理想社會的建設」（法鼓文理學院心靈環保研究中心 106 學年「心靈環保講座」第 1 場演講），網路影片資料：https://www.youtube.com/watch?v=i6FcqmESmHE。檢索日期：2020/3/29。

心」開始,其目的卻最終能達到「淨化社會」之緣故。

亦即,如學者鄧偉仁所指陳,「建設人間淨土」不僅建設人心,更是「社會改造」工程;隨著心靈資本之跨域傳布,「建設人間淨土」在社會制度之解構與重構上,當有其無盡發展潛力。

有鑑於聖嚴法師「心靈環保」、「心六倫」等建設人間淨土運動於社會制度及人文領域之貢獻,聖嚴法師於二〇〇八年獲頒美國設計與流程科學學會(SDPS)「李國鼎傑出經濟社會制度設計獎」,該獎成立以來,以往的受獎者,都是在經濟領域有卓越貢獻的人士,二〇〇八年打破先例,首度頒贈給非經濟領域人士,❻可以說是國際社會對聖嚴法師建設人間淨土運動於社會制度層面所生作用之肯定。

將「建設人間淨土」理念貢獻於現代社會制度之解構與重構,其本心仍在於上節所述奉獻、捨得之無我態度。以聖嚴法師念茲在茲之佛教教育制度為例,聖嚴法師有感於國內缺乏制度化培養佛法人才之教育體制,乃借鑑先進國家經驗,於一九八五年創設中華佛學研究所,致力於佛教教育及學術工作之發展。聖嚴法師說:

> 晚近以來的中國佛教,不是沒有教育,而是沒有制度化及現代化的教育,例如:楊仁山的祇洹精舍,歐陽竟無的支那內學院,太虛大師的武昌佛學院、漢藏教理院、閩南佛學院,都造就了不少僧才,都是模仿現代化,然均不是

現代化，尤其沒有一套完整的制度，不能維持長久；直到
抗戰勝利，臺灣光復以來的各佛學院，依舊如此，殊為可
惜。作為現代化及制度化而且有永久性的佛教教育機構而
言，應該說是自本所招收第一屆研究生為始。❻

　　由此可見，聖嚴法師於我國佛教教育制度之用心與貢
獻，由中華佛學研究所開始，聖嚴法師引領法鼓山之建設，
開創世界佛教教育園區，以團體的力量生產清淨佛法，推動
三大教育，更為法鼓大學之籌辦而不斷奔走努力，凡此，均
可見出「建設人間淨土」在教育制度所生之作用與貢獻，❻
亦可視為是如何在現代社會建設人間淨土實例之一。

　　聖嚴法師對教育制度之建設，如上所述，乃一貫秉持
奉獻、捨得之無我態度，聖嚴法師於一九九四年一場開示中
提到：

　　　兩個星期前，研究所有位助教來找我談一個問題，她
　　說：「師父，中部有一家佛研所要成立了，他們希望我們
　　把中華佛研所的制度規約章程給他們。」她問我說：「是

---

❻ 釋聖嚴，《教育‧文化‧文學》（臺北：法鼓文化，1999 年），頁
　223。

❻ 聖嚴法師說：「創辦法鼓大學、中華佛學研究所。前者是以淨化人心、
　淨化社會的佛教精神，培養提昇人的品質、建設人間淨土的各項專業性
　的領導人才；後者是以優良的佛學研究環境，培養以及儲蓄高水準的佛
　學研究人才，來帶動國內外的學術界及知識分子，重視佛學，尊重佛
　教，影響二十一世紀的人類世界，認同和接受提昇人的品質、建設人間
　淨土的大趨勢。」見釋聖嚴，《法鼓山的方向》，頁 134。

不是可以？」我說：「當然可以呀！」她說：「師父，我
們花了十多年時間，用了很多頭腦、人力物力，辛辛苦苦
把它建立起來的，我們白白給人家，不是很可惜嗎？為什
麼這樣子做？」我說：「阿彌陀佛！佛教都是一樣的啊！
我們做得那麼辛苦，難道我們忍心看人家也那麼辛苦地做
嗎？我們不要做唯一的，不做獨一的，我們只是要奉獻我
們自己，成就佛教，成就社會！」❻❻

　　以十多年時間及無數人力、物力建設起來的教育制度，
聖嚴法師並不以之為私己獨占之資本而自我標榜為唯一、獨
一，而是以無我無私的態度，將之奉獻於佛教，奉獻於社
會，奉獻於人類。

　　綜上，以無我奉獻的態度，將心靈環保理念跨域應用，
以從事於現代社會制度之解構與重構，為建設人間淨土可能
與時並進之展望。果光法師近年提出以「心靈環保」為主軸
的經濟思維，解構資本主義經濟社會追求物質欲望最大化之
生活模式，而回歸心靈環保，重構起少欲、利他的經濟生
活，朝向涅槃、離苦得樂之人生方向，❻❼是為可喜之實例。

五、結論

　　本文在「人生佛教」與「人間佛教」之歷史發展脈絡

---

❻❻　〈孤掌與鼓掌〉，《法鼓》雜誌，52 期，1994 年 4 月 15 日，版 4。轉
　　引自林其賢，《聖嚴法師年譜》，頁 939。
❻❼　見釋果光，《心靈環保經濟學》（臺北：法鼓文化，2014 年）。

下，詮解聖嚴法師「建設人間淨土」的理念，以人間性、場域性和解構性來論證聖嚴法師「心靈環保」思想，在現代社會與後現代社會接軌之際，開出重構當代社會的重要方向，期使現代人可以安頓身心，自在解脫。[68]

　　進一步言，「建設人間淨土」係以現代人心為弘化對象，以現代社會為實踐場域，並以「心靈環保」為實踐方法，由無我的立場，生產清淨性、解脫性之心靈資本，以解構內境的煩惱與外境之汙染，在心靈資本之跨域流通中，由淨化人心而能淨化社會，重構現代社會為人間淨土，使現代人自在解脫。就此而言，「建設人間淨土」已由漢傳佛教之現代化追求，邁向後現代性之解構與重構。

　　經由本文之論析，可以發現「建設人間淨土」回應著當代社會之需求，其「心靈環保」之核心方法，承繼著漢傳佛教現代化使命，同時由無我的解構性立場，接軌了後現代社會之時代精神。

---

[68] 本處結論，感謝匿名審查人之寶貴意見。

引用書目

一、聖嚴法師著作

釋聖嚴，《正信的佛教》，臺北：法鼓文化，1999 年。

釋聖嚴，《法鼓山的方向》，臺北：法鼓文化，1999 年。

釋聖嚴，《法鼓山的方向 II》，臺北：法鼓文化，1999 年。

釋聖嚴，《法鼓鐘聲》，臺北：法鼓文化，1999 年。

釋聖嚴，《禪門》，臺北：法鼓文化，1999 年。

釋聖嚴，《教育・文化・文學》，臺北：法鼓文化，1999 年。

釋聖嚴，《聖嚴法師心靈環保》，臺北：法鼓文化，1999 年。

釋聖嚴，《人間世》，臺北：法鼓文化，2005 年。

釋聖嚴，《動靜皆自在》，臺北：法鼓文化，2005 年。

釋聖嚴，《法鼓晨音》，臺北：法鼓文化，2005 年。

釋聖嚴，《找回自己》，臺北：法鼓文化，2005 年。

釋聖嚴，《平安的人間》，臺北：法鼓文化，2005 年。

釋聖嚴，《工作好修行——聖嚴法師的 38 則職場智慧》，臺北：法鼓文化，2008 年。

釋聖嚴，《真正的快樂》，臺北：法鼓文化，2008 年。

釋聖嚴，《聖嚴法師 108 自在語合輯（中文繁體平裝本）》，臺北：財團法人聖嚴教育基金會，2009 年。

釋聖嚴，《是非要溫柔——聖嚴法師的禪式管理學》，臺北：法鼓文化，2010 年二版。

釋聖嚴，《聖嚴法師教淨土法門》，臺北：法鼓文化，2010 年。

釋聖嚴，《美好的晚年》，臺北：法鼓文化，2010 年。

釋聖嚴，《我願無窮——美好的晚年開示集》，臺北：法鼓文化，2011 年。

二、專書

丁仁傑，《當代漢人民眾宗教研究：論述、認同與社會再生產》，臺北：聯經，2009 年。

白德滿（Don A. Pittman）著，鄭清榮譯，《太虛——人生佛教的追尋與實現》，臺北：法鼓文化，2008 年。

林其賢，《聖嚴法師年譜》，臺北：法鼓文化，2016 年。

林煌洲等合著，《聖嚴法師思想行誼》，臺北：法鼓文化，2004 年。

章英華等著，《中華民國發展史——社會發展》，臺北：聯經，2011 年。

韓炳哲（Byung-chul Han）著，莊雅慈（正文）、管中琪（講稿）譯，《倦怠社會》（*Müdigkeitsgesellschaft*），臺北：大塊文化，2015 年。

釋印順，《華雨集第四冊》，印順文教基金會推廣教育中心印順法師佛學著作集網站：http://yinshun-edu.org.tw/Master_yinshun/books。檢索日期：2019/4/7。

釋果光，《心靈環保經濟學》，臺北：法鼓文化，2014 年。

釋聖嚴等著，釋惠敏主編，《人間淨土與現代社會——第三屆中華國際佛學會議論文集》，臺北：法鼓文化，1998 年。

三、單篇論文

李玉珍，〈人間佛教研究之回顧與前瞻〉，收於慈惠法師總編輯，《二〇一四人間佛教高峰論壇輯二：人間佛教宗要》，高雄：佛光山人間佛教研究院，2015 年，頁 161-167。

杜文苓，〈電子產品製造的環境代價〉，《科學發展》484 期，2013 年 4 月，頁 6-11。

林其賢，〈聖嚴法師人間淨土思想的實踐與弘揚〉，收入聖嚴教育基金會學術研究部編，《聖嚴研究》第一輯，臺北：法鼓文

化，2010 年，頁 153-205。

林益仁，〈環境實踐的「全球」與「在地」辯證：以法鼓山的「環保」論述為例〉，《台灣社會研究季刊》55 期，2004 年 9 月，頁 1-46。

林建德，〈近二十年來臺灣地區「人間佛教」研究發展概述〉，收於《佛教圖書館學刊》52 期，2011 年 6 月，頁 6-17。

楊郁文，〈佛法的人間性與現實性〉，收於林煌洲等合著，《聖嚴法師思想行誼》，臺北：法鼓文化，2004 年，頁 113-149。

楊曾文，〈人間淨土思想與不二法門〉，收於釋聖嚴等著，釋惠敏主編，《人間淨土與現代社會——第三屆中華國際佛學會議論文集》，臺北：法鼓文化，1998 年，頁 181-205。

釋印順，〈契理契機之人間佛教〉，《華雨集第四冊》，印順文教基金會推廣教育中心印順法師佛學著作集網站：http://yinshun-edu.org.tw/Master_yinshun/books。檢索日期：2019/4/7。

釋果樸，〈聖嚴法師「建設人間淨土」理念根源——法師大陸出家學習與近代中國佛教興革〉，收於林煌洲等合著，《聖嚴法師思想行誼》，臺北：法鼓文化，2004 年，頁 345-504。

釋惠敏，〈「心淨則佛土淨」之考察〉，收於釋聖嚴等著，釋惠敏主編，《人間淨土與現代社會——第三屆中華國際佛學會議中文論文集》，臺北：法鼓文化，1998 年，頁 221-246。

釋聖嚴，〈戒律與人間淨土的建立〉，收於氏著，《學術論考》，臺北：法鼓文化，1999 年，頁 404-445。

蘇碩斌，〈休閒、運動與觀光〉，收於章英華等著，《中華民國發展史——社會發展》，臺北：聯經，2011 年，頁 621-653。

嚴瑋泓，〈聖嚴法師戒律思想之倫理學義蘊〉，收入聖嚴教育基金會學術研究部編，《聖嚴研究》第六輯，臺北：法鼓文化，2015 年，頁 413-448。

〈孤掌與鼓掌〉，《法鼓》雜誌，52 期，1994 年 4 月 15 日，版 4。

四、網路資料

鄧偉仁，「佛教倫理與理想社會的建設」（法鼓文理學院心靈環保研究中心 106 學年「心靈環保講座」第 1 場演講），網路影片資料：https://www.youtube.com/watch?v=i6FcqmESmHE。檢索日期：2020/3/29。

五、外文著作

Batchelor, Stephen, "The Other Enlightenment Project - Buddhism, Agnosticism and Postmodernity", in U. King ed., *Faith and Praxis in a Postmodern Age*, London: Cassell, 1998, pp. 113-127.

Chandler, Stuart, *Establishing a Pure Land on Earth: the Foguang Buddhist Perspective on Modernization and Globalization*, Honolulu: University of Hawai'i Press, 2004.

Jones, Charles Brewer, *Buddhism in Taiwan: religion and the state, 1660-1990*, Honolulu, HI: University of Hawai'i Press, 1999.

Mattis, Susan, "Introducing Buddhism in a Course on Postmodernism", in Victor Sōgen Hori, Richard P. Hayes, James Mark Shields ed., *Teaching Buddhism in the West: From the Wheel to the Web*, London: RoutledgeCurzon, - Curzon critical studies in Buddhism, 2002, pp. 141-152.

Pittman, Don A., *Toward a Modern Chinese Buddhism: Taixu's Reforms*, Honolulu: University of Hawai'i Press, 2001.

Verter, Bradford, "Spiritual Capital: Theorizing Religion with Bourdieu Against Bourdieu", *Sociological Theory* 21:2 (June 2003).

Human Domain, Practice Field, and Deconstruction:
Master Sheng Yen on How to Build a Pure Land in Modern Society

Hsuan-Li Wang

PhD in Religion, Columbia University

▎ Abstract

Master Sheng Yen had devoted himself to promoting the ideal of "building a pure land on earth". The ideal emphasizes that the "human domain" is the key concern of Buddhist soteriological enterprise and that our modern society is the main field of Buddhist practices. Moreover, as the method of building a pure land on earth, "spiritual environmentalism" implies the deconstruction of polluted fields to rebuild pure fields through spiritual purification with loving-kindness for our society.

The essay will firstly argue that the humanistic Buddhist ideals of Master Sheng Yen are aimed at the modern transformation of Chinese Buddhism which is not to secularize Buddhism, but to reorient it towards the "human domain", holding true to the original intents of Buddha, so that Buddhism could continue its soteriological enterprise in our secular modern society.

Secondly, the essay will suggest that the ideal of "building a pure land on earth" is to be realized in modern society (especially industrialized and urbanized capitalist society), taking it as the main field of humanistic Buddhist practices. Facing the social field structures developed by modernization, Master Sheng Yen observes and analyzes the causes of suffering in modern lives, and provides "spiritual environmentalism" as a solution. The essay will then investigate how "spiritual environmentalism" deconstructs the polluted fields to rebuild our modern society into a pure land on earth.

In conclusion, the essay will point out that because it emphasizes the "human domain" and the deconstruction of social fields, the ideal of "building a pure land on earth" has left the pursuit of the modernization of Chinese Buddhism behind and entered the contexts of post-modern Buddhist practices.

Keywords: Master Sheng Yen, Building a Pure Land on Earth, Deconstruction

The Social Origin of Creativity:
A Sociological Analysis of Master Taixu and Master Sheng Yen as Buddhist Thinkers

Rebecca S.K. Li*

Associate Professor, Department of Sociology and Anthropology, The College of New Jersey

▋ Abstract

Contrary to the belief that some thinkers are inherently creative who come up with self-evidently creative ideas, sociologist Randall Collins argues that creative ideas are co-created in intellectual networks that become more conducive to creativity under certain social conditions. Using Collins's theory of intellectual creativity, I explain why Master Taixu was deemed unoriginal in the 1960s but is regarded as one of the most important Buddhist thinkers decades later. First, I explain how political crises in late Qing shook up the organizational bases of Chinese intellectuals including that of Buddhist thinkers, resulting in the realignment of intellectual networks conducive to higher degree of creativity. Then, I demonstrate how Master Taixu's central position in overlapping intellectual networks in early 20th century China allowed him to be creative through exposure to and debates with

---

* I gratefully acknowledge the moderator, Dr. Richard Madsen, and discussant, Dr. Charles Jones, and the session participants at the "2019 International Conference on Buddhism and Social Science" for their thoughtful comments and questions. I would also like to thank Randy Collins for his feedback and the anonymous reviewers for their comments. All errors remain solely my responsibility.

thinkers in dynamic intellectual networks formed as organizational bases shifted. The horizontal ties with his contemporaries and vertical ties with his students and their students rendered his ideas significant through the process of intellectual debates among themselves. Using Collins's law of small numbers, I illustrate how the crowded attention space and the weak position occupied by Buddhist thinkers in early 20th century China resulted in Master Taixu's creativity of amalgamation. I then show how the social construction of Master Taixu as a creative thinker was facilitated by the communist takeover in China that brought Buddhist thinkers to Taiwan. I examine how the realigned and dense Buddhist intellectual networks in which Master Sheng Yen occupied a central location in turn made it possible for him to be creative. As Master Sheng Yen built his reputation in the emergent intellectual attention space by debating with Master Taixu and Master Yinshun, Master Taixu's ideas also gained significance, contributing to the recognition of Master Taixu as a creative thinker decades after the initial assessment. Lastly, I assess the future of Master Sheng Yen as a creative thinker in light of the network structure of Buddhist thinkers in Taiwan and the institutional conditions that can be cultivated to facilitate the continued circulation of Master Sheng Yen's ideas in future intellectual networks.

Keywords: Master Taixu, Master Sheng Yen, Chinese Buddhist thinkers, Chinese intellectual networks, Intellectual creativity, Social construction of creativity

1. Introduction

Great thinkers are socially constructed. Whether someone is considered a great thinker depends on whether their ideas stay in circulation by successive generations. This does not happen in the abstract, but through networks of people who have direct or indirect ties with the thinker. Having great teachers is important for one's education and network. Having great students with students going on to teach and publish is critical for one's ideas to survive in the marketplace of ideas and to thrive through rigorous debates of one's ideas. Collins's global theory of intellectual creativity articulates how the process works and the political and institutional conditions under which intellectual creativity emerges in networks and how resulting form of creativity is shaped by these social processes.

In this paper, I will start by explaining what Collins meant by social construction of intellectual creativity by using the case of Master Taixu. That is followed by an introduction of Collins's theory detailed in his monumental work, *The Sociology of Philosophies: A Global Theory of Intellectual Change,* a book of over a thousand pages to describe and explain the rise and decline of intellectual creativity in all major philosophical traditions from Asia to Europe from antiquity to the twentieth century. I then use Collins's theory to examine the intellectual networks that emerged in early twentieth-century China to explain the degree and form of intellectual creativity exhibited in Master Taixu. I argue that the crowded intellectual space of the early Republican Era brought together multiple intellectual lineages. Master Taixu's central location in these networks rendered it possible for him to be creative. The weak position of Chinese Buddhists in the crowded intellectual attention space compelled Master Taixu to adopt the strategy of combining seemingly incompatible positions, what Collins called "creativity of amalgamation" in time of weakness. I then examine the network of Chinese Buddhists who moved to Taiwan after 1949 to illustrate how the network of Master Taixu's students and their students kept his ideas in circulation by debating with these ideas. I argue that Master Sheng Yen's central location in the overlapping networks of Buddhist teachers in mid-century Taiwan made it possible for him to be creative. The opening intellectual attention space to be occupied by Buddhist thinkers allowed Master Sheng Yen to disagree with both established Buddhist thinkers, Master Taixu and Master Yinshun, and to establish his own position. Unlike Master Taixu's "creativity of amalgamation" in time of weakness, Master Sheng Yen's is the creativity of synthesis to a higher level of abstraction.

2. The Social Construction of Master Taixu as a Great Thinker

In his book, *The Sociology of Philosophies: A Global Theory of Intellectual Change*, Randall Collins argues that intellectual creativity is socially constructed. By this, he means that the ideas of philosophers are not inherently creative or uncreative. Whether their ideas are creative cannot be known until later generations of thinkers discuss and interpret their ideas and determine that their ideas are indeed creative and thus worth discussing. When their work continues to be read, cited and debated by many in generations after, they become "great" thinkers. This means there is no inherently creative thinker, nor is there inherently creative ideas. In order for someone's ideas to be recognized as creative, Collins argues that they need to be in the center of a dense network of intellectuals both for them to be exposed to different ideas that will serve as ingredients of their intellectual work, but equally importantly for their ideas to spread horizontally among contemporaries and to flow to future generations of thinkers who will collectively determine the contributions of their ideas. It is through this process that an intellectual comes be recognized as a "great thinker" and this is what Collins means by creativity being socially constructed.

To illustrate Collins's argument, Master Taixu's place in the intellectual world offers a good example. In his widely cited book on Chinese philosophy, Wing-tsit Chan (1963) asserted that Master Taixu offered nothing new and merely revived Yogācāra study in China and did not deem any of Taixu's works worth including in his anthology. ❶ Welch (1968) was equally unimpressed. In the chapter on Taixu, Welch mainly detailed ways in which Taixu was self-promoting in his organizing efforts and bluntly wrote that "there was nothing new" in his attempt to illustrate the compatibility of science and Buddhism (Welch 1968:51-71). ❷ Over the past two

---

❶ In his discussion on the Consciousness-only School, Chan mentioned Ouyang Jingwu and Master Taixu and wrote "they contributed little that was new except to revive the old (Chan 1963:374). On the Theory of Knowledge, Chan wrote "neither Ouyang nor Taixu added anything really new to Buddhist philosophy in spite of the latter's attempt to synthesize it with Western thought and modern science (Chan 1963:743). In his chapter on New Confuscianism, Chan again wrote "both Ouyang and Taixu only revived the Consciousness-Only philosophy and added nothing new (Chan 1963:765). From his vantage point in the early 1960s, Master Taixu was clearly not recognized as one of the creative thinkers.

❷ Welch (1968) devoted an entire chapter to Master Taixu in *The Buddhist Revival in China* to detail what considered "one extreme in the Chinese Buddhist response to the West" as personified in Master Taixu's organizing efforts inside and outside China (1968:51). Welch spent most of the chapter on Master Taixu's international organizing efforts and wrote "the World Buddhist Federation fell somewhat short of representing either Buddhism or the world" (1968:57) and "Taixu's efforts abroad had apparently come to very little" (1968:63). On Master Taixu's metaphysical thinking to illustrate the compatibility of Buddhism and science, Welch wrote "there was nothing new in his attempt to find common ground for Buddhism and science. It had been made before and would be made again—sometimes with ludicrous results" (1968:66). These words conveyed the feeling that Welch was not impressed with Taixu as a thinker and put him in the same category with Buddhist teachers of the time who made uninformed claims such as people in outer

decades, Master Taixu has emerged as one of the most important Chinese Buddhist monastics in the twentieth century (Pacey 2014; Pittman 2001). It may seem difficult to reconcile these two extremely different assessments of Taixu's contribution to Chinese Buddhism. Collins's theory offers a sociological explanation of the delayed recognition of Taixu's greatness. Pittman (2001) identifies Master Yinshun, Master Xingyun, Master Sheng Yen, and Master Zhengyan as the legacy left by Master Taixu. All four masters are highly accomplished figures in Chinese Buddhism in the twentieth century. Master Yinshun is considered the most important Buddhist thinker since Ming Dynasty (1368-1644) (Lai 1998; Sheng Yen 1979). ❸ Master Xingyun established Foguang Shan in Taiwan and studied at Master Taixu's course in Jiao Shan Buddhist Seminary in 1947, after which he committed himself to propagating Master Taixu's ideas (Pittman 2001). Master Sheng Yen became an accomplished scholar-monk and founded Dharma Drum Mountain in Taiwan. ❹ Master Zhengyan founded the Buddhist Compassion

---

space would be speaking Sanskrit. In the last section of the chapter, Welch characterized Master Taixu as a promoter and not in a positive sense. He wrote of Taixu's claim that he revived Buddhism in China as "an exaggeration almost as preposterous as some of the titles conferred upon him by the more impressionable foreigners" (1968:69), clearly conveying his disapproval of Taixu's approach.

❸ Master Yinshun is revered as a scholar-monk and consider the foremost Chinese Buddhist authority. His book *A History of Chinese Chan Buddhism* was awarded a doctorate degree by the recommendation of an established expert on the origin of Chan in Japan (Lai 1998; Shengyen 1979). As a student of Master Taixu, Master Yinshun was also the compiler of Master Taixu's chronology and the complete collection of his work.

❹ He explicitly identified Master Taixu, teacher of his master, Master Dongchu, as one of his key influences and he had frequent contact with Master Yinshun and his student, Master Yanpei, in 1950s when he was stationed in Taipei as part of the military (Shengyen 1979; Shengyen 2002).

Relief Tzu Chi Foundation which carries out emergency relief work and provide health care in many countries around the world❺ (Pittman 2001). Through the network of Master Taixu's students and their students who are themselves accomplished Buddhist teachers, Master Taixu's ideas were discussed and applied.

According to Collins (1998), it is the interactions among participants in the network of thinkers that allow ideas by individuals in the center of the network to take on significance. The intense emotional energy generated in these interactions propels individuals in the network to carry out their work. Hence, Collins argues that individuals who are not part of a network are unlikely to be very creative because they are unable to benefit from the opportunity to experience the emotional energy generated when thinkers interact. As one may be exposed to many ideas in one's course of education, only certain ideas take on sufficient significance to motivate one to think and write about them. Collins argues that attributed significance is not inherent in an idea or in the thinker per se. As an idea is discussed in a network of thinkers, if emotional energy is generated in these interactions, an idea takes on significance for the participants in these interactions and becomes part of their thinking process in which they may argue against or integrate the idea. An idea that is argued against or integrated by many due to the thinker's central position in an intellectual network becomes "significant" and thinker recognized as "creative." This is what Collins meant by intellectual creativity being socially constructed.

At the time of Chan's writing in 1963, students of Taixu and their students were still in the early stage of their career. Master Yinshun just finished his *The Way in Buddhahood* in 1960 and it will not be published in English until 1998. His award-winning

---

❺ She said she did her work as a way to actualize Master Yinshun's teachings to use Buddhism to bring benefits to all beings as his disciple (Pittman 2001). Master Yinshun is a student of Master Taixu.

A History of Chinese Chan Buddhism has yet to be published and recognized by Japanese scholars until the 1970s. The other three masters were in even earlier stages of their career although they have been exposed to Master Taixu's work by then. It would take a few more decades for the process of social construction of intellectual creativity to unfold. Reading the stories of these masters provides a glimpse of the process described by Collins. Master Xingyun recalled feeling the commitment to Master Taixu's ideas when he witnessed the opposition of conservative monastics to his ideas while attending his seminary (Pittman 2001). Master Sheng Yen retold the pride and excitement he felt when he involved himself in the process of the doctorate degree to be awarded to Master Yinshun for his book on the history of Chinese Chan Buddhism; he also attended Master Taixu's lectures when he was in Shanghai (Sheng Yen 1979). These interaction rituals, as well as the opportunities to engage in intellectual discussions, generate emotional energy that is attached to the ideas discussed which will give these ideas significance, turning them into crucial ingredients in the work of successive generations of thinkers. Ideas that are read in books without any emotional energy involved through interactions in these network ties, argues Collins, are much less likely to become key ingredients in one's thinking process. This is why people who became important thinkers also occupied the center of dense intellectual networks teaching and lecturing on their travels. According to Collins (1998), thinking is internal conversation of ideas one is exposed to through network ties, thus one's position in a network of thinkers shapes an individual's ability to think creatively.

Collins calls his perspective "sociological realism" of intellectual creativity. He rejects the idea of a creative philosopher coming up with creative ideas. To clarify his argument, Collins writes "My own arguments are located in my internal conversation filled by communications of intellectual networks. If social network exists, so do their material bases; so does the nonintellectual part of the world; so does the material world in which they live" (Collins 2000a:198). In other words, ideas come together in the mind of individuals in a network of intellectuals to be formed into arguments and these arguments become recognized as significant also through the network of intellectuals. That these intellectuals can gather and communicate in their networks is made possible by organizations and institutions that are in turn subject to political and economic forces of the society. This is the sociological articulation of how causes and conditions come together for ideas to be formed. While ideas are attributed to the authors of these ideas, Collins argues that they are really co-created by the participants in the network without whom communications of ideas would not happen. People have to comment on ideas for everyone involved to understand the ideas and to let these ideas take on significance as they continue to live on through the networks of collaborators and opponents and succeeding generations of students. Otherwise, ideas die on book shelves covered with dust. For this to happen, participants in the network have to invite or allow each other to lecture or discuss or publish for ideas to be shared, debated, clarified and elaborated. Institutions and organizational settings, such as university, school, research institute, seminary, monastery, conferences, publishers of journals and books provide organizational base crucial for network participants to congregate and engage in intellectual work. The formation and maintenance of these institutions and organizational settings are in turn made possible by economic and political conditions. It is the coming together of these causes and conditions where intellectual creativity emerges. In a way, Collins theory of intellectual creativity is more in accordance with the teachings of emptiness then our usual discussion of important thinkers to whom we project the narrative of an unusually creative thinker who think great thoughts.

3. Collins's Theory of Intellectual Creativity

Now that we understand what Collins meant by the social

construction of intellectual creativity, we can turn our attention to his theory. Collins (1998) asserts that the level of creativity in an intellectual network is a variable. In an intellectual network of thinkers, there are periods when the degree of creativity is high with many new philosophical positions competing with each other and/or synthesis by raising the level of abstraction. In periods of low degree of creativity, intellectuals write commentary on old texts using languages that are "unimaginative, hair-splitting, full of repetition and jargon" or play intellectual games to generate classifications and lists and argue about the accurate categorizations (Collins 1998:796). As Collins rejects that there are creative philosophers coming up with creative ideas, it is not the presence of inherently creative individuals that render a period creative. He argues that periods of shifting organizational base for thinkers, either in the form of expansion or contraction, are conducive to intellectual creativity. Shifts in organizational base happen in times of rapid political and/or economic changes. Organizational base such as monastery or academy provide material support for thinkers to engage in intellectual creativity. When Buddhist monks moved their monasteries outside urban China to avoid official persecution, argues Collins, a period of high creativity followed. Chan masters engaged in Chan discourse of increasing reflexivity reflected in their understanding yielded from enlightenment experiences. Located far from the political center provided safety from political purges and economic confiscations, hence allowing Chan Buddhism to survive and prosper while other Buddhist sects in China were struggling (Collins 1998:295).

Collins argues that intellectual creativity happens through the process of opposition among members of a network of thinkers who are connected through generations of teachers and students from different schools of thoughts. Members of the network come up with arguments in response to ideas of others in the network, emphasizing and often exaggerating disagreements with other thinkers in order to gain attention to one's argument. Attention to one's ideas in turn comes in the form of opposing arguments.

According to Collins, there is what he calls the "law of small numbers" that governs the number of positions that can occupy the attention space in an intellectual network. The minimum number of positions is three, which can consist of the original argument, an argument established in opposition to the original argument, and the third position that synthesizes the two positions. In periods of high degree of creativity, there can be numerous positions emerging, like the many philosophical positions in opposition to Confucianism that emerged in ancient China (Collins 1998:137-168). However, Collins argues, six is the upper limit of the number of positions that can be held and circulated in a network of thinkers owing to the limit of our cognitive capacity. When there are more than six opposing positions, some of them will drop off or combine with each other through creative synthesis. Hence, there are two forms of intellectual creativity. One is the factionalizing of intellectual positions in times of strength to fill up the available attention space. The other is what Collins calls "creativity of amalgamation" that takes place in time of weakness that involves the combining of positions through synthesis. This kind of synthesis is different from the synthesis to a higher level of abstraction that takes place in the factionalizing of intellectual positions to establish a new position rather than combining the existing ones. When attention space opens up owing to the expansion of organizational resources that support the network of thinkers, factionalizing of intellectual positions occurs to fill up the newly opened attention space. Collins argues that, for instance, the decline of Confucianism and Daoism when Chan Buddhism emerged in Tang China left newly opened attention space to be filled up by the Chan masters all to themselves. The resulting creativity took the form of factionalizing into the Five Houses of Chan ❻ (Collins 1998:295-296). When the attention space shrinks in times of shifting organizational basis,

---

❻ The Five Houses of Chan include Linji (Rinzai in Japanese), Caodong (Soto in Japanese), Yunmen, Guiyang and Fayan.

previously competing positions are combined and creativity takes the form of synthesis. Collins points out that synthesis can take the form of increasing level of abstraction to combine seemingly opposite positions or syncretism that combines different practices that decreases the level of abstraction. Hence, Collins's theory articulates the conditions under which the degree of intellectual creativity increases and explains the form of creativity that results in a period of high creativity.

To study the emergence of intellectual creativity and the form of creativity that emerges, Collins uses the network of philosophers, instead of individual thinkers, as the unit of analysis. In this paper, I use the same approach to examine the network of modern Chinese Buddhist thinkers that connects Master Taixu, Master Yinshun and Master Sheng Yen to help us make sense of the emergence of intellectual creativity and the ensuing form of creativity in twentieth-century Chinese Buddhism.

4. Conditions for intellectual creativity in early twentieth-century China

To illustrate his argument that political changes that shift organizational base result in rising intellectual creativity as networks realigns, Collins uses the development of Chinese Buddhist philosophies in the sixth to ninth centuries (1998:281-290). This period of high degree of creativity could be seen in the growing density of the intellectual field by 600 C.E. It started with Tiantai that synthesized an array of Buddhist schools brought to China thus far. After 600 C.E., according to Collins, Tiantai absorbed most of the earlier schools except Pure Land. A struggle between Buddhism and Daoism resumed in the Tang court in the 620s C.E.. In mid-7th century, Xuanzang (602-664) established the Consciousness-Only school after bringing the teachings of Yogācāra from India. In this period, growing creativity in this intellectual network manifested in the factionalizing of ideas as two of Xuanzang's students split off to create their own sects. Collins asserts that, with Xuanzang in the central node of this network of thinkers, the intellectual network was undergoing a transition. One important development in this transition was Fazang (643-712), associated with Xuanzang through his translation bureau, who developed Huayan school in opposition to the Consciousness-Only doctrine. This opposition by Fazang brought about a higher level of reflexivity in asserting that emptiness is itself also empty. This increase in the level of reflexivity, Collins argues, takes place during period of intellectual creativity characterized by factionalizing of ideas through competition in a crowded intellectual attention space. The success of Huayan philosophy allowed it to have internal split in the later part of 700s C.E. to occupy the attention space while other Buddhist schools were disappearing (Collins 1998:289).

In early 800s C.E., as Tang government crumbled and fell into political crisis, rendering Buddhism's position in the court precarious. The organizational base of Buddhism shifted again, leading to another period of intellectual creativity within Buddhism. As organizational base shrank amidst increasing persecution of Buddhism and the growth of Chan Buddhism that took advantage of its insulation from political persecution, Huayan found itself in a position of weakness. By the time Zongmi (780-841), the last important Huayan master, came along, his Huayan philosophy took the form of "creativity of amalgamation in time of weakness" (Collins 1998:290). With connection to Confucian thinkers in his days, Zongmi broadened the synthesis to combine Confucianism, Chan and Huayan by downplaying radical claims made by Chan (Collins 1998:289-290). In this analysis, Collins examined the network of intellectuals that included Tiantai masters, Xuanzang and his teachers and students, Fazsang and his teachers and students, as well as their network ties to Chan masters such as Hungren and Huineng and to Zongmi (Collins 1998: Fig.6.2, p.287). He illustrates how creativity takes the form of factionalizing of ideas as attention space opens up and the form of synthesis when in a position of weakness in the midst of shrinking organizational resources due to political crisis.

As Qing dynasty began to crumble in the final decades of the nineteenth century, we can see the emergence of conditions leading to a period of increased intellectual creativity as political crisis brought about shifts in the organizational base of Buddhism in China. The Qing (1644-1911) regime began crumbling in the aftermath of Taiping Rebellion (1850 to 1864), devasting much of economic centers of Qing China. During that period, Qing China was also defeated by imperialist powers from the West and Japan, prompting reform efforts led by Chinese intellectuals.

Most Buddhist monasteries lost their landholding during the Taiping Rebellion in 1860s and was only slowly rebuilding their landholding in late Qing and early 20th century. As a result of lost revenue from land rent, many had to rely more heavily on death rites for revenue in order to pay for expenses and taxes. After the end of Qing dynasty, official protection of monastery land ownership right ended and monasteries had to rely on good relationship with powerful friends in the Republican government to avoid having their assets confiscated (Welch 1967). During the first decades of the Republican rule, repeated attempts to confiscate the assets of Buddhist monasteries and take control away from monastics, not dissimilar to the repeated persecution in Tang dynasty, shook up the organization base of Chinese Buddhism. In 1911, there was an attempt by monastic reformists to appropriate the assets of Jinshan monastery, one of the largest landholding monasteries with the reputation of strict monastic code enforcement, to establish modern Buddhist education. While the attempt failed, it left monastic Buddhist leaders feeling threatened and vulnerable (Welch 1968:28-33; Pittman 2001). [7]
In 1912, Ouyang Jingwu, a prominent lay Buddhist teacher, drew up a charter to be approved by President Sun Yatsen, China's

---

[7] Taixu's master, Eight Fingers, was compelled to travel to Beijing to lobby for the protection of their assets (Welch 1968:33-38).

new leader, to place all properties and institutions of Buddhist organization in China under the control of Chinese Buddhist Association founded by him (Welch 1968:33-38). These crises prompted senior Buddhist monastic teachers ❽ to form Chinese General Buddhist Association ❾ to secure political protection. ❿ In 1915, the Parliament passed a bill to increase government control over ordination and monastic activities and personnel despite monastic lobby against the bill. While the bill was not implemented ⓫, another attempt to enforce the regulations in the bill was reactivated in 1919 which prompted another round of organizing efforts among the monastics that ended in failure. In 1927, after Jiang Jieshi (Chiang Kai-shek) defeated the warlords and consolidated control for the Nationalist, there was another wave of confiscation of monastery assets in Zhejiang area ⓬ and the ensuing effort became policy adopted by the Ministry of the Interior (Welch 1968:40-41).

The collapse of Qing dynasty also brought about drastic changes to Chinese intellectuals. The examination system for which Chinese intellectuals spent their life studying Confucian classics ended with the dynasty's collapse. This major shift in the organizational base of Chinese intellectuals prompted the establishment of new organizational base or expansion of recently established ones. Ouyang Jingwu (1871-1943), who found

---

❽ The effort was led by Eight Finger and joined by Master Xuyun (Welch 1968).

❾ Chinese General Buddhist Association (Zonghua fojiao zonghui) was the first national Buddhist organization in Chinese Buddhist history.

❿ They sought protection from Yuan Shikai, the Republican president who ascended to power using his control of the military, by committing financial support for his military (Welch 1968).

⓫ The bill was not implemented due to the abdication of President Yuan in 1916.

⓬ This effort gained further support by the elite educated abroad who advocated confiscating property of monasteries and temples to fund education at a conference in 1928 (Welch 1968:40-41).

himself no longer being able to pursue official position through examinations, devoted his life to the study of Yogācāra and to his teacher's, Yang Wenhui (1837-1911), mission to return Buddhism to its ancient root. Upon his death, Yang left his Jinling Sutra Press to Ouyang Jingwu to publish and distribute Buddhist literature across China, an organizational resource he used to promote his vision of Chinese Buddhism (Aviv 2014). In turn, Ouyang studied with Yang Wenhui at Jetavana Hermitage, a Buddhist academy established by Yang, to revive the study of Yogācāra philosophy❸ and the academy was an important organizational base where the next generation of Buddhist and Confucian thinkers studied with Yang and entered each other's networks.❹ With the end of the examination system, there was a new emphasis on university as the center for higher education (Pittman 2001:23).❺ University enrollment increased steadily as it attracted professors and students and increasingly became the center for elite intellectuals, thus opening up new organizational base for intellectual activities.

China's Western-educated intellectuals held up science and democracy as the key for building new China. They were anti-religion in general, dismissing religious beliefs and practices as

---

❸ Yogācāra study has disappeared from Buddhist monasteries and Yang Wenhui's academy studied and taught Yogācāra outside Buddhist monasteries.

❹ Taixu would meet Yang Wenhui and enter the same network with Ouyang Jingwu and Zhang Taiyan (1869-1936). They were in turn connected to Liang Qichao, a key reformist in late Qing and student of Kang Youwei who adapted Neo-Confucian ideas to his Hundred Day Reform in 1891 (Chan 1963). Liang studied with Ouyang for a short time and was deeply influenced by Ouyang (Aviv 2014:306).

❺ In 1916, Cai Yuanpei (1868-1940), a respected scholar educated in Germany and France, was invited to serve as chancellor of the National University of Beijing. He restructured the university based on the European model, emphasizing academic freedom and shared governance of faculty (Pittman 2001:23).

useless and prescientific remnants of the premodern world. As they declared Christianity as unsuitable for Chinese minds, they also questioned the relevance of Buddhist institutions and practices in modern world. ⓰ Because of this, as early as 1898, proposals were made to appropriate the assets of Buddhist monasteries to finance educational reform (Pittman 2001: 25-29). Political crises in this period shook up the organizational base for Chinese intellectuals in general, and for Chinese Buddhist thinkers in particular. Similar to the way persecution of Buddhists during the second half of Tang Dynasty shifted the organizational base of Buddhism that opened up space for intellectual creativity, the shifts in organizational resources for Chinese intellectuals and Buddhist thinkers in early twentieth-century brought about a period of increased intellectual creativity.

5. Intellectual network in early twentieth-century China

The treaties signed by the Qing government with Western powers in the second half of the 19th century required China to allow Christian missionaries to operate freely in China. Christian missionaries engaged in education, health care and charitable services that helped convert Chinese in rural areas. To influence officials to have a greater impact on Chinese society, missionaries established private boarding schools and colleges. These schools enrolled children of the elite who wanted their children to gain exposure to Western education as it was increasingly a mechanism for upward mobility as universities replaced the traditional

---

⓰ Even intellectuals such as Liang Qichao and Tan Sitong who were interested in Buddhist philosophy argued for the need of Buddhism to shed its traditional institution and practices in order to remain relevant. This was partly due to the perception that there were few learned Buddhist masters and monastics were mainly engaging in death rites (Pittman 2001:25-29).

examination system to for elite aspirants. With this came increasing acceptance of Christianity among the urban elite. ❿ The number of Protestants grew from a few hundreds in 1860 to 100,000 in 1900 and rapidly to 500,000 in 1920s after the collapse of the Qing state in 1911 (Bays 2012:77, 94). At the same time, after China's defeat by Japan in 1895, Chinese intellectuals increasingly saw the need to incorporate Western science in their effort to save China from threats of Western imperialism while fighting the encroachment of Christianity. The entrance of Western science along with materialism and rationalism as well as Christianity into the domain of Chinese intellectuals stimulated a period of intense intellectual competitions. In this section, I will focus on the dense network of Chinese intellectuals that emerged in the wake of these challenges to Confucianism and Buddhism that have enjoyed dominance in Chinese philosophy.

In this network, Yang Wenhui (1837-1911) was a key figure (see Figure 1). When he worked in the Chinese embassy in London, he met Nanjo Bun'yu and discovered Yogācāra philosophy. Facing the collapse of monastic Buddhism in late Qing, Yang was eager to revive Buddhism by reintroducing Yogācāra studies in China. He corresponded with Nanjo Bun'yu to arrange for Yogācāra texts to be sent to China and set up Jinling Sutra Press ❽ to publish

---

❿ President Sun Yat-sen and prominent families like the Song family, whose daughters married Dr. Sun and Chiang Kai-shek, are among the more well-known examples (Bays 2012).

❽ Jinling Sutra Press (Jinling kejingchu) an important source of Buddhist texts in China throughout the 20th century. It has a high reputation of publishing only texts of high accuracy. Buddhist teachers and scholars refer to texts published by this publisher as the "Jinling edition." Master Taixu considered theirs as the "finest editions" of the Buddhist works published (Wu 2006). In his research on Yogācāra and Mādhyamika, for instance, Master Huimin referenced all the primary sources using the page numbers in the Jinling edition (Shi Huimin 1986).

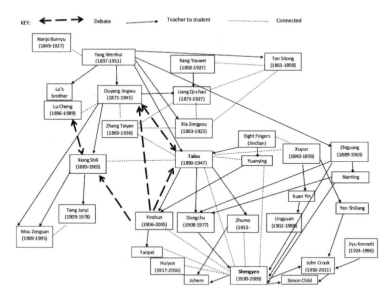

KEY: ← — → Debate ———→ Teacher to student ·········· Connected

Figure 1: Intellectual Networks of Chinese Buddhists in Early Twentieth-century China and Mid-Twentieth-century Taiwan

sutras and sastras. Yang began teaching Yogācāra philosophy at his academy, Jetavana Hermitage.

His academy educated a generation of Buddhist teachers, both lay and monastic, who will shape Chinese Buddhism in the twentieth century. Among his students were Ouyang Jingwu (1871-1943), Master Taixu (1890-1947), Xia Zongyou (1863-1927), Tan Sitong (1865-1898) and Master Zhiguang (1889-1963). Tan Sitong in turn was part of the "group of seven" along with Liang Qichao (1873-1927), reformers who tried to connect Buddhist doctrine with science (Jorgensen 2014). Kang Youwei (1858-1927) was another important figure during the last decades of Qing dynasty. He synthesized Confucian concept of humanity, *ren*, and was the first Chinese philosopher to extend this concept to the realm of natural science by asserting that *ren* is electricity and ether (Chan 1963:724). Tan Sitong, heavily influenced by Kang Youwei, elaborated Kang's doctrine and used his knowledge of Buddhism from his interactions with members of the "group of seven" to synthesize Buddhism, Christianity, Confucianism and Western science, albeit in a syncretistic way (Chan 1963:737). Liang Qichao was a student of Kang Youwei and they taught together in Guangdong in 1891. These Chinese thinkers at the turn of the twentieth century all engaged in intellectual synthesis in various forms, as would be predicted in Collins' theory. Collins argues that creativity of amalgamation tends to happen in time of weakness and/or when attention space becomes crowded, as was the situation of Confucianism and Buddhism in the early twentieth century when faced with influx of Western science and philosophy and Christianity brought by the invading powers from the West.

Overlapping of networks of thinkers from different philosophical schools promote creativity. This is exactly what happened in the network of intellectuals in early twentieth century China. Liang Qichao, a student of Kang Youwei, and Xia Zongyou, one of Yang Wenhui's students, occupied a central place in this network. Liang Qichao and Tan Sitong were part of the revolution society and "group of seven." Both Liang and Tan were friends with Xia Zongyou who was a loyal disciple of Yang Wenhui (Jorgensen 2014). Xia introduced Zhang Taiyan (1869-1936) to Buddhism and Zhang was also friends with Liang Qichao, Ouyang Jingwu and Master Taixu. Liang Qichao also studied with Ouyang for a short time which left a deep impression on him (Aviv 2014). Through these overlapping networks, the Confucian and Buddhist thinkers in early twentieth century China exchanged ideas and debated, contributing to intellectual creativity in their network. [19]

---

[19] In one example of these debates, with Xia Zongyou's influence, Zhang Taiyan criticized attempts to convert Buddhist monasteries into Western-style schools and advocated the study of Sanskrit and India as the source of Buddhism, planting the idea of returning to Indian Buddhis sources for Chinese Buddhist thinkers (Jorgensen 2014).

On the side of the New Confucians, Ouyang Jinwu (1871-1943) was an important node in the network. Xiong Shili ❷ (1885-1968), absorbed Ouyang's teachings on Yogācāra and developed New Confucianism. Mou Zongsan (1909-1995) studied with Ouyang and was opposed to him on Yogācāra. Mou also studied with Xiong at Peking University. Xiong treated Yogācāra as the best representative of Buddhism but Mou was unimpressed, deeming it as the second-poorest kind of Mahayana thought. Tang Junyi (1909-1978), another important New Confucian philosopher who also studied with Xiong in Nanjing in 1932, had even lower opinion of Yogācāra than Mou. Along with Ouyang, Xiong was an important node in the network of New Confucian thinkers who used Yogācāra, revived by Yang Wenhui, as the springboard of their philosophical creativity by opposing Yogācāra. After following the Yogācāra doctrine promoted by his teacher, Ouyang Jingwu, for instance, Xiong made a thorough critique of Yogācāra doctrine ❷ and established New Confucianism by synthesizing Yogācāra and Neo-Confucianism (Chan 1963; Clower 2014). ❷ Master

---

❷ Xiong Shili is one of Ouyang's best-known students. When asked to recommend one of his students to join the philosophy department at Peking University in 1920, Ouyang recommended Xiong (Chan 1963).

❷ Ouyang Jingwu was so impressed by Xiong's critique of Yogācāra doctrine in New Treatise of Consciousness-Only that when asked to recommend someone to the Department of Philosophy at Peking University, he recommended Xiong right away.

❷ After the communist party took over China in 1949, Mou and Tang went to Hong Kong and Taiwan and the two met and built their intellectual movement to revive Chinese civilization as professors at New Asia College that later became part of the Chinese University of Hong Kong. Before his death, Mou became a landmark figure in Chinese philosophy in Hong Kong and Taiwan and became the key interpreter of Buddhist philosophy in academic philosophy. His thoughts serve as the springboard for contemporary philosophers of Chinese thoughts (Chan 1963; Clower 2014).

Taixu's central position in these overlapping networks rendered his creativity possible and it is to this discussion I turn in the next section.

6. Explaining Intellectual Creativity: The Case of Master Taixu

Collins argues that creativity emerges in individuals occupying central positions in intellectual networks. These network ties are established through interactions as these individuals engage and associate themselves with different circles of people involved in various intellectual activities, what Collins calls "network mixture". Through the interaction rituals in these activities, such as teaching, debating and organizing, ideas discussed in emotionally arousing interaction rituals take on additional significance in the mind of the individuals involved and come together in their thinking process as internal conversations from which creative ideas can emerge. The shifting organization base in Chinese Buddhism prompted by political crisis and threats to Buddhism brought about the formation of the dense network of intellectuals in early twentieth century. This network was where Master Taixu found himself as he entered adulthood and decided to become a Buddhist monk.

Master Taixu studied with the most influential Buddhist teacher of the time, Yang Wenhui, that put him in the network of important Buddhist philosophers such as Ouyang Jingui, Zhang Taiyan and Xiong Shili. His ordination by Master Jichan, known as Eight Fingers, at Tiantong Monastery in Ningbo in 1904 brought him into the network of Buddhist monks who would be in the epicenter of the struggle between conservatives and reformers among Buddhist monastics in China. Through his master, in 1906 he met Yuanying (1878-1953), a disciple of Eight Fingers, with whom Master Taixu would develop a complex relationship as the former would become the first president of Chinese Buddhist Association (Zhongguo fojiao hui) formed in Shanghai in 1929 in response to the proposal to confiscate monastery assets to fund education. Master Taixu was also able to meet other disciples of Eight Fingers, such as Master Daojie (1866-1932) who would become abbot of an important monastery, Fayuan si, in Beijing in 1909 (Pittman 2014). In 1907, Yuanying encouraged Taixu to study at Xifang si in Cixi where he gained access to a larger Buddhist library. It was at Xifang si that Master Taixu had a powerful religious experience. At Xifang si in 1908, Taixu met the reformist monk Huashan who introduced him to the writings of Kang Youwei, Liang Qichao, Zhang Taiyan and Tan Sitong. Soon after, another student of Eight Finger, Qiyun, who was a member of the revolutionary society founded by Sun Yatsen, introduced Master Taixu to political writings of Sun Yat-sen and Zhang Taiyan and Liang Qichao (Pittman 2014).

After studying at Yang Wenhui's Jetavana Hermitage in 1909, Taixu was invited to lecture at Hualin si in Guangzhou in 1910. He helped organize a new Buddhist studies center at Shizi lin and his lectures there were his first scholarly publications on modern-day bodhisattva path and sangha reform. In the same year, he became the head monk of Shuangxi si in Guangzhou where he lectured constantly, while making friends with political radicals on the eve of the 1911 revolt in Wuchang. Taixu effort to organize an Association for the Advancement of Buddhism connected him with the radical monk Renshan (1887-1951), whom he met at Jetavana Hermitage when studying with Yang Wenhui. Their meeting led to what is known as "the invasion of Jin Shan" where Renshan proposed to use the revenue of Jin Shan monastery's landholding to fund education. The incident shocked the Buddhist establishment into action to defend monastery assets (Welch 1968). Taixu was asked by Eight Finger to form Chinese General Buddhist Association (Zhonghua fojiao zonghui) in 1912. ❷ The

---

❷ Chinese General Buddhist Association (Zhonghua fojiao zonghui) was the first national association to organize Buddhist monastics in Chinese history and the goal was to defend monastic property and improve sangha education in an effort to oppose a proposal by Ouyang Jingwu to take authority away from

effort brought together Eight Finger, Yuanying, Xuyun (1840-1959), among other monastic leaders. After that, Master Taixu engaged in numerous organizing efforts. In the 1920, he founded *Haichaoyin* (The Voice of Sea Waves)❷, a monthly Buddhist periodical. The journal became an important outlet for Master Taixu's publications to spread his ideas. In 1922, he founded Wuchang Buddhist Institute to promote monastic education. The graduates of the institute would go on to become teachers of China's Buddhist institutes in the following decades.❷ He travelled all over China to teach, founding more Buddhist institutes along the way. He established the Minnan Buddhist Seminary in 1926 to focus on Buddhist studies in Japanese and Sino-Tibetan Institute in Chongqing in 1932 that specialized in Tibetan studies (Pittman 2001; Hammerstrom 2014).❷

In his effort to promote a global Buddhism, Master Taixu organized conferences such as the World Buddhist Federation in 1924 in Lushan and, in 1928-29, he attended international conferences and engaged in lecture tours in Europe and North America. He met and collaborated with scholars on East Asian culture and Buddhism such as Russell Bernard and Christmas Humphreys on his organizing effort. He made connections with important scholars and got them to serve on the committee of his World Buddhist Institute; the recognition in turn got him elected

---

monastics in governing Buddhist organizations in China (Pittman 2001).

❷ *Haichaoyin* was an innovative effort aimed at modernizing Buddhism and its significance was noted by the editor of an influential international journal (Pittman 2001).

❷ Master Taixu's lectures at Wuchang Buddhist Institute inspired the establishment of the Right Faith Buddhist Society of Hankou, a modern lay Buddhist organization that engaged in publishing and educational activities (Pittman 2001).

❷ Master Taixu also initiated Buddhist ministries in prison in 1920s and involved his seminary and lay students to engage in social services.

to the executive committee of the German Research Academy for Chinese Culture (Pittman 2001:108-127). These activities put Master Taixu in situations where he could engage with Western intellectuals and Chinese Buddhists in interaction rituals of the kind described by Collins (1998) that renders creativity possible.

Collins argues that reputation in an intellectual community is built by disagreement, taking position in opposition to other thinkers who can be one's teachers, their rivals, or students of one's teachers. Master Taixu built his reputation, hence allowing him to compete in his intellectual community for attention, by debating against Ouyang Jingwu, a prominent student of Yang Wenhui. This is a classic pattern of how creativity emerges within an intellectual network, as described by Collins (1998), where intellectuals articulate their ideas that are opposed to their teacher and/or other students of the same teacher. According to Aviv (2014), Master Taixu objected to Ouyang Jingwu's on a number of issues and I will focus on two here. First, Master Taixu disagreed with Ouyang's view on the difference between two approaches in Yogācāra teachings. While Ouyang asserted that faxiang (characteristics of dharmas) and weishi (nothing but consciousness) are entirely separate, Taixu argued that the two cannot be separated and faxiang must be subsumed within weishi. Second, Master Taixu and Ouyang Jingwu also disagreed on the classification of scriptures as the former accused the latter of misinterpreting the meeting of the key concept of zong (the most major principle). Master Taixu favored the interpretation that equates weishi and faxing, the latter often seen as synonymous with tathata (Suchness). Master Taixu's creativity is a form of synthesis by combining seemingly incompatible positions (Collins 1998). ㉗

㉗ Master Taixu's position in his debate against Ouyang on the relationship between reality and Suchness as discussed in *Dasheng qixin lun* (Pacey 2014) put him in the same camp as Xiong Shili (1885-1968). Xiong Shili is a New Confucian thinker who critiqued the Yogācāra doctrine promoted by his teacher,

In the face of challenges from Western science, Taixu took an adaptive stance to demonstrate the ability of Buddhism to encompass emerging scientific knowledge from various disciplines. In the metaphysical argument of whether science embodies an outlook on life, Taixu took a Neo-Kantian position and used Buddhism to adjudicate the similarity and difference between different kinds of knowledge (Collins 1998:689-691). In response to argument putting science in opposition with religion, Taixu synthesized science and Buddhism. He argued that science and Buddhism complement each other, asserting that the materialist basis of empirical scientific observation can be supplemented by Buddhist insight of the relationship between the phenomenal world and mental cognition (Pacey 2014:156-7). Similarly, Taixu explained how psychology and Yogācāra could work together, claiming that Yogācāra provides a broader understanding of mental processes than psychology with its discussion of the seventh consciousness. Taixu incorporated Tan Sitong's integration of Western psychology with Buddhism and improved it by explaining memory retention using the concept of base consciousness (Pacey 2014:160). [28] With physics, Taixu took an assimilatory stance

---

Ouyang Jingwu, and then synthesized and transformed Yogācāra and Neo-Confucianism to articulate the doctrine of New Confucians (Chan 1963; Clower 2014; Makeham 2014). The debate between Master Taixu and Ouyang parallels that between Xiong Shili and Lu Cheng (1896-1989), a follower of Ouyang's teachings and dean of China Institute of Inner Learning that promoted Ouyang's view of Buddhist studies (Lin 2014). The formation of opposing intellectual camps among thinkers of the same teacher-student network is a common feature of intellectual creativity described by Collins (1998).

[28] Hammerstrom (2014) helpfully points out that the creative ideas on the integration of Buddhism and science often attributed to Taixu should be understood as a collective enterprise of Taixu and his students which Hammerstrom calls the Wuchang School. For instance, Zhang Huasheng,

by identifying that similarities between physics and Yogācāra while also asserting that Yogācāra is more comprehensive with its realization that both the physical and mental world are mental constructions (Pacey 2014:161-166).

Taixu's treatment of Buddhist teachings is another example of his strategy of synthesis. He viewed the different Buddhist vehicles as "expedient expressions of one Buddhayana" and not distinct vehicles. Similarly, Master Taixu saw that different schools of Buddhism, such as Madhyamika, Yogācāra, Tiantai, Chan, Huayan, Esoteric, are all different aspects of one true Dharma (Pittman 2001: 87). Instead of arguing for the superiority of Yogācāra, as did Ouyang Jingwu, or criticizing Chan's teaching of inherent enlightenment as false Buddhism, as did Lu Cheng, Master Taixu shifted to a higher level of abstraction to establish the notion of one true Dharma that encompasses all schools in his synthesis (Lin 2014:359).

It is in Taixu's theory of social evolution that his strategy of synthesis is the most obvious. In response to Spencer's theory of social evolution, Taixu came up with his classification of human knowledge and put them in various stages of social evolution. He put theism as the first stage of human development after survival is assured. This is followed by mathematics, ethics, science and rationality. The next stage in human development would be characterized by practice of mental cultivation such as Jainism, Yoga, Confucianism, Daoism and Chan. At the final stage, according to Taixu, scientific outlook of earlier stages would give way to outlooks representing schools of Buddhism such as Chan, Huayan and Tiantai (Pacey 2014: 161-3). Collins calls this form of

---

Taixu's student, played an important role in extending many of Taixu's ideas by explaining instinct using seeds in the eighth consciousness. This argument was further developed by another student of Taixu, Manzhi, who has also studied at the China Inner Learning Institute and thus had overlapping network ties between Taixu's and Ouyang Jingwu's circles.

creativity "hierarchical classification" with doctrinal classification in Chinese Buddhism such as Tiantai and Huayan as successful examples (Collins 1998: 795-9). Collins argues that this form of creativity, while not changing the level of abstraction very much, serves several possible functions. Among them are the attempt to claim attention space in the intellectual network by using the strategy of synthesis, as it did earn Taixu recognition, and to "assert superiority for one's own sect" which Taixu did consistently in asserting Buddhism's ability to offer a more comprehensive understanding in various scientific disciplines. This form of creativity also, according to Collins, allows "for syncretistic alliances" when in a position of weakness. Similar to Zongmi who had to include Confucianism in his hierarchical sequence of Buddhist cultivation and extend his classification to Chan, Taixu's sequence included theistic religions, such as Christianity, and science as early stages (Collins 1998:797-8; Gregory 1991). In the stage of cultivation, he included practices from Chinese as well as Indian traditions. In the Buddhist stage, he included all major Buddhist schools. It is an effort to form syncretistic alliance similar to that of Zongmi in the face of persecution of Buddhism in late Tang albeit with an international scope. While shifting organizational base during this period opened up space for intellectual creativity, the threat of Western science and Christianity brought by colonial power exerted pressure on Chinese Buddhist thinkers like Master Taixu to adopt the creativity of amalgamation to synthesize, as did others in time of weakness.

So far, I have demonstrated how we can apply Collins's theory of intellectual creativity to explain the emergence and the form of intellectual creativity in early twentieth-century China. Political crisis in late Qing China brought about shifting organizational base of Buddhism in China, promoting networks of intellectuals to realign. That results in what Collins calls "network mixture" with individuals who studied with teachers in different schools and "organizational movers" who established seminaries and founded periodicals and publishing houses (Collins 1998: 728-730). Ouyang

Jingwu and Master Taixu are examples of such individuals in this network. As reputations were built by disagreement, the intense disagreement between them turned them into key intellectual figures of the time. The struggle for attention space in the intellectual network in early twentieth-century China is manifested in these thinkers' response to Western science and Christianity by reconceptualizing Buddhism and Confucianism. The shifting organizational base brought by political crisis and the struggle of attention space in intellectual network explains the emergence of intellectual creativity during this period. As predicted by Collins, with the constant threat of confiscation of monastery assets, Buddhism was in a weak position in a crowded intellectual space filled with secular science, Christianity, New Confucianism as well as challenges from lay Buddhist thinkers such as Ouyang Jingwu promoting Yogācāra. To avoid being dismissed as the number of philosophical positions reached the upper limit of what Collins calls the law of small numbers, creativity of amalgamation through synthesis was the form of creativity taken in this period.

7. Explaining Intellectual Creativity: The Case of Master Sheng Yen

In the remainder of this paper, I would like to discuss how the emergence of the network of Buddhist thinkers after Master Taixu was shaped by organizational base he helped to build. In particular, I focus on how shifting organizational base after the communist revolution in China in 1949 helped place Master Sheng Yen in a central location of the overlapping networks of Buddhist thinkers in Taiwan. Collins's theory is then used to explain the mechanism and form of intellectual creativity that emerged in this network with a focus on Master Sheng Yen.

In the second half of Figure 1, we see the generation of Buddhist masters after Master Taixu, many of whom were students of Master Taixu. Among them, Master Yinshun (1906-2005) was a prominent scholar-monk, widely recognized for his scholarly achievements and had a multitude of ties with Master Taixu. Master Yinshun was tonsured by Qingnian, one of Master Taixu's ordination brothers, and took his monastic precepts at Tiantong si with Yuanying, a rival of Taixu's reform efforts. He studied with Master Taixu at Minnan Buddhist Institute in 1931 and at Wuchang Buddhist Institute in 1934 where he gave his first lecture on San-lun School. Furthermore, in 1938-39, Master Yinshun studied at Sino-Tibetan Buddhist Institute established by Master Taixu (Travagnin 2009:39). He edited the *Chronological Biography of Master Taixu's Life* and the *Collected Works of Master Taixu*. When he moved to Shandao si in Taipei in 1952, he became the editor of *Haichaoyin*, the influential Buddhist periodical established by Master Taixu at the time (Pittman 2001: 263-270). As a young scholar-monk, Master Yinshun has already engaged in a debate against Ouyang Jingwu's discussion on the Buddhist Canon and disagreed with his Mahayana Twofold system (Travagnin 2009: 40, 47). He also disagreed with Master Taixu on the relationship among the schools included in the Mahayana Threefold system. Specifically, Master Taixu conceptualized the three as starting with the Emptiness school, followed by the Consciousness-only school and perfected by Tathagatagarbha teaching. It was the traditional Chinese doctrinal classification that placed the schools in a hierarchy. Master Yinshun, while adopting the Threefold system, argued that only the first phase of the system represented pure and correct Dharma whereas the other two schools represented the "gradual corruption of the Dharma" (Travagnin 2009: 42). In these disagreements, Master Yinshun established his reputation as a Madhyamika scholar despite his refusal to identify with any specific school. His non-adherence to the traditional San-lun position and the adoption of Tibetan tradition of Madhyamika distinguishes him from Master Taixu's traditional Chinese Buddhist position (Travagnin 2009:124-6). ❷⁹

---

❷⁹ Master Yinshun's position stems from his disagreement with Master Taixu on

Master Sheng Yen admitted that he was deeply influenced by Master Yinshun who dominated Buddhist study in Taiwan. After being transferred to Taipei by the army in 1956, Sheng Yen visited Shandao si in Taipei during his time off and talked with Master Yinshun and his student Master Yanpei and borrowed books from them during these visits. Besides his visits to Shandao si, Sheng Yen would have interacted with Master Yinshun who was editor of *Haichaoyin* when he submitted his articles for the periodicals. Also, in 1956, Master Sheng Yen joined Master Yinshun and Master Zhuyun (1919-1986) in debating a Christian priest who launched an attack on Buddhism (Sheng Yen 2002). It was a good example of creative energy generated by intellectuals engaging in interaction rituals. Master Sheng Yen recalled attending lectures by Master Zhuyun in packed lecture hall where he spoke on the comparison between Buddhism and Christianity. The attack was a response to Master Zhuyun's book on Christianity. In their previous meetings, Master Zhuyun encouraged Sheng Yen to submit his writings to Buddhist magazines. He submitted articles to periodicals such as *Haichaoyin* and *Humanity* and received very positive reviews. These interaction rituals generated emotional energy that inspired Sheng Yen to write his own investigation of Christianity. The book earned him a reputation within the Buddhist circle and attracted more demand for articles from various Buddhist magazines (Sheng Yen 1993). It was clear that requests from magazines for his writings energized Master Sheng Yen and prompted his desire to investigate various subject matters through his writings. Buddhist periodicals, such as *Haichaoyin* that was founded by Master Taixu, served as important organizational base for Buddhist thinkers

---

how to save Buddhism in China. He did not believe that it could be accomplished by Master Taixu's reform of Buddhist education. Rather, Master Yinshun believed what was needed was correct understanding of the Dharma (Travagnin 2009:42-44). It is why he felt the need to delve into the texts outside traditional Chinese Buddhism in his study.

to publish their ideas and engage in discussions with each other. Through these writings in 1957-60, Master Sheng Yen debated with intellectuals criticizing Buddhism as passive and articulated his ideas on right view. He also wrote about the problem of monastics supporting themselves through performing rituals and articulated his views of the proper role of monastics (Sheng Yen 1993). This experience helped him develop a self-consciousness of being a thinker, a view of himself that he would articulate more explicitly in his later years. ❸

Master Dongchu (1908-1977) took Sheng Yen as his disciple after the latter has spent ten years in the military in Taiwan after leaving China in 1949. Dongchu, like Yinshun, studied with Master Taixu at Minnan Buddhist Institute in Xiamen. He also studied with Master Nanting at Zhulin Buddhist Institute in Zhejiang. Before moving to Taiwan, he was dean of Jiaoshan Buddhist Institute and abbot of Dinghui si in Jiaoshan. He founded *Humanity Magazine* in 1949 when arrived at Taiwan and founded Chunghwa Institute of Buddhist Culture in 1956. In 1960, Sheng Yen was made the editor of *Humanity Magazine*, where he and Master Dongchu published their writings, when he became Master Dongchu's disciple. During his two years as editor of *Humanity Magazine*, Sheng Yen wrote for the magazine and connected with Buddhist authors of his time. When he took his full monastic precepts, he was given the task of recording the lectures on precept proceedings. After publishing the details of the precept ceremony, he began to conduct research on the vinaya and submitted an article on the Bodhisattva precepts to the Buddhist periodical, *Wujindeng*, published in Malaysia. The editor, Master Zhumo (1913-1983) who, like Master Yinshun and Master Dongchu, also studied with Master Taixu at Minnan Buddhist Institute, encouraged Sheng Yen to publish the result of

---

❸ In his article discussing four most important Chinese Buddhist thinkers, Master Shengyen indicated this self-consciousness of being part of an intellectual community (Shengyen 1979).

this study into a book and promised to provide financial support (Sheng Yen 1993:69). Hence, Master Sheng Yen was connected with several students of Master Taixu; he also attended Master Taixu's lectures in Shanghai when he was a teenage monk. ❸

Political crisis created the unique situation in Taiwan in 1950s to 1970s where a high concentration of Buddhist masters established monasteries and institutes, published magazines, and taught there. Besides Master Yinshun and Master Dongchu, Master Sheng Yen became the disciple and protégé of a number of senior monks who moved from China to Taiwan after the communist revolution in 1949, allowing him to become the center of a dense network of Buddhist teachers from the generation that preceded him. Master Zhiguang (1889-1963), like Master Taixu and Ouyang Jingwu, studied under Yang Wenhui (Sheng Yen 1993). Sheng Yen's master, Master Dongchu, received Dharma transmission in the lineage of Caodong School in Chinese Chan from Master Zhiguang. Master Dongchu would in turn give Dharma transmission to Master Sheng Yen in 1976, asking him to inherit the Chung Hwa Institute of Buddhist Culture in Taipei (Sheng Yen 2002; Sheng Yen et al 2016). Master Sheng Yen began visiting Master Zhiguang in 1950 after moving to Taiwan and received emotional and financial support from the old master after rejoining monastic life (Sheng Yen 2002:13-23). Master Nanting, also a Huayan expert like Zhiguang, was a lecturer at Jing'an Monastery in Shanghai and taught Master Sheng Yen when he was a teenage monk. Sheng Yen reconnected with the master in Taiwan when Master Nanting and his master, Master Zhiguang, moved to Taiwan upon the communist takeover in China (Sheng Yen 2002:55-61). Master Nanting was also a teacher of Master Dongchu. Master Xuyun (1840-1959), who worked with Eight Fingers to defend monastery assets in the early years of the twentieth

---

❸ In Shanghai, Shengyen also attended lectures by Yuanying, Master Taixu's Dharma brother (Shengyen 2002:100).

century, was grandmaster of Master Lingyuan (1902-1988). ㉜ Sheng Yen met Master Lingyuan in 1958 when he practiced at a monastery in Gaoxiong while on vacation from the army and had an enlightenment experience during an exchange with the master. Sheng Yen received Dharma transmission from Master Lingyuan in 1978 in the lineage of Linji school (Sheng Yen 2002:68-73; Sheng Yen et al 2016). The concentration of Buddhist masters in Taiwan who used to be dispersed across China made it possible for Sheng Yen to be in the center of a dense intellectual network, engaging in discussion with them in person and benefiting from the intellectual energy generated in these interaction rituals.

Like Master Taixu, Master Sheng Yen became a network hybrid by moving around internationally, making network ties with intellectuals in multiple networks. Moving to Taiwan allowed him to connect with prominent Buddhist masters from China. His graduate studies in Japan allowed him to connect with graduate students from Taiwan. While studying at Rissho University, for instance, Master Sheng Yen met Master Huiyue (1917-2016), a Tiantai master, who was studying with the advisor of his doctorate research, Professor Yukio Sakamoto (Sheng Yen 1979:467-480; Sheng Yen 2002:214). ㉝ Master Sheng Yen also attended numerous academic conferences organized by competing schools of Japanese Buddhism and they each published their own journal, providing plentiful opportunities for Sheng Yen to publish. During his six years in Japan, he attended, and sometimes presented at,

---

㉜ Master Lingyuan was asked by Master Xuyun to be abbot of Nanhua si in Guangzhou in 1947. Like many monastics after the communist revolution in 1949, Master Lingyuan moved to Hong Kong and stayed at Baolian si. In 1953, the master moved to Taiwan upon the invitation of Nan Huaijin, a prominent lay Buddhist teacher (Shengyen 2002:68-73; Shengyen et al 2016).

㉝ Master Shengyen also met other students of Professor Yukio Sakamoto, a Huayan expert. These students were Liaozong, Tongmiao, Jinghai, Xiuguang, and Huiguang (Shengyen 2002: 214).

over twenty conferences, garnering sufficient recognition for his research on Buddhism in Ming Dynasty China to pass the rigorous dissertation review process in the Japanese system (Sheng Yen 1993:119-123). While in Japan, Master Sheng Yen also practiced at many important monasteries and received *inka* from Bantetsugu Roshi, a Dharma brother of Yasutani Roshi, authenticating his enlightenment experience. This connected him to the Japanese Zen lineage established in the United States by Yasutani's students such as Maezumi Roshi. For instance, Roshi Kapleau, one of Yasutani's students, invited Master Sheng Yen to lecture at Rochester Zen Center, and he was the first Chinese Chan master to visit the center (Lin 2000). By mid-1990s, Master Sheng Yen has taught and led practice at numerous Buddhist practice center in North America. Between late 1970s and late 1990s, Master Sheng Yen lectured on Buddhism and the practice and theory of Chan at numerous university campuses. In 1970s and 1980s, he also regularly presented his scholarly research on Buddhism in Ming China at international academic conferences, connecting him to the network of contemporary scholars on Buddhism (Lin 2000).

That Master Sheng Yen became a network hybrid of multiple intellectual networks and the unique situation of the intellectual network in Taiwan explain the form of intellectual creativity we see in his work. Invoking Durkheim's theory, Collins asserts that greater diversity in network tends to generate higher level of abstraction. On this, Collins writes, "debates at one level of abstraction are resolved by moving to a higher level of abstraction from which they can be judged and reinterpreted" and "the mind of a 'sophisticated' intellectual, heir to a historically complex network of oppositions and changes in level, internalizes an invisible community of diverse viewpoints, unified by looking on them from a yet more encompassing standpoint" (Collins 1998:790-791). Master Sheng Yen's participation in multiple networks of intellectuals exposed him to diverse viewpoints, prompting him to think at higher level of abstraction. Meanwhile, the political changes that prompted the departure of Buddhist masters from

China split up the intellectual network of which Master Taixu was a part. New Confucian scholars such as Xiong Shili, Lu Cheng, Tang Junyi and Mou Zongsan either remained in China or moved to Hong Kong, leaving the attention space for Chinese intellectuals largely to the Buddhists in Taiwan. In this network, Master Yinshun was a key figure. His opposition to Master Taixu's ideas turned the pair into intellectual rivals.❸ Rivalry drives creativity in intellectual networks and this can be seen in the prolific scholarship of Yinshun. The key disagreement lies in their view of the relationship among different philosophical schools in Buddhism. Master Taixu's view represents the Chinese Buddhist tradition of doctrinal classification, asserting that Tathagatagarbha is the most mature development in Buddhist philosophy. Master Yinshun's view departs from Chinese Buddhist tradition entirely and reconnects Chinese Buddhist teachings with Madhyamika philosophy from Indian Buddhism, leaving behind the complex system of Chinese Buddhist teachings (Sheng Yen 1979:453-466). Their debate is illustrated in Kent Lin's discussion of the relationship between the concepts of Śūnyatā (nature of emptiness) and Buddhatā (Buddha nature) (Lin 2017). In this debate, Master Taixu put the concept of Buddha nature as higher, or closer to the truth of Buddha's teachings, than the concept of nature of emptiness whereas Master Yinshun argued the opposite. Master Yinshun's opposition to Master Taixu's idea kept the latter's ideas in circulation within the intellectual network and established the former as an important thinker as reputations were made by disagreement (Collins 1998:730).

With the attention space all to themselves in Taiwan, Buddhist masters could afford to disagree among themselves. Master Sheng

---

❸ The intellectual rivalry prompted a robust volume of research debating whether Master Yinshun was Master Taixu's disciple, despite the fact that the former compiled the chronological biography and collected works of the former (Travagnin 2009).

Yen's framing of his argument in opposition to Master Taixu and Master Yinshun to establish a third position matches the pattern of intellectual creativity as discovered by Collins (1998). In fact, the law of small numbers articulated by Collins requires at least three different intellectual positions for sufficient energy to be generated within an intellectual community. Master Sheng Yen added a third position that is entirely different by shifting to a higher level of abstraction. He argued that Buddha nature is precisely nature of emptiness. The same applies for concepts such as Dharma realm or Dharma nature or true suchness used in other schools of Buddhism. Master Sheng Yen argues that these are merely different concepts but they are all in fact no different from the nature of emptiness. This standpoint encompasses all schools of Buddhism, recognizing each as an aspect of one Buddhadharma serving its function, without any need to rank them in terms of purity or maturity. It is a position articulated at a higher level of abstraction than either of Master Taixu's or Master Yinshun's. Collins's theory explains how the unique situation of Taiwan's intellectual community provides the attention space for Master Sheng Yen to articulate a drastically different position and why it is one of synthesis at higher level of abstraction.

8. Conclusion

To close, I would like to quote Collins's summary of his argument. He writes, "If we are in central locations in intellectual networks where redivisions of the attention space are taking place, we are energized to produce combinations and oppositions out of these internal conversations which result in creating ideas that the network will make significant by passing them much further along" (Collins 2000b:312-3). In this paper, I discussed the conditions that brought about the redivisions of attention space in early twentieth-century China and how Master Taixu's central location in intellectual networks of his time prompted him to create ideas through combinations and oppositions. I also examined the networks that passed along Master Taixu's ideas that turned them into significant ideas and Taixu a significant thinker. Collins's theory also sheds light on the form of Master Taixu's intellectual creativity; it was the creativity of amalgamation in synthesis when in time of weakness. In the last part of the paper, I discussed the realignment of intellectual networks as Buddhist masters moved to Taiwan in mid-century and Master Sheng Yen's connection to key figures in this network. Master Sheng Yen's central location in this network energized him to produce combinations and oppositions from ideas to which he was exposed. The openness of attention space at the time allowed Master Sheng Yen to engage in creativity in the form of factionalizing, by establishing a separate position from that of Taixu and Yinshun by synthesizing to a higher level of abstraction.

It is important not to misunderstand Collins's theory as asserting that the ideas of these thinkers were mediocre but only came to be recognized as great due to their networking effort. Rather, Collins argues that thinkers with great ideas are unlikely to be recognized as such without also being part of a dense network of intellectuals who incorporate and debate with each other's ideas. Furthermore, it is by being part of these networks that thinkers got the ingredients and emotional energy that fuel their intellectual activities. Collins also points out that the dense network of intellectuals conducive to creativity is not a given but emerges in times of changing political and economic conditions and shifting organizational bases. In this paper, I apply Collins's theory by examining the political, economic and institutional changes that shaped the intellectual networks to which Master Taixu and Master Sheng Yen belonged and in which their creativity emerged. The difference in the emergent intellectual attention spaces occupied by the two thinkers also provides us with an opportunity to test Collins's law of small numbers. The case comparison supports the prediction that crowded intellectual attention space tends to encourage "creativity of amalgamation" in times of weakness as was the case for Chinese Buddhists in Master Taixu's time. The open intellectual attention space in Master Sheng

Yen's time allowed him to establish a new position apart from those established by Master Taixu and Master Yinshun. The case comparison in this paper is by no means an adequate test of this part of Collins's theory. More cases will be needed for a robust test of Collins's law of small numbers.

Collins drew on networks of philosophers throughout history and across cultures to illustrate and substantiate his global theory of intellectual creativity. It was a monumental effort but not without flaws. Despite the broad scope and variety of cases included in his study, Collins's overall argument is weakened by the problem of case selection bias common in historical-comparative research. Case selection bias happens when only positive cases, those exhibiting the outcome being explained by the theory, are included in the study. The nature of the subject matter, social construction of intellectual creativity, as examined by Collins lends itself to this bias. For the ideas to even be included as cases of intellectual creativity, they would have to be debated and discussed by intellectuals through the generations to remain part of our cultural repertoire. That these ideas can be considered as creative today requires them to have been circulated in the networks of generations of intellectuals. Ideas generated in a dense intellectual network conducive to creativity in the past but did not remain in circulation due to the paucity of subsequent generations of intellectuals debating these ideas would have been excluded. Collins did identify thinkers who were popular among their contemporaries but were forgotten because their intellectual offspring, if they had any, did not constitute part of the intellectual network crucial for their ideas to remain in circulation and recognized. Since the unit of analysis here is network of intellectuals, these cases of individual thinkers whose ideas failed to survive do not qualify as negative cases. Examining only the positive cases—the intellectual networks that were sustained through the generations and kept the ideas generated in these networks in circulation and hence recognized as creative ideas—can be the first step in theory construction. Future research needs to include networks of intellectual creativity in history that did not produce any "great" thinkers for comparative analysis in order to offer a more rigorous test of Collins's entire theory. The inclusion of negative cases will allow us to test the specific hypotheses proposed by Collins on the conditions under which subsequent generations of intellectual offspring of thinkers in past networks of creativity succeeded or failed to keep these ideas in circulation and be potentially recognized as "great."

Collins would argue that it is still early to determine whether Master Sheng Yen's ideas are significant and him a significant thinker as that will be work of the network **❸** of intellectuals that follows. It will require his ideas to be debated, cited, applied by generations of thinkers in different networks. As can be seen in the dynamics of intellectual creativity discovered by Collins, disagreement with Master Sheng Yen's ideas is integral in the process of intellectual creativity and should not be suppressed. In fact, while the intellectual attention space in Taiwan is still open, we can use more disagreement to stimulate more debates to increase the intellectual energy for more creativity. For this to happen, organizational resources are needed for thinkers to engage in intellectual work, exchange ideas, publish their debates to form

---

❸ In Figure 1, I inserted the network ties of three of Master Shengyen's students to illustrate this point. It is by no means an exhaustive account and the network are still in the process of development. Collins would say that we are still in the fog of the present. Master Jichern studied with and received Dharma transmission from Master Shengyen. He is also a disciple of Master Zhumo, the editor of *Wujindeng* when Master Shengyen wrote about the vinaya. John Crook studied with and received Dharma transmission from Master Shengyen Before meeting Master Shengyen, John Crook studied with a teacher in the lineage of Master Xuyun in Hong Kong. After that he studied with Vajrayana teachers such as ChoygamTsungpa and Soto master Jiyu Kennet. John Crook's student, Simon Child, also studied with and received Dharma transmission from Master Shengyen (Shengyen et al 2016).

intellectual networks. Through these interaction rituals, intellectual energy is generated for creativity. Stability in organizational base can breed stagnation, lowering creativity by focusing on intellectual games of list-making, categorization or textual commentary using archaic jargons to shield the lack of new ideas. Shifting organization base in times of external shock or political and/economic crisis promotes network realignment that stimulates creativity.

While it may seem disrespectful to argue that Master Taixu and Master Sheng Yen were not inherently great thinkers and that their "greatness" or creativity is social constructed, this perspective is actually in accordance with the teachings of emptiness that there are no independent thinkers coming up with inherently creative ideas. Rather, through social interactions with others in a network, significant ideas come together in internal conversations in network nodes. The ideas of these thinkers were really co-created by participants in these intellectual networks. As indicated in his books detailing influences of his teachers and peers, I believe Master Sheng Yen would agree with this assessment.

Work Cited

Aviv, Eyal. 2014. "Ouyang Jingwu: From Yogācāra Scholasticism to Soteriology" in John Makeham (ed.) *Transforming Consciousness: Yogācāra Thought in Modern China.* Oxford & New York: Oxford University Press.

Bays, Daniel H. 2012. *A New History of Christianity in China.* West Sussex, U.K.: Wiley-Blackwell.

Chan, Wing-tsit. 1963. *A Source Book in Chinese Philosophy.* Princeton, NJ: Princeton University Press.

Clower, Jason. 2014. "Chinese *Ressentiment* and Why New Confucians Stopped Caring about Yogācāra" in John Makeham (ed.) *Transforming Consciousness: Yogācāra Thought in Modern China.* Oxford & New York: Oxford University Press.

Collins, Randall. 1998. *The Sociological of Philosophies: A Global Theory of Intellectual Change.* Cambridge, MA & London, England: Harvard University Press.

Collins, Randall. 2000a. "The Sociology of Philosophies: A Précis" *Philosophy of the Social Sciences* 30:157-201.

Collins, Randall. 2000b. "Reply to Reviewers and Symposium Commentators" *Philosophy of the Social Sciences* 30:299-325.

Gregory, Peter N. 1991, *Tsung-Mi and the Sinification of Buddhism.* Princeton, NJ: Princeton University Press.

Hammerstrom, Erik J. 2014. "Yogācāra and Science in the 1920s: The Wuchang Schools' Approach to Modern Mind Science" in John Makeham (ed.) *Transforming Consciousness: Yogācāra Thought in Modern China.* Oxford & New York: Oxford University Press.

Jorgensen, John. 2014. "Indra's Network: Zhang Taiyan's Sino-Japanese Personal Networks and the Rise of Yogācāra in Modern China" in John Makeham (ed.) *Transforming Consciousness: Yogācāra Thought in Modern China.* Oxford & New York: Oxford University Press.

Kessler, Lawrence D. 1992. *Introduction: Christianity and Chinese*

Nationalism in the Early Republican Period, Republican China—A Symposium, 17:2, 1-4, DOI: 10.1080/08932344.1992.11720195.

Lai, Whalen. 1998. "Introduction", in Master Yinshun's The Way to Buddhahood. Somerville, MA: Wisdom Publications.

Lin, Chen-Kuo. 2014. "The Uncompromising Quest for Genuine Buddhism" Lu Cheng's Critique of Original Enlightenment" in John Makeham (ed.) Transforming Consciousness: Yogācāra Thought in Modern China. Oxford & New York: Oxford University Press.

Lin, Kent. 2017. "Ven. Sheng-Yen's Exposition and Integration of the Concepts of Sunyata and Buddhata" Dharma Drum Journal of Buddhist Studies 21:131-180.

Lin, Qixian. 2000. Shengyanfashi qi shi nian pu (Chronological biography of Master Sheng Yen at 70). Taipei, ROC: Dharma Drum Culture.

Makeham, John. 2014. "Xiong Shili's Critique of Yogācāra Thought in the Context of Hist Constructive Philosophy" in John Makeham (ed.) Transforming Consciousness: Yogācāra Thought in Modern China. Oxford & New York: Oxford University Press.

Pacey, Scott. 2014. "Taixu, Yogācāra, and the Buddhist Approach to Modernity" in John Makeham (ed.) Transforming Consciousness: Yogācāra Thought in Modern China. Oxford & New York: Oxford University Press.

Pittman, Don A. 2001. Toward a Modern Chinese Buddhism: Taixu's Reforms. Honolulu, HI: University of Hawai'i Press.

Sheng Yen. 1979. Cong dongyang dao xiyang (From East to West). Taipei, ROC: Dongchu Publishing.

Sheng Yen. 1993. Sheng Yen Fashi xuesi lichen (Master Sheng Yen's Studies and Thoughts). Taipei, ROC: Zhengzong Bookstore.

Sheng Yen. 2002. Wode famen shiyou (My Dharma Teachers and Friends). Taipei, ROC: Dharma Drum Culture.

Sheng Yen. 2010. The Dharma Drum Lineage of Chan Buddhism: Inheriting the Past and Inspiring the Future. Taipei, Taiwan: Sheng Yen Education Foundation.

Sheng Yen, John Crook, Simon Child, Zarko Andricevic and Gilbert Gutierrez. 2016. Chan Comes West (2nd ed.) Elmhurst, NY: Dharma Drum Publication.

Shi Huimin. 1986. *Zongguang yu Yuxie* (Madhyamika and Yogācāra). Taipei, ROC: Dongchu Publishing.

Teng, Wei Jen. 2016. "Tradition and Innovation: On the Interpretation and Significance of Master Sheng Yen's Construction of "Chinese Chan Buddhism" with a Focus on the Tiantai's Thought" *Studies of Master Sheng Yen* 8:133-157.

Travagnin, Stefania. 2009. "The Madhymika Dimension of Yinshun: A Restatement of the School of Nagarjuna in 20th Century Chinese Buddhism." Unpublished Ph.D. Dissertation, Department of the Study of Religions, University of London.

Welch, Holmes. 1967. *The Practice of Chinese Buddhism: 1900-1950.* Cambridge, MA: Harvard University Press.

Welch, Holmes. 1968. *The Buddhist Revival in China.* Cambridge, MA: Harvard University Press.

Wu, Yankang. 2006. "Yang Renshan and the Jinling Buddhist Press" *The East Asian Library Journal* 12:49-98.

創造力的社會根源
——從社會學角度分析做為佛教思想者的太虛大師及聖嚴法師

李世娟

美國新澤西大學人文社會科學學院社會學與人類學系副教授

▋摘要

關於創意理念的產生，有一種觀點是，原本就富有創意的思想者，發想出明顯富有創意的理念。與此相反，社會學家蘭德爾・科林斯提出，創新思維是在特定的社會狀況中，在有利於產生創意的智識網絡中被共同創造的。本文應用科林斯的智識創造理論，解釋為什麼太虛大師於一九六〇年代被認為是無原創性的，但數十年之後卻被認為是最重要的佛教思想者之一。本文首先提出清末的政治危機，顛覆了包括佛教思想者在內的中國智識分子的組織基礎，重塑了知識網絡的聯繫，這種新的聯繫讓創造力更有可能生發。接著，本文演示太虛大師在中國二十世紀初期的多個交互聯繫的智識網絡中處於中心的位置，因此讓他在重組的動態智識網絡中能學習新知，參與辯論，成就了他的創意。通過與他同時代人的橫向網絡，以及與他的弟子及他們的弟子的垂直網絡，太虛大師的理念在這些網絡的智識辯論過程中被賦予了舉足輕重的意義。應用科林斯的小數法則，本文描繪了擁擠的關注空間和二十世紀初佛教思想者相對微弱的地位，產生了太

虛大師融合的創意。本文接著展示太虛大師做為一位創造型思想者的定位，是如何由因為共產黨在內戰中獲勝而遷移到臺灣的佛教思想者所構建的。本文也探討了在臺灣重整而密集的佛教智識網絡中，由於聖嚴法師處於中心位置，成就了他的創意。而聖嚴法師思辨太虛大師及印順法師的理念所產生的智識關注空間，也是太虛大師在早期的評斷數十年後，被認可為富有創意的思想者的增上緣。最後，本文分析臺灣佛教思想界的網絡結構，探討聖嚴法師繼續被認可為富有創意的思想者的前景，以及體制條件要如何形塑，方能讓其思想在未來的智識網絡中能繼續流通。（陳維武譯／澳洲墨爾本大學社會工作系研究員）

關鍵詞： 太虛大師、聖嚴法師、漢傳佛教思想者、華人智識網絡、智識創造力、創造力的社會構建

聖嚴思想論叢 13

聖嚴研究 第十三輯
——聖嚴法師圓寂十週年國際研討會論文集
Studies of Master Sheng Yen Vol.13:
Collection of Essays From the 2019 International Conference Commemorating
the 10th Anniversary of Master Sheng Yen's Passing

編者	聖嚴教育基金會學術研究部
出版	法鼓文化
主編	楊蓓
封面設計	胡琡珮
地址	臺北市北投區公館路186號5樓
電話	(02)2893-4646
傳真	(02)2896-0731
網址	http://www.ddc.com.tw
E-mail	market@ddc.com.tw
讀者服務專線	(02)2896-1600
初版一刷	2020年11月
建議售價	新臺幣650元
郵撥帳號	50013371
戶名	財團法人法鼓山文教基金會—法鼓文化
北美經銷處	紐約東初禪寺
	Chan Meditation Center (New York, USA)
	Tel: (718)592-6593 Fax: (718)592-0717

法鼓文化

國家圖書館出版品預行編目資料

聖嚴研究. 第十三輯：聖嚴法師圓寂十週年國際
研討會論文集 / 聖嚴教育基金會學術研究部編.
-- 初版. -- 臺北市：法鼓文化, 2020.11
面； 公分
ISBN 978-957-598-869-2（平裝）

1.釋聖嚴 2.學術思想 3.佛教哲學 4.文集

220.9208   109014125